BORIS JOHNSON

THE GAMBLER

TOM BOWER

WH
ALLEN

I

WH Allen, an imprint of Ebury Publishing,

20 Vauxhall Bridge Road,
London SW1V 2SA

WH Allen is part of the Penguin Random House group of companies
whose addresses can be found at global.penguinrandomhouse.com

Copyright © Tom Bower 2020

Tom Bower has asserted his right to be identified as the author of this
Work in accordance with the Copyright, Designs and Patents Act 1988

First published by WH Allen in 2020
This edition published by WH Allen in 2021

www.penguin.co.uk

A CIP catalogue record for this book is available from the British Library

ISBN 9780753554920

Printed and bound in Great Britain by Clays Ltd, Elcograf S.p.A.

The authorized representative in the EEA is Penguin Random House Ireland,
Morrison Chambers, 32 Nassau Street, Dublin D02 YH68

Penguin Random House is committed to a sustainable future
for our business, our readers and our planet. This book is made from
Forest Stewardship Council® certified paper.

To George and Sylvia Bower
Generous, inspirational and loyal

Contents

Prologue

A Family's Secret

On Friday 16 August 2019, Boris Johnson hosted a dinner at Chequers for his father's seventy-ninth birthday. Stanley Johnson was understandably proud that his son could entertain his family at the prime minister's official Buckinghamshire country estate. Elected by the members of the governing Conservative Party nearly four weeks earlier, Boris had fulfilled his childhood ambition to become the nation's leader. As the staff served dinner in the Jacobean wood-panelled dining room, Stanley's familiar bonhomie and the new prime minister's joviality could not conceal the tension. At the very moment when the famed Johnson clan should have been rejoicing, the family's relationships were splintering.

Just over a year earlier, when he resigned as Foreign Secretary, Boris and his wife Marina had left Carlton Gardens, the minister's formal St James's residence, in separate cars. After twenty-five years of marriage, they had agreed to divorce. Some were surprised that the marriage had lasted that long. After several humiliating exposés of Boris's adultery, Marina had tried to repair their relationship but those efforts were wrecked by his most recent affair with Carrie Symonds, the thirty-year-old Tory Party communications chief. Too many lies, betrayals, confessions and apologies had been offered over the years to make any credible amends. 'He's a shit. He's utterly selfish. He's destroyed the family,' exclaimed one of the Johnson clan. Those raw emotions were barely concealed during Stanley's birthday celebrations.

Rachel and Jo Johnson, Boris's younger sister and brother, the latter an MP, had both come with their spouses and children. (Leo, the fourth sibling, had not returned from holiday in Greece.) To Stanley's disappointment, Boris's and Marina's four children had rejected the invitation to the party. Not only were they angry about their grandfather shaking Carrie's hand at a public meeting about the environment, but they also refused to speak to their father. On top of that resentment was the friction between Stanley's older children and his new family, one that had simmered for years but only intensified in the wake of Boris's latest achievements. In recent months Jenny, Stanley's second wife, had openly denounced Boris and had even forbidden him to visit Nethercote, the Johnsons' family farm on Exmoor. Boris's brother and sister were understandably surprised that Jenny, an intelligent woman, and Max, her son, had agreed to come to Chequers. Stanley tried to brush the troubles aside and, to explain her presence at Chequers to the three older Johnson children, Jenny said that Stanley had insisted that she join his birthday celebrations and under duress she had agreed.

During all the media appearances over the previous years, the striking similarity of appearance, mannerisms and jokey tone shared by Stanley and Boris would suggest that the two men were closely bonded. Few people noticed during the Tory party's leadership campaign the cold stares Boris shot as he walked past his father, invariably standing in the front row. The ambiguity of Stanley seeking his son's recognition was partly explained by Boris's first wife, Allegra Mostyn-Owen. Boris's worst habits, she discovered, were inherited from his father. But even Allegra, after their eight-year relationship, was unaware of the real reason for Boris's deep anger towards Stanley. Only Charlotte Wahl, Boris's seventy-seven-year-old mother, could explain her son's cold stare. It reflected the family's great secret.

Stanley, the star after twenty days in the jungle of the 2017 series of *I'm a Celebrity – Get Me Out of Here!*, could not understand how his son had become prime minister. Earlier in 2019, he said that Boris, despite a masterly understanding from Pericles about risk and power, was not personally ambitious and never took risks. Looking across at his son during the dinner, Stanley imagined that in life everything happens spontaneously without much forethought. In his self-centred approach to life, Stanley misinterpreted much about the world, not least what his son had learnt from his father's mistakes.

As usual, Boris's enthusiasm and jokes during the Chequers dinner hid his own feelings. Secretive and untrusting, his accomplished performance concealed his vulnerability to stress. Compartmentalisation has been a key to his public success. Few outsiders could imagine any anxiety provoking an occasional meltdown. An extra gear in his life, fuelled by defiance, set him apart from his contemporaries. Ruthless ambition had allowed him to exploit the natural reserve of his competitors. Any sadness about his children's absence was cancelled out by his triumph. 'It's all about Boris,' many of those working with him would frequently assert. But even for his family that truism merely highlighted the enigma. Did anyone, they wondered, know the real Boris? They agreed he was a loner with few close friends. Among those few had been Marina, his anchor and consigliere, and the ghost at the feast. 'Marina's Magic' had held the Johnson clan together for years, especially more recently at the family parties in Chevening, the Foreign Secretary's official country home. Boris's disloyalty to Marina had generated intense hostility towards him and deep sympathy for her.

Marina blamed Stanley for her marriage's collapse and refused to speak to him. Like Allegra, she said that Boris's adultery and his other misdemeanours mirrored his father's habits. The same unhappiness Stanley had spread among his own children, she said, was being repeated by Boris towards his four children with Marina. 'Like father like son' echoed across the Chequers dining room.

To understand the new prime minister required forensic examination of his relations with his father, both as a child and as an adult. Naturally, the fracture of their close relations was concealed from the public. United by intelligence, charm and their blond hair, the Johnsons were lauded by the media as a dynasty of achievers although a profile written two years earlier by Prue White in *The Times* had, after focusing on Stanley's successful appearance on *I'm a Celebrity*, concluded 'All his wit, charm and self-deprecation were a smokescreen for narcissistic, rapacious ambition.' Stanley gave the impression that he was never hurt by the truth. That was an illusion. The seamless friendly competition generated by Stanley among his eldest children, endlessly described by the media, had been both remarkable and destructive. The first fractures of their relationships had appeared many years earlier but Brexit had become the public lightning rod for their disagreements.

Rachel was openly opposed to Boris's Brexit campaign and her husband had rarely missed an opportunity to express his dislike of his brother-in-law. By contrast, although Jo, the quietest and most intelligent of Stanley's six children, was a committed Europhile, he remained a loyal MP and minister in Boris's new government. His wife, Amelia Gentleman, a *Guardian* journalist, opposed Boris but she had remained silent in public. Likewise, Leo was a Europhile displeased by Boris's leadership of the Brexit campaign, but he also remained diplomatically silent. The major surprise was Stanley's stance. Unlike his children, the patriarch of a previously united family had abandoned his lifelong passion for a united Europe to share the limelight with his son. Anxious to stay close to the flame, he had switched from an ardent European to a Eurosceptic.

Amid so many conflicting emotions, especially the mix of Brexit and Marina, no Johnson family gathering could escape a meltdown argument, and that evening was no different.

Looking across the darkened fields at the end of the meal, Stanley was naturally proud that his eldest son was prime minister. His own political ambitions had largely failed but he enjoyed basking in his son's triumph. He had eagerly accepted the opportunity to stay the night at Chequers with all his family. The campaigner, adventurer and celebrity could not miss the chance to sleep under the same roof as Britain's past leaders and see the magnificent house's remarkable collection of paintings and artefacts, especially those from the Cromwellian era.

At breakfast the following morning, Boris expected everyone to stay for Stanley's birthday lunch. Instead, Rachel and Jo had other long-standing arrangements and departed with their families. To those who remained, their departure appeared ungracious. Suddenly, it was rather quiet. At lunchtime on the sunlit lawn, Boris was as usual in good spirits, pleased when the staff brought a birthday cake. After the traditional good wishes, Stanley blew out the candles and enjoyed the cake. Soon after, he too left.

One year later, on the eve of Stanley's eightieth birthday, the unforeseen circumstances of Boris's premiership had severely tested the nation and the Johnson family. During 2020, as the prime minister battled to save the nation from the Covid pandemic and bankruptcy, the family tensions simmering at Chequers erupted into an irreconcilable feud. Throughout extraordinary roller-coaster weeks in the spring, as Boris faced the possibility of his own death from the Covid virus and the birth of his sixth child, the tensions did not abate. The four older Johnson children had become more bewildered about their father's second marriage, just as they all queried Boris's relationship with his fiancée. As Boris struggled to protect 67 million Britons from disaster, his own family – still heralded by many as an enviable model of love, laughter and glory – was disintegrating in the shadows.

The question asked during those distressing summer months as Britain struggled to return to normality was whether the unseen collapse of the Johnson dynasty was a metaphor for Johnson's premiership. Besieged by critics that he had ignored the early warnings about the pandemic, that he had failed to oversee his ministers' chaotic mismanagement of the government's response, and finally that he ignored his own warnings and caught the virus himself, he emerged hollow-eyed from illness to complaints that he had lost energy and authority. Some of the more detailed complaints have proven to be unfounded, but the long-standing rebuke about his laziness, disorganisation and lack of attention to detail have come to haunt him. Some blame his divorce from Marina, who was 'unafraid to dispense home truths', for the absence of an anchor and reality in his life. Contrary to Stanley's imagination, Marina had held the dynasty together, and the prime minister's fate was determined by both his loyalty and disloyalty to his friends and family.

ACT I

Origins

Chapter 1

The Truth

The birth of the Johnson dynasty had a dreamlike quality. Amid the breathtaking beauty of Oxford, the citadel of Britain's self-confidence, the fellows of All Souls College hosted in summer 1962 a celebratory dinner. Among the guests was Charlotte Fawcett, an undergraduate studying English at Lady Margaret Hall. Seated next to her was Stanley Johnson, nearly two years older and studying English at Exeter College. Charming and amusing, Stanley instantly captured Charlotte's affection. In Stanley's opinion, it was not by chance that Sir James Fawcett, the college bursar and an outstanding international lawyer, had placed him next to his daughter. Well liked across the university, Stanley was also the winner of that year's Newdigate Prize for poetry. Winning the prize – an award he would still proudly mention nearly sixty years later – was a blessing for Stanley. Not only was it a passport to his career after Oxford, but it also introduced him to a remarkable woman.

One of five children, Charlotte was educated at Mayfield then Westminster Tutors and had enjoyed a happy, social childhood in a large house in St John's Wood, an affluent area in north-west London. The Fawcetts were politically active liberals and outspoken campaigners for human rights, women's equality and against racism. Beatrice Lowe, her mother, was the Jewish daughter of two distinguished academics. Financially and emotionally secure, Charlotte had been in love with another student, a left-wing president of the students' union, before meeting Stanley, but she quickly embraced her new boyfriend.

Stanley was exceptional. Dynamic, intelligent and intensely social, he had a wide range of friends in Oxford, had already travelled across the world and was sufficiently impressive to be identified as a recruit for MI6, the foreign intelligence service. He had, however, already discovered his intellectual limitations. He had entered Oxford to study Greats but had switched to English, an easier subject. The wisdom of his decision was not only the Newdigate Prize but also the award of a Harkness Fellowship which would finance a study trip to the USA after graduation.

Bowled over by Stanley's energy, Charlotte agreed in 1963 to delay her final year's study and exams and join him for one year in America. Before leaving, they married in Marylebone registry office and, with little money, spent their honeymoon at a friend's farm. Some years later, she realised that instead of a loving and deep friendship, she had become infatuated with a man who deliberately minimised the seriousness of anything and ridiculed intimacy. The intellectual and emotional values championed by the Fawcetts were scorned by her new husband. In the whirlwind of their romance, too headstrong to care for her family's reservations, she had also failed to notice that bluster and bonhomie camouflaged the scars of his own childhood.

Stanley was understandably intrigued by his family's history. In the nineteenth century in Anatolia, Turkey, his grandfather, Ali Kemal, a fearless Turkish journalist, became a famous opponent of the corrupt Ottoman Empire. After the empire's collapse in 1918, Kemal was appointed Turkey's interior minister. Vigorously but forlornly he campaigned against Kemal Ataturk, the ardent nationalist, to align Turkey with Britain, and was abruptly forced to resign. Returning to journalism in a febrile atmosphere, he continued as a newspaper editor to oppose Ataturk until, in November 1922, he was kidnapped by his enemies and lynched by a mob. His corpse was hung from a tree.

By then, his thirteen-year-old son Osman Ali was living in Britain. For her safety, Ali Kemal's first wife, half-British and half-Swiss, had given birth to her son in Bournemouth. She had died soon after his birth and her mother, Margaret Brun (née Johnson), adopted her grandson who was renamed Wilfred 'Johnny' Johnson.

After a truncated education, Johnny farmed in Canada, visited Switzerland and headed to Egypt to manage an estate. Standing in a Cairo bar in 1932, he spotted Irene Williams, a twenty-five-year-old Anglo-French Oxford graduate being accosted by a British serviceman. To everyone's surprise, Irene walloped the serviceman. As he hit the floor, Johnny walked across to offer his congratulations and Irene, instantly attracted to the cool Englishman, introduced herself as 'Buster'.

Johnny had struck lucky. Irene's father was a Lloyd's insurance investor whose wealth and status were inherited from his grandfather, Sir George Williams, the founder of the YMCA and a successful businessman, and her mother was a descendant of Baron de Pfeffel, a rich Alsatian family living in a grand Versailles house. Surrounded by maids, nannies and seemingly unlimited wealth to fund an exciting social life filled with music, Irene was educated at Cheltenham Ladies' College followed by Oxford. Uncertain about her future, the amusing dilettante was sent by her father to Cairo to escape some unsuitable relationships. After three years tutoring in Cairo, she returned to England in 1935. Johnny followed. Once he was employed by a City timber broker in 1936, they married.

Financed by Irene's family, Johnny had a comfortable life, commuting daily from Bromley to Cannon Street and returning with pleasure from London's smog to the luxury of domestic staff and his first two children. Soon after the war broke out, Johnny volunteered to fly for RAF Coastal Command and was absent when in 1940, in the midst of the Battle of Britain, Stanley was born. To escape the Blitz, Irene moved with her three children to live first with her parents in Cornwall and then in Devon. Her idyllic life snapped towards the end of the war. Standing on a hill to watch Johnny fly past and tip his wing in salute, Irene stood thrilled until she watched the plane crash following engine failure. Burnt and permanently lame, Johnny left the RAF in 1947 poor and unemployed. His good fortune was Irene's devotion and her family's money. Convinced that his best fate was to escape suburbia and return to farming, he bought West Nethercote, an isolated 250-acre sheep farm in a high but shady valley near Winsford on Exmoor by the River Exe.

Without reliable electricity, proper sanitation or adequate heating, the rapidly expanding family of four children shared their rambling, cold, stone house with cows, sheep, poultry, dogs, mice and the occasional horse. Seemingly, Buster's love for Johnny smothered any regret for the comforts she had abandoned.

Hard physical graft dominated Stanley's childhood. Daily, during his holidays from his boarding prep school, he helped his father with the sheep, collected hay, picked fruit and learned to survive on the hillside. There was no washing machine or fridge. Newborn lambs were kept warm by the kitchen wood-burning stove. The idyllic setting belied the truth that Nethercote was not a happy home. As well as being an unsuccessful farmer, Johnny was a silent alcoholic who never read books and ignored sickness. The sullen hangdog regularly whacked Stanley and his other children. And in front of his children, he often beat Irene. Stanley would tell Charlotte how he resented his father's behaviour, especially hitting Irene. In hindsight, Stanley's feelings were ignored by his parents and he in turn had little affection for his brothers and sister. 'He didn't think they were good enough,' observed Allegra Mostyn-Owen. In particular, Mostyn-Owen was struck by Stanley's poor relations with his brother Peter, whom she assumed was ruined by their father's cruelty. In contrast, Stanley found Irene's eccentricity endearing. Whenever cake crumbs fell onto the floor, Stanley watched her lie on the floor and blow the crumbs under a chair. 'I protested,' he recalled and she replied, 'I'll do what I want.' Seventy years later he reminisced, 'I learned from my mother that exaggeration with a purpose is a price well worth paying. She was always ready to do things, even if it looked ridiculous. Being contrary was what she taught me.'

In 1953, aged thirteen and with what would become the trademark mop of blond hair, Stanley was sent to Sherborne, a public school in Dorset. Irene's family paid the fees for this blimpish, third-rate teaching establishment, big on flogging and games, and mentally and sexually truncating. Adapting himself to the school's frenzied competitiveness, Stanley drilled in the army cadets in preparation for service in the empire, played sport every day but had enjoyed no artistic activities. Despite being regularly flogged, he won prizes and was appointed head boy. 'Whenever I walked through the school,' he would remember, '660 boys stood to attention and took their hands out of their pockets.' The result, he would admit, was a 'swollen head'.

Before going to Oxford, he set off in 1958 to Greece and Turkey, to trace his family roots, and then on an adventurous trip to Brazil and across South America. He returned to Nethercote with a taste for endless travel.

With that self-confidence, Stanley arrived in Oxford in 1959 eager to win what were called at the time 'the glittering prizes'. On graduating in 1963 and having secured the Harkness Fellowship, he sailed in August from Southampton with his new bride. On the New York quayside he was given a new Chevrolet and directions to drive to Iowa College to start a creative writing course.

Stanley is the first to admit that he wasted his opportunity to learn the craft of writing which undermined his lifelong ambition to become a bestselling author. With a short attention span and not able to master the detail of the course, he abandoned Iowa and headed for New York to study economics at Columbia. Their new home was a single-room loft near the Chelsea Hotel in mid-Manhattan. By then, Charlotte was pregnant and Stanley, always impatient to travel, suggested they head to Mexico for a holiday. Since their car was not licensed across the border, it was abandoned in Texas and they headed for Mexico City in a twenty-hour bus ride. Resisting Stanley's domineering enthusiasm was impossible for his amenable wife. Soon after arriving in the city, they introduced themselves to Boris Litwin, the generous parent of an Oxford friend. Stanley, as his family would discover, was a professional guest, always searching for a free bed. By then, Charlotte was suffering morning sickness. To save Charlotte the long return bus journey, Litwin bought the couple airline tickets back to Texas. 'If it's a boy,' said Charlotte with relief, 'we'll call him Boris.' On 19 June 1964, Alexander Boris de Pfeffel Johnson, weighing just over nine pounds, was born in a New York hospital used mostly by Puerto Ricans. His father missed the birth while out buying a pizza. 'De Pfeffel' was added as a marker of Boris's mother's aristocratic background. To the family, he was always known as 'Al' or Alexander.

As had happened at Oxford, Stanley once again failed to follow the meticulous study course at Columbia. He wanted to resume travelling but Charlotte persuaded him that they return to Oxford with Boris so that she could complete her degree. By autumn 1964, Charlotte was once again studying English at Lady Margaret Hall. Baby Boris often slept in a drawer in her room. Occasionally, he was fed boiled eggs, creating a lifetime aversion. After Christmas, Charlotte was again pregnant and her relationship with Stanley changed.

The return to Oxford and fatherhood did not suit Stanley, nor did his lifestyle. Unable to focus on establishing a career, twenty-four-year-old Stanley had started teaching in a state school. Dissatisfied, he switched to an Oxford graduate course in agricultural economics and earned a small amount as an editor of a technical quarterly. Although he relied on the Fawcetts' money to survive, he mocked them. 'They're champagne socialists,' he told Charlotte. He derided their thoughtful, socially responsible intellectualism and their affection for the *Guardian*. 'He was rude to them and made fun of them,' said Charlotte. 'He didn't like their Catholicism or their support for Labour but without them, we would never have had enough money.' But there was worse. During a series of bitter arguments, Stanley accused Charlotte of seeing too much of her friends. 'He resented that I cared about my friends,' she recalls, 'and that's when he first hit me.' Boris was asleep in the same room. Charlotte blamed herself for Stanley's anger and continued her studies.

The incident was buried after Stanley was approached to join MI6 and began an intensive training course which separated him and Charlotte during the week. In June, she passed her degree and celebrated that Boris had walked in the kitchen at eleven months. By the time Rachel was born in September, the fifteen-month-old boy understood exactly that he would need to share his mother's attention. Boris's expression on seeing his sister for the first time was not joyous: 'When Boris arrived at the hospital to see Rachel in my arms,' Charlotte recalls, 'his look was shock, disbelief and fear.'

By then, the Johnsons had moved to north London and Stanley was once again edgy. The anonymous spy world did not suit a man ambitious for fame. He successfully applied for a job at the World Bank in Washington. At twenty-five, he would finally be able to support his family.

The four Johnsons flew to Washington in February 1966. Boris was proving to be a temperate, smiling baby, keen to sleep even when his cot collapsed. Eighteen months after arriving in Washington, Leo, their third child, was born. Despite being a mother to three young children, Charlotte went to art classes and encouraged her children to paint. Boris seemed particularly keen on drawing and painting buses in oils. His mother would keep his sketchbooks in a box together with other momentos of his early life including his hair and milk teeth. Even before he was two years old, Boris told his mother colourful stories about bad children at nursery school. 'And then he would answer my questions in an amusing and creative way.' Aged three, Boris had begun to read, in particular he enjoyed a 'Look and Learn' comic strip depicting the science-fiction story of the Trigan Empire, based on Ancient Greece. 'He was gripped by that,' said Charlotte, 'and that gave him an idea. He said to me, "I want to be world king."'

Stanley missed those milestones. He was flying around the world seeking to improve the condition of poverty-stricken countries. But within two years he was bored once again. After pulling a prank on his boss, he quickly moved on in 1968 to research global overpopulation for the Rockefeller Foundation in New York. While Charlotte and their three children lived by the sea in Connecticut, Stanley flew thousands of miles across the world to produce *Life Without Birth*, a polemic denouncing the lack of birth control and the dangers of the Pope's ban on contraception. Bursting with indignation and pride, he would claim that his book paved the way for a UN agency to control the world's population.

He returned to Connecticut and a troubled relationship with Charlotte. Although in their hectic social life, Stanley was adept at placing himself at the centre of attention as the life and soul of any gathering, Charlotte noticed his impatience with those who were neither intellectual nor rich. Status was important for Stanley and he was unusually selective of whom he liked. For those he favoured, he speedily spotted the moment to break the ice and start conversations with a joke. But back at home, the humour disappeared. 'He was always hitting me,' says Charlotte, 'and Boris saw it.' Ignoring the unhappiness caused by his violence, Stanley has described that American period of his life as 'wonderful', not least because he also wrote *Presidential Plot*, a novel about the assassination of Lyndon B. Johnson. Although published, it was not successful.

In 1969 Charlotte demanded that the family return to London. After a series of violent arguments, he relented to her ultimatum that she would travel without him. Renting a house near her parents' London home in Little Venice, Stanley used his friendships to find a temporary and unpaid job at Conservative Central Office to produce the party's 1970 election programme on the environment. Since his only income was a grant from the Ford Foundation for a programme about population, the family could not afford to send the children to a nursery. Happily, Charlotte taught Boris and Rachel English, history and maths at home. At five years old, Boris had started to read the *Daily Telegraph*'s editorial column. Although the Fawcetts were again helping financially, Stanley grudgingly admitted that his income was insufficient to support his family. The solution, he decided, was that his family should live with his parents at Nethercote. To fulfil his Ford Fellowship, he would travel for one year around the world, leaving Charlotte to bring up the three children. On the eve of his departure from Exmoor, there was another violent argument in front of Boris.

'You're selfish,' Charlotte told Stanley. 'You only do what you want.'

'No, you're selfish,' replied Stanley, 'not wanting me to do what I want.'

'Stanley was very bad-tempered,' says Charlotte. 'He was always shouting, angry and then he hit me.' Without apologies, Stanley drove off from Nethercote for his next adventure. As Rachel

Johnson would write nearly fifty years later, 'He is never happier than setting off to live with some remote tribe many thousands of miles from his loved ones . . . He cares far more about other animals than even his own family.'

Being left behind at Nethercote, in those days an eight-hour drive from London, was a punishment for his wife and, as Charlotte believed, an opportunity for serial adultery. Asked many years later if he was, as Charlotte believed, 'completely unfaithful' and 'an amazing womaniser', Stanley replied, 'Total garbage. Honestly.' In his self-deprecating way, Stanley has also said that 'Human relations remain a mystery to me.' His ebullient personality always winning new friends, he loved to travel and, despite any discomfort, seemed unaware of anyone else's feelings. Selfishness was a criticism Stanley could not understand.

*

Life at Nethercote was chaotic. As Boris approached the start of school, the family moved into a dilapidated, unheated house next to his grandparents, Johnny and 'Granny Butter' as 'Buster' became known. With little money, Charlotte was marooned. 'Stanley left me there for a year without a car,' she recalls. Once a month, Buster drove Charlotte in a battered Volkswagen to the cash-and-carry in Minehead to stock up on food. Long before she returned to Minehead four weeks later, their remaining food was stale, damp and mouldy. 'There was no point saying to Stanley, "Give me a car",' Charlotte explains. 'He wouldn't.' In that isolation, she taught her children friendship and loyalty to each other. While they played or read, she painted dark, troubled and remarkable images in oils that reflected her anguish. Nearby, Boris would sit on the unswept floor enthusiastically painting and fluently replying to Charlotte's questions. When asked to play, he would reply: 'Let's play reading,' or 'Let's see who can be quietest for longest.' Untidiness became a way of life. Toys were strewn around the home just as in his later life, rubbish was either thrown into the back of his car or out of the window. Their domesticity was frequently interrupted by sickness. While

Stanley was saving the rainforests, his family were sick because Nethercote's water was contaminated by lead pipes. 'We were all lying ill on the floor,' says Charlotte. Compounding that sickness, Boris often screamed with pain from agonising earaches caused by grommets. If camphorated vapours and aspirin failed to work, the ever stoical Buster agreed as a last resort to drive through the night to a hospital for antibiotics. The consequence for Boris was periods of deafness.

Getting three children to Winsford's village school every day was a problem, especially in winter. Without a car, Charlotte walked with them nearly two miles to the main road to wait for a lift from Phil, owner of a local garage, who regularly passed in his Land Rover. Charlotte returned home and repeated the walk in the afternoon to collect the children. There was no chance that Johnny would allow Charlotte to use his Land Rover. It had smashed head-lights, severely dented bumpers, its roof squashed after a cow pushed it over into a ditch and a piece of twisted metal as replacement for the ignition key. Johnny did not trust her to preserve the wreck. Moreover, he needed the vehicle. Most evenings, he left his wife alone and drove down to the village pub and, after closing time, went to see his girlfriend Kate nearby. His affair had lasted twelve years and, as Charlotte knew, he had simultaneous relationships with other women. Throughout their marriage, Stanley's mother tolerated Johnny's serial adultery – and his miserliness. She was allowed just one new dress every year which he chose and bought without her being present. Similarly, Stanley refused to conform. To adultery and violence, his family could add deserter. Charlotte's only relief were the visits by her parents, James and Beatrice Fawcett.

During those days and over the following years, James Fawcett, a classicist who had won a double first at Oxford, introduced ancient Greece and Rome to his grandson. From the books they read together, Boris learned to admire their civilisation and literature. He became fascinated by the ceaseless competition between macho males driven by self-belief. He learned to adore Rome's heroes, worshipped by the crowds in the Forum and on the battlefield, and was intrigued by the Greeks' exaltation of their gods. 'It was a world,' he would write, 'that believed above all in winners and losers, in death and glory.' While other boys imagined themselves as football players, rock stars or doctors, Boris's introduction to the classics conjured a dream of victory and the spotlight shining on the leader. 'As the oldest,' he later wrote, 'I've always known that my position is unchallengeable. It is the fixed point about which my cosmos is organised. I smile indulgently on everybody else's attempts to compete with me. Bring it on, I say.'

In that isolation, the only constant male influence was Johnny, the grandfather. Unaware of his misconduct, his grandchildren loved him, all proudly bearing the special names he gave them. Boris was Beetle, Rachel was Spider, Leo was Fly. Jo, born later, was Flea. Unlike Stanley, Johnny did not smack his grandchildren nor criticise their appearance.

In summer 1970, Stanley returned to Nethercote. He remained frustrated that he had found neither fame nor fortune. In their shambolic world, Boris saw his father write a book about his recent trip and occasionally emerge from his study to teach his children to love the beauty and natural harshness of country life – animals being born and slaughtered and stags hunted to their death. He also told gripping tales about his family's remarkable background – his Muslim father and Boris baptised as a Catholic. Still to come was the discovery that Buster's grandmother, Karoline von Rothenburg, was the illegitimate daughter of a nineteenth-century German prince directly related to Britain's Hanoverian king, George II. For Stanley, an impoverished writer and humanitarian campaigner dependent on his in-laws, the exotic family tree partly satisfied his aspiration for status in a class-conscious society which frowned on foreigners.

Success, Stanley believed, was generated by competition. Instinctively, he pitted his three children against each other – at snooker, reading, maths and table tennis. After Rachel beat Boris at table tennis, she watched his fury: 'he kicked the garage door so hard he broke his toe'. Once, after Rachel got onto a table to make a speech, Boris, with uncontrolled anger, pushed her off to make his own speech. There was even Stanley's film to prove Boris's defiance. Sitting calmly alone in a yellow inflatable boat, his six-year-old son was recorded being swept down the river Exe and dropping over a weir. The celluloid does not reveal a glimmer of fear.

The coloured images of a small boy's determination concealed the family's suffering. Charlotte had openly confronted Stanley about his affairs and he denied it. 'Stanley wanted to be loved,' she recalls, 'and wanted sex and he wanted power. And when I contradicted him, it threatened his power.' Charlotte never thought of leaving: 'I stayed because I loved him, despite the abuse.' She sympathised with the frustrations in his life, especially his inability to become a famous writer. 'He wanted to be as famous and successful as his hero, P. G. Wodehouse,' says Charlotte. Stanley found anonymity intolerable. His family understood he would go to the ends of the earth to find fame and new relationships.

Boris agonised over his mother's fate. Not only had he watched his mother suffer from being regularly hit, but he also saw his father blatantly deny the truth. Unwilling to confide in others about his father's violence, he became a loner. In his solitariness, his competitiveness was off-set by self-doubt. To mask the misery and hurt, he demanded attention. Just as his father wilfully amused friends and strangers to conceal the wretched chaos at Nethercote, Boris adopted his father's performance. Rachel, his only confidante, did the same. The beauty of rural life at Nethercote, plus their grandparents' love, inspired their overwhelming resilience. Their survival was assured. Their parents' secret was protected. After many more arguments, Stanley bowed to Charlotte's demand that the family should return to London for the children's education.

With the Fawcetts' financial help, Stanley bought a house in Primrose Hill and Boris went to Princess Road Primary, the local state school. To earn a living, Stanley accepted a job with the International Planned Parenthood Federation (IPPF) to encourage birth control. The natural attraction was endless global travel at his employer's expense. The irony was that Jo, Charlotte's fourth child, had just been born. The IPPF was yet another temporary job while Stanley pursued his latest ambition, to be elected to Parliament.

Joke Aarnink, the Johnsons' Dutch au pair, was the eyewitness to that ambition. One evening, she opened Stanley's front door to Ted Heath, the Tory leader, and Alec Douglas-Home, the former prime minister, for dinner. The evening failed to secure a safe Commons seat for Stanley. But Aarnink's brief employment did seal her memory of Boris as 'insecure and very sensitive'. His lack of self-confidence was well concealed. Any display of vulnerability, Boris learned from his father, was unacceptable.

Finally, in 1972 there was good news. Aged thirty-two, Stanley was offered a well-paid job. Britain had just joined the Common Market (the EEC) and Stanley, as a passionate environmentalist, was asked to be the head of the Prevention of Pollution and Nuisance Division at the EEC's headquarters in Brussels. At public expense, the Johnsons moved in 1973 to Belgium and rented a splendid house. With a good income, Stanley had status, Charlotte was painting and the four children were healthier than previously. In the prestigious social world which the Johnsons now enjoyed, they were reunited with Charles Wheeler, an outstanding BBC broadcast journalist. The families had previously met in Washington. In the small British community, the Johnsons and Wheelers became further united by their children at the European School. Boris (aged nine) and Rachel (eight) met Charles's daughter Marina, although Marina would later say that she was not impressed by Boris's flamboyant showmanship. He would roll around on the ground and throw hard balls at children. Her disapproval was echoed by Mary Kidd, a Norland nanny employed by the family. Some families in Brussels, she said, banned their children from playing with the 'too rough' Johnsons. Nevertheless, after ten years of marriage, the Johnsons appeared a picture of stability. Few guessed from his performance that Stanley revelled in any opportunity to be an unconventional rule-breaker. At parties, Stanley's bonhomie delivered a stream of opinions, occasionally suffocating any chance of a reply. No speech, Stanley believed, was worthy without a succession of jokes. Across the international community, his charm and comic act were appreciated – although Stanley, they learnt, was always about Stanley. 'I can count the seconds,' Rachel would write in 2017 about meeting her father for lunch, 'until he says, "So what I've been up to . . . ".' Only a few registered the unfortunate impression that beyond his generosity and good-natured friendship, he seemed to lack sympathy and judicious contemplation. Imitating Stanley, Boris assumed that his life was always going to be about Boris. Like his father, he would entertain to get the laughs and become the leader.

Visitors to the Johnsons' home in Brussels marked out Boris as extraordinary. Aged ten, he read *The Times*, *The Economist* and an eclectic range of novels, not least by P. G. Wodehouse. During that year's holiday in Greece, Boris asked a group of visiting classicists if he could join their game of Scrabble. They agreed, only to be beaten. Believing their defeat to be an aberration, they agreed to a second game only to be beaten again.

The boy's excitement masked deep unhappiness. His parents' marriage had become irredeemably fractured. Charlotte was convinced that Stanley was rampantly unfaithful and a serial womaniser. Images of scantily clad au pair girls were mentioned. Charlotte found the pressure of his neglect and philandering overwhelming. He was inaccessible, neither a friend nor a confidant. 'He hit me,' she says. 'And hit me.' Boris aged ten and nine-year-old Rachel became the guardians of the secret. His family was safer if outsiders did not know.

That year, 1974, the dam broke. Overwhelmed by severe depression, Charlotte suffered a nervous breakdown. She was rushed from Brussels to the Maudsley Hospital in south London. Isolated from her children, she felt wretched. For her four children, the circumstances were unusually difficult.

On an overcast day forty-five years later, in autumn 2019, handicapped by Parkinson's and other illnesses, the accomplished artist who lives with a carer in a small but comfortable Notting Hill Gate flat, disclosed that their marriage 'was ghastly, terrible'. In particular, Charlotte describes the 'difficult times' at the Maudsley. 'I want the truth told,' she said.

Over the years, Stanley has professed ignorance about the causes of his wife's depression. 'I never got to the bottom of it,' he said in

2019. 'It was too complicated for me and a mystery. Charlotte also never understood the causes. Freud and the mind is a particular mystery.' Strangely, Stanley also feigned ignorance about Charlotte's paintings completed at the hospital. One shows her at the top of a tree, her small children below, arms outstretched while Stanley, standing apart, looks on, completely uninterested.

Charlotte corrects Stanley's recollection: 'The doctors at the Maudsley spoke to Stanley about his abuse of me. He had hit me. He hit me many times, over many years.' On one occasion, Stanley had hit Charlotte especially hard. 'He beat me up and broke my nose,' she recalls. After that attack, Charlotte was treated in the St John & St Elizabeth Hospital in north-west London. The children were told that a car door had hit their mother's face. Boris, however, knew the truth.

'Although Stanley hit me, he made me feel I deserved it,' she explains. Her parents, who lived near the hospital, visited their daughter daily. 'My parents confronted Stanley about it,' she continued, 'but he denied it.' Although Boris was just ten years old, Charlotte forensically discussed her marriage and condition with her eldest son. On the one hand, she realised, her son 'admired his father's humour and dash'. With some sadness, she recalled that Boris had witnessed her being hit by Stanley. 'That was terrible for the children,' Charlotte admitted. 'Unfortunately,' she told Boris, 'I'm driving your father mad.' Her stoic bravery and silence taught Boris never to reveal vindictiveness or bear grudges. He learned to act without revealing his motives. Most important, Boris has never revealed how those events permanently influenced his life, character and personality. Psychologists agree that the children of battered women are worried, frightened, confused and vulnerable. Without sufficient stability, security and protection, they are exposed to substantial risk.

While Charlotte was in hospital, Stanley was responsible for his children. But he was absent from their home in Brussels for much of the time, leaving an au pair in charge. The young children were often expected to look after themselves, even making the arrangements to travel from Brussels to London to visit their mother.

Neither then nor later did Stanley voice any sympathy for Charlotte's illness. 'Depression wasn't allowed in Stanley's book,' Allegra Mostyn-Owen would discover. Even now, Rachel refuses to blame Stanley. 'It was difficult for my dad too,' she wrote. 'I can't pretend it wasn't bleak, but he did brilliantly to keep it all going. He very much kept the show on the road. And my mother is a brilliant, brilliant mother . . . I feel fiercely protective towards my parents.' Boris understood the cause of his mother's condition. 'I have often thought,' Charlotte would later say, 'that his being "world king" was a wish to make himself unhurtable, invincible, somehow safe from the pains of your mother disappearing for eight months.' Her stoic acceptance of her fate during Boris's visits to the Maudsley imbued in him an absence of malice. If his mother was not angry, then Boris could not be angry. After all, Stanley had promised him that he would never leave his beloved mother. The lesson he did draw from witnessing the violence was to avoid overt confrontation.

On Charlotte's return to Brussels, Boris assumed that she was cured. Among her first paintings was a self-portrait. Sitting in a chair surrounded by her family, Charlotte's head is thrown back and her mouth is wide open, screaming. She called her painting *Hasn't Worked*.

During those weeks, Stanley decided that his children needed a better education than was available in Brussels. His ambition was they should all follow him to Oxford. Based on his own upbringing, it was quite natural to send very young children to boarding school and, in his words, leave their upbringing to the school. Charlotte had no alternative but to agree. He chose Ashdown House in East Sussex, a prep school renowned for teaching classics and coaching its best pupils to win a place at Eton.

Aged eleven, Boris arrived with Rachel, the school's first girl. Stanley cannot remember whether he delivered his children on their first day. He assumes that Boris and Rachel travelled alone from Brussels. In the pre-Channel Tunnel era that meant a train to Ostend, a boat to Dover and then a train to the school – carrying luggage from train to boat to train. 'It was tough,' wrote Rachel.

'We were in the throes of my parents' ice-stormesque open marriage and that was the end of family life. We learnt very quickly, very early, not to have emotional needs.' Boris has never spoken publicly about his feelings at that time. Charlotte is certain that her suffering played on him. He was happy reading, going alone to museums or painting. The untidiness of his childhood was deeply embedded. Unlike his siblings, he could never shed Nethercote's chaos. At Ashdown House, denied his mother's embrace and the absence of any home warmth, there was a vast emotional hole. Some called the result, the 'frozen child'. Stanley however dismissed the notion that his children were abandoned or suffered pain: 'It's a strange idea that parents should talk to their children at home. I didn't have much influence on my children. I never read to them or asked about their homework. I relied on the schools.'

The introduction into Boris's life of Clive Williams, Ashdown's classics teacher, was fortunate. Sitting at the back of the class for the first days, Boris remained unnoticed until an English teacher brought his first essay – a laugh-aloud piece – into the common room. The teachers agreed that their new pupil was exceptionally well read and a potential scholar. After the first Latin and Greek lessons, Williams declared that his new pupil could master the classics from scratch and could, with hard work, be sufficiently proficient within two years to get a place at Eton. 'He was better and faster than anyone else I had taught,' Williams would report – not only in the tests, but Boris also quickly learnt the lines of the king in the Greek play *Rhesus*, for example, and acted with 'a sense of drama and understanding of the language'. His personal qualities also emerged – warm hearted and competitive to perform at the centre of the stage, unable like his father, to bear anonymity.

At the heart of his performance was an adaptation of Bertie Wooster, P. G. Wodehouse's buffoonish upper-class character. Wooster is repeatedly saved from disaster by Jeeves, his erudite manservant. There is good reason to adore Wodehouse, one of the finest and funniest prose writers of his time. His plots and dialogue are remarkable. Imitating Wooster, however, is to confess to being a bit of a life's clown oneself. Wooster makes light of everything and gets away with everything. Absolution is always at hand. The question raised in later years was whether Boris was really an unserious, spontaneous Wooster-like buffoon or rather was presenting himself as a clown in a calculated act to conceal that at his core, his serious life was best approached with invincible optimism and indefatigable hope. He played it both ways by adopting Wodehouse's mantra that those who are principled and clever should wear their learning lightly.

The summer of 1976 in Nethercote was memorable for the extraordinary heat and nudity. Sometimes Stanley and Charlotte walked around their homes without clothes. That summer, Stanley told the two au pairs that since there was a water shortage – the river had run dry – they would be unable to wash their clothes so they should just as well not wear any. Both complied and walked around in the nude. Stanley insisted on two au pairs in case one resigned. In the event, both stayed for the summer not least because Stanley, in the knowledge of his children, embarked on an affair with one of the girls.

At the end of two years at Ashdown, Boris's mastery of classics was acknowledged by his entry into Eton as a King's Scholar, a remarkable achievement which classed him among Eton's elite. He left Ashdown House with a glowing testimonial praising his optimism, gamesmanship, debating skills, and with no criticism about his character or morals. Charlotte credited the school for instilling his ferocious ambition. His critics would later say that feeding that ambition damaged his character. His own only criticism of Ashdown was corporal punishment. 'I remember being so enraged at being whacked for talking at the wrong moment,' he wrote, 'that it has probably given me a lifelong distrust of authority.' His other legacy was to arrive at Eton in 1977 with a perfected Wodehousean performance.

Chapter 2

Effortlessly Superior

With his mop of blond hair, wearing his scholar's gown over his tails and white tie, Alexander Johnson stood out among Eton's 1,200 pupils. For more than most of the entrants, the school exposed him to a new world. Boris's ambitions were transformed. The provost's introductory speech encouraged the scholar to regard himself as a future leader. No fewer than eighteen Old Etonians had been prime minister and, as Robert Birley, a famous former head master had said, 'We are turning out the human material to run the nation.' With brutal expectations, Eton chose its elite with an emphasis on winning. Each pupil was bestowed with a 'sense of his own importance' and instilled with a conviction that nothing was impossible. While emphasising courtesy, bearing and a duty to care for society, scholars felt protected by a glass ceiling through which others could not break.

Eton liberated Boris. During the ransack of his room by other pupils, his passport was found and defaced – de Pfeffel became Pee-Pee – and his fellow pupils, amused by his non-establishment second name, decided to call him Boris rather than Alexander. Charlotte noticed how Eton changed him. He became a bare-knuckle boy, anxious in full public view to get everything out of life. 'He was a very good member of College,' said John Lewis, his housemaster. 'Humorous, loyal and, in the politest possible way, irreverent.' These qualities were attractive to others, who enjoyed him quoting Nigel Molesworth ('girly swot', 'down with skool'), and shared his obsession for *Private Eye*. Combined with P. G. Wodehouse, a new person was emerging.

The happiness was interrupted during his summer holidays at Nethercote in 1978. Stanley told his children that he and Charlotte were divorcing. They had been married for fifteen years. 'Why did you have us?' Boris asked his father alongside the three other children. Stanley would subsequently claim not to understand why his marriage collapsed, or whether his children suffered, 'because I never asked them'. Charlotte made no secret to their friends about her reason for demanding an end: 'I couldn't stay with him. He was inaccessible, not to say completely unfaithful.' His flippant insincerity, she said, was intolerable. Her close friends in Brussels knew that the fact that she was no longer prepared to put up with the violence was the tipping point. She also revealed Stanley's violence to Nick Wahl, a charming American academic whom she had met that year in Brussels at a dinner hosted by Roy Jenkins, the Labour politician serving as the European Commission's president. The following morning, Wahl came to see her paintings and then invited her to Paris where he lived. Since Stanley was, as usual, away, she accepted and began a regular commute. Her children endured benign neglect. Clive Williams, the classics teacher at Ashdown, noticed that Jo, the most gifted of the four children, 'became very quiet'.

'I was upset when they broke up,' was the limit of Boris's disclosure in 2004, adding, 'It had some effect. They handled it brilliantly.' In truth, Stanley's violence has forever haunted Boris. 'My father promised me that they wouldn't divorce,' he told a girlfriend years later, 'and I could never forgive him for that.' The 'divorce' was code for Stanley's rage towards Charlotte. What followed compounded the damage. They were abandoned as children after the divorce. They had to bring themselves up. They had no home.

The family house in Primrose Hill was sold and Charlotte bought a two-bedroom maisonette in Elgin Crescent, Notting Hill Gate, for herself and the four children. By installing partitions, three extra bedrooms were created. With little money, Charlotte survived by selling her paintings and letting out the bedrooms during term time. 'There was nothing in the fridge,' recalled Rachel.

'There wasn't much to eat.' Thereafter, Stanley declared, he had little influence on his children. 'I paid for all the children's education,' he insisted. Financed by his EU salary, the school payments were reduced by Eton's and Bryanston's scholarships. But, Charlotte recalls, the Fawcetts also made regular contributions. The schools, said Stanley, were responsible for his children's fate. The children disagreed. During the holidays they were often alone in Notting Hill Gate while Charlotte was in Paris, or they travelled unaccompanied to Brussels, and later to New York after Wahl moved there, joined by Charlotte.

Before his return to Eton at the end of the summer, Rachel noticed Boris's insecurity, as did a visitor who entered the table-tennis room at Nethercote and saw Boris banging Leo's head into the wall because his younger brother had just beaten him. In Boris's world, winning was essential. Etonians were about to witness his determination to defeat others.

The contrasts in the school were unique. Boris found himself surrounded by the children of Britain's aristocracy with seemingly unlimited wealth who had also suffered difficult childhoods. 'We were the children of fathers who failed their sons and created troubled boys,' recalled one early friend. Boris shared that destabilising neglect. The pain, said Rachel, made him impetuous. The romanticism of his beloved classics justified his recklessness. In Greek and Roman literature, there is contempt for the risk averse: fortune favours the bold, sacrifice is noble and even the brave are prepared to die in the ditch. Like magic, after reading Jasper Griffin's lucid *Homer on Life and Death*, he had understood the *Iliad* and the *Odyssey*, the principal characters of Athens, their relationship between death and glory, and that there could be no glory without death. According to Homer's *Iliad*, heroes are more virtuous than the gods because mortality compels them to develop the supreme virtue of courage.

Boris also found a hero, Pericles, a revered Athenian who, with charisma and shameless populism, pleased the crowds to win constant re-election. Blending the influences – Wooster, Molesworth, *Just William* and Pericles – Boris developed a unique oratorical style in the school debates combined with the belief that every speech must include humour. But unlike Stanley, he remained noticeably sensitive about his audience, always searching for approval. In the same way, he was loyal in sport, leading the charge in rugby, a zealous overperformer, excising his unstable background.

Poor, scruffy, haunted yet shrewd and able to conceal his self-doubt, Boris gradually emerged as a leader, usually captain of the team. He chose his friends, not for their wealth, but to share their 'parentlessness'. Roger Clarke, at Eton thanks to his adopted parents' sacrifice, enjoyed long discussions about literature and admired Boris's 'slightly wonky poetry jukebox'. Blessed with an excellent memory, Boris could recite hundreds of poems, Shakespeare sonnets and the first hundred lines of the *Iliad* in Greek. His more infamous friends were Charles Spencer, the brother of Diana, later Princess of Wales, and Darius Guppy, a louche, iconoclastic Anglo-Iranian. All three shared emotional hardship during their childhood.

Boris and Charles Spencer shared an interest in writing. Frequently, Boris mentioned his father – dubbed 'Stanley the Steel' – as a writer, mirroring his need to emulate and outperform Stanley. As in all his friendships with men, Boris disguised his hurt and solitude beneath brash humour and personal warmth. Without revealing his true thoughts, especially to Spencer, he nevertheless sought his approval. That summer, Spencer invited Boris to Spain. He returned dazzled by Spencer's fame and fortune. In return, Spencer was invited to Nethercote. The viscount was noticeably appalled by the conditions but soon enjoyed the games – especially 'Murder in the Dark' – and the drinking. Darius Guppy was not invited to Nethercote. Boris's relationship with that 'exotic creature' was unconventional. Byronic and romantic about mysterious cult forces, Guppy's exaggerated qualities amused Boris, especially his obsession with ghosts and witches. Like Boris, Guppy sought reassurance. Some doubted whether in Eton's fiercely competitive atmosphere those were genuine friendships. Etonians were not encouraged to be mutually supportive, but rather to take each other down. In any event, unlike his contemporaries in the school, in 1979 Boris was not just a romantic adolescent but also was beguiled by politics.

On 4 June, Founder's Day, Stanley paid a rare visit to Eton, to watch the annual cricket match on Agar's Plough. Parking his dilapidated Fiat alongside Bentleys and Rolls-Royces, his car stood out for many reasons, especially because the scratched paintwork was covered with 'Vote Johnson' stickers. For some months, Stanley had sought a parliamentary seat. The Labour government was collapsing and Margaret Thatcher was on the eve of entering Downing Street that May. To have become a candidate required Stanley to cultivate relationships. His early efforts had been sabotaged by his own risky language and careless attitudes. When asked in Leicester whether he had ever previously visited the city, he replied, 'No, but I have often walked through Leicester Square.' Charlotte noticed that while Stanley had always chortled about rejection, Boris learned not to tread on people's toes and, unlike his father, to be kind. Charlotte credited herself with inculcating in her children genuine politeness.

After repeated failures, Stanley was finally placed that year on the shortlist for East Hampshire in Europe's first parliamentary elections. His competitor was Bill Cash, an old friend from Oxford. Johnson won the nomination for the safe Tory seat. 'Stanley,' recalled Cash, 'was not a Tory and he had no political convictions. He was just passionate about environmental laws.' Three days after the cricket match, Stanley won the election. He drove Boris down to Portsmouth for the count. On the way, the Fiat caught fire and all the rosettes were singed. Just days before his fifteenth birthday, Boris watched his father, wearing a burnt rosette, claim victory and, as the new MEP, bask in the applause. There was no prepared speech, merely an outpouring of words intended only to grip the audience's attention and without much care about their accuracy. Success, Boris evidently concluded, depended on an energetic performance and good jokes.

Within months, Stanley was disillusioned with politics. Life in the impotent European Parliament, he discovered, was uninteresting. He applied again to be a candidate for election to Westminster.

'I made some silly jokes,' he admitted, 'and didn't get the seat.' He abandoned his parliamentary ambitions and returned to a post in the Brussels Commission. By then, Boris had learned some of the lessons of his father's failure. Unlike Stanley, he recognised the importance of concentration, beliefs and principles; and details were more valuable than generalities, although as the master of opportunism he often struggled to implement all those lessons. When faced with unfortunate difficulties, Boris embraced one motto that Stanley preached: 'Nothing matters very much and most things don't matter at all.' And, he could add, avoid apologising.

At school, Boris had established a relationship with one particular teacher – Martin Hammond, a noted classicist. Hammond was delighted to encounter a student who not only shared his enthusiasm for Latin and Greek but also shone as an outstanding intellect. In September 1980, he wrote to Stanley: 'I've found Boris a quite delightful person, a real life-enhancer. I like his open friendliness of manner and his ready wit.' Seven months later, Hammond again wrote to praise Boris for 'asserting his intellectual ascendancy powerfully but modestly'. His caveat was that the sixteen-year-old could undermine his ability as a 'considerable scholar' and 'a classicist of real distinction, one of the best we've had for years' by a lack of focus and tardiness to deliver his homework on time.

Proud of what he called 'my benevolent disinterest', Stanley ignored the warning. 'I didn't read Hammond's reports,' he says, 'or perhaps I gave them a cursory read, but I never sat with the children to discuss their reports or told Boris to behave.' He rarely went to 'tedious' parents' evenings. 'I wouldn't want to take up the teachers' time,' he explained. Regarding his eldest son's education, Stanley's only stricture to Boris was, 'If you're working hard, don't show it. You should be paddling underneath but show effortless superiority.' Hammond was invited once for dinner with Stanley but Boris was not mentioned.

Stanley was focused on his new marriage to Jenny Kidd, a young widow and the stepdaughter of Teddy Sieff, the chairman of Marks & Spencer. Within one year, Jenny gave birth to Julia. Between his marriage and daughter's birth, Stanley's relationship with his other four children changed. They found that there was no bedroom provided at their father's new home in Brussels. All four blamed Jenny for the rupture. Jo in particular found the distancing from Stanley difficult. Over the following years, Stanley and his new family would create a separate existence, whitewashing the reasons for the breakdown of Stanley's first marriage and rejecting any description of Stanley which did not accord with their version.

In 1981 Boris was elected to Pop, the society for Eton's most popular and outstanding pupils. Spencer joined him, as did Guppy who, unlike Boris, was forced as a Non-PLU – 'Not People Like Us' – to campaign for his election to Pop. For some, Guppy was 'exotic' while for others he was 'slimy'. For his admirers, Guppy's self-mythologising was electric. Working himself into a frenzy, he held his audience's attention by boasting, 'I'm off to fight the Russians.' On another occasion, proffering his pilot's licence, he related how in mid-air he had frightened a passenger by turning off the plane's engine. Styling himself as a poet and womaniser – he had sex before anyone else in his year – he beguiled Boris by his adventures with the mother of a London friend. Still a virgin, Boris was impressed by Guppy's account of regularly slipping through a garden window into the married woman's Chelsea house. Later, Boris offered stories about himself, boasting about sex with some of the family's au pairs and about a relationship with Alex de Ferranti, a school friend of Rachel's. Sex had become ever more important in his life. The wonder of male superiority in ancient civilisations was free sex and unrestrained relationships enjoyed without rancour or guilt. In ancient Greece, endless sex was perfectly acceptable. Christianity, Boris would later curse, suppressed that idyllic world.

Fortunate that he could read and absorb textbooks much faster than others, he began busking his studies. Disliking solitariness, he was immersed in rugby, cricket, debating, acting, learning to play the piano and running the Political Society. In everything, Boris sought to excel and, with the exception of the piano, succeeded. In rugby and the wall game, Eton's unique test of brawn and courage, he led the pack, renowned for hurling himself – do or die – at his opponents. Reckless to some, he loved the uncontrolled aggression – breaking bones and egos – with one objective: to win. The price for his hyperactivity was angry teachers, annoyed by his tardiness and waning diligence. Conformity had become for him an anathema.

'Rubbish,' growled Eric Anderson, a remarkable English teacher and later head master of Eton, while Boris was reading an essay about a subject which bored him. And if he was bored he was idle. 'Unacceptable,' carped the drama teacher after Boris failed to learn his lines for his part as the king in *Richard III* and stuck slips of paper on the props across the stage. 'Johnson's atrocious acting did not quite destroy this production,' was the sentiment of the review. Boris was perfecting the art of playing himself, but as an actor he was wooden. Busking and cutting corners annoyed some, but his jokes and good nature appeased the rest. The casualties were miffed. Roger Clarke, the joint editor for three months with Boris of *Chronicle*, the school magazine, was shocked when Boris disappeared leaving Clarke to do all the work. If the choice was sport or engaging in the solitary editorship of the magazine, Boris chose the fun. Clarke paid a high price. He failed exams to win a school scholarship – which still rankles forty years later.

In April 1982, Hammond issued a stark warning to Boris's parents about their unconventional showman son: 'Boris really has adopted a disgracefully cavalier attitude to his classical studies and the scandal . . . would be if he did drop a grade at A level through sheer fecklessness.' Hammond concluded that his prize pupil 'sometimes seems affronted when criticised for what amounts to a gross failure of responsibility (and surprised at the same time that he was not appointed Captain of School for next half) . . . I think he honestly believes that it is churlish of us not to regard him as an exception, one who should be free of the network of obligation which binds everyone else.'

Stanley did not read the report, while Charlotte urged Boris to improve but that did not influence his teacher's stark conclusion at the end of the academic year: 'Boris has something of a tendency to assume that success and honours will drop into his lap: not so, he must work for them.' Nevertheless, as one of the school's most popular pupils, a charmer and a friend to everyone, Boris was elected a member of Pop, Eton's elite club of elected prefects. The appointment brought duties and influence, the first rung on the 'greasy pole' to power.

Hammond's criticism spoke of Eton's ambition to stretch pupils and juggle their lives so they learned the true sense of self-worth. 'You have to give them the tools to shape their destiny and change the world,' said a later head master. 'We should be unashamed about excellence and celebrate elitism. But also teach how to deal with failure and sticking with it. Be ambitious, have self-belief but don't be arrogant.'

With Hammond's encouragement, Boris won a place to study classics at Balliol, one of Oxford's top colleges. A first in Greats, classics teachers believed, was a passport to a dignified life, not necessarily rich but correct in a social and moral sense. That myth hardly matched Boris's lifestyle or his aspirations. He did not seek a conventional, dignified life. Content to be the insider's outsider, he sought to be flamboyantly exceptional, a trait Hammond recognised and condemned. Winning the Balliol scholarship irritated his teacher. Hammond disliked his pupil's 'effortless superiority', excelling without apparently much effort. 'My fear,' wrote Hammond in his last message to Stanley in January 1983, 'is that Boris may take his easy-going ways with him to Balliol and add to the statistics of Etonians who do little work at Oxbridge.' Anticipating that Boris would not work hard enough to win a first, Hammond concluded that despite his 'very sharp intelligence . . . I think it true to say that Boris has no real academic bent, and he'll be an easier prey than some to the temptations of Oxford life.'

Hammond's judgement was accurate. In his farewell to Eton, Boris inserted in the leaving book a photograph of himself wearing two scarves and holding a machine gun, with his pledge to score 'more notches on my phallocratic phallus'. A bold gesture, bordering on inappropriate, but nothing if not memorable. Two years later, the relatively invisible David Cameron recorded a forgotten message in Eton's leaving book.

Chapter 3

Uncertain Star

Fellow students would later say that Boris arrived in Oxford in 1983 planning to reach the Cabinet by the age of thirty-five. Eton and Balliol are enviable starts for those with political ambitions. Eton has produced innumerable Cabinet ministers and dozens of Balliol graduates have become famous statesmen. The added ingredients to fuel Boris's ambition were observing Stanley's attempts to become a politician and his own admiration of Roman and Greek history. Students of history often become mesmerised by a particular character. For Boris, fascinated by the two ancient civilisations' outstanding leaders, he unashamedly sought to emulate his heroes. Adopting not only their ideas but also their oratorical style to win popular appeal, he dreamt of hearing millions applaud his achievements. The first steps to advance his ambitions coincided with an unusual burst of heroics and leadership.

The year 1983 was a watershed in Britain – the eve of a revolution. In the wake of her victory in the Falklands the previous year, Margaret Thatcher won a landslide general election and the country was about to shake off the shackles of a socialist economy and the label as 'the sick man of Europe'. The nightmare of the 1970s was over. Starting with Ted Heath's 'three-day week', through endless strikes, shortages and devaluation ending with the destructive Winter of Discontent in 1979, the decade had been worse than a waste. Ever since Harold Wilson imposed socialism on Britain after 1964, the country's decline had been marked by a crippling brain drain. To escape confiscatory taxation and punitive state control, the most talented of Britain's wealth creators had fled abroad to earn their fortunes. For Boris, bred as a natural Conservative by his father and Eton, Thatcher was the harbinger of a new dawn and new hope. Boris had just enjoyed a gap year in Australia with Hillie, his father's sister and his cousins, teaching Latin and English in Geelong Grammar, the country's leading private school. He returned with little to say about his experience but proudly wearing Stubbies shorts and R. M. Williams boots.

Balliol excelled in teaching classics. Jasper Griffin, the author of *Homer on Life and Death*, was the college's fellow in classical literature. To be taught by a cult figure famous for his wit, enthusiasm and scholarship, enthused the new arrival. Less exciting were Boris's fellow students in the common room. Most were 'to the left of the Communist Party', observed Anthony Kenny, a philosophy teacher and Balliol's master, and 'Trots were the main people so Boris did not find it congenial. As a conventional Tory, he preferred palling up with fellow Etonians.' The most notable were Charles Spencer and Darius Guppy at Magdalen. Eventually, Boris also met David Cameron. Since Cameron was two years younger and had been neither a King's Scholar nor elected to Pop, Boris would honestly claim to have only the vaguest memory of his new acquaintance. Boris's most notable friend was Justin Rushbrooke, a Harrovian living in the neighbouring room at Balliol and also studying classics. Unlike Boris, Rushbrooke was not ambitious and uninterested in fame.

Drawing on his experiences at Eton then perfected in front of elite students in Australia, Boris arrived with a mature showman's hunger for celebrity and ultimately election as president of the Oxford Union, the student debating society. Famous throughout the world for the high quality of debates and the star guests invited to stand in its hallowed chamber, the Union cast a spell over every student aspiring to impress themselves upon history. The Union was a natural magnet for Boris. Standing in raffish clothes at the Union bar, he entertained his audience as the life and soul of the party (although he was markedly reluctant to pay for drinks). Some would say that his routine was a camouflage to protect himself from rejection but they would be mistaken. Although sensitive to criticism, he was fearless when he challenged his opponents in Union debates.

Facing other students and occasionally famous guests, the new arrival immediately demonstrated his established and repeated music-hall routine rehearsed at Eton. After patting his pockets to ask his audience 'Where am I? Am I in the wrong place?', he started off in the rhythm and deliberate hesitation of Churchill's speeches to support one side of the argument, then switched to advocate the opposing argument leaving the audience baffled but intrigued. Next, he appealed to the audience's sympathy by highlighting his own emotional vulnerability. To win laughs and applause, he appeared to forget his lines, although that was often a well-concealed truth to manage the repetition of old jokes. 'Humour is a utensil that you can use to sugar the pill and get important points across,' he would say. While his opponents stuck to the normal Oxford Union rules, posing as veteran politicians to make themselves appear as authentic, Boris set his own rules to appear more honest than his rivals. Then, with the audience's attention and embrace, he made his pitch as a trustworthy orator who would not try to fool them. Debating at the union about the abolition of capital punishment, he impressed Toby Young, a fellow student, as 'something of Nietzsche's *Übermensch*. He had an electrifying, charismatic presence of a kind I'd only read about in books before.' With his imposing build and huge head decked with an unruly mop of blond hair, his way of speaking projected, recalled Young, 'a state of advanced dishevelment and a sense of coiled strength, of an almost tangible will to power. He was the finished article.'

Within weeks of the new term, as the unrivalled star at the Union, the student gossip was about 'this amazing person just up from Eton'. Even at this stage, a few mentioned him as a future prime minister. He was not the cleverest but possessed a magic combination of intelligence, wit, cunning and exhibitionism.

His showmanship disturbed Charlotte when she visited Boris at Balliol with Nick Wahl, a graduate of Nuffield College. Beneath her son's sparkle, she saw that his childhood grief about his parents' relationship lingered. Ignoring his mother's new happiness and Wahl's warmth towards the Johnson children, Charlotte noticed how Boris 'hated Nick'. Normally shy in one-to-one encounters and uneasy to look people in the eye, he was, Charlotte concludes, 'jealous about Stanley. He wanted his parents to be married. Boris's reaction was primitive.'

Boris needed a soulmate, someone with whom he could speak heart-to-heart. That, he found, was impossible with men. Only a woman could ever be his confidante. His requirements rarely changed: good-looking, intelligent and sophisticated. On that scale, few girls in Oxford exceeded Allegra Mostyn-Owen, a student at the neighbouring Trinity College. Students spoke of Allegra as one of Oxford's most beautiful women, a judgement confirmed when she was photographed by David Bailey for the cover of the re-vamped aristocratic *Tatler* magazine, which transformed her into the most desirable trophy. Her father, William Mostyn-Owen, was a landowner and a director of the auction house Christie's; her mother, Gaia Servadio, was a well-known Italian journalist. The family lived in an imposing house at Woodhouse in Shropshire, and also owned Aberuchill, a seventeenth-century castle in Scotland. 'I don't know how many bedrooms there are,' Gaia Servadio had once said about the castle, conjuring the impression that her Eton- and Cambridge-educated husband was rich.

Allegra was an amazing catch way beyond any student's approach. Except for Boris. During the first term, he arrived in her room with a bottle of wine for a party, only to discover it was the wrong night. He stayed, they shared the bottle and Allegra, despite her many boyfriends in London, became attracted because 'I'd never met anyone like Boris. I felt happy and relaxed. He was non-threatening, so easy and he made me laugh.' His striking hair, use of absurdly unusual words and his self-entitlement as an Eton scholar and head of Pop made her feel special: 'I felt secure with Boris.'

He was also cool. Unlike the proposals and declarations of love from others, Boris just made endless jokes. Over the following weeks, he dispatched funny messages through the colleges' internal mail to his new girlfriend in the self-conscious style described in

Evelyn Waugh's *Brideshead Revisited*. As they established a close relationship, Allegra's attraction to Boris intensified.

*

After a trip to Turkey to trace his family history and some time at a kibbutz, Boris returned to Oxford for his second year ready to be shaped by his classical education and become a confident politician. Sincerity is not always relevant to classical studies. Originality of thought is prized, even though it can occasionally lead to flights of fancy that have little purchase on evidence. As in chess, the pieces are there, and new and ingenious ways to move them and dismay others can become an obsessive goal for bright students. Verses and prose are marked by teachers according to the quality of the rendering, not for innovation; but a critical understanding of great poetry and literature requires intensive thought and sympathetic engagement. More than other subjects in the Humanities, classics supplies a framework for thought, accuracy and self-confidence. In the classics, there is grammar, there is scansion, there is an apt quotation and a wealth of historical and political teaching concerned not just with winners but with the foundational ideas of society and civilisation. As a grammarian and student of rhetoric, the classicist is a master of language, seeking to persuade others of the merit of his case and of himself. In short, the classicist cannot be phoney; but a lesser student may be something of a bluffer, as a good chess player can be, by giving the impression to his or her opponent by mere verbal dexterity that they are pursuing a deep and well-thought-out plan.

In drawing on the classics, Boris's critics would say he replaced sincerity with parody, an act and a promise where his ruthlessness was dressed up as integrity. That would become Boris's smokescreen while concealing the weakness of his classical education. Unlike other classical scholars, however eloquent, Boris failed to master the dialectic and forensically destroy his opponent's arguments. Like Cicero, when Boris lacked a good case, he relied on improvisation, bluster and playing to the gallery.

Boris's goal now was to be elected president of the Union, a milestone for many aspiring politicians. His plan coincided with Margaret Thatcher's new government being threatened by Marxist trade unionists, especially the miners, in a febrile political atmosphere.

Like his predecessors, Boris ignored the Union's rule expressly forbidding canvassing for support. He recruited what he called 'a disciplined and deluded collection of stooges' to gather the vote. The delusion, he admitted, was to promise his 'stooges' a return favour to help their own election campaign for other posts. Their relationship, he later admitted, was 'founded on duplicity' because he could not support every stooge who helped him. Each of them 'wants so much to believe that his relationship with the candidate is special that he shuts out the truth . . . The terrible art of the candidate is to coddle the self-deception of the stooge.'

Boris entered the presidential race to win. His defeat taught him a salutary lesson. He had limited his appeal to Etonians and other public-school undergraduates, isolating himself from the majority of students. That was folly. 'Boris hated losing,' recalled Allegra. 'I was uninterested in his Union stuff but I agreed that he could invite potential supporters to my parties. Hacking to get their vote.' Allegra was also reluctant to hear Boris speak at the Union. She went just twice, once to listen to the Greek actress and politician Melina Mercouri. 'I wasn't interested,' says the strong-willed Allegra. Her steely demeanour added to her attraction for Boris, if not for his close friends. The antipathy was mutual. 'Charles Spencer,' she declares, 'wasn't charming or popular so it was hard to understand the basis of his friendship with Boris – except that he was useful.' She was also critical of Darius Guppy: 'He was an irritant who needed reassurance that he was liked, but his exaggerated qualities amused Boris.'

More than ever, bohemian rule-breakers like Guppy attracted Boris. Despite Boris's financial constraints and middle-class background, Boris shared with Guppy an Old Etonian's aristocratic indifference to bourgeois conventions. Together with Charles Spencer, they jointly edited *Tributary*, a magazine inherited from Toby

Young. Boris firmly refused to continue its seditious exposure of students' embarrassments. Aiming to stand for election again, he did not want any enemies. He wanted to be loved. The exception were the victims of the Bullingdon Club.

Limited to about twenty-four members, the club united Old Etonians and rich progenies to a night of excessive drinking and riotous behaviour to enjoy wrecking restaurants, bars and bedrooms. This was occasionally accompanied by performances of buxom strippers. Among the well-known members were David Cameron and George Osborne. As a pinnacle of reckless fun and debauchery, Boris adored the club's notoriety. Among his victims was Matthew Leeming who spotted Boris arriving to destroy his flat. 'I'm calling the police,' he shouted to protect himself. Radek Sikorski recalled that while asleep in the middle of the night, about twelve students led by Boris burst into his room, trashed all his belongings and, at the end, he heard Boris announce, 'Congratulations man, you've been elected.' Boris was also present when a flowerpot was thrown through a restaurant window and the premises wrecked. 'The party ended up,' he would later say, 'with a number of us crawling on all fours through the hedges of the Botanical Gardens and trying to escape police dogs. And once we were in the cells, we became namby-pambies.'

Boris's enthusiasm for the Bullingdon's raucous world stemmed partly from P. G. Wodehouse's portrayal of the Drones Club, in which loyalty to one's old school chums is the principal and unbreakable law. To outsiders, the Bullingdon cast were rich Old Etonian idiots who had never grown up, behaved like hooligans, treated women as goddesses or monsters, had no apparent parents, and were alienated from the lower classes. Boris was different. The Bullingdon mix for him was not to eulogise the exceptional qualities of Etonians but about embracing an anarchic passion to break rules, undoubtedly inherited from his father.

In 2013, Boris admitted that he looked back at the Bullingdon days with a sense of 'deep, deep self-loathing'. He added, 'This is a truly shameful vignette of almost superhuman undergraduate arrogance, toffishness and twittishness. But at the time you felt it was wonderful to be going round swanking it up. Actually I remember the dinners being incredibly drunken.' Since it was hard to get Boris to pay for drinks, extracting money to compensate for his vandalism proved impossible.

Membership of the Bullingdon did not harm his second attempt to be elected Union president in November 1985. He had learned the lesson. Since hardline Tories had an impossible hurdle to overcome, he would pose as a member of the new Social Democrat Party which combined right-wing deserters from the Labour Party and some Liberals. He also spoke in favour of Israel in order to get the Jewish vote and, to get the nascent green vote, about his passion for the environment. Grasping the crudity of elections, Boris, like Stanley, was not a conviction politician. 'He wasn't entrenched in his opinions,' recalls Allegra. 'I was an SDP Keynesian and he was a Thatcherite spouting trickle-down nonsense. He wasn't a libertarian.' Some, including Frank Luntz, an American student who would become a famous pollster and who had initially supported his efforts, were shocked by Boris's opportunism. But as so often in Boris's life, his critics' anger was fuelled by their own dissatisfaction. Luntz, called 'Frank Y Fronts' by Boris, did not enjoy Oxford. Unsuccessful with girls, he could not understand the class system and eventually resented helping Boris.

Among Boris's stooges was Michael Gove, the adopted son of the owner of a fish-processing business. Educated at a Scottish independent school and studying English at Lady Margaret Hall, a minor college compared to Balliol, Gove was lower in Oxford's social hierarchy than Boris, but nevertheless eagerly supported his election. During his strategic campaign, Boris was hyper-conscious of attacks on his own character, especially by Lloyd Evans and Aidan Hartley, the joint student editors of a satirical magazine. They planned to ridicule Boris as an incompetent exiled Armenian chicken farmer. In the middle of the night, Boris stormed into Hartley's Oxford home and demanded that the piece should not be published. Being a chicken farmer, Boris declared, was acceptable, but 'incompetent' was outlawed. The article was dropped. The two students – who would later write for the *Spectator* under Boris's editorship – understood that

Boris saw himself in Oxford as special. He wanted others to believe in his destiny and favoured those prepared to empower his myths. Damage to his image was intolerable.

Boris convincingly won the election. In the aftermath, he wrote an unbeatable account of campaigning for the post in *Oxford Myth*, a witty anthology edited by his sister Rachel. Some have damned his elegant description of how he recruited gullible students including Gove to work for his campaign in return for false promises as Boris congratulating himself for the deception, but that's foolish. In 2003 he explained: 'I think my essay remains the *locus classicus* of the English genre of bogus self-deception.' He captured the unique self-absorbed madness of student politics. Yet, critics insist, his essay is a confession of dishonest politicking. Whether he told lies or allowed the electorate to be deceived depends on the mindset of the commentator. Anthony Kenny was equivocal: 'So far as I know, he told no actual lies, but his strategy recalled Macaulay's words about the difference between lying and deceiving.' Talleyrand, the French diplomat, 'never told a lie and deceived the whole world'. Boris's final sentence summarised the truth: 'The key thing seems to me that you pick up a load of self-knowledge.'

That summer, Boris went with his sister and Sebastian Shakespeare, another undergraduate who would become a noted journalist, to Spain and Portugal. Allegra came for part of the time, watching Boris and his sister filming wildlife, especially a chimpanzee sanctuary, for a charity campaigning against cruelty to animals. Allegra found the experience 'bizarre', and made arrangements to spend the nights with Boris at the homes of rich friends of her parents, leaving Rachel and Shakespeare to fend for themselves. 'It was awkward,' Allegra admits. She was 'not fond of Rachel' and decided to keep her distance. The stern woman found Rachel 'boastful. She was always projecting herself.'

Allegra returned early to Britain. Unknown to Rachel and Sebastian, Boris had proposed marriage to Allegra, although thirty-six years later she could not recall the circumstances. Insecure, with a fear of homelessness, Boris was to fulfil his ambition to marry up. Because his proposal was couched in uncertainties, she had agreed but was not completely committed. 'Boris's game plan,' she was convinced, 'was influenced by what Stanley had done.' His father had married a wealthy woman early and Boris decided to follow suit. In her absence, Boris was unsure whether his offer was wise. 'Should I marry Allegra?' Boris asked Shakespeare every night. 'You're too young,' Shakespeare replied, unaware that the marriage had already been agreed.

Boris's concealment and uncertainty illustrated a trait running throughout his life – his vacillation during his relationships with women. After agreeing to an idea, he then feared being trapped by reality and had second thoughts. Over the following decades, women would discover that Boris inhabited an inner or fantasy world. In those circumstances, they questioned whether his commitment was genuine. There was no doubt about his love for Allegra. His uncertainty was fear that he could not cope with her moods or with a permanent relationship. Even on the night before the wedding ceremony, he would ask a friend whether he should marry Allegra. 'Bit late now,' his friend replied.

After Christmas, Allegra's parents invited Boris skiing in La Plagne, France. To her mother's surprise, Boris arrived at the resort with a suitcase full of dirty sheets and no ski clothes. Standing at the top of a challenging black run in his tweeds, he launched himself downhill, zooming without fear or style over icy moguls to survive unscathed, thrilled by the danger. 'I am more or less addicted to the joy of hurtling myself down the slopes,' he would confess. Irritated by his appearance, Gaia Servadio was insulted by his disdain for Italian politics during dinner conversation, casting the government in Rome as a joke. Allegra's father shared Gaia's disapproval of their guest. 'What societies did you join?' Boris asked the fellow Old Etonian, knowing that William Mostyn-Owen had been neither a King's Scholar nor a member of Pop. Needling his host with one-upmanship delighted Boris. 'He's rapacious,' Mostyn-Owen warned his daughter. 'What do you see in him?' Servadio asked, a question she regularly repeated. At the end of the academic year and finals, Allegra announced their engagement. Both were still just twenty-three.

Insensitive about others, and even incurious about his future wife's character and limited ambition, Boris failed to grasp the reason Allegra rejected a job in Washington DC which had been arranged by her parents. 'I wasn't interested in that career stuff,' said Allegra, whose family wealth meant work was not essential. 'I wasn't ambitious and I needed reassurance,' she admitted. To relieve her solitariness and neediness, she relied on Boris's self-confidence. She did, however, reluctantly agree to work at the *Evening Standard* in London edited by Charles Wintour, her mother's close friend.

Towards the end of his final year, Boris had feared he would not get a first-class degree. Instead of entirely focusing during those last months on his studies, he had been diverted into Union politics, social life and sport. By then, his reputation among his tutors was mixed. Oliver Lyne, a Horatian scholar, was one of several unimpressed teachers. At a tutorial he told Boris, 'I'm not going to teach you, with you sitting there all drunk and crapulous.' Boris later recalled obtusely 'I dimly formed the thought that I could not logically be both drunk and crapulous at once, but somehow it wouldn't come out.'

'Probably the worst scholar Eton ever sent us – a buffoon and an idler,' the ancient historian Oswyn Murray declared. Neither were impressed by a student who either arrived unprepared or relied on his remarkable memory to recite passages but failed to show deep understanding. Others were sincerely positive. Jonathan Barnes, another tutor in ancient history, called Boris 'a good egg' while Jasper Griffin, the tutorial fellow of classical literature, was enthusiastic. Griffin and Anthony Kenny agreed to give Boris extra tuition to achieve a first, but it was too late. He was awarded an upper second. Forever, he was disappointed.

Chapter 4

Awakening

Two hundred guests were invited to Boris's wedding to Allegra on 5 September 1987 at West Felton church in Shropshire. Woodhouse, the Mostyn-Owens' country house, sitting in 1,500 acres, was the perfect setting for the reception. 'It was a very happy wedding day,' recalls Allegra, 'although my parents didn't like Boris.' Giving Guppy the task of collecting their wedding rings from Hatton Garden in London, Allegra sensed, was 'just inauspicious. I was side-tracked by Etonians.' The tension between the two families was a foreboding.

Unknown to Allegra, an argument had blown up the previous night. Stanley and Boris had stayed at the home of John Biffen, a well-known slightly eccentric Tory MP. Sarah Biffen was shocked by the Johnsons' behaviour at the pre-wedding dinner hosted by Lord Gowrie, also educated at Eton and Balliol, and his wife Alexandra. 'Stanley behaved disgracefully,' Sarah Biffen complained, 'sticking a sort of cine camera up everyone's nose.' He would compound his tactlessness by trying to make an impromptu speech at the wedding reception until Sarah Biffen abruptly silenced him. In the morning, Boris revealed that he did not have the required morning suit. Biffen agreed to lend him an old one and then Boris discovered he had no cufflinks. In Sarah Biffen's immortal damnation, 'The reason he didn't get married in my husband's shoes is that his feet were larger – he would have limped to the altar.' Boris wore his own shoes with holes in the soles. Both Boris and Stanley were insensitive to those blunders, just as Stanley was unaware of the Mostyn-Owens' disquiet about Stanley's flagrant infidelities. Since Allegra's parents were on the verge of separation for similar and other reasons, their sentiments may have been sanctimonious but Charlotte sensed their disapproval.

On the morning of the wedding, Charlotte arrived with her other children to a 'grand but uneasy' atmosphere. Gaia was 'difficult' and 'a terrible snob' casting 'her dissatisfied mood over everything'. Gaia disliked other women, Charlotte noticed; she spoke only about people's wealth and clearly disapproved of Boris. 'Gaia wanted Allegra to marry a lord or a rich man,' Charlotte knew. The premonitions were muddied. While Charlotte 'liked Allegra' and Allegra 'loved' Charlotte, Boris and Allegra seemed to expect the world at their feet. Allegra, Charlotte spotted, 'was strong-minded and would not compromise. There would be trouble. But because I liked her I did not warn Boris.' The best man was Leo, his younger brother and a favourite. After returning from a happy two-week honeymoon in Egypt, Boris was told that John Biffen had found their marriage certificate in his trousers. Boris had also lost his own wedding ring. 'I know where it is,' he reassured his bride, but never produced it.

Their first weeks living in unfashionable Olympia were unstable. Allegra found life on the *Evening Standard*'s famed Londoner's Diary irksome. Success as a journalist depends on survival in the gutter and swimming in the sewer. Allegra was unsuited to cajoling and charming the rich, famous and scurrilous to divulge embarrassing secrets. She left Fleet Street to become a solicitor. Boris was equally dissatisfied. Within one hour on his first day as a management consultant at £18,000 p.a. he admitted defeat. 'Try as I might,' he would recall, 'I could not look at an overhead projection of a growth-profit matrix and stay conscious.' Unlike his wife, to escape the commercial world he had discovered a sudden passion to be a journalist. Personable, masterful with words and intrigued by the exercise of power, it was a natural next step. By chance, he bumped into Miriam Gross, the arts editor of the *Daily Telegraph*. Impressed by his charisma and intelligence, Gross arranged for Boris to be introduced to *The Times*'s editor, Charlie Wilson. Hired as a trainee,

Boris was sent to the *Wolverhampton Express & Star* to learn the craft. Living in provincial lodgings was neither fun nor healthy for his new marriage, but did expose the Old Etonian to the reality of Britain's working class. Too many, he thought, lacked ambition and relied on benefits. Margaret Thatcher's glory was to destroy the poisonous welfarism of the 1970s and she became his hero.

His reunions in London with Allegra were uneasy. Seemingly depressed, she saw the glass was always half empty. Unlike their friends, she refused to host dinner parties and preferred restaurants but, conditioned by his parents' marriage, Boris was unaware of the brewing problems.

His arrival at the headquarters of *The Times* hardly improved their spirits. Working at the end of the news desk – the bottom of the heap – his chore was to rewrite stories supplied by news agencies, an unglamorous life for a man of destiny. Through graft, trial and error, he needed to master the skill of devising an 'angle' to enliven a dull story. So it was that the glamour boy was asked to rewrite a tedious report about the discovery of the 'Rosary', the palace of Edward II, at Hay's Wharf on the Thames Embankment. Boris decided that the story needed sexing up. In his rewrite he added, 'According to Dr Colin Lucas of Balliol College, Oxford, this is where the king enjoyed a reign of dissolution with his catamite Piers Gaveston, before he was gruesomely murdered.' A catamite is a boy kept for gay sex.

In his insubordinate manner, Boris ignored a salient fact – Piers Gaveston had been murdered in 1312 and construction of Edward's palace began in 1325. Not only could the catamite story not be true but Colin Lucas, Boris's godfather and Stanley's best friend, was not an expert in medieval Britain but in modern history, especially France in the eighteenth century. At the time, Lucas was a lowly tutor at Sheffield University but he was a Balliol graduate with ambitions to become a pre-eminent scholar.

Hurt by his fellow academics' scorn about his ignorance as reported by *The Times*, Lucas complained to Charlie Wilson. After hearing from Boris that the quotation was accurate, Lucas's objection was rejected. But after compounding his lie in a second article,

Boris was summoned by the editor. In his defence, Boris declaimed that most of the quotations in *The Times* were fabricated. Shocked by his insolence, the editor fired the anarchist. 'I was angry that Lucas complained to Wilson,' said Stanley indignantly. 'He put a whole new interpretation on the word "Godfather".'

Boris's good fortune was Miriam Gross, willing to help him escape from a sticky corner. She appealed to Max Hastings, her editor at the *Daily Telegraph*, to meet Boris. Since his appointment in December 1985, Hastings had notably improved the conservative newspaper. The military historian and formidable journalist appreciated fast-thinking mavericks and was unfussed by Boris's abrupt departure from *The Times*. As an individualist himself, Hastings appreciated that every young journalist learns from their mistakes. Just as he had been given chances through personal connections, Hastings was willing, in 1988, to give Boris an opportunity to shine, and to be booted out if he failed. The result was positive. Boris proved himself to be a remarkably fluent, unconventional fast writer with a self-confident style of writing, identifying himself with the contemporary *Telegraph* reader's political opinions – middle class and middle of the road. And he offered eccentricity. Asked to write an article for a skiing supplement, he focused on the importance of clipping the ski sticks behind before schussing down the piste. The only complaint was his congenital untidiness and unpunctuality.

Within a few months, Hastings decided that Boris would be an ideal correspondent in Brussels: French-speaking, knowledgeable about the EU and eager to puncture the EU's growing complacency and corruption. He arrived in summer 1988 just as Thatcher's Britain was booming and she had denounced in Bruges the EU's plan to transform the continent into a federalist state. Behind a smokescreen, Jacques Delors, the French president of the Commission, was plotting to build a European super-state with its own borders, its own currency, and eventually its own army. For the moment, the EU's bureaucrats were intent on imposing unwanted regulations on Britain, and that, Boris rightly sensed, was just the beginning. Welcoming him to Brussels were his father and Jenny, his stepmother.

While Boris was excited by the posting, Allegra was ambivalent.

First, she delayed her departure to Brussels by two months until her law exams were completed. Then, on arriving in Brussels, she disliked the apartment Boris had rented. To save money, he had rejected the flat used by his predecessor in the francophone town centre near other journalists and had chosen a dismal flat in a miserable Flemish suburb. 'Why did you do it?' asked Allegra, but she never extracted an explanation. Disheartened, she lacked the energy to even put up curtains. 'He was tight with money and he gave me none,' she says. 'He would always forget his wallet when we went shopping. I had to buy the food.' She relied on her income from family investments and her new job, promoting Italian cotton in the EU. Annoyingly, Boris also always used the red Fiat, a wedding present from her parents, so she was marooned. Yet, Allegra would always believe that Boris had married out of genuine love and not for money.

Dressed in a torn jacket, dirty trousers and a crumpled shirt, Boris began the daily routine of arriving at the Berlaymont, the European Commission's headquarters, for the briefing by the EU's spokesmen to over one hundred journalists representing the world's media. The club's rules dictated that being taken seriously by the Commission's staff was critical. But unlike other British besuited journalists, Boris did not feel beholden to curry favour with the well-paid Commission spokesmen serving platitudes about the EU's seamless achievements. With long experience of the institution and the Eurocrats' machinations during his school years when Stanley was employed as a Eurocrat, he felt no compunction to report uncritically the spokesmen's pronouncements. Why, he asked, should the EU's bureaucrats be assumed to be honest just because they were serious? Extracting the unvarnished truth about the Commission was difficult. First, because Commission officials often lied to protect their activities; and second, there was no single truth but just a conflict of policies between competing power groups.

Initially, to find his way, Boris charmed his competitors to give him help and advice. Acting the bumbling English gentleman, his image undermined his credibility. Joking, never malicious and always self-deprecating, his fellow journalists assumed as he glided past with a smile that he was an unthreatening innocent.

A succession of his reports overturned their assumption. 'Brussels recruits sniffers to ensure that Euro-manure smells the same,' appeared on the *Telegraph*'s front page. 'Threat to British pink sausages' was followed by reports from Boris about Eurocrats dictating the acceptable curve of bananas, the size of condoms, an order that women must return their old sex toys, that euro notes make people impotent, that euro coins make people sick, and a plan to blow up the Berlaymont because asbestos cladding made the building too dangerous to inhabit. Berated by their editors in London for missing good stories, Boris's rivals spluttered in outrage, 'Boris is making the stories up.' Embellishing was usually more accurate, but that was a charge rejected by his opponents. 'He was fundamentally intellectually dishonest,' said David Usborne of the *Independent*. 'He was serving his masters in a very skilful way . . . He was writing things without really believing in his heart what he was writing.' Sarah Helm, also of the *Independent*, agreed: Boris was 'a complete charlatan . . . His writing was a cheap thrill – a stunt and quite a dangerous stunt actually.' James Landale of *The Times* blasted: 'Boris told such dreadful lies, it made one gasp.' Their anger that his imprecision had become secondary to witticisms was ignored by the *Telegraph*'s editors. Max Hastings was a Eurosceptic keen to expose the idiocies of the Brussels bureaucrats. Boris's real success, ignored by his carping rivals, was to dredge up documents and decisions made by unknown Eurocrats intended to propel the EU into a federal state. 'Put that on page one,' his editors ordered. 'We never had a single complaint that Boris was lying,' says Jeremy Deedes, the newspaper's managing editor. 'Boris understood better than anyone what was going on in Brussels.' Their correspondent might be 'exaggerating but it was all too good to check. His reports were all correct in spirit if not in detail.'

Untroubled by the accusations, Boris was on a roll. For a man in a hurry to impress the world, his accusers were an undistinguished pack, regularly seen in the middle of the day gossiping in bars. He ignored those destined to be forgotten and constantly trawled the

Commission buildings looking for more scurrilous tales to feed his insurgency. Beating his competitors, he told Allegra, was bliss. 'He never lied,' she says loyally. 'He just has his own attitude to the truth.' Turning the circus upside down promised stardom, a mantra supported by Stanley.

'Exaggeration is OK,' said his father, the Eurocrat, 'because Boris had to ask, "How do I make my mark?"' An ironic herogram from Hastings was stuck on Boris's office wall: 'You know how highly I think of you but you must learn to be more pompous.' In return, Boris hero-worshipped Hastings, grateful for being catapulted to prominence.

Among Boris's most serious critics was Sonia Purnell, the number two in the *Telegraph*'s Brussels office. She would later write about 'rumours' that Douglas Hurd, the Foreign Secretary, had asked Hastings to fire Boris, but that was inaccurate. She would also write that 'the Foreign Office even set up a Boris unit, a team of people tasked with rebutting negative Boris stories or trying to stop them appearing in the first place'. That was an exaggeration. The European Commission, according to Charlie Pownall of the Foreign Office's communications team, did establish the 'Rapid Response Unit' to combat Euromyths but that was directed more against Christopher Booker and Richard Littlejohn, two other prominent British journalists. In Brussels, Purnell would later summarise Boris's demeanour as: 'under a well-cultivated veneer of disorganisation lay not so much a streak of aspiration as a torrent of almost frightening focus and drive'. That antagonism would later prompt Jeremy Deedes to visit Brussels. 'Purnell,' he concluded, 'always behaved as if the cards were dealt to her from the bottom of the pack. She was permanently disgruntled. She was tricky with a capital T.' Having agreed to lunch with Boris, Deedes went to the Commission's daily briefing. While one hundred journalists carefully wrote down the spokesman's announcements, Boris stood at the back, hands in his pockets not taking a single note. To Deedes's surprise, at the end, many journalists queued to ask Boris in different languages to explain what it all meant. For thirty minutes, he held court and belatedly the two went for an oyster lunch.

In the same year, Bill Cash, the Tory MP for Stafford and an early Eurosceptic, began to travel regularly to Brussels. His soulmate in the capital to explain the creeping federalism was Boris, whom he had known as a child. 'Boris was a fish out of water in Brussels,' says Cash, 'but he was buried in the detail. He was the only journalist who knew the detail of what was happening.' Boris believed in the idea of Europe – intellectually and emotionally – but as a committed libertarian was suspicious about the EU's ambitions to interfere in people's lives. On his return to London, Cash reported to Thatcher that Boris was 'in the game and on the game and telling things from the front line that are true'. Cash became so close to Boris that he would appoint the journalist as his literary executor and invited him to stay in his Shropshire manor house. 'We were never sure how many rooms he slept in,' he sighed cryptically.

In summer 1989, Boris and Allegra flew to Sharm El Sheikh for a holiday. 'The relationship was already creaking,' she says. Distressed by the break-up of her parents' marriage, she needed Boris's support but he, flippant and emotionally superficial, was indifferent to his depressed wife's low self-esteem. Living in his own space, his head swam with ideas and problems. His generosity of spirit, his desire to believe the best of people and a lack of pettiness and envy, did not extend to Allegra. That was 'girly blouse' and women's feelings did not matter. Lonely, self-doubting and locked in a competitive boys' game, he was reluctant to discuss his ambitions and never revealed to Allegra the pains of his childhood. To conceal his vulnerability, the guard never dropped. Oblivious to his wife's quirks, two needy and insecure people sat on an Egyptian beach and could not help each other.

Allegra had arranged to learn scuba-diving but became ill. Boris reported to her that the staff wanted to know what she did. 'I told them that your job is to keep Egyptian cotton out of Europe.' Later she wrote, 'This shows his spiteful side quite clearly.' As a half-Italian, she was also irked by what she called his 'ridiculous' Euroscepticism, and they disagreed about his support for Thatcher. Finally, she would be angry that Boris included diving as a hobby in

Who's Who despite failing to dive because, according to the instructor, he could not control his breathing.

On their return to Brussels, Boris made himself busy. 'He's married to his job,' concluded Allegra. 'He needs the adulation of others. He cannot thrive without that.' Spotting Allegra, one British journalist approached her, 'Could you please ask Boris to stop ruining my weekends?' 'He's ruining my weekends too,' she replied. The only diversion from work was visiting Stanley and Jenny in a Brussels suburb for Sunday lunch and a game of tennis. On reflection she realised that Boris's interest in culture and travel was limited. Other than the ancient classics, Shakespeare and Wodehouse, he barely read contemporary literature; he was uninterested in classical music, preferring the Rolling Stones, and seldom went to museums and art galleries. Moreover, he never took the opportunity to drive to Amsterdam or Paris: 'He wasn't interested in art. He was too interested in frantically writing about crisps or rushing off to Strasbourg.' When Allegra was fired from her job, he showed neither sympathy nor interest. Sitting alone in her undesirable flat, she couldn't find a career to satisfy herself but had enough money not to work. 'We rarely spent an evening together,' she muses. His refusal to be with her, she decided, was a blind spot he had inherited from Stanley: 'an inability to take women seriously'.

The final straw came in February 1990 when she cooked dinner for him one evening and he failed to return home. The following morning, she bought the *Telegraph* and read his story with a byline in Zagreb. Without telephoning her, he had accepted the offer of a trip on a special EU flight. His passport and a suitcase were kept in the office for that eventuality. Out to enjoy himself, he didn't really care what others thought. He telephoned his wife only after he returned to his office in Brussels. 'I didn't give him a hard time,' says Allegra. 'I didn't even ask why he hadn't called.' Unemployed, lonely and occasionally drinking herself to sleep, she quietly fumed about his selfishness and feared she was heading towards a breakdown similar to Charlotte's because of Stanley's behaviour. She returned alone to London.

In reality, she could not understand a competitive workaholic so unlike her own father. Gaia Servadio would blame Boris's demand for someone obedient and silent. 'My daughter wasn't that kind of person. Lacking self-confidence but strong-minded, she is very sensitive while Boris was very ambitious.' Allegra disagreed. Boris, she said, did not want a submissive wife. He wanted someone who enjoyed sharing the rough-and-tumble of life. But his selfish terms did not match her special needs. 'I was lonely in the marriage,' she told Matthew Leeming, a friend from Oxford, on what Leeming calls 'a manic high' in London.

Tearfully, Boris called Roger Clarke, his school friend, to fume that the public image of Allegra as the broken blossom, the Virginia Woolf-type, passive and aesthetic, was phoney. Under extreme emotional pressure, Boris's friends would discover, he sobbed. He next called Matthew Leeming to discuss how to repair the relationship. Losing public esteem because of her rejection, he feared, would be intolerable. 'He's an actor,' Leeming concluded, 'and actors remember the one person in the audience who didn't clap.' Briefly Boris and Allegra discussed divorce but agreed to try again. She would try to complete her interrupted law studies in London and commute to Brussels for weekends. At the law school she was seen with a boyfriend. Charlotte also heard from a friend that Boris was spotted with a woman in a Brussels restaurant. 'I was shocked,' she says. The marriage had unravelled fast. 'But I did nothing because Allegra wasn't easy and his own parents were not a shining example.'

During that summer of 1990, Boris was telephoned by Darius Guppy. His school friend had run into trouble. Earlier that year, he had called the New York police to claim that he had been tied up by thieves in a hotel room and they had stolen jewels worth £1.8 million. After convincing the police that a genuine theft had occurred, Guppy successfully claimed compensation from Lloyd's, the London insurers. Three months later, Guppy heard that Stuart Collier, a journalist on the *News of the World*, was investigating that the 'theft' had been staged by Guppy and a friend. After pocketing the profits from his fraud, Collier had been told, Guppy was offering the 'stolen' gems to Hatton Garden dealers.

In his telephone call to Boris, Guppy asked his friend to provide Collier's home address and telephone number. His purpose, he explained, was either to threaten Collier or have him beaten up. At the end of Guppy's first call, Boris refused to help. Guppy persisted. Responding to Guppy's demands for loyalty in their last conversation, Boris asked 'how badly' Collier would be injured. 'He will not have a broken limb or broken arm,' Guppy replied. 'He will not be put into intensive care or anything like that. He will probably get a couple of black eyes and a cracked rib or something like that.' As the conversation continued, Boris said, 'OK, Darry, I said I'll do it and I'll do it.' But Boris did not 'do it'. Collier remained unaware of the threat and was unharmed; and Boris forgot the call.

A second seminal moment came two weeks later. Unlike the Guppy call, Boris realised at the time how much it would influence his future, albeit for very different reasons. By then, Allegra had been persuaded by Boris to attempt a permanent reconciliation. Returning to Brussels at the end of September 1990, she started a new course in European law. She had barely settled in before Boris flew to Rome for a summit of EU leaders. In a critical moment, Boris witnessed Helmut Kohl and François Mitterrand, the leaders of Germany and France, trap or 'handbag' Thatcher. Both countries wanted her approval for Europe to forge an economic and monetary union. Robustly, she refused. That would lead, she said, to a political union. She walked out. Kohl and Mitterrand illegally dismissed the British veto and agreed to launch Europe towards a single currency through the exchange rate mechanism (ERM). Boris saw for himself the power wielded by Berlin and the humiliation of Thatcher. 'I was there,' he would write, 'when they ambushed Margaret Thatcher with conclusions that the British thought had been explicitly rejected.' The two men had treated Britain's veto with disdain. Europe, Boris realised, would no longer remain the economic free trade area Britain had joined in 1972 but, guided by the Commission's centralising mission, was heading towards a European federal state. Despite her protest and against Britain's interests, Thatcher was squeezed by her Chancellor John Major and other Europhiles to join the ERM. In mid-November, as the power struggle intensified, the senior Tory and former Defence Secretary Michael Heseltine, desperate to succeed Thatcher, forced a leadership contest leading to Thatcher's resignation. Distrusted by many, Heseltine lost the election and Major, the least talented, slipped through to become prime minister.

Electrified, Boris followed those events in Brussels. As ever, they occupied far more of his attention than his troubled wife, whom he'd persuaded to attempt a permanent reconciliation. Allegra now once again returned to London. Morose, Boris met Matthew Leeming in Dublin. 'I've been living a lie,' he told their Oxford friend. He wanted Allegra's Italian cooking and sex but it wasn't working. 'How long does this awful feeling last?' he asked. 'Two to three months and then you'll be out of it' replied Leeming. Rather than ending the marriage, Boris once again persuaded Allegra to commute between the two capitals.

Amid the see-saw of their emotions, Boris was reporting from the front line about the EU's fate. In 1991 John Major, a passionate supporter of the EU, signed the Maastricht agreement and paved the way for Britain to join the Economic and Monetary Union (EMU). Except that Major distorted the treaty's intended outcome, calling it a 'decentralising treaty' and pledged there was no prospect of a single currency.

Implementation of the Maastricht agreement depended on approval by all the EU's member countries. Some required a referendum. In Britain, there was a vote in the Commons. With a majority of just eighteen after the 1992 general election, Major was fighting a tight battle against twenty-two Tory Eurosceptics including Bill Cash. Maastricht, the rebels protested, would inevitably transfer Westminster's powers to a federal European state ruled from Brussels. British sovereignty and democracy was in peril, they argued, an assertion denied by Major. During that ferocious party battle, Major complained about Boris's sceptical reports in the *Telegraph* exposing the Brussels bureaucrats' plans to forge an ever closer union. To Boris's glee, Major even voiced his anger about his reports at a meeting of EU leaders. 'That cured Boris's insecurity,' said Allegra. 'For a time anyway.'

As his marriage deteriorated further, Boris spotted Louisa

Gosling, a friend of Allegra, on a street in Brussels. Convinced that Gosling would spread stories about his aggressive behaviour towards Allegra, he warned her against doing so. Gosling denied doing anything of the sort. An allegation of shocking behaviour towards Allegra would later be repeated by Sonia Purnell to enhance her description of Boris's temper in their office. 'He is capable of a very bad temper,' agreed Allegra, 'but he doesn't hit out.' Charlotte agreed: 'His temper is his anger directed against himself.'

Depressed and moody, Allegra was again persuaded to return to Brussels permanently. Soon after, she regretted her decision. 'He couldn't change,' she realised. Only recognition made Boris happy. 'The same energy and enthusiasm which could make things happen was also exasperating,' she sighed. Their final argument was about education. He believed public schools epitomised education. 'Oh God,' thought Allegra. 'He's got no political baggage and no ideals. And that did it for me.' Her husband (whom she called Alexander at Oxford), she concluded, was three different personalities: Alexander, Al and Boris. 'Boris is the public person, but did I meet Al, the private person, or Alexander, a mixture of the private and public person, or had I lived with Boris? I never knew.' Even Boris, at any given moment, appeared unable to decide who he was playing.

Boris told his mother about the end. 'I'm unhappy,' he told her, 'but Allegra is too demanding.' After hearing about the break-up, Stanley called Allegra and suggested that they meet. Allegra found the venue he selected, a hamburger bar, underwhelming. 'A bum rap,' said Stanley unwilling to acknowledge that Allegra was rejecting his son. 'Rejection is not in the Johnsons' vocabulary,' she realised. 'There wasn't even a bunch of flowers to apologise.'

One evening in early 1992, Boris returned from work and found the flat empty except for one mattress on the floor. 'That's all he bought,' Allegra would say. The rest of the furniture had been moved into storage. 'When we got married,' Allegra concluded years later, 'that was the end of the relationship instead of the beginning.'

By the time of the break-up, Boris was in a relationship with Marina Wheeler. They had first met at school in Brussels and had much in common – the children of two journalist families and long time friends were neither pompous nor class ridden. Most important, as the daughter of Charles Wheeler, Marina was accustomed to a journalist's frequent absences and Boris's preoccupation to fulfil his ambition.

Grounded, happy, secure and intelligent, Marina could provide the substance and emotional interpretation of his life in the world he required. She had read law at Cambridge, studied European law, qualified as a British barrister in 1987 and was working in Brussels as a lawyer. Charlotte was thrilled. Marina was a loving, honest and practical person. And Boris got on well with Charles Wheeler and Dip, his Indian wife. The only possible hazard was the Wheelers' support for Labour, and Marina's Labour friends. On arriving at the London birthday party of Philippe Sands, a Labour-supporting lawyer and academic, Boris was not greeted as a friend. In uncompromising terms, Sands described the Tory's arrival as 'painful, hilarious and devastating all at the same time'. Sands was 'totally appalled' by Boris. He was not only 'fucking ugly', said Sands, but his support of Thatcher was a 'ghastly moment'. Sonia Purnell also personally warned Marina about the danger: 'I delivered a judgement more candid than careful – "I think he is the most ruthless, ambitious person I have ever met." ' Ignoring that hostility, Marina embraced Boris and never fussed when he left the city to report from EU summits. Few were more important than a foreign ministers' meeting in Portugal in May 1992. Maastricht had not yet been fully ratified. Denmark was due to hold a referendum on 2 June.

For Boris, the bogeyman in Brussels was the Frenchman Jacques Delors, the well-educated and savvy president of the European Commission. Boris was convinced that Delors' furtive ambition was to create a federal Europe state ruled from Brussels. That was not the opinion of John Palmer, the *Guardian*'s correspondent in Brussels. In advance of the meeting in Portugal, Palmer wrote a lengthy scene-setter. Boris asked his rival whether his account was based on official documents. 'Yes,' replied Palmer. To Palmer's anger, the following day, under the front-page headline 'Delors Plans to Rule Europe', Boris asserted that the president's ambition for monetary union was a smokescreen to strip away the veto rights of individual states in order to ultimately create a political union. Palmer was outraged by that report, a gross distortion and untrue, he said. Boris would say that he understood Delors' ambitions better than Palmer, because that precisely became the Commission's formal proposal. By contrast, Palmer appeared to write what he was told. History remembers Boris. His *Telegraph* report was widely discussed in Denmark and, in a tight race, the marginal majority that had been predicted for 'Yes' to Maastricht switched to 'No'. Boris became famous. Charles Moore, editor of the *Sunday Telegraph*, warned him that Douglas Hurd, the Foreign Secretary, was urging Hastings to dismiss his Brussels correspondent. Both Hurd and Hastings robustly denied Moore's assertion. The notoriety thrilled Boris. Thirteen years later, he confessed to the excitement of 'Sort of chucking these rocks over the garden wall and I listened to this amazing crash from the greenhouse next door over in England as everything I wrote from Brussels was having this amazing, explosive effect on the Tory Party. And it really gave me this, I suppose, rather weird sense of power.'

The horror for Boris and most Britons struck on 16 September 1992, 'Black Wednesday'. After days of financial turmoil, Britain was forced to leave the ERM. The value of the pound collapsed, interest rates soared and Britain was humiliated. Norman Lamont, the Chancellor of the Exchequer, blamed Germany for selfishly refusing to modify the ERM's rules. From the front line in Brussels, Boris's reports about Europe's perfidy strengthened the Tory Eurosceptics against John Major, blamed for foolishly ignoring the warnings, destroying Britain's economy and crippling the Tory Party.

A few months later, the insurgent was becalmed. Not only had Boris become a renowned journalist but he was also happy with Marina, who was now pregnant, and they had decided to marry on 8 May 1993. Arranging the divorce from Allegra was complicated by Boris's failure to submit the forms on time, a familiar habit like botching his tax returns or insurance policy payments – a recurring problem, and arguably a hangover from the chaos of his childhood. With just twelve days before his marriage and one month before

Marina gave birth, Boris struggled to find Allegra and obtain her signature on the divorce papers. To track her down, he called Candida, her sister-in-law. 'Why are you divorcing?' asked Candida. 'What happened?'

'It was God,' replied Boris. Nothing more. Despite the chaos, Allegra generously ensured the signed papers were delivered in time.

The wedding with just family and a few friends at a registry office in Horsham, West Sussex, was followed by a reception at the Wheelers' nearby home. 'We've had a Sikh wedding,' Marina announced, describing the preceding Sikh blessing. 'Suck and you'll find,' Boris added cryptically. The omens were good. In Marina, Boris found a soulmate. The most important ingredient in their relationship, as with all Boris's subsequent affairs, was the absence of competition. Unlike his instinctive rivalry with men, Boris trusted Marina, an old friend, not to cause him any harm and not get in his way. One month later, Lara Lettice was born in Brussels. To the Johnson mixture of Muslim, Jewish and Christian, his first child was also part Indian.

One friend not invited was Darius Guppy. Three months earlier, Guppy had been convicted at Snaresbrook Crown Court of fraud after Collier had exposed Guppy's crime in the *News of the World*. Guppy was jailed for five years. One month later he was again convicted, this time of a tax fraud. Shortly after, Boris described his friend's virtues and vices in the *Telegraph*. 'He lives by an Homeric code of honour, loyalty and revenge,' he wrote, adding that 'the joy of knowing Darius is the humourless self-deprecation beneath the idiotic flamboyance'.

Later that year, Max Hastings received a tape from Peter Ridson, a co-conspirator with Guppy in New York. Ridson had secretly recorded the last conversation when Guppy asked Boris for Collier's address in 1990. After Hastings listened to the tape, he summoned Boris from Brussels. Unaware of the reason, Boris looked surprised when told there was an incriminating tape. Pushing his hand through his hair, he explained to Hastings and Jeremy Deedes, 'Darius was a good, old friend and he was upset but I just wanted to get rid of him. I had nothing more to do with it.' By the end, the interview petered out. Boris had persuaded both men that he had done nothing to help Guppy, and just because he had not refused his request outright did not mean that he condoned or co-operated in the plan. Deedes agreed. The tone of the recorded conversation convinced him that Boris just wanted Guppy off his back after several telephone calls without genuinely offering any help. In Hastings' words, 'We sent him back to Brussels bearing only a strongly worded note from me, suggesting that he would be rash to make such an error of judgement again, or even indulge such a man as Guppy down the telephone. As a virtue, loyalty to friends has its limits.'

Twenty-five years later, Hastings was less generous to Boris. The Guppy affair, he would conclude, confirmed two facets of Boris's character: 'First he will say absolutely anything to man, woman or child that will give him pleasure at that moment, heedless of whether he may be obliged to contradict it ten minutes later. Second, having registered his wild-card status as a brand, he exploits it to secure absolution for a procession of follies, gaffes, idiocies, scoundrelisms, such as would destroy the career of any other man or woman in journalism, let alone in government.'

In 2005, Sue Lawley had anticipated Hastings' criticism. On *Desert Island Discs*, she asked Boris 'whether the charm is all a bit of a ruse . . . to sort of get you by?'

'I suppose that could be something,' he replied and unconvincingly blamed his childhood earaches and deafness: 'I think I must have developed then a certain sort of evasiveness, because often really I couldn't follow what was going on at all.'

In his unworldly way, Boris returned to Brussels without considering what Ridson might do with the tape. His narcissism blinded him to consider other people's motives, or what made people tick. Quentin Letts, the *Telegraph*'s diary editor, noticed that Boris never provided any gossip stories: 'He doesn't notice peoples' quirks and their embarrassments.'

Boris's last day in Brussels in 1994 was marked by a half-generous farewell from the Commission spokesman followed by the press corps rising to applaud their departing rival. He moved back to London as the *Telegraph*'s assistant editor, leader writer and chief political columnist. He and Marina bought a house in Islington.

In the *Telegraph*'s office in South Quay, Canary Wharf, he appeared as a cheerful, brazen bumbler. Not part of the club, he separated himself, ignorant about who was up or down and without insight into or interest in the people with whom he worked. Behind the smokescreen of a disorganised, untidy, unpunctual and unreliable eccentric, he was concerned only for himself, promoting his own personality but not in a hateful way. 'Who's Clinton?' he asked in a conference, shocking those unaware of the ploy. In the Commons lobby, he would act the fool and ask 'Bernard, do you know what's going on?' 'As a general tactic in life,' he later explained, 'it is useful to give the slight impression that you are deliberately pretending not to know what is going on – because the reality may be that you don't know what is going on, but people won't be able to tell the difference.' His shambles, the critics stressed, exposed him as an amateur compared to their professionalism. To their irritation, he never seemed bothered or prepared for anything, and attracted adoring women.

Few insiders forget the *Telegraph*'s cricket match at Radley that year where Boris's determination to win showed his class as a sportsman and a trophy hunter. His success sparked envy among many of his fellow journalists. Here was a man who made life look easy, even effortless. Not only had he enjoyed success at Eton and Oxford but he could write remarkable articles in a fraction of the time his colleagues needed. Unknown to them, he was also coming to the conclusion that journalism was an insubstantial career.

Chapter 5

Defying the Critics

Life in the *Daily Telegraph*'s new glass tower office in Canary Wharf had become routine and unchallenging. After contributing to the daily editorial conferences in the morning, Boris was expected to deliver an editorial or feature by the end of the day. While he loved journalism, that was hardly a challenge. His real ambition had never changed. He wanted to become prime minister or 'world king'. That dream had intensified while watching Europe's leaders from the sideline as a journalist. As they basked in the spotlight at international conferences, stepping out of polished limousines and asserting their importance at press conferences, his desire to be a player rather than a reporter of events became fixed. Through his position at the *Telegraph*, he had easy access to Tory party officials and, aided by his established fame in Brussels, his chance of securing nomination as an MP gave him an advantage over his rivals. Unsurprisingly he frequently discussed his ambitions with Bill Deedes, the eighty-year-old former Tory government minister and past editor of the *Telegraph* with whom he shared a desk at the newspaper. Deedes, a legend in his lifetime, was unenthusiastic about his experience during the Macmillan government. 'It's better being on the outside firing in,' Deedes told the younger man, 'rather than being inside being shot at.' Boris thought of the advantages of being on both sides, and shooting both ways, simultaneously employed as a journalist and politician. Quietly, he applied to be a Tory candidate at the next election.

Some leftish neighbours in Islington did not appreciate that their

Old Etonian friend was a committed Conservative. Suspicious of Islington's liberals, Boris rarely discussed politics at their parties. Moreover, disliking inane gossip, he refused to share any intimacies. Their suspicions were mutual. But his home in Calabria Road was happy chaos. After the birth of his second child, Milo Arthur in February 1995 (Cassia Peaches was born in September 1997 and Theodore Apollo in July 1999), the scratched furniture would soon be surrounded by bikes, sports gear, books and paintings balanced on shelves. The bliss was dented by the *Mail on Sunday*'s publication in July 1995 of the Guppy tape provided by Ridson. 'I certainly did not attempt to find the address,' Boris told the newspaper. That, he assumed, buried the story forever.

In September 1995, Max Hastings resigned after a series of disagreements with Conrad Black, the newspaper's owner, about Europe and Black's interference in the newspaper's content. Among Hastings' last words to Boris was advice to avoid a career in politics because 'a penchant for comedy is an almost insuperable obstacle to achieving high political office'. Naturally, Boris ignored the advice from a man with whom he had little in common. In theory, Boris's relationship with Charles Moore, the new editor, should have been better. Moore, himself an Old Etonian and former editor of the *Spectator* and *Sunday Telegraph*, respected Tory politicians more than his predecessor. But unlike Max Hastings, Moore did not respect mavericks and aspired to conform as a member of the Tory establishment. While Moore valued Boris's ability to write speedily a good profile, political analysis or feature, his chronic unpunctuality caused him despair. Boris, summarised Moore, was like David Niven's description of Errol Flynn: 'You always knew precisely where you stood with him because he *always* let you down.'

Boris's unreliability was a matter of choice. In an important cause, he took no chances. Getting into Parliament was such a cause. By the end of 1995 his application to be nominated as a Tory candidate had progressed, although an unexpected and considerable obstacle, he was told, remained.

In his favour was Andrew Mitchell, a thirty-nine-year-old MP and a member of the candidates' selection board, willing to advance Boris's political ambition. Against Boris were Douglas Hurd, John Major and MEPs annoyed by his Euroscepticism. 'What are you doing thinking of putting Boris on the list?' Major told Mitchell. 'He made my life a misery from Brussels.'

'If you don't back me, I'll resign,' replied Mitchell. 'Boris is bright and he's a Tory. And he's promised me not to try for a safe seat. If you start to interfere you'll undermine the candidates' committee.' At the end of a 'real fight', Mitchell won. 'Boris was among the best,' he decided. 'And there was no doubt that Boris wanted to be prime minister,' he says. Later that year, Boris was selected as the Tory candidate at Clwyd South, a safe Labour constituency in Wales. He was certain to lose at the election due in 1997. Mindful of his promise to Mitchell, he had eventually rejected an offer from Peter Lilley, a Eurosceptic MP and Cabinet minister, to be nominated for a safe seat in St Albans.

Under John Major, the party had become divided and discredited. Ever since Britain's withdrawal from the ERM, the party's reputation for economic competence had been shattered. By contrast, Tony Blair's New Labour promised an exciting new era. With a certain Labour landslide, it would be better to wait at the *Telegraph* until the Tory Party's fortunes changed, although he found the prospect of churning out articles frustrating.

Nevertheless, eager to impress Tory Central Office during the 1997 election campaign, he energetically toured through the constituency and addressed a meeting partly in Welsh. 'I say,' said a man when he finished, 'nobody understood a word you were saying. We don't speak Welsh in Wales.' Predictably trounced in the Labour landslide that May, the agent's positive report qualified him for a safe seat in the next election. That was no compensation for a man obsessed with being a winner. As always in his life, defeat or personal disaster provoked a well-concealed depression. Marina had become accustomed to cope with those moods.

One year later, in 1998, Boris was having lunch on a restaurant terrace near the *Telegraph*'s office with his old school friend Roger Clarke. Surrounded by baying bankers in the sunshine by the river,

Boris unveiled his misery: financially stretched, at war with his editors and fearful that he would not be promoted. His contemporaries, Boris moaned, were earning zillions in the City and he saw no prospect of fame or fortune. Unexpectedly, he spoke about his sudden desperation to move on from the *Telegraph*. The move, he complained, had been stymied. Aged thirty-four, his hope to be close to being in the Cabinet by then had evaporated. At the end of Boris's lament, Clarke spoke. 'I was hurt,' he said, 'about a column you wrote ridiculing "tank-topped bum boys". You see, I'm gay,' Clarke revealed. Boris, he saw, was visibly 'shocked'. By the end of their conversation, Clarke concluded, 'He wasn't homophobic, just not emotionally acute.' Clarke left their lunch depressed. Boris, he decided, could be generous to some and mean and tight-fisted with others. Filled with complexities and contradictions, he was just not normal, thought Clarke.

Salvation from conformist predictability was delivered to Boris later that year. The invitation to appear on the BBC's *Have I Got News for You*, a popular TV comedy news quiz, was a good wheeze. Eager for the fame, he failed to consider the motives for making the offer. To his surprise, during the programme he was ambushed by regular panellist Ian Hislop, the editor of *Private Eye*, a magazine he had admired, who played an edited version of the Guppy tape. Clearly shaken, Boris proved incapable of an instant crushing reply. Many personalities might have been fatally damaged, but Boris's subsequent response embarrassed his adversary. Under the headline 'I was Stitched Up', he denounced the programme in the *Spectator* as 'a fraud on the viewing public'. Contrary to the image of slick spontaneity, he wrote, the producers ponderously rehearsed, staged and then edited everything to disguise the plodding truth. Ungrateful for that revelation, Hislop nevertheless maintained the relationship. Although he judged Boris to be unprincipled and amoral, he was also valuable entertainment. Repeatedly re-invited, first as a contestant and then as the presenter, Boris relied on his 'spontaneous' delivery from autocue and instinctive jokey jabs at Hislop to win the audience's coronation as a national celebrity. The downside of his cultivated performance was disapproval from those whom he categorised as pompous and envious. Comedians, they carped, were good entertainment but unacceptable in politics. One exception to that censure was Conrad Black, a dishonest Canadian newspaper proprietor eager for acceptance by London's fashionable patricians.

Ever since Conrad Black had bought the *Telegraph* in 1985 and the *Spectator* in 1987, his status had risen in London despite his notoriety in Canada as a financial charlatan. 'While Mr Black grows ever richer,' wrote the Canadian political philosopher John Ralston Saul, 'some of his companies grow ever poorer.' Like every other employee, Boris applauded Black's ownership of the revived *Telegraph* in spite of Black – a self-important fantasist – damning journalists as 'a very degenerate group' who 'are revenging, money-grabbing know-nothings'. To prove his mastery of language, he added that journalists were 'temperamental, tiresome and nauseatingly eccentric and simply just obnoxious'. In the past as in the future, Black had good reason to fear journalists' investigation of his own financial skulduggery.

There was one exception to his congenital dislike. In 1992, Black married Barbara Amiel, a glamorous and trenchant journalist. Boris became a regular social guest at their Kensington home. As his celebrity grew, Amiel appreciated Boris's style and ensured he was seated near her at their dinners. 'I love Barbara. I venerate her,' he would later say. In parallel to Boris's rise, the Blacks became disillusioned with Frank Johnson (not related to Boris), the *Spectator's* editor. Although the magazine's circulation had risen to over 50,000, Algy Cluff, its chairman and previous owner, disliked Frank Johnson. 'We need a new free spirit,' Cluff told Black and urged that he appoint Boris as editor. Despite Boris's reputation for a basketful of sins, Black agreed that Boris's mercurial temperament and unconventional attitudes suited a weekly magazine. In Boris, Black recognised a fellow careerist, ruthless for power and wealth and conveniently uninterested in exposing swindlers in Westminster or the City. Reassured by his Etonian polish, Black assumed he could trust the seemingly unconfrontational Boris not to rock the boat.

Black's offer to Boris in spring 1999 was not a surprise to Boris, although it was to Frank Johnson. Black made his offer conditional on Boris promising not to pursue his political ambitions. Boris brazenly gave that undertaking knowing that it was false. At that moment, several applications to constituencies were being considered but success was not guaranteed. If he told Black the truth he would not get the job, so it was better, he calculated, to take the risk. Only by breaking rules, Boris was convinced, could exceptional men like himself fulfil their ambitions. Black, he assumed, respected those who behaved like himself – politely merciless and brazen. Each thought he played the other well, but Boris played the game better and got what he wanted.

He moved from the *Telegraph*'s modern offices in Canary Wharf to a seedy town house in Doughty Street, Bloomsbury. The appointment was not universally welcomed. Simon Heffer, the ineffably pompous *Telegraph* writer, was outraged. Ambitious for the job himself, he would never forgive either Black or Boris for the snub. Another envious rival judged Boris's appointment as 'entrusting a Ming vase to the hands of an ape'.

To secure Boris's agreement, Cluff vetoed Black's proposal to cut the editor's salary by 20 per cent. 'I need to pay my mortgage,' Boris had pleaded. The salary would be maintained by also writing a column for the *Telegraph*. But Boris did agree to Black's appointment of Stuart Reid, a calm, professional journalist, as his deputy to make sure that the magazine came out on time. Boris told Reid that in the big picture he opposed sanctimony about sex, favoured legalising drugs and was pro-enjoyment of life. Extolling his liberal ideology – pro-capitalism, elitism, good education, tolerance of immigrants, and anti-Blair – Boris wanted the magazine to be a haven for uncensored entertainers, with a ban on 'preachers'. No one welcomed Boris's anarchic spirit more than Rod Liddle. The chain-smoking drinker, former editor of BBC Radio 4's *Today* and *Spectator* columnist loved the 'convivial, clubbable and naughty' atmosphere overseen by a dishevelled editor who wore plimsolls, with his shirt hanging out and shapeless trousers. Looking hopeless, Boris's short telephone conversations to brief journalists were nevertheless precise and efficient. He refused to be immersed in detail. His job was to give direction and be open to ideas. 'I know that Tony Blair and Alastair Campbell went stag hunting,' asserted a political writer. 'Great,' gushed Boris and commissioned the fictitious story. 'I'm going to draw a cartoon of Muhammad,' said another contributor hoping to emulate a notorious Danish cartoon. 'Crikes, great, yes, hammer the bastards.' Occasionally, suggestions were stonewalled. Unable to make many decisions on the spot, he needed time to resolve complicated ideas. Precision was often inconvenient. His strength was enthusiasm for having a crowd around him to give support and structures without them feeling any intellectual intimidation.

Soon after his appointment, he telephoned Adam Zamoyski, a renowned historian, asking him to write an article pegged to the sixtieth anniversary of the outbreak of war in August 1939. 'Say that the Poles should have done a deal with Germany,' suggested Boris, 'and then the war would not have happened.'

'I can't do that,' replied the historian. Hitler, Zamoyski explained, wanted to destroy Poland, and the Poles could never have tolerated an alliance with the Nazis. Clearly dissatisfied, Boris prevaricated until he reluctantly agreed to publish a historically accurate article.

The pattern emerged of an editor constantly testing people, especially their loyalty. He demanded their adulation, and even if he had betrayed them, he expected their forgiveness – and love. Inevitably editors make mistakes or need to clear up a mess caused by a writer. If justified, Boris pleaded guilty, expressed undying remorse, admitted his expectation of instant dismissal and in turn begged forgiveness for himself. Every time it worked.

In late 2000 Mark Amory, the *Spectator*'s elitist literary editor, commissioned an especially negative review of *The Constant Gardener*, John le Carré's new novel due to be published in January. Boris disliked Amory's assault and, before the review's publication, arrived unannounced at le Carré's home in Hampstead, north London. Removing his cycle helmet, he introduced himself to le Carré, whose real name is David Cornwell, and they drank a cup of tea. Although Boris perhaps planned the visit to mitigate the dreadful

review, that was not mentioned in their conversation. 'Old Etonians are fascinated that I taught there,' recalls Cornwell, 'and we
talked a bit about it. His visit showed he didn't like criticism and
feared making an enemy out of me.' The review's publication a few
days later 'came as a complete shock' to Cornwell. Although a
scathing critic of Boris, the author remembers the visit as 'a thor-
oughly decent act'.

The incident also reflected Boris's fear of confrontation. As the
magazine's editor, he could have refused to publish the review but
he preferred not to argue with Amory, a difficult employee. Endorsing the abusive review reflected to some extent his lazy absenteeism
and lack of principle but also his liberal belief against censorship.
His operation, insiders knew, depended on appointment, trust and
delegation, not on diktat. Singing 'Tubthumping' ('I get knocked
down, but I get up again') by Chumbawamba, or a song by Dire
Straits, the new editor preferred not to interfere and focused on
maintaining good relations throughout Doughty Street. Certain
of his own abilities, he liked smart, talented people around the
building.

At parties and long drunken lunches, Boris enhanced the magazine's existing hierarchy. The officer class – pompous and flaky
with double-barrelled names – were separated from the ranks.
Liddle, the son of a Darlington train driver, was good company but
his undisguised chippy class-consciousness ruled out friendship.
Conversely, young beautiful women, especially if they were
Oxbridge-educated like Lady Annunziata Asquith, were welcomed.
Applications for employment bereft of nepotism or patronage were
automatically binned. When the circulation had risen above 50,000,
not everyone was gleeful. 'I remember when circulation was 18,000,'
sniffed Mark Amory, 'and that was everyone' (by which Amory
meant that the new readers did not rank among those he valued as
the elite).

That atmosphere suited Boris. His talent was to make each
member of his staff feel they were special. Although always friendly,
he lived behind a barrier – both of class and a refusal to allow anyone too close. Among the ranks, his theatrical delivery, quoting

Latin and Greek to show his genius and the public's stupidity, was quietly questioned. Few knew whether Boris's Latin was accurate or relevant. Like his buffoonery, the classics were a smokescreen. Among the aristos, his declamations were a delight but they still wanted to probe his camouflage. During a *Spectator* lunch a favoured woman guest heard Roger Clarke mention that he had been at Eton with Boris. 'Tell me about that,' she said to Clarke. 'Don't tell her anything,' ordered Boris sharply. Secrets about his personal life had to be protected.

The evasiveness about his past mirrored his refusal to commit to an ideology. Frustratingly for those who hoped that the magazine would renew Tory beliefs to defeat New Labour, he rarely took a line about Conservatism. Political principles barely interested him. Clearly committed to Toryism, he remained unattached to any faction or tribe – other than his own. The nuances of the Tory Party's internal politics were ignored. Other than proclaiming liberalism and opposing the Tory far right, especially the Monday Club, he was unpredictable after considering the arguments about which side the magazine would support. 'He believed in free speech,' complains Liddle. 'But while he supported the sign "I'm gay, get over it" on the bus, he opposed a sign which supported Christianity.'

Liddle's interest in the limitations of free speech became an issue in 2000 while he and Boris investigated Unicef's suspicious aid operations in Uganda. Driven in an air-conditioned Mercedes by two humourless Swedish women from one impoverished village to the next, Boris raged about the UN's neo-imperialism. Both journalists were aghast at the sight of privileged condescending whites dishing out aid to the local people. To both, the experience resembled the worst of the bygone colonialist era. 'Onwards to the next bunch of grinning piccaninnies,' Boris said in mockery of the corrupt UN executives. On the following day, in a truck heading to another village with white UN administrators, Boris began singing 'Money for nothing and chickens for free.' To illustrate their prejudice, he parodied their racism. When they dished out aid, he said, they would expect 'watermelon smiles' in return. His illustration of what he perceived to be the UN's racism would be later construed as his personal bias.

Two years later, on the eve of a visit by Blair to the Congo, Boris witnessed what he regarded as the very same hypocrisy of Europeans descending on Africa in the same manner as their imperialist predecessors. 'What a relief it must be for Blair to get out of England,' he wrote in the *Telegraph*. 'No doubt the AK47s will fall silent, and the pangas will stop their hacking of human flesh, and the tribal warriors will all break out in watermelon smiles to see the big white chief touch down in his big white British taxpayer-funded bird.' In the same article, he wrote 'The Queen has come to love the Commonwealth, partly because it supplies her with regular cheering crowds of flag-waving piccaninnies.' Boris would claim that he was satirising neocolonialism.

Johnson's marriage to a half-Indian woman, and his own Muslim, Jewish and Christian ancestry, would be an unusual background for a racist, an accusation which did not arise among his left-wing neighbours in Islington – also employed in the media and law. Their particular gripe was that the Johnsons did not continue to send their children to Canonbury Primary, the local state school. The Johnsons were unconvinced. Education in Islington was appalling – practically the nation's worst – and despite the efforts of middle-class parents, the teaching at Canonbury Primary was particularly bad. Like many other parents of pupils at the school, the Johnsons moved their children to private schools. Eventually, an Ofsted inspection failed Canonbury and its head was sacked for viewing porn on a school computer. During those debates that year, few of the Johnsons' friends suspected Boris had serious political ambitions.

At the *Spectator*, he rebuffed politicians. Those who called to beg for a story to be either promoted or buried were usually snubbed. He won brownie points among his staff when he enthusiastically published an account of a member of the royal family shooting a wild animal. After the story was deleted from the magazine's website, Boris loudly ordered for the item's restoration. For those journalists who despaired about jargon or political correctness,

Boris's willingness to take a blunt risk and cause offence, often with humour, was a tonic. Few recalled that he had stood as a Tory candidate in the 1997 election or knew that his ambition to become prime minister remained as strong as ever. Their enthusiasm dampened after Boris revealed that he thought the *Spectator* was a mere stepping-stone to Downing Street.

Unknown to his staff, in spring 2000, Peter Sutherland, the president of Henley Conservatives, formally invited Boris to apply for the seat. Michael Heseltine, the MP for twenty-seven years, had decided to step down bequeathing an 11,167 majority. Over the previous decade, the former deputy prime minister and Europhile had forlornly regretted his missed opportunities to become prime minister. Heseltine's misfortune was Boris's chance. A safe seat in a picturesque location by the Thames and close to London, was an aspiring politician's dream. The constituency had a relevant historical connection. Valentine Fleming, the MP a century earlier and the father of the famous spy writer Ian, was described by Winston Churchill, his obituarist in *The Times*, as a 'lovable and charming personality . . . a man of thoughtful and tolerant opinions, which were not the less strongly or clearly held because they were not loudly or frequently asserted'.

Inevitably, Conrad Black heard about Boris's application and scolded the editor for lying to him or, in his maleficent language, being 'ineffably duplicitous', a tag which would three years later be attached to Black himself after being accused of fraud. After a series of rants against the editor, Black succumbed to Boris's apologies and charm. He was too good to lose. 'He's a very cunning operator,' Black would say. 'He is a fox disguised as a teddy bear. I don't know how he's kept it going for so long. He knows the people, he understands public sensibilities.' Boris would admit lying to Black. 'The blessed sponge of amnesia has wiped the chalkboard of history,' he later told the *New York Times*. 'I want to have my cake and eat it,' he admitted to Charles Moore.

Once his plan was known, Boris asked Rod Liddle if he should go for the seat. 'But you're the editor,' replied Liddle angrily. That, Liddle then realised, was not a barrier. As an unrestrained ambitious enthusiast, nothing was ever enough for Boris. 'I don't think he believes in anything other than his self-advancement,' Liddle reflected.

Andrew Mitchell also protested. 'You promised me that you wouldn't go for a safe seat,' he told Boris, apparently convinced that he should fight marginal seats until the Tory high command decided otherwise. 'I'm so sorry,' replied Boris with staged humility. Mitchell was not deceived. 'In politics,' Mitchell knew, 'you must look sincere, but that doesn't mean you are.'

From Westminster, David Davis, the Conservative MP and future Cabinet minister, was intrigued by the spectacle. 'It was a mistake to judge Boris like others. They all wriggled up the greasy pole. He leapt over the pole at a great height.'

In July 2000 Boris arrived with Marina for the final selection meeting. David Platt, a pro-Europe solicitor, was his principal rival. Backed by Heseltine, Platt expected to be rewarded for gathering many supporters over the previous months. He suffered a double misfortune. Not only the arriviste's celebrity but his Euroscepticism appealed to many local Conservatives disenchanted by Heseltine. Ever since his failed bids for the leadership during the 1990s and the rise of the Eurosceptics, Heseltine had disregarded his constituents' opinions. In retaliation, the members who disliked him wanted another star to restore the association's vitality. The result was a bitterly divided constituency. At a crowded, acrimonious selection meeting, Boris's opponents threw all the dirt at the candidate, including the Guppy tape. 'In so far as you accuse me of keeping this Guppy business a secret,' replied Boris, 'well, that seems a bit thin since I have actually been questioned about it on a TV game show watched by I don't know how many millions.' Asked about his editorship, he replied that he would remain at the *Spectator* 'not least because I would be broke' otherwise. 'My greatest advantage over David Platt,' Boris would later admit about his gay opponent, 'was that I had a wife, beaming up at me from the front row, with every appearance of interest, wearing a suitably colourful flowery coat.'

Heseltine was furious about the Eurosceptic's success. His anger was shared by Max Hastings, his good friend and now the editor of the *Evening Standard*. Hastings had become disenchanted with his former employee. Puzzled that the party would choose a celebrity, Hastings predicted that 'Johnson, for all his gifts, is unlikely to grace any future Tory Cabinet . . . To maintain his funny-man reputation he will no doubt find himself refining his Bertie Wooster interpretation to the point where the impersonation becomes the man.'

Boris's misfortune was that, unlike other politicians, his long association with fellow journalists exposed him to particular scrutiny. Few journalists could associate Boris's untidiness, last-minute delivery of copy, colourful vocabulary and reporting, fabrications and inventions, especially when he was the *Telegraph* correspondent in Brussels, with the seriousness expected of a politician. 'I was shocked by his ambition when he was adopted and would become MP,' says Liddle. How could a journalist, asked A. A. Gill in the *Sunday Times*, cross the line into politics? Although that was a familiar career path, Gill, a hyper-critical purist, was nevertheless appalled. Under the headline 'It's Boris, the worst politician in the world', Gill described a chaotic morning canvassing with Boris in the constituency and an interview in a pub where the candidate was 'like a man drowning in porridge and he's really not enjoying this'. At the end of the morning, Boris asked Gill, 'You're going to stitch me up, aren't you?' To which Gill honestly replied, 'Yes.' 'Boris Johnson,' Gill concluded, 'is without doubt the worst putative politician I've ever seen in action. He is utterly, chronically useless – and I can't think of a higher compliment.' Denigrating Boris became a competition. Among his bitterest critics, Boris was said to be profoundly duplicitous and insincere. His emotional reaction to the onslaught, motivated he assumed by envy, appeared to be mute. In private, his hypersensitivity drove him to despair. Only Marina and one particular friend witnessed his anger.

Chapter 6

'It's all a mess'

Boris's life in Islington with Marina and their four young children was becoming routine. Marina, he later confided to one person, was no longer a woman much interested in a close relationship or spirited conversations. Another was given the opposite impression: that Marina remained his best friend and a rock in difficult times. A third eyewitness simply concluded that the nine-year-old girl he first met in Brussels had transformed from a sister-like friend into a fun-loving party girl, and was now a homemaker, mother and lawyer. She was no longer the full-time, uncritical confidante he required. Too often, she told him the unpleasant truth. Despite enjoying time with his children, he discovered that fame had attracted other women. The agitator had become 'untrustworthy'. He felt waning loyalty towards Marina. Convinced their relationship was secure, his appetite fuelled him to risk a new challenge. Ann Sindall, his sulphurous gatekeeper in the Doughty Street office, knew how to protect her employer from demanding women. One called to confirm an appointment. 'He's not coming,' Sindall declared. 'You know Boris. He only agreed to make you happy. He didn't mean it.' But he needed friendship, comfort, support and consolation. During 2000 he found that at the *Spectator*.

Ever since he became editor, his relationship with Petronella Wyatt, the magazine's thirty-two-year-old deputy editor whom he had inherited from Frank Johnson, had become closer. Good-looking, vivacious and intelligent, she was the daughter of the late Woodrow Wyatt, a former Labour MP and peer, and Verushka, her

Hungarian mother, both of whom enjoyed the turf and mixing with royalty and celebrities. Petronella wrote witty articles, but her critics carped that she was not wholly committed to journalism; and even she would admit that she was a well-connected young woman who enjoyed being chased by eligible men. 'All Petronella wanted,' said a boyfriend, 'was to get married and have children. And that's what her mother wanted too.' Naturally, Petronella's racy articles about her elusive matrimony concealed her burning ambition. 'No one expected me to settle down,' she would colourfully write about her first engagement, in 2009, to a 'gloriously unsuitable man'. 'This is because of my repeated protestations over the years that I would never, ever, live with a man, let alone get engaged.'

Over lunches and in the office, her friendship with Boris intensified. Discovering a mutual interest in ancient history, poetry and later music, Boris taught his deputy to read Greek and occasionally they exchanged messages in Latin. Petronella discovered his affections for her by accident. Rummaging through his untidy desk for a *Spectator* lunch's guest list, she found a handwritten love letter to her from him. In his shy manner towards women he found attractive, he had never revealed his passion, not even by a physical gesture. Boris was certainly not a groper. Those who would claim the opposite, Petronella believed, were lying. But, she realised, he had no problem renouncing any conscience about Marina.

The mutual attraction for two vulnerable people was companionship. 'You are the first woman friend I have ever had,' Boris said to Petronella. 'He was a loner with few friends,' she later wrote, 'and like many loners, he has a compensating need to be liked . . . he wants to be loved by the entire world.' During those first months, Boris hinted at emotional fractures of his childhood with violent swings between happiness, hilarity, moodiness and depression. Stopping on the way to his home, he found someone to impress who welcomed him. 'I've been waiting for you all day, and you're wonderful,' Petronella mused. He thought he was safe, but he was completely unsafe. After their affair started, he revealed intense jealousy about Petronella's friendship with two famous historians. Convinced that she was unfaithful, his rage exposed insecurity, especially about his own intellectual inferiority, his stretched finances and what he perceived were his inadequate looks. Recklessly, he poured out his emotions in reams of letters and poems. During that first summer, Boris telephoned Petronella on holiday in Italy. 'I want to marry you,' he said. On her return, he discussed the prospect with Petronella's mother. Nothing happened. Unwilling to be a mistress, Petronella demanded action. In 2001, about eight months after their relationship began, Petronella was pregnant.

Attracted by the notion of a second family, Boris urged Petronella to have the child. She was torn. Unwilling to be a single mother, she insisted that they should marry. Boris visited her mother's house in Cavendish Avenue, St John's Wood, and discussed marriage. He saw a divorce lawyer and then he confessed to Marina. His wife was shocked, moved out to stay with her parents and then persuaded him, she thought, to end the affair. As the guarantee of his promise, he wrote a cheque for a large amount, handing all his savings to his wife. The next morning, after looking at his four young children eating breakfast, Boris was faced with reality: his family's certain disapproval, the prospect of confrontation and poverty too. Remembering his own horror of his parents' divorce, he retreated. His marriage, he decided, was not over. Petronella had an abortion. Solemnly, he again promised Marina that his affair was over. In the nature of Marina's love for Boris, she chose to believe him. He lied. His disloyalty to Marina, Petronella wrote later, was justified by being 'inordinately proud of his Turkish ancestry and his views on matters such as monogamy are decidedly Eastern'. Boris believed it was 'genuinely unreasonable' that men should be 'confined' to one woman, said Petronella. Inexplicably and recklessly, he imagined that he could continue his affair even as a famous politician.

*

At the general election on 7 June 2001 Boris won his seat in Henley with a majority of 8,458. That was just over 2,700 votes fewer than

Heseltine's majority had been in 1997, and Boris's share of the vote slightly decreased too. In the midst of another Labour landslide majority of 167 with the loss of just five seats, Boris's election was hardly noticed. Blair's magnetism had crushed a rotten Tory campaign led by William Hague under the slogan 'Last chance to save the pound'. Boris was thrilled to have 'MP' after his name. 'Someone,' he later wrote, 'it may have been Trollope, once said that a man could have no higher honour than to have those letters after his name. He was right.'

Days after the election, Graham Brady, the chairman of the Conservative backbenchers' 1922 Committee, invited the new arrivals to an introductory speech about the behaviour expected in Westminster. In a world suffocated by conceit, Boris stood out, not as the *Spectator*'s celebrity editor, but as a dishevelled interloper. Elsewhere in the room were George Osborne and David Cameron, also newly elected. Hugo Swire, the new MP for East Devon, sat opposite Boris. As Brady drawled on, Swire was impressed that Boris was busy writing. 'Bit keen aren't you, taking all those notes?' Swire asked him at the end. 'I'm twenty-four hours late for my *GQ* column and getting stick from the editor,' explained Boris.

The Conservative MPs' first task was to elect a new leader. Among those who approached Boris was Oliver Letwin, a leading Eurosceptic canvassing for Michael Portillo against Ken Clarke, a passionate pro-European. Over the previous decade, Letwin had written over one hundred articles for the *Daily Telegraph*, critically scrutinising line by line the consequences of Maastricht; ironically he would later become Cameron's fixer to avoid Brexit. 'I'm supporting Ken,' Boris told Letwin.

'If Ken wins, the party will split on Europe,' Letwin countered.

'Nonsense,' Boris replied.

Letwin put Boris down as pro-Europe. Over the following seven years while Boris was an MP, Letwin would never encounter him among the small passionate band of EU critics. 'He was invisible in the Commons,' noted Letwin, 'he was politically light, there was no ideology and the *Spectator* was not anti-EU.' Boris told the Commons in 2003, 'I am not by any means a Eurosceptic. In some ways

I am a bit of a fan of the European Union. If we did not have one, we would invent something like it.'

Michael Portillo also sought Boris's support. Boris refused. In pique, Portillo replied that Boris should decide between being a serious politician and a joke. Outraged, Boris never forgave the wayward Tory. In the third ballot, Portillo was one vote behind Iain Duncan Smith and was eliminated. Boris's vote would have given Portillo a chance for the leadership in the final round.

From the outset, Boris was depressed by the House of Commons, dominated as it was by Labour. The political prospects for the new Tory MP were grim, and having failed to make an initially positive impression, Boris's reputation in the Commons slid downwards. Appointed to shadow the government on culture, Boris never turned up to David Davis's Tuesday meetings. Nor did he arrive on time for a lunch date with Davis, then shadowing the deputy prime minister. 'Many apologies,' he spluttered after appearing nearly one hour late. 'At the time,' recalls Davis, 'I put it down to a mistake in my diary but later I realised it was a pattern. He was a needy character and gave the impression you were unimportant because, with a sense of his own importance, he had no time for the rest of the world.' Unless Boris was the captain, he refused to play in the team.

Ignoring the whips, he often missed votes to fly off on fact-finding trips, edit the *Spectator*, write his column for the *Telegraph*, appear on TV or test cars for *GQ* magazine – and even the *Guardian*. *GQ*'s editor complained that Boris's parking tickets had cost £4,500 while the *Guardian* calculated that his test drive of a Kia had generated £500-worth of unpaid parking tickets and congestion charges. In answer as to why he spent so much time on extra-parliamentary work, Boris replied that he was no different from scores of MPs with directorships or Labour MPs working for their trade unions; and no different from Churchill, Disraeli and many other lesser-known MPs who wrote books and articles. Unspoken was his need for money. Four children could not be privately educated on a parliamentary salary.

The niggling was compounded by his poor performance in the

Commons. (One notable exception was his passionate defence of pig farmers in Henley.) He could neither think on his feet nor dominate an arena packed with enemies armed with a range of tricks. He stutteringly failed to master the art of flattering previous speakers, or showing the necessary humility. Rarely seen mingling with MPs in the tea room, he occasionally appeared as required in a standing committee processing a long crime bill or squeezed into the benches for the regular Wednesday Prime Minister's Questions. 'Boris did not enjoy Parliament,' concluded Iain Duncan Smith. 'He was only interested in what would get him attention. Boris was always about Boris.' Even his weekly chore alongside Cameron and Osborne to prepare Duncan Smith for PMQs was laboured. Duncan Smith assumed that Boris, the outstanding celebrity, could conjure up brilliant one-liners, but lacking Cameron's ability to do so, Boris did not find it easy and gave up, uninterested in political principles or puncturing Blair. 'Hey, Dave, what's the plan,' he asked after one depressing session. Having struggled to get a parliamentary seat, it was all rather an anticlimax. Everyone agreed he was a fish out of water. Over time, MPs said that the more they got to know Boris, the less he was liked.

The glamour was outside Westminster, and couldn't have been more of a contrast to the drudgery of being an MP. Indeed in November 2001, Conrad Black hosted a party in Kensington to celebrate the 'Boris Phenomenon' – he had evidently got away with lying to his host about his political ambitions. One hundred and fifty guests were greeted with champagne, life-size cardboard cutouts of Boris and a comic act. For the Blacks, always seeking an opportunity to flaunt their own importance, their editor was an exceptional celebrity. For the hero, the party was marred only by Marina's insistence that Petronella could not be invited. There would be violence, she warned, if Petronella was there. Petronella was disinvited.

In his unworldly way, Boris was unaware that the champagne was financed with stolen money. At the annual meeting five months later in New York of Hollinger Inc., Black's company, shareholders publicly called Black a 'thief'. Grubby criminality did not interest the *Spectator*'s editor. Instead, he was entranced by Barbara Amiel, famous for her low-cut dresses. 'I'm always worried about cleavage,' Amiel confessed during an interview with *Vogue*. 'I seem to keep spilling out of things.' Shimmering in an Oscar de la Renta ballgown, Amiel confided during a tour of her vast wardrobe in her extraordinary house, 'Now I have an extravagance that knows no bounds.' Excess of a different kind had become attractive to Boris – politician, editor, columnist, TV celebrity, author, father – and adulterer.

The caprice extended to his professional life. After the *Spectator* alleged that Alastair Campbell, the prime minister's spokesman, had interfered in arrangements for the Queen Mother's funeral to promote Tony Blair, Campbell lodged a protest with the Press Complaints Commission, the media's watchdog. To settle the matter, the PCC's executives asked Boris to publish a correction. 'OK,' agreed Boris. But then he somersaulted. 'We'll fight this,' he announced. 'Boris failed to do as he's promised,' reported a PCC executive. The atmosphere in Doughty Street encouraged impulsive bravado.

Soon after his election, Boris bought a small, unmodernised remote house in Thame, about twenty miles from Henley. With the permanent excuse that constituency business demanded that he sleep away from his Islington home, he and Petronella resumed their affair. In their love nest, Boris was clearly happy. He ate his favourite dish – sausages and roast potatoes – recited Greek poetry, enjoyed excursions and especially picnics in West Wycombe Park, a favourite destination of John Wilkes, an eighteenth-century radical, journalist, MP, member of the Hellfire Club and champion of liberty. The more he read about Wilkes, Petronella's hero, the more he realised the pleasures of eighteenth-century life, especially the tolerance of politicians enjoying relationships with a mistress, and using journalism to promote political ambitions. As their affair became known among the magazine's staff, Boris grew even more reckless. Together they went on trips to Paris and to a conference in Moscow. In the hotel restaurant, they spotted Bruce Anderson, a *Spectator* journalist (Anderson had borscht all over his shirt, and he seemed more preoccupied by his meal than by the sight of his editor).

Back in London, Boris and Petronella were surprised during a lunch at Wheeler's with David Blunkett, the Labour Home Secretary, by the unexpected arrival of the American Kimberly Fortier, the *Spectator*'s publisher. 'I've always wondered what it's like to have sex with a blind man,' Fortier said after sitting down. As Blunkett's head jerked, she added, 'Since I realise that a blind man cannot see me, I've put on special perfume so you can smell me.'

In that extraordinary atmosphere, Boris's affair appeared to be encouraged by Conrad Black or his wife. At their dinners, guests noticed how Boris would be seated next to Petronella. 'Boris's adultery,' says his mother Charlotte, 'is just like his father's. The motives were lack of love for their wives, boredom, selfishness and insecurity.' To Boris's good fortune no one at that time raised the parallel between him and Stanley. The reasons for Boris's parents' divorce remained unknown.

In midst of that affair, Mary Wakefield, a commissioning editor at the *Spectator*, developed a crush on Boris and Boris, it appeared, was swooning for Mary, 'one of the loveliest people', according to Rod Liddle. Jeremy Deedes, a director of the Telegraph Group which owned the *Spectator*, also noticed that 'Mary was besotted with Boris. She was like a spaniel on heat. Boris was scratching his head: "What are we going to do?" he asked me.' If there was no danger, Boris did not feel he was travelling. In a *Daily Mirror* interview, he hinted about his recklessness: 'I am a juggler. I can have it all.' He could not control his impulses – what he wanted, he could justify. Dancing with danger, he was engaged in a rhetorical dialogue with the gods: 'If I do this, will I get away with it? If I do get away with it, and the gamble comes off, I won because I am blessed.' The relationship with Petronella proved to him that he was special.

Inevitably, his reckless lifestyle imploded. In the summer of 2002, Petronella was suffering from the pressure and secrecy of their relationship. If Boris refused to marry her, she said, they should stop seeing each other. That horrified Boris. 'He threatened suicide and cried – buckets full,' a close friend of Boris witnessed. Expelled from Verushka Wyatt's home in St John's Wood, he walked down the street. Fearful of what he might do, Petronella ran after him. A rapid conversation produced no solution. Soon after, Petronella headed for a holiday in Porto Ercole in Tuscany. Boris was with his family in Sardinia. Abruptly, he left Marina and his children and flew to the mainland. After arriving in Porto Ercole, he climbed a wall to enter Petronella's villa and declared that his impulsiveness and bravery proved his love. But again, nothing happened. He returned to Marina.

On her return to London, Petronella sought to rebuild her life and met an interesting American. Since the relationship with Boris had reached deadlock and she was exhausted by all the lies, she moved to Virginia in the USA to live with her new friend. The chance of a new permanent relationship and marriage was shattered by Boris's constant telephone calls. Unable to be alone, he needed Petronella's friendship and support. Eventually she returned to London. At midnight soon after, Boris was standing at her mother's front door. 'Don't let him in,' he heard Petronella shout. Verushka liked Boris and opened the door. Their relationship was reignited.

Rumours about his affair with Petronella were reported to the *Telegraph*'s executives by Mary Wakefield, who also brought news of other affairs in Doughty Street. Rod Liddle had a close relationship with Alicia Monckton, the magazine's sassy young receptionist. At the same time, Liddle was planning his wedding to Rachel Royce, his long-term partner and the mother of his two children. On another floor was Kimberly Fortier – she had begun her affair with David Blunkett. Their relationship would be exposed after Blunkett's phone was hacked by the *News of the World*. Shortly after, Blunkett was identified as the father of Fortier's unborn child. Petronella would write about their introductory lunch, 'Mr Blunkett and I ate Dover sole. Miss Fortier ate Mr Blunkett.'

Soon after marrying Rachel Royce, Rod Liddle pondered whether he should divorce her and marry Alicia Monckton. 'You should never leave your wife,' Boris reprimanded his columnist, ignoring his own imbroglio. At the same time, Fortier reprimanded

Alicia Monckton for having an affair, even though Fortier was also having an affair with Simon Hoggart, the magazine's columnist and *Guardian* writer. In the most graphic language, she also moaned to Liddle that John Humphrys, the BBC broadcaster, had spurned her seduction.

*

None of that turmoil seeped into Westminster. Boris's appearances passed without any mention that Doughty Street resembled a sexual madhouse. For his own part, despite hating a backbencher's routine drudgery, Boris had no doubt about his destiny – to be prime minister. 'All politicians in the end,' he admitted in an interview, 'are like crazed wasps in a jam jar, each individually convinced that they're going to make it.' That was not an opinion shared at the *Spectator*. When the prospect of Boris as prime minister was uttered at the magazine's editorial conference, it provoked universal roars of laughter – except from Boris. He bore the insult silently. Naturally, he feared their lack of faith in his own vision of his destiny. As ever, most people underestimated his talent. Undoubtedly, their scepticism was shaped by his poor reputation in the Commons. His ponderous set pieces – just oral manifestations of a good article – fell flat. And yet with so few stars among the Tory MPs, no party leader felt they could afford not to use his talents.

The parliamentary party's decision to remove Iain Duncan Smith on 29 October 2003 after a disastrous party conference was followed by the unopposed election of Michael Howard as leader. Intelligent, articulate and forensic as a lawyer, Howard's prospects of winning the next general election were enhanced by Blair's unpopularity after the Iraq War. One personal weakness was his intolerance of critics. In his authoritarian manner, Howard was wary of Boris's media celebrity and his liberal instincts. He was especially apprehensive about Boris's support of immigration. To park him safely outside the tent, he made Boris a party vice chairman with responsibility for campaigning. Soon after, he promoted him to a Shadow arts minister under John Whittingdale, a lifelong politician. The normally anti-Tory arts luvvies, Howard calculated, would approve of Boris.

Grabbing the opportunity, Boris fired in all directions. He championed better education, a halt to local authorities selling sports fields for housing, improved broadband, more radio stations, more encouragement for the arts and the bizarre idea of presenting replica Elgin Marbles to Greece to end their demand for the originals' return. That hyperactivity was crammed into other obligations including frequent demands from Tory MPs that he help raise funds for their local constituency with after-dinner speeches. His celebrity promised a sell-out. 'Just remind me what this charity/ organisation does,' he usually said as he sat down late and began writing his speech. Nervous before speeches yet demanding to be the centre of attention, he disliked circulating a room, slapping backs. Arriving deliberately late, some would say, was a shy man avoiding conversation. Others assumed his native cunning was playing as a curtain-raiser to his humour. Most concluded that he was just winging it, improvising again and again with the same ingredients, accompanied by jokey mannerisms underneath the haystack hair. At the end of the performance, wherever he was, even hundreds of miles from London, he would refuse an offer of a hotel for the night. 'I must get back to the wife,' he explained. Usually, he jumped into a high-performance car provided by GQ, including once a Bentley, and raced back to London.

Amid all these manic activities, he also found time to write a comic thriller, *Seventy-Two Virgins*. The plot focused on a terrorist bid to capture the US president while he was addressing parliament in London. His hero, Roger Barlow, is a dishevelled back-bench Tory MP who cycles to Westminster, is unfaithful to his wife, is flippantly racist and politically opportunistic. Throughout the novel, Barlow fears that his political career is about to be ended by a tabloid scandal because his investment in a lingerie business was actually a cover for a brothel.

Art imitating life was risky but Boris had an urge to reveal himself in a fictional confession. The anger and envy directed against him, he thought, was designed to diminish his glory. 'That great prodigious tree in the forest,' Stanley called Boris, 'under the shade of which the smaller trees must either perish or struggle to find their own place in the sun.' Stanley spoke about success as having 'skipped a generation' in the family, regretting that he, the father, had not won the garlands. Boris's fame could even irritate the *Spectator*'s jealous directors. After a board meeting, everyone headed to the Cipriani off Berkeley Square for dinner. Many of the directors were standing outside the restaurant as Boris arrived on his bike. 'Hello Boris,' said a passer-by, 'can I have a go on your bike?' 'No you can't Elton,' laughed Boris to none other than Elton John. 'You'll go off with it.' Boris was amused by the directors' discomfort about his fame. In his expectation of loyalty from them and everyone else, he occasionally forgot the need to show appreciation.

In April 2003, the irrefutable accusations of fraud against Black had forced the sale of his British newspapers. 'I seem to have understated what Conrad did,' admitted Boris. In his artless briefing to Rod Liddle, he explained 'Basically Conrad bought a nice big chocolate cake to share with the family, and put it in the fridge, and then got up during the night and ate a lot of it.' 'Conrad will rebound faster than a cannonball express,' he told others. That proved foolishly optimistic. Four years later, after conviction of fraud by a Chicago jury in July 2007, Boris sent a letter to Black's trial judge seeking leniency. Black, he wrote, is 'a man of high intelligence and considerable literary interests and energies.' But on the critical issue of Black's honesty, Boris remained silent: 'I cannot comment on his present predicament.'

Boris's enjoyable status changed after the secretive Barclay brothers bought the *Spectator* in June 2004. 'I'm looking forward to meeting the Ribbentrop brothers,' Boris quipped injudiciously about the billionaire twins whose controversial rise from poverty to living offshore in a castle on Sark in the Channel Islands, was protected by sharp legal threats to newspapers. Andrew Neil, the magazine's new managing director, renowned as a former *Sunday Times* editor and broadcaster, was unimpressed by Boris's commitments outside editing the magazine. Regardless of the high circulation, he wanted the editor's full attention when he called.

Too often, the background noise of their conversations was traffic while Boris cycled somewhere. That was particularly grating on Wednesdays as the magazine was prepared for printing. The *Spectator*, Neil believed, could no longer be 'run on a whim and a prayer' – he wanted someone commercially minded. The plan, Neil told Boris, was to abandon the shabby premises in Doughty Street where the pursuit of money was deemed to be vulgar and establish a more profitable expanded business in Westminster. Boris felt the skids under his feet. One month later, the colliding elements of his packed life began to implode.

First, Rod Liddle's affair with Alicia Monckton was publicly exposed. Rachel Royce, his new wife, was miffed and blamed Boris for employing beautiful young girls instead of staid middle-aged women. Hosting fantastic parties in Doughty Street, Royce fumed, was outrageous. Her hatred for Boris was echoed by the sisterhood. 'My impression of *Spectator* parties,' wrote Royce, was 'full of young things in short dresses, high heels and lipstick, and the men flirting with them and ignoring their wives. I just felt Boris was running the whole place as a knocking shop.' Shortly after, she sent ten sacks of manure to the *Spectator*'s office. One month later, Fortier's affair with the Home Secretary was exposed. Not only was her husband Stephen Quinn wounded, but Blunkett, the father of her baby, was compromised. Questions surfaced about whether Blunkett had involved himself improperly in speeding up the Home Office procedure to obtain a visa for Fortier's nanny. The debacle led to David Blunkett's resignation irrespective of his protestation of propriety, accompanied by Tony Blair's hilarious eulogy that Blunkett's 'integrity was intact'. Andrew Neil did not complain as the circulation of the *Sextator*, as it was now called, 'went through the roof', he conceded. 'It gave Boris breathing space.'

The moratorium ended abruptly when Petronella, now thirty-six, discovered in September 2004 that she was again pregnant. For months she had believed Boris's promises to leave Marina and marry her. Her pregnancy forced him to make a decision. In her support, Verushka Wyatt, who strangely accompanied her daughter to parties and even chose her underwear when she travelled with her boyfriends, persistently telephoned Boris urging that he marry her daughter – a habit familiar to many of Petronella's more desirable suitors. Boris could have refused to take her calls but he listened. He and Verushka got on well. However, while he refused to divorce Marina, he did not urge Petronella to have an abortion. On the contrary, he encouraged her to have their 'daughter' – they decided on the spur of the moment that it was a girl – and they would raise her together. The final decision was left to Petronella. Trusting Boris would be a good father, she decided to have a full-term pregnancy.

Everything in Boris's life was being done in an exceptional hurry – under pressure, late and often furtively. But there was nothing especially unusual in Boris's call on Tuesday evening, 12 October 2004, asking Simon Heffer to write a leader for the following day, just before the *Spectator*'s final print deadline. Heffer suggested an editorial criticising Liverpool's excessively emotional reaction to the murder in Iraq of Ken Bigley, a British aid worker, by Islamic terrorists. In Heffer's words, Liverpool had expressed 'a mawkish sentimentality' about the death and the city suffered the same problem over its self-inflicted downfall since its glorious pre-war era. Constant strikes and Marxist militants had destroyed the great port and the city's industries.

As promised, the editorial not only criticised Liverpool's excessive emotion about Bigley's murder but also condemned Liverpudlians as 'hooked on grief' by succumbing to victimhood rather than accepting responsibility for their self-inflicted poverty. 'Their misfortunes,' stated the editorial, were compounded because they 'seek to blame someone else for it [sic], thereby deepening their sense of shared tribal grievance against the rest of society'.

That controversial opinion was corrupted by an outright distortion. Heffer blamed the city for not accepting the responsibility of drunken Liverpool football fans causing the death of 'more than 50 Liverpool football supporters at Hillsborough', a disaster before a football match in Sheffield in 1989. Liverpool, stated the *Spectator*, had wrongly blamed the *Sun* newspaper for exposing that harsh truth. The magazine also excused the police at Hillsborough for any wrongdoing. Those 'facts' were totally false. Liverpool's fans were not drunk. The *Sun's* accusation was an outrageous calumny, and the paper had itself apologised in July, three months before the *Spectator* piece was published. Moreover, police negligence was responsible for the horrendous deaths of ninety-six fans, not fifty as Heffer carelessly threw in. Worse, to protect themselves, the police had lied about their own conduct and the fans' behaviour.

Normally, a newspaper's inaccuracy would be ignored, but this was special. The magazine's editor, a high-profile politician, had deliberately disregarded the *Sun's* earlier apology to the bereaved for its gross defamation of 'drunken' fans.

Michael Howard was incensed, 'turbo-charged and bashing the table' according to one eyewitness. He was also fearful. As a passionate supporter of Liverpool football club, Howard anticipated being booed on his next visit to Anfield. The calumny coincided with good opinion polls for the Tories, especially in the crucial north-west where the party needed gains. One year before the election, everything could be lost.

Knowing he was not at his best when angry, Howard refused to speak to Boris. 'He's too difficult to deal with,' he complained about a man who was so very different from himself. While Howard liked to exercise total control, Boris delighted in delegating. Those who suggested to Howard that the best solution was the 'dead-cat strategy' – invent a ridiculous story to divert the media's attention – were ignored. To show that he was honest compared to the mendacious Tony Blair and his henchman Alastair Campbell, Howard ordered Boris to issue a grovelling apology – and not just through the magazine, he agreed with Rachel Whetstone, his senior adviser: Boris, he ordered, should apologise in person to Liverpudlians. Whetstone called Boris with Howard's demand. Public self-flagellation was Howard's price for him remaining as a junior spokesman.

Boris had several choices. He had not written the editorial but to use that excuse would be weasly. He could also have refused Howard's demand that he participate in what he would later call 'a pilgrimage of penitence'. Howard was after all a disciplinarian with a limited sense of humour. But he was the Tories' only hope to defeat Labour, so the honourable Etonian team player agreed to perform. His force of personality, he anticipated, would get people back on side. Without fuss, he listened to the lines of homage he was expected to deliver.

'You do realise that Michael is out to destroy you?' the Tory MP Bernard Jenkin asked Boris as they walked into the Commons chamber.

'Really? Why?' asked Boris.

'Because he can't stand you,' explained Jenkin.

Boris shrugged. He was committed. He knew exactly how he would play matters to his advantage, raising his profile with a quality appearance. Only later would Howard realise that Boris had made apologising into an art form. He underestimated Boris's ability to turn his own flaws to his advantage.

But first there was another crisis. On Monday 18 October, Petronella had a miscarriage. Distraught in the Portland Hospital, she waited for Boris's visit. In an attempted disguise, he entered the hospital. Together, in genuine misery for both Petronella and their lost child, they sat for some time. The following day, Petronella went to the country to recover. Few could imagine the secret juggling that followed. Stanley's homily for survival – 'Nothing matters very much and most things don't matter at all' – would be tested.

On Wednesday 20 October, Boris went alone to Liverpool. No other editor and MP would have travelled unprotected and unaccompanied. That was Boris – a loner convinced that his courage would outsmart his foes.

Within minutes of his appearance in the city, Howard's plan for a decorous apology fell apart. Surrounded by a scrum of journalists without a Liverpudlian in sight, Boris claimed that Howard could not have read the whole article and asserted that some parts of the editorial were accurate. Since he was fighting for his political career, the performance was polished. There were no jokes, the buffoon act was buried and he did not ruffle his hair. Narrowing his eyes, he calculated how to swerve from incoming attacks. But for once, his performance could not entirely deflect his accusers. A nasty blow landed during a radio interview. 'You're a self-centred pompous twit,' Paul Bigley, the brother of the victim, told Boris. 'You don't look right, never mind act right. Get out of public life!' As he left Liverpool, Boris's refusal to make a full apology left everyone dissatisfied – except Boris. Endless interviews, explanations and his celebrity had exhausted the controversy. There was barely time to gather his breath before the next ambush.

Two and a half weeks later on Saturday morning, 6 November, Tina Weaver, the editor of the *Sunday Mirror*, called Howard's office. Her newspaper had paid a member of the Portland's staff for the tip of Boris's visit. Weaver asked Howard's spokesman whether Boris had paid for Petronella's 'abortion'. When contacted, Boris blustered and denied any affair. 'Poor, poor Marina,' he wailed with his wife standing nearby. 'Why does she have to be put through this?' Weaver was given Boris's denial and decided to publish the allegation about an affair between Petronella and an unnamed MP – without naming Boris.

Early that same evening, Simon Walters of the *Mail on Sunday* heard about the *Sunday Mirror*'s scoop. By then, Boris had discussed the leak with Petronella. At her insistence, he agreed that he would lie. When Walters called, he asked Boris whether he would resign as Shadow arts minister because of allegations about his private life. 'I have not had an affair with Petronella,' replied Boris. 'It is complete balderdash. It is an inverted pyramid of piffle. It is all completely untrue and ludicrous conjecture. I am amazed people can write this drivel.' Combined with Verushka's denial about the affair and that her daughter had had an abortion, Boris's fate was left dangling.

During the following week, Verushka Wyatt became incensed about the treatment of her daughter. Finally, she snapped and confirmed to the *Mail on Sunday* that there had been a long affair and an 'abortion' of Boris's child. Michael Howard heard the news late that Saturday afternoon. Conscious of the lies Blair had told about the Iraq War and the recent report by Judge Hutton into the BBC's exposé of Alastair Campbell's nefarious operation to 'sex up' the intelligence about weapons of mass destruction, Howard was hypersensitive about politicians telling truth. 'If it's true,' he ordered, 'and he's lied to the media, he'll have to go.'

'Did you lie last week?' Howard's emissary asked Boris that afternoon.

'It's my private life and I have the right to lie about my private life,' Boris replied.

'Tell him to resign,' Howard ordered.

'I won't resign,' Boris retorted.

'Then Michael says you're sacked,' he was told.

'I have the right to lie,' he said. 'My private life is just that – private.'

'Then you're sacked.'

Shortly after, Boris was seen in Rachel Whetstone's office with 'his head in his hands, looking awful'. Boris was furious. He had not lied to Howard, an impetuous and blinkered man, but to a journalist. 'People always lie about their affairs,' he fumed. But he had learnt a lasting lesson. In future, when asked about his private life, he would never lie – a major error – but refuse to comment by saying, 'I'm not getting into this.'

'I'm sorry, I'm off,' Boris told John Whittingdale, the Shadow culture minister. 'It's all a mess.' On reflection, Howard regretted firing Boris. After all, Boris was just weak – an adulterer who lied – but he was not corrupt or evil. Howard blamed his advisers.

Before the Sunday newspapers including the *Mail on Sunday* were delivered, Boris was ordered by Marina to leave their house. For months, she had wanted to believe Boris's promise that his affair with Petronella was over, but his lies had now become intolerable. Hurt and humiliated, she changed the locks and took off her wedding ring. He lodged in Camden Town with Justin Rushbrooke, his Balliol friend, and Nell, Justin's wife, the daughter of Robin Butler, the former Cabinet Secretary. Several times, he begged Marina to have him back but she refused. 'Notwithstanding his reputation as a rake,' Petronella wrote later, 'Boris is a home-body, and uxorious, who would prefer to be at home with Marina.' Marina attracted

universal sympathy, but not Petronella. She was accused by some
of selfishly wrecking Boris's marriage. Few politicians caught in a
similar storm survived. Women particularly began to loathe Boris.

Contemplating his fate in Camden Town, Boris did not ask
'What did I do wrong?' His predicament was not a mistake. Life in
his opinion was about taking risks and challenging oneself. 'There
comes a point where you've got to put the dynamite under your
own tracks . . . derail yourself. See what happens,' he had earlier
explained. The Petronella affair was just a risk gone wrong. 'My
great-grandfather had four wives,' he fancifully told Rushbrooke. 'I
don't see why I should be faithful.' Monogamy did not appeal to
him. No marriage, he reasoned, would survive if husbands or wives
always told the truth, and politicians should not be judged on their
adultery. They were not elected to be paragons of sexual virtue.
Loyalty and moral virtue towards Marina were irrelevant to him.
Later he blamed newspapers for feeding 'public prurience and jealousy' by demanding that politicians, including Bill Clinton, had no
right to have girlfriends. Those private relations, he insisted, were
no business of the media or the electorate. He could not change his
character. Exaggeration and masquerade were his means of communication against his critics' hypocrisy. Especially by those
mocking BBC commentators. In anger he called Christopher
Bland, the BBC's spirited chairman. 'It's utterly disgraceful what
your reporters are doing on screen about my private life,' complained Boris. 'It's time you realised that I know all about your
private life. If the BBC goes on reporting my affairs like this, you'll
be reading all about yours in the *Spectator*.' 'That's blackmail,'
replied Bland. Boris never fulfilled his threat.

The fallout produced a cascade of casualties. 'It was a truly hor-
rible time for us,' said Liddle. Rachel Royce, Liddle's estranged wife,
tried to make it worse. Commiserating with Marina and lambast-
ing *Spectator* men, she publicly attacked men like Boris who, 'with
their power and celebrity, are so puffed up with their own egos
they end up living in a parallel universe, where they think they can
do what they please'.

Four days after sacking Boris, Michael Howard turned the mess to some advantage. By chance, he was the star at the *Spectator*'s Parliamentarian of the Year lunch. After Boris briefly introduced his former boss, Howard delighted in delivering a well-rehearsed quip about the magazine: 'In all senses of the word it could best be described as political Viagra. And I must take this opportunity of congratulating Boris on the tremendous enthusiasm with which you have approached your various front-bench duties. You were keen to make your mark with the City of Culture [Liverpool]. And you succeeded beyond my wildest dreams. All I can say is, Boris, keep it up.' The only person not roaring with laughter was Boris.

Many MPs assumed Boris's political career was finished. In limbo, Boris told Andrew Gimson at the *Spectator*'s offices, with familiar inconsistency, 'I'm getting fed up with it. Obviously I've been very selfish and stupid, but it's not me . . . There were things in the papers yesterday.' Marina's anger, he sensed, was softening. She loved him and he relied on her. Eventually, he believed, they would be reconciled. His relationship with Petronella was over, but only for the moment. He still needed her friendship.

Elsewhere in the *Sextator*, columnists Toby Young and Lloyd Evans were writing *Who's the Daddy?*, a farce about an oversexed editor and his libidinous staff. 'They wrote the play because they weren't getting any sex while Boris was always surrounded by girls,' carped another writer at the magazine, convinced that Boris was already immersed in another relationship. Their play featured three affairs, Boris and Petronella, Fortier and Blunkett, and Rod Liddle and Alicia Monckton. The magazine's publisher was lampooned giving birth to triplets all with thick blond hair. 'I always knew my life would be turned into a farce,' Boris told Young and Evans. 'I'm just glad it's been entrusted to two such distinguished men of letters.' Neither was reprimanded. Boris, everyone agreed, was a free spirit who trusted his staff beyond expectations. Sales of the magazine soared.

Soon after, Boris was booked to be the guest speaker at the annual dinner of Peter Lilley's constituency. Although arranged long before, Boris cancelled at the last minute and offered to send Petronella in his place. She spoke about political mistresses. Witty and well informed, her speech was a hit, especially with the men in the audience. 'They assumed,' said Lilley, 'that it was a tradition for all *Spectator* editors to bonk Petronella.' Petronella was forgiving. 'Boris,' she wrote years later, 'never sets out to lie. It is just he will do anything to avoid an argument, which leads to a degree of duplicity.' Nor was he vain, she revealed: 'He regards himself as rather ugly.'

After one week's punishment, Marina allowed Boris to return home. By then, Boris had revealed his innermost secret to Marina: witnessing Stanley hit Charlotte. So much about Boris was explained by that experience. Thereafter, she unhesitatingly rebuked Stanley for her husband's sins. Any contrition on Boris's part was not publicised. In a later newspaper interview with Lynn Barber, Boris explained, 'I'm a bit of an optimist so it doesn't tend to occur to me to resign . . . I tend to think of a way of Sellotaping everything together and quietly finding a way through if I can.' The scandals revealed the unusual potency of the 'Boris Phenomenon'. The bulldog test would be his fate in the May 2005 general election.

By most accounts, the Tories were well placed. Despite vast expenditure of taxpayers' money, Blair had failed to improve education, made the NHS less productive and had lost control of immigration. Blair's own position was undermined first by Gordon Brown's incessant demand for his resignation, and second by official inquiries in the aftermath of the Iraq War which questioned the prime minister's honesty. Most would have agreed with Boris that the war had been 'massively corrosive' to the public's trust in politicians. Tasked to win that trust, Michael Howard focused on immigration and crime. This, however, failed to resonate with the electorate. His cause was further harmed by his dismissal, in a flash of temper, of Howard Flight, a deputy party chairman, for telling the truth about the Tories' intention to cut spending. For ambitious Tories, the result of the election was dire. Although the Conservatives won thirty-three more seats, Labour won its third consecutive election victory with a majority of sixty-four – still healthy, although a long way down from a majority of 167 in 2001. Boris's reward for his energetic campaign was an increased majority (over the Liberal Democrats) of 12,793. Hours after Blair declared victory, Michael Howard resigned. Without an obvious successor, the Tory leadership was an open race.

Chapter 7

Downfall and Resurrection

'You've got to run for this thing, Dave,' Boris urged David Cameron immediately after Michael Howard's announcement, 'or else I will.' The threat, Boris would recall, forced Cameron to declare his candidacy. That version of a conversation was Boris's. Not surprisingly, Cameron has never acknowledged Boris's influence on his careful plot to beat his competitors over the following seven months. Michael Howard had deliberately contrived a long campaign to facilitate Cameron's success. Boris was never a contender. During that hiatus, he told an interviewer, 'I am backing David Cameron's campaign out of pure, cynical self-interest'. He expected to be rewarded after the new leader was named at the party conference. In the political vacuum, Boris felt vulnerable.

Soon after the election, Boris met Andrew Neil for breakfast at a Chelsea brasserie. Neil's plans to close Doughty Street and expand commercialisation of the *Spectator* were complete. 'I need a full-time editor,' said Neil. Despite increasing the circulation to 70,000, Boris had too many masters for Neil's liking. 'I've had a good innings,' said Boris cheerfully. 'I'll be gone by Christmas.' Boris was out. Under his replacement, the magazine lost its glamour and the circulation fell.

In his developing habit of introspection, Boris's interview on *Desert Island Discs* in October 2005 revealed both his aspirations and uncertainty. Between choosing the Beatles, the Rolling Stones, the Clash and his favourite, Johann Sebastian Bach's *St Matthew Passion*, he candidly told Sue Lawley, 'My ambition silicon chip has been programmed to try and scrabble my way up this *cursus honorum*, this ladder of things, and so you do feel a kind of sense you've got to [go for it] . . . I think British society is designed like that.' Asked to choose between journalism and politics, he admitted 'I have successfully ridden two horses for quite a long time, but I have to admit there have been moments when the distance between the two horses has grown terrifyingly wide . . . and I did momentarily come off.' Taking risks, he admitted, included the possibility of being caught out. To avoid the consequences of exposure, he revealed, his calculated tactic was to make a joke or a deflective comment. 'I think the profound truth of the matter is that it would be very, very hard to do it in any other way.' He could not endure the 'sheer mental strain' to always have a 'snappy, inspiring sound bite on my lips' because he would 'explode'. Therefore, it was 'much easier for me to play what shots I have as freely as I can'. In the future, he said, his political ambition would take precedence over journalism.

His vulnerability increased after the thirty-nine-year-old Cameron convincingly won the leadership on 6 December against David Davis, the fifty-six-year-old Yorkshire MP. 'I was with Boris on the day Cameron was elected leader,' Stephen Glover, a critic of Boris, wrote in the *Daily Mail* five years later. 'He was shocked to his foundations that the man whom he claimed to have outshone at Eton and Oxford could have leapt over him in this way. It was as though a cosmic injustice had occurred.' That exaggerated observation – Boris had expected Cameron to win – nevertheless accurately reflected the politicians' rivalry.

Unlike Boris, Cameron was not an arriviste. Reflecting his family's traditional City stockbroker background, Cameron enjoyed shooting with the aristocracy and regularly holidaying with the Notting Hill Gate set – a group of friends, many from Eton or Oxford, who met frequently and were godparents to each other's children. To those members of the new establishment, blessing themselves as the modern Camelot, Boris, the loner from Islington, was an outsider more anxious about his income and his mistresses. To hype his social status, Boris occasionally flourished his de Pfeffel aristocratic background or blew hot about his association with Charles (now Earl) Spencer, even though their friendship was not close. His misfortune was his image as an untrustworthy and uncontrollable celebrity unwilling to obey anyone unless he deemed it to be in his own interest.

Planning to rebuild the party, Cameron decided not to rely on Boris. Whatever his charms, he was judged to be a man without convictions – or just one, recently for speeding. Intensely disappointed not to be appointed to the Shadow Cabinet, Boris accepted a minor post as Shadow higher education minister. The snub provoked a riposte to a fellow MP. 'I dimly remember Cameron as a tiny chap known as Cameron minor,' said Boris, contemptuous of that 'second-rate' man. Those like Cameron who got firsts at Oxford were 'girly swots who wasted their time at university', he scoffed, still privately incensed that he had failed to make that grade.

Although passionate about education and equally ardent against worthless degrees like wind surfing, Boris found the tour of universities, soliciting inquiries about student loans and coursework, hardly fulfilling. Uninspired both by David Willetts, the Shadow education minister, and Cameron's failure to develop a robust alternative to Labour, his indifference was ill-concealed. Asked in a BBC TV interview who he supported in a university strike – the staff or the local authorities – Boris waffled, desperate not to take sides. Invited to deliver a key speech to a distinguished audience at King's College London, he arrived unprepared. In his familiar cavalier manner, he treated his audience as fodder without a proper speech. They interpreted his behaviour as a gross insult to their status and intelligence. Some even heckled. In the aftermath, Max Hastings wrote an excoriating criticism of Boris's offence. In reply, Boris sent Hastings a letter with a threat of revenge, from which Hastings concluded, Boris is 'not nice'.

Veering between carelessness and recklessness in his political life, his eagerness to promote himself never faltered. Making money out of notoriety, he wrote *Life in the Fast Lane*, a book in praise of gas-guzzling cars. To summarise his life, he pumped up the pleasure of speeding in expensive sports cars, and chortled about the curse of parking tickets, tow-aways, and running out of fuel. Driving a Ferrari through London 'like some racehorse trying to weave though a herd of cows', he damned the obstacles thrown up by 'our namby-pamby, mollycoddled air-bagged society'. Speaking on a mobile phone while driving, he spouted, was not seriously dangerous – no different from scratching your nose. To advertise a Lexus, the seventeen-stone writer sat on the roof. The dent cost £5,000 to repair. Shamelessly, the MP even admitted that he could imagine an affair with Cherie Blair and confessed to having taken cocaine: 'I remember it vividly. And it achieved no pharmacological, psychotropic or any effect on me whatsoever.' Previously, he had said that none went up his nose because he sneezed, and added, 'In fact, I might have been doing icing sugar.'

The hyper-publicity reflected his frustration. In politics and journalism he had hit a brick wall. Emotionally, he was also dissatisfied. Life with Marina was difficult and he missed Petronella. Despite the exposé of that relationship, he had started another affair, with Anna Fazackerley, a twenty-nine-year-old political reporter on the *Times Higher Education Supplement*. His misfortune was that the *News of the World* was employing an expert to hack their mobile telephones. Their photographer was waiting when he walked out of Fazackerley's Chelsea home. The affair was exposed while he was abroad filming a two-part TV series on ancient Rome. Marina was doorstepped and Fazackerley resigned from the supplement. Reflecting the state of his marriage, Marina did not order her husband to leave the house. For the sake of the children and convenience it was best to once again accept his apologies and get on with life. One year later, Boris would express his admiration of France's management of adultery during the break-up of Nicolas Sarkozy's marriage. One morning, Madame Sarkozy had stood next to the French president in Paris and by nightfall the following day she was with her lover in New York. 'It's vastly superior to our approach,' gushed Boris.

Four years after he had entered Parliament, and in the wake of yet another sexual scandal, there was neither balance nor consideration in Boris's world. Nor any care about the electoral consequence – especially to women voters – of being a serial adulterer. Ghosts, past and present, cast a gloomy fate over his life. His career had again hit the buffers. This time, there was little reason to hope for resuscitation.

*

Unknown to Boris, during 2007, the Tories would choose their candidate for London's mayor. The elections were due on 1 May 2008.

In mid-2006, Cameron had not thought about the contest. In the previous two elections, Ken Livingstone, the former Labour MP, had humiliated the Tory challenger Steve Norris, and Livingstone was expected to win the third election. Cameron was in no hurry to find a new candidate. Despite the prestige of the position, the mayor's responsibilities and powers were limited to London's transport network, the Metropolitan Police, social improvements and planning. Most of the £11 billion budget was spent on transport. Most else depended on pushing the thirty-two London boroughs to build houses, creating the right atmosphere for generating more public and private investment and encouraging charitable donations. Persuasion through publicity and grants had been Livingstone's weapon to change London.

Veronica Wadley, the editor of the *Evening Standard*, then a newspaper of considerable influence in London, was frustrated by Cameron's indifference to challenging Livingstone's tired regime. In the 2006 London borough elections, the Tories had won 35 per cent of the vote against Labour's 28 per cent, their best showing since 1982. Livingstone was vulnerable about fare increases and the congestion charge. Wadley had suggested that Michael Portillo should stand but, convinced a Tory would lose, he refused. To defeat Livingstone required an unusual personality able to cross party loyalties and attract dissatisfied Labour voters. After considering the limited options, Wadley fixed on the only Tory matching her requirements. She had worked with Boris at the *Telegraph* and understood his potential. At a summer party in Carlton

Gardens, she cornered Boris and suggested that he run for mayor. Although surprised, he agreed to consider it.

Some months later, she told Cameron that the newspaper would support Boris and no one else. 'He's optimistic, he makes people feel good and he has a serious political agenda,' she told him, overselling the only candidate with a chance to beat Livingstone. Cameron dismissed the idea. Boris, he believed, was 'useless' and could not be trusted to run anything. After approaching an eclectic group of wholly unsuitable personalities, he landed on Nick Boles, the ambitious director of Policy Exchange, a leftish Tory think tank. Boles's selection was bizarre. As a paid-up member of the Notting Hill Gate set, the intelligent Wykehamist was known as an overemotional prima donna. Worse, he lacked any political profile at the time. Livingstone would have little difficulty crushing another Tory dud. Wadley told Cameron that only a character like Boris could defeat Livingstone. In the event, Boles was saved from the *Standard*'s veto after he fell victim to cancer and withdrew. While Cameron cast around for alternatives and proposed more duds, Boris protected himself by remaining 'uncertain'. Their mutual distrust was not helped after Cameron's office leaked that Boris could be the Tory candidate. That leak was followed by a formal announcement: 'Boris is definitely not a candidate.' In reply, Boris issued a statement that he was 'honoured' to be considered as the candidate 'but I'm greatly enjoying what I'm doing'. Then, George Eustace, Cameron's press spokesman, left a message on Boris's answerphone asking him to call back. Before Eustace replaced the receiver, he inadvertently said to someone in his office, 'That man is a complete cunt.' After hearing the recorded curse, Boris called Eustace: 'I suppose I am behaving like a bit of a cunt.'

Boris was agonising about his future. The Commons was a disappointment. He disliked the reprimands for ignoring the whip's discipline and Cameron seemed intent on squashing him. Against that, the prospect of victory in London was slim. With Labour's lead in the national polls increasing – 40 per cent against 33 per cent for the Tories – there could be a general election in 2008. If that occurred, he would face the risk of resigning from the Commons before the mayoral election. Then, if he lost, he would be neither the mayor nor an MP. Finally, even with the *Standard*'s support, Livingstone seemed impregnable. On the other hand, with the promise of the newspaper's support, his higher profile would improve his status in the Commons. To settle the matter, Marina's advice was decisive: he should run. With no alternative, Cameron reluctantly agreed to support Boris.

On 4 July 2007 – one week after Gordon Brown succeeded Tony Blair as prime minister – the *Evening Standard* revealed that Boris, forty-three, had emerged 'as a surprise Tory contender'. For a week he 'agonised' about the decision. On 16 July, in an article for the *Standard*, he officially declared himself a candidate. Publicly, Cameron's office welcomed his candidature, but privately briefed against their accident-prone colleague. Westminster was surprised by his decision. Boris's candidature, said Steve Norris, 'smacks of a certain desperation'. Peter Sutherland, the Henley constituency chairman, was doubtful about Boris's ability to govern the city. Few believed that he possessed the self-discipline. Boris did not deny the challenge: 'The political risk for me is considerable. Ken is the favourite.' Not quite. The first opinion poll in July showed a 'Boris Bounce' with his lead over Livingstone at 46 per cent to 40 per cent – paradoxically the same percentage of voters who favoured Gordon Brown over Cameron, and Brown's lead soon rose to 10 per cent, the benefit of a honeymoon early in his premiership. The trick for Boris would be to exploit London's particular interests.

In his *Evening Standard* article, Boris explained his decision: 'I have found myself brooding – like all paranoid politicians – on the negative voices, the people who say that the great King Newt [i.e. Livingstone, famously a newt-fancier] is too dug in, that his positions are impregnable, his machine is too vast and well oiled . . . I say phooey . . . the prize [is] too wonderful to miss.' Next, he set out his agenda: 'When I look at the streets of London, I see the future for the planet, a model of co-operation and harmony between races and religions, in which the barriers are broken down by tolerance and humour and respect – without giving way either to bigotry or the petty Balkanisation of the race-relations industry.' Appalled by the rise in crime, the disparity of wealth, the empty foreign-owned homes and overcrowding on the Tube, there was much to be done. However, his flaws were obvious. 'I suppose I will be pilloried for being a toff, representing a small section of society,' he wrote. 'And all I can say is, be my guest.' After setting out his Muslim, Jewish and Christian background qualifications to be 'a one-man melting pot', he appealed to Londoners as a supporter of immigration and diversity. Athens, he said, thrived while Sparta collapsed because Sparta forbade immigration.

In contrast to this rousing call to arms, Boris's first media appearance on 16 July was not encouraging. Pushing a dilapidated bike, he arrived late in front of City Hall. Disappearing into a scrum of journalists and photographers, his blond mop occasionally bobbed up amid the morass heading slowly towards the river. 'What do you stand for, Boris?' they asked, convinced that he lacked any core beliefs and his only ambition was for himself. Finally, he called a halt, got on his bike and after colliding with the TV crew, wobbled away. His only policies, according to the newspaper reports, were to abolish speed bumps, ban car booster seats for children and kill the bendy buses – 'the 18-metre-long socialist Frankfurters'. The overwhelming mood that day about a man accused of being unreliable and opportunistic was negative. Few gave him much chance against Livingstone's machine.

That pessimism was endorsed by John Ross of the think tank Social Action Team: 'It's a mathematical impossibility for Boris to win.' The presumption, agreed Professor Tony Travers, the London School of Economics' expert on the capital's politics, was that the lightweight would be defeated by the entrenched wily operator. 'What should I be doing?' Boris asked Travers when they met in Westminster. Boris, it appeared to Travers, had no particular policy interests and relied on a sense of wanting to make London better. 'He's like Stanley Baldwin,' thought Travers: 'I'd rather be an opportunist and float than go to the bottom with my principles around my neck.' Just how, wondered Travers, could Boris survive the rich reservoir of prejudice which Livingstone and the *Guardian* had instantly unearthed from his *Telegraph* articles? Their vitriol was vehement.

As an Old Etonian, Livingstone's press office relayed, Boris had supported fox hunting, the Iraq War, and voted against adoption by gay couples (although he had voted in 2003 to end the discriminatory Section 28). He had also opposed extra tax breaks to single-parent families, insisted that young Muslims must be taught only in English to force their integration, and spoke of his fear that religious zealots were ruling 'large chunks of the Muslim population' in Tower Hamlets with sharia law. He had spoken against 'carpet-bombing some of the loveliest places in [south-east] England' with housing developments, against 'the persecution of smokers', and against forcing schoolchildren to eat healthy meals. That left the race card. Livingstone's officials had dug up the articles mentioning 'piccaninnies' and 'watermelon smiles' and a 'racist' quote from the *Telegraph* in 2006: 'For ten years, we in the Tory Party have become used to Papua New Guinea-style orgies of cannibalism and chief killing.' Papua's ambassador in London had complained that her modern country should not be compared to the Tory party's antics.

Another blast was fired by Doreen Lawrence, the mother of the murdered teenager Stephen Lawrence. The negligent Scotland Yard investigation of her son's murder had been criticised by Sir William Macpherson, the retired judge who conducted the inquiry into the killing, as 'institutionally racist'. With the background of a long campaign for justice, Doreen Lawrence condemned Boris as a rabid racist for criticising Macpherson's recommendation that racist language in a home or private place should be a crime. Mrs Lawrence forgot that the Labour government had also opposed that Orwellian recommendation. Some readers of her denunciation may not have realised that her organisation had received £1.9 million from Ken Livingstone to build a campaign headquarters.

Chuka Umunna, a lawyer whose grandfather, Sir Helenus Milmo, was an accomplished barrister and High Court judge, compiled a dossier of Boris's quotations on behalf of Compass, a left-wing think tank. Among his allegedly incriminatory discoveries was Boris's 'fanatical' backing for George W. Bush. In the article, Boris had actually written that the re-election of the 'cross-eyed warmonger' had been 'the most dismal awakening of my life'. Besides misquoting Boris, Umunna had also in his search missed a priceless Boris sentiment: 'Some dream of their teeth falling out as they are about to be executed with the scimitar by a beautiful black woman.' Inevitably, some were convinced that Boris was a racist, not least Polly Toynbee, the *Guardian*'s matriarchal loather of Tories. No one matched Toynbee's predictions of doom for an Old Etonian personifying intellectual, social and educational elitism. Cameron, she wrote, 'has just made his worst mistake . . . It would be as much a disaster for Cameron's Tories as for Londoners if this buffoon, jester, serial liar and self-absorbed sociopath got to run the great global city.' Fearing the potential lure of Boris's 'humour and wit', Toynbee damned a man 'who has never run anything except his own image' for treating 'this mighty financial centre' as 'a celebrity Eton wall game' without any care for 'ordinary Londoners'. Worst of all for Toynbee, Boris embraced excellence in education, although she had sent her own children to private schools for a time. The Camerons, Toynbee concluded, 'are struggling for gravitas but Boris will strip it away from them'. As a finale, she condemned the *Standard*'s bias towards Boris. Her newspaper's support for Livingstone was naturally different.

Boris spat out a reply to Toynbee: 'She incarnates all the nannying, high-taxing, high-spending, schoolmarminess of Blair's Britain. She is the defender and friend of . . . every gay and lesbian outreach worker, every clipboard-toter and pen-pusher and form-filler whose function has been generated by mindless regulation. Polly is the high priestess of our paranoid, mollycoddled, risk-averse, airbagged, booster-seated culture of political correctness.'

More soberly, Cameron acknowledged that Boris was a problem. To curb his irrepressible contradictions and mistakes, he asked Nick Boles, now in recovery, to mastermind Boris's campaign. Boris rejected Boles. Others were recruited – all young and inexperienced about leadership, strategy and running a campaign. 'A bunch of crusties,' their replacement would later judge. 'Stray dogs and also-rans.'

Their first test was the launch of Boris's campaign at County

Hall on 3 September. Organised by James Cleverly, a publisher and territorial officer who was standing for the London Assembly in the same 2008 elections, it proved his team to be amateurs. After a long delay, *Boris the Movie* started. Looking dishevelled, Boris spoke but there was no sound. Stopping the film, Cleverly announced 'I give you the original political blond bombshell', and pointed at the main door. There was no dramatic entrance because Boris was slouching towards the stage from the corner of the room. In an uncharacteristically dull speech, he promised to replace the bendy buses – 'the jack-knifing, traffic-blocking, self-combusting, cyclist crusher' and a magnet for fare dodgers – with a new Routemaster; Livingstone's new rabbit-hutch dwellings would be replaced by bigger homes; the west London congestion zone would be reviewed; and he would terminate Livingstone's barter deals with Hugo Chavez, Venezuela's Marxist dictator. Finally, Boris added 'I reserve the right in the course of this campaign to make jokes.' Asked about the racism exposed by Livingstone and others, Boris appeared to be trapped. He believed in free speech, hated to be told to use politically correct language but the journalist knew that protesting politicians dug their own graves. 'If you're the incumbent,' he replied, 'you don't big up the challenger. I really can't believe it. It's a classic political goof.' Unlike Livingstone, he would preach openness and optimism: 'I will always defend the use of humour in politics . . . It's a great utensil for bringing people together.'

Eight weeks later, Boris had made no impact. Many wondered whether a campaign even existed. Instead of focusing on winning votes, the candidate was earning money from journalism, TV appearances and after-dinner speeches. His key pledge remained to scrap the flammable, road-blocking bendy buses and restore the iconic red Routemaster double-decker 'hop on, hop off' bus. 'I want to give Londoners a bus they can be proud of,' he said with childlike nostalgia. Challenged about the cost of conductors on 600 buses, he invented a figure of £8 million. The true cost would be at least £70 million. When exposed, he assumed, he could ignore the mistake as harmless. Wadley's patience was exhausted. At the *Spectator*'s annual lunch in November she sat next to Boris.

'You're pathetic,' she said loudly. 'You need to pull your finger out.' In her subsequent conversations with George Osborne, the Shadow Chancellor, she repeated the warning.

Facing chaos, Cameron stepped in. He called Jonathan Marland, a no-nonsense successful businessman and the Tory Party's treasurer: 'The campaign's no good and there's no money. Take over.'

'Why me?'

'Because you're the only person Boris will be frightened of.'

Marland called Lynton Crosby, an Australian political strategist famed for masterminding John Howard's four successful campaigns to be elected Australia's prime minister. 'You need a win in the UK,' Marland said, reminding Crosby of his failure in 2005 to secure Michael Howard's victory. Crosby was blamed for focusing excessively on immigration. 'We'll pay you £75,000 and we'll get you rent-free accommodation in Chelsea,' said Marland. 'It's an odd campaign so far,' he added. 'It's as if Boris is unwilling to mow the lawn, hoping his popularity will carry him through.' George Osborne was the next to call Crosby. 'The campaign's going nowhere,' he said. Finally, Boris emerged. He asked Crosby to take over but noticeably did not admit that there were problems.

'I watched his declaration of running,' Crosby said later, 'and I thought he had no chance of winning. There was no clear message. No grip. He's not lazy, just ill-disciplined. He wasn't applying himself and was unaware what was required.' The good news was that initial research reported that Boris was an admired celebrity.

They agreed to meet in Quirinale, a restaurant in Westminster, at 8 p.m. Boris arrived at 8.25.

'If you ever come late again,' said Crosby, 'I'll cut your legs off.'

'I know what you're going to say,' replied Boris, 'I'll get my hair cut.'

Over the following two hours, Crosby and Marland read the Riot Act. 'There'll be no more womanising,' ordered Marland convinced that Boris was having affairs all over town and *News of the World* reporters were tailing him. 'You've failed at everything so far. You need a win. This is your last-chance saloon in your political career.'

Boris became downcast. The race, he acknowledged, was his redemption rather than a stepping stone to something greater. Even if he won, he could not decide whether he would remain in City Hall for one term or two. Like a butterfly, his conversation darted around, committing himself to prove he was serious and competent. Other than promising symbols – bikes and bendy buses – he didn't have a narrative about his vision for London.

'The voters on polling day,' said Crosby, 'must have a strong idea why they should buy from you. They need a story.' Next, Crosby unveiled the winning strategy: 'We're going to target the Tories in outer London. Either they've never voted in local elections or they voted for Ken because they didn't like Norris.' Crosby had learned from Norris's defeat. Mistakenly, Norris had focused on outbidding Livingstone with undeliverable election promises and he had ignored London's suburbs. Success for the Tories' cross-generational candidate depended on the second preference votes from the minor parties, and his appeal to traditional Tory outer-London boroughs like Bromley as well as the rich in Notting Hill Gate. Analysis of elections was a novelty for Boris. He was gripped. Finally he was interested and listened.

'I'm taking total control,' said Crosby. The current team would be replaced by himself and James McGrath, another Australian. Boris, he decided, 'was like a puppy dog running around the farm, and sometimes I'd need to whack him with a rolled-up newspaper'. Boris was ordered to stop writing his *Telegraph* column. 'I am laying down my pen and taking up the sword full time,' he wrote, cringing about the financial loss. At their next meeting two days later, Boris arrived twenty minutes early, a shambolic figure drenched from cycling in the rain.

Crosby taking 'total control' transformed Boris's chances. First priority was to agree on a simple campaign promise. Livingstone's many flaws, not least his anti-Semitism, would play a part in the campaign, but the achievements of London's first mayor could not be entirely dismissed. Public transport had improved, the congestion charge had been a success, he had supported the Blair government's bid for the Olympics and he had not opposed

Thatcherite reforms to enhance London's global financial status. Above all, Livingstone had made a huge success of Blair's proposal that cities would prosper with self-governing mayors.

Crosby identified Livingstone's weaknesses. Knife crime was increasing, London suffered huge inequality of wealth and, despite encouraging unlimited immigration, Livingstone's housing record was dismal. Construction of new homes in 2008 would fall to just 12,300 compared to 28,800 just one year earlier. Livingstone's 'raw deal from Gordon Brown' meant Treasury grants had fallen while Livingstone had increased rates by 152 per cent over his eight years. Livingstone also made many bogus claims, especially about transport and housing.

Nearly all the new overground train and Tube extensions and improvements across London had been commissioned under the last Tory government. Crossrail had been conceived by Margaret Thatcher's government and was still struggling to start construction during the Labour era. Livingstone's bendy buses had increased fare dodging and blocked London's roads. Many were running 80 per cent empty. Even the congestion charge, invented by a White-hall civil servant, was faltering – traffic levels had surged back to pre-charge levels. Aesthetically, Livingstone had damaged London by approving multiple tower blocks in the City and along the Thames. He was damned for his love of towers by Eddie Lister, the Tory leader of Wandsworth, as the obsession of a 'one-man dictatorship' for the edifice complex. Boris would publicly pledge to disallow any proposed tower threatening London's historic beauty.

On Crosby's orders, few of those truths would be mentioned in the campaign. Boris was told not to speak about social justice, a 'fairer city' and repairing the 'fractures' because those issues would not win votes. Instead, he was to focus solely on the environment, Livingstone's rate increases, rising Tube fares, bendy buses and especially the growth of gangs and street crime. Focus on the murders – shootings and stabbings – Crosby ordered Boris after Christmas. Livingstone was accused of spending more time with property developers than with the victims' mothers. The statistic that violent crime had fallen in London by 8 per cent to a ten-year low was buried.

For a man eager to entertain and offer something new, the order of constant repetition offended Boris's authenticity. 'I can't keep giving them the same old stuff,' he complained to Crosby.

'You have to, that's what you must do,' ordered Crosby. 'The message must be consistent. It's not dog whistle but a fog horn – everyone must hear what we're saying.' A furious argument erupted in a taxi after Lionel Barber, the editor of the *Financial Times*, acknowledged receipt of an article purportedly by Boris. 'How dare you,' Boris shouted at Crosby, who had submitted an article in Boris's name but written by a staffer. 'It's no good. My words are my currency and that's not me.'

'We haven't got time, Boris,' snapped Crosby closing the argument. The Australian had given up discussing what Boris should wear. He had laughed after hearing that Cameron had held four meetings to decide what he would wear for a photo shoot at the Taj Mahal.

At the beginning of 2008, the election result was uncertain. Boris's hope for a roller-coaster campaign was stalled. Opinion polls put Livingstone ahead. Everything depended on the preference vote, persuading Lib Dems to choose Boris for their second vote. Then unexpectedly the mood began to swing against Labour. Gordon Brown had missed his chance of victory by opting not to call a snap general election and was riding into the financial crisis. As so often with Boris, events beyond his control, a gambler's luck, conspired to work to his advantage. To his further advantage, his contact with voters spread optimism. Like Bill Clinton and Ronald Reagan, he made people feel good. His genius was to persuade people to like him. Unlike most politicians, he was stopped in the street. Funny, tactless, ironic, posh, vague and genial, he did not refuse any demand for a selfie. Having got her selfie, one woman walked away and said loudly to her friend, 'I'd never vote for him.' Boris was nonplussed. Crosby mentioned the benefit of being underestimated: 'You'll always surprise people. And if you surprise them at the right time, that can be very powerful.'

Occasionally, Boris behaved suspiciously. He disappeared on his bike or, just after he and his team got into a Tube carriage, he jumped out at the last moment. 'He's given us the slip,' a staffer shouted. Although he would arrive at the destination, his team were puzzled. Was he just a loner fond of saying 'I cycle because no one can tell me what to do'? Or was he calling in to see a girlfriend? Asked by a newspaper whether he had any secret children, he replied 'Not as far as I am aware.'

'Are there any other affairs?' he was asked

'Not that I know of,' he said.

Boris's affairs, Crosby discovered, did not dent his popularity and remained unmentioned because Livingstone himself had three undisclosed children from previous relationships. Some called it the Clinton effect – the president's ratings had increased during the Monica Lewinsky scandal – and Boris championed Clinton's right to privacy about his sexual relationships. Politics, wrote Boris, was being 'turned into hell for so many of its practitioners by the public's belief in the "democratic right" to insist on its leaders taking no mistresses'.

*

The election's momentum and tone dramatically changed in early 2008. Andrew Gilligan – the sharp investigative journalist who at the BBC in 2003 had broken the story about the 'sexed up' dossier into Iraq's military capabilities – had been directed by the *Evening Standard*'s editor to investigate suspected corruption at City Hall. The centre of the spider's web, he discovered, was the London Development Agency (LDA), established by Livingstone to create jobs and generate business. Since 2000, the LDA had spent £2.6 billion. Livingstone claimed that the LDA had 'created or safeguarded' 90,800 jobs but Gilligan had discovered that City Hall could only identify a few hundred additional jobs. The LDA's real beneficiaries were race, environmental and peace groups, especially in migrant communities which supported Livingstone. Christian community groups received barely any money. Huge sums of LDA grants, Gilligan discovered, had disappeared through bankruptcies and waste. Among the beneficiaries was a Greater London Authority (GLA) employee: she enjoyed a holiday to Nigeria paid from public funds. The victims of Livingstone's cronyism, the newspaper claimed, were London's children living in poverty in the East End. They had received none of the LDA's money to improve their education to avoid poor jobs or unemployment.

The *Standard*'s principal target was Lee Jasper, the mayor's equalities adviser. According to Gilligan, Jasper had handed over between £2.5 million and £3.3 million of LDA money to allies. Among the beneficiaries was a group managed by a woman employed as a community worker with whom Jasper had apparently enjoyed a sexual relationship. Jasper had given the group £100,000.

Boris demanded that Livingstone account for the £2.6 billion. 'There is something chilling and Stalinist about his refusal to comply,' Boris said.

Livingstone's supporters, especially in the *Guardian*, protested that Boris's racism had fuelled the attacks on Jasper. Boris, they said, was endangering Livingstone's 'progressive' policies to build a multicultural city. 'It is an utter disgrace,' replied Boris about the 'slush fund' for Jasper's 'cronies', that 'anyone who dares question the order of things is denounced as a "racist" . . . It is the politics of the skunk.' Accused of breaking City Hall rules, Jasper resigned but Livingstone loyally insisted that Jasper was innocent and would be re-employed if Livingstone won the election. (A subsequent official inquiry would condemn Jasper's behaviour as 'entirely inappropriate' and 'improper'.)

In answer to the racist charge against himself, Boris apologised on a website for having used the terms 'piccaninnies' and 'watermelon smiles' in his journalism: 'Of course I am sorry because it does not represent what I have in my heart. I think people have a political motive to try and take something out of twenty years of journalism – millions of words – and they have found a few phrases that they think they can spin to prove that this guy harbours old-fashioned thinking. It's absolute nonsense.' At hustings he repeated that he supported immigration and an amnesty for illegal immigrants – 'I'm absolutely 100 per cent anti-racist. I despise and loathe racism' – and lamented that the debate had been 'reduced' to misquoting his article. Invariably, he recited his family background: Muslim, Jewish and Christian with a Catholic baptism. In reply, the *Standard* highlighted Livingstone's association with Muslim extremists who denounced western liberalism and shared his anti-Semitism; and also his tirade against the Jewish property developers David and Simon Reuben. After an argument about a site they owned near the Olympic Park, Livingstone had told the brothers, who were British citizens born in Bombay, 'Go back to Iran.' (Livingstone's reference to Iran was doubly wrong, as the Reubens' parents were actually Iraqi Jews.) In retaliation, the brothers contributed to Boris's election fund.

As the race turned increasingly acrimonious, Crosby discovered that most of London's voters were, to his relief, unconvinced by the allegations of racism levelled at Boris. Crime and transport were, as he'd predicted, the dominant issues. The balance was tilted by the *Standard*'s characterisation of Livingstone as 'a phoney, a charlatan and a fraud' and his re-election as a 'frightening prospect'. Daily, the newspapers' 500 street billboards across the city screamed 'Ken-fraud', 'Ken-lies', 'Ken-scandal', 'Suicide bomb backer runs Ken campaign' and 'Ken – drunk on power'. Johnson suffered only marginal criticism in the newspaper. 'I'm not working to get a Tory elected,' Andrew Gilligan said. 'I'm working to get Ken unelected.'

Looking exhausted with eight weeks of campaigning still ahead of him, Livingstone's vulnerability was reflected in the polls. By mid-March 2008, the *Standard*'s poll placed Boris 12 per cent ahead of Livingstone. The voters thought Livingstone was more dishonest than Boris; and in a surprising insight into voter psychology, Boris was particularly popular among women. Unexpectedly for Livingstone, some working-class voters in the suburbs targeted by Crosby were attracted to Boris; and painfully for Livingstone, Lib Dem and Green supporters were tempted to cast their second preference vote for Boris rather than him. With Labour running about 15 per cent behind the Tories in the national polls, the hammer blow fell as Livingstone became an unforeseen casualty of Gordon Brown's personal unpopularity. Nevertheless, with a loyal following, some polls put Livingstone slightly ahead. As election day loomed, the *Guardian* reported uncertainty about the outcome and Boris's own belief that he would lose. Those doubts were echoed by *The Times* and even the *Telegraph*, both lukewarm about Boris. Envy poisoned some natural Tories. 'Mr Johnson,' wrote Simon Heffer, 'is not a politician. He is an act. For some of us the joke has worn not thin, but out.' Among other Tories who refused to vote for Boris was Michael Portillo. Both critics would have been scathing about a riotous fundraising dinner for Boris's campaign in Notting Hill Gate organised by Boris's Bullingdon friends including David Cameron. At the end of Boris's speech, his toast was to 'Mayor Leavingsoon'.

In late March, Gordon Brown had written off Livingstone's chances while Livingstone himself continued to live in hope. Although Crosby's and the *Standard*'s polls predicted that Boris had a real chance of winning, Boris himself still feared he might lose the prize by making an inappropriate joke or an unfortunate revelation about his personal life. Nervous and tired, in the last days he chose to be dull. He pledged to ban alcohol from the Tube, stop drug-taking on buses and, overruling the Tube's managers, not to close any ticket offices. The flurry was in fact a smokescreen following an embarrassing encounter of exactly the kind Boris had feared might derail him at the last moment. A. A. Gill, the acerbic *Sunday Times* columnist, asked Boris, 'What are you going to do on your first day in City Hall?' Boris was stuck. There was no plan. 'Put conductors and policemen on buses,' he stuttered. He also failed to name a single member of his future team. Unlike Livingstone, he had no court of fellow travellers with whom he had worked in Parliament or the party. Crosby had wanted Boris to focus on the campaign and avoid appearing complacent by anticipating appointments. Other than put on a serious face, Boris genuinely did not know what he would do. In desperation, he announced that he would appoint Bob Diamond, Barclays Bank's former chief executive, to run the Mayor's Fund, his new charity for young Londoners. Diamond had earned £21 million in the previous year despite Barclays writing off £1.6 billion in losses.

'Boris was freaked out by the prospect of becoming mayor,' Jonathan Marland noticed as election day neared. 'His self-confidence fell.' There was no team. No one had prepared for victory. Boris did not understand the process of public appointments and managing state organisations. 'I've got an £11 billion budget,' he said in panic. Marland, Francis Maude, a cerebral senior Tory MP, and George Osborne discussed how to save the still unelected mayor. Boles, they agreed, should be responsible for choosing the transition team with Boris as chairman of the board. No one believed Boris could actually manage.

On election day, Thursday 1 May, the *Standard*'s headline over a photo of Boris pointing Kitchener-like at the camera was 'Honesty and competence'. The *Guardian*'s headline was: 'Be afraid. Be very afraid . . . Imagine what it would be like if this bigoted, lying Old Etonian got his hands on our diverse and liberal capital!' Their columnist Zoe Williams derided the 'floppy hair, that sodding bicycle and big gob'. Boris, 'a snob' she wrote, 'despises gays, provincials, Liverpudlians, Muslims, Congolese and Africans'. London, she lamented, would become an international 'laughing stock' because Boris would make 'a mess of the whole thing'.

The results would not be announced until the following evening. At 5 p.m. on Friday 2 May, Tessa Jowell, the Labour MP, telephoned the *Standard*'s editor with an insider's tip that Livingstone had lost. One hour later, with victory almost certain, Wadley ordered the final edition to be printed before the result was confirmed. 'Boris has won' was the headline of a special edition on sale across London by 6 p.m. She was taking a risk, she told her staff, without admitting that if Boris lost she would probably be fired. Five hours later, Boris, with Marina beside him, stood in City Hall to take applause. After the second preference votes were redistributed, Boris got 1,168,738 votes against Livingstone's 1,028,966 – 53 per cent to 47 per cent. Livingstone was shocked. Despite losing in white working-class areas like Barking and Dagenham because they disliked his race card, he blamed the *Standard*'s campaign. In truth, the Tories were trusted by a multiracial city. (In the nationwide local elections, which had taken place on the same day as the

London mayoral election, the Tories won 44 per cent of the vote with Labour struggling on 24 per cent.) In his victory speech, Boris praised Livingstone's 'transparent love of London', courage and 'sheer exuberant nerve'. Len Duvall, a Labour member of the London Assembly who would be a vocal critic of the new mayor, saw the dawn of a different epoch: 'Ken's a twentieth-century politician, Boris is twenty-first century. Celebrity won.'

Beside her husband, Marina stood pensive and composed, shunning the spotlight. Throughout much of the campaign, she had been away fighting a complex case in the north and, as in Henley, she was rarely seen. Their children were looked after by a nanny and housekeeper. Barely looking at each other, they left the hall and headed to a champagne celebration at Millbank Tower. In the cheering crowd, Stanley Johnson revealed that he would try to inherit his son's seat in Henley. Cameron firmly crushed that idea. 'We need a local candidate,' he swiftly ordered. Watching Stanley, a friend commented, 'Every time Boris succeeds, a little bit of Stanley dies.'

'Let's get cracking tomorrow – let's have a drink tonight,' Boris said in a short speech. Down below stood the Festival Hall. Exactly eleven years earlier, Tony Blair had stood in front of delirious supporters to hail the 'New Dawn'. Now, the shell-shocked *Guardian* editors composed a report under the headline 'New Dusk'. Obsessed by networks, privilege and money, they puzzled how an Old Etonian could win London with another Old Etonian favourite to be prime minister. Decay, the newspaper predicted, would spread from City Hall until the Tories were defeated in the 2010 general election.

In City Hall, Livingstone's key staff were also shocked, unable to believe their defeat. 'Please call me Boris,' said the victor as he toured the building the following morning. 'You'll discover I'm not a crazed Thatcherite neocon,' he smiled as he shook hands in the canteen. Since he was derided by the *Guardian* as an 'inexperienced buffoon', the expectations of those trained to obey Livingstone's edicts were low. Deploying his natural gift to make each person feel special, regardless of class or race, even the antagonistic staff became inclined to like Boris. At least his first orders – to destroy Livingstone's conspiratorial atmosphere by removing the partitions, and banning alcohol on the Tube – were inoffensive.

The jubilation was followed by nastiness. Floating above the confusion, Boris seemed oblivious to his responsibilities. His instinct for leadership was missing. 'Leave it to Nick,' Boris had told Crosby, persuaded by Cameron that Boles could be trusted as Boris's chief of staff. To assert himself, Boles did not tell Crosby about when Boris's swearing-in ceremony would be held. The Australian was furious. Before the end of the first week, Crosby observed, the mayoralty was all about Boles, not least because Boles did not trust Boris. Bewitched by his new role, Boris failed to wrest control from the prima donna. Amid that uncertainty, Marland suggested to Boris that they appoint a chief operating officer to undertake the executive chores. Boris would be a figurehead mayor and chairman of the board. Francis Maude nominated Tim Parker, a friend known for cost-cutting at Kwik-Fit and the AA, to be appointed the deputy mayor to supervise and initiate all the day-to-day administration including transport. 'Right,' agreed Boris, reflecting his naivety and lack of self-confidence. He had never met Parker and was unaware that Parker, aka the Prince of Darkness due to his reputation for slashing workforces, was impatient and sceptical of politicians and government. Hired for an annual salary of £1, Parker assumed that Boris would cut ribbons while he, like Mayor Michael Bloomberg in New York, would dominate London. Boris, who hitherto would play only as the captain of the team, had temporarily lost his nerve, scared of the challenge.

The combination of Boles and Parker shocked City Hall's officials. Neither knew anything about local government. Their antagonism was unfair to Boles. With experience at Westminster Council and the Policy Exchange, he selected three critically important members of Boris's new team. Kit Malthouse, an accountant and deputy leader of Westminster Council, would be the deputy mayor responsible for the police; Munira Mirza, thirty, state-educated in Oldham and an Oxford graduate, was given responsibility for culture and arts; and Simon Milton, the outstanding leader of Westminster Council, was appointed as a consultant for housing and planning. Educated at St Paul's and Cambridge, Milton was the perfect administrator. With twenty years' experience at Westminster, the son of a German Jewish refugee who created the London patisserie chain Sharaton's, Milton understood how to negotiate with Whitehall, especially the Treasury. Alongside him was Eddie Lister, fifty-eight, the leader of Wandsworth Council, where he had successfully cut costs and privatised council services. The former corporate executive was recruited to undertake a financial audit of City Hall.

Seemingly oblivious to all those appointments and facing the greatest challenge of his life with great trepidation, Boris focused on his own wallet. In panic, he told Marland that he faced a crisis, namely the sharp reduction of his personal income. The mayor's salary of £137,579, he pleaded, was insufficient to pay for his children's private education. His instant solution was a newspaper column. Marland called Rupert Murdoch. 'Hire Boris,' Marland said. 'It won't do you any harm in the long term.' Murdoch refused. Marland's next call was to Aidan Barclay of the *Telegraph*, son of the co-owner David Barclay. Barclay quickly agreed Marland's demand of a £250,000 fee for a weekly column. Boles was shocked by the agreement. Boris was persuaded to give £50,000 of the fee to fund media and classics scholarships. Asked by the media whether the donation was ordered by Cameron, Boris replied 'If you put that I was forced to do it by some fucking Cameron bollocks, I'll be extremely annoyed.' The precise amount finally donated by Boris would remain unclear. The *Telegraph* column was to prove, over the following years, an invaluable platform to explore and express his political ideology. In self-justification, Boris would later write 'Any columnist is engaged in a dialogue. What you are doing is emerging from the wings and diving onto the stage for five minutes, doing a twirl before shooting off into the wings. You are then listening to see if anyone's paid any attention . . . You get screeds of abuse or praise.' Leading the critics of the deal was Sonia Purnell. Boris's 'puzzling preoccupation' with his 'pursuit of money', wrote Purnell, was insatiable: 'All the riches, the power and the glory are never quite enough, it seems.' Not least, she wrote, because the Johnsons were rich, owning 'valuable houses or large tracts of land in London's Islington, Regent's Park, Notting Hill Gate, as well as Oxfordshire, Somerset and Greece'. By 'the Johnsons', Purnell meant Stanley and his four eldest children. All five Johnson families saw themselves as hard-working, living in modest accommodation and financially challenged. Everything was relative. Glued together by optimism and competition, the Johnsons could not believe their luck about their newly elevated social status thanks to Boris's unexpected triumph.

As Boris admitted, there was a pertinent resemblance between himself and Mercury, the god of eloquence, theft, sharp-wittedness, luck and getting away with it. By a quirk of fate, Boris had unintentionally anticipated his eventual resurrection four years earlier. Just two days after his dismissal in disgrace by Michael Howard in 2004, Boris had fulfilled a long-standing engagement to address the Horatian Society in Lincoln's Inn, London. For Britain's devoted classicists, the gathering was an eagerly awaited event to enjoy a new interpretation of Rome's favoured lyrical poet and satirist. Boris had not disappointed his audience. To roars of approval, his forty-minute witty analysis of Horace displayed profound knowledge of the texts, outclassing the academic who followed him. During his unusually fluent speech, Boris identified with Horace's own association with Mercury – not only the guide of souls to the underworld, but also the god of communication. From Lincoln's Inn, he headed home, and as usual before he went to sleep, he read Greek poems in the original.

ACT II

'The first time he'd had to work in his life'

Chapter 8

The Challenge

Just days after Boris's election, Bernard Jenkin, the Tory MP, spotted the new mayor standing alone in Westminster's Great Hall, glued to the spot where Charles I had stood for his trial in 1649.

'What are you doing here?' asked Jenkin.

'I can't believe I'm giving this up,' Boris explained, just before submitting his resignation from the Commons.

'Don't worry, you'll be back,' said Jenkin as consolation.

Boris looked unconvinced. As a man of energetic enthusiasm, for once he looked lost. Parliament had been a disappointment. Without any achievements or progress up the greasy pole, he had left no impression other than as an unreliable chancer. Now he was even unsure whether the mayoralty would improve his route to Downing Street.

In a trance or perhaps in haste, he cycled that night back to Islington. On the way, he passed through six red lights, failed to stop at a zebra crossing, cycled on the pavement and finally through a no-cycling park. He was followed by a *Sunday Mirror* journalist. The publication of his lawlessness was a warning of the new peril of his life in the spotlight. He no longer enjoyed a journalist's licence to act frivolously, or feign a backbencher's powerlessness. He had become the representative and lawmaker of one the world's great cities with the power to influence millions of lives. For the first time, his decisions mattered.

*

For Boris's formal inauguration, he arranged that Livingstone's key executives for the mayor's principal responsibilities – planning, police, transport – should be seated together in the front row. All had good reason to feel anxious. Manny Lewis, the chief executive of the London Development Authority (LDA), Peter Hendy, the commissioner of Transport for London, and Ian Blair, the Metropolitan Police commissioner, were dogged by allegations of partisanship, chaos, overstaffing and financial mismanagement.

Known as 'Ken's chequebook', the LDA had spent £1.5 billion over four years on 'community projects'. In the previous months, at least £159 million had been handed over to phoney 'diversity' projects including to extremist Muslims with few attempts to monitor whether the money was justified. Lewis was fired by Boris for misspending 'tens of millions of pounds'. He did not protest when Boris terminated his contract.

Peter Hendy, a privately educated graduate trainee of London Transport, had astutely anticipated Boris's antagonism. As a Livingstone loyalist, he had publicly opposed the Routemaster buses. To avoid dismissal, just before the inauguration ceremony, he had presented Boris with a transport plan to help him implement his manifesto. Astutely, he had included Boris's beloved Routemaster. He also proposed to reverse much that he had done for Livingstone. 'A number of people were looking for my neck,' said Hendy, 'including the *Evening Standard*, so I was always insecure. But Boris's perverse streak decided to do the opposite. One of the great things about Boris is his generosity.'

With one gone and another hanging on, Ian Blair, the Met commissioner since January 2005, had good reason to fear dismissal. In July 2005, after Islamic extremists had murdered fifty-two people in a series of bomb attacks on the London Underground and on a bus, Met detectives had shot Jean Charles de Menezes at Stockwell Tube station. Seven bullets were fired into the Brazilian's head. Soon after, Blair had told a press conference that Menezes' death was 'directly linked to the ongoing anti-terrorist operation' even though his senior officers already knew that Menezes was innocent. During a BBC radio interview that day, Boris condemned the police for being 'too trigger-happy'. Before he could finish fully articulating the line of thought, he was cut off by the BBC. Blair wrote to Boris that his remarks were 'outrageous' and 'offensive' and demanded 'in the strongest possible terms that you withdraw your remarks'.

'I have absolutely no intention of doing so,' replied Boris, repeating that the police were 'trigger-happy'. Blair was accused of hampering the independent investigation of the shooting. Two years later in 2007, after the truth of the Menezes shooting had been exposed, the GLA assembly passed a vote of no confidence in Blair. The commissioner's position, said Boris, was 'untenable'. He added, 'A paralysing culture of health and safety lies at the heart of the Met Police.'

One year later on his inauguration day, Boris knew that Scotland Yard had become dysfunctional. An investigation into a corrupt senior officer had spun out of control and several officers were using their police Amex cards for personal use including payments for holidays and one even for his wife's breast implants. London was also engulfed by a wave of knife crime. Among the mayor's few powers was policing. But with Parker's appointment as chief operating officer, Boris remained uncertain how to handle Blair, let alone the Yard. Insensitive to politics and without experience of public administration, Parker's abrasive manner had quickly paralysed City Hall. Parker didn't understand that he needed to work with the bureaucrats, not break them.

Boris returned to his new office in City Hall, a glass egg with stunning views across the Thames to the Tower of London and the City, and opened a cupboard to discover bottles of Châteauneuf-du-Pape. 'Rows and rows of glistening bottles,' chortled Boris, 'left behind by Mayor Livingstone.' Boris would drink the wine. He also cancelled City Hall's daily subscription for forty copies of the *Morning Star* and closed down the *Londoner*, a newspaper published by Livingstone to promote Livingstone. That saved £1 million a year. Finally, he fired one hundred GLA staff including Emma Beal, Livingstone's partner and the mother of their two children. Paid £96,000 a year as an 'administration manager', Beale had, at Livingstone's request, facilitated first-class travel to Cuba and numerous destinations, and delivery of a £2,500 crate of fine wine. Boris's new media spokesman, Guto Harri, discovered that many of Livingstone's records had been shredded but some invoices for his entertainment and travel had been overlooked in filing cabinets. They were kept just in case Livingstone stood in the next election. His humiliated cronies left City Hall waiting for their revenge.

In July, just eight weeks after his victory, Boris became headline news again.

In the rush to recruit his team, Boris was unaware of the process and pitfalls of public appointments. Vetting each person's background was crucial. Among the first appointments was Ray Lewis, the founder of an academy in east London for Caribbean youths, victims of parental neglect which had led to a life of crime. Lewis, a jovial Samaritan, exposed the left's refusal to admit the special needs of black youths. Lewis had presented himself as a priest and a magistrate, but soon after his appearance with Boris, his official CV unravelled. Although he had been approved to sit as a magistrate, his appointment had not passed the final hurdle. More importantly, east London church leaders claimed that Lewis had been defrocked because of allegations of financial and sexual misconduct. Although Boris believed the accusations were politically motivated, Lewis resigned. Distraught about asking for Lewis's departure, Boris telephoned to commiserate. 'I really regretted it,' Boris would later say, 'because he's a man with a fantastic amount to offer and I felt we should have handled it better . . . I could have protected him better.'

Soon after, Bob Diamond, the former chief executive of Barclays Bank, resigned as his charity adviser. More trouble followed when James McGrath, a political adviser working with Lynton Crosby, made an ill-advised comment. In a conversation with Marc Wadsworth, a Labour activist, McGrath was told by Wadsworth that some immigrants disliked their lives in Tory London. 'If they don't like it here,' replied McGrath, the dissatisfied immigrants 'can go home'. Wadsworth accused McGrath of racism. Instead of supporting McGrath who was not racist, Boris fired him. Again, Boris had clearly made a mistake. In 2016, Wadsworth, all the while proclaiming his innocence, was expelled from the Labour Party when charges of anti-Semitic incidents that were deemed 'grossly detrimental to the party' were upheld.

Three high-profile casualties in the new mayor's first nine weeks persuaded Simon Milton, his senior planning adviser, to tell Boris the truth. City Hall was chaotic. Boris looked puzzled. 'Boles doesn't understand local government or London,' continued Milton, 'and you can't decide what to do.' Boris was already failing to engage with his responsibilities – planning and transport – and his administration was in turmoil. 'You're supposed to be in charge,' said Milton. Boris, he realised, did not understand the machinery of government – how to staff it with loyal, talented advisers and, more important, how to get City Hall's roughly 700 officials to make and implement the right decisions – the decisions that he, as mayor, wanted. During his study of the classics and even as a journalist, he had never been exposed to the bureaucrats' decision-making processes. He sat in his office without an inkling where to find a single lever of power. Administration was an unknown science. 'Mr Johnson's summer honeymoon,' declared the *Standard*, 'is fast ending. The autumn will decide whether he can really govern the city.' Just as his critics predicted, Boris appeared to be 'an inexperienced blunderer'.

First Boles left. 'Boles failed,' concluded Marland, 'because his life was all about Boles.' Then Milton focused on Parker's manner. 'I'll go if this continues,' warned Milton. Faced with that ultimatum, Boris agreed to Parker's departure.

In the midst of City Hall's turmoil, that year's twentieth stabbing victim had died. Six men had been murdered in six days. All those deaths, Boris acknowledged, had been 'endlessly ignored'. One hundred days after his victory, he conceded the job was 'bigger than I expected. Much, much bigger, more intellectually challenging than anything I've ever done.' Then followed a surprising confession: 'Over the past few weeks, it has become increasingly apparent that the nature of the decisions that need to be taken are hugely political and there is no substitute for me, as directly elected mayor, being in charge.'

To the surprise of Professor Travers – the LSE professor who had agreed with the verdict that a Boris mayoralty was unlikely – the chaos did not damage Boris's popularity. Boris was seen as a good man. 'The public,' recorded Travers, 'saw the mistakes as evidence of Boris's authenticity.'

After the debris had been cleared, the mood in City Hall's Monday morning meetings changed. Centre of attention and acting as the host of a good party, Boris alternated between jokes and seriousness to steady his administration. 'My manifesto is for London to be happy, green, clean and safe,' he said. In a relaxed and friendly atmosphere, he listened to his team's opinions, asked questions, wrote notes and preferred to follow the mood music so as not to be isolated or disliked. His style was not coercive but inspiring, encouraging the group to support him. As a speed reader, he had usually mastered the details of a proposal. If uncertain because he did not have the facts, he tended to follow the last person he spoke to. 'No, you can't do that,' Milton would say, 'because last week we agreed the opposite.' 'He wants to be loved,' some would say. His new ally, Guto Harri, an Oxford friend and experienced BBC journalist recruited as his communications director, became with Simon Milton a key aide.

*

Sitting outside Boris's office, Milton began rebuilding the administrative machine. The agenda was to cut spending by 15 per cent, reduce knife crime, create more apprenticeships, boost tourism and protect the City's global dominance. Four weeks later he would tell the *Standard* that he had underestimated Boris: 'My job is to translate into action the ten ideas Boris has while he cycles to City Hall.' Boris's foremost priority was to develop the Olympic Park.

Beating the intense international competition to stage the 2012 Olympics in London had won Tony Blair and Ken Livingstone huge accolades. Once the excitement passed, sceptics competed to predict that London would fail to deliver the project on time and on budget, and that like other host cities, the huge area in east London designated for the Olympic Park would be permanently blighted by derelict stadiums and the capital burdened by huge debts. As a keen fan of sport and mindful of the Olympics' origins in ancient Greece, Boris took upon himself the challenge to prove the doubters wrong. Being the mayor during a successful Olympics, he calculated, would boost his profile and his popularity for the party's leadership. He cast around to find a mastermind to build the Olympic legacy, not only for London but also a permanent memorial to himself.

Livingstone, he recalled, had advised him to employ Neale Coleman, a Marxist and close ally of the former mayor. Coleman had been automatically fired after Livingstone's defeat but three weeks later Boris telephoned him. Although ten years older than Boris, Coleman had a lot in common with the new mayor. Both had studied classics at Balliol, both were taught Homer by Jasper Griffin, and both had the same tutors for Virgil and history. Intelligent and politically savvy, Coleman had opposed Boris but was enticed by his vision. Livingstone had failed to conceive a master plan for the future use of the Olympic stadium, the Aquatic Centre and the £490 million Media Centre. His LDA had not signed up a single tenant for the complex after the Games. Equally alarming, the Olympic Development Authority (ODA) had failed to raise £450 million from the private sector to build the Olympic village. Without construction contracts and agreements to subsequently sell the 17,000 athletes' apartments, the ODA was responsible for a £1 billion project without any money. The biggest problem was the fate of the Olympic stadium after the Games – a potential financial albatross once the Labour government and Livingstone had agreed that the stadium should remain unaltered as a venue for athletics. In reality, the stadium was only financially viable if sold or leased to a Premier League football club, and the only realistic tenant was West Ham, a local club.

Boris told Coleman that, unlike all other Olympic cities, London's Games would come in on budget. 'I'm determined about that.' Money must be saved, he said, not least by abandoning Livingstone's plans for temporary arenas and by using Wembley stadium. More important, he must get the legacy powers to develop the Olympic zone, a key aspect which Livingstone had disregarded. 'We must get this sorted out,' Boris told Coleman. At the heart of Boris's personal vision was to develop Stratford as a new metropolis like Canary Wharf, the futuristic development enabled by Margaret Thatcher in the 1980s. The challenge twenty-odd years later was just as enormous. To transfer the debt and land after the Games to a new corporation required complicated negotiations and legislation. In the nature of bureaucratic turf wars, that would be opposed by Whitehall, the local authorities and Transport for London (TfL). Overcoming their obstruction would require Boris's personal engagement and mastery of the details. 'The biggest problem will be TfL,' said Coleman with bitter experience. Hendy was told to prepare a plan while Boris headed for the Beijing Olympics.

Boris's excitement about the potential of the Olympics reflected the difference between himself and Livingstone. Unlike his predecessor, Boris was a sports fanatic. Not only did he enjoy playing tennis, table tennis and cricket, but he had been a keen rugby player. He hated the left's denunciation of character-building through sport and gruelling hikes. Britain's educational establishment, he fumed, had developed an aversion to games and a damaging obsession with 'elf and safety', denying that competitive sport taught resilience, teamwork, trust and leadership. 'The only sport we're excelling in,' he said on the eve of flying to Beijing, 'is the national sport of running ourselves down.' Among the cynics, Boris included David Cameron, who had just cast Britain as a 'broken society' because 'welfarism and political correctness' had sapped young people's courage and morals. 'Piffle,' countered Boris, refreshed after curtailing his City Hall troubles and keen to assert himself as an independent warlord. 'Britain is a decent, compassionate and vibrant nation,' said the proud patriot. 'No one has broken Britain and no one ever will.'

The publication of the 'piffle' snipe appeared as Boris flew economy class to China. His flight coincided with the TV broadcast of the episode of the BBC's genealogy series *Who Do You Think You Are?* in which he starred. Trawling through Boris's background including Turkish, German, French, Muslim and Jewish ancestors, the researchers had discovered that through the de Pfeffels, his eight-times grandfather was George II of England. Like Cameron, he was a genuine toff after all.

Stepping off the plane somewhat dishevelled after eleven hours in an economy seat, the mayor was immediately asked about deriding Cameron's opinion as 'piffle'. Was that a bid to be prime minister? 'Were I to be pulled like Cincinnatus from my plough,' he replied, 'then obviously it would be a great privilege,' and headed for the Olympic stadium. The line was drawn. Unwilling to hide his impatience, Boris still could not understand how someone as boring as Cameron could be a potential prime minister. For his part, Cameron could not understand how a shambolic character could be so popular. Cameron's bewilderment was about to escalate.

In the days before Boris's appearance at the closing ceremony on 24 August, his Chinese hosts had become perplexed. Among Boris's sayings, they were told, was 'Love is a pyramid composed of bullshit and stupid deeds'; and 'The chances of my becoming prime minister are as great as my finding Elvis Presley or being reincarnated into an olive.' They were uncertain what to expect when he walked towards the podium, watched by 1.6 billion people worldwide. Undoubtedly they had also heard of the British cynics carping that he would inevitably drop the Olympic flag or say something foolish during the handover ceremony.

In anticipation of that drama, Boris had taken some care. At lunch, Guto Harri was surprised to watch him for the first time put a napkin over his shirt before he began eating noodle soup. 'Why?' asked Harri. 'Because I can't appear in front of a billion people with soup stains,' replied Boris. As he entered the stadium with his hand in the pocket of a rumpled open jacket, he strode untidily towards the immaculately dressed, stiff-backed Chinese officials standing on a podium proud of their world-beating extravaganza. 'There is no Olympic jacket button protocol,' he later wrote. 'Open or shut it's up to you. I was going to follow a policy of openness, transparency and individual freedom. No disrespect intended. It's just there

are times when you have to take a stand.' Others surmised he was
too fat to do up the button. Later at a party for the British delegation to celebrate the handover, amid relief that Boris had not
dropped the flag, he made a speech informing his audience how
Britain had either invented or codified most international sports,
including table tennis, arguably China's national game: 'Ping-pong
was invented on the dining tables of England, ladies and gentle-
men, in the nineteenth century, it was, and it was called wiff waff.
And there I think you have the essential difference between us and
the rest of the world. Other nations, the French, looked at a dining
table and saw an opportunity to have dinner. We looked at a dining
table and saw an opportunity to play wiff waff . . . and I say to the
Chinese and the world, ping-pong is coming home.' The hilarity
won Boris the celebrity he yearned. He regretted forgetting to
mention that the pankration event of the ancient Greek games
should have featured in Beijing but would hopefully feature in London. 'The chief exponent,' he later told his hosts, 'was Milo of
Croton whose signature performance involved carrying a living ox
the length of the stadium, killing it with his bare hands and then
eating it on the same day.' At the end of that day, his only moan was
about the cost of the phenomenal firework finale. 'Probably cost
more than the London Olympics' entire £3.4 billion budget,' he
sighed.

After Beijing's success, London's Olympic budget was increased
to a more realistic £9.3 billion. The project was ahead of schedule
but the plans for the Olympic Park and the arenas were in danger of
being crippled by the 2008 banking crash. The housing market had
collapsed and the prospect of private investment in the Olympic
village was wiped out. London house prices fell by 15 per cent and
the cranes disappeared overnight. Some 7,000 small builders and
developers were declared bankrupt or disappeared. London had a
housing crisis.

Chapter 9

Exposing Vipers

Ten years earlier, in the infancy of Tony Blair's government, London had no housing crisis. Although Big Bang and Canary Wharf had reversed the city's falling population and London was no longer a tired city, Blair ignored the inevitable demand for more homes after he encouraged immigration. Young Britons and Europeans flocked to the capital. As the 2011 census would show, London's population would grow faster than predicted from 7.5 million to 10 million by 2031. Tony Blair, reported Rick Blakeway, Boris's new housing chief, had created London's housing crisis. Livingstone's revised 'London Plan' published in early 2008 was redundant.

The new Greater London Authority (GLA) created by Tony Blair in 2000 denied the mayor any power or money to build houses. The mayor's only power was planning. Livingstone's solution was to draft a planning scheme for a particular area of the capital and cajole the local authority to build homes to match his proposal. With a combative manner which alienated the people he needed, Livingstone's success was limited. 'Ken's always looking for a fight,' noted Peter John at Southwark Council, echoing other boroughs' housing directors. Those prepared to co-operate were usually unable to satisfy Livingstone's demand for 'affordable homes' – a crunch issue in the city. In exchange for obtaining planning permission, Livingstone wanted developers to subsidise 50 per cent of the homes they built to be sold at lower, affordable prices. The result of his demands disappointed him. In Barking Riverside, a new town of 11,000 homes created in 2000, only 600 homes would be built in the first ten years. In effect, Livingstone's 'affordable homes' target had become 50 per cent of almost nothing.

The problem was money. Public authority housing depended on attracting finance from private developers. Facing high costs for infrastructure and resolving complex legal ownership on brownfield sites, most developers rejected Livingstone's demand that 50 per cent of any development be 'affordable'. They saw his schemes as a recipe for losses. Livingstone's demands had become especially self-destructive in areas like Dagenham where land was available but where few people wanted to live at that time.

A further complication was added by the Labour government. All the finance for civic housing required Whitehall's approval. London was limited to 20,000 new homes annually. To achieve that number, Livingstone abandoned quality and built what David Lunts, his own housing official previously employed as an expert by Prince Charles, called 'ugly, minimalist rabbit-hutch flats'.

Before his election, Boris had not understood the mayor's limited powers to influence the construction of new homes. Since he had never asked the questions, he had not considered how to exercise the mayor's solitary but critical power to approve or reject planning applications. In the recent past, he had simply attacked all planning regulations. Developers, he had urged, should be free to build anything – except tower blocks, other than in clusters at 'appropriate locations' like Croydon and Docklands. Under pressure during the election, he had modified his personal prejudices but maintained his disdain for the pastiche classical buildings designed by architects like Quinlan Terry.

Those ideas put Boris at odds with Prince Charles, a passionate advocate of Quinlan Terry and an opponent of towers. Soon after Boris's election, Charles invited the mayor to Clarence House. The prince urged him to protect London's skyline and reverse Livingstone's collaboration with Richard Rogers, a modernist architect Charles disliked, to build huge skyscrapers in the City and along the Thames. The river would soon flow through a valley of twenty-one towers, complained Charles. He had good reason to recruit Boris as an ally. During his election campaign, Boris had told questioners, 'I'll stop this madness.' Towers, he agreed, were eye-sores and destroyed residential communities. Approval for a further twenty-one 'drab and featureless . . . phallocratic buildings', said Boris, would be stopped by overruling the local authorities. The development of three towers in Waterloo, blocking the views of Westminster, had been immediately frozen. 'This fetish for tall buildings anywhere and everywhere,' Simon Milton agreed just after the election, 'will be a disaster in London.' But by early August, Boris changed his mind. He decided, without giving any reason, that he favoured a thirty-one-storey tower block at Queen's Market in Upton Park, east London. The 2,600 objectors, including all the local shopkeepers, suspected commercial pressure. Was the mayor, some wondered, persuaded by the last person he spoke to? Boris rushed to reassure the protestors. 'Planning is central to my vision for London,' he promised. Every building he approved 'will be won-derful for one hundred years'. Eventually he would reject the Queen's Market tower but two weeks later he ignored the guidelines to protect the skyline and allowed a high-rise luxury development in Doon Street, Lambeth.

Politics dictated his U-turn. Having pledged to build 50,000 homes in three years to answer the housing crisis created by Blair, he realised that his headline promise was undermined by the bank-ing crash and the bankruptcy of builders. Moreover, all his plans were subject to scrutiny and approval by Bob Kerslake, the chief executive of the Homes and Communities Agency (HCA), a bur-eaucratic quango recently established by Labour to dispense grants for housing across the country. Obtaining money from Kerslake was complicated for a Tory mayor. To overcome those obstacles, he understood, the tower blocks became a more attractive propos-ition. Not only did they deliver politically advantageous numbers of homes but they were favoured by developers. To entice the few remaining solvent developers, he reduced the number of 'afforda-ble homes' required in every project to 30 per cent. He also hinted that, if pushed, he would agree to an even lower target.

The biggest prospective development was Nine Elms in Batter-sea, a site four times the size of Canary Wharf and blighted by a redundant power station. Several developers had already been ruined by the site's complicated finances. The government had stipulated that the iconic four cooling towers be preserved. Developers were also burdened by lower house prices and rents south of the river. Negotiating a realistic package to encourage a developer to accept the challenge demanded exceptional expertise and, critically, the construction of a new Tube line.

To understand that new world, Boris began touring building sites, asking technical questions about construction. Unlike Livingstone, he tried to establish good relations with the boroughs and Whitehall. 'He doesn't do nasty,' Tony Travers realised. Sucking in information at meetings with developers, he sat like a student, sleeves rolled up, writing notes on an A4 pad. With the help of Rick Blakeway, the housing director, and David Lunts, he checked to make sure he could speak with conviction. 'He can do detail,' Lunts reported, 'but doesn't necessarily enjoy it.' Livingstone's rabbit-hutch flats were to be replaced by homes large enough to be comfortable, and often with balconies. 'The meetings were enjoyable,' Lunts found, 'because there were lots of jokes.' In November, Boris was interviewed about housing by John Humphrys on the *Today* programme. The famously aggressive journalist was silenced as the mayor reeled off statistics. 'It's all a question of energy,' he later explained about his attitude to detail. 'If you're interested in getting something done, by God you focus on the detail.' By contrast, while briefed about waste disposal as he munched a packet of crisps or an apple, his eyes glazed over.

Five months after the election, a relaxed rhythm was spreading throughout City Hall. The familiar daily dramas sparked by his predecessor had disappeared. Even the most fervent members of Livingstone's clique were converted because Boris, unlike Livingstone, ate in the canteen and spoke to everyone while queuing for lunch or travelling in the lift up to his eighth-floor office with views of the Tower of London. On a wall hung a painting by his mother. Beyond City Hall, John Humphrys was not the only frustrated sceptic. Boris's detractors remained convinced that the reign of the blond bumbler would end in a car crash, and even seemed miffed that the wicked racist they had prophesied had not yet materialised. Defying the caricature, ethnic festivals continued and Boris called for an amnesty of 500,000 illegal migrants estimated to be living in London. 'They would pay taxes,' he explained. He also introduced a minimum wage for City Hall employees, a third higher than the government's minimum wage: 'It's about people who are struggling to put bread on the table for their families, people on low incomes who are working hard and who are ambitious.' He even professed enthusiasm for electric cars.

The so-called 'lazy buffoon' got up at 5.30 a.m. to read the briefs and documents for that day's meetings, to set off before 7.30 a.m. to speak at one or two breakfast meetings on most days and arrive by 9 a.m. in City Hall. On weekdays, he was usually invited to two lunches and two dinners but seldom ate the meals. After making his speech, he would leave. Guarded by Ann Sindall, his loyal PA imported from the *Spectator*, he usually took a thirty-minute nap in the afternoon. Sindall particularly enjoyed repelling visiting Tories, a tribe she hated. 'Fuck off, he's got no time for you,' she snapped. 'Stop that,' ordered Guto Harri. 'We need those people.'

Londoners were his strength. Walking along the pavement, on the Tube or cycling, he was regularly accosted by strangers eager to shake his hand and express their affection. His popularity was enhanced by appearing on TV programmes including *Top Gear* and a series about Rome. Even Andy Beckett of the *Guardian*, a natural critic, was begrudgingly impressed after following him at a careers fair in the East End. 'Boris we love you,' the teenagers shouted as they surrounded him. Boris's initial apprehension had been replaced by delight.

In contrast to the drudgery of being a dispensable MP, as mayor Boris had a platform to develop his own image and political ideas. He could express his ideology in conventional sound bites – spending taxpayers' money did not automatically improve people's lives, and dependency on social benefits by healthy people was unacceptable – and offer his own solutions. Tory success depended on proposing a solution to poverty, housing, the NHS and multiculturalism. To narrow London's wealth gap, he would seek philanthropy from the super-rich to train the disadvantaged. Civic Conservatism would mobilise the voluntary sector to help and train people into productive lives. Labour, he argued, would not be allowed to own the answers to those social problems. His inspiration remained Pericles, the general of Athens in its golden age. 'He was a real genius of municipal politics in action,' said Boris. To those who assumed that Cameron was giving the orders, Boris replied 'We're doing our own thing.' His proof in 2009 was to decide the fate of the Metropolitan Police.

Few Londoners understood Livingstone's iniquitous legacy at Scotland Yard. London's police force was dysfunctional. Commissioner Ian Blair was accused of allowing warring factions of maverick and disloyal officers to disrupt the Yard's management. Blair's control of crime in London had also failed. The city's teenage murder rate had spiralled. 'How can this happen in the richest city in the world?' Boris asked Blair. The commissioner provided no satisfactory explanation for closing down a successful specialist anti-gang unit. But Boris's dissatisfaction went deeper. The Yard had lied about the shooting of Jean Charles de Menezes at Stockwell Tube station in July 2005 and Blair was accused by a newspaper of favouring a friend with police contracts (which he denied), of being obsessed with public relations and being politically aligned with the Labour government. Scotland Yard, Boris said just before the election, needed 'a yank on the steering wheel and that's what I intend to provide.' Blair had replied that he supported 'continuity'.

In hindsight, Ian Blair should have been suspicious as he walked into the mayor's office on 1 October 2008 for a routine consultation with Boris, acting as the chairman of the Metropolitan Police Authority. Not least, as he later said, 'because Boris's hair was combed'. Blair was taken by surprise by what followed: 'There's no easy way of saying this Ian but I want a change of leadership at the Met. You've lost the confidence of the locker room and Londoners. You've reached the end of the line. I want new leadership. I want you to leave by Christmas.' Blair reeled. He told Boris the mayor did not have the power to dismiss the commissioner. Not one had been forced to resign in 120 years. Boris did not retreat.

The mayor's decision took Whitehall by surprise. Neither Jacqui Smith, the home secretary, nor her officials had been consulted. 'Only I have the power to fire and hire,' said Smith. Gordon Brown, the prime minister, urged Blair not to resign. Both Labour politicians were impotent. Boris demanded 'a clean break and a new start for policing in London'. They reluctantly agreed. On his retirement day, Blair accused Boris of making 'a very political move'. Boris did not disagree. The criticism of 'Bumbling Boris' would, he hoped, be heard less often. In the interim, Sir Paul Stephenson, Blair's deputy, would be the acting commissioner. Stephenson's appointment had been unusual. Three years earlier, on the eve of his retirement as the chief constable of Lancashire, he had been asked by the Home Office to move to London. Not one of Scotland Yard's senior officers was trusted to act as Ian Blair's deputy. After thirty years' service, Stephenson was the favourite to become commissioner and radically reform the Yard. Blair and Scotland Yard's politics tested his credibility on his first day as the acting commissioner.

At 10 a.m. on 27 November 2008, the same day as Ian Blair finally departed, Boris's fear about Scotland Yard's politicisation materialised. Stephenson called Boris with a warning. Later that day, he said, the police would raid the homes and offices of an unnamed MP. At 1.19 p.m., Stephenson called Boris and identified the target as Damian Green, the Tory MP for Ashford. Fifteen minutes later, Green was arrested and taken to Belgravia police station for nine hours' questioning. Meanwhile, police officers searched his homes, his constituency office and his Westminster office. They took away a stash of private documents and his computers.

The raids were led by Assistant Commissioner Bob Quick, the counter-terrorism chief. The reason for the raids was Green's embarrassing questions to government ministers in the Commons about failed immigration policies. Green's questions were clearly based on confidential government documents received from a Home Office civil servant. Quick needed Stephenson's authority to arrest the MP. The justification, Quick explained, was Downing Street's declaration that the leak was a matter of 'national security'.

At 2 p.m., after Green's arrest, Boris called Stephenson and 'expressed outrage'. Using the anti-terrorist squad to target an MP for receiving leaked documents was not 'proportionate', protested Boris. This, to Boris, was further proof of the Yard's political prejudice, revenge for Ian Blair's dismissal and evidence that the Yard was out of control. Leaks from Whitehall to MPs, said Boris, had been an element of countless MPs' careers, especially Gordon Brown's from Treasury civil servants during the Conservative government. But none had been arrested and subjected to an intensive search. As the uproar increased, Quick openly denounced Boris for illegally warning Green about the raid. He would later call the Tory Party 'wholly corrupt'. Quick lacked any evidence that Boris had alerted Green and a formal investigation would clear Boris of that accusation.

By the end of the day, Stephenson and Scotland Yard were mired in accusations of political bias. Jacqui Smith had been told about the investigation by David Normington, the permanent secretary; and the Speaker, Michael Martin, a Labour MP, had approved the unprecedented search of an MP's office and the closure of Green's email address. Within days, Stephenson admitted to Boris that the arrest was politically motivated and national security was not an issue. 'This will cause trouble,' replied Boris. 'This was exactly why Blair had to go.'

'Stephenson told me it's a mess,' Boris told colleagues, 'and he's ordered an external inquiry.'

Boris was now in uncharted territory. Although sceptical about Scotland Yard, he did not properly grasp the contagion of incompetence among senior officers. He'd naively assumed that getting rid of Blair would be sufficient, and failed to see that the problem was infinitely more complex. He'd missed the bigger picture. Nor did he realise how his reaction would be exploited by Labour and the police to tarnish him. As the police authority chairman, he was expected to remain utterly neutral. Instead, four days after the raid, he called Green. In a short conversation, Green explained that no one had been bribed and there was no breach of the Official Secrets Act. 'I hope they haven't taken your passport,' said Boris, 'so you can still go skiing.' Regardless of its innocence, Boris was unwise to have made the call. He provided his enemies with grounds to accuse him of prejudice.

Jacqui Smith bowed to Boris's demand that he join the selection panel to interview candidates to be the new commissioner. The choice was between Stephenson and Hugh Orde, the successful and outspoken Ulster police chief. Unlike Stephenson, Orde had served twenty-six years in London and had better skills to cure the Yard's malaise. Yet surprisingly neither candidate at the selection interview was asked for his plan to restore the Yard's integrity. Reflecting his ignorance about government machinery, Boris wanted a police chief to reduce murders and violent crime and shun the limelight. As a retail politician, his priority was favourable crime statistics, not the unglamorous resolution of the Yard's internecine feuds. Stephenson was the 'safe pair of hands' and got the job.

Relations with Stephenson started well. Asking sharp questions and writing the officer's answers into his A4 notebook, Boris urged Stephenson to copy New York's zero tolerance. 'Give me 8,000 more policemen on the streets and I can deliver that,' Stephenson told Boris. 'There's no money for that,' sighed Boris, still unaware of the Yard's staggering financial profligacy. Instead of ordering a forensic investigation of the Yard itself, he demanded announcements on knife crime. Stephenson introduced Operation Blunt, a new stop-and-search dragnet of mostly black youths to curb gang warfare. Thereafter, every week Stephenson reported his increasingly successful results.

'Ping-pong,' exclaimed Boris after they finished a satisfactory briefing. Two tables were cleared and pushed together. At the end of the match, Stephenson acknowledged Boris's victory. 'Boris cheated,' he later told Nick Ferrari, the LBC radio host. 'He put a line of law books as the net, but they were on his side of the table split, so he had the advantage.' 'What are you going to do?' Stephenson was asked. 'I'll challenge him to a swimming competition.'

Boris was heard to decline. 'I don't want to be seen in my budgie smugglers,' replied the seventeen-stone mayor.

Boris hoped he was beginning to solve Livingstone's legacy at the Yard. Next on his agenda was the city's transport system, crippled by an appalling deficit.

Chapter 10

Birth of 'Borisism'

As the new year approached, Boris was still struggling to understand the scale of his task. The three-hour mayoral question sessions for Assembly members was called by him 'medieval torture', and 'unhelpful' by the members. Too often he was unwilling to give a clear answer. Either he would sidetrack issues with a joke, or seek to divert attention from what he thought were banal questions. To his good fortune, he was never exposed during the first term to forensic scrutiny. In the sterile atmosphere of the Assembly, few of the politicians forged a relationship with him. The exception was Len Duvall, a tough Londoner representing the best of Labour's traditional passion for his community. Boris, Duvall decided, was 'not lazy but being mayor was the first time he'd had to work in his life. He didn't think journalism was a job. He could knock anything off and still have time for lunch. Being mayor was different.' Boris did not resent the sharp east Londoner's needling but gave nothing away. 'What sort of Tory are you?' asked Duvall. 'One Nation Tory, European Christian Democrat, or Thatcherite?' Boris did not reply. 'He doesn't want to be pigeon-holed,' Duvall concluded. With over a year before the general election, Boris refused to identify himself with Cameron. Promoting himself was the priority.

Plans for the mayor's £2 million firework celebrations on New Year's Eve were underway. A 200-foot image of himself would be projected on to a building by the river. Some carped that the celebration was an ego trip, but unlike other politicians, Boris was a celebrity without spending money. Livingstone's £1 million annual contract with Matthew Freud, the publicist, had been cancelled by Guto Harri as an expensive irrelevance. Boris could promote himself, and reassure the world that the city would be ready for the Olympics, for nothing. His message to the revellers was optimistic: 'The recession will end. Let's go forward into 2009 with enthusiasm and purpose.'

Mindful of Boris's ambition 'to go all the way to Downing Street', Harri suggested that he meet Paul Dacre, the *Daily Mail*'s influential editor, 'to clean up'. Even though Dacre wielded potent influence on the Tory Party, Boris was hesitant. Dacre was clearly delighted that Livingstone had been defeated, but given Petronella's 'abortion', Marina's humiliation and the four Johnson children's discomfort, the editor of a newspaper that championed family values would be an unlikely cheerleader. Especially because, unlike Boris's adoration of clever women, Dacre was reputedly a misogynist. Finally, they did meet for lunch at Mark's Club in Mayfair. Boris returned to City Hall looking miserable. He rarely got on with people who did not approve of him.

'Was it that bad?' Harri asked.

'I resisted the urge to brain him with my bike clamp. Dacre is like putting Dracula in charge of a blood bank.' At least, Boris discovered, Dacre was lukewarm about Cameron and was unaware of his latest affair.

In late January 2009, Boris stood in Westminster Abbey with Marina at a memorial service for Charles Wheeler, her accomplished father, who had died the previous July. To the packed congregation, the couple appeared united. Past difficulties had been overcome. They were searching for a new house in Islington which they would buy in May. Yet Boris was in the midst of an affair with Helen Macintyre, a thirty-five-year-old art dealer whom he had first met at a theatre in Watlington, near his house in Thame.

Sparky and good company, Macintyre had admired Boris for years. After their affair started about six months earlier, Boris appointed her as an unpaid adviser in City Hall. She was spotted instantly by a friend of Boris's at a mayoral presentation to London property developers about investment in the Olympic Park.

Smiling and sexy, Macintyre was encouraging interest among the audience which included the Reuben brothers, Gerald Ronson and Lakshmi Mittal. 'I took one look at her,' said one of the guests, 'and I warned Boris not to touch Helen. "You have an excess of enthusiasm for women," I told him and he just laughed.' Engaging with Macintyre despite all the risks to his marriage and mayoralty revealed the paradox of Boris. Although a loner, he craved company. Loneliness plunged him into a depression, only relieved by conversations with his current mistress. 'What's the difference between a wife and a bad job?' he asked an aide. 'After several years a bad job still sucks.' He also quipped, 'The moment you stop lying to your wife, your marriage is over.'

Marina loved Boris working at City Hall. Unlike the random working hours at the *Spectator* or the Commons, she believed that the mayor was fixed to a rigid timetable. Every hour was accounted for. She believed that his closest staff would always know his movements. At the Tory Party conference, she was told, a man stood outside his bedroom to prevent women entering. Marina was not told that Boris frequently disappeared, or arrived late at functions, with his shirt-tails hanging out, having stopped somewhere on the way.

Boris's treatment of Marina was a private judgement but his relationship with Macintyre was subject to a formal employment code of conduct designed to prevent favouritism and corruption. Boris had signed the code promising to declare any private interest relating to his public duty. Even Macintyre's unpaid employment at City Hall should, in the spirit of the code, have been declared. Not for the first time, Boris had no qualms about breaking rules.

Just as he had with Petronella Wyatt, Boris arranged to meet Macintyre in various locations including her Belgravia flat. The only complication was the flat's owner. Pierre Rolin, a Canadian financier, was Macintyre's live-in boyfriend. Fortunately, he travelled a lot, so in his absences, the mayor cycled across London to Belgravia. With his blond mop concealed beneath a woolly hat, he ignored the CCTV at the block's entrance. His visits were logged by the porter. Over Christmas, they agreed to meet in January at the annual world economic forum in Davos. Boris was not concerned that she would be travelling with Rolin.

'This will not be a normal year at Davos,' said one senior banker looking forward to endless parties. Bankers were being stigmatised amid the ongoing financial meltdown but Boris ranked among their few champions. Faced with a shrinking economy and rising unemployment, Boris posed as a fierce advocate of London as the world's financial centre. Banks, he agreed, had been 'hideously' greedy but they contributed 9 per cent to Britain's GDP and the taxes on bankers' bonuses helped to relieve poverty. 'Don't get carried away by neo-socialist claptrap,' he had warned the Labour government at the Tory Party conference the previous September. Acknowledging the inevitability of inequality, he believed in rewarding ambition, talent and achievement. But his sensitivity to the ungenerous rich was raw. 'A load of selfish cunts,' he said loudly after he left a lunch at a major city law firm who had refused to contribute to the Mayor's Fund for underprivileged children. Critics accused him of lacking 'vision' because his capitalism was not expressed in ideological jargon. But he did support wealth creation and in return expected the wealthy to be charitable.

Lakshmi Mittal, ranked as Britain's richest man, counted among Boris's angels. During a chance forty-five-second encounter in a Davos cloakroom, Boris persuaded the Indian steel tycoon to finance a £15 million tower for the Olympic Park. Boris had started the competition for a folly to distinguish east London's skyline. Enthusiastically he spoke of a rival to the Eiffel Tower. Helen Macintyre was also soliciting funds for the tower. Callously, Boris also accepted £80,000 from the unwitting Pierre Rolin negotiated by Macintyre. 'I saw him in the lift,' Rolin recalled later about a chance meeting in Davos. 'He knew who I was and he suddenly got really nervous, his eyes darting all over the place.' Macintyre became pregnant soon after.

Boris returned to London focused on the Olympics legacy, especially the development of Stratford. All the previous Olympics, Boris knew, were cursed by costly white elephants. Summoning

Peter Hendy, he listened for two hours to a presentation. 'He sucked it in,' said Hendy, 'understood everything.' Next, to prevent any obstruction by TfL, he discussed the detail with Neale Coleman. 'He likes big flashy projects,' Coleman discovered. 'Transforming Stratford was substantially due to Boris's willpower. He inspired and executed the concrete steps to make it happen. Nothing would have happened without his drive.' There was more. To transform the Olympic Park into a cultural destination, he directed Coleman to recruit the director of the V&A museum (a subsequent director, the German Martin Roth, would become energetically involved in 2011), the director of Sadler's Wells theatre Alistair Spalding, and others from the Smithsonian in Washington and University College London to build auditoriums, exhibition venues and a new student campus within the park. Alongside was a scheme to build 7,000 homes, schools and a £1.5 billion Westfield shopping centre. Never daunted by obstacles and crushing naysayers, Boris presented to the world a rational plan for an unprecedented development. Sheer willpower brought the Olympic Park into existence.

With the same passion, he raced across the capital to community centres, cultural events, workplaces and especially schools, spurred by his discovery that being mayor empowered him to improve peoples' lives. Hoping to break down barriers, re-knit British society and end isolation, he launched the 'Big Lunch' across London to care for the lonely and elderly; and to signal that City Hall would devote money and manpower to reduce rough sleeping, he went on to London's streets at night to persuade the homeless to move into hostels. Not for want of trying, his pledge to end rough sleeping by the end of 2012 failed. Official surveys reported that newly arrived migrants from eastern Europe rejected offers of accommodation. The numbers of rough sleepers would double to 964 in 2016. Undoubtedly he brought a feel-good factor to the city, increasing support for his administration. Unlike most politicians, he genuinely enjoyed listening to people's stories. His frequent appearances with gays, immigrants, the isolated and the ignored had disarmed some critics. Each engagement prompted more initiatives.

Shocked during one visit to a good grammar school that not one of the sixth-formers could recite a poem – 'not so much as a sonnet had lodged in their skulls', he wrote – he committed time and money to literacy, numeracy and to 'spread the benefits I had as a child', despite education not being a mayoral responsibility. With the London Curriculum, schools accepted the mayor's offer to encourage children to learn more about their city.

Nothing made Boris more angry than the state of the capital's schools. One-third of London's eleven-year-old children could not properly read and write. A million Londoners bordered on illiteracy. Lefty educationalists, he believed, were the culprits. Their rejection of synthetic phonics – to learn how sounds make up a word like c-a-t – was authoritarian. London's schoolchildren, he fumed, were forced by those ideologues to rely on self-learning. The inevitable result was that the life opportunities of disadvantaged children were crushed. Among those he blamed was Ed Balls, the education minister, who had dismissed Latin and Greek as unimportant and was unconcerned that advanced maths was not taught in Camden. The mayor damned Balls's 'tragic and wilful ignorance' as 'viciously elitist' for denying 'our children the chief glories of their inheritance'. From 2012, although he possessed no formal powers over education, he relied on his deputy mayor Munira Mirza to recruit donors to help establish free schools and academies, introduce talented teachers into classrooms and fund a variety of educational experiences. To resist the advancing 'barbarian hordes around us', he urged the British to wage a *Kulturkampf* – a struggle to retain control of schools – and simultaneously demand that schools protect beleaguered teachers from bullying parents, supine education authorities and 'the crazed culture of health and safety'.

In those passionate appeals, he anticipated being 'denounced by the left as the last word in bug-eyed, foam-flecked capillary-popping reactionary conservatism'. His blast at political correctness won him unexpected support. He was to be no longer automatically ridiculed as a buffoon. Even Dave Hill, the *Guardian*'s cantankerous columnist, was disarmed by Boris exceeding expectations.

'Johnson,' he grumbled, 'has emerged as a more interesting and appealing politician than the cartoon reactionary depicted by his foes.' Livingstone's Marxism had been replaced by Borisism, a Napoleonic liking for the spotlight and establishment of a grandiose legacy, which bemused his critics and supporters alike.

Part of this was a fondness for monuments: bridges to Ulster and France, tunnels under the Thames and a cable car over it. James Murdoch of News International, he hoped, would sponsor the first cable car in exchange for permission to build a new headquarters in Newham. With the same tenacity, he denounced the government's plans for a third runway at Heathrow and proposed an airport on an artificial island on the Thames Estuary, three times as big as Heathrow. The cost of the so-called 'Boris Island', he said, would be £40 billion and completion within eight years. Critics countered it would take thirty years to build and cost £70 billion. Every airline opposed the scheme; environmentalists were shocked by the inevitable destruction of bird habitats; and an overwhelming proportion of Londoners agreed with the government's edict, 'Heathrow is vital to our economy and is operating at full capacity.' Nevertheless, Boris committed £15,000 to fight the government in the courts. All that grandstanding deflected the critics from his failure to solve London's deteriorating transport system.

Peter Hendy, the transport commissioner, was an accomplished survivor. Steve Norris (newly appointed to the board of Transport for London) said the thirty-page report Hendy presented to Boris after the election sounded 'Like a Soviet tractor report. "Everything is wonderful in London. TfL is succeeding on every front."' Norris's scepticism about Hendy was also levelled at Boris for not carefully reading Hendy's report: 'Boris was skating on thin ice but he skated fast and got away with it. 'As the failed Tory mayoral candidate, Norris was not surprisingly uncharitable about Boris; but he could not deny that Boris had inherited a poisoned chalice.

Burdened by a £3 billion debt, the London Tube risked serious disruption without essential improvements which would cost £1.4 billion. Simultaneously, Crossrail was paralysed by an unrealistically low budget. Close to financial collapse, there was insufficient money to cover an immediate £84 million black hole in TfL's finances. During his last weeks in office, Livingstone had committed the same money three times over: to finance Crossrail, to commission essential Tube repairs, and to freeze fares as an election giveaway. He blamed Gordon Brown for the mess.

The prime minister loathed Livingstone and had shown little interest in London. Together with Shriti 'The Shriek' Vadera, an unpopular banker and his personal adviser, Brown had imposed on the Tube a flawed privatisation scheme. Over the previous five years, two corporations contracted to rebuild the Tube had received £8 billion from the Treasury. After pocketing huge profits, one corporation collapsed and the other tottered on the edge of insolvency – and the network had been barely improved. Relying on Bakelite switches installed in 1926, signals and tunnels were seriously dangerous. Trains regularly broke down and thousands of passengers were trapped in the dark by fire alerts and power failures. Brown handed the responsibility for resolving the chaos to the mayor. Livingstone was stymied. He had opposed the Brown/ Vadera privatisation scheme because under Brown's privatisation contracts, the state was left with all the risk. Unable to shed the Treasury's control over London's finances, City Hall engaged in endless hand-to-mouth negotiations while Brown stubbornly denied London any certainty about the Tube's future. That was Livingstone's legacy to Boris. Among the problems was the Jubilee Line, entrusted to the care of Bechtel, the American construction and engineering corporation, and other contractors.

Bechtel insisted that the Jubilee Line be closed down while essential repairs were undertaken. Boris refused and started a war of attrition to recover control of maintenance of the line. Bechtel and the other contractors demanded £2.5 billion to give up the contract. Boris refused. 'We must carry on shaking the tree until we win,' Daniel Moylan, his deputy chairman of the TfL board, told Boris, 'although I don't know how we will win.' Finally, all the contractors settled for £310 million. But Brown still refused to pay £1.4 billion for the repairs. That 'gloomy old nail-biting misery guts', wrote Boris, 'is a manic meddler who treats Londoners as a bunch of overweight and exhausted laboratory rats'. Boris accused him of 'gambling with the fortunes of the capital like some sherry-crazed old dowager who has lost the family silver at roulette and who now decides to double up by betting the house as well'.

Livingstone had not mentioned his battle with Brown during his re-election campaign. Instead, he claimed credit for the new rail lines across London, especially Thameslink, the Docklands Light Railway and the new St Pancras station. In reality, all three had been designed under Conservative governments. Crossrail, proposed by Margaret Thatcher in 1989, was a seventy-three-mile east–west railway, including twenty-six miles of new tunnels running a hundred feet below London with ten new stations to transport 200 million people a year at 100 mph. The plan was cancelled in 1994 but revived by Livingstone. Approval depended on Gordon Brown providing at least £17.6 billion. In anticipation of a general election, Brown approved Crossrail but committed only £14.8 billion. Completion was set for 2017. That fantasy was Livingstone's legacy, and Boris's burdersome inheritance.

'How many votes are you going to lose me?' Boris had asked at his first meeting with the small Crossrail team in their Canary Wharf office in 2008. Reading from his notes just scribbled on a scrap of paper, he spoke enthusiastically about Crossrail, constantly looking across the room at Gordon Brown, nervously studying his own notes in the corner. Weeks after the election, Brown had not congratulated Boris on his victory. Brown had, however, succumbed to Boris's pressure to take some responsibility for delivering Crossrail.

In his speech, Brown refused to make any genuine financial commitment but did agree that an Act of Parliament should be passed in 2009 which would empower Crossrail to buy land and underground access along the route. Without a financial agreement, Bechtel withdrew from the project. The risk and responsibility was transferred to the Department of Transport and TfL. In the first auditor's review of Crossrail that year, the project was criticised as out of control. Nevertheless, as a symbol of his determination, on 15 May 2009 in Canary Wharf, Boris pressed a button to drive the first concrete pile into place. The construction of Crossrail had begun – a meaningful gesture. Nothing more could be done until David Cameron won the 2010 election even though the future prime minister was himself opposed to Crossrail. His opposition was supported by Simon Jenkins, the former editor of the *Evening Standard* and *The Times*, as 'a costly white elephant that even the government no longer wants'. Crossrail, Jenkins added, was 'no longer a railway that makes sense'. The money should be spent on restoring the Tube. Boris demanded the government should finance both. But at the end of 2008, he had had no money for the Tube or Crossrail. Scrabbling for cash, he abandoned Livingstone's plans for trams and new bridges to save £3 billion, and increased fares by 10 per cent, a breach of his election pledge.

On his first anniversary as mayor, his popularity had increased. An opinion poll reported that 46 per cent were satisfied. Boris gave himself 6.5 out of 10. A *Time Out* survey reported that 22 per cent of women and 29 per cent of men would not be interested in having sex with him. In other words, over 70 per cent *would* be interested. His achievements remained slim: alcohol was banned on public transport, knife crime had fallen by 12 per cent, and Londoners enjoyed a freeze of the GLA's share of the council tax. Nevertheless, as the most visible elected Tory, he praised himself. 'I am a nightmare for Labour, the worst thing that could happen,' he declared, knowing that he was equally a mixed blessing for his party's leaders.

To placate them before the pre-election party conference, he told the *Evening Standard's* new editor that he intended to fight for a second term as London's mayor. 'Oh my God. Weird,' he sighed when he read the newspaper's front-page headline declaring the opposite: that he would not run. Instead, the newspaper speculated, he intended to challenge Cameron. Boris knew the opposite. Cameron could not be ousted, but he could be embarrassed.

Chapter 11

The Messiah Complex

As the nation's senior elected Tory, Boris planned to tease his party's leaders at the October 2009 party conference in Manchester. Over the previous year, the party's popularity had declined, a clear indictment of Cameron's leadership. 'He doesn't stand for anything,' Boris told Guto Harri. 'Dave wants to be prime minister because he thinks he'll be good at it but he's not giving people a positive reason to vote Conservative.' As an untested, smooth operator with few remarkable ideas and misdirected passion, Cameron was not giving anyone a reason to vote Tory. He hoped, complained Boris, to create the mood music to win the 2010 election by default.

In his conference speech, Boris intended to denounce Labour's high taxation state and to trumpet capitalism. He would 'stick up for the pariahs' and condemn the 'banker-bashers' like Cameron. Boris had always liked the rich, especially foreign millionaires. He had been easily lured to meet Evgeny Lebedev, the *Standard*'s new Russian owner, in spite of the direct link of Lebedev's father's fortune to the KGB's plunder of Russia. On trips to Lebedev's house in Italy, Boris 'behaved like a naughty schoolboy', according to an aide. Socialising with billionaires was even better fun, especially New York's mayor Michael Bloomberg, a hero for London's scrimping mayor. At a party in Bloomberg's Upper East Side mansion in 2009, Boris was the centre of attention. He had been born in New York, he liked to remind his audience, under a Puerto Rican health scheme because his parents were uninsured. Then he repeated a quip about the British in New York: 'We have been easily distinguishable by our accents, by our irritating charm and by our inferior dentistry.'

Mixing with New York's rich had been unexpectedly illuminating; Wall Street was under attack. Back in London, he no longer sympathised with bankers. Goldman Sachs announced that 5,000 senior staff would receive bonuses. 'Unbelievable,' wrote Boris in the *Telegraph*. Instead of protecting good businesses from bankruptcy, the bankers had ignored their social duty. London's best houses, the media reported under negative headlines, were being snapped up at bargain prices. After surviving because of the taxpayers' bailout, he sniped, the bankers' hands, 'stuffed with money – bulging, busting, ballooning with the biggest bonuses you ever saw [were] piling back into the yachts and villas'. Unfortunately, he was completely wrong: Goldman Sachs had not been bailed out by the British taxpayer and their London bankers paid taxes on their bonuses. He would not repeat his mistake. When George Osborne, a rival for the throne after Cameron, later complained about Boris protecting the bankers, he counter-attacked, paraphrasing Pastor Niemöller's poem 'First they came . . .' about people staying silent while the Nazis murdered one group of victims after another. 'First they came for the bankers and I said nothing,' he wrote; 'when they came for the trustafarian sons of wealthy wallpaper manufacturers, there was no one left,' referring to Osborne's family business. That rivalry between Boris against both Cameron and Osborne had set the scene for Manchester.

Unlike any other politician, Boris's image was the result of extraordinary casualness. Even wearing a formal blue suit, he looked dishevelled. Tie askew, collar up, odd socks, a shoelace undone on his scuffed shoes was his normal appearance. The real man was reflected in his jogging outfit. Unwilling to spend money on unnecessary clothes, he emerged from his home or office wearing a woolly hat, an old shirt, shorts of a variety of colours and patterns, tatty trainers and occasionally a fleece of unknown provenance, not only looking a mess but also unhealthy. No one could contrive such an unattractive image: a pale-skinned man with a slightly bloated face, wide girth and chubby white legs. Altogether, he offered unrivalled authenticity.

While Cameron fretted about his image as a rich Old Etonian detached from the pain of normal life, Boris planned to mingle in the conference centre as a joker among the common man. To embarrass Osborne, he would praise wealth creation, promote low taxes as the only way out of the recession and denounce the 50p income tax for harming London's financial industry. Boris boasted that 48,000 people in London were employed in tech. But, he questioned, why had no Briton created Facebook, Twitter, Google and the rest? Why, he wondered, did Britons not pocket billions like American inventors? The reason, he believed, was making money in America is 'a good thing' while in Britain it excited 'chippiness and disgust'. No one, he said, had yet come up with a better way to run an economy than capitalism but the Tories were too fearful: 'We are hostile to risk and more hostile to reward.' And now, thanks to Gordon Brown's high taxes, unopposed by Osborne, Switzerland was successfully luring British hedge-fund managers and oil traders with low taxes. A trip to Brussels three weeks earlier had aggravated his fears.

In his first visit after a twenty-year absence, his anger was reawakened. An extravaganza of new glass palaces were, he commented, 'filled with overpaid, underworked, anonymous power-hungry Eurocrats' led by a Spanish socialist who was pioneering regulations to stymie the City and Mayfair's £400 billion hedge-fund business. Neither the Labour government nor Whitehall were combating the EU's grab. Mindful of how Margaret Thatcher's objections to Euro-federalism in Rome in 1990 had been ignored, Boris became agitated by the growing euro crisis. Forty per cent of Greece's workforce was unemployed and its youth was fleeing north to find jobs. Berlin's refusal to help the Greeks justified the Eurosceptics' resistance to Britain joining the euro. The stakes in 2009 were just as serious. Britain, urged the Eurosceptics, should veto the Lisbon treaty formally agreed in June 2008 but still not ratified by Ireland and some other countries. Until *all* the EU member states had ratified the treaty, it did not come into force. Tory Brexiteers hung on the hope that Ireland would vote a second time against ratification.

Europe's federalists rejoiced that the latest EU treaty further integrated the members into a European state. After Maastricht, Amsterdam and Nice, Lisbon increased once again Brussels' authority. Not only did the EU's officials and parliament receive enhanced powers but the ability of member nations to veto EU proposals had been severely curtailed. Decisions taken by the British government about asylum, justice, health and social security could be overruled by the European Court of Justice (ECJ) in Luxembourg. With EU embassies established across the world, Britain's sovereignty was marginalised in foreign affairs. Several countries were obliged to hold a referendum to ratify the Lisbon treaty. Under its 2005 manifesto, Labour had been committed to a referendum but Tony Blair jettisoned that pledge in the hope of becoming the EU's first president. Cameron refused to commit himself to a referendum to withdraw from the Lisbon treaty if every other EU country approved the agreement before he became prime minister. Boris arrived in Manchester prepared to challenge Cameron and demand a referendum.

Boris was not at that stage demanding a referendum to leave the EU. Quitting Europe was not his agenda. Rather, he wanted to stop the Eurocrats' power-grab and Britain 'being ripped off by Europe'. His latest complaint was the one-way traffic of EU students to get free university education in Britain – 62,000 EU students were studying in Britain and not paying any fees. And Britain was training EU citizens to be nurses for free. No EU country was training Britons to become nurses without payment. Europe, said Boris, was a 'force for good' but there should be limits.

'It's absolutely wonderful to be here in Manchester,' Boris told the conference, 'one of the few great British cities I have yet to insult.' Then followed a masterclass in populism. The audience laughed both at Boris's jokes and lapped up his delivery – the dramatic emphases, the pauses, and the ridiculous. Rhetorically, the audience was urged to agree with him and then were congratulated for sharing his opinion. To irritate Osborne, he urged British politicians to say loudly 'we need bankers'. The rapturous applause annoyed the *Telegraph*'s journalists. Charles Moore regurgitated his story that Boris was always late with his column, while Simon Heffer predicted that Mayor Boris was 'yet one more chapter in an epic of charlatanry'. The biggest critic was Cameron, fuming about being upstaged. As Boris got off the train in Euston on his return from Manchester, he read a text from Nick Boles, responsible for the future transition of the party into government. 'Thanks a lot for your help this week, you cunt.' Boles continued, '*La vendetta è un piatto che va mangiato freddo*' (Revenge is a dish best eaten cold).

Boles's fury was a pleasure to behold for Boris's supporters. *When Boris met Dave*, a TV documentary broadcast during the conference, suggested their rivalry stemmed from the Bullingdon Club. Initially, Boris denied a split but the publication of Boles's text in a newspaper encouraged him to be candid: 'All politicians are fed by their mad vanity and suffer from the necessary delusion that they can rise further up the greasy pole. I think there are two things going on. One, it is fun to see if you can make sure people are ambitious and then watch them fail. But the other is a great group of people who are endlessly trying like wasps in a jam jar to be the survivor, because what politicians are doing is competing.' His own abilities, he admitted, gave him a 'Messiah complex'.

Unlike Cameron, Boris wielded real power as mayor, and sought to bask in his few successes, not least the introduction of bikes for hire across central London. On 12 September 2007, the Tory Quality of Life Group had publicised in an 800-page document a proposal to copy Paris's rent-a-bike scheme. Livingstone had seized the Tories' idea in February 2008 as an election promise but had done nothing more. He had not even sent a memo to TfL to research a scheme. No 'bike file' existed when Boris had told Peter Hendy that TfL should find a contractor and a sponsor. One year later, in August 2009, TfL signed a £140 million six-year contract with Bixi, the Canadian designer of the French bikes, to provide 6,000 bikes 'at no cost to the taxpayer'. Forty-one improvements would be added by Kulveer Ranger, Boris's bike tsar responsible for setting up the scheme, to prevent their theft and make them more attractive.

'Boris Bikes' produced a huge flutter of publicity. Asked whether he suffered any doubts, Boris replied, 'I'm not very big on self-doubt. What was my biggest anxiety? God . . . I don't want to sound as if I am a monstrous zeppelin of self-confidence, because obviously one constantly worries that something is going to go wrong . . . but that doesn't mean that I don't worry and I don't work very hard because I do.'

No one was allowed to tell Boris that his bikes could not be self-financing. The five-year sponsorship deal with Barclays Bank would deliver only £25 million a year, a quarter of City Hall's expectations. The ratepayers' burden over the next eight years would be over £100 million. His manifesto pledge that the scheme would be 'at no cost to the taxpayer' would be broken. 'We always knew that as public transport the bikes would need a subsidy,' acknowledged Kulveer Ranger. The bad news was ignored in his pitch to launch not only the new bikes but also two major cycle highways across London and a £116 million campaign to promote cycling. For Boris this was a genuine cause. As more cyclists crowded onto the streets, an increasing number were being crushed underneath lorries. Better visibility from lorries' cabs would help protect cyclists but, Boris discovered, EU laws prevented the British unilaterally ordering modifications. Brussels bureaucrats, beholden to the truck manufacturers, were refusing to impose new regulations. That became another reason to wage war against the EU but would not hamper the publicity blitz to unveil his innovation. Some commentators carped that the idea was inherited from Livingstone, which was untrue. The success entirely belonged to Boris. Two years later, Barclays chairman Marcus Agius complained that despite their £50 million sponsorship since the start of the scheme, they were known as 'Boris Bikes'. 'Give me another £50 million,' Boris snapped back, 'and I will change my name by deed poll to Barclays.'

Boris Bikes gave him a temporary high. Re-election, however, depended on building new homes. Overcoming the obstacles required political compromises. Builders were going bankrupt in the ongoing fallout of the financial crash, and the handful of surviving developers would only submit plans for luxury flats in tower blocks. Before the election Boris had said about tower blocks, 'I'll stop this madness.' One year later, fearing that no homes would be built in London, his opposition to tower blocks waned. A conversation with the mayor of Denver persuaded him about political reality. Elected mayors, said the American, were judged 'through the warped crystal of the city's downtown skyline'. Electors wanted to 'see the glowing red lights on cranes'.

At his regular Friday morning meetings, Boris listened to the presentation of big schemes. Steve Norris witnessed the process: 'He had never sat with a developer before, or ever considered planning. At one of the early meetings, the folder was opened and it was clear that Boris had not read it. He took decisions on the hoof and delegated the implementation to others.' In rapid succession, he approved three towers in Waterloo, a forty-two-storey tower at Wandsworth, the sixty-three-storey Columbus Tower in Canary Wharf, and a twenty-five-storey tower in Ealing. 'Boris is not keeping his promises,' complained Simon Jenkins, the National Trust's new chairman. He was fearful that Boris would also approve a 300-metre tower in Battersea, part of the Nine Elms redevelopment, visible from Hyde Park.

Prince Charles also intervened. Over the previous year, Charles had invited Boris to Clarence House to tell the mayor of his opposition to developers' modernist plans. In 2009, Charles sought Boris's support to stop the emir of Qatar's £3 billion philistine development of Chelsea Barracks designed by Richard Rogers. Boris contributed to Charles's success in changing the architect and the design, but he ignored Charles's opposition to the 180-metre Gherkin in the City and approved a 150-metre tower in the Paddington Basin developed by the Reuben brothers. Campaigners would battle to reduce those heights but the outcome was delegated to Simon Milton. 'I'll sort it out,' Milton reassured Boris. Milton's skill, tact, intelligence and political expertise were invaluable to Boris, as was his wit on watching a video of Boris falling into a muddy river in Catford while trying to clear litter. 'I've got the *Standard*'s headline,' Milton quipped. ' "River Crisis – Mayor steps in".'

Boris's reliance on Milton was a template for his style of

government. Unlike most politicians, he knew his own vulnerabilities and identified Milton as a man who could protect him. Milton had expertise, and delivered advice and criticism in a way which enhanced Boris's self-esteem. Milton knew the trick was to deliver advice palatably. Boris stepped away from anyone who suggested that he didn't know his facts. The messenger was instantly scrutinised for loyalty, and judged whether to be allowed back into the room. Many critics failed the test and were jettisoned. Loyalty was rewarded but ultimately Boris would turn 180 degrees if necessary, because at the end of the day Boris was always and only loyal to himself. As Number One, he chose when to be generous and when to keep people out.

For the Tories' most popular politician, the scene was set for the general election in May.

Chapter 12

'I'm standing by to fill the gap'

The two Old Etonians appeared together at the Royal Hospital in Chelsea. Standing in front of the red-uniformed pensioners, both knew that the dozens of journalists and photographers were waiting for the moment – a phrase or grimace – that would expose their rivalry. Boris had already ridiculed Cameron's election showpiece – 'Big Society' – as 'piffle'. 'Any questions for the mayor?' asked Cameron angling to score a revenge point. A pensioner demanded a better service from the 211 bus. Unfortunately, although Boris was stuck for an answer, he was not embarrassed. 'Ask whether Dave will fund Crossrail,' Boris urged another pensioner. Cameron ignored the comment. His opposition was well known. The sparring match ended in a bloodless draw. Cheekily, Boris wrote the following day an article praising Cameron for building a happy, united party for Europhiles and Eurosceptics to work in harmony.

*

'Shouldn't you send Dave a text wishing him well?' Guto Harri asked Boris on election day.

'Why?'

'Because you're old friends.'

'I don't see why I should wish him well.'

After some persuasion Boris sent a text: 'Good luck Dave and don't worry, if you bog it up I'm standing by to fill the gap.' To reinforce his own qualifications, Boris listed the previous four prime ministers who, like himself but not Cameron, had been King's Scholars at Eton.

'It's all gone tits up – call for Boris,' Rachel Johnson tweeted as the prospect of a Tory majority faded. Vapid and unfocused, the Tory campaign against an unpopular government failed to secure an overall majority. Cameron could become prime minister only if he formed a coalition with Nick Clegg, the Lib Dem leader. Pouring poison, Clegg claimed that Cameron's people operated a Boris loyalty test: 'If you don't like Boris you're in.' In reply, Boris dubbed the Lib Dems 'a bunch of Euro-loving road-hump fetishists who changed their opinions in midstream like so many hermaphroditic parrotfish'. He said nothing publicly about Cameron beating him to Downing Street. Despite their common cause, Cameron regarded Boris as 'full of jealousies and paranoias, which so often influenced his behaviour'. There was an unreliability and habitual mess about Boris which made Cameron laugh but also fuelled his unequivocal declaration: 'I didn't always trust him.' That distrust also stemmed from Boris's habit of speaking in sound bites and not following through on the substance. 'I have a nine-point plan,' Boris explained about driverless Tube trains, but he could not remember the points. Some assumed 'nine points' was an invention. Boris shared the same low regard for Cameron. After the new prime minister declared 'I want a Boris in every city,' the mayor replied, 'I hope I can survive your endorsement.' After he was once again beaten at tennis by Cameron, Boris quipped, 'He needs to sink a few thousand in his backhand,' proving in Cameron's opinion that although Boris was funny and attention-seeking he was keen to embarrass others to save face. As for Osborne, with whom he had little in common, Boris knew that he owed the new Chancellor a debt for helping to organise his mayoral election campaign and, although they were potential rivals for the leadership, he could not now squander the possibility of getting significantly more money for the capital.

Soon after the election, Boris cycled to Downing Street for what was later described as a 'social call'. Looking as scruffy as usual, he parked his bike against the railings, took off his helmet and, carrying his rucksack, entered Cameron's headquarters. The agreed agenda was money for Crossrail, the Tube and housing.

Quickly, they agreed to change the GLA Act which forbade the mayor spending money on housing. A new law would devolve power and guarantee money for housing to London's mayor. That was an easy victory for Boris. The real battle was about transport. In Boris's opinion, Cameron, like many politicians, used too many taxis and chauffeured cars and so was unsympathetic to funding improvements of public transport including Crossrail. Getting more money for London was obstructed by Osborne's austerity cuts. Although the budget cuts in London were lower than in the rest of the country, Osborne had so far not allocated any new money for Crossrail or the Tube. During their conversation, Boris could see that Cameron was looking at the Treasury's briefing paper setting out his opening offer and the maximum Boris could receive. Naturally Boris wanted to see it and Cameron refused. Lunging to grab it, Boris fell on the desk and Cameron pulled away. Wrestling on the ground to get hold of the document, both would later claim to have won 'the battle of the paper' but either way Boris left the building defeated. Continuing Labour's policy, the government would not fund the Tube's £1.4 billion repair programme and would frustrate Crossrail by cutting £5 billion from its budget.

In retaliation, Boris publicly threatened a 'Stalingrad defence' – presumably he meant that everyone would die in the ditch (except himself). Next, as his arguments with Osborne and Cameron intensified, he told newspapers that he was considering not running for a second term and returning to the Commons. In a mayoral election, Boris said, the Tories would be vulnerable to Labour unless he secured the money. The arguments became further embittered with the inclusion of Philip Hammond, the class-conscious Transport Secretary. In his opinion, Boris was a buffoon. Puzzled that Osborne bothered to take Boris seriously, Hammond, a dry accountant, pressed the Treasury's demand that London's transport budget be cut by between 25 and 40 per cent and Crossrail be cancelled. 'I cannot and will not accept that,' retorted Boris in an open declaration of war. 'We have no choice but to make these improvements and any delay is a false economy.'

In the midst of those negotiations, Boris displayed his seditious art of communication. Invited to address the Structure Finance Association, he arrived with his shirt hanging out, just thirty seconds before he was due to speak. 'Now what's this all about?' he asked looking at a room of crusty financial experts. 'Anyone got a pen?' As he scribbled, he heard, 'Pray silence for Boris Johnson, the mayor of London.' Boris bounded to the lectern holding a scrap of paper. 'I'm delighted to be here,' he said, glancing behind him to read out the name of his hosts. In a speech about London, he included three jokes, one of which was his current favourite about Larry Vaughn, the mayor of Amity. In the film *Jaws*, the mayor refused to close the beach despite the shark, to protect the town from economic catastrophe. 'OK, in that instance he was actually wrong,' chuckled Boris, 'but in principle, we need more politicians like that mayor!' As a libertarian, he hated the 'health and safety' brigade's imposition of limits on free choice despite the danger. He got a standing ovation.

This was very different from his performance at BP's annual champagne celebration at the Victoria and Albert museum. He winged the twenty minutes with chunks of Latin and said nothing about the fate of oil or anything else, leaving the audience puzzled.

Prone to sudden bouts of depression, Boris's performances varied hugely, reflecting his internalised torment. Not surprisingly for a man defeated twice in his bid to be London's mayor, Steve Norris's explanation was less sympathetic: 'There was a recklessness in his approach and his language, not fuelled by malice but simply the greed of a polymath eager to consume every dish on the table, even though there was no possibility to digest them all. So he was not just the mayor, but a key national politician, and also a journalist, author and ran a mistress. He grabbed every opportunity.' Boris's hosts never knew what problem was uppermost in their speaker's mind in the moments before he arrived – and at around this time Boris was having to deal with another dilemma of his own making.

In June, he had taken Marina to watch the football World Cup in South Africa. To their friends sharing the trip, they appeared a close couple. But the image of a contented family man was shattered by the *Mirror*'s headline on 15 July: 'Is Bonking Boris to Blame?' The newspaper reported that Pierre Rolin had left Helen Macintyre after he had taken a DNA test. Contrary to Macintyre's assertion, Rolin discovered that he was not the father of Stephanie, her blonde-haired baby daughter, born in November 2009. 'I can't stop,' shouted Boris at journalists as he cycled from his home. 'I need to go and give a speech.' Hours later, Boris appeared at a street party and, amid laughter, was photographed holding a baby girl. Lacking any contrition, he was angry that what he saw as prurient hypocrites had another excuse to seize his scalp.

Rolin had discovered Macintyre's deception while coping with the debris of his collapsed business. 'I was completely snowballed. I think he has no moral compass,' Rolin said about Boris. 'He thinks he is completely entitled and thinks he's above it all. He will one day be accountable for all this and one day the truth will catch up with him.' On Stephanie's birth certificate, Macintyre had omitted the father's identity.

The routine in Islington was familiar. On Marina's orders, Boris moved into a rented flat, a hundred yards away. 'Kicked out of the house like a tom cat,' said a friend. From there, Boris ordered take-away curries, waited for his housekeeper to bring his ironed clothes and occasionally, when Marina was out, returned to the house to see his children. Tough and stoical, Marina appeared soon after at Rachel Johnson's book launch near Covent Garden. She ignored Boris while he ebulliently posed for photographs. Asked why Boris had left the party without her, she smiled 'There's only one seat on his bicycle . . . It's just the way we do things.' Boris remained silent. After his denial six years earlier of the affair with Petronella, he explained, 'I took a sort of vow ages ago that when bowled any sort of ball like that, the great thing to do is to watch it very carefully for as long as possible as it flies through the air, and then you stick your bat straight out, put your foot forward, block it and return to your crease.'

Paul Dacre, the *Daily Mail*'s editor, would not tolerate Boris's silence. To uphold family values, Dacre believed, 'Politicians with scandalous private lives cannot hold high office.' He was contemptuous of a man with 'the morals of an alley cat'. He encouraged Stephen Glover, a columnist, to pour scorn on the adulterer. Under the headline 'Selfish, lazy, arrogant', Glover declared 'My friend Boris thinks he can get away with anything (but I don't think he'll ever be PM)'. While admitting that Boris had never claimed to be virtuous, Glover denounced on Dacre's behalf Boris's 'wild recklessness . . . born of a monumental arrogance'. Dacre was furious about Boris's 'utter conviction that he is a genius – and has persuaded others and the whole nation of his myth'. Anyone entering the jungle with Boris would not last fifteen minutes before he 'ate . . . you, but with a smile on his face'. Echoing Dacre's opinion, Glover concluded that 'we expect little of Boris, other than to be entertained. He has a Mickey Mouse job as mayor of London, and his finger (thank God) is very far from the nuclear button.' In Dacre's opinion, Boris was 'impossibly far from being prime minister'.

In public, Boris agreed with Dacre's conclusion. In a live radio interview on the same day, he refused to answer questions about Stephanie's paternity but agreed that his ambitions were torpedoed. 'I've got more chance of being reincarnated as Elvis Presley or as an olive as being prime minister,' he admitted, reusing a familiar expression.

Quite deliberately, in his own unceasing search for publicity, Stanley Johnson found himself in the spotlight. Asked for the first time whether Boris had merely copied his father and whether he, Stanley, had been unfaithful to Charlotte, Stanley replied, 'These questions are not good. I was wholly faithful to Charlotte in all important respects.' Adultery was not the only habit Boris inherited from Stanley.

Unexpectedly, Len Duvall, a Labour member of the London Assembly, was sympathetic. Boris, he said, clearly wanted to show his 'appreciation' of Helen and thought he would not get found out. The affair, said Duvall, did not expose Boris as bad but vulnerable – a man craving love and attention. Although Duvall's perception of

human weakness was rejected by the *Daily Mail*, the GLA standards committee was more tolerant. Hiring Macintyre on GLA
business was described as an undeclared conflict of interest. Boris's
promise to 'bear in mind the definition of a close associate for the
future', concluded the GLA's investigation but not the saga. Helen's
application for an injunction to prevent the media naming Boris as
Stephanie's father was rejected by a High Court judge. The judge
decided that Helen had already publicly disclosed the father's identity through the media and that it was 'a matter of public interest
which the electorate was entitled to know when considering his
fitness for office'. During her evidence, Helen had accepted that by
embarking on an affair with Boris, she was 'playing with fire' and
the affair was certain to attract media attention. Nevertheless, she
appealed against the judgement and delayed any media reports. By
then, Boris appeared to be immune to embarrassment. 'I now see
all these disasters are temporary, you can move on,' he said, adding:
'As I discovered myself, there are no disasters, only opportunities,
and indeed opportunities for fresh disasters.'

Luck always played a big part in Boris's career and to his further
good fortune, the debate about his adultery and the questionable
record of his administration was knocked off the front pages by
the revelation that Andy Coulson, the head of communications
for David Cameron since 2007, was accused of telephone hacking
while editor of the *News of the World*. Rocked by the outrage,
Cameron held on to Coulson. Osborne, equally responsible for
hiring Coulson, was also vulnerable. Downing Street's instability
boosted Boris's struggle to overcome Osborne's refusal to fund
Crossrail.

Sheer willpower finally secured the Chancellor's agreement in
mid-October 2010 to approve the project, on condition that completion was delayed by one year and the budget reduced by £1.5 billion.
In addition, Osborne agreed to fund the Tube's improvements on
condition that TfL staff would be reduced by 3,000 people, to save
£5 billion over four years. 'If you see a desk for sale in the Holloway
Road,' Boris told the next party conference, 'it very likely comes
from Transport for London,' 4,232 TfL desks, he claimed, were

sold. To help Boris's re-election, Osborne would say, he agreed that Boris could claim to have won a bloody victory. The Chancellor was also pleased with his triumph. At Boris's suggestion, the government had closed the LDA, saving £500 million a year but the Treasury returned only £130 million to London. Whitehall civil servants would chortle to the media that Boris had lost the money by failing to master the details. Insiders doubted that Simon Milton was so foolish and assumed it was all part of the deal.

Immediately, the jubilant Crossrail team ordered six 1,000-tonne machines to bore two tunnels under central London. Completion of the tunnels was set for 2015, nearly thirty years after Margaret Thatcher had initiated the project. There would be no political kudos for Boris in time for the 2012 election. His media celebrity sustained his political popularity but his re-election depended on proving substantial achievements as mayor. He needed to remove the negatives.

For months he had wavered whether to fulfil his election pledge and abolish the western congestion zone covering Notting Hill Gate and Kensington. Opposed by the majority of residents and businesses, TfL had alleged that it generated £55 million a year. Uncertain of the bogus benefits, Boris needed to win re-election and so reluctantly abolished it. The traders rejoiced.

He had also failed to honour his pledge to open three rape crisis centres. A summons from Clarence House solved that dilemma. Just as he was parking his bike, Camilla, Duchess of Cornwall, appeared. Taking Boris by the wrist, she said 'You and me, upstairs now.' In the course of the next hour, she told Boris how she had been assaulted on a train when she was seventeen. 'I did what my mother told me. I took my shoe off and hit him in the nuts. And then I reported him to the police at Paddington.' If Boris financed two rape centres, she promised, she would open them. 'Oh God, what a woman,' Boris told Guto Harri as they cycled back to City Hall. The ducks were falling into a row for the next election.

In another stroke of luck, Livingstone was reselected as the Labour candidate. The living ghost refused to disappear. Since there was no chance of Cameron departing before the 2015 general election, and as mayor he would shine during the Olympics, Boris declared he would run for a second term. The polls predicted a Boris victory. He would campaign, he said, to make London a 'less selfish' place by persuading more citizens to sign up as volunteers for charities and good causes. The issues on which Livingstone could attack him were the Tube and housing.

To save money, Boris had announced that he would close the Tube's ticket offices, a clear breach of his election pledge to keep them all open. Since the general election, Hendy had persuaded him that Oyster and debit cards had removed the need for tickets. To save £400 million a year, the 800 staff should be sent on to the concourse to help passengers, to replace staff who resigned.

Coinciding with his re-election announcement, Bob Crow, the Marxist leader of the RMT, the Tube's principal trade union, declared a strike to retain the ticket offices. In an obvious political manoeuvre to take revenge for Gordon Brown's election defeat, the militants aimed to sabotage Boris's chance of re-election. The strike would paralyse London. 'Can't we fire them all?' Boris asked. 'No, I can't replace them all,' Hendy replied. Attrition and recruiting more women was the only answer. In a bloody, bare-knuckle struggle with Crow, Hendy was determined never to let Boris negotiate with the trade unions. 'If you let Crow into your office,' Hendy told Boris, 'he'll never leave. You can't trust what Crow says. He never ends a dispute, he just ends the strike. You have to call their bluff.' Livingstone naturally ridiculed Boris's refusal to meet Crow, although Livingstone's own negotiations with the militant had not prevented countless strikes. To disarm Crow, Boris urged Cameron to pass a law deeming that a strike was legitimate only if 50 per cent of the entire workforce voted in favour, rather than a straight majority of those voting – in the current strike about 14 per cent voted to strike. Cameron agreed but then reneged. 'A lily-livered government,' pronounced Boris. Hours later, Boris received a text from Cameron: 'Remind me to be helpful to you on May 3', referring to the date of the mayoral election. The strike crippled London and then talks resumed. The cycle was endless. With rising fares, Boris was vulnerable.

That vulnerability increased after the government announced a cap on housing benefits which cost £15 billion a year. In London, a single mother with six children by different fathers was photographed outside her multimillion-pound home in Kensington, funded by the taxpayer. The government proposed to limit the total benefits to £21,000 a year. Welfare beneficiaries should not enjoy a lifestyle denied to the employed working class. Those working, said Cameron, should not subsidise those who chose to be unemployed or had children recklessly. With estimates that 82,000 households could be forced to relocate out of central London, Boris criticised Cameron's policy as 'draconian'. Fighting for every vote, his rhetoric became exaggerated. In a BBC radio interview, he damned the government's 'Kosovo-style social cleansing'. That struck home. The prime minister, said Cameron's spokesman, was 'bristling with anger'.

Cameron delivered his revenge at the *Spectator*'s awards ceremony two weeks later. The magazine, said the prime minister, had been praised for writing seriously about sex: 'After all, there's been enough of that going on in your office.' He focused on Ian Gilmour, who edited the magazine in the late 1950s and went on to become a Tory MP and Cabinet minister. Gilmour, educated at Eton and Oxford, was a man of inestimable charm with an enviable head of hair, always bursting with brilliant turns of phrase, yet dismissed by Margaret Thatcher. 'But what went wrong for Ian?' asked Cameron. 'I suppose he rubbed up the prime minister the wrong way and never really recovered. Shit happens. Anyway there's always the chance of Boris becoming our ambassador in Pristina, I suppose.' Boris hated being the target of laughter. Even worse, he had by then been under pressure to recant. His words about 'Kosovo-style social cleansing' in the BBC radio interview, he said, were distorted. To divert attention from the humiliation, he blamed the BBC. 'I don't listen to *Today* or watch *Newsnight* or BBC News,' he wrote. 'It's just not important anymore.' One of the mayor's subsequent aides observed, 'To Cameron, Boris was a cuddly irritating shit like a brother; a man who drove a hard bargain with good and bad ideas. Both Cameron and Osborne had to indulge Boris because he was a huge asset and everything good he did was good for the Tories.'

*

Walking across the road from Southwark Council's headquarters to City Hall in early summer 2010, Peter John, the newly elected council leader, had been looking forward to meeting the mayor. A political earthquake had altered their shared priority in housing. As part of austerity, the Tory government had cut £6 billion from the budget of affordable housing. Boris would lose £100,000 for each new home built in London. The upside was his agreement with Osborne that under the proposed Localism Act, Bob Kerslake's Homes and Community agency would be marginalised and the government's powers over housing would be devolved to London. In an agreement between Boris and Osborne, the GLA was given for the first time a £3 billion annual housing budget and 625 hectares of land. Eighty specialist staff were recruited to manage development and boost building without Whitehall's control. Boris also negotiated for London to keep a larger share of the business rates. With real power and money, Boris welcomed Peter John as an ally. For his part, John approved of Boris 'love bombing' developers to get investment. 'He was flirting with you,' an aide told John as they walked back to their offices. 'Must be because I laughed at his jokes,' replied John.

Boris had entered what he called a 'parallel universe'. All his decisions on housing were criticised by the media but the boroughs and the building industry were supportive. His challenge was to persuade the boroughs and developers to start building houses. At a property exhibition in Cannes, Peter John surged towards Boris. 'We could build 20,000 homes and more if you extend the Bakerloo Line from Elephant & Castle down to Lewisham and then towards Bromley.' Boris stopped and listened. 'We would call it the Boris Line,' said John. 'Absolutely, let's do it,' said Boris. He had already persuaded the government to fund a branch of the Northern Line to Battersea and also support the Silvertown tunnel under the

Thames to North Greenwich. The next victory was an Act of Parliament to extend the Bakerloo Line. New housing would follow. The downside was those projects wouldn't be completed for twenty years, long after his mayoralty.

Pulling levers fed his hunger for instant gratification. With great fanfare, he arrived in the Olympic Park to unveil his 'Eiffel Tower'. The competition for the sculptural observation tower, financed by Lakshmi Mittal (his initial £10 million loan had increased to £16 million), had been won by Anish Kapoor, the Anglo-Indian sculptor. Kapoor was Boris's second choice after Antony Gormley refused to make his tower accessible to the handicapped and then became 'catastrophically difficult'. Most in Boris's office, including Neale Coleman, sympathised with Gormley. 'Boris has a weakness and enthusiasm for huge projects,' recalled Coleman. 'In Kapoor's case, he had an excess of energy for an ill-conceived and worthless flashy project. Everyone thought it was crazy and too expensive.'

The result was a 115-metre red tower, called 'The Hubble Bubble' by Boris because of its similarity to a shisha pipe, but officially called 'Orbit'. Costing £19.1 million, it was described by critics as a 'towering, twisted mass of metal', 'Meccano on Crack', 'gruesomely awful', 'meaningless, ugly, banal, clunky, downright embarrassing', and a piece of art which is 'useable' and so 'lost any integrity'. Undaunted, Boris hailed the tower as the symbol of 'a city coming out of recession and the embodiment of the cross-fertilisation of cultures and styles that makes London the world capital of the arts and the creative industries'. Without telling Kapoor, he planned to turn the sculpture into a helter-skelter for paying visitors. When Kapoor found out, he was not pleased.

In his passion for 'big things', as Peter Hendy called them, Boris remained captivated by the idea of a cable car across the Thames. In unison, his close advisers led by Coleman knocked the idea but their advice was ignored. Once attached to a scheme, Boris could not be moved. Having initially sought sponsorship from James Murdoch of News International, in the end the £25 million cable car across the Thames was approved without Murdoch's money after the hacking scandal broke, and the Emirates Air Line, operated by TfL, opened in June 2012.

Soon after, while cycling at 10.30 p.m. across London, Boris called Hendy.

'Let's build another cable car.'

'Let's not,' replied Hendy. 'Let's do Crossrail 2.'

'You think so?'

'Yes.'

'OK,' said the mayor.

That did not deter his plans for a pontoon promenade with buildings along the Thames from St Paul's to the Tower, a fifteen-acre floating 'town on stilts' around the Royal Victoria Dock and, later, a twenty-two-mile ring road under London. Not surprisingly his usual critics lampooned his unreality. His reaction to those decrying his zany vision was unorthodox. So often, he complained, the loudest objectors to all his ideas were the socialist prophets of doom who ignored life's improvements since 1950. The protestors refused to acknowledge that most people were richer, taller, healthier and their incomes had increased. Infant mortality was down, and life expectancy was up. The world had become a better place. He associated that progress with diluting state control and removing regulations. As a libertarian, he decried as anti-liberals those demanding health warnings on wine bottles, a ban on smoking in parks, forbidding an unaccompanied male to sit next to a child on an airplane, and demanding booster seats for ten-year-olds in cars. Imposing regulations, he believed, was the madness of a 'bossy and nannying' state. He associated his critics with antisocial extremists. The Occupy movement of 'hemp-smoking fornicating hippies' was less attractive to him than bankers; prison sentences, he argued, should be longer; and he ridiculed the 'Stone Age religion' obsessives about global warming. He applauded President George W. Bush for his 'decision to crumple up the Kyoto protocol'. He was outraged that government lawyers were supporting British Airways' refusal to allow a female employee to wear her small crucifix. Even the victims of hacking by the *News of the World* were lambasted for complaining. Believing that the allegations were politically motivated by Labour against News International, he dismissed the scandal as 'codswallop'. After Andy Coulson resigned from Downing Street in January 2011, Boris refused to pursue a claim against News International for hacking his own telephone, through which they discovered his affair with Anna Fazackerley. He feared the publicity would expose 'some extremely unpleasant interference in my private life'. Revisiting his adultery was unappealing. No other British politician spouted so many competing and sometimes illogical opinions, especially from one lauded as a master communicator.

Finding a common thread in all those activities and ideas was a challenge. As a man on a mission to establish his unique electoral appeal, or 'Borisism', and simultaneously understand for the first time the issues facing the less fortunate was an unusual political adventure. Unconventional and untainted by a fabricated morality, Boris's free spirit was beyond Cameron's comprehension. Despite the formal bonds of Eton, Oxford and the party, Cameron's secure English traditionalism had nothing in common with a mixed-race outsider shooting daily from the hip to survive. Naturally, Cameron did not trust a man he could not understand. At the time, the gulf of misunderstanding between the two did not matter. In his ineffable manner, Cameron's gift was to make the coalition work. But having failed utterly to rout Labour, Cameron's mistakes made Boris's re-election harder.

*

By spring 2011, one year before the next mayoral election, the mayor's initiatives had been resonating with some Labour voters. Boris, the *Guardian* grieved, had defied those 'convinced that the gaffe-prone Johnson would make a hash of it'. But in April, he suffered a serious blow. Simon Milton, his chief of staff responsible for saving his reputation, died of cancer aged forty-nine. No one could entirely replace the wisdom and experience of the former president of the Cambridge Union. The best substitute was Eddie Lister, the leader of Wandsworth Council for nineteen years. Lister, a Thatcherite cost-cutter, had the experience to protect Boris, solve problems and implement decisions. He inherited an efficient machine but with limited achievements to present to the electorate. Better things than bikes and improved Tube services would need to be promised for a second term. Winning, however, had become uncertain. Boris feared that Londoners were fickle and his future was on a knife edge.

David Cameron understood the importance of Boris's victory. Although Boris's 7 per cent lead over Livingstone was encouraging, austerity was damaging the Tory Party. In the capital, the Tories were running 20 per cent behind Labour. In May, Cameron invited Boris and Marina to dinner. There was no hint of the Johnsons' estrangement the previous year. Their reconciliation had been sealed with a family holiday in India and Boris's declaration after his return to the marital home, 'I think I am very lucky and happy.' Cameron, the perfect gentleman, made no reference to their personal troubles. His purpose was to remove the disruptive rivalry with the mayor, aggravated by a poll making Boris more popular than Cameron, at 57 per cent to 43 per cent. Cameron's initiative failed.

To win re-election, Boris had decided to decouple from the government. He had already criticised Cameron's intervention in Libya, warning against repeating the 'appalling mistakes of Iraq' by boasting 'mission accomplished'. On the eve of more Tube strikes, he once again accused ministers of being 'adolescents' for failing to introduce tougher anti-strike laws. Only 11 per cent of the Tube's 3,429 drivers had voted for the latest strike. The law, Boris advocated, should impose a 50 per cent threshold. At the last moment, the strike was called off but Bob Crow won the final round. To prevent strikes during the Olympics, Boris agreed that the drivers' basic pay would be increased to £52,000 plus a bonus. For sitting in a cab while a computer controlled the train, most drivers were earning £65,000 plus long holidays and other perks. To Boris's anger, Cameron was not prepared to take on the trade unions and the trains were still unreliable. Just after he was photographed in a Jubilee Line train to publicise the new signalling system, another train on the same line broke down in the morning rush hour, causing misery for thousands travelling to Canary Wharf. That would inevitably risk votes.

Getting positive attention was not always easy. The media kept repeating the same negative anecdotes and occasionally he even had to push his way through a crowd towards the photographers. At an event in west London's Botwell Green Library with Peter Andre, the singer, he could see the photographers deliberately cutting him out of the photo. Determined not to be outshone, he sat himself right next to Andre. Even so, most newspapers featured photos without him. He certainly would not invite Cameron to help his election campaign. In fact, soon after their dinner, Boris addressed 780 former members of Pop, the society of Eton prefects distinguished by their spongebag trousers and brightly coloured waistcoats, on their 200th anniversary. Not having been elected to Pop, Cameron was not among them. Inevitably, Boris could never resist highlighting Cameron's invisibility at the school. 'Never apologise to the ordinary members of the school,' Boris said in his after-dinner speech alluding to Cameron. 'Greasing is the key to success in life.'

Soon after, as a goodwill gesture to Marina, Boris booked a summer holiday, driving a Winnebago motorhome with his family through the Canadian Rockies. As he set off at the end of July, he had overseen massive turmoil at Scotland Yard. The problems, he hoped, were resolved. Instead, the unforeseen presented the greatest threat to his re-election.

Under Met commissioner Paul Stephenson, he believed, the headlines had improved. Operation Blunt Two, the police's stop-and-search exercise, had curbed knife crime and the murder rate had reduced by 50 per cent to just one hundred per year, the lowest since 1969. In six weeks, 26,777 people had been searched, 1,214 had been arrested and 528 weapons were seized. During the year, over 10,000 knives had been confiscated. These were good headlines. As usual, there was also bad news. Sky News had followed Stephenson and an army of policemen in a drugs raid. The police burst into the wrong address. 'Don't worry,' Boris told the apologetic commissioner, 'you're speaking to the great custard-pie man of British politicians – just lick it off.'

Relations with Stephenson had been temporarily shaken after a special constable read Boris's description in a *Telegraph* article of his purloin of Saddam Hussein's cigar case during a visit to post-war Baghdad. 'You must give it up,' he was told by the constable, citing the crime of seizing an antiquity. 'This is political correctness gone mad,' replied Boris. 'No, it's the law,' insisted the policeman. For several weeks, Boris resisted and then surrendered. The cigar case's fate remains unknown.

That triviality was overshadowed by substance. Contrary to his election pledge, he was forced by Osborne's austerity immediately to reduce the force by 455 policemen. 'Barking,' he said. Within a £3.4 billion budget for London's police, the saving was a gesture but alarming before an election. Police numbers would influence crime statistics and headlines were his priority. Notably, in his discussions with Stephenson, he never raised the fundamental changes required to eliminate Scotland Yard's incompetence. In spite of the evidence in 2011 that the Yard was still reluctant to reform itself, Boris remained uninterested in the flaws of its governance.

First, Scotland Yard had lied about the death of Ian Tomlinson, a gentle, elderly newspaper vendor. In the midst of policing a demonstration in central London in April 2009, a policeman had fatally struck Tomlinson from behind. For a week, Scotland Yard had denied the truth until the *Guardian* produced a handheld video of the assault. Stephenson took one week to suspend the delinquent police officer, not for the assault but because he had been previously disbarred from employment by the Met. To avoid embarrassing Stephenson, Boris did not demand an inquiry into Tomlinson's death.

The Yard's ineptitude had also been exposed after the conviction in March 2009 of John Worboys, a London black cab driver. He had raped nearly a hundred women passengers after offering them spiked drinks. Dozens of women had reported Worboys' attacks to the police but had been ignored. The officers in question were not fired by Stephenson and Boris did not insist they were sacked.

Finally, in April 2009 Assistant Commissioner Bob Quick had

been photographed walking along Downing Street holding an open folder revealing the details of an imminent secret anti-terrorist operation. In the furore, Quick's home was identified by the media as the base for his family's wedding business. To City Hall's surprise, Stephenson did not want to fire Quick for that double breach of security. Instead, he proposed to promote him to run the Territorial Support Group of 800 specialist police officers. Hearing that Theresa May, the Home Secretary, had mentioned, 'Quick must go', Boris summoned the BBC and announced Quick's resignation before the policeman had a chance to submit it. 'It's a matter of sadness,' Boris told the BBC, 'as he had a very, very distinguished career in counter-terrorism.' Quick's departure was not a signal of City Hall's uncompromising purification of the Yard. Rather, Boris was taking revenge for Damian Green's arrest and a recent embarrassment in Parliament.

Despite his impulse to win people's affection, there were some characters who excited Boris's unmitigated venom. One was Keith Vaz, the dishonest Labour chairman of the Commons Home Affairs Select Committee. During his editorship of the *Spectator*, Boris had shamed the 'ludicrous' MP with his 'snout in the trough' over his family's management of a questionable visa business and his month's suspension from Parliament for misconduct in 2002. Not surprisingly, Vaz had long sought his revenge, and Boris's involvement after Green's arrest in November 2008 was a good reason to summon him before the committee the following February to settle some scores. The mayor was asked whether, in conflict with his role as chairman of the Metropolitan Police Authority, he had spoken to Green after his arrest. 'I must invoke the doctrine of the Holy Trinity here,' replied Boris. 'I am all three-in-one and one-in-three.' The MPs were left speechless. By refusing to answer the question, Boris appeared to incriminate himself. Worse, asked whether he had discussed Green's arrest with David Cameron when they met later that same day at a church service, Boris gave the wrong answer.

At first, Boris denied making any comments to Cameron. Later, he admitted in a letter to Vaz that he had made a mistake. They had spoken about Green both at the church service and also earlier on the same day on the telephone after the arrest had taken place. Either deliberately or because he failed to prepare himself, Boris had given the committee false information. Boris's admission was publicised. Accused of lying, the media reported he would be recalled by the committee.

At 7.10 p.m. that same day, Boris telephoned Vaz. 'I'm so fucking angry,' Boris screamed at Vaz for making him look a fool. Unaware that Vaz had allowed someone to record their conversation, a transcript of their heated exchange was quickly released. Boris was caught out. Although he was cleared of a conflict of interest, he was exposed as unreliable and unwise.

To avoid future embarrassment and manage his other commitments, in January 2010 Boris handed over the chairmanship of the police authority to Kit Malthouse, the deputy mayor for police since 2008. Malthouse, a former accountant and one of Simon Milton's protégés at Westminster Council, shared Boris's indifference about cleaning up the Yard. Without their fingers firmly on the Yard's pulse, neither anticipated how matters could quickly get out of control.

After delegating his power, Boris was not troubled about Stephenson's battle with Home Secretary Theresa May over Operation Blunt. Convinced that stop-and-search was disproportionately targeting black youths, she accepted her civil servants' advice that the Met remained racist. In her meetings with Stephenson, May voiced her doubts that the senior officer was enforcing diversity. Fearful that 55 per cent of London's young blacks were unemployed, Boris had attempted to discuss the festering violence with May but, hiding behind her officials, she refused to engage with the mayor. Boris retreated, unaware that her anti-police rhetoric and demand for a reduction of police numbers had reignited a schism between Stephenson and his ranks. Her obduracy was undermining Stephenson's faltering attempts to cure his tarnished inheritance from Ian Blair. And then, in November 2010, the wobbly edifice was shaken by the abrupt departure of Stephenson. Struck by cancer, he took leave for treatment. His temporary replacement was Tim

Godwin, an intelligent but inexperienced officer. Over the following seven months, neither Boris nor Malthouse was aware that Stephenson's absence had sparked the resumption of acrimonious warfare among the Yard's senior officers. As Godwin's credibility evaporated, morale deteriorated. Theresa May was similarly blind to the disarray. Fearing dire consequences of Godwin's waning authority, Stephenson returned prematurely to the Yard. Although still manifestly weak from cancer, the decent officer walked into a storm.

For some months, there had been suspicion that Scotland Yard's investigation of the *News of the World* hacking operation against hundreds of celebrities had been deliberately buried. There had been few criminal convictions and News International's emphatic denials of any wrongdoing had been corroborated by Scotland Yard's announcement that the allegations of a cover-up were not supported by the evidence. That changed in January 2011. Under pressure from the victims, politicians and the *Guardian*, Scotland Yard reluctantly reopened its inquiry. By July, a series of discoveries and arrests had enmeshed Rupert Murdoch's empire in serious crimes, not least hacking the phone of Milly Dowler, a thirteen-year-old Surrey schoolgirl, soon after her murder in 2002. Dowler's phone had been hacked with the knowledge of the *News of the World*'s senior staff including Andy Coulson, the editor.

Tim Godwin and Stephenson underestimated the gravity of the hacking. Neither could grasp that a handful of senior Scotland Yard officers had repeatedly failed to discover the truth. They were not helped by Boris's affection for Murdoch, encouraged no doubt by his need for the tycoon's media support, and his perfunctory dismissal of the victims of bugging. 'I bet that virtually the whole of Fleet Street was involved (and may still be involved),' he wrote inaccurately. In that vein, Stephenson dismissed the cover-up allegations as 'white noise' and a distraction from investigating terrorism and murder.

On 14 July 2011, Neil Wallis, the former executive editor of the *News of the World*, was arrested as a hacking suspect. On the same day, Stephenson admitted that in 2009 he had hired Wallis, alias the

The troubled Johnson family in January 1973: Aged nine, Boris (above, left), was an eyewitness to his mother's unhappiness. Charlotte and Stanley finally divorced in 1978.

Boris shone at Eton – but he walked a tightrope. Fired with ambition to succeed, he threw himself into everything with gusto – studies, sports, debating, journalism, acting. He was a King's Scholar and became a member of Pop, the College's elite group of Prefects, but was criticised at the end for laziness.

Controversial friends: At Eton and Oxford, Boris's friends included Darius Guppy (above, left) and Charles Spencer. Guppy went to prison while Spencer publicly denounced the Royal Family at the 1997 funeral of Princess Diana, his sister.

Boris's defiant pose just before leading his team into Eton's wall game.

Launch pad: Oxford set up Boris for life. He dated and then wed Allegra Mostyn-Owen, acclaimed as the university's most attractive undergraduate; and was elected President of the Oxford Union on his second attempt.

Party: Boris, with Allegra and his sister Rachel (right) at Charles Spencer's 21st birthday party in 1985.

Boris and Allegra in 1986.

The *Spectator* days: The magazine's circulation soared under Boris's editorship, not least after the exposure of Boris's relationship with deputy editor, Petronella Wyatt, a trusted confidante and good friend.

In trouble again: Boris's editorship and political career crashed after the *Spectator* published a scurrilous and untruthful attack on Liverpool. Boris's 'apology' to the city was a PR masterstroke but left him in the wilderness.

Success: Boris's election as London's Mayor in 2008 resurrected his political career. Anchored to reality by Marina Wheeler, his wife, Boris posed as the family man, usually with Stanley eager to share the spotlight. At the end of a bitter personalised campaign, he had no affection for Ken Livingstone.

Victory night: Boris's family, including his wife Marina Wheeler (in white top), sit in the front row at City Hall before the announcement of his victory in the 2012 London Mayoral election. His success owed much to Lynton Crosby (top row, fourth from right).

Close friends: Boris finds life difficult without a secret soulmate. Despite the danger of inevitable exposure, he had a serious relationship with Helen Macintyre (left), with whom he had a daughter, then with Anna Fazackerley (below), a journalist, and an intense four year relationship with Jennifer Arcuri, an American entrepreneur.

Boris with Jennifer Arcuri.

Refuge: Exposure of his affairs was usually followed by expulsion from the family home. On the first occasion, he lived with Justin Rushbrooke, his close friend from Balliol.

Heading for the top: The 2012 London Olympics sealed Boris's reputation. As David Cameron, prime minister at the time, said 'If any other politician in the world got stuck on a zip wire it would be a disaster. For Boris it's a triumph. He defies all forms of gravity.'

Boris's rivalry with Cameron and George Osborne (pictured together on a fraught trip to China in 2013) was never concealed – and became the foundation of Boris's bid for the party leadership.

'Wolfman', as a speech-writer and adviser. For some, that link between Scotland Yard and News International explained the police's refusal to investigate the hacking. The crisis at the Yard could no longer be ignored. The Met had recently been criticised for allowing violent anarchist demonstrators to attack Tory Party headquarters and later dangerously threaten Camilla, the Duchess of Cornwall, in her car. In the commissioner's absence, his loss of control over the Yard had become glaring. Summoned by Boris, Stephenson's explanations of the Yard's conduct were unconvincing. At the end of the ninety-minute meeting, no instant solution had been agreed. Pertinently, Boris refused to take responsibility for the Yard's conduct and Malthouse remained silent.

Hours after their meeting, Stephenson admitted to a media inquiry that he had accepted three weeks' hospitality in a friend's health resort to recover from his illness. In normal circumstances that gift could have been brushed aside but Neil Wallis was also the resort's public relations executive. Wallis's double relationship with Stephenson was damning. On Sunday 17 July, Stephenson resigned. 'This will go down as the most honourable resignation since Carrington,' Boris told Stephenson, the fourth commissioner in ten years, referring to the Foreign Secretary's resignation in 1982 for failing to anticipate the Argentine invasion of the Falkland Islands.

Andy Coulson's employment as the Downing Street spokesman now linked David Cameron to the *News of the World*'s sleaze. In City Hall, Boris denied any error of judgement or responsibility for the crisis. But he lacked any track record to demonstrate his attempts to cure the Yard's malaise. With his back to the wall, he needed a scapegoat. The media had alighted on John Yates, the Yard's assistant commissioner. In 2009, after a cursory search through the records, Yates had declared that there was no reason to reopen the hacking inquiry. Two years later, Yates's mistake appeared inexcusable. 'You're affecting my brand,' Boris told Yates. 'You'll have to go too.' Malthouse added, 'Resign or you'll be suspended.' To his lasting regret, Yates resigned on Monday 18 July, the day after Stephenson's resignation. Shortly after, Boris invited the loyal officer for a drink in City Hall. 'I'm terribly, terribly sorry,' said Boris, giving the impression, as he had years earlier while politely drinking tea with John le Carré, that while plunging the knife he still wanted to be loved.

The hacking storm headed off in other directions, searching for other culprits. Stephenson returned to sick leave, while Boris, unconcerned by the Yard's disarray and Godwin acting again as commissioner, set off with Marina and their four children for their summer holidays in the Canadian Rockies. On the eve of departing, he had agreed without protest that London's police numbers would be reduced by 1,900 – another breach of his election pledge to increase the number of officers to above 32,500.

With unfortunate policies and unsuitable people in authority, Boris had not properly understood the consequence of ignoring explicit warnings. The mishaps of Ian Tomlinson, John Worboys, Bob Quick and the *News of the World*'s hacking all signalled the decay at Scotland Yard but Boris and Malthouse failed to come to the obvious conclusion. A few days later, on 4 August 2011, an undercover policeman shot Mark Duggan, a twenty-nine-year-old black criminal, in Tottenham, north London. No one had foreseen the outcome of failing to remove the putrefaction at the Yard.

Chapter 13

Playing with Fire

Two days after Mark Duggan's death, a small protest by his friends accelerated into riots across north London. With no experience of civil unrest, Godwin reassured Kit Malthouse at the end of the first day that the situation was under control. The following day, a Sunday, the riots spread to north-east London and then down to Brixton in south London. Despite indiscriminate looting and burning, the police failed to intervene effectively and a police commander in north London went on holiday. At the end of the weekend, Godwin resisted asking outside forces to send reinforcements to the capital. That night, in a telephone conversation Malthouse reassured Boris that there was no reason to abandon his holiday. Neither man grasped that Stephenson's and Yates's departures had destabilised the Yard. Nor did they consider their reliance on Godwin, who had emerged as an artless officer whom Stephenson no longer trusted. Without considering their successive misjudgements over the previous two years, Boris was relieved to be told that the police had London's streets under control, and for the next hours he continued to drive through the Rockies without questioning his reliance on Godwin. Naturally, the same questions should have been asked by Theresa May and the Home Office, but the department, still unreformed since John Reid the Labour Home Secretary judged it 'unfit for purpose' in 2006, was incapable of taking any initiative.

On Monday morning, thousands of masked looters began to rampage across the capital, setting buildings alight and attacking people. Among the targets in flames was a beloved family-run furniture store in Croydon which had survived the Blitz. Cowed, 6,000 police abandoned areas to the mob, doing nothing but watch rampant criminality. That night, Cameron and May headed back from their holidays to London. In Canada, Boris realised the severity of the situation and decided to return to Britain on his own. 'I was watching the TV news in Calgary waiting for a plane,' he wrote. 'I felt a sickening sense of incredulity that this could really be happening in our city . . . I felt ashamed.'

On Tuesday, the prime minister chaired an emergency Cobra meeting in the Cabinet Office. Theresa May was there but, since Boris was still flying back to London, he was represented by Malthouse. Godwin's mistakes had heaped humiliation onto the three politicians but the police chiefs at the meeting were unapologetic about their failure to restore order. While Malthouse endorsed the Yard's strategy of retreat from the mob, Cameron was extremely critical. He ordered an extra 10,000 police to be deployed on the streets immediately. To promote herself after the meeting, May told the waiting media that she had cancelled all police leave.

After Boris arrived at Heathrow, he joined May and headed for Clapham, a scene of shocking destruction. Together they listened with glazed looks to the residents' fury about the police absence as bricks had smashed through their windows. As the crowd began to jeer and heckle, May walked backwards and then disappeared. Boris was left to take the blame although the final responsibility for the police failure was in fact hers. On the street, Boris refused to criticise the police. They had, he said, performed 'brilliantly'. The fault, he said, was the government's, and especially May's, for cutting police budgets and officers.

That night, the police struck back at the politicians. Scotland Yard described Cameron's criticism of the police as a 'miscalculation'. On BBC TV, Hugh Orde, the president of the Association of Chief Police Officers, declared that the three politicians' dramatic return to London was 'an irrelevance in terms of tactics that were by then developing'. He continued, 'The vital distinction between policing and politics remains. The police service will make the tactical decisions.' Brusquely, he scolded May about cancelling police leave. 'She can't do that,' said Orde. 'She doesn't have that power.' The extra police, he added, had been ordered not by Cameron but by Godwin. In dealing with the riots, he said, the police had been hampered by the European human rights laws. No one accepted that feeble and inaccurate excuse. Everyone was outraged by the TV footage showing police officers idly watching the rioters and not using their statutory powers to impose law and order. Orde's reproach on TV coincided with the end of Cameron's dinner with Boris in Downing Street.

Among Cameron's positive qualities were his integrity and friendship, regardless of Boris's disruptive opposition. Cameron had cooked steak and potatoes for the two of them. Yet, despite their laughter and teasing, at the end Boris refused to abandon his own interests.

On morning radio hours later, Boris criticised the government for imposing the police cuts – by then 1,126 had gone. The cuts, he said, saved £2 billion, which represented a 20 per cent reduction in the police budget. 'Mayors always want more money,' Cameron replied angrily. Boris, he discovered, was irked by the accusation that the riots were his 'Hurricane Katrina moment' (referring to George W. Bush's failure to act speedily in 2005 after New Orleans was deluged), a charge that would be used against him in the following year's mayoral elections. Boris assumed the media story deriding his late return to London from his holiday was put out by the government. In reality, it originated in the *Guardian*. 'He was being paranoid,' Cameron recalled in his memoirs, 'and frankly at this stage of the proceedings a massive irritation.' The mayor, continued Cameron, 'was veering all over the place'. Cameron refused to cancel the police cuts.

The mayor arrived ten minutes late at that Wednesday's Cobra meeting, or as one police chief smiled, 'fashionably late, performing to show that he was independent of the government'. The sight of the mayor, sweaty and puffing as he took off his cycle helmet and protective clothing, irritated Theresa May. Cameron was also visibly annoyed. The mayor had missed Godwin's briefing and then contributed to a moment of farce. People in east London, the politicians were told, were suspicious of officers whose uniforms carried the word 'Heddlu'. 'What's Heddlu?' asked Boris. 'You should know,' snapped Cameron. 'You once stood in a Welsh seat. It's "police".'

The next day, 11 August, the riots in London were over. Thousands of extra police and mass arrests suppressed the mob. The costs were an estimated £200 million, but the damage to Boris's reputation at that moment was incalculable. Criticised for delaying his return from holiday, he was also attacked on the BBC for lacking sympathy for both the rioters and their victims. His behaviour appeared to endorse the caricature of him as a lazy toff. In truth, his continuing incomprehension about Scotland Yard's dysfunction reflected his misunderstanding of governance. Typically in these serious circumstances, no one would dare to explain his mistakes to his face. Critics were not readmitted to his office.

Boris did not blame Kit Malthouse for his late return from Canada. Instead, he turned on the BBC for calling the looters 'protestors' against politicians and bankers. 'People were not stealing because Gerald Kaufman, a Labour MP, had claimed a flat-screen TV on his expenses,' he wrote. Seventy-five per cent of those charged had previous convictions. They were known criminals, members of 'a feral underclass', not rioting to alleviate their poverty. 'The young rioters were betrayed by the educational system and their families who failed to give them discipline or hope or ambition.' He blamed London's 'chillingly bad' schools, turning out illiterate and innumerate youths, for creating rioters. He refused to blame the police. They were the victims of 'squeamishness', he believed. 'We politicians speak with forked tongue to the police.' His solution: 'Robust policing is essential.'

With that mindset, Boris's priority in choosing a new commissioner, with Theresa May, was again to reduce crime. Once again, he showed no interest in transforming the Yard. He agreed with May to exclude the ideal candidate for that task – Hugh Orde, Ulster's successful police chief. Orde was not forgiven for criticising Boris, Cameron and May in his BBC TV interview. That left Bernard Hogan-Howe from Merseyside as the last man standing. Once again, Boris failed to scrutinise the candidate's qualifications: he had never served as a senior front-line policeman or as a detective but had been responsible for human resources. He was also regarded by some police critics as a bully who, said many in the Yard, 'always thinks he's right'. Although Hogan-Howe disliked politicians, he skilfully conceded to them, especially their demands for cuts. There was neither boldness nor pragmatism in Boris's choice. Hogan-Howe was appointed to fill a void.

Only Boris understood that his lack of interest in Scotland Yard's fate was influenced by his obsession with the party's leadership. So often, he was focused on his rival George Osborne, and the recurring fear that his dream of entering Downing Street with a wave to the flashing cameras might end as a nightmare, cheated of the chance. Just before the party conference in October 2011, Osborne called Boris. 'Please, no fireworks,' the Chancellor pleaded.

'What's it worth?' asked Boris.

'What do you mean?' asked Osborne.

'Well I'm sitting in front of a blank screen and I'll write to support an EU referendum on Lisbon if you don't give an additional £93 million to the Met.'

'Are you joking?' asked Osborne.

'I need to fulfil an election pledge,' replied Boris.

Osborne succumbed.

'The best-paid column I've never written,' quipped the mayor.

The party conference was a lull before the storm. In his showcase speech, Boris delighted his fans. 'Pay your car tax or it will be towed away,' he warned. 'You'll get it back in a small box for Christmas.' Pause. 'From crusher with love.' His great pleasure was Theresa May's embarrassment after she claimed, in a rant about immigration, that one particular illegal immigrant could not be deported because their human rights to stay in Britain were protected by the court's refusal to separate them from their pet cat. That was untrue. Seeing a rival crumble always pleased Boris.

His crunch moment was a fringe meeting on the EU. His promise to Osborne was forgotten. Europe's leaders, he believed, were living in 'a fool's paradise' advocating a closer union to solve the euro crisis. That, he told his admirers, was 'absolutely crazy'. To halt the federalism, he called for a referendum on the Lisbon treaty and, for the first time, an in-out vote. Reports of the speech quickly reached Cameron. Boris, he said in fury, was playing with fire, pandering to the party's Eurosceptics. David Nuttall, a Tory MP, was planning to introduce a motion in the Commons to hold an EU referendum. Cameron intended to order a three-line whip to defeat the Eurosceptics. Boris was not aligned with Nuttall but he wanted to be recognised as a contender for the leadership. Asked whether he would run for Parliament in 2015 and be the next party leader, Boris replied, 'There's not a snowball's chance in Hades of a return . . . I don't think I'll do another big job in politics after this.' Naturally, he was not believed.

In Westminster, meanwhile, Cameron was struggling to control his party. Although Nuttall's motion was defeated, the EU's crisis emboldened the Eurosceptics. To save the euro, the EU leaders decided in November to strengthen their fiscal union. Without consulting Britain, they proposed a new treaty with new regulations to be imposed on the City, including extra transaction taxes. Cameron's protests were ignored. To save himself, on 11 December, Cameron vetoed the treaty. The 26-to-1 vote marked another step on Britain's drift away from the EU.

Boris praised Cameron for 'playing a blinder' and predicted that the eurozone would break up within one year. To reinforce his position, he attacked EU regulations protecting European sugar-beet producers. Tate & Lyle, the famous British sugar refiner, needed sugar cane and not sugar beet to make its golden syrup. But the EU's high tariffs on imported sugar cane, Boris protested, penalised the company. To prove his Euroscepticism, he joined Iain Duncan Smith at the end of January 2012 in Downing Street, to urge Cameron to resist the EU's latest treaty changes and agree to an in-out referendum. Cameron rejected the idea. After the meeting, both Duncan Smith and Cameron were puzzled about Boris's Euroscepticism. His real motive, they suspected, was self-interest. At that moment, everything was focused on Boris being re-elected mayor for the second term.

Over Christmas, Ken Livingstone had leapt to an 8-point lead. Boris was panicking. Grandstanding was the only way he knew to win back voters, even at Cameron's expense. During a visit to the Olympic Park, Cameron watched Boris climb up to a ten-metre diving platform to promote his successful legacy plans. Down below, Cameron swallowed his irritation about being upstaged.

Chapter 14

'Jealousies and paranoias'

Three months before the 2012 mayoral election, Boris faced the prospect of watching the Olympics on TV, rather than in the stadium as mayor. The chance of defeat was real. London had endured days of rioting, repeated Tube strikes, fares had increased by 40 per cent and the polls put the Tories 17 per cent behind Labour in the capital. To be certain of victory, however, Livingstone still needed to land some punches. Boris's good fortune was Livingstone's inability to find new angles to malign his opponent, both politically and as a person.

Boris had originally intended to campaign on building Boris Island, his Estuary airport, the cable car across the Thames and a pledge to finance more culture and street parties. Then he summoned Lynton Crosby. The Australian derided Boris's ideas. The real issues, he pronounced, were the police, crime, housing, transport and the economy. Just stick to five points, he ordered his client. Stay on message, focus on limited issues and suppress your instincts. 'Lynton's taking the bubbles out of the champagne,' Guto Harri later reflected, making the campaign more tribal and less interesting. Occasionally, the authentic Boris did burst out of Crosby's shackles.

Walking along the pavement or as he cycled across London, excited pedestrians shook Boris's hand, took a selfie or shouted their opinions during what he called 'a rolling focus group'. Cartoon caricature or celebrity, they loved his star quality. Regardless of his personal life and betrayal of his wife, women liked the rogue.

Cheered by taxi drivers and multimillionaires, his raw political instincts offered optimism. Passionate, unafraid and never seemingly cruel, voters did not necessarily believe he was the mayor for the poor but people trusted him because of his scruffy appearance. Neither waxen nor a stereotype, he appeared to speak honestly, avoiding politicians' clichés. The best rhetorical approach, Boris believed, was to use simple words that people understood. 'If you want to be heard you have to speak plainly.' 'It doesn't matter where you come from as long as you know where you're going,' said a man who never apologised for his Etonian background. He certainly never mentioned his childhood suffering.

London was thriving. The City was recovering after the 2008 crash, and cranes filled the skyline. Boris's critics gave him no credit for that revival and he was forbidden by Crosby to stray off his script. The simplicity of Boris's message was the daily target of the metropolitan moralisers. Left-wingers highlighted the absence of any political ideology or 'core message'. The critics on the right, especially Matthew Parris and Max Hastings, agreed that his charisma alone might bring victory, but nothing else. They disliked the man and denied there was a message. His critics were deaf to his compassionate, cosmopolitan Conservatism – an amnesty to illegal immigrants, a higher minimum wage, lower taxes, better education and Euroscepticism. That message did appeal to some Labour voters and he relied on them to reject Livingstone. 'You can't trust Ken,' Boris repeated again and again. Livingstone had left City Hall in a toxic atmosphere and his key promise to cut fares depended on Cameron supporting a £1.2 billion Labour giveaway. That, said Boris, was unlikely.

'Don't vote for a joke' was Livingstone's line in 2008, but few now believed Boris was a joke. In his search for new weapons, Livingstone deployed the class card. Four years earlier, Boris had referred to his £250,000 annual *Telegraph* fee as 'chicken feed'. That comment, and Boris's support for bankers, was flagged widely by Livingstone in interviews. Livingstone also attacked the Routemaster buses, which suffered from design faults including ventilation failures. In late February, the campaign was a stalemate.

The *Evening Standard*, by then a freesheet with declining influence, provided little support. Crosby launched the nuclear option.

By undisclosed means, Andrew Gilligan, Livingstone's nemesis, discovered that Livingstone charged for his work through a limited company. Rather than paying 50 per cent income tax, Livingstone was liable only for the lesser 20 per cent corporation tax on his profits. His effective tax rate was 14.5 per cent. Although his scheme was wholly legitimate, Livingstone had waged war against 'rich bastards' and 'tax dodgers' who should 'not be allowed to vote'. Combined with the creeping realisation that Livingstone's association with Muslim extremists reflected his anti-Semitism, his exposure as a hypocrite hit his poll ratings.

Sensitive to his fate four years earlier, Livingstone struck back. During a live radio discussion Livingstone accused Boris of also avoiding taxes. 'You are absolutely lying,' Boris told Livingstone. 'You're a bare-faced liar.' As the two descended in a lift after the programme, Boris screamed 'You're a fucking liar.' Livingstone's allegation was completely false. As the idea of 'Livingstone the tax dodger' took hold, Boris pulled 6 points ahead in the polls.

And then the polls during late April swung against him again. Newspaper headlines in March 2012 about Osborne's 'omnishambles' budget highlighted a flawed 'Granny' tax penalising thrifty pensioners, a costly charity tax, punitive North Sea oil taxes, a cut of the top rate of tax to help the rich, and VAT levied on pasties. In addition, there was a strike by fuel delivery men, horrendous queues at Heathrow and talk of a double-dip or even triple-dip recession. Boris could only be grateful that, on Cameron's orders, Osborne had abandoned a mansion tax, an annual levy on homes regardless of income or ability to pay. 'Two arrogant posh boys who don't know the price of milk,' scorned a disgusted Tory MP. 'George is doing this to sabotage my campaign,' Boris quipped to Guto Harri. Was Crosby conflicted, Boris wondered, because Osborne was paying him more for the next Conservative general election campaign?

'You're overdoing the gloom,' Boris told the prime minister. Cameron, Boris believed, was not a proper capitalist. He should ease up on austerity and encourage employment and investment in infrastructure. Cameron saw it differently. Boris, he sighed, was 'full of jealousies and paranoias'. City Hall, Cameron believed, was 'dysfunctional'.

At times Boris struggled against not only Cameron but also the BBC. 'I sometimes felt,' he wrote, 'that my chief opponent was the local BBC News', whose reporters in his view were 'statist, corporatist, defeatist, anti-business, Europhile and above all over-whelmingly biased to the left'. Under Chris Patten, the BBC's presumptuous chairman, the Corporation had become unstable. Patten's reckless interference in the management was failing to restore professional editorial control of news and current affairs. One solution, Boris urged, was the appointment of a Tory as the BBC's next director general who did not believe that the taxpayer should pay for everything. 'If we can't change the BBC,' he wrote, 'we can't change the country.' Haplessly, Patten would appoint George Entwistle as the director general, a disastrous choice. Entwistle lasted just fifty-four days before he was forced to resign after his gaffe during a radio interview about his mismanagement of the BBC's defamation of the senior Tory Alistair McAlpine.

After the election polls closed on 3 May, Boris and his supporters headed to a West End club. His confidence of victory was rattled by reports from various counts that the vote was tilting towards Liv-ingstone. Boris waited nervously with Crosby. In City Hall, some officials began clearing their desks, convinced he had lost. Sud-denly, two batches of uncounted votes from Tory wards in Brent, a Labour council, were discovered. They had been 'accidentally' placed in a store by council employees. Victory was confirmed at midnight. He had won by just 62,538 votes, a 3 per cent victory thanks to support from traditional Labour areas. 'Only Boris could have won a second time,' said Stephen Greenhalgh, a Tory council leader. 'Boris told me, "We kind of got by in the first term, now we must focus on what we can deliver."'

The following year, Livingstone recounted that after the elec-tion Boris wanted to make up about their argument about tax avoidance: 'He was worried that I was angry with him, and this is a breathtaking weakness in a politician. He wants to be loved even by the people he's destroying.' Others would say it was more nuanced. Boris clasped his enemies close to defuse the antagonism.

Boris's victory protected Cameron from humiliation. In the local elections nationally, Labour won 38 per cent of the votes against the Tories' 31 per cent. Middle England was angry about Cameron's obsession with gay marriage and wind turbines. He had ignored their opinions, especially their Euroscepticism. Boris was their hero. The polls showed that only Boris, as the party leader, could defeat Labour. Asked by ITV whether his next ambition was to be prime minister, Boris denied it 'Definitively, categorically, emphatically, without hesitation or doubt. Will that do?' The next day, Max Hastings wrote, 'It is dismaying that he has become the most popular Conservative in Britain . . . It is crazy to speak of him as a prospective prime minister. If Boris reached Downing Street, government would become a permanent pier-end panto, probably with a striptease thrown in . . . Surely the British people deserve better than a comic, cad and a serial bonker, however entertaining.' Hastings would have been relieved to have heard a conversation between Cameron and Boris at City Hall. 'I'm going to do this job,' Boris told Cameron, 'and that's me done with public life. I'm leaving public life after this. People say I want to be an MP. I don't. I'm not going to do that.'

Six weeks later in New York, Boris revealed in an interview that his true ambition was to be prime minister: 'That's the awful fact.' He counted on the Olympics to boost that ambition.

Chapter 15

'Alexander the Great'

Any other British politician would have been flailed by the gloom and doom dominating the media in the weeks before the Olympic Games. After predictions that London's ageing transport system would collapse, that businesses would be crippled because tourists were warned to stay away, and that Britain would be embarrassed by its failure to match Beijing's extravaganza, the German newspaper *Der Spiegel* forecast that an almighty deluge was certain to drown the event. Then Senator Mitt Romney, the Republican nominee for US president, agreed the Games would be a disaster, an opinion endorsed by the Anglophobe *New York Times*. Their pessimism appeared to be justified after an unfortunate sequence of events. There was the failure of G4S, the security company, to provide the 10,000 guards needed for the stadium. Boris directly blamed that on Theresa May. Then the Hammersmith flyover was closed, cutting a vital route into London from Heathrow, and the American Olympic team was mistakenly driven to Southend. The doomsters, however, were wrong. Led by John Armitt, chairman of the Olympic Delivery Authority, the Olympic Park was completed, pristine, on budget, and was an outstanding testament to British skill.

'Get happy,' Boris ordered London. 'See the sunny uplands.' In his welcoming speech at the arrival of the Olympic flame from Athens to the Tower of London in bright sunshine, he chortled: 'As Henry VIII discovered with at least two of his wives, this is a perfect place to bring an old flame.' While the capital partied, he described a 'contagion of joy' spreading across London. 'The Geiger counter of

Olympo-mania will go zoik – off the scale.' Rarely was a politician more suited to an event. Boris's political instincts were born from competitive sport. Games, he chanted, were the supreme human achievement. 'Ruthlessly and dazzlingly elitist', they were 'the antithesis of the "all must win prizes"' mindset. The Olympics were all about character. Winning required 'not just physical genius but also colossal intellectual and emotional effort'. Drawing on his love of ancient Greece, he worshipped the grand moral of the Games. Athletes were confronted by 'the glory of winning, the pathos of losing and the toil that can make the difference'. That was, he exhorted, the key to a healthy society and also to economic growth.

On the morning of the opening ceremony on 27 July, the Olympic Committee was invited to a momentous celebration at Covent Garden. From the stage, Boris read in classical Greek a poem specially written by Armand D'Angour, an Oxford classicist, in the style of Pindar, a poet in fifth-century BC Greece who celebrated the beauty and mystery of athletic achievements. The mayor's flamboyant delivery to 1,000 people was hailed as outstanding.

That evening, nearly a billion people watched a dazzling opening ceremony which included James Bond (Daniel Craig) taking the Queen from Buckingham Palace to the Olympic stadium by helicopter, and appearing to parachute together into the stadium. Then followed a few nail-biting days before the British athletes began to win medals. Amid huge cheers as Boris walked to the Aquatic Centre to watch Britain's swimmers win more events, and said to an aide: 'It may not get any better than this, but this is good enough for me.' He made the Games his success, exalting that the trade at tattoo parlours was roaring, and semi-naked women 'glistening like wet otters' were playing beach volleyball in the rain in Horse Guards Parade. 'The whole thing,' he roared, 'is magnificent and bonkers.' The following day, the crowds in Hyde Park chanted his name and his popularity soared further. Back in the Olympic Park, Princess Anne was greeted by Boris before making her speech. 'It's always good not to come after Boris,' she confessed.

A sense of reckless fun filled City Hall. At the Foreign Office's request, Boris agreed to receive the mayor of Ulan Batur, the

Mongolian capital. 'I've just been to the Gulf,' said Boris, 'and they put lipstick on their camels. Do you put lipstick on your camels in Mongolia?' The mayor was thrilled.

Less thrilled were those who had helped Boris win the mayoralty, given him money and hospitality but did not receive his invitation to the Olympics. 'That's what's strange about Boris,' complained one prominent benefactor. 'It's all about Boris. He never thinks about repaying debts or hospitality, or even appreciating help and generosity.'

On 1 August, Boris visited the £60 million cable car over the Thames. Emirates Airlines had contributed £36 million and £8 million had come from the EU. 180,000 people were using it every week. Afterwards he headed to Victoria Park to publicise a zip wire. In theory, he should have zoomed across. Instead, having understated his weight, he came to a standstill before reaching the end of the wire and, clutching two Union flags, pleaded 'Get me a ladder.' Dangling helplessly, no help arrived. 'Is there anything you can do?' he shouted at Karl, his bodyguard, concealing the pain he was in. Slowly Karl reached into his inside pocket. 'I thought he was taking out a gun,' Boris said later. Instead, Karl took out his phone to take a photograph. 'If any other politician in the world got stuck on a zip wire,' said Cameron, 'it would be a disaster. For Boris it's a triumph. He defies all forms of gravity.'

On 10 September, the day after the Paralympics ended, a million people crowded into the Mall for a victory parade. 'You brought the country together,' Boris said to the athletes. 'You routed the doubters and you scattered the gloomsters, [producing] paroxysms of tears and joy on the sofas of Britain.' The crowd chanted his name. Beside him was Cameron. The prime minister was a bystander watching the mayor's triumph. 'What comes next?' asked Gerard Lyons, his economic adviser. 'City Hall is his stepping stone to Downing Street,' replied Peter Hendy.

By then, Boris's attention was distracted by a new relationship. On the opening night of the Paralympics, no one had spotted the mayor slipping away from the stadium and head to a flat in Shoreditch, east London. It was rented by a blonde twenty-seven-year-old Californian digital entrepreneur he had met the previous year. Intelligent and vivacious, her name was Jennifer Arcuri.

Jennifer Arcuri had settled in London to make her fortune in the tech industry. With sassy humour, she flaunted her looks to ingratiate herself with anyone deemed potentially able to help her build Innotech, her fledgling business that introduced aspiring entrepreneurs to policymakers. It was during a routine hunt for clients at a British Venture Capital Association reception in a Marylebone hotel in 2011 that she had stood among a group of expectant bankers. 'What's up?' she asked.

'We're waiting for the mayor,' one banker replied.

'Who's that?'

'Boris. If you stand right here he might notice you.'

In her words, 'a chubby guy arrives with his shirt hanging out and I watched him turn that group of sweaty old men into something on speed. I walked right up to him, shook his hand and said, "You should come to speak to my group." "Yes I will," he said. "Email me."'

Nothing happened until 3 March 2012. Arcuri's business had grown and she needed official endorsement. She talked her way onto Boris's election campaign bus as a volunteer and sat so close that the mayor could not help seeing her. 'She clearly targeted him,' a Boris aide realised later. 'She will just bulldoze her way into anything because she has that self-belief.' To Arcuri's delight, Boris turned every thirty seconds to look at her. 'I realised he was interested,' she recalled nearly a decade later. 'I was flirtatious, I mentioned Shakespeare, I made him smile, intrigued him and got him to laugh. I had him hooked.' At the end of the journey, Arcuri gave Boris her card. 'No, no. I just want to contact you directly,' he insisted. She gave him her telephone number and soon after he called. She indexed his number under 'Alexander the Great'.

About a month later, Arcuri faced a crisis. Jimmy Wales, the founder of Wikipedia, had agreed to address an Innotech reception for a £25,000 fee. She had hired an expensive venue in Covent Garden and attracted a large fee-paying audience. 'I used sex to get people to come to my events,' Arcuri admits. 'It was all emotionally charged.' At the last moment, Wales cancelled. In search of a special speaker she called Boris. 'You said you'd talk at an event,' she said. 'I need you on 18 April.' He agreed. As he spoke to her audience, Arcuri realised 'That's the first time he's spoken about tech and he knows nothing about it.' To her close friends on Facebook, she congratulated herself: 'We made Boris look like a rock star at our event.' In the aftermath, Arcuri was thrilled by the profit her event had generated by 'the man of the hour'. To her further delight, 'whenever I called him, he would call me back'. Conveniently, her Shoreditch flat was on his cycle route from City Hall to Islington.

Arcuri's presence in Boris's life could not be kept secret from his closest staff for long. Although he 'swore blind' to Marina after his affair with Helen Macintyre that he would be faithful, some could see that while he worshipped Marina as a soulmate, their relationship, they mistakenly speculated, had become platonic. Emotionally weak, he would never leave Marina. Among the first to have scented a problem had been Lynton Crosby. He had extracted a promise that Boris would not start an affair until after the election. Thereafter, he was unconcerned.

Soon after the election, having been head-hunted by News International, Guto Harri left City Hall (although he remained an unofficial adviser to Boris). Boris chose Will Walden, an experienced BBC journalist, as his replacement. Walden changed the media operation. While Harri had cultivated the media to sell Boris mercilessly, Walden wanted less fuss, less noise and more consensual journalism. He preferred not to ask Boris about his personal life, and in any event Boris refused to discuss it.

In the wake of the Olympics, Britain's most popular politician left no one in doubt about his ambitions. Outmanoeuvring George Osborne, his principal rival, had been much easier after the omnishambles budget but he had been spooked by reports of Osborne appointing supporters to key positions in the party across the country. Suspiciously, invitations by constituencies for after-dinner speeches had been withdrawn to deny Boris's access to the grass roots. On the other hand, Osborne's own prospects looked bleak. After the Chancellor was booed at the Olympic stadium, the leadership polls put him on 2 per cent against Boris's 32 per cent. He was unelectable. Boris's only opponent was Cameron. 'I can't possibly do a worse job than he's doing,' he had told Guto Harri while they discussed his tactics for the leadership in Boris's Islington home.

'Stop it, Guto,' shouted Marina playfully, 'you're giving him this mad idea,' convinced it was highly improbable.

'This is his destiny,' replied Guto. 'He's wanted to do it since his schooldays.'

Anyone who failed to accept his need to exert his power would get burned.

★

In anticipation of the party conference that October, Boris's target was the media. He needed the newspaper editors to rein in their hostile columnists. Back in early August, following a thunderclap of Borismania at the Olympics, Philip Collins in *The Times* had written 'Boris will never be prime minister . . . He is a clown who happens to run a major city, the opposite of the leadership that Britain wants.' And on the same day Quentin Letts wrote in the *Mail*, 'Boris is not a prime minister.'

Boris had invited Rupert Murdoch to a swimming event at the Olympics as his personal guest, despite News International being under criminal investigation. They had previously met in New York for lunch. Murdoch had never concealed his dislike of Cameron and his enthusiasm for Boris. In return, Boris had written 'There's a sort of demonisation of Rupert Murdoch. He's not a convicted criminal.' He added, 'He's not even under any criminal investigation.' That was wrong. After the arrest of his company's executives and former employees for phone hacking in 2011 and being charged with conspiracy in May 2012, Scotland Yard's investigation could have still led to Murdoch himself. Boris's carelessness with key facts was among the reasons, despite his Olympic triumph, the *Daily Mail* dubbed him a 'jester' not suited to the 'serious business of governing the country'.

Dacre, Boris heard, had become gripped by Boris's 'box-office appeal' and obsessed with the mayor's private life. He was demanding to know whether there were any undiscovered illegitimate children and about his behaviour as a father. Recently, the *Mail* had mentioned publishing a photograph of Boris's teenage daughter drinking from a bottle in a field near Oxford; and the newspaper had also obtained a photo of his son Milo holding his fingers as a gun. 'Aren't they entitled to have a childhood?' Boris fumed, relieved when the newspaper agreed to back down. But nevertheless, Dacre commissioned a profile to discover whether Boris was a serious contender for Downing Street. Boris feared it would simply be an exposé of his sex and home life. In Boris's view, his *Telegraph* column was a 'never decommissioned weapon' to be used if necessary 'to get my own back against Dacre'. But he lacked the spite to ever use it, even after a meeting which Dacre would later describe as a 'lachrymose lunch (his tears not mine) with Boris bewailing that the *Mail* was destroying his marriage'. The mayor could not stop the newspapers' hostility, and taking on Dacre and Murdoch, Boris knew, was considerably more dangerous than taking on Cameron.

Just before the party conference, Boris and Marina had lunch with the Camerons at a pub near Chequers. Once again, the prime minister hoped that Boris's disruptive desire for the spotlight could be contained. Sensitive to the YouGov opinion poll putting Boris substantially ahead of him, Cameron had not been displeased when Grant Shapps, the party chairman, openly said that Boris lacked the right 'set of skills' to be prime minister. In what could be seen as an admission of his own vulnerability, Cameron quipped, 'No point in trying to contain Boris. I'm relaxed about having the blond-haired mop sounding off from time to time.'

The rivalry between Cameron and Boris – initially played out in banter about their respective careers first at Eton (Boris a King's Scholar and head of Pop, Cameron neither) and then Oxford (Cameron had got a first, but in PPE, which Boris disparaged as an inferior degree to his own subject, Classics) – had become more profound during Cameron's premiership. Cameron had overseen muddled NHS reforms, not understood the public's growing disenchantment with Brussels and worst, worshipped Tony Blair, whom he called 'The Master'. Admiring Blair's presidential style and his team's slick media manipulation in order to generate favourable headlines, Cameron had unquestioningly accepted too much of his inheritance from Labour. For Boris, Blair offered no redeeming features, especially after Blair asserted that the Iraq invasion was not responsible for the rise of al-Qaeda or the huge number of Iraqi deaths. 'Tony Blair has finally gone mad', he wrote. 'He surely needs professional psychiatric help.' The war, Boris concluded, was 'a tragic mistake' by a flawed man who had approved the invasion without a plan for the aftermath. For all those reasons, Cameron's bid to be reconciled with Boris over lunch near Chequers would be difficult.

During their conversation, they disagreed about Cameron's decision to appoint a commission under Howard Davies to report on Heathrow's third runway. 'A fudge-a-rama,' said Boris. In his reckoning, Davies was a lacklustre has-been. Formerly the deputy governor of the Bank of England, in 2011 he had resigned as the director of the London School of Economics after questions had been raised about the sources of funding that the institution had accepted. But Boris's own position had shifted. Having promoted an airport on 'Boris Island', he now favoured a £65 billion airport on the Isle of Grain on the Hoo Peninsula in Kent, to be designed by Norman Foster. That change of direction, however, troubled Cameron far less than Boris and Europe.

An opinion poll had reported that 83 per cent of grass-roots party members wanted an EU referendum and 70 per cent would vote to leave. To prevent a fatal split of the party, Cameron had pledged in July that the next manifesto would include a commitment to hold a referendum. During the Chequers lunch, Cameron concluded that Boris had no idea what sort of referendum there should be. His ideas were undeveloped, which was 'potentially dangerous'. But, Cameron believed, Boris opposed an in-out referendum. He preferred, Cameron assumed, for the government to negotiate to repatriate powers and veto a bigger budget. Then, a referendum would seek approval for the new relationship with Europe. But for his part,

Boris knew that he had recently proposed an in-out referendum but did not repeat that over lunch. The confusion was perfect. Cameron was famous for best understanding his own point of view. With that misunderstanding, lunch was followed by football: the children against the adults. The children won, despite Boris's aggressive tackling forcing one of his own children to leave the field.

Boris returned to London pleased. His popularity reflected the public's dislike of conventional politicians, especially by the middle classes who felt 'utterly ignored'. Cameron's fuzzy talk, failing to promote Conservative values, spurred 150 donors towards Boris's mayoral election fund to gather the following evening at a Berkeley Street gallery. To them, their moribund party led by Cameron risked losing the next election. To keep his flame burning, Boris refused in interviews to endorse Cameron as the best prime minister. Instead, he praised competition for the job. 'My wife keeps saying all this is very bad for my ego,' he said. 'It puffs it all up.'

When Boris arrived at Birmingham's New Street station in early October for the party conference and was welcomed by a chanting crowd, Cameron's worst fears were confirmed. The following day, the prime minister's forty-third birthday, Boris mounted the stage at the conference, and asked 'Where is Dave?' From the seventh row, the victim smiled wanly. As Boris made a humdinger of a speech, Cameron accepted the difficulty of forging a deal with him. Accuracy was unimportant to the audience in the hall. They were eager to be entertained by Boris's boasts and self-deprecation. Britain, he told them, was a paradise. The terrific Routemaster was made in Britain; the Dutch were buying British bicycles; and the French were buying British cakes. And London, he would add later, had more Michelin-starred restaurants than Paris – 'Yes, a fact too good to check,' he gasped. He knew it wasn't true, but his speech spread happiness. Patriotism always was a trump card at the party conference. 'Self-deprecation is a very cunning device,' he explained later for the first time, 'all about understanding that basically people regard politicians as a bunch of shysters, so you've got to be understood ... that's what it's all about I suppose.' Cameron left

Birmingham deflated. Boris stood at plus 30 in opinion polls and Cameron was minus 21.

That night, responding to Boris's conference triumph, Paul Dacre signed off on an Exocet fired by Max Hastings: 'If the day ever comes that Boris Johnson becomes tenant of Downing Street, I shall be among those packing my bags for a new life in Buenos Aires or suchlike because it means that Britain has abandoned its last pretensions to be a serious country . . . Most politicians are ambitious and ruthless, but Boris is a gold-medal egomaniac. I would not trust him with my wife nor – from painful experience – with my wallet . . . He is a far more ruthless, and frankly nastier figure than the public appreciates.' Hastings' conclusion was withering: 'He would be a wretched prime minister. He is not a man to believe in, to trust or respect save as a superlative exhibitionist. He is bereft of judgement, loyalty and discretion.'

Hurt by his former editor's vitriol, Boris never uttered a public rebuke. He knew Hastings was outraged by Boris's refusal to honour a £1,000 bet on the outcome of the 2010 election. Hastings had asked for his money. Boris stalled and then sent a letter with a note saying 'Cheque enclosed'. It wasn't. Johnson, Hastings later wrote, is a 'welsher, one who does not pay his debts'. Hastings would also describe Boris as resembling Gussie Fink-Nottle, a character in P. G. Wodehouse's novels. The comparison was odd. Fink-Nottle was an antisocial, bespectacled, tongue-tied dreamer obsessed by newts and terrified of women.

Boris's relationship with Jennifer Arcuri belied that comparison. At her request, he agreed to be listed as a reference for her application for a £100,000 job as chief executive of Tech City, a quango placed under the control of London & Partners, the mayor's official promotional organisation. Only 'proven business leaders' were qualified for the job. Arcuri's application was outrightly rejected. Boris had not promoted Arcuri's application, but his intimate relationship with her did require him to declare his interest under the GLA's code of conduct. He didn't.

Three days after his conference speech, Boris flew to Perugia in Italy in the private jet owned by Alexander Lebedev, the former

KGB officer turned oligarch. His host for two nights was Alexander's son Evgeny, the socialite owner of the *Evening Standard* since 2009. Several people warned Boris not to take hospitality from the son of a man relying on a dubious fortune apparently amassed with the blessing of the KGB and the Kremlin, but the risk was outweighed by the promise of luxurious fun in Lebedev's hilltop house. Free hospitality was an irresistible attraction to Boris. Asked if he wanted to be prime minister, he quoted Clint Eastwood's character Harry Callahan in *Magnum Force*: 'A man's gotta know his limitations.' In the movie, Callahan delivers the line just after he has killed his boss.

Chapter 16

'Transparently self-defeating policies'

In late January 2013, Boris, Cameron and Osborne were sharing cheese fondue at the Alte Post in Davos. Three men, united in leading the Tory Party and utterly divided by their ambition, had exhibited their childlike rivalries at the previous night's dinner hosted by Martin Sorrell, the advertising executive. Inevitably, Boris was late. 'Oh look,' shouted Osborne, 'the leader of municipal government in England has arrived.'

'Would you like a drink?' Boris asked.

'Yes please,' replied Osborne.

'Then get one,' snapped Boris.

The banter could not camouflage their insoluble dilemma – to find a route out of the party's EU maze.

Two days earlier, one hundred Tory MPs had threatened to vote in the Commons to leave the EU unless Cameron negotiated to repatriate sovereign powers. Responding to that threat, Cameron believed he could rely on the German Chancellor Angela Merkel to agree to favourable terms for Britain's future membership. In particular, Cameron wanted the immigration rules changed. Both in private and in a speech before visiting Britain, Merkel and her officials had given encouraging assurances to Cameron.

Boris's position before Davos was, as ever, unclear. In some speeches before Christmas, he supported a referendum on a new treaty while explicitly opposing a straightforward in-out referendum. In other speeches he said, 'It's between staying in on our terms or getting out.' His antagonism towards the EU, an organisation he said was 'riddled with fraud', had been fuelled by Merkel's sophistry. While she pledged to do whatever necessary to keep Britain inside the EU, she had also agreed that Cameron's veto on the fiscal union should be ignored to save the euro. Closer integration of the eurozone nations, she believed, was vital. Then matters worsened. Osborne's attempt to defeat the EU imposing a limit on bankers' bonuses was defeated by twenty-six votes. The EU's blatant disregard of vital British interests was another watershed in Britain's relations with Europe. 'Brussels cannot control the global market,' cursed Boris, unfashionably championing the City. 'These are transparently self-defeating policies.'

Although Germany was prepared to negotiate, the French government was stubbornly against. Not only did Paris deny Britain's right to renegotiate its EU membership, but the socialist government led by François Hollande demanded that after the new fiscal union was created, the City would be banned from trading euros. Over 40 per cent of euro trades were done in London but the French wanted the trading compulsorily transferred to Paris. If the relationships were that sour, Boris commented, Britain should walk away. Leaving 'would not be the end of the world'. But then, just before arriving in Davos, he declared that he hoped Cameron could negotiate a new treaty placing Britain as an active member of the single market on the 'outer tier'. In the hope of a deal, he added, 'I think this option [of leaving] is neither particularly necessary nor particularly desirable nor particularly likely.'

Now, as he gossiped with his two unloved friends – Cameron and Osborne, both Remainers – he lacked their certainty. The majority of their party members were Eurosceptics. Boris straddled the two sides. Neither his opportunism nor Cameron's referendum pledge appeared to compensate for the party's unpopularity among electors. Their conversation failed to clarify how they could win an outright majority in the next general election. Squaring the circle appeared to be impossible. Boris, the government's antagonist-in-chief, left the restaurant first, without paying his share. 'I have got to cough up,' he said later unconvincingly. He had rushed off to meet an Englishwoman. She would never forgive him for making it a one-night stand.

Four weeks later, the electors' judgement about Cameron's European policy was devastating. A by-election at Eastleigh in Hampshire had been triggered by the resignation of Chris Huhne, a prominent Lib Dem MP, who had been charged with perverting the course of justice having lied to the police to avoid a driving offence. Despite Huhne's comfortable majority, Cameron expected to win the seat. During Boris's campaigning visits to the constituency, he confidently attacked the 'yellow albatross around the Tory neck', the disloyal coalition partners who constantly undermined the Tories. The Lib Dems' only function, he said, was 'to fulfil a very important ceremonial function as David Cameron's kind of lapdog-cum-prophylactic protection device'. He sensed the unspoken disenchantment among Tory voters with Cameron on several issues: austerity; pandering to the Greens by increasing electricity prices despite the devastating effect on industry; giving billions of pounds to the Third World rather than helping deprived Britons; and most of all, his enthusiasm for Europe. Indignant about Cameron's slur that UKIP supporters were 'closet racists', many Tory voters were lured by UKIP's leader Nigel Farage. The result was a seismic shock. The Tory vote fell by 13.9 per cent and UKIP's rose by 24.2 per cent. With the Conservatives divided, the Lib Dems narrowly won the by-election despite a fall of 14.4 per cent in their vote.

Boris watched Cameron, beleaguered and baffled, flap helplessly. Under pressure from the party supporters he loathed – the Eurosceptics – Cameron had no option but to again agree to an in-out referendum. The alternative would be the party's disintegration. For the moment, Boris remained faithful, urging Tories not to panic about Farage, an 'engaging geezer'. Only the Tories, he said, could deliver UKIP's ambition to leave the EU. In that seminal moment, he asked 'Do I want in or out?', and presented the arguments for both views. On the one hand, Britain should stay in the EU to attract investment, frictionless trade and global influence. On the other, Britain should leave to save money, make its own laws and no longer blame Brussels for being much less productive than Germany. That last reason, he thought, was critical. Most of Britain's problems, he said, were self-made by 'chronic short-termism, inadequate management, sloth, low skills, a culture of easy gratification and underinvestment in both human and physical capital and infrastructure'. Britain needed to reform itself.

With two years to the next election, Boris needed to convince doubters that he was not a buffoon but a substantial alternative to Cameron – a Eurosceptic Thatcherite in tune with the disillusioned Tory heartlands. Britain's fate depended on renegotiating its relationship with the EU. 'We must threaten to leave if the EU refuses to give us what we want,' he concluded. To those who dismissed him as a narcissist without a strategy or beliefs but simply an actor making up the lines as he played himself, he offered the alternatives to prove he was a genuine politician prepared to listen.

In that mood, he arrived in Paris in mid-March 2013 to address a meeting hosted by Bertrand Delanoë, the capital's mayor. First, there was lunch with Peter Ricketts, the British ambassador. Boris pumped the ambassador for information and interrupted lunch to dispatch an aide to buy a toy red London double-decker bus. During his speech that afternoon, in a mixture of English and 'Churchillian French', he spoke about London's open welcome for business. Holding up the toy bus, he told his audience that London's biggest bus company, RATP, was French-owned. The applause was warm.

Back in London, the Court of Appeal ruled that in the public interest the electorate was entitled to know about his child with Helen Macintyre. By then, Boris was regularly visiting his daughter, encouraging her interest in music. When considering Boris's fitness for office, decided the judges, 'It is fanciful to expect the public to forget the fact that . . . a major public figure had fathered a child after a brief adulterous affair (not for the first time).' The judgement mentioned Boris's responsibility for 'two conceptions'. Many would deduce that the judges meant there was another 'unknown' child fathered by him. Others realised that the judges were referring to his and Petronella's aborted child. Nevertheless, since he refused to state how many children he had fathered, the hunt for the 'unknown' child continued.

His current lover, Jennifer Arcuri, had secured £10,000 sponsorship from London & Partners for an event in October 2013 at the

ExCel convention centre where Boris would be speaking. Arcuri's company would get another £1,500 from London & Partners for an event in the Commons. There was no evidence that Boris influenced the London & Partners employees to award that money, but the two women responsible heard Arcuri boast about her friendship with the mayor. Since he was visiting Arcuri's Shoreditch flat, sometimes after a drink in a bar, he should have declared their relationship. 'Validate me,' Arcuri asked him by declaring the GLA's approval of her company. He refused. 'I'd have to declare an interest,' he told her. Boris would later tell BBC TV, 'There was no interest to declare.'

By the end of the year, Arcuri had decided that Boris was not a womaniser but just after her because, as he said, 'I feel so horny.' Instinctive and sensitive, she saw a self-obsessed man for whom relationships were difficult. He lacked close male friends and relied on her, but only on conditions. Until he was certain of his emotions and could trust her, allowing anyone into his personal life was regarded by him as a weakness. She would need time to persuade him to lower his guard. But any affection or love, she realised, would become a double-edged sword. She saw him as an introvert, a depressive who enjoyed solitude, and someone who needed to be alone. Paradoxically, particularly on those days of his greatest public successes, he could decline into an intense depression. His moodiness reflected the frustration of his thwarted ambition. 'Do you want to be prime minister?' she asked. 'I'm a very competitive person, so it's natural,' he replied.

Natural, perhaps, but Will Walden's charm offensive had not sealed the deal with the media, especially the BBC. That became pressing as Theresa May's popularity as the 'Stop Boris' candidate rose. Posing as the successor to Cameron, May dismissed the mayor as a ridiculous figure who changed his mind every five minutes. In an attempt to counter that narrative, he reluctantly agreed that his family should co-operate with Michael Cockerell, a BBC political documentary reporter, for a fifty-minute profile. Among the obvious risks was the hazard that Stanley would use Boris's fame to promote his own journalistic career. Similar fears were expressed about his sister Rachel. 'There are no boundaries,' advised one City Hall aide, 'about how RJ and SJ will exploit you for their own profit. They do anything to live off you.' Occasionally, their antics were excessive. In the *Star* newspaper, Rachel had recalled as children noticing while showering with Boris that he was impressively endowed. And during the Dominique Strauss-Kahn scandal in New York in 2011, in which Strauss-Kahn was accused of sexually assaulting a hotel maid, Rachel had written in the *Spectator* that she found the French politician sexy. Boris, she added, had told her that 'Women cannot resist men who obviously like women.' By implication, the chambermaid who alleged that she had been attacked by Strauss-Kahn was asking for it. Labour politicians piled into Boris. 'What the fuck are you doing?' Boris shouted at Rachel. 'You've ruined me.' Rachel retreated, admitting her 'embarrassment' over the 'terrible confusion about the comments'. Despite all this, he agreed to the BBC documentary without considering other good reasons for caution.

At the end of the formal inquiry into phone hacking and the tabloid newspapers, Lord Justice Leveson had recommended severe restrictions on the media. Boris was outraged. Leveson's proposals, he wrote, would end press freedom and delight Vladimir Putin. To his further disgust, the BBC was reporting Leveson in approving terms. That was the same BBC, he wrote, which had suppressed its own investigation into Jimmy Savile's paedophilia in 2011, 'luxuriated' in the downfall of the bankers, enjoyed the humiliation of MPs over their ill-gotten expenses and 'felt tremendous satisfaction' as the hacking scandal unfolded. His anger against the Corporation's political prejudice and sloppy journalism was aggravated by the BBC's refusal to be embarrassed by revelations of its 'blind-eye culture' as the Jimmy Savile scandal unfolded. Dismissive about any culpability, in November 2012 the same tainted senior BBC executives approved the broadcast of *Newsnight*'s accusation of child abuse committed by a 'senior Conservative', named in off-the-record briefings by some involved in producing the programme as Alistair McAlpine, the seventy-year-old former Tory treasurer and close associate of Margaret Thatcher. The story was totally untrue, broadcast, despite warnings, by the BBC. Wracked by misery, the innocent art-lover died from a heart condition fourteen months later. Boris denounced the senior BBC executives for approving transmission because, for those left-wing producers, McAlpine was a guilty Thatcherite toff. 'The story was too good to check,' complained Boris. 'It's a tragedy,' chimed the denizens in Broadcasting House – by which they meant it was tragic for the BBC. Boris noted that Chris Patten, the BBC's self-important chairman, had not properly acknowledged 'the appalling calumny which hastened McAlpine's death'. Patten, demanded Boris, should apologise 'on his knees' and all the BBC producers responsible for the defamation be sacked. In the event, no BBC executive was publicly censored or dismissed, and the director general, George Entwistle, was forced to resign only after doing a radio interview in which he compounded the impression that he was not in charge of the organisation he was supposed to be running.

In spite of all this, Boris was persuaded to trust Cockerell to produce a fair documentary. The result was genuinely endearing. Stanley found his 8 mm cine film of Boris as a young child and Rachel revealed that her brother had said 'I want to be world king.' Max Hastings performed his traditional cameo. 'Lock up your willy,' he had told Boris and, since all his sensible advice had been ignored, he believed that Boris could not be trusted near the nuclear button in case he confused it for the bell to summon the maid.

The documentary generated huge media attention ahead of its transmission on 25 March 2013. In anticipation, Boris accepted an invitation to appear on the BBC TV's Sunday morning *The Andrew Marr Show*, the day before the documentary was broadcast. The interview, he was told, would be about 'the Olympic legacy, housing and general politics'. He was ambushed. Eddie Mair, the interviewer standing in for Marr, who was recovering from a stroke, proved not to be an admirer. Reciting the depressing miscellany of duplicity (including Boris's fabricated quotation in *The Times* and the alleged conspiracy with Darius Guppy), Mair continued, 'Let me ask you about a barefaced lie,' referring to his denial to Michael Howard about the affair with Petronella, 'Why did you lie to your party leader?'

Boris was floored. He could not deploy his usual defences: deviation, run his hands through his hair, crack a joke, or recite a Latin phrase. He looked shaken, even wounded, his dignity dented as Mair delivered the verdict: 'Aren't you in fact making up quotes, lying to your party leader, wanting to be part of someone being physically assaulted? You're a nasty piece of work, aren't you?'

Mair's conclusion – 'nasty piece of work' – was dynamite on live TV. In the past, Boris would have disrupted an interviewer's artistic impertinence with a quizzical look: 'I know what you're doing here, but I'm in control.' But Mair suffocated that tactic. Unable to think on his feet, he retreated, too confused to retaliate. After taking a minute to recover, he replied with remarkable self-control that Mair's questions were 'trivial' and 'hysterical', and the interpretation of events was not 'wholly fair'. The allegations were old – two of them happened over twenty years earlier. On *The Times* fabrication, Boris replied 'I mildly sandpapered something somebody said, and yes it's very embarrassing and I'm very sorry about it.' For the Boris haters, Mair's performance was heroic. The *Guardian* declared Boris was politically dead. Simon Heffer twisted the knife: 'Mr Johnson is selfish, two-faced, a proven liar and has a private life too baroque for one who aspires to the highest office.' Only Stanley came to his aid. The interview, said his father, was 'disgusting' and his son's private life was irrelevant. 'It was a stitch-up,' Will Walden complained. The BBC producers had lied to tempt Boris on to their programme – to accuse him of lying.

Forty-eight hours later, the storm had passed. Mair was praised by Boris for 'a splendid job' and 'a fair interview'. Mair, he said, 'was perfectly within his rights to have a bash at me – in fact it would have been shocking if he hadn't . . . If a BBC presenter can't attack a nasty Tory politician, what's the world coming to?' As he said a year later during a speech in the City: 'It's been an amazing day for me as it began, as it has so often in my life, with me finding myself in a colossal hole partly of my own making.'

*

'The great trick in politics is never to talk about your opponents,' Boris later explained. 'Don't give them oxygen.' Contradicting his own homily, he nevertheless spoke a lot about UKIP's Nigel Farage and the danger posed by Labour's Ed Miliband. Labour's hateful reaction to Margaret Thatcher's death in April 2013 displayed raw enmity. Reflecting the broadcaster's bias, the BBC's editors embraced those hissing that Thatcher was a byword for selfishness and bigotry. Contributors were chosen by the BBC to dismiss Thatcher's transformation of Britain from the sick man of Europe into a dynamic trading centre. The preponderance of voices ignored the booming City, the Channel Tunnel, construction of Canary Wharf and the reduction of personal taxation from 83 per cent to 40 per cent, and instead emphasised Thatcher's legacy, as portrayed by Labour, of destroying Britain's industry and society itself. For Boris, the BBC epitomised the enemy, echoing Miliband's sermons of protest and protection of special interest groups in the public sector. Crucially, the opinion polls showed that for many Tories, only Boris, not Cameron, could replicate Thatcher's promise to reverse Britain's decline since the 2008 crash and renew the country's enterprise and aspiration.

In an attempt to sharpen this perceived contrast between himself and the prime minister, Boris wrote '2020 Vision: The Greatest City on Earth – Ambitions for London'. The eighty-four-page glossy document promised new rail connections across London including Crossrail 1 and 2, new crossings over and under the Thames, hundreds of thousands of new homes, improved schools, more apprenticeships and volunteers, London as the world's tech capital and even fracking for natural gas. He opposed HS2, the high speed train to the north. As a Heseltine Tory supporting state intervention when necessary, he also praised the free market economy, wealth creation and help for the needy. Regularly, he chaired the London Enterprise Panel in order to attract investment, create 250,000 new apprenticeships and install superfast broadband.

There was substance to that ambition. Six months after the Olympics, the Park was a vast construction site for Boris's 'Olympicopolis'. Beside homes, schools, offices, tech centres, museums and parks, there would be a university campus and a theatre.

Livingstone's accusation that Boris's record had produced no achievements was rebuffed.*

Ed Lister, Boris's chief of staff, matched that mood of expansion and confidence – conjuring the grandiose romanticism of Olympicopolis across the capital. Walking down Blackfriars Road with Peter John, he excitedly imagined the thoroughfare redeveloped with 'a canyon of towers, just like Manhattan'. Shortly after, looking over the Old Kent Road, Eddie Lister lamented, 'it's so low, undeveloped'. Restricting clusters of skyscrapers to the City, Paddington or Croydon had previously been acceptable but Lister wanted to abandon those limitations. He did not seem concerned that the fifty-storey Cheesegrater in the City approved by Livingstone had ruined the view of St Paul's from the west, or that the wall of tower blocks along the Thames approved in 2005 had destroyed communities. Tasked in 2013 by Boris to build 100,000 new affordable homes by the end of his mayoralty, to overtake Livingstone's 90,000 homes, Lister approved the construction of more towers. Failure to build the additional homes, he feared, would accelerate the surge of young families joining the white flight from London. High house prices and bad schools would hollow out the city.

The obstacles inherited from the Labour government were substantial. City Hall calculated after the 2011 Localism Act that historic failures by Whitehall to release derelict land and unused buildings owned by the NHS and the Ministry of Defence across London had prevented the construction of 25,000 homes, plus 2.5 million square metres of office space, and more schools and community centres. The new Act empowered the mayor to designate five abandoned hospitals to be designated for homes.

---

* One outstanding problem was the £430 million stadium. The choice was either tumbleweed or a further £150 million to secure its future for a Premier League football club combined with a permanent athletics venue. The estimated additional cost for a roof, retractable seats and corporate facilities was £752 million. Since West Ham was the only prospective tenant, there was no alternative but to accept their very low offer of £15 million plus £2.5 million annual rent without paying for its maintenance. To hide the embarrassment, Boris predicted that the rent would cover the costs. His optimism was a fantasy. The annual bill would be £20 million, but the headlines were hopeful.

By 2013, permission had been granted to build 200,000 homes but only half were under construction. Without government money, no British developer could build them. Only foreign investors, Lister persuaded Boris, would finance the towers. Accompanied by British builders and developers, the mayor flew to India and China to sell new luxury homes with rents up by 20 per cent in one year. 'Don't beat up foreigners coming to London,' Boris told his Labour critics. 'They bring money and jobs. Don't collapse in a xenophobic frenzy.' The choice was either taking their money or 'Mumbai, Dubai and bye bye'.

In that expansionary mood, David Cameron was attracted in 2013 to stand alongside Boris and the Malaysian prime minister to open the £8 billion Battersea project for 3,992 homes. Boris was proud that he had convinced a Malaysian developer to commit to the project with the promise of a £1 billion government-funded extension of the Northern Line into the redeveloped Battersea power station. He was untroubled that Battersea was a development for the foreign super-rich with just 550 affordable homes, or that mostly overseas non-taxpayers were lured to the buy-to-leave investments priced at £350,000 for a studio flat and £6 million for a penthouse. Without foreign investment, he reasoned, there would be fewer new homes and fewer new jobs. He was not worried either by the fate of a fifty-storey tower just completed at St George's Wharf, Vauxhall. One hundred and thirty flats sold to foreigners could be left empty and the five-storey penthouse, bought by a Russian for £51 million, might remain unoccupied or rented. None of the 214 flats were 'affordable'.* Knight Frank, the estate agents, revealed that 69 per cent of new flats in London were sold to foreigners over the previous two years. Critics screamed in dismay. 'They're gloomadon-poppers,' snorted Boris, asserting that only 7 per cent of all homes in Britain were bought by foreigners. Building statistics, everyone knew, were totally unreliable. The need to house an additional million people in the near future was, however, irrefutable. To satisfy

---

* The luxury block was part of a project for 1,400 homes of which 380 were 'affordable'.

that demand, Boris accepted Lister's advice and approved gigantic towers in White City, on the Shell Centre site opposite Westminster, and the partial demolition of the Spitalfields Fruit & Wool Exchange built in the 1920s. On Lister's recommendation, Boris even met Richard Desmond. Desmond, a deeply unpleasant and dangerous businessman prone to swearing, who had impersonated Nazi goose-stepping with colleagues and published a defamatory article in his newspaper in a vendetta with a fund manager, was eager to develop a large site on the Isle of Dogs. As with his holiday trips courtesy of Evgeny Lebedev, Boris ignored the warning that any association with Desmond would end badly. By March 2014, 256 towers were proposed, approved or under construction. Two years later, critics claimed that Boris, alias 'the lackey of London's development lobby', was building over 400 towers.

The battle between luxury and affordable homes, and between the Labour boroughs and Boris, became particularly fierce over the fate of the huge Post Office site at Mount Pleasant in central London. Lister stipulated that only 14.4 per cent of the 681 homes would be affordable, and even those tenants would pay £2,800 per month for a four-bedroom flat. Wanting 30 per cent affordable homes, Camden's Labour councillors delayed the project with endless appeals. By contrast in Southwark, Peter John was relaxed about a £50 million penthouse in the Shard tower: 'I wouldn't turn away the 10,000 jobs the Shard brought to Southwark.'

By 2016, Boris would have completed 94,001 homes, near to his 100,000 target; and the boroughs built a further 101,525 'affordable' homes over his eight years. City Hall's statistics recorded that Livingstone had completed 24,009 houses in 2005 while Boris finished 41,371 houses in 2016 and 18,270 affordable homes in 2015, the highest since 1981. Chasing headlines bore a cost.

One great casualty of Lister's affection for towers and Boris's emphasis on numbers for political kudos was potentially the biggest prize in west London. Old Oak Common was a vast 650-hectare wasteland sprawling from Wormwood Scrubs prison up to the North Circular road. Crossed by railway lines, roads and a canal, Old Oak Common was a decaying industrial zone and the headquarters of Cargiant, a multimillion-pound car dealership employing 800 people. At his own expense in 2011, Terry Farrell, a prominent architect, had produced a development plan for Old Oak Common. Presented to Stephen Greenhalgh, Hammersmith Council's Tory leader, Farrell showed how 24,000 homes and 55,000 jobs could be created on the site. Excited by the same rich possibilities as had been identified at Canary Wharf thirty years earlier, Greenhalgh sought to enlist Lister and Boris. They replied with polite disdain. To transform that area demanded a detailed plan, political commitment and money. After Boris's re-election in 2012, Lister was more sympathetic to the project but knowing that Boris was uninterested, he was reluctant to engage the mayor.

Unlike Margaret Thatcher who 'seized' ownership of Canary Wharf, an abandoned area bedevilled by the debris of old docks and industrial waste, Boris was deterred by Old Oak Common's complexity. Designated in 2012 as the possible transport interchange point for Crossrail, the Tube and HS2, Boris was unenthusiastic about also transforming the area into a residential and commercial metropolis, like the King's Cross of West London.

That changed in 2013. Stephen Greenhalgh had joined the mayor's team in City Hall. Under his pressure, Boris finally published a thirty-year plan to develop Old Oak Common following Farrell's outline. To make it happen, he needed to lobby the government to create a development corporation similar to the Olympic Park's. By then, his relations with Cameron and Osborne were strained by their disagreements over the EU and his constant demand for finance for houses and the Tube. He could have dispatched Lister to gather support in Whitehall for Old Oak Common but he had yet again become distracted, this time by the fluttering eyelids of the actress Joanna Lumley.

Six days after his re-election, Lumley – who was an old friend of Stanley Johnson – had sent a flattering letter to Boris offering 'a thousand congratulations' about 'the wonderful news for London'. In her letter, she urged Boris to support a 'green pedestrian bridge' with trees and plants that would bestow 'great loveliness' across the Thames between Temple and Lambeth. She concluded, 'Please say yes.' Asked how Boris reacted, she explained: 'I've known Boris since he was four, so he was largely quite amenable.'

After the success of the Olympics, the 'Living Bridge' matched Boris's longing for more grand projects around London. Thomas Heatherwick – who had designed Boris's Routemaster and the acclaimed Olympic cauldron with 1,000 moving parts – had already been chosen by Lumley to design the bridge. Building a new 366-metre link between the north and south banks of the Thames, Heatherwick told Boris, would bring 'human nourishment' to those who used it. With naive enthusiasm, Boris exclaimed, 'Surely, we can build a bridge?' and set the hare running. At Davos in January 2013, he met Tim Cook, Apple's chief executive. The two agreed to meet in California to discuss Apple sponsoring the project.

Nine weeks later, clutching Heatherwick's rough drawing, Boris and Lister flew to California to seek £60 million, the bridge's total estimated cost. By 'chance', Heatherwick appeared in the Apple building. Cook agreed to Boris's proposal on condition that an Apple shop was located on the bridge. Heatherwick rejected any branding and negotiations broke down.

On his return to London, Boris refused to disclose to elected members of the Assembly why he had travelled to California and who had accompanied him. Knowing that he had broken the rules regarding public procurement, which required a formal tendering process, he wanted to conceal Heatherwick's presence. The secret did not last long. 'Boris told me that he had bumped into Heatherwick in California,' Len Duvall would recall, 'and he had said to him, "Come with us to Apple."' Lister also said, 'It was just he was there.' Duvall described that 'improbable' explanation as 'immature rather than a lie'. Eventually, Boris admitted on LBC that he had arranged to meet Heatherwick in the Apple building because the bridge was 'my idea' and it was 'essential' that Heatherwick gave Apple a detailed description.

Once that plot unravelled, Boris set out to raise money from private individuals. At the same time, Heatherwick and Lumley asked George Osborne for money. Flattered by the pair, the Chancellor visited Heatherwick's studio. The pitch was sublime. Seven million people were expected to cross the bridge every year, more than visited the Eiffel Tower. The inevitable congestion generated by people queuing to see 270 trees and thousands of plants, and the annual £3 million maintenance costs, were not discussed. After being presented with a unique chair designed by Heatherwick, Osborne committed £30 million of taxpayers' money to the project.

'I've got a great deal from Osborne,' Boris told Duvall, 'so we'll go ahead.' By the end of 2013, the estimated cost had risen to £150 million. Just as his original pledge for the bikes, which included the commitment of 'no cost to the taxpayer' had evaporated and London's ratepayers were billed £11 million annually for the bikes (compared to zero public funding in Paris); and the cable car's estimated £25 million cost had soared to £60 million and was losing £50,000 a week because no one was using it; his promise to fund the bridge entirely through private money also disappeared. Boris persuaded Peter Hendy that TfL should contribute £30 million. Hendy did not dare to contradict the mayor's enthusiasm.

Committed to build the bridge, Boris again circumvented the official rules. Contractors should by law be chosen by public tender. To protect Heatherwick and Arup, the favoured engineers, Lister and his officials did not override Boris's decision to bypass the legal tender process and appointed his favoured team.

In the time spent on the bridge, housing and so much more, Old Oak Common, and the great, enduring opportunity it represented, was simply pushed aside. In summer 2013, Boris's focus switched again to the party conference and his positioning for the leadership. With a general election due in eighteen months, there was every reason to show loyalty to Cameron – for now.

Chapter 17

'A blithering, Bullingdon, Bollinger-drinking buffoon'

In the circle of fortune, Ed Miliband was losing support and Nick Clegg was shipwrecked, accused of betraying his principles by agreeing to tuition fees, austerity and much more. Clegg, wrote Boris, was 'some cut-price edition of David Cameron hastily knocked off by a Shanghai sweatshop to satisfy market demand'. Both opposition parties' support for a mansion tax helped the Tories.

Even though Cameron welcomed Boris's future return to Westminster in 2015, Boris posed as the coy, undecided bride. His unremitting competition with Cameron and Osborne would, he knew, once again be played out – this time in China; but only after what had become an annual bacchanalian blowout with Evgeny Lebedev in Italy. Shortly after his return from Umbria, looking unusually scruffy, he flew to Beijing.

The trip had been suggested earlier in the year by Gerard Lyons, his economic adviser at City Hall. Soon after his arrangements were made, both Osborne and Cameron clambered to fix their own visits to China. Keen to get there before Boris, Osborne succeeded in putting his plan in place, only to be horrified. The Chinese government announced that the three politicians were visiting in reverse order of their standing – Osborne, Boris and finally Cameron. Osborne protested, but could rearrange only that he and Boris arrived together. The Chinese were confused; and Osborne looked piqued after Boris attracted huge media attention during an unscheduled trip on Beijing's subway. Visibly nervous, Osborne arrived at Beijing University with Boris. The Chancellor spoke first, a fatal mistake, explaining in serious tones that his daughter was studying Mandarin. Next, the mayor, a considerably better speaker, stood up. Not only was his daughter also studying Mandarin, he said, but 'She's coming to Beijing next week. How about that George?' Osborne winced as Boris love-bombed the audience. 'Who was Harry Potter's first girlfriend? Who is the first person he kisses? That's right, Cho Chang, who is a Chinese overseas student at Hogwarts School.' The laughter grew as Boris offered an example of British openness. The Chinese, he said, were rebuilding the tower used as MI6 headquarters in *Skyfall*. 'We have sold you our offices of the secret service. Saves time I imagine.'

That night, the Chinese hosted a dinner for Osborne and Boris. At the end, the two men stepped into a small lift. Osborne's body-guard decided to walk down the stairs. During the short ride down, the two men grabbed each other and fought. When the doors opened on the ground floor, both walked out without showing any emotion. Boris returned to London impressed by China, not least after travelling from Beijing to Shanghai – 819 miles – on a high-speed train which took just two years to build. 'It's terrible that Labour opposes the HS2 project to win Tory votes in marginal areas,' he commented and somersaulted. HS2 was now a priority as 'investment for long-term growth'.

Back in London, everything was again focused on establishing his leadership qualities. Burying the critics' derision was essential. Opponents like Sadiq Khan, Labour's mayoral candidate for the 2016 election, had joined the chorus to call Boris a 'blithering, Bull-ingdon, Bollinger-drinking buffoon'. To prove his credentials as a visionary, Boris's theme in that year's Margaret Thatcher Lecture at the Centre for Policy Studies, titled 'What Would Maggie Do Today?', was the advantage of inequality. Appealing to London's Gordon Gekkos, he lauded the 'spirit of envy' as a 'valuable spur' to growth and wealth creation. London, he said, was booming again. Don't kill the talented, he urged. Nurture them. Cut taxes and renegotiate with Europe. Of Thatcher's position on the EU, he said 'I don't think she would pull out of the single market that she helped to create.' But, he continued, the British would remain in the EU only if negotiations produced membership on new terms, followed by a referendum. The controversy in his speech was his unashamed acceptance of inequality, elitism and excellence. Society should prioritise opportunities for those likely to succeed and accept that 16 per cent of Britons with an IQ below 85 could never succeed. The Guardianistas were outraged, seeing this as proof of a conspiracy by the rich to exploit the poor and the less intelligent. Boris challenged the leftists: explain why half of Britain's state schools failed to produce a single pupil who went on to study medicine; and explain why half of all medical students came from public and grammar schools – which educated just 7 per cent of all Britain's children. Teachers in state schools, he kept repeating, were failing children. Social engineering rather than disciplined education was their priority. Provoking an uproar suited Boris but Cameron and Osborne distanced themselves.

Education was troubling the government. Michael Gove, the education minister, was under attack from both teachers and parents for making the curriculum more demanding. Inadequate teachers and the extremist National Union of Teachers described Gove as 'a demented Dalek on speed, who wants to exterminate everything good in education'. Some parents who feared that their children would fail exams disliked Gove's demands for higher standards. His approval of excellence was popular among Conservatives who disliked the left's advocacy of social engineering even at the cost of lower standards. In Boris's opinion, Gove did not go far enough. The mayor wanted control over London's schools and the children's lunches. Gove refused and retained control to authorise more free schools and academies. To spite Boris, he also introduced his own healthy menu for school lunches.

The feuding among the four leading Tories – Cameron, Osborne, Gove and Boris – publicly erupted in March 2014. The cause was reports of a dinner at Rupert Murdoch's London home. Gove told Murdoch that Boris was not suitable to be prime minister. The best candidate, he suggested, was Osborne. Gove's advice leaked and Boris was incandescent. At the same time, Boris believed that

Cameron and Osborne were plotting against him. There was, he suspected, something sinister in Osborne's public exhortation that Boris should stand for Parliament in the next election. The Chancellor had emerged with a new look – sleek, even thin, and with a strange new haircut. Was it, Boris wondered, a new look for an heir apparent? To muddy the waters, Boris hinted that he might after all stand for Parliament in 2015. The mutual suspicion was provocatively stirred by Fraser Nelson, the *Spectator* editor. 'The seeds of Cameron's destruction are there,' he wrote. He would bet £1,000 that Labour would win the general election. Ed Miliband, he warned, 'is terribly underrated by Conservatives'. The fault, he concluded, was Cameron's for being alternately complacent or in a panic. Without a clear ideological purpose and fearing public opinion, he relied on focus groups and his trusted friends. As the rumours of dissent among party members spread, Gove hosted a dinner to reconcile Boris and Osborne, while Lynton Crosby organised a dinner between Boris and Cameron. Finally, to disprove the negative rumours about their relationship, Boris and Cameron campaigned together at a by-election in Newark. 'He's had a haircut. He's looking very good,' said Cameron. 'I'm always well turned out,' replied Boris. 'It's all going horribly well.'

That was not quite true, however. While Boris had been focusing on higher-level manoeuvrings, City Hall had become besieged on several fronts. For a start, fourteen cyclists had been killed in London in 2013 and more were dying in 2014. 'You're letting people die,' the cycle lobby accused Boris. 'That hit Boris hard,' observed a close aide. 'As a cyclist he wanted to encourage people away from private transport on to bikes. Arguing the safety case wasn't helped by a minority – generally young, male, Lycra-clad louts – who continued to behave recklessly, largely immune from prosecution, whilst innocent casual cyclists were dying under the wheels of lorries because cab designs made them invisible to drivers. He felt he couldn't win because he couldn't tell the real story, which was more nuanced than the headlines. On the one hand the pro-cycling lobby hated him – staging 'die-in' protests daily – whilst on the other business and the government – who loathed cycling – were screaming don't build the fucking cycle lanes.' His ambition to build cycle highways across London was being stymied by TfL and was opposed by London's drivers who feared longer journey times. Even Eddie Lister was being obstructive, opposing Boris's appointment of Andrew Gilligan as his cycling tsar. Their disagreement was resolved by a press release issued on Boris's orders announcing Gilligan's employment.

Boris's battle against Heathrow's third runway had also run into the sand. Passionate about building the Estuary airport, he had mastered all the engineering details to promote his cause. In response, Howard Davies treated him shabbily. To humiliate the mayor, Davies arrived thirty minutes late at a public meeting in East Ham town hall, pointedly ignored Boris and highlighted that only 16 per cent of the public supported closing Heathrow. Predictably, Davies's interim report advocated the third runway. Boris Island would be damned as a 'reckless' waste of £100 billion. 'Scandalous,' said Boris. He accused the government of 'pussyfooting and fannying around'. After a telephone conversation, Boris and Davies engaged in a public slanging match. Boris accused Davies of predicting a fourth runway. 'That's a complete lie,' said Davies. Boris released his notes of their conversation. They did not refer to a 'fourth runway'.

Boris was also fighting Bob Crow. The trade union leader, photographed holidaying on a Brazilian beach in January 2014, had ordered a strike to stop the closure of the Tube ticket offices even though only 3 per cent of passengers used them. The strike halted 60 per cent of the trains. On his return to Britain, Crow hailed the strike as another victory. One month later, Crow, aged fifty-two, died of a heart attack. Although Crow had scoffed on Thatcher's death that 'She should rot in hell', Boris was silent about the Marxist's malignant career. Instead, he described Crow's death as 'Tragic . . . He played a big part in the success of the Tube and he shared my goal to make transport in London an even greater success.' Some wondered whether Boris had missed an opportunity to demythologise the man who blackmailed London, sabotaged the modernisation of the Tube and humiliated the mayor himself.

Shortly after Crow's funeral, Mick Cash, Crow's successor, called a forty-eight-hour strike. Fifty per cent of the network was paralysed. Peter Hendy claimed that as victory because more trains were running and, despite the union, 1,600 jobs had gradually disappeared. Even if attrition was beginning to work, commuters were unforgiving towards Boris. But the biggest (and as yet unseen) calamity was again at Scotland Yard.

At their dinner at the fashionable Cinnamon Club in Westminster in June 2012, nine months after his appointment, Bernard Hogan-Howe had asked, 'What do you want, Boris?'

'I want no more riots, police numbers to stay at 32,000 and crime to come down by 30 per cent,' he replied.

Crime was falling by 3 per cent across Britain but only 1 per cent in London.

'I can't do 30 per cent,' said Hogan-Howe. 'Let's say 15 per cent.' They agreed 20 per cent by 2016.

Neither mentioned the ongoing problems at the Yard. A survey which reported that 60 per cent of staff did not have confidence in the commissioner wasn't brought up. As predicted, Hogan-Howe's appointment had been a mistake. He was proving incapable of rooting out incompetence. 'He's a traffic cop on the second time round,' Boris admitted. But as usual, Boris was not too concerned about the Yard's morale and internal strife. The governance of an important institution remained alien to the mayor. (Running City Hall was largely delegated to Eddie Lister.) He had never discussed the Yard's inertia with Paul Stephenson and he never thought of discussing that legacy with Hogan-Howe. His 'reform' agenda was solely about reducing crime and saving money.

Austerity, decreed Osborne, demanded that London's police budget would be reduced by 20 per cent every year over the next four years, by which time the annual budget would be £400 million less.

The problem was undisguised. Long before the election, Boris had pledged not to cut police numbers below about 33,000 officers. In early 2014, London had 30,085 officers. 'Bobbies before buildings,' Boris stipulated. Police stations did not make arrests, he said. Fewer people were seeking help at police stations and there was no evidence that they deterred crime. To save money, he ordered nine police stations to close and the sale of Scotland Yard, the Met's headquarters. Communities became alarmed by the closures, fearing a rise in street crime. The statistics suggested the opposite. Crime in London, reported *The Times* in early 2014, was 'falling steeply'. In November 2013, crime fell by 9 per cent and knife crime had fallen by 11 per cent which had 'beaten the rest of the country'. Other statistics, however, proved the opposite. If the classification of 'woundings through GBH' was altered to plain 'woundings', the crime rate had risen between 2012 and 2014 in some areas by 118 per cent. And if domestic crime with an injury was included, the increase was even higher. Crime statistics could be and were manipulated to suit the political agenda. 'If you can't measure it you can't manage it,' Boris had told Greenhalgh. Boris was not measuring an explosion of cyber crime and fraud, both ignored by Scotland Yard. Although 81,631 frauds were reported during 2013/14, only nine were successfully prosecuted. Boris never mentioned that failure to Hogan-Howe. Either out of fear or fickleness, Boris never questioned the commissioner's conduct, even after a fellow Tory MP was traduced in what became known as 'Plebgate'.

In early 2012, Andrew Mitchell, the Tory chief whip, had been involved in an argument after police officers refused to open the main Downing Street gates to allow him to cycle out into Whitehall. He was accused of swearing and of calling the police officers 'plebs'. Mitchell apologised for swearing but denied he said 'plebs'. After the police leaked the incident to a newspaper, the dispute escalated into a serious public battle between politicians and Scotland Yard. Cameron ordered Jeremy Heywood, the Cabinet Secretary, to investigate but Britain's top civil servant was an inept sleuth. Eventually, the CCTV emerged, confirming that the police officer's version of a 'blazing row' between himself and Mitchell in front of members of the public at the gates was untrue. The footage showed no members of the public were at the gates. One policeman was exposed as a liar and another had falsified his notes. Yet in 2014, Hogan-Howe claimed that Scotland Yard had undertaken 'a ruthless search for the truth' about Plebgate. His statement was flawed.

Eventually, Hogan-Howe apologised to Mitchell, but to Mitchell's surprise Boris had consistently supported Hogan-Howe instead of the Tory MP. Was Boris, some MPs wondered, fearful that the police might seek revenge against himself? No one dared to openly ask the question.

Boris offered similar support to Hogan-Howe to continue to conceal corruption in the Yard. Ever since Daniel Morgan, a private investigator, had been found dead in 1987 with an axe wound across the back of his head, the Yard had failed to prosecute the suspected murderer. 'We'll do what we can,' Boris told Morgan's family in City Hall twenty-six years later. But he sought no assurances from Hogan-Howe that the crime would be solved and the suspected murderer remained unprosecuted. Nor did he express anger that the files of the Yard's anti-corruption unit investigating the suspected police officers had been shredded.

His lack of interest in internal Met affairs was also shown by his reaction to new revelations about the Yard's investigation of the 1993 murder of Stephen Lawrence, the eighteen-year-old black student, by white racists in south-east London. The Met, Boris heard, instead of pursuing the identified murderers, had placed a spy among the Lawrence family. 'I'm utterly fed up with attacks on the Met,' exclaimed Boris. The past did not interest him. His concern was that no new case of corruption was exposed on his watch. The police could be effective, he believed, only if they were respected and not criticised. The intruder into Boris's smooth relationship with Hogan-Howe was Theresa May, the Home Secretary.

Boris and May shared nothing in common except membership of the party. Even their understanding of Toryism was different. The Home Office posters plastered across cities in 2013, directing illegal immigrants to 'go home or face arrest', irritated Boris. 'Blunt and uncompromising,' he wrote. They should have been 'more gently drafted'. Although illegal immigrants, he thought, should be deported, they were unfortunately protected by 'eloquent lefty lawyers' funded by the taxpayer, May's tactics had failed to repatriate large numbers. May disliked any reproach, especially from Boris. In 2011, he had criticised her for diluting the anti-terror laws by abandoning the power to force suspected terrorists to move from their homes. They had also argued about police numbers. 'Boris, are you threatening me?' May had asked during a meeting. 'They clearly don't trust each other,' judged Greenhalgh. Their most bitter argument followed the murder of Fusilier Lee Rigby by two Muslim extremists in Woolwich on 22 May 2013. That evening, at a meeting of Cobra chaired by May, she announced that soldiers should be ordered not to wear uniforms outside their barracks. 'No,' said Boris aggressively. 'We cannot do this. We should take those extremists down, not kow-tow to them.' At the end of the meeting, May insisted that Boris should not be allowed to speak to the waiting media. Craig Oliver, Cameron's director of communications, overruled her. As London's mayor, ordered Oliver, Boris should speak on the government's behalf. In a huff, May walked off. To everyone's surprise, that night she posed as the government's spokesman on TV, but was silent about uniformed soldiers. The following year, with her own ambitions set on Downing Street, May spotted an opportunity to trounce her rival. Her vehicle was the aftermath of the 2011 riots.

Addressing a Commons Home Affairs Select Committee inquiry into the riots in 2011, Boris had opposed the introduction of water cannons on the grounds that they were 'un-British'. Mindful that Hugh Orde, who had used them in Ulster, had dismissed their use on the mainland, he had bowed to the officer's expertise that they 'buy you space but they're useless when the crowds are not static as in the London riots'. At the same Commons inquiry, May made no comment about the cannons. Two years later, Hogan-Howe pressed for the purchase of water cannons as a weapon of last resort. They were preferable, he said, to horses and rubber bullets. Again Boris was reluctant but, under pressure from Cameron and the Home Office, he relented. 'Like you,' wrote May in agreement, 'I am keen to ensure that forces have the tools and powers they need to maintain order on our streets.' With May's support, Boris paid £85,000 for three second-hand cannons from Germany for use by all of England's police forces. The refit would cost £218,000. Once completed, May was expected to license their use.

In May 2014, May unofficially launched her leadership campaign. At the annual meeting of the Police Federation, she denounced police failings, citing the Yard's ill-fated investigations into the deaths of Stephen Lawrence and Ian Tomlinson. Police reform, she said, was long overdue. 'It is time to face up to reality,' she concluded and cut off the Federation's government funds. Her speech coincided with the dismissal of a fourth policeman guilty of lying about Plebgate. The media's spectacular headlines glorified May. Her political coup outclassed Boris. The mayor had not only defended Hogan-Howe but inexplicably recommended that his term be extended by two years. In tune with the public's criticism of Hogan-Howe, May was praised by the *Daily Mail* and she soared 12 per cent ahead of Boris in the poll of Tory members. Bookmakers placed her as the favourite as the Tories' next leader. Shortly after, without telling Boris, she decided to postpone her decision whether to license the water cannon until after the general election – even though Scotland Yard had satisfied all the Home Office's safety requirements.

*

In the summer of 2014, the capital was still booming, with record numbers of tourists and the recession over. With more billionaires than any other European city, London had also become the tech capital of Europe. Britain was creating more new jobs than all the other EU countries combined, not least because living on welfare had become harder; and London had become a haven for the non-tax paying plutocrats benefiting from the fall of average wages. In an *Evening Standard* poll, 64 per cent of Londoners approved of Boris, and the Tory Party's popularity had risen to 35 per cent. The Lib Dems languished at 8 per cent.

Personally, Boris was also riding high. He and Marina celebrated their twenty-first wedding anniversary and five weeks later headed for Althorp House for the annual Johnson family cricket match against Charles Spencer's team. Delivered by helicopter, Kevin Pietersen was the surprise player recruited by the Johnsons to win the match. The following weekend, Boris hosted his fiftieth birthday party at Thame. Compared to George Osborne's party four weeks earlier for his forty-third birthday, which included a *Who's Who* of Britain's power brokers, Boris had invited only a small group: two MPs, two close friends, the whole Johnson family plus Jasper Griffin. His Oxford tutor read a Greek ode composed in his honour. The highlight, as usual at a Johnson party, were some ferociously competitive games of rounders and tennis.

Over the rest of the summer, he was rushing to complete a biography of Winston Churchill. Before embarking on the project, some of his aides had spoken about his 'Churchill fetish'. Like Churchill, Boris believed that a good leader, relying on flair, panache and passion could, if necessary, sometimes wing it and change his mind with integrity. But writing the book had revealed to him a mass of detail about the politician's extraordinary roller-coaster career. The insight was a seminal moment.

The offer to write the book was made by the Churchill estate. Aware that many young people believed that Churchill was the pug dog featured in advertisements for an insurance company, the estate's trustees had looked for a popular writer to take Churchill's story to a wide audience. Boris would be helped by an expert historian.

In his vivid style, Boris wrote admiringly of Churchill's stubbornness and bravery to overcome the experience of being bullied at school. As a war correspondent, the Duke of Marlborough's grandson took enormous risks with his life. 'The spirit of derring-do coursed through his veins,' wrote Boris. 'Having vanquished his own cowardice, it was easy to vanquish everything else.' Churchill's remarkable bravery in the Boer War, in Sudan, and while attacking from the trenches in France across no man's land, had all fed Churchill's imagination to be the 'greatest man in the history of the world'. Boris wrote with admiration and even envy that Churchill could pack so much into his life. He could dictate 2,000 words at 10 p.m. (often fortified by drink), and his speeches had music as well as substance. 'It's the sizzle not the sausage,' concluded Boris. With that unique background, Churchill, the wild card, had stood against Britain's establishment in 1940 to prevent a deal with Hitler. Respectable Tories dismissed Churchill, wrote Boris, as 'a Goering, an adventurer, a half-breed, a traitor, a fat baby and a disaster for the country'. His political enemies thought he was worse, 'a blowhard, an egoist, a rotter, a bounder, a cad and on several well-attested occasions a downright drunk'. By overcoming all that adversity and going on to beat the Nazis, Boris concluded, the world owed Churchill thanks.

While writing the book, describing Churchill's response to each challenge, success and disaster, Boris engaged in a conversation with himself. He tested his fantasy of his own image and the cards to play to secure his own destiny. Churchill, Boris realised, had made many mistakes, not least dispatching the British army to Norway in 1940, a disastrous expedition which nevertheless iron-ically accelerated his own passage to Downing Street after Chamberlain's resignation. Churchill never admitted his errors. He simply ignored or silently learnt from them – and he never stopped taking risks. The trick was to surround yourself with intelligent, loyal critics, listen to their advice and then decide. That arrange-ment collapsed for Boris when the personal pressure became excessive. When up against the wall, he sometimes rejected criti-cism. That, he assumed, was also Churchill's way. Some assumed that in self-glorification, Boris exclaimed 'I'll be the next Churchill.' Publicly, he disparaged the copy-cats: 'Pathetically they try to emu-late him and wear floppy bow ties but nobody can pull it off. He was one of a kind.' Self-identification is common for an illusion-ist. Boris behaved as if he was the exception.

On the eve of publication in 2014, Boris was assured of a global bestseller translated into thirty-six languages. He would earn £612,583 that year, including £127,505 as mayor, enough to excite considerable envy. Any self-doubt disappeared during the book's promotional tour. 'Women threw themselves at Boris,' recalled an eyewitness. Nancy Dell'Olio, the Italian socialite, kept pestering an aide to get Boris's phone number. Even *Guardian* women were attracted by his animal magnetism, Boris discovered, although there were exceptions. The mayor, wrote Tanya Gold in the

Guardian, had no beliefs. Everything was focused on his hair, 'deliberately tousled – and now he's going bald'. She asked: 'Will his ambition outlive his hair? I think not. He lives by narcissism; he will die by it.' Inevitably, there was also some professional envy. Richard Evans, the historian, condemned the book's narrative as 'like being cornered in the Drones Club and harangued for hours by Bertie Wooster'. But unlike Boris's book, Evans's own works did not sell 160,000 hardbacks in Britain in just six months. There was also political carping. 'In his second term,' observed Len Duvall, 'he became a part-time mayor. He delegated more to Lister and he wrote books because he needed the money.' Boris's next contract was a £500,000 advance for a biography of Shakespeare titled *The Riddle of Genius*, a story of 'illicit sex and the power struggles, the fratricide and matricide . . . the racism, jealousy and political corruption'.

In the autumn, Boris found time to meet Jennifer Arcuri. Earlier that year, he had declined to speak at another tech event she had organised, and she then asked him to speak at a subsequent event, which he did. Later they met in a hotel and after an hour, he agreed to speak at another event. Plodding around the room in his underwear, eating cheese, conscious about his looks and his need to lose weight, she felt a bond was being forged. He was clearly attracted to her interest in power, conflict, intellectual strength, and especially in Shakespeare. Between his expressions of affection, he asked whether he had hurt her, what he could do for her, how he could make her happy? Eager to see more of him, Arcuri later arrived at a reception to promote the Churchill book. She found him in a hotel room writing his speech. He spoke about his loneliness and need for her friendship. He also spoke about going away together or at least she should come to Thame, his Oxfordshire house. She demanded a car to collect her. Fearful of being spotted, he refused, and also declined her invitation to meet for lunch at the Royal Thames Yacht Club. Unwilling to give Arcuri the emotional security she demanded, they parted. Unaware of that background, Janice Turner interviewed Boris about his Churchill book for *The Times*: 'I asked what kind of father are you? "Swerve," he cried.

"Avoid. I'm entitled to take the Fifth [Amendment] on all that." ' She concluded, 'It was bizarre.'

The accumulation of all those events – his wedding anniversary, fiftieth birthday, the publication of the Churchill biography and his growing affection for Arcuri – marked a milestone in his life and a curtain-raiser to calculated gambles in an increasingly uncertain political climate. More disillusioned Tory Eurosceptics were moving towards UKIP and Cameron feared the Tories could once again fail to win a majority.

With the general election due in a matter of months, Boris was approached by Ben Wallace, a former soldier and the MP for Wyre and Preston North, with a proposition. Aggrieved that he had not been promoted by Cameron, Wallace explained that he and Jake Berry, a former solicitor and Lancashire MP, wanted to further Boris's ambitions to be the party's next leader. They volunteered to search for a safe seat for him in London and since he lacked a close relationship with most Tory MPs, they would organise introductory meetings with possible supporters. With gratitude, he agreed.

By this time Boris had received the 'Euro report' he had commissioned from Gerard Lyons, his economic adviser and a renowned Eurosceptic. Lyons set out two options: why Britain could stay in a truly reformed EU or should leave an unreformed EU; and how that would affect the country. Lyons' recommendation was that since the EU refused to reform, Britain should leave.

In recent months, more reasons to leave the EU had emerged. Added to Europe's high unemployment, a new euro crisis and the annual arrival of over 2 million migrants, the European Parliament had severely limited British doctors' working hours, the European Court of Justice had imposed a Robin Hood tax on City trades (which Britain rejected), and Jean-Claude Juncker had become the favourite candidate as the EU's next president. Since Juncker, a former prime minister of Luxembourg and a federalist, had Merkel's support, Boris ridiculed Cameron's attempt to block the appointment of a known drunkard, supported by every other EU government, as the 'quintessence of turd-polishing pointlessness'. To add to Cameron's woes, a tape emerged of senior Polish government officials mocking Cameron's bid to secure EU reforms. Finally, a new Euromyth had surfaced. The Commission, it was reported, had ordered cows to wear nappies.

Lyons' report was adapted for a speech that Boris was to deliver at Bloomberg's London headquarters on Wednesday 6 August. Cameron would be challenged to leave the EU if Brussels refused to negotiate a good deal. Boris's demands from the EU would be difficult to meet: Britain would take back control of its borders and restore controls over social, environmental, agricultural and migration laws. 'You've got to go in hard and low,' Boris explained, using a rugby analogy. There was nothing to fear about leaving the EU, he would say, except 'a great and glorious future'.

In the days before his speech, the political mood changed. Rumours spread that Tory MPs had threatened to defect to UKIP. An opinion poll predicted that Cameron would lose the next election and Boris was named as the most popular successor – with double the support for Theresa May. Only with Boris as leader, the poll reported, could the Tories win the election. Boris was easily persuaded to accept an offer negotiated by Wallace.

The Tory MP in Uxbridge and South Ruislip, west London, had decided to retire at the next election. With a 11,216 majority at the 2010 election, it was a safe seat. The constituency chairman, Wallace told Boris, could no longer delay the selection process. With Marina's approval, Boris agreed to announce at Bloomberg's headquarters that his indecision was over. The evening before, he had a haircut. The following morning, the atrium in the City venue was packed.

With his hair dishevelled and wearing a crumpled suit, he pulled out his notes and after some comments about Europe said, 'I think we have danced around it for an awfully long time now. I'm clear I cannot endlessly dodge this question as I have tried to do. So . . .' and then he revealed his return to Westminster, adding: 'It's highly likely that I will be successful in that venture, by the way.' The announcement completely overshadowed his European demands, which would be later ignored by Cameron, as was his pledge to support Leave if Cameron's EU deal was unacceptable.

In the excitement which followed, the journalist and former Tory MP Matthew Parris predicted that Boris's chance of 'ever leading the Tory Party are less than 10 per cent'. If he did defy the odds, 'the first thing he'd do is betray the Tory right'. It was easy to take no notice of Parris, who rarely visited Westminster to witness the strength of those organising Boris's return. For them, Boris had legitimised himself as a liberal to attract Londoners and as a nationalist to win back Eurosceptic Tories minded to vote UKIP. Three weeks later, Douglas Carswell, a Tory MP, defected to UKIP and triggered a by-election in Clacton. Identifying the only person with a chance to defeat Carswell, Lynton Crosby asked Boris whether he wanted to stand. 'Thank you, no,' replied Boris.

That exchange coincided with a buffet dinner in Islington for key City Hall staff. Several sat with him in a corner discussing his future. 'How Eurosceptic are you?' asked one aide. Angrily he replied, 'I'm the second most Eurosceptic politician after Daniel Hannan. It's just that he's written more than me.' To prove his credentials, he set out his history of disenchantment with the EU and how he witnessed Margaret Thatcher handbagged in Rome in 1990. Two weeks earlier, he reminded them, he had told BBC TV that if Cameron's negotiations failed, 'I think we should campaign to come out.'

Cameron approached October's party conference in Birmingham weakened by his leadership of the Scottish independence referendum. Blamed for a clumsy campaign, he had turned the original 22 per cent lead against independence into 10 per cent. Criticised for flying by the seat of his pants, many wondered whether he could negotiate adeptly with the EU, especially after Mark Reckless, another Tory MP, defected to UKIP. Cameron's saviour was Ed Miliband. The Labour leader's conference performance, also in Birmingham, damagingly portrayed Britain as a broken country. One appalling speech had slashed Labour's chances of victory.

Boris arrived in Birmingham committed to a display of utmost loyalty. He cheered Cameron's rousing speech promising more controls over immigration, and delivered thirty minutes of jokey entertainment, but nothing more. Theresa May was given an open field to pitch for the leadership. Plans for his own campaign were more sophisticated. After two nights in Umbria with Evgeny Lebedev, he planned a trip to Malaysia, Singapore and Indonesia to promote himself and to attract investors for property developments in Elephant and Castle, Vauxhall and Battersea. With the approval of London & Partners, Jennifer Arcuri was accredited as a member of the official party.

By then Arcuri had established herself in London, appearing in the magazine *Business Insider's* list of 'The Coolest Women in UK Tech'. The magazine described Innotech as a company which 'helps bring together London's technology scene with the British government. Thanks to her close ties with London mayor Boris Johnson, the shaggy-haired politician has repeatedly agreed to speak at her events, which also shows the government's interest in the east London tech cluster.' Arcuri's grip on Boris was tightening. Nevertheless, she had to work hard to secure his fourth appearance at an Innotech meeting on 14 October in Piccadilly. Arcuri sold tickets for £1,000 a head. 'Viva Innotech folks, and forward with all your deliberations,' Boris said at the end of his short speech. Seconds later, he asked 'Will that do Jennifer? Can I go now? Thank you very much.' Somewhat ashamed of the pressure she had exerted, she never asked him to speak again. But in November, she was alongside not only Boris in Singapore, but also Max Johnson, his half-brother, employed as a banker in Hong Kong. As soon as Arcuri was aware that Boris had seen her speaking to Max, she realised there was a problem. 'It was such an awkward moment,' she said later. An arrangement for private drinks with Boris was cancelled: 'He didn't want any more suspicious gossip being spread.'

Boris flew on alone to Jakarta. 'Your people love you,' Boris fawningly told President Joko Widodo. 'They say great things about you.'

'Yes,' replied the president. 'And what do they say to you in London?'

'Usually, Tory tosser,' replied Boris.

Back in London, on 18 December, Boris and Marina were the

star guests at Mark's Club for drinks and dinner with a hundred northern Tory MPs and businessmen who funded the event. At the end of a successful evening, Boris agreed with Ben Wallace and Jake Berry that he would host regular meetings in Islington to meet more potentially supportive MPs.

The following night, Boris hosted a boisterous staff party in City Hall. He generated genuine loyalty through encouragement, praise and gratitude for his staff's hard work, often in sincere handwritten notes and thoughtful gifts. At Boris's insistence, the climax was a table-tennis competition. His desk was cleared, books erected as the net and Stephen Greenhalgh was selected as the victim. Naturally Boris won. As they congratulated each other at 10 p.m., Boris announced that he had to go to another event. 'I work so hard,' he told everyone. His next stop was Jennifer Arcuri's Shoreditch flat.

The American's home had become his haven. As always, Boris trusted a woman as his confidante. First, he was able to talk about the stress of being in a position of authority in City Hall, the flip side of which was the boredom of the same people telling him the same things every day. And secondly, as a sanctuary from the sadness in his own home. Marina, he said, was often away. Not only had she become distant but he feared that his family life was withering. The cure to his depression, he said, was Jennifer Arcuri. Although the moment he arrived at her flat he would say he couldn't stay, her direct manner soothed him. Cool and in command, she never pressured him. The chase was his. The dalliance appeared to have become his only real friendship. Partly mother and partly lover, she claimed to understand his mind, and that he felt safe in her company. In return, he expressed affection but she could never be certain whether he was truthful. Despite his ability to quote Shakespeare and Wordsworth, she was falling in love with an unromantic man. He could never love women in the way a woman wanted to be loved. 'I fell in love. I never admitted how much I loved him,' Arcuri said. Whereas his texts were recklessly amorous, and his crazy propositions – like setting up a ski centre in Bulgaria or even the two of them becoming a political team in New York – were the product of often being alone in the evenings, there was what some might judge to be foolishness to invite her to his empty Islington home. Boris's displays of emotion were puzzling. Despite being surrounded by family photographs, he was already divorced from that life. 'Will you hoist sail, sir? Here lies your way,' he recited from *Twelfth Night*.

By Christmas 2014, Boris did not conceal the relationship from advisers in Conservative Central Office and City Hall. With his help, Arcuri was invited to a party in Buckingham Palace celebrating technology. Dropping his name, she had also received £15,000 from the international trade department to encourage foreign entrepreneurs to set up in Britain. Pushing as usual at both ends, she persuaded Boris to allow her official access to an event he would host in New York in the new year.

'We need to see Boston's tunnels,' Boris announced. Boris and ten City Hall staff crossed the Atlantic in January 2015 to search for answers to problems with London's connections under the Thames. The other purpose of the £40,000 trip was to have a photograph of himself next to Hillary Clinton, the favourite to win the presidential election. Perhaps he hoped that Clinton's staff remained unaware of his description of her in 2007 as having 'dyed blonde hair and pouty lips, and a steely blue stare, like a sadistic nurse in a mental hospital'. In the brief but fun meeting in her office, Boris reminded Clinton of his birth in New York. He omitted to say that he had given up his American citizenship following his discovery that he was liable for about £100,000 in American capital gains tax after the recent sale of his Islington home had produced a £730,000 profit.

During that trip, Boris hosted a breakfast at a Manhattan hotel for potential investors in London. Having been present at one event, Arcuri asked London & Partners whether she could attend the breakfast. Her request was declined. Innotech, she was told, did not qualify. Undeterred, she spoke to Boris's staff and soon after a London & Partners executive emailed, 'Please put her on the list . . . she has been speaking to Boris.' 'Boris was kind of hilarious,' Arcuri told an American friend. 'He's kind of got to the point that I am not some kind of floozy.'

Just as Boris had little interest in the governance of institutions, or complex long-term projects, he was brazenly dismissive of the City Hall rules. In breach of the code of conduct, Boris again did not declare his relationship with Arcuri. Asked four years later about the invitation to the breakfast, Boris said 'I can tell you that absolutely everything was done with full propriety . . . and in accordance with proper procedures.' He was however honest about calculating his response to those difficult questions: 'In cricket, when the ball comes down you tell yourself over and over again, "I must not try to whack this ball. I must advance the bat and pad together and play it correctly." But when the ball bounces, it hangs there for a millisecond, tempting and beautiful, and you want to whack it. That's what I try to do and quite often I am out . . . My approach to politics and to life is to try to play the shots I have as naturally as I can.'

On his return to Britain, his agenda was packed. While continuing as mayor for the next sixteen months he would also fight the general election in May, speak at innumerable events to get support for his leadership bid and then he would consider his position for the inevitable EU referendum.

Chapter 18

'The next PM will be Miliband if you don't fucking shut up'

Scattering leaflets, smiling for selfies, waving at drivers who stopped to shout his name, the candidate marched down Uxbridge high street thrilled by the adulation. 'Can we count on your vote in the election?' he asked, wearing odd socks and a crumpled jacket. 'Wonderful,' gushed Eton's celebrated 'pleb'. Everywhere across the country, roaring crowds gathered to watch the spectacle. On the Ramsgate sea front to campaign for Craig Mackinlay against Nigel Farage, he stood outside the Royal pub enjoying his rock star celebrity. 'Totally unbelievable,' swooned Mackinlay. In Chippenham's town centre, Nigel Adams, the Tory candidate, witnessed 'the incredible impact'. Boris, realised the Yorkshireman expelled from a grammar school, was a man without doubts. 'He wanted to win.' Boris returned the compliment: 'I like you and if the ball comes out of the scrum in the near future, I'd like you to help me.'

Cameron felt rather differently. While he did the hard work, Cameron complained, Boris was unreliable, untrustworthy, crass, bumbling, 'and loving twisting the knife'. His wrath rose after Boris wrote an article describing all the Old Etonian prime ministers. 'The next PM will be Miliband if you don't fucking shut up,' he texted Boris. Face to face with Miliband on BBC TV, Boris failed to land a punch with a critical one-liner to explain the difference between capitalism and Miliband's socialism. To prevent any embarrassment, Boris was kept away from the manifesto launch – 'A brighter, more secure future' – but to display their unity on the

campaign's twenty-fifth day, he appeared for the media with Cameron in a south London nursery making a jigsaw. 'A jigsaw crisis,'
cried Boris, unable to finish the puzzle quickly. Afterwards they
agreed that the election's outcome was uncertain even though the
Lib Dems were struggling. Boris willed the coalition to collapse. 'Is
the Clegger heading for the oubliette of history?' he asked. 'I don't
know. I have the feelings of ordinary compassion just as I might feel
a twinge if I accidentally trod on a wasp or a slug . . . There is a terrible pop if you do it in bare feet.' The Lib Dem vote, Boris feared,
would switch to Miliband. If Cameron lost, all bets were off. The
leadership would be contested but Boris was not attracted to serve
as leader of the opposition for five years and any way he would still
be mayor for another year. Hiding from that possibility became
impossible once Cameron revealed that he would not run for a
third term. Boris had no choice but to admit on Sky TV his aspiration to be the leader. Among his first calls was to Lynton Crosby.
Without Crosby, he could not mount a campaign. Then he contacted Rupert Murdoch. They agreed to meet for dinner.

Rapidly, Boris reconsidered his philosophy. His 'inequality is
good' theory outlined in his 2013 Margaret Thatcher Lecture had
been unpopular. He needed to reposition himself as a One Nation
Tory – providing opportunity for everyone, a welfare net for those
in need, full employment and fair taxation – rather than as a
defender of the rich. In a series of articles, he somersaulted and
damned the gap in earnings between those at the top and their staff
under them as 'outrageous'. Top executives, earning 'eye-watering'
salaries 130 times more than their employees' average wage,
offended his new 'moral purpose'. Chief executives, he wrote, were
engaged in a 'racket' and 'an orgy of mutual back-scratching' while
the poor he had met during his seven years as mayor could not survive on the minimum wage. 'We've got to look after those people
who can't help themselves,' he said. 'I don't mind people in club
class quaffing champagne provided that the people at the back of
the plane don't feel their standards are falling behind. That's what
worries me.' Life expectancy, he knew, dropped by a year with
every Tube stop from prosperous Westminster to impoverished

Canning Town. 'We cannot just shrug at the wealth gap,' he wrote, and would campaign in favour of the living wage.

The opinion polls on the eve of election day predicted a hung parliament. Some even forecast a small Labour majority. The exit polls proved the pundits wrong. Sipping Red Bull, Boris and Marina watched the final votes for Uxbridge and South Ruislip counted at Brunel University in the early hours of 8 May. It was their wedding anniversary and Marina looked noticeably unemotional as Boris hailed his 10,695 majority in his victory speech. In the TV studios, George Osborne was credited with orchestrating the victory, thereby improving his prospects as Cameron's successor.

Despite being elected with the first outright Tory majority since 1992, Cameron's weaknesses were immediately debated. Criticised for complacency and failing to make people feel good, insiders complained, 'Nobody came out of Dave's office feeling better than when they went in.' Fingers were pointed at the unpleasant group of public school snobs in Downing Street who had distanced Cameron from the party faithful. Together, they failed to advance a compelling Conservative vision of society. Cameron was personally blamed for breaking his promise to reduce immigration to the tens of thousands. Instead, net immigration in 2015/16 was 323,000 people. His good fortune, after Ed Miliband resigned, was Labour's selection as leader of Jeremy Corbyn, a 66-year-old anti-Semitic Marxist.*

---

* Corbyn was closely associated with militant Islamists who he knew expressed outrightly anti-Semitic opinions and, as Labour's leader, allowed anti-Semitism to erupt for the first time within the party and then delayed the expulsion of outright anti-Semitic party members. In 2012, Corbyn had protested on the grounds of 'free speech' after Lambeth council removed 'Freedom for Humanity', a large mural painted by an American artist. The mural portrayed Jewish financiers playing Monopoly on a board supported by the naked backs of the world's oppressed – mostly blacks. Even after a snapshot glance, Corbyn could not have failed to grasp the familiar caricature of grotesque-looking Jewish bankers engaged in a worldwide conspiracy to manipulate subjugated slaves. In addition, Margaret Hodge, Ian Austin and the Board of Deputies accused Corbyn of anti-Semitism. All of this in spite of an insistence that there is no place for anti-Semitism in the Labour Party.

Most greeted Boris's return to Westminster as a celebrity outsider discredited for not being a team player. He did not find many
new admirers within the parliamentary party. The resentment
towards him was noticeable. Among those who spoke disparag-
ingly in the Commons tea room were Philip Hammond, Nick Boles
and Nicholas Soames, the grandson of Winston Churchill. Despite
Boris's achievements as mayor, these critics spoke only about his
flaws – and his worst it seemed was to be one of life's winners.
Everything seemed to come too easily. Whatever the bounder
wanted, he secured. He wanted a platform at the *Telegraph* and got
it. He wanted to be editor of the *Spectator* and, despite a dishonest
undertaking to Conrad Black that he wasn't going to pursue a political career, he was appointed. He then got the Henley seat, said he
could do both jobs and he did. Not content with two jobs he also
had two women, and more. He not only attracted women but could
even shrug off adultery. He wanted to be mayor of London and,
despite the odds, he was elected. Then he wanted to return to the
Commons and he was handed Uxbridge. Now, they assumed, he
aimed for Downing Street, and with his popularity he was in danger of succeeding. Boris was charmed.

The envy among some MPs was not shared by those who
resumed their meetings in Boris's Islington home. 'My amigos,' as
Boris called them, were led by Jake Berry and Ben Wallace. Over
takeaway curries bought by his City Hall PR adviser Will Walden,
Boris gathered his core team: Eddie Lister, plus three more MPs –
Nigel Adams, Amanda Milling (to attract women MPs) and Nigel
Powers. To identify other potential supporters, Boris met his long-
standing City Hall political secretary Ben Gascoigne on Wednesdays
to agree the Islington dinner invitation list. Every week, three
MPs, usually liberal metropolitans, asked the same question:
'What's this all about?' 'We're not plotting Cameron's downfall,'
replied Boris, careful never to criticise the prime minister. 'Just discussing what will happen before 2020.' Boris listened to a
thirty-minute discussion and then spelled out his views – optimism
in the age of austerity, the living wage and One Nation compassionate Conservatism. Occasionally Marina entered to say 'Hello'.

Although Brexit was never discussed, Nigel Adams, a Brexiteer, was convinced that Boris would side with out.

For Berry and Wallace, what they called the 'Granita moment', confirming Boris as the right person to lead the party, dawned during a three-day summer break with Marina in Rhoscolyn, a small village by the sea in Anglesey. Staying in Wallace's house, Boris listened to his host's anger – 'I'm really pissed off that I haven't been promoted' – planned a second reception at Mark's Club, and discussed his leadership campaign. In between, they played cricket on the beach. On his first ball, Berry's seven-year-old nephew bowled Boris out. 'No,' shouted Boris. 'I wasn't ready.' Boris also tried to water ski in a creek. 'Will you teach me?' Boris asked Berry although he had water-skied as a teenager in Greece. Now, despite repeated determined attempts to get up, he was too heavy and fell. Rather than letting go of the rope, he was dragged through the water. Sightseers came by boat to gaze at the star floating in the water.

To seal their relationship, the two MPs were invited to play in the annual Johnsons versus Spencers cricket match on 12 July. The Conservative MP Nigel Adams, who was a keen cricketer and had scored a century at Lord's, also played. He, along with Amanda Milling, Berry and Wallace, were the self-named 'awesome foursome' who began laying the foundations for Boris's leadership bid.

To other MPs, Boris remained a distant figure. Having rejected the offer of a Cabinet post as incompatible with remaining mayor, he participated only in the regular meetings of the political Cabinet, sitting amiably but isolated at the end of the table. Cameron was friendly, while others like Oliver Letwin were suspicious. Letwin, the Dorset MP responsible for the Cabinet Office, had been irritated in 2011 by Boris's public distortion of his opposition to the idea of the Estuary airport. Letwin had argued that it was financially unsustainable because only holidaymakers and not businessmen would use it. Boris refused to apologise to Letwin. Now he sat in the Cabinet Room making no contribution. Boris, Letwin assumed, was calculating how his leadership hopes would be influenced by the referendum. After all, in 2001 Boris was the pro-EU politician who rebuffed Letwin's Euroscepticism. Self-interest, Letwin assumed, would guide Boris's ultimate position about the EU.

The Tory manifesto had promised that Cameron would renegotiate the terms of Britain's EU membership followed by an in-out referendum before the end of 2017. One month after the election, the hard-line Eurosceptics became disenchanted by Cameron's weak demands to the EU leaders. 'You need to be bold,' urged Boris. 'You have to show them that you are serious. Be prepared to walk away if the EU rejects your terms.' Cameron's refusal to please the Eurosceptics coincided with George Osborne cutting tax credits to reduce the welfare budget by £4.4 billion. To Osborne's surprise, some Tory MPs voted against the government. Boris was among the rebels. The reason, he said, was to protect low earners but others assumed he was delighted to damage Osborne's leadership chances. Defeated in the Lords, Osborne retreated. Tarred as a politician who lacked empathy for the disadvantaged, Osborne's misfortune enlivened the atmosphere at Jake Berry's 'End of Term Christmas Party' at Mark's Club in early November 2015. One hundred MPs, the entire 2015 new intake, were invited to meet Boris. Since most did not know him personally and also had no grounds for envy, Boris felt he was among potential friends who would not try to pull him down.

Three weeks later, at a Brussels summit, Cameron's tepid proposals to the EU leaders, including a short-term ban on benefits for newly arrived EU migrants in Britain, were rejected. Cameron's original list of fundamental reforms had disappeared. Without securing any concessions, Cameron nevertheless accelerated the referendum to 2016. 'There is much, much more that needs to be done,' said Boris, exasperated by Cameron's idleness. The latest madness of the EU, Boris added, was a new regulation to ban the recycling of teabags.

His frustration was expressed to Peter Ricketts, the British ambassador in Paris. Boris was visiting the French capital to lay a wreath to remember the victims who died at the Bataclan concert hall in November. Boris spoke in French about the tragedy of the 129 murdered by Muslim extremists across Paris that night. On the drive back to the airport, they discussed Brexit. 'I can see both sides,' said Boris. 'Honestly Peter, I'm torn.' He expressed the same dilemma at Liam Fox's New Year's Eve party in the Carlton Club. For thirty minutes he stood in a corner with Osborne discussing the possibility of a second referendum, favoured by the Leavers in case they lost the first referendum. 'I would vote to stay in the single market,' Boris had said. 'I'm in favour of the single market.' Like Letwin, Osborne judged that Boris was waiting for his opportunity to realise his dream: addressing the nation as prime minister.

Chapter 19

The Legacy

Cycling home at night through Clerkenwell in mid-June 2015, Boris was accosted by a black-cab driver. The driver ranted that the mayor was failing to stop 100,000 Uber drivers swamping the capital and not paying any taxes. 'Why don't you fuck off and die, and not in that order,' Boris shouted back, unaware that he was being recorded. Boris refused to apologise: 'I think it comes under the heading of getting the ball back over the net,' he explained. Despite the affection many cab drivers had for him, Boris regarded the trade as 'Luddites' who staged loud protests inside City Hall. Yet by the end of the year, his sympathies had changed. Both the Home Office and Downing Street refused to engage with the cab drivers' legitimate complaints. Cameron, he suspected, had been influenced by Rachel Whetstone, a close friend of Cameron's and recently employed as Uber's director of communications. As for Theresa May, she had declared war.

In mid-July, Boris was telephoned by May. In ten minutes, she said, she would be making an announcement in the Commons that she had refused to license the three water cannons. Rushing over to Westminster, he sat on the back benches while the Home Secretary, adopting a dramatically serious voice, told MPs that the vehicles were not only blighted by sixty-seven faults but the British police would never willingly 'hide behind military-style equipment'. Whatever was acceptable in Belfast, she said, Londoners were policed by consent and would resent being pounded by water. 'Silly cow,' said Boris to a colleague, forlornly shrugging off the humiliation.

'Absolute nonsense,' he wrote the following day in the *Sun*. London's police use tasers, clubs and firearms, so what's dangerous about water? he asked. 'Does anyone consent to be tasered, for heaven's sake?' May's intention to damage his bid for the leadership was blatant. 'She wants to blunt the end of your nose,' said Will Walden. In a telephone conversation with Cameron, the prime minister explained that he would instantly license the cannon if they were required, but it was pointless to overrule her that day. In public, it appeared that Cameron had switched to support May as revenge for Boris's unhelpful attitude towards the EU; while Osborne, the principal rival, announced a £9.35 living wage to undermine Boris's £8.80 living wage in London. (Five months later, Boris increased his London living wage to £9.40.) On that day, compared to the substance of May and Osborne, Boris was cast as a fool. He consoled himself that Churchill was sixty-five when he became prime minister.

By focusing his ambitions in Westminster, once again the latest chicanery at Scotland Yard had been allowed to develop unchecked. Bernard Hogan-Howe's senior officers were destroying the lives of eminent men. Claiming to possess evidence which was 'credible and true', the Yard had committed a team of detectives to Operation Midland, which got underway in November 2014. Their task was to investigate the allegations that a group of prominent public servants – including the former prime minister Edward Heath, and Lord Bramall, the former head of the army – had participated in a VIP paedophile ring which tortured boys. By early 2015, the Yard's 'credible and true' evidence was proven to be wholly fabricated. The lives of the public figures had been destroyed by the Yard's misconduct. Among the casualties was Leon Brittan, the former Home Secretary. Not only was Brittan wholly innocent but he had died in January 2015 before being told he was cleared. 'I cannot honestly remember,' Hogan-Howe replied about whether the Yard had apologised to Brittan. Hogan-Howe also refused to apologise immediately to Lord Bramall, even though twenty policemen had raided his home with a search warrant obtained with an untrue statement. Bramall had been accused of participating in an orgy at the very moment he was laying a wreath on Remembrance Sunday. Belatedly, Boris whispered that Bramall deserved a 'full and heartfelt apology' but Hogan-Howe resisted. Thereafter, Boris mysteriously remained silent about those gross injustices. By contrast, in his chase for headlines, he was vocal about soaring knife crime but silent about the crime detection rate falling by 21 per cent since 2008. He would blame May for denying any connection between rising crime and declining police numbers and her 'politically correct squeamishness' for ending stop-and-search. 'That turned out to be a very grave mistake,' he said. Hogan-Howe, however, escaped censure.

Boris's reluctance to hold openly officials or political opponents to account for their errors undermined his claims to be a principled standard-bearer. There seemed to be a link between concealing his own transgressions, especially his adultery and his lies, and his refusal to censure accountable public servants for their wrongdoing. To his good fortune, no one in the media mentioned that weak link in Boris as a politician. Staging celebrations became his smokescreen for avoiding bad news and not challenging those responsible for creating problems.

The good news he celebrated on 4 June 2015 was the near completion of Crossrail's tunnelling. Forty metres beneath London, Boris and Cameron acknowledged a remarkable feat of engineering. During their performance for the media, Boris was assured by Andrew Wolstenholme, Crossrail's chief executive, that Crossrail was 'being delivered on time and within budget'. By then, Boris knew that was not quite accurate. At the regular Thursday meetings, Terry Morgan, Crossrail's chairman since 2009, explained a series of problems. 'Bombardier's trains,' said Morgan, 'are awful.' Built in Derby in a £1 billion contract, the trains would be delivered late, not least because they could not meet the special requirements for Crossrail's unique computerised signalling system. Every train needed to automatically shift between three different computerised signalling systems along the seventy-three miles. Boris was told that Crossrail's mechanical engineers had underestimated the problems and their software writers in Scandinavia and Italy had made a succession of serious mistakes which they were still unable to rectify.

Another problem, Morgan knew, were the Underground stations. In Bond Street, Costain, the contractors, possessed neither the skills nor the finance to deliver their promises of completing on time and on budget, made worse by the Jubilee Line tunnel sinking. The costs of their badly run contract were increasing by over 300 per cent. Similarly, the costs of Whitechapel station were rising by 600 per cent. To complete the project by 2018, Crossrail's executives adopted a 'can-do' mentality and minimised their financial controls over the contractors. As Daniel Moylan, Boris's representative on Crossrail's board, warned, 'In big projects you can't take anything at face value. There is a psychological tendency to believe that everything is going well.' Boris preferred to ignore Moylan's warning.

During the Thursday meetings, Morgan discovered that Boris was prepared to hear everyone's opinion and in turn emphasised the importance of controlling costs. But he was not keen to hear about difficulties. 'I had to be careful when telling him about the problems,' recalls Morgan, 'because he didn't understand risk.' Mindful of his political reputation, Boris asked, 'Why are you telling me this? Are you passing the problem to me?' Morgan recoiled. 'I had to give him confidence. I had to leave him optimistic that we could fix the problems. I never told Boris it would be late or over-cost.' In telling Boris what he wanted to hear, Morgan minimised the risks. 'The project is on-time and on budget,' he reported. Crossrail's assumption of progress, a subsequent NAO report concluded, 'bore little resemblance' to the truth. 'Can-do became unrealistic.'

Boris's refusal to hear bad news reflected his reliance on Mike Brown, TfL's new chief executive. Amid new strikes on the Tube, aimed to prevent the introduction of all-night trains despite the promise of extra pay, Boris relied on Brown to supervise Crossrail on his behalf. Just as Brown, a surveyor, could not overcome the Tube unions' obduracy, he also could not resolve Crossrail's engineering problems. He was not entirely to blame. The government had assigned the supervision of the project to the Department of Transport, staffed by notoriously incompetent civil servants. All these were familiar frustrations for government ministers, but Boris appeared to be uninterested in the grinding administrative chore of holding Brown or anyone at Crossrail to account.

With the same 'can-do had become unrealistic' attitude, Boris had fallen into a trap of his own making with the Garden Bridge. At the end of 2014, construction of the bridge had been approved by Westminster Council and Lambeth on condition that the bridge's upkeep would be privately funded. To hasten the project's construction, Eddie Lister had spent large sums to swiftly obtain engineering reports to match planning regulations, in spite of the pledge of Sadiq Khan, Boris's expected successor, to scrap the 'white elephant'. Furious about Khan's opposition, Boris snapped, 'The garden bridge is ringed by demented enemies . . . Surely London can have another iconic landmark?' After opinion polls showed that a majority of Londoners endorsed the project, Khan switched. 'I fully support the bridge,' he said. Even Nick Clegg became a reluctant enthusiast, as did Simon Jenkins, albeit he suggested that the bridge should be built at Battersea because there was no apparent demand for a footbridge at Temple.

Originally, Boris had pledged that no public money would be spent on the Garden Bridge. That vow was broken once he relied on £60 million from the Treasury and TfL towards the total cost of £175 million (£85 million had been pledged by private donors). He still called his £60 million cable car 'a howling success' although only 300 passengers a day were using it at a loss of £6 million a year; and he waved aside the Boris Bikes' subsidy of about £3 for each journey. Rather than being free for ratepayers, the bill by the end of eight years was £195 million. To deliver his legacy, obstacles were pushed aside, even legal requirements identified by Lister. One key obligation was that before construction of the bridge could begin, all the 'funding is in place'. At the last minute, Boris was told, the trustees of the bridge could no longer provide a cast-iron guarantee of private funding for the bridge's maintenance for the first five years. The solution devised by the mayor's office was to substitute that a 'funding strategy [was] in place'. No one was fooled. The project was jeopardised.

All the effort put into the bridge, the cable car and other iconic schemes dreamt up by Boris provided useful media headlines, promoting City Hall as a hive of creativity and activity. Boris loved to dream that his legacy as mayor would be remembered by future generations. Proposals spewed from City Hall. Plans for thirteen new Thames crossings – bridges, ferries and tunnels, including a tunnel to replace Hammersmith Bridge – plus Crossrail 2, a new concert hall, 400,000 homes and ultrafast broadband. But there was silence about Old Oak Common, considerably more important for London than a bridge or a cable car. At stake were not only 24,000 new homes but a huge transport hub. Daily, about 250,000 people would be passing through the interchange of HS2, the Tube, Crossrail and the GWR railway line from west England to Paddington. The west London wasteland was Boris's greatest potential legacy. In early December 2014, Steve Norris mentioned to him a meeting due to be held near Whitehall and chaired by Patrick McGoughlin, the Transport Secretary. 'This meeting will decide Old Oak's fate,' said Norris. 'You must come.'

Crossrail had won permission to build a vast marshalling yard in the centre of the Old Oak Common site, its most valuable area. On behalf of a consortium of builders and developers, Norris wanted the government to deck over the marshalling yard with concrete platforms to allow the construction of shops, offices and 12,000 homes. To support the decking, deep concrete piles would be poured into the ground. The estimated cost was £200 million. Everyone at the meeting on 17 December knew the advantages of the proposed development. To deliver the financial and social advantages, George Osborne would need to approve the investment. But to Norris's horror, 'Boris showed no enthusiasm or even interest. He took little part in the meeting. He said practically nothing. He just let Peter Hendy present an absurd argument to fob us off and then just handed it over to Lister. Lister was keen but unusually Boris overruled him. "We can't delay Crossrail," Boris said. After that meeting, it was a dead duck.' None of the cast in the meeting – Boris and the representatives of the Transport Department, the Treasury and Crossrail – were prepared to take the initiative. Instead of a stunning £10 billion development, Old Oak Common was relegated to become a railway depot with a few tower blocks.

Boris's reluctance was personal and political. The benefits, he calculated, would not happen during his era – meaning there was no immediate reputational legacy – and all three local authorities were Labour councils. Regeneration for those politicians meant rich people – not Labour voters – buying the new homes. Without any electoral advantage, the Labour council leaders would stymie the private developers. 'Old Oak,' concluded Terry Farrell, 'is probably the biggest cock-up I have seen in my career of fifty years in London. Over the past five years everyone just talked and talked. It's just been five wasted years of pass the parcel.' If only, he lamented, Boris had devoted as much attention to Old Oak Common as his Estuary airport or the Garden Bridge, 24,000 new homes might have been built. 'You spent too much time on the bridge instead of Old Oak,' Len Duvall complained to Boris. 'Just because Lumley fluttered her eyelashes.'

No actress or major developer was lobbying to transform Old Oak Common. Unlike Paul Reichmann, the Canadian visionary who lobbied Margaret Thatcher to develop Canary Wharf, Boris was not targeted, despite *New London Architecture* magazine labelling him 'the lackey of London's development lobby'. Tilting in the developers' favour, he had approved nearly 400 towers. 'It's all about numbers,' observed an aide. 'Nothing else mattered.' To deliver Boris's pledge of completing the construction of 100,000 homes before his mayoralty ended, Lister had even endorsed a monstrous tower developed by Irvine Sellar, overshadowing Little Venice where Boris's maternal grandparents had lived. Other potential casualties included the demolition of historic buildings in Spitalfields including Norton Folgate, a street dating from the 1530s. Supporting the developers of forty-three-storey tower blocks in Bishopsgate, Boris overruled the local council anxious to protect an ancient viaduct. 'The bloated, bulging light-blocking buildings,' wrote Rowan Moore, the architectural expert, would cast swathes of London in a permanent shadow. Ironically, the damage caused to London's heritage by the towers coincided with Boris's protests against the destruction by Muslim extremists of Palmyra, the city in Syria founded 5,000 years earlier.

His plea for Palmyra justified a dash to Israel to mark the end of his mayoralty and his re-emergence into national politics. Having worked on a kibbutz as a student, Boris's sympathy for Israel was unconditional: 'Whatever the criticisms of Israel may be,' he said on arriving in Tel Aviv, 'some of them justified and some of them less so, it is still the case that Israel is the only democracy in the region, the only free country, the only pluralist society.' After opening the stock exchange and cycling around Tel Aviv, he vocally opposed the boycott of Israel organised by 'snaggle-toothed, corduroy-wearing lefty academics'. Then he headed to the West Bank to meet the Palestinian leaders – and trouble. To his surprise, the Palestinians were upset by his opposition to the boycott and his praise of Israel as 'a remarkable country justified by an incontestable goal: to provide a persecuted people with a safe and secure homeland'. His visit to Ramallah was cancelled on 'security grounds'. Visibly distressed by the imbroglio, he discovered that pleasing everyone, especially the BBC, was impossible. Norman Smith, the BBC's correspondent in Jerusalem, announced that the Palestinians' snub amounted to 'the death of Boris Johnson'. Boris's misfortune was compounded by his inability to meet Jennifer Arcuri. She had travelled separately to Israel to use Boris's name for establishing business contacts. They had hoped to meet at his hotel but tight security prevented Arcuri getting to his room.

The end of Boris's eight-year term could have been heralded by a list of his considerable achievements. London had overtaken New York as the world's most popular city; he had built 94,001 affordable homes in eight years, slightly more than Livingstone despite the 2008 crash, and bequeathed a construction boom to produce a total of about 40,000 homes a year to meet London's annual population increase of 100,000 people; the Tube was vastly more efficient with sound finances and the drivers had finally agreed to all-night trains; the Olympic Park was under construction; Routemasters had replaced the bendy buses; and, by raising the living wage, increasing apprenticeships, mobilising thousands of volunteers and encouraging education and culture, especially the Mayor's Music Fund to help talented children from low-income families, he had reduced the capital's poverty. In 2008, four of Britain's six poorest boroughs were in London. After Boris's terms, none of the nation's poorest ten boroughs were in London.

Success came at a price. With the approval of 71 per cent of Londoners, cycle superhighways stretched across the inner city despite the uproar of wealthy City denizens stuck in their stationary limousines. To seal his success, in February 2016 Boris welcomed the Queen at Bond Street to open Crossrail and name it the Elizabeth Line. Part of it, he announced, would be opened the following year. Crossrail's executives standing near him knew that was untrue. Several stations were not yet built, none of the trains had been tested and the signalling problems remained unsolved. Completion was further delayed by a transformer erupting in flames.

Despite his achievements, his legacy was about to be buried. Just as in 2008, David Cameron's choice of Tory mayoral candidate was bizarre: Zac Goldsmith. The attraction to Londoners of a multi-millionaire who had never worked in his life was questionable. Goldsmith's only advantage as the MP for Richmond was his passion for the environment, hardly a pressing issue for those Labour voters who had supported Boris. Boris did not raise any doubts about Goldsmith's selection and encouraged his use of Lynton Crosby against Sadiq Khan, the MP for Tooting. As a product of Labour's political machine, Khan lacked the appeal of Boris or Livingstone. Indeed, he could boast few outstanding qualities except his background as the self-made son of Pakistani immigrants, an advantage in a city where about 60 per cent of the population were immigrants. Lynton Crosby, who was automatically hired to run Goldsmith's campaign, thought otherwise. Labelling Khan an extremists' ally, he highlighted Khan's appearance on platforms with anti-Semites. Crosby's campaign backfired. The lacklustre Goldsmith was written off by the metro-elite. Khan was elected with 57 per cent of the vote. In turn, the metro-elite and Labour voters gave Boris no credit for anything.

Even committed Tories barely praised Boris. Writing in *The Times*, Clare Foges described his legacy as 'curiously slim . . . he has been pretty useless as a public administrator'. The bikes, she wrote, were Livingstone's idea; Livingstone secured the funding for Crossrail; and Johnson delivered affordable housing only because Livingstone obtained the funding from the Labour government. Each of Foges' assertions was completely untrue. 'Horror stories', wrote Matthew Parris, circulated about negotiations with government departments by Boris 'where he so failed that he left having conceded hundreds of millions more in cuts than the department had planned to be in its final offer'. That was not a complaint heard from Cameron or Osborne. Once again, misinterpretation overrode any balanced judgement, thereby underestimating his achievements as mayor. Few wanted to accept that over time he could improve. Some also misjudged the realities of his ambitions. 'I think I'm totally different from eight years ago as an MP,' said Boris, recognising the lessons he had learned as mayor. 'More interested in making government work.' The last thought would prove to be wishful thinking.

His departure from City Hall coincided with Jennifer Arcuri's exit. Their last meeting was at his house. 'I'll see you later,' she said stepping into the street and without revealing her decision to move on. Wanting a child, she had found her future husband and they moved to Cheshire. Soon pregnant, she decided there would be closure and blocked his calls. 'I assumed that Boris would stay married,' she would say, 'and I made sure he wasn't caught.' His last text message would be sent on 29 December 2018. 'I miss you and I need you,' he'd write. She deleted the text. Silently, a passionate relationship ended.

On his last day as mayor in May 2016, Boris opened the cycle superhighway along the Victoria Embankment. Smiling as he watched the first bikes zoom along, a Lycra-clad cyclist shouted at him, 'You're a prick.' Then he had lunch with Lynton Crosby, the architect of his election victory in 2008. Uppermost in their minds was the next leadership campaign. What about a book about his achievements as mayor? he was asked. 'I don't believe in booster-ism,' he replied. Back full-time in Westminster, Boris's first task would be to build support among Tory MPs.

Chapter 20

'He's ruined my life'

The exchange in the House of Commons chamber in late 2015 was quintessential Westminster politics. The Tory benches were packed for the weekly Prime Minister's Questions. Boris had just asked David Cameron a forgettable question and received an innocuous reply. The backbencher sat down, pleased to have reminded the prime minister of his presence. As Boris waited for the session to end, Bernard Jenkin, a Tory MP since 1992 and prominent Eurosceptic, turned and asked, 'What are you going to do?' referring to the referendum.

'I'm not a quitter,' replied Boris. Jenkin believed him.

Around the same time, Boris had told Len Duvall 'I'm marginally for staying.' Both politicians believed that Boris would support Cameron to remain in the EU. The in-out referendum was due on 23 June 2016. Remain had a substantial lead over Leave. The unanswered question was the Labour Party's position under Jeremy Corbyn.

Since 2009, Boris's attitude towards Europe had been clear and principled. As an internationalist and European, he was appalled by EU federalism and the Brussels bureaucrats. He wanted Cameron to renegotiate the terms of Britain's EU membership and submit the result to a referendum. As a long-term Eurosceptic, he was sympathetic to the complaints of the hard-line Tory critics but not, critically, to their ultimate ambition of leaving the EU regardless of any new agreement. The crunch meeting was on 18 February 2016, the deadline for Cameron and the EU to finalise the renegotiated terms of Britain's membership. That would be the basis of the referendum.

Among the many seeking to influence Boris was Anthony Kenny, the Oxford philosopher and former master of Balliol: 'I write to you now because at this moment you are in a remarkably influential position. Whatever happens at this week's summit, the PM is bound to say that he has achieved a great deal, and the Eurosceptics will say that it is not enough. You are one of the very few people whose personal decision could affect the outcome. You are respected by both parties to the debate, and you have kept your stance impartial between them both. Please use your influence in favour of a vote to remain.' Prophetically, Kenny urged Boris not to associate with the 'populist and xenophobe tabloid' Brexiteers. 'Remember your Europhile youth,' he concluded. Unusually for Boris, the letter remained unanswered.

In his pledge on 23 January 2013, Cameron had declared that a referendum by the end of 2017 would be about a 'full-on treaty change'. The Commons voted in 2015 by 544 to 53 in favour of a referendum and all three major national parties campaigned in that year's election to implement the referendum result. The unravelling began with the final deal Cameron presented to Parliament in February 2016.

On every issue in the draft deal, Cameron had failed. France and the Euro MEPs were blocking meaningful concessions. Worse, contrary to Merkel's explicit promises in April 2013 to Cameron during a family weekend in Schloss Meseberg, her official country residence outside Berlin, the German Chancellor at a critical moment had refused to support Britain. The result was dire for Cameron. Europe's leaders refused to substantially change migrants' welfare rights, limit the European Court of Justice's infringement of Britain's sovereignty and respect Britain's veto over ever closer union. Cameron had been outwitted, even betrayed, by Merkel. These were not the 'fundamental' changes which Cameron had promised in 2015. 'It's a crap deal,' Ed Llewellyn, Cameron's chief of staff and a friend from Eton, told Rodney Leach, a leading Eurosceptic, at an Open Europe dinner. 'The dilemma in a nutshell', wrote Boris, was the EU's refusal to reform. Staying in a reformed EU would be good, he continued, but to escape an increasingly federal Europe where Britain was constantly outvoted was the alternative for 'a great future outside'.

Fearing Boris's opposition could be fatal, Cameron invited him for a game of tennis at the American ambassador's residence in Regent's Park in the last week of February. Cameron described Boris's tennis as 'aggressive, wildly unorthodox . . . and extremely competitive'. Jonathan Marland, an old ally, was less complimentary, and could have been describing more than just his game: 'Keen but not very good. He runs everywhere, chases every ball, has bad footwork and occasionally serves underarm to make a good shot look effortless.'

In their conversation after their match, Cameron acknowledged that Boris might find the negotiations were 'disappointing' but urged him to support Remain to allow a 'fight for more change in the future'. If he supported the government, suggested Cameron, Boris was promised a key job in the government, probably Defence. Cameron could not grasp the consequence of his failed negotiations. 'I'm deeply conflicted,' Boris told journalists and promised to 'come off the fence with deafening eclat'.

Just before that tennis match, Boris had met Lynton Crosby, Jonathan Marland and Eddie Lister, now employed by Marland in a property development company, for dinner in the alcove of 'M', a restaurant in Victoria Street. The Brexit campaign, he was told, needed him as a leader. 'It will show the difference between you and Dave,' said Crosby. 'You're the next leader after Dave.' Conflicted, Boris said: 'I'm not going to do it. I can take Dave and George down anytime.' Interrupted by bottles of champagne sent over by other admiring diners, the conversation ended after four hours with no resolution. Boris, Crosby decided, could be persuaded but he would need Marina's approval.

Boris had not resolved his dilemma when, shortly after the EU summit, Iain Duncan Smith, a veteran leading Eurosceptic, spoke to Cameron in Downing Street.

Duncan Smith had watched Cameron and Osborne rush, botch

and misjudge the negotiations. On civil servants' advice, they had restricted their demands to what they were told was possible, and even they were rejected. Neither really understood the EU's historic intransigence or their own MPs' opposition to the deal. In the class divide which characterised the debate within the Tory Party – the Notting Hill Gate leadership versus the red-brick arrivistes – Cameron relied on Ed Llewellyn to report on the mood of Tory MPs. But Llewellyn rarely spoke to MPs. He preferred to relay what Cameron wanted to hear. And that week, he confirmed Cameron's belief that Boris, the metropolitan moderniser, would not want to associate with right-wing proselytisers like Bernard Jenkin, Bill Cash and Iain Duncan Smith. Boris, Llewellyn was convinced, could be persuaded to support Cameron. That reassurance inspired Cameron's reply to the warning from Ken Clarke, the veteran Tory former minister and Remainer. Clarke foresaw that Cameron could lose the referendum: 'Don't worry Ken, I always win.' Llewellyn had failed to report that the majority of Tory MPs either supported Leave or were undecided. Duncan Smith surprisingly also urged caution. 'You don't need to hurry,' he told Cameron. 'You have another year to say to the EU "Give us a better deal".'

'I'm not prepared to let this issue dominate my legacy,' Cameron replied.

'You'll be astonished by the emotional outbreak the referendum will have,' warned Duncan Smith.

Cameron dismissed the advice.

'Cameron's drunk his own Kool-Aid,' Duncan Smith told his fellow Eurosceptics. Having won the Scottish referendum, the prime minister believed that he could win again. He was a lucky man. Blessed by family wealth, a good education, a happy marriage and natural charm, Cameron had slain his foes – Gordon Brown, Ed Miliband, and was now trumping Jeremy Corbyn. Neither Cameron nor his advisers could anticipate a potential leader of the Brexit campaign. Relying on Crosby's assurance that Michael Gove was unelectable as Tory leader, Cameron firmly believed Gove's repeated assurances despite being a well-known Eurosceptic. 'I won't campaign against you,' Gove promised. He relied on similar promises about Gove from Sarah Vine, Gove's wife and a *Daily Mail* columnist.

'What do you think Michael will do?' Boris asked Oliver Letwin, the Old Etonian Eurosceptic. Gove's position, Letwin acknowledged, was truly important for Cameron. As close friends, Cameron expected Gove to place loyalty above ideology and support Remain. 'I feel the same,' Letwin told Boris. Despite being a lifelong Eurosceptic, Letwin could not bring himself to vote against Cameron. 'I'll live with the deal,' Letwin said. Most commentators assumed that Boris would also support Remain. Similarly, Cameron made the same assumption. That certainty was shaken when, to his surprise, Marina spelled out the case against Europe in a well-argued article in the *Spectator*.

The lawyer focused on the European Court of Justice. Cameron's deal, she wrote, 'raises more questions than [it answers]'. In plain prose, she described two identical and phoney promises. Both Blair in 2007 after the Lisbon treaty was agreed and Ken Clarke in 2011 as Justice Secretary had assured Parliament that the European Court of Justice could not enforce the European Charter of Fundamental Rights on Britain. The opposite, Marina wrote, had happened. Contrary to their express assurances, British employment, immigration and asylum laws had been overruled. Acting capriciously, the European Court had thwarted Acts of Parliament and crushed British sovereignty. Cameron's proposed deal did not reverse the court's opaque and uncontrolled accumulation of power against which there was no appeal. Those close to Boris would say that Marina's article and their conversations had a profound influence on him.

Ever since he had witnessed Margaret Thatcher being handbagged in Rome in 1990, Boris had argued for a legal guarantee of Parliament's sovereignty. Over twenty-five years, there had been repeated examples of British influence in the EU being eroded. The latest was the 'Five Presidents' Report' written to save the euro. Britain would be outvoted 27 to 1 and thus was unable to veto centralised EU economic decisions even if they damaged British interests.

Greece's plight had intensified Boris's antagonism towards the EU. His love for the country, not only through his study of ancient Greece but from the many holidays he spent in his father's house on the Pelion peninsula, had intensified his shock about what he regarded as a conspiracy between the European Commission, the European Bank, Goldman Sachs and the German government to protect the euro at Greece's expense. Consequently, 40 per cent of young Greeks were unemployed. Seeing their suffering led to a Damascene conversion towards Boris favouring Leave. This influenced his discussions with Oliver Letwin, Cameron's intermediary.

'What can you do to bring Boris round?' Cameron asked Letwin. Boris was invited to Downing Street to discuss a bill to enshrine Britain's sovereignty into law. The principal issue for Boris, Letwin discovered, was to define the relationship between Britain and the European Court of Justice. How, Boris wanted to know, could British courts prevent 'ever closer union'? In the course of five meetings, Boris, advised by Martin Howe, a lawyer specialising in EU law, debated the precise words of a new law empowering British courts to reject the European Court's rulings and interpretation of treaties. Letwin, by turns charming and emotional, did not give up, but to no avail. 'I don't think there's much there,' Boris reported to friends. The obstacle, as Cameron acknowledged, was that each time Letwin and Boris agreed the terms, Whitehall's Europhile lawyers 'kept watering down the wording' to protect the European Court. Cameron weakly refused to overrule the officials, a familiar predicament throughout Britain's membership of the EU. In the countdown to the official launch of campaigning on the referendum, Boris's imminent decision became crucial.

In one last attempt, Letwin called Boris at home on Tuesday evening, 16 February. To his surprise, Boris was eating a dinner of slow-roasted lamb with Gove and Sarah Vine. With a government lawyer on speakerphone, they discussed once again Britain's sovereignty: could the European Court overrule Cameron's deal on migrant rights? 'Boris was agitated, genuinely tortured as to which way to go,' reported Vine. Letwin noted the opposite. During their conversation, the inflections of Boris's voice suggested that he was considering his own and not Britain's interests, and that was Leave. Letwin's next call was to Cameron. Boris and Gove are together, he reported. That was, he concluded, a game-changer. He was unaware that Evgeny Lebedev was also at the dinner. The son of a former KGB officer who had been close to the Kremlin, was an intimate observer of a British government crisis.

Cameron, the architect of the crisis, was struggling to find a solution. Gove was a close friend (they were godfathers to each other's children), but he had fired Gove as Education Secretary in July 2014 on Lynton Crosby's advice that Gove was unpopular with the electorate. Gove was outraged that his success against the teachers' unions should be rewarded by Cameron's disloyalty. As for Boris, Cameron could not believe that Marina's legal arguments had conclusively swung her husband against the deal. The truth would probably never be known but that is what the eyewitnesses in Islington were reporting. The danger, Cameron feared, was Boris as a Leaver. He would 'legitimise the cause and help detoxify the Brexit brand'.

Cameron's disbelief that Boris could be guided by principles was shared by the *Guardian*. Just as Zoe Williams predicted in 2008 that London would be destroyed by Boris as mayor, Rafael Behr accused Boris of 'cunning and cowardice' to suggest he faced a dilemma. As a pro-EU politician, wrote Behr, Boris 'recognises that complete severance is neither possible nor desirable ... The unappealing alternative is diminished status as a quitter and saboteur.' Boris, Behr concluded, 'does not want to be on the side of the mavericks and also-rans'. His ambition would 'not trump belief' just 'to reap the career dividend'. Boris would choose, Behr concluded, to remain in the EU although the idea that Boris's 'opinion matters at all ... is absurd'. Underestimating Boris had become a media illness.

Over the following hours, Boris was bombarded by messages and telephone calls, especially from the group of MPs organising his leadership bid. In an email, Ben Wallace warned Boris that support for Leave would class him with 'a cast of clowns' including Nigel Farage, and would damage his chance of becoming leader.

Jake Berry also urged him to support Remain. If Boris campaigned for Leave and Remain won, Berry warned, 'you won't recover'. Not all the Brexiteers were fans. Bernard Jenkin told a newspaper: 'He's dishonest, a philanderer and unpredictable.' If Boris became leader, he added, he 'would be a disaster'.

During conversations with allies on the morning of 17 February, Boris sounded to Berry 'genuinely torn. His desire was to be loyal to Cameron but he genuinely believed in Leave.' Their conversations were interrupted by a summons to Downing Street.

Cameron was baffled, even angry when Boris arrived. One of the prime minister's weaknesses was to project his own values onto others, a failing he later admitted. Convinced he understood Boris, he interpreted his rival's motives as political calculation rather than principle. Boris, he believed, was primarily motivated by 'the best outcome for him'. Boris would not want to risk Gove usurping his bid for the crown. With Leave certain to lose, Cameron suspected that Boris would take 'a risk-free bet on himself' and, 'making doubly sure he would be the next leader', would go for Leave. Even if Remain won, Boris would be the champion of the party's Leavers, a majority of party members. And, in Cameron's opinion, if Leave won, Boris expected to renegotiate a better deal with the EU. Either way, it was win-win.

Pertinently, Cameron failed to understand how Boris in recent years had learned to deliberately conceal his lodestar. As a loner, his character had become impenetrable to other men. He revealed his true feelings only to a few selected women, namely Marina and his secret girlfriends. Accordingly, during their forty-minute conversation, Cameron dismissed Boris's despair about Greece as irrelevant. In trying to persuade Boris to support the deal, Cameron did not mention the economic and social advantages of EU membership, especially for the City's access to the single market. The conversation focused on the unaccountable power of Brussels and the European Court. 'People want to feel they have control,' said Boris. Fifty-nine per cent of British laws are EU regulations and directives, he added. No, countered Cameron, 'It's just 15 per cent.' Nevertheless, Cameron promised, Parliament would enact a bill to allow Westminster and the British Supreme Court to over-rule Brussels and the European Court. Cameron's proposal did not alter the supremacy of Brussels. As a final throw, Cameron promised that after Remain won, he would appoint Boris as the Foreign Secretary. 'No deal as far as I know,' said Boris as he left Downing Street.

Soon after, Boris called Gerard Lyons, his economic adviser. Usually their conversations lasted two minutes but this one continued for fifty minutes. Methodically, Boris recited each argument made by Cameron to support Remain. On each point, Lyons gave the rebuttal – 'I hit a six on everyone,' he would later say. 'Exactly,' Boris exclaimed at the end of their conversation, convinced by the Leave argument. 'Why don't you write two articles,' Lyons suggested. 'One for Remain and one to Leave, and at the end you'll see that Leave is right.' 'Exactly,' Boris repeated.

Two days later, Gove declared that he would campaign to leave. Cameron was horrified. A real friend had forsaken their friendship and lied to him. All eyes swung onto Boris, the stardust in any campaign. Although the polls showed that Remain's lead was 15 per cent, the polls also reported that Boris was the key to Cameron's certain victory. The arch-Brexiteers including Bill Cash and Iain Duncan Smith had no contact with Boris but both did expect him to join their cause. They wrongly assumed that unlike Gove, Boris did not meet Cameron and Osborne socially and the same dilemma would not arise. The following day, Boris drove to his Oxfordshire house to write the two articles.

Boris had reached a Thatcher moment. For years he had praised her for showing absolute ruthlessness in defence of British interests: dispatching the Royal Navy to liberate the Falkland Islands in 1982, confronting the Marxist-led miners in 1984, and abolishing the socialist state economy. 'She was a liberator,' Boris later wrote. Her opponents were intellectually thrashed. To survive, the rival parties had changed their names to New Labour and Liberal Democrats. Boris lauded her bravery to break 'the conspiracy by cowardly politicians to dodge the hard questions'. She did not fear dividing the people or her party. Few other British politicians would have quoted

Samuel Johnson to argue the cause of liberal capitalism: 'How small, of all that human hearts endure, / That part which laws or kings can cause or cure.'

Some would say that Thatcher defined herself by choosing her enemies. Boris was not in that league. He disliked confrontation and was more sensitive to criticism of himself. Unlike Thatcher, he did not invite critics into his inner circle in order to thrash out ideological positions. That did not mean that his antagonism to the EU was not ideological. It was, but he needed to write it down to be certain.

During Saturday, writing the two articles, Boris was in constant contact with Cameron about British sovereignty. 'It looks like Out,' said Cameron reading a message on his BlackBerry. Another message suggested Boris felt tortured and feared he would be crucified by the 'hate machine' but he would 'go with his heart' although Leave would lose. Late that night, Cameron had new hope that Boris might after all decide to remain. Boris is 'genuinely in turmoil', concluded Craig Oliver, Cameron's director of communications. In Cameron's opinion, Boris 'seemed to change his mind substantially at least twice' and he had told a journalist that he was 'veering all over the place like a broken shopping trolley'.

As he wrote the Remain article favouring loyalty to the party, he later explained, it 'came down overwhelmingly in favour of leaving. I then thought I'd better see if I can make the alternative case for myself so I then wrote a sort of semi-parodic article in the opposite sense.' Set side by side, Leave was 'blindingly obvious'. The Remain article 'stuck in my craw to write'. On Cameron's deal with the EU, he said 'We got absolutely zilch, effectively.' The two articles were sent to Will Walden and Ben Wallace. 'It's not worth the paper it was written on,' he told Walden about the Remain article. 'This is going to make me vomit. I just don't think it's good enough.'

On Sunday morning, Rachel Johnson arrived to read the articles. As a Remainer, she asked him 'Why would you want to associate yourself with Farage and Brexit types?' Boris replied that any decision would be dictated by what was right and not his ambition. Moreover, while he believed the opinion polls pointed conclusively to a Remain win, Cameron's failure to get a deal had finally converted him to become a Leaver. Holding a referendum is what he had said since 2009. He was consistent. Throughout his life he had gambled – either for his career or with women. This time, the stakes certainly appeared high, but either way he felt he had little to lose. With that, after lunch – burned lasagne – he drove back to London.

'Al is about to do something stupid,' Rachel told Guto Harri, who was abroad skiing. 'You're the only person who can stop him.'

'I'm still deciding,' Boris told Harri a few minutes later.

'Are you happy to be known for the rest of your life as the fellow traveller of [John] Redwood and [Bill] Cash?' asked Harri. 'You can lead Europe rather than leave Europe. You'd be doing something for the wrong reason.'

Subsequently, Boris told Harri that his call had been counterproductive: 'You pushed me because you suggested that Britain could not stand alone, and that's a defeatist attitude I reject. We're a great country. Britain should believe in self-rule.'

At 4.40 p.m. on Sunday afternoon Boris texted Cameron that Brexit would be 'crushed like the toad beneath the harrow' (an adaptation of a line from Kipling), and 'It's not about you, it's about doing the right thing.'

At 4.49 p.m., Jake Berry called again to urge Boris to side with Remain. 'Too late,' said Will Walden. 'He's just gone outside to say Leave.'

In the scrum outside his house, the snatches caught by the media of Boris's announcement that he would join the Leave campaign included, 'The last thing I wanted was to go against David Cameron . . . once in a lifetime chance to end the erosion of democracy . . . I want a better deal for the people of this country, to save them money and to take back control . . . people are enraged by the inability of British politicians to control immigration.'

'He'll need balls of steel,' Rachel texted Marina. 'A careershattering move,' Stanley puffed. In Boris's mind, he was the decisive politician at a defining moment in the battle between the people and the elite. 'I accept there will be a risk,' he had written in his Leave article, 'This is the moment to be brave – not to hug the skirts of the Nurse in Brussels.'

'He's ruined my life,' Cameron was heard to say. Cameron and Letwin were certain about his motives: Boris was thinking what was best for Boris. 'He always thinks how do I get some advantage out of this?' Letwin mused. Politicians, Letwin believed, were bound to consult their own interests but should also think what is the right thing to do. Boris was not part of the team and therefore did not consider compromise. His leadership ambitions were at the heart of that decision. Cameron agreed. Boris was an opportunist. He did not believe that erecting tariffs against the EU would benefit Britain. He supported Leave to advance his own career, Letwin believed.

On Monday 22 February, Boris's article in favour of Leave was published in the *Daily Telegraph*. Many realised that it could change the course of Britain's history.

The same morning, Boris was shocked to find crowds seething with hatred outside his front door. Curses were yelled at him. As he cycled away, he looked hurt. Later he would say the abuse was 'water off a duck's back', but that was untrue. His destination was a meeting of the London Enterprise Panel. He was visibly surprised by the businessmen's frosty reception. Unanimously, he was criticised as an opportunist. The businessmen who highlighted his constant praise of London as the centre of Europe were shrugged off. He departed without making any attempt to justify himself.

Overnight, his enemies had lined up – especially at *The Times* – to demolish the man. Leading the pack was Jenni Russell. Characterising Boris as a bad-tempered, deceitful, failed mayor whose only successes – the bikes and Crossrail – were inherited from Livingstone, Russell lambasted what she said was his failure to build any homes and wondered how he hoped to get deals with Putin and the EU if he was beaten by the RMT union. As a passionate Remainer, Russell appeared to be particularly outraged that Boris had told unnamed 'friends' that he would support Remain, which proved his inability to 'distinguish truth from fantasy'.

'I know for a fact he's not an Outer,' raged Nicholas Soames, 'because he told me.' Cameron, he suggested, should treat Boris like a growling Alsatian and 'kick it really hard in the balls, in which case it will run away'. In similar apoplexy, Michael Heseltine attacked Boris for destroying the City and jobs.

That afternoon in the Commons, Cameron asked peevishly how the City's champion could destroy that golden egg. Boris's notion, mocked Cameron, of new negotiations followed by a second referendum was 'one for the birds'. 'Rubbish,' retorted Boris, already 2/1 favourite as next prime minister. Cameron's anger was personal. 'I've known a number of couples who have begun divorce proceedings. But I don't know any who have begun divorce proceedings in order to renew their marriage vows.' Amid the laughter, Boris puffed, shook his head and waved off an attack on a position he had long abandoned. In the aftermath, some criticised Cameron for 'bigging up' Boris.

Convinced that Leave would lose and he would play only a minor role in the referendum campaign, Boris was 'downbeat' in conversations with friends. But since he was committed to Leave, he refused to countenance defeat. That was his special quality: his determination to smash down the most intimidating wall. He summoned his self-belief: 'We can win.'

Boris's prospects rose after the resignation of Iain Duncan Smith as Secretary of State for Work and Pensions on 18 March. George Osborne was blamed by Duncan Smith for cutting welfare benefits, hurting the poor and helping the rich. In reply, Osborne highlighted contradictions in Duncan Smith's protests and accused the Eurosceptic of incompetence during his six years as the minister. Boris supported Duncan Smith. In the climax of the Tory Party's defining battle, Osborne revealed their rivalry. In an after-dinner speech, he mentioned an exchange between Boris and George W. Bush. Spotting that Boris was wearing a watch with Che Guevara's image on its face, the president chided, 'Boris, in Texas we execute people who wear Che Guevara watches.' Osborne jibed, 'Unfortunately Bush was bluffing.' With the Chancellor's leadership hopes faded, the public scrutiny of Boris intensified. The first venue was at Westminster's Treasury Select Committee, chaired by Tory MP Andrew Tyrie.

Boris repeated his line that 59 per cent of British laws emanated from Brussels. 'This is all very interesting, Boris,' said Tyrie. 'Except none of it is true.' The committee focused on his claim that an EU regulation had banned the recycling of teabags. 'Can you remember which country asked the EU to issue it?' asked John Mann, the Labour MP. Boris looked baffled. 'It was Britain,' said Mann, explaining it was part of the anti-foot-and-mouth regulations imposed in 2002. Boris replied, astonished: 'Then I'm sure the French have never obeyed it.' Carelessly, he threw in that the EU forbade sales of bananas in bunches of three. The EU edict said four bananas, a silly mistake by a tabloid journalist clearly not concerned that his enemies would highlight any slip. The MPs concluded that Boris's only consistency was his inconsistency. He also adopted an old habit of speaking without pause, with the odd joke thrown in, to delay their questions. Following that disastrous performance, he fell into more traps in bruising TV interviews. 'This is very hard, very hard,' he confessed to an MP.

His car-crash appearances led to *The Times* renewing their attack, this time by Matthew Parris. Appalled that Boris was playing to win, Parris, who had been a *Spectator* columnist during Boris's editorship, wrote 'Where else in politics can such self-validating, self-inflating nonsense be found that Britain could ever want Boris Johnson as prime minister? . . . There's a pattern to Boris's life: it's the casual dishonesty, the cruelty, the betrayal and beneath the betrayal, the emptiness of real ambition: the ambition to do anything useful with office once it is attained.' Parris's evidence for that damnation was 'almost no mayoral achievements at all'. He concluded, 'If Mr Johnson had the sense of nemesis I suspect he has, he should stop now.' Fearful that the Brexiteers would destroy moderate Conservatism and hand the party to right-wingers, Parris saw in the 'zealots a streak of madness'. Four days later, walking in St James's, Jake Berry spotted in a window a quote by Pericles: 'Freedom is the sure possession of those alone who have the courage to defend it.' He sent Boris a copy of the quotation.

In the battle of Boris's reputation, his old friend Petronella Wyatt was lured to defend her ex's 'gamble of his career'. Boris, she wrote, 'isn't lazy. The suggestion is preposterous . . . Boris works hard.' He was also 'entirely without malice [and] both soulful and a man of strong beliefs' blighted only by occasional 'erratic judgement'. But, she did admit, 'he will do anything to avoid an argument, which leads to a degree of duplicity . . . His untruths are generally harmless and get him into more trouble than the person he directs them at.' She concluded that his ambition to be prime minister was motivated by a desire to be loved by more people.

To his critics' fury, the greater the attack, the more popular he became. After letting the criticism 'kick around in his head', as Will Walden observed, he did not dwell on his plight but simply moved on. The critics underestimated his credibility among electors, and his resolve. In retaliation, Boris became emboldened and personal. Cameron and the pro-EU campaigners, he said, were the 'Gerald Ratners' of British politics. (In a self-destructive joke in 1991, Ratner had said in a speech to his employees and others that some of the products his company sold were 'total crap'.) During April, the Remainers' worst fears materialised. Trust in Cameron plummeted among Tory voters and the referendum's outcome became less certain.

In desperation, Cameron asked President Obama to visit London and warn about the dire consequences if Britain voted Leave. Boris's favourite American politician was Ronald Reagan, a conservative former actor with a winning, folksy manner. In 2008, Boris had supported Obama as the next president because 'He visibly incarnates change and hope' in the wake of the Iraq War and the banking crisis. But eight years later after a disappointing Obama presidency Boris concluded that Obama was fluent but phoney. Introducing Obama into the debate, exploded Boris, was a 'piece of outrageous and exorbitant hypocrisy' because America refuses to 'kneel to almost any kind of international jurisdiction'. America would never accept rule by the EU. One week later, Boris attacked Obama again for having removed Churchill's bust from the Oval Office and returning it to the British Embassy. 'Some said it was a snub to Britain,' complained Boris. 'Some said it was a symbol of the part-Kenyan president's ancestral dislike of the British Empire.' In his autobiography written in 1995, Obama had criticised the imprisonment of his Kenyan grandfather by the British colonial administration. Nicholas Soames carped that Boris's 'deeply offensive' remarks showed 'remarkable disregard for the facts, the truth and for all judgement'. Boris, he declared, was unfit to be prime minister. John McDonnell, the senior Labour politician, called it 'dog-whistle racism', and Andrew Gimson, Boris's biographer, denounced 'a disaster for Boris because Obama is pro-British'.

Obama was furious. He had replaced Churchill with a bust of Martin Luther King, appropriate for America's first black president. But there was another Churchill bust in his private quarters. 'I love the guy,' he said.

To Cameron's delight, during his visit to Britain, the president warned that if Britain left the EU, the country would wait ten years 'at the back of the queue' in the trade negotiations with the USA. In another setback for Leave, President Macron of France sniped that outside the EU, the UK would be reduced to the status of Jersey and Guernsey. The putative Leave campaign could not produce a single report proving that Britain would be richer outside the EU. 'The Remainers think the game is over,' snapped Boris, and have 'bombed us into submission . . . They are crowing too soon.'

Boris was right. Leave supporters were repelled by Obama's interference and believed that the president disliked colonial Britain. The 'racist' jibe against Boris was bogus. The next polls showed an increase of support for Leave and more trust in Boris. 'We'll win,' Boris texted Jake Berry. The MP went immediately to William Hill and bet on Leave at 5/2.

Two months into the campaign, Boris was in full flow. At the outset, he had assumed a minor role but Leave's organisers deployed him as their front man. On the stump, in town centres, Boris was gold dust. 'Like taking Harry Styles into the school yard,' swooned Nigel Adams, a Tory MP. Unexpectedly popular in the north, he appealed to Labour voters to break the deadlock. 'What's it like driving Boris round?' an MP asked the driver of Leave's battle bus. 'It's like going around with Beyoncé,' he replied.

Standing by the side of a bright red bus covered with the slogan 'We send the EU £350 million a week. Let's fund our NHS instead', Boris adored the adulation. He knew the Remainers' protests about the inaccuracy of '£350 million' were justified. That was a gross figure ignoring the money returned to Britain by the EU. The net payment to the EU estimated by the Treasury for 2015 varied between £160 million and £248 million a week. Even Iain Duncan Smith and Andrea Leadsom, a Brexiteer MP, disapproved of the slogan. 'I will not campaign on a lie,' protested Leadsom. But Boris cared only about winning and expected others to follow. After watching David Davis tell a televised parliamentary committee 'I've never used that figure,' Boris immediately texted the Brexiteer, 'Dont dis the Leave campaign'. Hyperbole stole the oxygen from the Remainers' arguments. The battleground was cleared against a foe without anyone equal to Boris to argue their case. During a conversation with Gove, Boris agreed to intensify the pressure. The issues would be immigration and the single market.

In mid-May, the Office of National Statistics revealed that between 2010 and 2015, possibly 1.4 million more migrants had settled in Britain from the EU than the 1 million they had registered, making the official total 2.4 million. Even that was a considerable underestimate according to Migration Watch, the lobby group. In 2015, 630,000 migrants had arrived in Britain, including 77,000 from the EU without a job. The backdrop to the record net increase of 333,000 migrants arriving in Britain that year was the daily media footage of thousands of young Africans being pulled out of the Mediterranean and taken to Italy after their small boats sank. Thousands of others were crossing from Turkey to Greece. Theoretically, all of them could eventually be eligible to live in Britain. Recalling Tony Blair's deceit which admitted millions of migrants after 1997, Boris accused Cameron of equal 'terrible dishonesty' and the 'corrosion of popular trust in democracy' by claiming he would cut immigration to 'tens of thousands'. 'It's depressing beyond belief,' said Cameron, insulted by the slur against his integrity. 'Deeply maddening.'

In the exchange of insults in interviews and open letters, Boris accused Cameron's descriptions of the single market as 'increasingly fraudulent' while Cameron called a vote against the EU 'immoral' and likely to trigger 'war'. In what Boris called 'Project

Fear', Cameron approved the Treasury's forecast that Brexit would cost Britain 820,000 jobs in the first two years, the pound would drop 15 per cent, house prices would fall by 18 per cent and GDP decrease by 6 per cent. Boris called that forecast 'scaremongering' because there were 'no good economic arguments' against Brexit. On the instructions of Leave's strategist, Dominic Cummings, Boris avoided offering a detailed economic argument in favour of Brexit.

Iain Duncan Smith had been the first Tory to spot Cummings' abilities. In January 2002, after a brief spell as a would-be entrepreneur in Moscow, Cummings became Duncan Smith's director of strategy at Business for Sterling, a lobby group opposed to the euro. Their relationship collapsed after eight months and Cummings departed. He redeemed himself by organising the successful opposition to Labour's proposal for regional governments. Then, as chief of staff to Gove both as Shadow education minister and later in the Department of Education, he challenged the left-wing educational establishment's belief that schools should be vehicles for social engineering rather than to champion excellence in classrooms. Running the department as an autonomous wing of the government, Cummings redesigned the education curriculum and planned to expand the number of academies and set up free schools. Exposure to incompetent and lazy civil servants turned him into a coruscating opponent of Whitehall's 'dodgy accountancy' and their officials' failure to manage projects. He also scoffed at Cameron who, in response to Cummings' personal aggression, labelled him a 'career psychopath'. With an impassioned sense of vengeance, he became Leave's strategist and turned the tables on Cameron. His slogan 'Take Back Control' was hailed as the game-changer but his personality deterred many Tory Brexiteers joining Leave's campaign. Boris took the opposite view. Cummings had qualities he admired. In particular he liked Cummings' advice to avoid difficult arguments. Leavers, said Cummings, were under no obligation to produce a post-Brexit scenario. 'Creating an exit plan that makes sense,' wrote Cummings, 'and which all reasonable people could unite around seems an almost insuperable task . . . There is so much to be gained by swerving the whole issue . . . The sheer complexity of leaving would involve endless questions of detail that cannot be answered in such a place even were it to be 20,000 pages long, and the longer it is, the more errors are likely.' That was exactly Boris's criticism of Blair's invasion of Iraq – that there was no plan for the aftermath and the result was catastrophic. But like Blair before the invasion, Cummings' advice to say as little as possible suited Boris. Brexit's advantages were restricted to slogans – except when Boris approved a nuclear option.

To halt more refugees coming to Europe, Angela Merkel had offered Turkey visa-free access to the Schengen area. On that basis, Vote Leave warned that 77 million Turks could come to Britain if their country joined the EU. Cameron was outraged. Boris knew that Turkey had no chance of joining the EU, not least because Britain could veto Turkey's accession. Moreover, in 2008 Boris had made a TV documentary which advocated Turkey's accession to the EU. In combination with the Leave slogans 'Take Back Control' and 'We want our country back', the campaign was pitched against immigration. Nigel Farage entered the fray. Standing by a poster headed 'Breaking Point', the photo showed thousands of swarthy migrants walking across fields. Although Farage was not part of the official Leave campaign, Boris did not protest. He was now damned for leading a right-wing nationalist, populist movement. Boris would dispute that immigration had become the key issue. Rather, he said, it was about 'control' – the sense that British democracy was being undermined by the EU.

Remarkably, in the midst of their bitter war, Cameron appeared at the London Transport Museum to celebrate the end of Boris's mayoralty. Surrounded by a collection of old buses, Cameron spoke warmly of his rival and mentioned their struggle on the floor in Downing Street over the briefing paper. 'That came as a great surprise to my PPS [principal private secretary],' said Cameron, 'who walked in to find two grown-up men wrestling on the floor.' He added, 'I'm not quite sure who got the piece of paper.' 'I did,' Boris yelled. In his speech, Boris acknowledged he had not been Cameron's favourite candidate to be mayor and relations had not always been perfect. Glancing at Cameron, he allowed a pause for laughter. No one would have guessed that the two were immersed in a struggle to decide the country's future.

After the speeches, the two spoke briefly. Cameron's hope that the referendum would unify a modernised party had failed, yet he was encouraged by Andrew Cooper, his pollster and co-founder of Populus, that Remain would win 59 per cent of the vote. Cooper had also predicted that Cameron would lose the 2015 election. Boris began to doubt Cooper's figures, which aligned with Lynton Crosby's prediction that Remain would win. Outside London, Boris had discovered, Cameron had misjudged the electorate and the working class trusted him more than Cameron. They were not moved by Cameron's warning that leaving the EU would cost Britons money. Either they were prepared to suffer the loss or had no money to lose.

Tapping into working-class anger against the elite, especially Goldman Sachs and the other Wall Street banks who urged Britain to remain, Boris reminded his audiences that the fat cats did not face the overcrowding in the NHS and schools, or suffer from overcrowded homes and low wages, because of immigration. In tabloid language, he ratcheted up the vitriol by drawing historical comparisons to EU officials in Brussels seeking to unify Europe: 'Napoleon, Hitler tried this out, and it ends tragically. The EU is an attempt to do this by different methods.' Once again, the Boris haters sprayed their scorn. Boris has 'gone too far', snarled Nicholas Soames. Boris's 'preposterous, obscene political remarks', said Heseltine, meant he would be 'very surprised' if Boris ever became prime minister. Martin Selmayr, Jean-Claude Juncker's German chief of staff, described the prospect of Boris as prime minister as a 'horror scenario', like Trump and Marie Le Pen as possible leaders. Others called Boris 'desperate and offensive'.

'It's an artificial media twit storm,' replied Boris, adding to the opprobrium after reading that prosecutors in Germany had indicted a local comedian for accusing Recep Erdogan, Turkey's leader, of bestiality. In a limerick, Boris ridiculed Erdogan: 'There was a young fellow from Ankara / Who was a terrific wankerer / Till he sowed his wild oats / With the help of a goat / But he didn't even stop to thankera.' Boris would win a £1,000 prize for the poem in a *Spectator* competition.

In the closing weeks before the vote, politics became dirtier, even venal. As Boris became the linchpin of the Leave campaign, unethical personalities in the Remain camp sought revenge against a man they reviled as an unprincipled, opportunist turncoat. To take down the star of the show, a wholly untrue story was spread that Boris was very close to the drunken female barrister who had been caught the previous summer in a daytime clinch with a fellow lawyer under a bridge near Waterloo station. Marina, who is not a serious drinker, knew precisely the source of that lie: 'It's a Downing Street black ops,' she confidently told her friends.

The nastiness became blatant. A TV audience mauled Cameron as a 'hypocrite' and 'scaremonger' for praising the EU's contribution to Britain's prosperity. In retaliation, John Major screeched on TV: Boris 'is a court jester' leading a 'fundamentally dishonest … squalid campaign'. Moments later, Boris sat in the same TV studio chair. He refused to engage in 'blue-on-blue' soap opera to question Major's credentials – a prime minister who in 1997 left behind a wrecked party, and who launched a moralistic 'Back to Basics' campaign having secretly enjoyed an adulterous affair. The vitriol intensified in a TV debate just days before the vote. Boris was pitched alongside five women politicians. The poison was spread by three women opponents led by Amber Rudd, a plausible and appealing Tory MP. Before her election to Parliament, Rudd's business career was linked to offshore tax havens and the imprisonment of a co-director of a suspicious internet company. In normal circumstances, Rudd's conduct in the City would have disqualified her from questioning Boris's infidelity. But normal rules did not apply if the accused was Boris. He was on trial. The result was hysteria.

Unashamedly, Rudd tried to destroy Boris's character. In her prepared lines, she quipped, 'The only number Boris is interested in is Number 10'; 'Boris is the life and soul of the party, but not the man you want driving you home at the end of the evening'; and 'If you want an expert on jokes, I'll ask Boris. If I want an expert on the economy, I'll ask an economist.' When cued about the £350 million on the bus, Rudd joined the women's chorus 'lie, lie, lie'. Calmly, Boris refused to 'reduce the debate to a lot of personal stuff'. To his followers, Rudd was desperate. She represented Jean-Claude Juncker and the sterile Eurocrats who had sacrificed millions of young Europeans to unemployment to save the discredited euro. She promised neither reform nor an exciting vision of Britain within the EU.

'Let Thursday be our Independence Day,' Boris shouted as he zipped around the country in a helicopter on the last days. 'When I think of the champagne-guzzling orgy of backslapping in Brussels that would follow a Remain vote on Friday, I want to weep.' In London's Billingsgate Market, he resisted a fish merchant's urge to kiss a large fresh salmon, and at a warehouse in Kent, he said, 'Thanks for coming' to a woman in the audience who replied, 'We have to come. We work here.' On the eve of the vote, exhausted but still fighting, he sighed 'We're on the verge of an extraordinary event.'

On polling day, Andrew Cooper, Cameron's pollster, called Downing Street to report that Remain had a 20 per cent lead. Other polls predicted Remain leads of between 4 per cent and 7 per cent. Some bookies gave 3/1 against Leave. Only the Tory leaders of the Brexit campaign – Bill Cash, Iain Duncan Smith and Bernard Jenkin – expected to win, but they were disbelieved by the media.

Boris had spent the day at his daughter's graduation ceremony at St Andrews University in Scotland. After a delayed flight back to London, he rushed to vote in Islington at 9.30 p.m., just thirty minutes before the polls closed. By the time he returned home to watch the result, a casual conversation he had had with a passenger on the train from the airport was on the news. Boris had told the undeclared Labour activist that he expected Leave to lose. Along with other Leave MPs, Boris had signed a letter to Cameron urging him to remain as prime minister and reunite the party.

A large group had gathered in the Johnsons' den overlooking the garden, including Ben Wallace, Ben Gascoigne, Will Walden and some of the Johnson children. At 10.03 p.m., Nigel Farage appeared on the big TV screen to concede defeat. Unlike general elections, there was no exit poll. In Downing Street, there was satisfaction that Boris and Gove were finished. Glued to his seat over the following two hours, Boris was following the spread betting. 'A good indicator,' he said, as the odds improved. At twenty minutes past midnight, the die was cast. Sunderland voted overwhelmingly to leave. 'Holy shit, we've done it,' shouted Boris, genuinely happy; 17.4 million voted for leave and 16.1 million to remain. On a 72.2 per cent turnout, Britain was near evenly divided. 'The mood was celebratory but not over-the-top euphoric,' according to one eyewitness. At 4 a.m., Boris was ordered to get some sleep in anticipation of a big day ahead. Forty-five minutes later he reappeared wearing a Brazilian football shirt and shorts: 'I can't sleep.'

In Downing Street, Cameron did not conceal his anger. Boris and Gove, he cursed, had 'behaved appallingly' for betraying him and the government, and for aligning themselves with liars and racists. As the victor, Boris was poised to seize the prize.

Chapter 21

Leadership and Treachery

'Oh God. Poor Dave. Poor Sam. Jesus,' said Boris as he watched David Cameron emerge into Downing Street at 8.45 a.m. on Friday morning, 24 June. He had not anticipated Cameron's resignation, or expected to watch Sam Cameron, dazed by the unexpected result, wrestling with her emotions. At the end of his announcement, the couple turned and walked back into Number 10 leaving the Tory Brexiteers surprised, shattered and even angry.

'Go upstairs and focus on what you're going to say,' Boris was ordered. 'It's going to be the most important speech you've ever made.' After writing his speech, he rattled off an article for the following day's *Telegraph*.

Outside Boris's house, an angry crowd had gathered screaming obscenities at a man accused of dividing the country. None trusted him to pick up the pieces. Inside, Boris was not receiving congratulatory calls. Tory Brexiteers were not prepared to declare immediately their support for Boris, the clear favourite as prime minister at 4/6. On the other side, Tory Remainers had already swung behind May.

Exhausted and bewildered, and despite the sheer acrimony of the campaigns, Boris was not prepared for the antagonism sweeping the country. After telephoning Lynton Crosby to secure his help for the leadership campaign, he cautiously emerged from the house. Twenty policemen had arrived to protect him from the mob. On the railings of his house were underpants adorned with his face. Being demonised for 'a special place in hell' was not what he imagined. Squeezed into a waiting car, the driver was told, 'Don't stop at any lights. It'll be too dangerous.' As the first set of traffic lights turned from green to red, the driver stopped. Within seconds, a mob was beating on the car and preventing it moving. Over the next minutes, waiting for the police, Boris was told by Will Walden to rewrite his speech: 'Insert an appeal to youth that we will unite.' Once freed from the protestors, heading towards Leave's headquarters, he texted Cameron: 'Dave. I am so sorry to have been out of touch but I couldn't think what to say and now I am absolutely miserable about your decision. You have been a superb PM and leader and the country owes you eternally.'

Shortly after, he appeared on a stage with Gove and Gisela Stuart, the Labour MP, to celebrate their victory. After a series of fractious disagreements among the Leave organisers, all three looked miserable. The markets had slumped, the pound had hit a thirty-one-year low, there were predictions that Britain would break up (Scotland voted 62 per cent to remain), City bankers were aghast and Juncker petulantly demanded immediate talks to negotiate Brexit. Speaking for many, the chef Jamie Oliver said 'I'm out of Britain if Boris becomes prime minister.' Unprepared for that vitriol, Boris told the crowd that Cameron was 'a brave and principled man'. Without his normal conviction, he extolled the restoration of parliamentary democracy, condemned 'those who would play politics with immigration', and pledged that 'Britain will continue to be a great European power . . . I believe we now have a glorious opportunity.' Head fallen, he moved to the back of the stage. Clearly shocked, Gove spoke next. He did not disguise his guilt about Cameron's resignation. That sucked the joy out of the victory. To avoid the protestors in London, Boris headed for Thame. Suspecting a media stake-out on the road, he walked across fields to his house.

By nightfall, however, he no longer felt so bad about Cameron's demise. He buried his quip that his chance of becoming prime minister was as good as being 'reincarnated as an olive'. Speaking to Ben Wallace and his group, they agreed to meet the following day at Althorp for the annual Johnsons vs Spencers cricket match.

'Are you sure that you should go?' Boris was asked. 'It won't look good.'

'I've made the commitment and I won't break it,' he replied. 'It'll be fine.'

The Johnson team, captained by MP Nigel Adams, was boosted by Herschelle Gibbs, the outstanding South African batsman. During the game, Boris drank wine and optimistically discussed his prospects. After twice defying the odds and winning in London and, contrary to the polling forecasts, winning the referendum, his chances of securing the party leadership appeared overwhelming. To enhance his chances, they agreed, as the Spencers beat the Johnsons, that he would seek a pact with Gove.

The two had first met in Oxford. During Boris's second attempt to become the Union president, Gove had acted as one of his 'stooges' to 'rustle up support' in his college. The relationship, Boris admitted in *The Oxford Myth*, 'is founded on duplicity'. Gove fell for Boris's unfulfillable promises about the future and delivered his college's votes for Boris. Over the next thirty years, Gove rarely featured in Boris's life. Although they frequently met at party meetings, in Westminster and Gove had vigorously campaigned for Boris in 2008, there was no special bond. Gove's close relationship with Cameron not only precluded friendship with Boris but he shared Cameron's disdain for Boris's character. Unlike Boris, reform was Gove's passion. By relentless focus on detail, Gove had pushed his ideas through Whitehall's resistant bureaucracy and could deliver outstanding sixty-minute speeches on complicated issues without hesitation or even notes. So although the two had little in common they were united on the big issue of the moment.

In a teleconference that evening, Boris, Gove and Will Walden discussed Boris's leadership bid. The fourth participant was Dominic Cummings. Boris understood that Gove would not move without Cummings by his side. Boris also knew that the forty-four-year-old was famous as unremittingly bombastic, volatile, aggressive, and occasionally depressed. As a proud iconoclast, Cummings cherished creative destruction. The son of an oil-rig project manager and brought up in Durham, he had studied history in Oxford under the outstanding Norman Stone who introduced him to Euroscepticism. Uncompromising and unwilling to take prisoners, some appreciated Cummings' extraordinary ability to shape political judgements based on perceptive understanding of effects and consequences of actions. As a congenital rule-breaker, he was more interested in delivering policies than converting voters to new ideologies. The majority of Tories with personal experience of working alongside him agreed that his outstanding characteristic was his talent to alienate those he sought to influence. Many Tory Brexiteer MPs, Boris knew, would refuse to support him if Cummings was part of his team.

Towards the end of the four-way teleconference, Boris accepted Gove's offer of collaboration. He also agreed that Gove would be the Chancellor of the Exchequer, in charge of Brexit negotiations and responsible for reforming the Civil Service. He refused Gove's demand that Osborne be made Foreign Secretary. 'I'm not committing to anything more,' Boris insisted, but then made another concession. With mixed feelings, Boris agreed to Gove's nonnegotiable demand that Cummings be included in their team. He had no choice and believed he could resist his intellectual intimidation. 'That was an example of two people parking their tanks on your lawn,' Walden texted to Boris. Gove, Walden was convinced, assumed that Boris would be prime minister just in name and could be rolled. As Gove's chances to be leader were rated at 11/2, Boris ignored Walden's warning. After all, Gove had repeatedly pronounced himself over previous years unsuitable to be prime minister. 'I could not be prime minister,' Gove had told BBC TV. 'I'm not equipped to be prime minister. I do not want to be prime minister.' Boris did accept Walden's advice to call Lynton Crosby. 'Gove will support me,' Boris told the Australian. 'Our deal is that Michael will be deputy prime minister and Chancellor and Brexit negotiator. Dominic will be head of policy in Downing Street.' But, he added 'Dom must be invisible' during the leadership campaign. Boris and Crosby agreed to meet on Monday morning after a planned secret summit between Boris and Gove arranged for the following day at Boris's house in Thame.

The Sunday morning newspaper photographs of Boris enjoying

the Althorp cricket match outraged the Remainers. While half the nation grieved, the man who had convulsed Britain had been frolicking with his Etonian chums. Why, they shrieked, was he not at work to repair the destruction? Boris ignored the losers' carping. With his loyal team – Will Walden, Jake Berry, Ben Wallace, Nigel Adams, Eddie Lister and Amanda Milling – he considered the pledges of support. 'According to our data,' said Nigel Adams, 'we have sixty-four definites. We'll need 111 to get over the line into the final round.' He expected at least twenty-five more commitments over the next two days.

'How come the TV cameras are here?' Gove asked when he arrived.

'Because your wife told them,' Walden replied. 'The TV crew told me that Sarah [Vine] tipped them off.'

Over the barbeque lunch, the atmosphere became 'frosty'. 'Who supports you?' Gove asked. 'No, you tell us who supports you,' replied Adams. 'Eighteen,' he replied, including Jacob Rees-Mogg and Dominic Raab. Numbers, in Gove's opinion, did not matter. As a Cabinet minister with a proven record, he assumed his superiority over Boris while Boris saw no reason to suspect his friend from Oxford of plotting.

'Let's see your list,' said Gove. Wallace resisted but Boris agreed. 'I'll run your leadership campaign,' announced Gove. Wallace became angrier but Boris did not protest. 'And we'll run the media operation,' added Gove. 'That's my job,' Walden interjected. Boris's key aides were being sidelined. Gove and his team assumed control. Wallace handed over his spreadsheet of supporters. Despite winning on every score, Gove left in a huff. 'This is all very odd,' said Adams.

'I'll sort Michael out,' said Boris, insensitive to what had happened, which in his unfocused manner, he did not try to understand. Too often, for convenience's sake he took people at face value. He was unaware that Gove had earlier confided to Rod Liddle, 'Boris can't be trusted.' Nor did he suspect that Nick Boles, who had previously described himself as 'a vague Remainer', had become a Brexiteer helping Gove. But others became suspicious after Boles described the lunch as 'boozy'. No one drank alcohol, there were no jokes, and anyway, Boles was not at Thame that day. The only link to alcohol was Boles's endorsement of Boris as 'the Heineken candidate'.

That night, Boris wrote his column for Monday's *Telegraph*. Having divided Britain, he posed as the agent of reunification to the 16 million Remainers with a plan, not least to prevent Scotland breaking away. 'We must reach out, we must heal, we must build bridges.' He praised co-operation with Europe for culture, education and the environment; he promised to protect the rights of EU citizens living in the UK; and he insisted that Britain would have access to the single market thanks to a special arrangement to stay within the EU's 'internal market': 'There is every case for optimism: a Britain rebooted, reset, renewed and able to engage with the whole world.' Pledged to pursue One Nation policies, he would end the discrepancy that FTSE 100 chiefs earned 150 times more than the 'forgotten people'. Before submitting the article, he sent it to Gove for comment. 'Overall very, very good,' Gove replied. He suggested minor changes to present a more 'inclusive, positive and optimistic message'.

The article caused mayhem among Boris's potential supporters. To Iain Duncan Smith and other seasoned Brexiteer MPs, Boris seemed to have gone soft about the single market. He wrote: 'The only change – and it will not come in any great rush – is that the UK will extricate itself from the EU's extraordinary and opaque system of legislation.' That was not the Brexiteers' Gospel. Britain, they preached, would have access to the single market but would not be part of the 'internal market'. Unlike Boris's 'have the cake and eat it', they did not expect to leave and enjoy the benefits.

Before he had absorbed this fundamental disagreement, Boris was sitting on Monday morning in Lynton Crosby's Pimlico office. The good news, said Crosby, was that his calls to donors had produced money for Boris's campaign. The rest was bad news. Gove arrived with Cummings, despite Boris having stipulated that Cummings was not to be present. Nick Boles also arrived. Crosby had already warned Boris: 'I wouldn't trust Boles. He has no political judgement.' The mutual suspicion increased because Gove hated

Crosby. In the summer of 2014, the pollster had advised Cameron to remove Gove as Education Secretary. Gove's anger had been restoked by Sarah Vine, his ambitious wife. And because Crosby distrusted Boles, Boles distrusted Crosby. Despite that tension, all that mattered was finding more MPs to support Boris. By then, Wallace had listed commitments from nearly one hundred MPs including Nicholas Soames – a surprise after he recently called Boris, 'an ocean-going clot'. Wallace did not know which MPs supported Gove. They would need to switch to Boris.

In Pimlico, the heat was rising. Crosby decided to bang heads together: 'There's only one fucking list – both of you hand yours over to me and I'll merge them.' To everyone's surprise, Gove refused. 'I'm running the campaign,' snapped Crosby, 'and we're focusing on Boris.' Gove hated that and knew that his wife would be outraged. In the pandemonium, Gove told Boris 'I'll run the campaign and Lynton can help.' Without any questions, Boris flapped and guffawed. Slow to think on his feet, he preferred not to sully the atmosphere with an argument. He failed to reflect about the similarity of the demands and protests the previous Saturday. He allowed the momentous decisions to be rushed through rather than demand time to reflect about the barrage of disagreements that had emerged over the previous twenty-four hours. For a man who had for years survived despite consistently ignoring deadlines, there was on this occasion no safety net. He agreed to Gove's demand. 'Nick will submit the formal nomination papers,' continued Gove, clearly in charge. In return for his support, Gove again demanded that George Osborne would be Foreign Secretary, and Andrea Leadsom, a former banking bureaucrat, would be Chancellor of the Exchequer. Forty-eight hours earlier, Gove had said *he* would be the Chancellor. Now he was promoting an unknown energy minister with a peculiar passion, as she would highlight in a speech, for the benefits of massaging babies' brains. Since some Brexiteer MPs were mentioning her as their favourite to be prime minister and she had confirmed her own ambitions for the leadership, Boris just nodded.

Arriving later that morning in Westminster, Boris knew that his success depended on converting the sceptics to favour him rather than Theresa May, his principal rival. A well-functioning election machine would have smoothly conveyed the uncommitted MPs into his office. He would listen to their demands, pledge sympathy for their interests, assure them that with him as prime minister they would keep their seats in the next election and that, with confidence, they could rely on his plan for Brexit and government. The most important group to seduce were the fifty hardcore Brexiteers – some of whom had campaigned for Britain's departure from the EU since the 1980s.

Most Brexiteers were sceptical about Boris as prime minister. He had no ministerial experience; he had never been a true Brexiteer; and many were cross about the £350 million slogan on the bus. 'I don't think he is intellectually ready,' reflected one Brexiteer. 'He isn't well organised and does not realise it. He's only been mayor and he's never run a Whitehall department. He doesn't have enough experience.' As shrewd politicians, they also looked at his closest aides as an indication of his administration. All they saw were Gove and Boles. Although Boris had denied that Cummings would be part of the government, few believed him and Gove aroused suspicions. In personal meetings with Boris, they made requests and were angered by his confusing answers. Andrew Mitchell was among many to criticise the campaign. 'We know what we're doing,' replied Wallace. By Wednesday, the muddle had increased.

Boris the Buffoon, reported *The Times*, had turned into Boris the Brave Brexiteer, but even some Leave voters saw him as Boris the Betrayer. 'He's completely untrustworthy,' reported the newspaper, 'or rather you can trust him completely to always let you down.' There was also despair about assertions by Brexiteers. David Davis predicted that the day after Parliament approved of Brexit, a British government minister would fly to Berlin and conclude a new trade deal with all the same benefits of EU membership. 'The cards', he said, were 'incredibly stacked our way'. Liam Fox asserted that fixing a new deal with the EU would be 'the easiest in human history' and that the day after Parliament's Brexit vote, he would sign 'forty new trade deals'.

During the morning, May summoned Boris. Neither trusted the other and during the referendum she had behaved suspiciously. 'Submarine May', said Cameron, was 'an enemy agent'. Unlike Boris, she had played her cards close to her chest, in her own interest, ignoring the country and the party, not least by rejecting Cameron's demands for immigration controls. Until the very end, she had refused to campaign for Remain. Her opportunism was paying off. YouGov reported that morning that May was the favourite among Tory voters at 31 per cent against 24 per cent for Boris. As the stop-Boris candidate, she could assume the support of Remainer MPs.

Boris ignored her command. Two hours later, Gavin Williamson, an ambitious but lowly MP employed as her campaign manager, delivered her offer: 'Step down. You can be my deputy.' Her terms were rejected. Boris was playing to win. Looking for allies, he summoned Amber Rudd. Even calling Rudd exposed Boris's artlessness. In the event, she offered her support on the condition she would be the Chancellor of the Exchequer.

'Why are you bothering with Amber?' he was asked by one of his key MP aides. 'She brings no supporters. You should speak to Andrea [Leadsom].'

'Andrea's on board,' replied Boris. Patting his pocket, he added, 'I've got a letter for her.' The letter confirmed that Leadsom would abandon her own leadership bid in exchange for being the Chancellor in Boris's government. 'But I've got a problem,' Boris added. 'Michael [Gove] also says that he wants to be Chancellor.' In his solitary state, Boris could no longer make sense of events as gossip about his offer to Leadsom flew around Westminster. Brexiteers could not understand why Boris cared about Leadsom. She was stubborn, not particularly intelligent and had exaggerated her banking career. Blind to the turmoil, Boris, a one-man band without a consigliere, moved fast towards the climax of the drama. Before noon the following day, he would formally declare his candidature for the leadership.

That night, the Tory Party's leaders and donors met at the annual summer party at the Hurlingham Club in Fulham, a black-tie dinner. As usual Boris was late. While he was hurrying back to Islington to change, Jake Berry was texting with Gove about the choreography for the following morning. Amber Rudd, it was agreed, would introduce Boris to his supporters at the St Ermin's Hotel in Westminster. Boles, it was agreed, would drive Boris after the dinner at the Hurlingham from Fulham to Islington to write his declaration speech.

Boris arrived at the Hurlingham to find a toxic, mournful and tearful atmosphere. Among the most emotional was Cameron. The most hated person in the room was Boris. Amid that emotional bedlam, a series of conspiracies was born. The first was the fate of Boris's letter to Leadsom guaranteeing she would be the Chancellor. She had demanded a letter in exchange for not declaring her leadership bid the following day. In Boris's version, he gave the letter to Boles to hand to Leadsom. In the account by Gove's team, Boris admitted that the letter was left at his home when he changed clothes.

At the end of the evening, Boles and Boris drove back from Fulham to Islington. 'Give me your mobile,' said Boles, 'so you can focus on writing.' Unknown to Boris, among the text messages received on his mobile during the journey was one from Leadsom asking about the promised letter. Boles, it appears, deleted that text. As he got out of the car in Islington, Boris said 'See you at St Ermin's tomorrow.'

'Yes,' replied Boles.

The car sped away, not to Boles's home but to Michael Gove's west London house. The plotters did not sleep much that night.

*

Despite denying any ambition to be prime minister, Gove hankered for the job, especially after working so close to Cameron. For years, his ambition had been encouraged by Rupert Murdoch. Over the past days, Gove's team of advisers encouraged his disdain for Boris, even as a figurehead. Cummings was against Boris in anger that he had been banned from a future government. Boles, filled with self-important delusions, could not forgive Boris for his success. He joined Cummings to persuade Gove to dump Boris, especially after Osborne had been recruited to be Foreign Secretary. The seal had been set in an email from Sarah Vine to her husband. Both Paul Dacre and Rupert Murdoch, she wrote, 'instinctively dislike Boris' and would support him, Gove, as prime minister. In Gove's negotiations with Boris, Vine ended, 'Do not concede any ground. Be your stubborn best. Good luck.' Vine was described as Lady Macbeth without the charm.

At 8.53 a.m. on Thursday morning, Gove called Crosby who was eating breakfast at the Corinthia hotel by the Embankment. 'I thought I'd call you first,' said Gove. 'I'm running.'

'I know you're running,' replied Crosby, puzzled. 'You're the campaign manager.'

'No. I'm running for the leadership.'

'Have you told Boris?'

'No.'

One minute later, Boles emailed Boris's office that, despite their agreement the previous night, he would not be submitting Boris's nomination papers.

At that moment, Boris was stepping out of the shower. The phone rang. Crosby relayed the news.

'It's over,' puffed Boris. 'That's it. I can't go on. I can't run.'

'Don't make any decisions,' ordered Crosby. 'Don't tell anyone you're not running. Come over with Marina to the office.'

At 9.02, Gove's office emailed journalists: 'Events since last Thursday have weighed heavily with me . . . I have come, reluctantly, to the conclusion that Boris cannot provide the leadership or build the team for the task ahead.' Gove declared he would run for leader.

Will Walden was at Crosby's office by the time Boris arrived. Like the others, Walden was shocked by the treachery of Gove, Vine and Cummings.

'Gove has done the dirty on us,' Boris told Jake Berry on the phone.

'If you both run,' replied Berry, 'you'll destroy each other.' His parliamentary team were already calling ninety MPs to check whether they remained pledged to Boris.

'We should have been suspicious when Gove asked for the list of our supporters,' Wallace told David Davis in the Commons. 'It's been a spectacular betrayal.'

'We're losing people,' Boris was told. Even Michael Howard, a Boris supporter, switched to Gove. Only sixty MPs were likely and just thirty were firm. Their constituency associations were supporting May with her Thatcherite image of safety and security. Boris's decades of gaffes cemented MPs' conviction that he was flakey.

'You haven't got enough support,' declared Crosby.

'Bad for your image if you fight,' added Walden.

'It's your call,' Crosby said. 'We can't win. Keep your powder dry for another day. But if you decide to run, we'll stay in the trench with you to the end. You and Marina, go to a room and discuss it.'

Fifteen minutes later, they emerged. Marina had persuaded Boris to pull out.

'It's not your time,' agreed Mark Fullbrook, Crosby's associate. 'Let Gove spend his time hitting you.'

'I was a fool to trust him,' admitted Boris. 'Some of you told me I should never have done so and I'm sorry I didn't listen.'

At midday, Boris entered the Cloister's Suite at the St Ermin's Hotel. One hundred politicians, journalists and supporters were waiting to hear the declaration of his candidature. None had spotted that his staff had covered the 'Exit' sign over the tradesman's entrance through which he would leave. The photographers would be denied an open goal.

Boris stepped towards the lectern to speak about steadying nerves and unifying the country. Now, he continued, quoting Shakespeare's *Julius Caesar*, was 'a time not to fight the tide of history but to take that tide at the flood and sail on to fortune'. Britain's new leader would need to unify the party and represent the country. And then came the bombshell: 'But I must tell you my friends . . . I have concluded that that person cannot be me.' Silence followed. Shocked and speechless, his supporters watched Boris walk away.

Without a murmur, he left the room. Mindful of the perils, he said nothing more to the media. He resisted lashing out at those who betrayed him and those who now piled in, speculating about unrevealed skeletons. Was it his past relations with women, or other secrets? Leaving some mystery camouflaged his weakness.

'Holy shit, I'm glad it's over but it was a mistake to pull out,' he said as his car drove away. 'You should have stuck with me, mate,' Cameron texted, bemused by the shock announcement. 'Blimey, is he [Michael] a bit cracked or something?' Boris replied. 'Great speech last night,' referring to the dinner at the Hurlingham. 'Everyone watched and thought we'd gone insane to lose you and people were looking at me as if I was a leper, but you had eleven hard years of party leadership and six superbly as PM, more than I will ever do.' Within the hour, Crosby had emptied the campaign office. Boris's presence had been wiped out.

Thirty minutes after Boris's exit, May launched her bid. Mocking 'showy' politicians and their 'gimmicks', she derided her former rival: 'Boris negotiated in Europe. I seem to remember last time he did a deal with the Germans, he came back with three nearly-new water cannons.' (They would be sold as scrap by Sadiq Khan for £11,025 in 2018.) Boris was a target for point-scoring and Gove joined the crowd.

Accompanied by Nick Boles, his campaign manager, Gove announced his candidature to a small audience including just five MPs, not the fifty he had expected. Careless about the hostility towards himself and deluded he could beat May, Gove had not anticipated Boris pulling out. His speech was not about Britain's future but justification of his conduct. 'In the last four days I had a chance to see up close and personal how Boris dealt with some of the decisions we needed to make in order to take this country forward. During that period, I had hoped that Boris would rise to the occasion . . . but I saw him seek to meet and not pass those tests.' Boris, said Gove, lacked the necessary experience and leadership qualities to 'unite the team and lead the party and the country' and he did not 'believe heart and soul' in Brexit.

Gove would later claim that the Sunday barbeque in Thame was shambolic, that Boris's *Telegraph* article was a 'sloppy' appeal to both sides, and that the non-delivery of the Leadsom letter was typical of Boris's disorganisation and lack of attention to detail. Those misrepresentations would provoke Boris to denounce Gove as 'deeply Machiavellian and flawed'. He accused Boles of 'stealing' his phone to sabotage his link with Leadsom. But the ultimate passage of Gove's speech was the most wounding because, as Boris later learnt, it was crafted by Clare Foges who had worked for Boris in City Hall. That, he felt, was the ultimate betrayal: 'I also thought ultimately, can I recommend to my friends that this person is right to be prime minister? The answer was no.' He added, 'I think I am the right person to be prime minister.' Then followed a uniquely self-destructive reason for his candidature: 'I did not want it. Indeed, I did almost everything I could not to be a candidate for the leadership . . . I was so very reluctant because I know my limitations. Whatever charisma is – I don't have it – whatever glamour may be, I don't think anyone could ever associate me with it.' The instant vituperation against Gove was widespread.

Gove, wrote Rachel Johnson, had 'executed the most egregious reverse ferret and act of treachery in modern political history'. Jake Berry tweeted, 'There is a very deep pit reserved in hell for such as he.' Others spoke of a 'calculated plot', a 'venal backstabbing liar', 'a political psychopath run by his wife', and 'a total cuckoo-in-the-nest operation from the beginning'.

Boris's exit was welcomed by Ruth Davidson, the Scottish Tory leader. Others were appalled that the architects of Brexit had fled. 'He ripped the Tory Party apart,' wrote Michael Heseltine, 'he has created the greatest constitutional crisis of modern times. He is like a general who led his army to the sound of guns and at the sight of the battlefield abandoned the field. I have never seen such a contemptible and irresponsible situation . . . He must live with the shame of what he has done.' Max Hastings was grateful that an 'amiable cove's' withdrawal had saved him 'having to fulfil my 2012 pledge that I would catch a plane to Buenos Aires if this essentially brutal buffoon became prime minister'.

The following day, Boris fulfilled a long-standing engagement at a constituency dinner. He drove four hours to Devon to speak for Mel Stride, a Tory MP, even though Stride had not supported his leadership. During the journey, he contemplated the end of his career. Instead of negotiating Brexit, he was gone. Hated by Tory Remainers and not supported by Leavers, he plunged into a deep depression. Not one of the 150 Tories at the dinner that night sensed their speaker's humiliation or his personal devastation. Compartmentalising his emotions, his performance was perfect. At the end, they cheered a speech that in the circumstances had been surprisingly jokey.

Boris returned to London and backed Leadsom in the leadership stakes. Paul Dacre at the *Daily Mail* backed May. *The Times* did not outrightly endorse Gove. In the first round, May won 50.2 per cent of the votes with 165 MPs while Gove had 48 votes. In the second round, Gove dropped to 46 votes and was eliminated. After serious inconsistencies were exposed in Leadsom's version of her own career, she withdrew. On 11 July, May was elected unopposed.

Isolated and lonely, Boris was not consoled by the Remainers' misery. Their dream had been shattered by the people (or voters) they pretended to represent. Instead of blaming themselves, they cursed Boris. The Brexiteers' success sowed a deep hatred of him.

ACT III

The Cabinet

Chapter 22

'We're being stitched up'

'I don't know if she'll offer me a job,' Boris confessed to Jake Berry on 13 July, sitting in his Westminster office, 'and if she did, I don't know which I would accept.' Googling the size of all the government departments, Boris listed the options. 'I wouldn't take DCMS [Department of Culture, Media and Sport], that would be less than being the mayor, but I would take Health or Welfare.' His chances, he sighed, were nil. He had not concealed his dislike of May as a characterless phantom, and she had snatched every opportunity to humiliate him.

'You're as popular as the man who's just told his wife that he's got a dose of genital herpes,' laughed Berry.

Their conversation was interrupted by a call – a summons to Downing Street.

The vicar's daughter enjoyed mocking men. 'You and I have a patchy history,' May said to Boris with a schoolmarm's disdain, 'but I know there are two Borises: a serious intellectual, a capable and effective person; and a play-around Boris. I want this to be your opportunity to show you can be the good Boris.' In normal circumstances, Boris would have snapped that unlike her, he had won two elections in London and successfully led the Leave campaign. She had won nothing except the leadership by default. But what followed stunned him: 'I want you to be Foreign Secretary.'

'I was very, very surprised,' he admitted. 'You could have knocked me down with a feather.' Stunned by the offer, he did not hesitate to consider whether it was a poisoned chalice. Clearly, May wanted him in the tent pissing out. He failed to ask what limitations would be imposed on him. Nor did he ask what she had meant by 'Brexit means Brexit'. She had already cast doubt on the automatic right of EU citizens to remain in Britain and suggested that corporations make lists of foreign employees. He did not question how her protectionism would match his belief in global, open Britain. May had already publicly said, 'Leave means leave' and 'No deal is better than a bad deal'. The largely monosyllabic jargon had complicated her negotiating position. Some Brexiteers had hoped to do a trade deal which left Britain in the single market. May wanted the same, but by saying 'No deal is better than a bad deal' she appeared to exclude any chance of an accommodation with the EU. It was a bad place to start, not least because the EU had refused the Brexiteers' preference. In truth, May herself had no idea of her final destination. Instead of questioning her confusion, Boris grabbed the unexpected lifebelt and the lure of his first ministerial job. The chance to sit in the Cabinet was priceless. Others realised that he had walked into a trap set to destroy him.

From Downing Street to the Foreign and Commonwealth Office is a very short walk. In his excitement, Boris is unlikely to have noticed the faded splendour of the building's grand entrance and the shabby carpets. Instead, he was thrilled to enter his huge personal office – the very room where outstanding statesmen had taken critical decisions about Britain's fate. More mundanely, he would assume the political responsibility over 14,000 employees in 270 postings across the world.

Standing by his side was Simon McDonald, the Foreign Office's senior official, the permanent undersecretary. With a big smile, McDonald had welcomed Boris and escorted him up the wide curved staircase to his hallowed office. Unctuous and fluent, McDonald was well trained to camouflage his true sentiments. For good reason, his welcome glowed with insincerity. Over the past forty-three years, the Foreign Office had integrated itself into the EU. To remain in lockstep with the EU was the diplomats' life mission. Foreign Office officials were seconded to Brussels, and in most international dilemmas, their first call was to consult Brussels as well as other European capitals. In parallel, the officials prided themselves that Washington's first call to discover the EU's policy was often to the Foreign Office. Now the 'buffoon' responsible for destroying their life's work was inside their citadel. The leader of those who neither trusted nor respected Boris was McDonald himself. Yet, McDonald's department was the architect of its own misfortune. Despite their boasts of orchestrating a Rolls-Royce machine, McDonald's diplomats had failed to persuade the twenty-seven EU governments to make the obvious concessions to Cameron in order to secure a Remain vote. Naturally, their anger was not directed at themselves. McDonald's clan blamed Boris. McDonald, a fifty-five year old from Salford, had little reason to protect Boris from his own mistakes during his period as Foreign Secretary.

In his unsuspecting manner, Boris did not appreciate that McDonald had married into the Foreign Office's aristocracy. Sir Patrick Wright, his father-in-law, had also been the Foreign Office's top official. Gossips suggested that McDonald had secured the senior post in 2015 because 'he knew which way the wind was going'. He pledged to improve diversity. Ever since, his annual reports and tweets focused on the numbers of female, black, Asian and minority ethnic (BAME) recruits, and disabled staff. Just before Boris's arrival, McDonald boasted, 'I was delighted to appoint Joanna Roper as the FCO's Special Envoy for Gender Equality. I have resolved to place gender equality at the heart of all we do.' McDonald's tweets never mentioned Britain's policy on Syria, Russia or the Gulf. Grinding down the complicated options on foreign policy was sacrificed to his 'personal priorities'. Unlike Boris's belief in excellence in education, McDonald espoused social engineering even if that meant diluting his diplomats' collective intellectual qualifications. Running the Foreign Office's supervisory board – the department's management forum – was McDonald's fiefdom. Boris would be excluded. In his tick-box process, McDonald dictated the line to take. While he supported Boris's attempts to secure more money from the Treasury, he resisted any interference in the quality of those recruited from university.

McDonald was not to blame for his inheritance. During the

Blair decade, the Foreign Office had been stripped of responsibility
by Downing Street. Under weak leadership, McDonald's predecessors had avoided any challenge of the government's lies to justify
the wars in Iraq and Afghanistan. Under McDonald's predecessors, the Foreign Office's famed Camel Corps of Arabists had
disappeared and the strict requirement for linguists was diluted.
Officials were dispatched to capitals unable to speak the local language and with superficial knowledge about the culture.
Spellbound by the EU, some of Britain's diplomats had lost their
way, and became tumbleweed upset about the reduction of knight-
hoods for ambassadors. In recent years, crippled by severe budget
cuts, especially under Gordon Brown, their diminished department's ability to host international conferences, seduce potential
allies with favours and hospitality, and intervene in Britain's interests had robbed the Foreign Office of its historic self-confidence.
The decline had gathered pace in the wake of David Cameron losing the Commons vote in 2013 to bomb Syria in retaliation for a
chemical-weapons attack on civilians. Under Philip Hammond,
Boris's predecessor as Foreign Secretary, the decline had accelerated. 'The Foreign Office has had its limbs amputated,' wrote Peter
Ricketts, the former head of the Diplomatic Service, about the
Hammond era. 'Institutionally, the Foreign Office is a bit timid,'
admitted Simon Fraser, McDonald's immediate predecessor.
McDonald never appeared concerned that the Foreign Office had
become a shadow of its former greatness.

Boris was only marginally aware of those problems. Still not genuinely interested in the machinery of government – a puzzling
attribute for someone eager for new responsibilities – his first priority was to attract his staff's affection. For that purpose, he immediately
rescinded Philip Hammond's veto and allowed the rainbow flag for
the LGBT community to be flown. Next, he eagerly accepted
McDonald's invitation to address the Foreign Office staff in the
atrium known as Durbar Court. On occasions such as this, Boris
excelled. His enthusiasm, voice, delivery and humour combined to
give a great pep talk. Faced with a suspicious audience who viewed
Brexit with horror, he memorably spelt out a vision of the Foreign

Office, no longer a supplicant to Brussels but entrusted with new authority to assert 'Global Britain' – a revived nation pursuing its own interests and policies through a reconstituted network of international relationships. To transform 'Global Britain' from a slogan into substance depended upon leadership, expertise and intellect. Since Theresa May was not interested in foreign policy and Boris lacked the expertise, the new minister would expect his officials to help restore Britain's role in the world.

None of his audience understood Boris's method of exercising power. After eight years at City Hall, he had perfected the art of setting out an agenda, asking pertinent questions, encouraging discussion, issuing an instruction and then delegating the execution of his policy to his team. His senior team had performed that task smoothly and efficiently. He expected Foreign Office officials to follow that practice. McDonald's duty was to craft 'Global Britain' into a substantive policy.

By nature, diplomats tend to be cautious, conservative – and identified by an insider's chuckle. With a self-satisfied smirk, McDonald declared 'diplomacy is the art of letting other people have your way'. Except the opposite had happened. Boris's expectation to reassert British influence in the Middle East and elsewhere was, McDonald thought, risible. Instinctively, most of his senior officials were similarly antagonistic. Compared to those 'analogues', the converts to 'Global Britain' were the 'digitals', the younger elite enthused by the prospect of reversing the decline of British influence. The sight of Boris eating lunch in the canteen and chatting with everyone persuaded them that former ambassador Christopher Meyer's judgement might possibly be right: 'It's an inspired appointment. Imaginative, clever, bold and offering Britain just the voice it needs at a time of major rebuilding of our foreign policy.' Meyer's only caution was Boris's 'need to erase the gaffes'.

Boris's first hurdle was to work out how the Foreign Office functioned. Assuming it would be similar to City Hall, and in stark contrast to his absorption of the complexities of the property world when mayor, he failed to ask the right questions at the right time. Gradually he slipped into Whitehall's swamp.

At the end of his first week, the gloss of the job began to fade. The straitjacket imposed by May became obvious. Downing Street forbade the employment of his trusted aides, including Will Walden. Only Ben Gasgoine, his private aide, could join him. Not only was Boris deliberately isolated but May appointed Alan Duncan, her key supporter and friend from Oxford, as a junior Foreign Office minister. Elected to the Commons in 1992 after a successful career in the oil industry, Duncan had been irritated by Boris's arrival in Westminster in 2001. While Duncan's political career was flatlining, Boris basked endlessly in the media. Unimpressed by that success, Duncan had referred during the recent leadership elections to 'the theatrical and comic antics of Silvio Borisconi', an allusion to Silvio Berlusconi, the Italian former prime minister, infamous for his 'bunga bunga' sex parties and allegations of corruption. Weeks later, soon after his own appointment, Duncan told BBC TV that Boris had only joined the Leave campaign to position himself for the leadership. In truth, said Duncan, Boris had hoped Leave would lose. Among those watching Duncan's performance was Steve Baker, the Brexiteer Tory MP. Baker was surprised. He recalled Duncan approaching him in 2015 to ask if he, Duncan, could be the 'chairman of Vote Leave'. During their conversation, Baker assumed that Duncan now wanted to replace Boris. Not only was Duncan an unfriendly critic and May's spy within the Foreign Office, but, to enhance his own position, he appointed himself as Boris's deputy.

With mischievous glee, the cuckoo in Boris's nest watched the dismay of European politicians to Boris's appointment. Preceded by his reputation for reckless hyperbole and clownish self-promotion – not least hanging from the zip wire during the Olympics – the Brussels bureaucrats cancelled an informal dinner for all twenty-eight foreign ministers. At a Bastille Day reception in the French Embassy, Boris was booed, reflecting the ridicule heaped on him by Jean-Marc Ayrault, France's foreign minister. 'During the [referendum] campaign,' said Ayrault, 'Boris lied a lot to the British people.' Ayrault doubted whether Boris was 'clear, credible and reliable'. Echoing that disdain, a German TV presenter had laughed while he read the news of his appointment. Frank-Walter Steinmeier, the German foreign minister, criticised Boris for failing to take his responsibilities seriously in the immediate aftermath of the referendum result: 'Instead he played cricket. To be honest, I find this outrageous.' Similarly, Carl Bildt, the Swedish former prime minister, tweeted 'Wish it was a joke.' Undaunted, Boris replied, 'It is inevitable there is going to be a certain amount of plaster coming off the ceiling in the chancelleries of Europe.'

Influenced by that scorn, Caroline Wilson, the Foreign Office's newly appointed director of Europe, did not appear as Boris's natural friend. In her opinion, he lacked a grip on reality, especially in his conviction that a Brexit deal would be easy. In despair, she told her colleagues, her efforts were to ensure 'he does not go off the rails'. Wilson knew that Boris and the Foreign Office would be excluded from the Brexit negotiations by May. The Foreign Secretary would not receive key official papers and would be encouraged to scrabble with Liam Fox and David Davis, the other Brexiteer ministers appointed by May to negotiate the withdrawal and the new trade agreements.

At the outset, May denied him the sole use of Chevening, the Foreign Secretary's grace-and-favour seventeenth-century, 115-room neoclassical mansion near Sevenoaks. Her order that he share it with Liam Fox and David Davis would eventually be overthrown by Chevening's trustees.

Like Boris, Fox was set up to fail. Whitehall had lost the expertise to negotiate trade deals after the UK joined the EU. Forty-three years later, the government could not even agree a trade policy – whether Britain should be protectionist or liberalise its tariff barriers. To further muddy the waters, Philip Hammond, the new Chancellor and a Remainer who disliked both Boris and Fox, announced that a British tariff system would be too expensive. Hammond, David Davis realised, was intentionally 'undermining the Brexit talks as a desperate strategy to keep Britain in the single market'. The Treasury was empowered by May's indecision to block Britain leaving the single market.

The confusion was compounded by disagreements between the

Brexit ministers. David Davis had told senior European politicians that Britain would stay in the single market, probably by paying for access. At the same time, Boris told a Czech newspaper that Britain would 'probably' leave the single market. On the same day, a Foreign Office spokesman contradicted Boris: 'No decision has been taken. It will be a matter for future discussion.'

'We're being stitched up,' Fox said to Davis after a Cabinet meeting. 'They're conspiring against us.' Davis agreed. The Remainers would not accept the referendum result and May refused to thwart the Remainers. Secretive and duplicitous, as Davis discovered, May agreed in the Cabinet to propose a temporary customs arrangement to the EU but, he discovered, her agreement was not included in the Cabinet minutes. 'I objected,' recalled Davis, 'but it wasn't changed.' Just as May sidelined Boris and Fox, she had also isolated Davis by telling the Irish government to deal with David Liddington, her deputy, and not Davis. May planned to survive by divide and rule. In the first weeks, her strategy was successful.

Frustrated by the prime minister's refusal to delegate any authority to his limited staff, Fox asked Boris to transfer the Foreign Office's trade and investment teams to his department. Boris refused. Fox, said the Foreign Office spokesman, was 'nutty and obsessive. There's something strange about him.' To humiliate Fox further, Downing Street criticised the Brexiteer for spending his time drinking champagne with friends on the Commons terrace. In retaliation, Fox attacked the Foreign Office as a department with a 'cartographer's view of the world' – too interested in politics at the expense of trade – and mocked British businessmen as 'fat and lazy'. Just three months after her election, with the Treasury, the Foreign Office and Downing Street pursuing different objectives, May's Brexit policy was in chaos.

To overcome Downing Street's marginalisation, Boris appointed David Frost, a career diplomat, as his special Brexit adviser. (Frost had left the Foreign Office in 2014 to become the Scottish Whisky Association's chief executive.) Simultaneously, he and David Davis agreed to disregard Ivan Rogers, the Foreign Office's representative to the EU in Brussels. As an uncompromising Remainer, Rogers'

singular failure was to negotiate on Cameron's behalf a good deal
with the EU. Impervious to his own deficiencies, Rogers constantly
berated Boris and Davis for misunderstanding the EU. He said the
same about the prime minister. May puzzled the Europeans. Over
lunch in Paris with Jean-Marc Ayrault, Boris was told that there was
a need for clarity from London. May was uncertain what she
wanted in the withdrawal agreement. On his return to London, to
fill the vacuum Boris listed to May his red lines for an agreement
with the EU: she must reject calls to stay in the single market, veto
any compulsory payment into EU budgets, impose proper immigration controls with an Australian-style points-based system,
remove the authority of the European Court of Justice, and stop
any EU legislation applying to the UK. By sheer willpower, he
hoped that by pushing against May – rather like in Eton's wall
game – he would win. Whitehall's fissures were apparent. May listened and said nothing; David Davis complained that Boris was not
a tactician with a strategy; and Liam Fox, ignoring reality, set off on
a global tour to sign trade agreements.

The Brexiteers' shenanigans did not impress Simon McDonald
and his senior staff. As the officials waited in Boris's outer office to
attend the regular Wednesday morning 'Prayer Meetings' to brief
the minister, the staid Foreign Office mandarins gazed at the por-
traits of Foreign Secretaries over the past centuries and reflected
about their current minister. Despite Philip Hammond's limitations, they had welcomed his scrupulous perusal of every file,
scribbling comments of appreciation of an official's deep thoughts
and purposefully approving a recommendation. In contrast to
Hammond's dry freakery, officials watched Boris speed-read
through their files. Pages were rarely scrutinised, they muttered,
and key points were not diligently underlined. Tellingly, Boris seldom demanded the background files. Their wariness became
apparent during the Wednesday meetings. After cracking a joke,
Boris asked questions and wanted a discussion about the Big Picture, the presentation and where he could pounce. In his
unconventional manner, he refused to discuss 'the desired outcome' in Foreign Office patter. In response, McDonald led the

officials' lack of enthusiasm to engage. In foreign affairs, McDonald liked to imagine, there was no absolutely fireproof opinion and, unlike in City Hall, the Foreign Secretary was not the master able to take a clear-cut decision. Boris, he decided, failed to realise the scale of difference between the mayor's responsibility to keep the Tube running and maintaining relations with over one hundred governments. Even David Davis was struck by the Foreign Office's disloyalty: 'If May sacked Boris,' one British ambassador told him, 'that would take £10 billion off the price of Brexit.' Boris's manner made him easy to mock, but while German and French politicians belittled him, the foreign ministers of Denmark, Hungary and the smaller countries liked him (they even jogged together at summit meetings). Sensing his lack of power and the atmosphere of malice, Boris was cautious at the regular meetings of Whitehall's National Security Council.

Seated next to May – not an ideal position – Boris broke with his predecessors' performance and refused to take the lead. To his officials' disappointment, he chose not to be assertive and shape the discussion. Hammond and other ministers were allowed to have their say and only at the end did Boris read the Foreign Office brief, adding a few comments. By avoiding dissent and debate, he gave the impression that he lacked any ideas. In reality, he was playing the game. Horrified to be working for a dull leader, he decided to avoid arguing with May in public. She remained uninterested in foreign affairs and rarely revealed her own opinion – either because she did not have an opinion, or if she did, was uncertain whether it was right. She had also let slip that the top-secret briefings Boris received from the heads of MI6 and GCHQ should be limited 'in case he blurts it out'. To avoid humiliation, the best course was to remain neutral but that was difficult. On the eve of the Tory Party conference, only 16 per cent approved of May's performance on Brexit. So, with unexpected honesty Boris replied when asked about his ambition to be prime minister: 'If the ball comes loose from the back of the scrum, it would be a great thing to have a crack at.'

For the moment that was a forlorn hope but his lifestyle offered comfortable compensation. Although the Foreign Secretary's spacious private flat on the top floors of the official residence in Carlton Gardens overlooking the Mall was shabby, Marina and their children found a similarity with their Islington home. Being Foreign Secretary also offered many advantages. The house was staffed, a chauffeured car was always available, the foreign trips were often fun, the frequent official dinners with interesting foreign visitors were stimulating, and jogging in St James's Park was pleasant. The only disappointment was the Foreign Office itself.

Just as he could not master the machinery of government within the Foreign Office, he lacked empathy with foreign-policy experts. Instead of acknowledging the seriousness of their subject and communicating with them about themes and policies in their special language, he tended to speak light-heartedly from notes on scraps of paper, winging it with familiar jokes. Needing laughs for reassurance, he looked uncertain if his audience gazed back stony-faced. Regardless of his virtues, Boris soon discovered that his tabloid tactics incited gossip from his officials.

During a visit to Rome in November 2016, Boris told the Italian government that Italy should back London as a financial centre after Brexit. The alternative, he declared, would be tariffs on Prosecco, 'and every year we drink 300 million litres of Prosecco'. His statement accurately summarised the mutual advantages of a trade deal but his reputation encouraged the Italians to make out they were 'insulted'. If Prosecco was taxed, the foreign ministry said, Britain would sell less fish and chips in Europe. 'Outraged' Foreign Office officials sniggered to the media about the Foreign Secretary's clumsiness.

Soon after, Boris arrived in Ankara to 'make it up with the Turks' after his 'wankerer' limerick. 'I am delighted to say,' he said after meeting the Turkish foreign minister, 'that the trivial issue did not come up. Much to my amazement it has not come up at all.' Having blitzed Turks with praise, including 'I am certainly the proud possessor of a beautiful, well-functioning Turkish washing machine,' he then baffled them about his fondness for Jaffa cakes manufactured by a Turkish corporation in Britain. So far, no new problems had arisen. But then he advocated Turkey's right to enter the EU.

Foreign Office officials were quick to publicly highlight that he said the opposite during the referendum, and to add that he had also defended Turkey's right to reintroduce the death penalty.

Next, during a visit to Cairo, a Foreign Office official leaked to the BBC that Boris's flippancy had insulted President Sisi of Egypt who abruptly got up and walked out of the room. That report was never confirmed by the Egyptian government and the British official responsible consistently refused to confirm his slur.

Reports of those incidents reaching London encouraged Alan Duncan to describe his task as the 'deputy' Foreign Secretary to the media: 'I'm Boris's pooper-scooper – clearing up the mess he leaves behind,' he declared.

Perfectionists of the Foreign Office's black arts were thrilled when another spat erupted in Germany.

During a visit to the United Nations in New York in late September 2016, Boris had predicted that Article 50 to trigger Brexit would be invoked in early 2017. 'We should go for a jumbo free trade deal and take back control of immigration policy,' he said. Sceptics told him that Britain could not get a free trade deal with the EU's single market and also limit free movement. 'Cobblers,' he struck back. 'Complete baloney, absolute baloney.' Wolfgang Schäuble, Germany's finance minister, was scathing. 'He should read the Lisbon treaty,' Schäuble said. 'The link between the single market and the EU's four core principles – including free movement – is unbreakable.' Boris hit back: 'Freedom of movement' as one of the EU's fundamental freedoms was, he barked, a 'total myth' and 'bollocks'. People don't have a 'fundamental God-given right to move wherever they want'. Angela Merkel told Boris publicly he was wrong. The Foreign Secretary, she said, did not understand the implications of Brexit.

Two months later, Boris arrived with Alan Duncan in Berlin. Frank-Walter Steinmeier, the German foreign minister, was openly contemptuous of Boris. For the Protestant civil servant, embodying the Prussian tradition of civic duty, the bumbling English gentleman who, in his opinion, treated life as a joke excited the German's visceral dislike. Antagonistic anyway towards Britain,

Steinmeier did not bother to understand Boris's point of view. His uncompromising purpose was to promote German interests. Just as he had crushed Greece during its economic crisis, Steinmeier was certainly not prepared to contemplate that many Britons had voted Leave to escape Berlin's diktat.

Boris was warned before his visit that Germans do not understand British humour, but he insisted on deliberately misquoting John F. Kennedy's 1963 phrase '*Ich bin ein Berliner*' as '*Ich bin nicht ein Berliner*'. 'He's a clown,' muttered Steinmeier loudly. At their press conference, Steinmeier made clear his disapproval: 'You were on the side of those who saw the future of Britain outside the EU. I am making no secret of the fact, and you know that, that I was not particularly amused about this.' Boris laughed off the insult and went with Alan Duncan to see Angela Merkel. 'Please don't make any public-schoolboy jokes with her,' Duncan warned. Boris smiled. 'Agar's Plough,' Boris said to Merkel, referring to one of Eton's games fields, 'reminds me of Berlin.' Merkel looked puzzled – and Duncan was infuriated. Playing games with the Chancellor was not clever. Two weeks later, Boris's joke came back to haunt Theresa May. During her visit to Berlin to meet Merkel, she was told to wait at the British Embassy until she was summoned to the Chancellery. By then, the Chancellor's aides had discovered what 'Agar's Plough' referred to.

The Brussels bureaucrats joined the attack. Pascal Lamy, a fierce federalist in the European Commission, recalled: 'We had known Mr Johnson as a child in Brussels . . . I saw Boris as a nasty young kid – and he never changed.' Boris, he believed, had been appointed as 'a fake foreign minister' to make sure that Brexit didn't happen.

On her return to London, May reasserted herself. Downing Street leaked to newspapers that at a Cabinet Brexit committee meeting Boris had read from the wrong briefing papers and May was 'coming to the end of her tether' over Boris's 'gaffes' and 'bungles'. It was just the latest of May's put-downs. In her party conference speech in October, she had sniped 'When we came to Birmingham this week, some big questions were hanging in the air . . . Can Boris stay on message for a full four days? Just about.' More recently, at the *Spectator* Parliamentarian of the Year event in November, she watched Boris win the 'Comeback of the Year' award. 'I hope my comeback will be a bit longer than Kim the Alsatian,' he said, comparing his feat with Heseltine's recent story of how he had accidentally choked his mother's Alsatian, Kim,who survived but was put down shortly after. Theresa May spoke next. Boris's reference to Heseltine's story, May accurately commented, missed the salient point: 'Boris, the dog was put down . . . when its master decided it wasn't needed anymore.'

Added to May's contempt had been Sadiq Khan's decision to abandon the Routemaster and the Garden Bridge, despite adequate finance. Mocked and under pressure, Boris toughened up. 'If I'm hated, I'll have to get used to it,' he told a City Hall confidant. 'I'm not going to let them rob me of the referendum.'

'You must stop making gaffes,' Bernard Jenkin suggested.

'It's my personality,' Boris replied. 'I gaffe.'

Both May and McDonald, he felt, were robbing him of authority. On 2 December, he made a well-considered speech at Chatham House summarising 'Global Britain': 'I believe this country is overwhelmingly a force for the good with the potential to do even more and we should not be nervous in the projection of our values and our priorities. We have our own distinctive identity and contribution. We should never underestimate the catalytic power of our creativity and the sheer concentration of intellectual resources to be found on this island. It is in the interests of global order that we are at the centre of a network of relationships and alliances that span the world to promote British interests.'

Despite Boris's clear presentation, Robin Niblett, Chatham House's director, had already categorised his guest as a blustering buffoon. In self-interest, Niblett avoided finding fault with Simon McDonald, who had not directed his staff to offer a substantive interpretation of the choices for 'Global Britain'. 'Clearly,' McDonald would later admit, 'there have been shortcomings with the label because other people are in charge of interpretation' and 'we have to make choices'. The permanent undersecretary had shifted the responsibility of reassessing Britain's foreign policy into the ether.

Rather than addressing Britain's fate after Brexit, McDonald left London to frenetically visit British embassies around the world. Excited tweets devoid of foreign policy recounted his breakneck adventures. He left behind Karen Pierce, the feisty fifty-seven-year-old who would be promoted as the political director. Unlike McDonald, Pierce was impressed by Boris's focus and grasp of detail when required and on issues which interested him, but she could not save him from the Marmite prejudice dividing the Foreign Office.

That hostility hurt, particularly as he watched the destruction of Syria. Under bombardment, Aleppo, a breathtaking ancient city, was burning. Ten million Syrians had been forced from their homes and hundreds of thousands had been killed. Ever since Labour refused to vote in favour of retaliation for President Assad's use of sarin in 2013 and President Obama lost his nerve to destroy Syria's stores of nerve gas, Russia had exploited the vacuum and protected Assad's position. As Foreign Secretary, Boris found himself relying on diplomats lacking any influence to prevent Russia and Iran collaborating against western interests, or to negotiate Britain's alignment with Israel to sway events. Worse, he faced McDonald's advocacy of Britain meekly supporting Obama, a president without self-confidence, to change Syria's fate. Forlornly, Boris relied on an empty husk which had abandoned any influence in the Middle East. Instead of admitting their own errors, the foreign affairs club led by Simon McDonald and Robin Niblett preferred to blame Boris for their impotence.

Although now anxious to stop the slaughter in Syria, Boris had written the previous year, 'Let's deal with the Devil – we should work with Vladimir Putin and Bashar al-Assad.' While acknowledging that Putin was a 'ruthless and manipulative tyrant' and Assad was 'a monster, a dictator', he had supported both for attacking the murderous ISIS groups (and later for saving the ancient site of Palmyra from total destruction). As Foreign Secretary, he wanted to improve relations with Russia. In August 2016, he had contacted

Sergei Lavrov, the veteran Russian foreign minister. Ever since the Russians had murdered the former KGB officer Alexander Litvinenko in London in 2006, Britain's diplomacy with Moscow had been frozen. Relations had become even worse after Philip Hammond, as Foreign Secretary, had accused Putin of being a wife-beater. Hammond had also issued a pointless demand that Russia return Crimea to Ukraine. In Boris's opinion, that hard line should be tempered. He had learned a valuable lesson during his visit to Baghdad in 2003 after Saddam was deposed: 'It is better sometimes to have a tyrant than not to have a ruler at all.' That truth was revealed in Libya after Muammar Gaddafi's overthrow and, he thought, applied to Assad too. But Aleppo's destruction in the later months of 2016 persuaded him to reconsider. Nearly 5 million people had fled the city. In 'The agony of Aleppo', Boris wrote, 'we are forced to watch one of the most ancient homes of civilisation being literally pulverised, the lives of innocent families shattered by every kind of munition from barrel bombs to chlorine gas.' It was 'enough to make you weep that 400,000 have been killed'. Putin's rocket launchers had been targeted against civilians yet Jeremy Corbyn, the Labour leader, refused to protest about Russia's war crimes. Now Boris supported military intervention but Obama refused. In frustration, Boris publicly called for demonstrations outside the Russian embassy, a gesture which outraged the Foreign Office mandarins for endangering British diplomats in Moscow. The only result was the Kremlin's curse of Boris's 'Russophobic hysteria'. Undeterred, Boris proposed to visit Moscow. Britain, he said, must challenge Russia. His idea was instantly rejected by Theresa May. She would not allow the Foreign Secretary to stand on principle. That would be her task.

Without dwelling on the rebuke, Boris headed to the Gulf in December. At a regional security summit in Bahrain, he was cheered by the officials and politicians in the audience, an unusual response to speakers at those formal meetings. His success annoyed Downing Street. Retaliation was swift. In a private conversation, he correctly observed that Saudi Arabia and Iran were 'twisting and abusing' Islam for political objectives in the Yemen war. Instantly

Downing Street leaked that Boris had been summoned by May for a reprimand. Saudi Arabia, she told the 'schoolboy Foreign Secretary', must not be criticised. Boris refused to back down. Every serious attempt he made to re-establish Britain's independent foreign policy was crushed by Downing Street. Her personal vendetta, he said, had to stop. 'Instead of letting it die,' he complained, 'they put paraffin on the fire.' Through a newspaper interview, Boris warned, 'It's time to call off the dogs or Boris will snap.'

His hope to restore any understanding with May was dead. His chance of a leadership bid at the time was also hopeless. May's popularity was rising in the polls, helped by the public's distaste of Jeremy Corbyn. Walking through a Commons corridor, Conor Burns, a friendly MP whom Boris had met in 2016, watched him pass some Tory MPs. Boris's hands were in his pockets and his head was down. 'Why don't you say hi to them?' Burns asked. 'I don't know them,' he replied. To another MP, Boris admitted that since Brexit he had lost friends and was separated from the people he loved most, especially his family. In his loneliness, he regularly called Petronella Wyatt. Over one lunch while he was still mayor she had asked whether he was doing anything stupid, like having another affair. No, he replied. Good, she said. You must stay domesticated. As his affair with Jennifer Arcuri had ended, he asked Petronella whether she wanted to revive their relationship. She declined. That meant there was a vacancy. He headed to Chevening for Christmas to contemplate his future.

Among his many irritations was Alan Duncan, the prime minister's ally. In the days before Christmas, Boris discovered that Duncan had been sending text messages to Chris Bryant, a Labour MP and foreign-affairs specialist. 'Give him hell,' Duncan texted Bryant, a contemporary of Boris's at Oxford. 'I thought Boris was a fraud then,' says Bryant, who when a student was 'a proper Tory'. Bryant was grateful for the information Duncan supplied to question Boris in the Commons. Unaccustomed to hostile manoeuvring within his own office, Boris was flummoxed. There was no solution. He could only wait for events to unfold.

Chevening at Christmas offered temporary respite from the

Foreign Office's malignancy. Over twenty Johnsons – including Charlotte, his mother, her four children and her grandchildren – descended on the house to enjoy 'Marina's Magic' – days of good food, dancing and party games including Assassination, a game invented by the Wheeler family. The Johnsons would look back at that Christmas and their other visits to the house as probably their happiest reunions. More than in recent years, the relationship between Boris and Marina appeared to be calm and stable. Rachel and Stanley were enjoying considerable success writing for newspapers and appearing on TV; while Jo had become a high-profile minister responsible for universities. Looking at their youngest sibling, neither Boris nor Rachel could forget their telephone conversation twenty-two years earlier at the end of Jo's studies in Oxford. 'Have you heard the bad news about Jo?' Rachel had asked Boris. 'He got a first.' Even in 2013, when asked about Jo's appointment as the head of Cameron's policy unit in Downing Street, Boris said, 'A little piece of me dies but otherwise I rejoice in his success.' Only Leo had kept himself out of the spotlight and uninvolved in the family's frantic competitiveness. None of the family leaving the house after the holiday imagined that Boris's happiness would soon end.

In the first days of 2017, Boris heard that the Foreign Office officials were unable to establish a relationship with the key staff close to Donald Trump, the newly elected president, ahead of his inauguration on 20 January. One of the reasons was Trump's antagonism towards Kim Darroch, the British ambassador. In his secret reports to the Foreign Office, Darroch had not only predicted that Hillary Clinton would win the election but was also disparaging about the Republican candidate. Darroch's opinions were leaked to Trump, possibly by Nigel Farage, the UKIP leader. To Farage's glee, Steve Bannon, Trump's mercurial strategist, had invited Farage to meet Trump. The result in December was an embarrassment for Simon McDonald. The Trump team was ignoring Darroch's attempts to arrange for Theresa May to be among the first leaders called after the new president's inauguration. For the cheerleaders of the 'special relationship', to be one of the first to receive Trump's call was vital. To remedy Darroch's failure, in December May had sent her closest advisers, Nick Timothy and Fiona Hill, to Washington. Both had sat in the embassy only to discover that they too were unable to establish any contacts with Trump's staff, and returned to London. Their embarrassment was compounded after a photograph appeared of Farage with Trump. May realised that the only person who might be able to protect her from humiliation was Boris – not because he and Trump had much in common, but because instinctively Boris made friends rather than enemies; and although she hated the idea of Boris meeting Trump, the two mavericks did already have a relationship.

At the outset, that relationship had been fractious. In the wake of an Islamic terrorist attack in California in December 2015, Trump had called for a 'total shutdown' of Muslims entering America. He added that parts of London were so radicalised that the police feared for their lives. 'Complete and utter nonsense,' replied Mayor Johnson. 'When Donald Trump says there are parts of London that are "no-go" areas, I think he's betraying a quite stupefying ignorance that makes him frankly unfit to hold the office of president of the United States. I would invite him to see the whole of London and take him around the city except that I wouldn't want to expose Londoners to any unnecessary risk of meeting Donald Trump.' Eleven months later, with Bannon's help, relations between Boris and Trump had been repaired. During a visit to Scotland after the referendum, Trump praised Brexit as a 'beautiful, beautiful thing' and promised if he became president, Britain would be 'at the front' of the queue in trade talks. 'Congratulations to Donald Trump' Boris tweeted in November 2016 after the US election. 'We are much looking forward to working with his administration on global stability and prosperity.' Provocatively, he criticised the EU's 'hysteria' and 'collective whinge-o-rama' about Trump: 'There is every reason to be positive about a liberal guy from New York who believes firmly in the values I believe in too – freedom and democracy.' In early January 2017, May asked Boris to approach Trump.

On 8 January, Boris met Jared Kushner, Trump's son-in-law, and Steve Bannon in New York's Trump Tower. After a robust discussion about the advantages of free trade (they agreed about the EU's vices) and Iran (they disagreed about lifting sanctions), Boris emerged to declare that the UK had been pushed to 'the front of the queue'. To underline Britain's commitment to the new president, Boris refused to sign an EU declaration at a Middle East conference critical of Israel. But despite his best efforts, Theresa May was the tenth world leader Trump called after his inauguration. The leaders of Egypt, India and Ireland preceded her.

Britain's prime minister was her own worst enemy. With limited emotional intelligence, she struggled to forge personal relationships with foreign leaders, especially the Europeans. Not only was she unsympathetic towards Europe, but she misunderstood Brexit – not least because she did not really believe in its benefits. Six months after becoming prime minister, the confusion continued. In her varying demands for a hard Brexit and Britain's departure from the single market, she outlined no meaningful trade deal to Brussels. Occasionally, she even suggested that Britain might after all remain in the single market. May, briefed Downing Street, had 'an open mind' but others concluded she had no idea about how to fashion an acceptable trade deal. Nor was she certain whether EU nationals living in Britain could stay. Without formulated policies, her three Brexit ministers also failed to agree a negotiating plan for a defined relationship with the EU.

Contemptuous of the government's 'muddled thinking', Ivan Rogers resigned from the Foreign Office in early January. Davis, Boris and Fox, he complained, were ignorant about the single market and inexperienced in negotiations. The politicians, he warned, had not listened to his warnings about the chaos of a no-deal Brexit. Nor had May. She had said 'No deal would be better than a bad deal'. Boris endorsed that fatalism. 'It would be perfectly OK,' he said, 'if we aren't able to get an agreement and leave without a deal.' The consequences, he added, would 'not be as apocalyptic as some people like to pretend'. Boris shared Davis's irritation about Rogers, whom both believed was intent on reversing the referendum. Like so many civil servants, Rogers's anger encouraged the BBC to denigrate Brexiteers as 'populists' and 'racists' who had 'lied' to win the

Leave vote. In the irreconcilable division between Brexiteers and Remainers, the absence of leadership from Downing Street left many questions unasked. Neither May nor Boris questioned why David Davis had not costed or made any contingency preparations for a no-deal Brexit.

In the vacuum, Boris assessed his tactics – and resorted to doing exactly the opposite to expectations. Exasperated by the clichés popular among diplomats, he resorted to gung-ho banter towards Europe. Asked to comment about President François Hollande's truism that Britain could not expect the same trading relationship with the EU after Brexit, Boris stuck the boot in: 'If Monsieur Hollande wants to administer punishment beatings to anyone who chooses to escape, rather in the manner of some World War Two movie, then I don't think that's the way forward.' European politicians were outraged. 'Abhorrent and deeply unhelpful,' said Belgium's Guy Verhofstadt, the European Parliament's chief negotiator. 'There is no government policy of not mentioning the war,' said Downing Street, for once defending Boris. Still intent on annoying the Europeans, in February 2017 Boris arrived with Alan Duncan at the annual Munich security conference. In that serious forum, Boris was unwilling to engage in foreign-policy discussions. Rather, he joked, 'Brexit is liberation', like Europe's liberation from the Nazis. 'He can never resist a gag,' Duncan told the appalled audience. 'Boris is rude, offensive and dumb,' Frank-Walter Steinmeier told Labour MP Chris Bryant.

Unable to unite her Cabinet and without sufficient preparation, May ordered the delivery of the letter to the EU on 29 March 2017 to trigger Article 50, the two-year countdown to Britain's departure. 'A magnificent moment,' said Boris, although he had been forbidden until the last moment to read the letter. In a mix of messages, May warned the EU that a punitive approach would be 'an act of calamitous self-harm' and urged them to agree 'a deep and special partnership'. If the EU demanded a hefty divorce bill, she wrote, then Britain would cease co-operating on security. 'Blackmail,' screeched the Eurocrats. Britain, said Juncker, would 'regret' its decision, forecasting gridlock at Dover and the disruption of

flights. His Eurocrats demanded a £100 billion payment while Liam
Fox estimated £3 billion was appropriate. 'The EU can go whistle
if it wants £100 billion for exit payment,' said Boris. 'It's extortion-
ate. We'll leave and pay nothing.' Sniping at Boris, Philip Hammond,
who had read the letter, said 'We can't cherry-pick, and we can't
have our cake and eat it.' Boris's no-deal exit, he added, was 'Ridiculous'. Parliament would never agree to a no-deal exit and he refused
to spend billions of pounds planning for the event.

Amid that dissent, May fell at the first hurdle. Although Article
50 stipulated that the negotiations for the exit terms and the future
trade relationship should be simultaneous, Angela Merkel instantly
rejected that provision. Britain would have to settle its debts first,
ordered the German Chancellor, and then proceed to its future
trade relations with Europe, including the City's access. Foolishly,
May had failed to fix the sequencing before triggering Article 50.
Worse, Whitehall had failed to produce a detailed proposal for Britain's future relationship with the EU. Solutions would be needed to
a myriad of contradictions. With her usual lack of anticipation, May
had sown the seeds for a constitutional crisis.

The Leavers wanted Britain to have the power to walk away
from a bad deal. Only that threat, they argued, would force the EU
at the last moment to agree to tolerable terms. The Remainers
wanted Parliament to retain the power to prevent a no-deal Brexit.
To prevent a no-deal Brexit, the Remainers started judicial proceedings to compel the government to abide by Parliament's wishes. A
constitutional time bomb was triggered.

Fighting on so many fronts, Downing Street was keen to deny
Boris opportunities to destabilise the government. With a quiet
word, the Foreign Office was encouraged to keep him away from
Europe. At McDonald's suggestion, Boris flew to East Africa, visiting Somalia, Uganda and Kenya, and then on to Washington where
he hoped to agree with Rex Tillerson, the new Secretary of State,
that Assad should be removed. Tillerson was puzzled.

For months, Boris had praised Assad for protecting Palmyra
from ISIS – 'The terrorists are on the run. I say bravo – and keep
going,' he wrote – and he had also praised Putin's support for Assad.

But shortly before he arrived in Washington, he somersaulted. On 4 April, Assad had dropped sarin on civilians, killing about eighty people. Four days later, American bombers struck a Syrian airbase. Boris planned to visit Moscow one week later. In their discussions, Boris told Tillerson he intended to threaten Russia with sanctions for its direct complicity in Assad's war crime. He returned to London anticipating his visit to Russia, the first by a British Foreign Secretary in five years. But at the last moment, he was ordered to stay put. Tillerson insisted on visiting Moscow first. He arrived with a foolish demand that Putin remove Assad. Russia had supported Syria against Israel since the early 1950s. Putin would never abandon Syria, just as America would not forsake Israel.

Still eager, in spite of May's endorsement of Tillerson's snub, to show his effectiveness, in April Boris next headed for a G7 meeting in Lucca, Italy. In advance, he said he was a man with a plan to punish the Russian and Syrian warmongers. The German and French governments, he was told by his officials, were 'four-square' behind him. Instead, he discovered that both countries and Italy opposed sanctions. The responsibility for making him look foolish at the conference was unclear but Downing Street was delighted by his humiliation. May, said the prime minister's spokesman, was 'unimpressed with Boris'. After hearing that Downing Street described the Foreign Secretary's influence as 'neutralised', he was cast by Labour as 'the figurehead of Britain's floundering foreign policy . . . the cartoon character at the helm' orchestrating 'another pratfall'. What followed was bizarre. Boris told the Commons that Assad was 'a monster' in need of 'decapitating' and Britain would support future American attacks against Syria. Hours later, Downing Street contradicted 'Bungling Boris'. Britain would not support American bombing, said May's spokesman. However hard he tried, lamented Boris to a senior official, Downing Street contrived to make him fail.

Squashing Boris had become an amusing sideshow for Theresa May's calculations. Her rising popularity against Jeremy Corbyn had produced outstanding victories in recent local elections. With opinion polls recording a 24 per cent Tory lead, David Davis was among many urging May to call a snap general election. This was, she thought, the ideal moment to increase the Tory majority of just seventeen MPs to push Brexit through the Commons. Among the few urging her to resist was Lynton Crosby. Boris ranked among the many who were told of her plan only at the last moment. He was not among the few fearful of the result of the election set for 8 June. Nor did he warn about the prospect of a seven-week campaign focused on an uncharismatic leader without the common touch.

Surrounded by her praetorian guard, Boris and other Cabinet ministers were denied the opportunity to read and discuss the party's manifesto in advance. There was good reason for May's unusual secrecy. Her pledge of higher taxes and more regulation was distinctly un-Conservative. Boris's impotence was aggravated by further humiliation. Downing Street leaked that, in a panic, Boris had asked May for reassurance he would not be sacked after the expected landslide. She refused to give him that comfort.

Over the following weeks, May's arrogance crumbled. While she addressed small, selected audiences offering neither inspiration nor excitement, Jeremy Corbyn was taking the country by storm. Reawakening the idealism of Old Labour, thousands of voters – young and old – were enthusiastically packing into arenas aroused by his vision of an egalitarian socialist state. Four days after her manifesto launch, May self-destructed. The manifesto referred to legislation to compel old-age homeowners to sell their homes to pay for their care. Hammered as the 'dementia tax', May retreated, abandoned the proposal, and thereafter struggled to survive. Against her, Corbyn's vision of glorious socialism included the cancellation of student debts, the promise of cheap housing and a wages bonanza for all public workers.

In the final week, the Tories' original 24 per cent lead fell towards zero. Boris's own campaign was struggling. On May's orders, he had been excluded from the spotlight. His critics pounced whenever possible. At a Sikh temple in Bristol, he enthusiastically predicted increased whisky exports to India. The media focused on the anger of teetotal Sikhs in his audience, but ignored the Sikhs who drank alcohol. Then the news broke that Rachel Johnson had joined the Lib Dems to fight against Brexit. The Tories, she complained, treated her 'like a brainwashed member of a cult'. That unfortunate headline was eclipsed by a painful sting during his return to Balliol to celebrate the eightieth birthday of his favourite tutor, Jasper Griffin. In the middle of the campaign, Boris composed a witty poem written in Griffin's honour. While he read it out loud, he was shunned by several guests opposed to Brexit. In particular, Oswyn Murray, his ancient-history tutor, was openly incensed by Boris's presence. 'Probably the worst scholar Eton ever sent us,' he said shortly after. 'A buffoon and an idler.'

As Boris left the college, undergraduates hissed and booed. Anthony Kenny, Balliol's former master, reflected ruefully on the college's part in Boris's education: 'We had been privileged to be given the task of bringing up members of the nation's political elite. But what had we done for Boris? Had we taught him truthfulness? No. Had we taught him wisdom? No. What had we taught? Was it only how to make witty and brilliant speeches? I comforted myself with the thought that even Socrates was very doubtful whether virtue could be taught.'

Eight days later, Boris was asked to give the warm-up speech in Birmingham for May's last appearance before polling day. In his speech, he warned, Jeremy Corbyn was not the 'mutton-headed old mugwump' tending his allotment that Boris had described in April, but a dangerous Marxist. Salvation, said Boris, depended on 'Our wonderful prime minister.'

Over the previous seven weeks, 'Maybot' had proven to be reluctant to risk exposure to the public. The last YouGov opinion poll accurately predicted the outcome. Fifty-eight hours later, on 9 June, the final results confirmed that the Tories had lost thirteen seats and were eight seats short of an overall majority. Corbyn had done spectacularly well. The Labour Party had won 3.5 million more votes than in 2015. The Tories, even with a record 42 per cent of the vote, were saved from total humiliation by a popular wave in Scotland. In revenge for the manner of May's dismissal of him as Chancellor in July the previous year, George Osborne (now editor of the *Evening Standard*) wrote: 'Theresa May is a dead woman walking. It's just how long she's going to remain on death row.' Osborne also attacked Boris for being 'in a permanent leadership campaign'.

During that night, many assumed that May, humiliated and tearful, would resign. Several Cabinet ministers phoned or texted Boris to urge him to bid for the leadership. Opinion polls cast him as the firm favourite to beat David Davis as the next leader. Boris, however, feared that little had changed over the past year. Too many MPs did not trust him. There were rumours that Hammond and Davis were already aligning against him. Indeed, at the *Spectator*'s summer party one month later, Davis told Boris openly, 'You're a failure.'

'I'll kick you in the bollocks,' retorted Boris, suspecting Davis of spreading rumours about Boris's affairs.

Uncertain of his prospects, Boris decided to await May's resignation. The ghost of Michael Heseltine – the unsuccessful plotter against Thatcher for the leadership – haunted Boris. A display of his ultra loyalty was required.

That night, Boris texted May that he would not force her departure. Relieved, the shell-shocked woman held up her phone to show the message to her advisers. In return, Boris would remain at the Foreign Office. 'Folks,' Boris emailed some MPs, 'we need to calm down and get behind the prime minister.' Despite Corbyn's demands that May resign, Labour had been defeated. The public, Boris wrote two days later in the *Sun*, 'are fed up to the back teeth' after three elections in three years. They did not want any more turmoil. He supported May – 'a woman of extraordinary qualities'. She could remain because there was no obvious, outright successor.

The government's fate now depended on forging an agreement with Ulster's DUP party. With the DUP's ten MPs, the Tories would have a Commons majority. The hazards of any deal with them were well known. The Ulster Unionists were opposed to a Brexit agreement which made a united Ireland more likely. That presented May with a near-insoluble problem. The DUP's version of Brexit meant that a trade border would be resurrected across Ireland. But, at Dublin's behest, Brussels insisted on free movement between the two parts of Ireland. Despite warnings, Boris had ignored the Irish border while campaigning for Brexit. But since the DUP loathed Corbyn for supporting the IRA, a deal with the Conservatives was certain.

'I'm the one who got us into this mess,' May told Tory MPs four days after the election, 'and I'm the one who will get us out of it.' As a public duty, she had offered unselfishly to serve the national interest and keep the job she always yearned to have. Her hollow crown left her powerless to control her rebel ministers, her Cabinet, or Parliament.

Chapter 23

'Boris is Boris'

Boris returned to the Foreign Office weakened by the election result. The government's inability to agree a soft or hard Brexit and the disdain directed at him in Parliament, Whitehall and across the EU undermined his credibility.

At the regular Friday morning meeting, Simon McDonald and his senior officials still regarded Boris as an intellectual vandal for destroying their Eurocentric statecraft. Encouraged by Tony Blair and other Remainers, they now hoped that the weak minority government could not prevent Brexit being reversed. If the EU could be spurred to reform itself, the reasons for Brexit would be undermined.

Their tactics were first to encourage their European colleagues to remain uncompromising towards a divided government. And then to take every opportunity to undermine Boris. The truculent officials were encouraged by the junior foreign ministers, Alan Duncan and Alistair Burt, responsible for the Middle East. Both were Remainers. Boris's only ally was the Brexiteer Conor Burns, his new parliamentary private secretary, who had replaced Andrew Stephenson, viewed as May's 'spy'. 'We'll be an amazing partnership and have fun,' Boris had told Burns.

At those regular Foreign Office meetings, Boris gave no hint of his suspicions. Despite finally being in Cabinet, he still shied away from confronting those suspected of sabotage. At the head of the list of the marked men was Simon McDonald, followed by many peers, the CBI's leaders, the BBC and certain newspapers, especially the pro-Remain *Times*. As his declared opponent, *The Times* pronounced, 'Not a single foreign minister in Europe takes [him] seriously.' In their view, stated the editorial, Boris was 'totally unreliable', a 'liar' and 'dangerous'. Even worse, Boris said, was the BBC. To his bemusement, the BBC chose to ignore the Treasury's forecasts frequently broadcast before the referendum of an immediate rise of unemployment of between 500,000 and 800,000 if Britain voted Leave. Those forecasts proved to be wrong. The BBC's journalists were clearly irritated that since the referendum, 400,000 new jobs had been created and unemployment was the lowest for forty-two years. The proof of their bias, scoffed Boris, was that their reports about Britain's successful economy were invariably prefaced 'In spite of Brexit . . .' Winning the propaganda battle would depend upon his leadership.

'Tomorrow the Brexit negotiations begin,' Boris wrote in the *Sunday Times*, a pro-Brexit newspaper, soon after the election. 'I urge the EU to work together with Britain.' His ideal settlement was 'open Britain' enjoying zero tariffs and frictionless trade for on-time delivery and production as previously within the EU. Negotiating that free trade deal with the EU, David Davis had promised, would be 'simple'. Officials in London and Europe shared frustrated anger with both Davis and Boris. Davis, said Juncker, was 'lazy and unstable'. Firstly, because he had not recruited any civil servants to manage the increase of customs declarations after Brexit – estimated to rise from 55 million declarations to 255 million – and secondly, because frictionless trade – especially for the motor, aerospace and pharmaceutical industries – depended on British exports to the EU complying with EU regulations. Davis and Boris were deaf to the importance of non-tariff barriers. Instead of understanding the complexity, they both threatened to leave the EU without a deal, preferring to assume that problems could be resolved during the negotiations, and seemingly unconcerned by the prospect of failure. Britain, they envisaged, would be a Singapore-style deregulated, offshore tax haven. Their scenario provoked rage in Brussels, especially Michel Barnier's, the EU's French chief negotiator. Creating mayhem, Foreign Office officials conjectured – without evidence – reflected Boris's wish for the negotiations to fail so he could overthrow May.

The officials' scenario came sooner than expected. On 14 June, Grenfell, a twenty-four storey block of flats in Kensington, west London, burst into flames. Incompetent firefighters inadvertently allowed the flames to take hold in the new cladding and then ordered the roughly 250 residents to remain in their homes while they fought the inferno. They failed, and seventy-two people died. The following day, May visited the disaster scene. Insensitive and scared, she stood briefly inside a cordon and avoided meeting any survivors. Jeremy Corbyn arrived soon after and hugged the distraught families. He was hailed a hero. Many Tories were aghast. All May's flaws revealed during the recent election were confirmed in the shadow of the burnt-out tower block. Several Tory associations demanded her resignation. Boris, the bookies' favourite, might have been poised to take over but he was stumbling after attacks from various quarters.

Tainted by the bogus '£350 million' slogan on the bus, a majority of Tory MPs, all Remainers, spread doubts about his veracity. Their argument was strengthened by David Norgrove of the UK Statistics Authority who criticised a 'clear misuse of data'. In the constituencies, the members may have loved his entertaining speeches but they questioned his judgement after the leadership fiasco in 2016. Why did he pull out? Was there more to it than just Gove? Was it a loss of self-confidence? Was he also an unpredictable risk? Was he just too much of a gambler? Rightly, he sensed his enemies were poised to attack the man rather than just his politics. It was best, Boris decided, to keep a low profile as Britain lurched into unusual turmoil.

Theresa May's unpopularity had encouraged the left to weaponise the Grenfell disaster. To Corbyn's satisfaction, the BBC and Channel 4 presented the tragedy as a capitalist conspiracy against downtrodden workers. The TV news reports of desperate survivors and '200' deaths, the victims of heartless Tories, emboldened Corbyn's supporters to chant 'murderers'. Trotskyist agitators spread the message that the dispossessed should grab power. Across the capital, Corbyn and his group spoke about 'mobilising the masses', a general strike, and revolution. This was the moment, Corbyn said, to topple May. In the excitement, a BBC commentator described the Labour leader's appearance at the Glastonbury festival at the end of June as 'brilliant'. But the left's revolution fizzled out in two weeks after Labour's 'March of One Million' through London attracted just 20,000 protestors. Throughout those unsettled weeks, May offered no reassuring leadership and then disappeared for a three-week holiday in the Alps. She left behind debris – of her party, her government and her ministers' reputations. At the end of August, Boris returned to the Foreign Office weaker than ever. Downing Street's beleaguered occupant declared a war for her own survival soon after.

On 6 September, Hurricane Irma devastated the Caribbean. Anguilla, a British protectorate, was hit particularly hard. Within two hours of the storm passing, Boris telephoned the chief minister and by the following day a Royal Navy ship was offshore with supplies. As soon as aircraft could land safely, Boris arrived on the stricken island with more troops, supplies for reconstruction and the promise of more money. His conduct was blameless.

Watching Boris's TV interviews in the Downing Street gloom, May complained that her rival was as usual not promoting the national interest but himself. Hours later, he was accused of 'bluster' and providing insufficient help to the island. A group of journalists reported that Boris was a grandstanding fool ill-prepared to focus on detail. In the *Telegraph*, one week after the hurricane, Fraser Nelson speculated that Boris was hiding and silent because he had nothing to say, was lazy, had been over-promoted, or was playing dead until May's leadership was over to avoid being labelled as a plotter. In any event, concluded Nelson, Boris's chance to be prime minister 'came and went last year'. On the same day, Iain Martin in *The Times* declared 'Boris seems done for.' And Oliver Kamm, also in *The Times*, damned the Foreign Secretary as 'idle and incompetent' and someone who 'inspires derision among Britain's allies'. The seemingly coordinated onslaught, Boris suspected, had a purpose.

He returned from the Caribbean to discover that May had excluded him from crucial discussions to agree Britain's Brexit proposals. In a series of meetings, she had sided with Hammond's preference for a soft Brexit. After leaving the EU, Britain would pay an annual fee for at least five years to stay in the customs union and single market. Britain's re-engineered position, Boris was told, would be presented by the prime minister on 22 September in Florence. Opposed to that deal, and convinced that May was incapable of negotiating *any* deal, Boris declared war.

On 16 September, he published 'My Brexit Vision', a 4,200-word manifesto for 'Glorious Brexit'. The substance was drawn from a speech, banned by May. In the *Telegraph* article, he described Britain, freed from the EU, becoming a low-tax and low-regulation economy. Avoiding jingoistic arguments, he wrote that too often Brussels was blamed for Britain's inferior education and low productivity. In reality, these were home-made defects. After Brexit, he envisaged an explosion of investment in science and technology which had eluded Britain while constrained by European regulations. He recalled the experience of Damijan Vnuk, a Slovenian farmer knocked off his ladder by a tractor in 2007. Vnuk's action for damages against the tractor's driver failed because it was an off-road incident and under Slovenian law, insurance was unnecessary. In 2014 the European Court of Justice overruled Slovenian law. Off-road vehicles were ordered to be insured. So, without any appeal, all Europeans were compelled to insure their quad bikes, Segways and scooters for use on their private land. Brexit, wrote Boris, would end that over-regulation. 'Our destiny will be in our own hands,' he concluded. Cheekily, he then tweeted, 'Looking forward to PM's Florence speech. All behind Theresa for a glorious Brexit.' As intended, the party's divisions were once again aggravated. The spotlight shone on him during a four-day media firestorm led by Remain-supporting newspapers.

The *Daily Mail* raged about a 'self-indulgent and divisive' attention-seeker; the *Mail on Sunday* described a 'ruthless, flaky opportunist ... to whom ambition is like a flesh-eating disease coursing through his body'; in *The Times*, he had 'blundered in with a series of egomaniacal meanderings'; others wrote about 'this insecure champion of the nationalist right'. In private, May damned Boris's treachery but in public she just lamented, 'Boris is Boris.' She did not dare fire him and risk his challenge from the back benches.

To recover control over Brexit, May demoted David Davis on 18 September, and Olly Robbins, Britain's senior Brexit negotiator and a Remainer, moved into Downing Street. Whitehall's machine was reorganised to develop a soft Brexit. On the same morning, May held a special Cabinet ostensibly to reconcile Hammond's and Boris's demands. Conveniently, Boris was in New York for a United Nations meeting but he threw a grenade across the Atlantic. His *Telegraph* article, he said, was 'a bit of an opening drum roll'. Inevitably, May failed to resolve her ministers' disagreements. Hammond refused to countenance Boris's threat of a no-deal crash out. 'He doesn't understand supply chains,' said Hammond, aghast at the inevitable destruction of the economy that would follow a no-deal exit. Later that day, on her way to the UN meeting in New York, May said wanly, 'We are all going in the same direction.' At the same time, outside Manhattan's Westin hotel, Boris was asked by TV journalists whether he would resign. With his eyes darting nervously from side to side, rapidly calculating his predicament, he replied 'I think you may be barking slightly up the wrong tree here.'

During the morning, while May was crossing the Atlantic, Boris sat among Commonwealth foreign ministers and afterwards met the Ugandan president. The French, Boris heard, were encroaching into Britain's traditional spheres of influence. 'We must beat the French,' he told his officials when he returned to the British delegation's office. International conferences should be held in London, not Paris. 'Why are they so beastly?' he asked, punchily displaying his suspicions. 'Because the French have their own interests,' an official replied. 'We shouldn't roll over,' said Boris. 'We must take their interests into account,' the official insisted. His officials' submission to Europe appeared to be irreversible.

Later that day, Boris drove out to JFK airport to meet May in the VIP lounge. Unexpectedly, the Jordanian foreign minister walked in, spotted Boris and joined them for a fifteen-minute conversation. Many appreciated meeting Boris. The prime minister was not one of them. On their journey into Manhattan, she issued an ultimatum: stay loyal or resign. He countered that Hammond's five-year transition was unacceptable. By the time they arrived at the Westin, there was no agreement. 'Boris,' she told Sky TV, 'is doing a good job as Foreign Secretary.' The following morning, as Boris returned sweaty from a run, he concealed their latest battle. 'The Cabinet is a nest of singing birds,' he told journalists. The next day, on the flight back to London, they agreed a compromise. In Florence, May could offer a two-year transition until 2021 and a payment of £20 billion. In a choreographed show of unity after the next Cabinet meeting, Boris and Hammond emerged from 10 Downing Street together. Both feigned enthusiasm and both were dissatisfied.

Three days after May's Florence speech, warfare broke out again. Michel Barnier dismissed May's offer as unsatisfactory while Boris reneged on their agreement and denounced the proposed transition arrangements. The Tory Party was slipping towards a nervous breakdown. Boris appeared isolated but May knew that to dismiss him to the back benches would create an even bigger threat. Her survival depended on damaging the rebel. Accordingly, her spokesman denounced Boris's insatiable ego as 'posturing', dismissed his 'straw' threats as self-publicity, and released a statement by May: 'I'm in it for the long term.' Privately, Boris doubted she could last more than one year. To prepare for the next leadership battle, his loyal team of MPs were continuing to host receptions to win more support. But their task was not made easy by their candidate. Boris could not stop handing his enemies opportunities to highlight his 'gaffes'.

To keep him out of London, the Foreign Office had arranged a visit to Myanmar (formerly Burma). Standing at the Shwedagon Pagoda, a 2,600-year-old gold Buddhist temple in the capital, Boris began to recite the opening verse of Rudyard Kipling's 'The Road to Mandalay', a British serviceman's nostalgic recollection of kissing a Burmese girl during the era of colonial rule. 'Not appropriate,' said Andrew Patrick, the ambassador standing nearby. 'Good stuff,' replied Boris. The exchange was recorded by Channel 4. With delight, the Foreign Office encouraged the media to watch the video and ridicule the Foreign Secretary. Alan Duncan, still the 'deputy' Foreign Secretary, also reminded the public of his role as Monsieur Le Poop Scoop, always rushing to placate angry Europeans about Boris's 'diplomatic mess'. Curiously, Duncan's services were not required after Simon McDonald referred to the Golden Temple in Amritsar, India, as the 'Golden Mosque'. The temple is a Sikh shrine. 'I am wrong. I am sorry,' wrote McDonald.

Boris's next stop was the party conference in Manchester. After her election disaster, Theresa May could not expect a rapturous welcome. Leading their familiar chorus, Ruth Davidson, the popular Scottish Tory leader, urged May to appoint 'serious people' to negotiate with the EU. She echoed outraged German politicians like Manfred Weber, a German MEP. 'Please sack Johnson,' Weber implored May. Boris's approach was to avoid reacting to his enemies, especially in his conference speeches.

Plotting his position carefully so as not to appear disloyal, he uttered only praise about May to the packed hall. In a speech headed 'Let the Lion Roar', he told his adoring audience 'The whole country owes her a debt for her steadfastness.' To those 'sunk in gloom', he said 'we can win the future'. Britain would not 'bottle out of Brexit'. The audience rejoiced. The challenger enjoyed the spotlight, despite Michael Heseltine's ridicule of him in the media as a populist feeding on 'the emotional nostalgia of a dying generation'. In his prime, Heseltine could have turned the audience against Boris but May lacked Heseltine's skills. As she walked onto the same platform the following day, the odds were stacked against her.

Twenty-five minutes late, she was suffering from a sore throat and bad cold. Wooden, she watched in silence from the lectern as a man approached the stage. 'Prime minister,' said the prankster, 'Boris asked me to give this to you.' He handed her a large cardboard P45. She then started her speech. Sipping and spilling water, her voice trailed off into coughs, croaks, a whisper and then into silence. Cheered by the audience, she resumed her speech until, behind her, the letters of the slogan 'Building a country that works for everyone', began one by one to fall. The catastrophe symbolised her decaying premiership. In the audience, Boris was transfixed. Abruptly, she ended her speech and left the stage. Within hours, Boris's enemies were on manoeuvres. Fearful that May's demise would lead to Corbyn's victory in another election, they focused once again on undermining him. Boris had handed them the opportunity with another apparent gaffe.

At a fringe event the previous night, Boris had referred to his visit to Libya in August. The Foreign Office, he explained, was providing £3 million to clear 5,000 improvised explosive devices (IEDs) left by ISIS fighters around Sirte, a major city on the coast. Many of the IEDs had been planted as booby traps beneath corpses of militants. 'There's a group of UK business people,' said Boris, 'wonderful guys, who literally have a brilliant vision to turn Sirte into the next Dubai. The only thing they've got to do is clear the dead bodies away and then they'll be there.' Within hours, Boris's critics accused him of a heinous crime.

'Why is anyone having a problem condemning these comments?' twittered justice minister Phillip Lee. 'I do. Anyone decent would.' Jeremy Hunt, the Health Secretary, was equally damning: 'Boris is Boris and that was very unfortunate language. I don't want to defend that.' Tory backbencher Anna Soubry said he was 'embarrassing'. Sarah Wollaston, a Remainer Tory, called the remarks 'crass, poorly judged and grossly insensitive'. All called on him to resign. Lee and both women would cross to the Opposition benches in the Commons in 2019 to vote against Brexit.

Foreign Office mandarins were equally scathing about his 'disrespect of Libyan suffering'. His 'after dinner' language, they scoffed, 'showed a tin ear to history' which might suit the *Telegraph* but not the foreign-ministers' club. Unrepentant, Boris returned to the Foreign Office to contemplate the prospects of a zombie government.

One month earlier, Conor Burns had brokered peace between Boris and Michael Gove, the new Environment Secretary. Meeting in Boris's office for twenty-five minutes, Gove poured forth as he later explained, 'Sometimes, my judgement has been faulty. Sometimes, horrendously faulty.' The result, he added, was 'me driving 100 mph and crashing into a brick wall'. Unwilling by nature to harbour resentment, Boris had accepted Gove's personal apology. 'He is a man of great talent,' explained Boris, 'and my job is to bring the party together. I am not a vindictive person at all. I bear no grudges.' 'Caesar forgave Brutus after the first betrayal,' Boris was warned, but he laughed. The two now united to prevent Hammond overturning Brexit, while puzzling about the Home Secretary, Amber Rudd. She was on manoeuvres. On one day, she attacked Boris for 'back-seat driving' on the EU negotiations and damned no-deal as 'unthinkable', but soon after she had secretly approached him to offer her support for his leadership. In return, she wanted to be his deputy. Forthright but flaky, Rudd had admirers but was best ignored as a perfidious lightweight.

Challenging May, Boris and Gove agreed, was blighted until Hammond was neutralised. His refusal to prepare for a no-deal walk-out, 'sabotaging' the no-deal threat in their opinion, kept Britain 'over the EU's barrel'. Together, they composed an ultimatum to May: 'We are profoundly worried that in some parts of the government, the current preparations are not proceeding with anything like sufficient energy.' Hammond and other Remainers, they demanded, should be disciplined to agree to the threat of no-deal. Their message ended with menacing sycophancy: 'And congratulations again on the clarity and courage you have shown.' The intermediary was Lee Cain, a former tabloid journalist newly employed as Boris's press adviser. Employed on shifts for the *Sun* and *Mirror* and seemingly unable to get a full-time job, Cain was best known for dressing up as the *Mirror*'s 'chicken' to taunt David Cameron in the 2010 election. After an allegation ended his shift work at the *Sun*, he was given a junior media position for Gove and May. Without good intentions, May allocated Cain to work for Boris. Regularly, Boris relied on Cain to patrol Portcullis House, spreading the word among Tory MPs that the Foreign Secretary was fighting back against Downing Street's malicious rumours.

The prime minister did not need to be reminded about her precarious position.

On 20 October, May had dinner with Jean-Claude Juncker. As ever uncertain, she pleaded with the hard-drinking Luxembourger to withdraw the EU's demand for £100 billion from Britain before trade negotiations could begin. If the EU persisted, she warned, her government would fall and they would face Boris and no-deal. Instead of sympathy, she received ridicule. Encouraged by the Remainers, Juncker's office later described May, 'with dark rings under her eyes', as 'despondent' and 'begging' for help. She returned home empty-handed.

May's new vulnerability terrified Remainer MPs, the majority in the Commons. Once again, the Tory Remainers contemplated the poisoned chalice: either another election and the chance of a Corbyn government, or Boris's election as leader. The safest route to avoiding either outcome was to protect May by damaging Boris. A new supposed gaffe presented that opportunity.

The briefing papers for Boris's appearance on 1 November 2017 before the parliamentary Select Committee on Foreign Affairs featured a description of the arrest at Tehran airport in July 2016 of Nazanin Zaghari-Ratcliffe, a thirty-eight-year-old Iranian-born woman. She had been returning to her home in London with her two-year-old daughter after visiting her parents. Although British by marriage, she possessed an Iranian passport and was regarded by the Tehran government as Iranian. Immediately jailed, she had in desperation after one year's solitary confinement signed a confession. At her brief trial, she was sentenced to five years' imprisonment in the notorious Evin prison for disseminating 'propaganda' and plotting to overthrow the Iranian regime. Naturally, her husband demanded that the British government secure the release of his innocent Iranian wife.

The responsibility for seeking Zaghari-Ratcliffe's release fell to the Foreign Office. It had failed to discover whether Zaghari-Ratcliffe had committed any offence in Iran or was just a casualty of Iran's familiar hostage taking – in this instance to recover £400 million held by the British government after a failed commercial deal. For years, Whitehall had refused to return the money. In their lackadaisical manner, Simon McDonald's officials could report no progress when compiling their briefing paper for Boris's appearance at the select committee. As usual, the report was in two parts. Above the line was information in the public domain. Below the line was restricted information for Boris headed 'Not for public disclosure'. Zaghari-Ratcliffe's employment as a project manager at Thomson Reuters, a news agency, was in the public domain. By all accounts, she was not involved in journalism and not responsible for Reuters' reports about Iran, classified by the Iranians as criminal 'propaganda'.

Unusually fluent during his testimony, Boris sat between Simon McDonald and the Foreign Office's political director Karen Pierce. During the session, both would be expected to alert Boris to any potential problems, not least because Tom Tugendhat, the committee's Tory chairman, was an outspoken critic of Boris.

During questioning by MPs about Zaghari-Ratcliffe's fate, Boris could not provide any reassurance. His officials had achieved absolutely nothing. However, in his customary manner to keep speaking to fill time and reduce the opportunity for more questions, Boris deplored what had happened and assured MPs that he had made many representations to secure her release. Then he said, 'She was simply teaching journalism as I understand it, at that very limit.' The remark departed from the Foreign Office official line that she was an innocent on holiday and had no connection to journalism. Pertinently, nobody – not one of the committee MPs, including Tugendhat, nor McDonald or Pierce – showed any concern at that answer. For twenty-four hours, nothing was said in London. Inevitably, in Tehran, government officials were constantly searching for any excuse to embarrass the British. Their purpose was served by seizing on Boris's statement about Zaghari-Ratcliffe 'simply teaching journalism'. That, the Iranian government announced, was 'proof' that she was a spy, a detail already confirmed in her forced confession. She was threatened with another five years' imprisonment.

Instead of accusing the Iranians of inhumanity, Foreign Office officials turned on Boris. Although they had failed to secure Zaghari-Ratcliffe's release, the Tehran regime's exploitation of a mistake served their purpose to pour scorn on the politician. Every day, this gaffe was dredged up in off-the-record briefings in Westminster and Whitehall to prove Boris's unsuitability as prime minister. Former Foreign Office officials joined the hunt. Arthur Snell, a former high commissioner in Trinidad and Tobago, quoted the Sirte and Zaghari-Ratcliffe incidents as evidence that Boris was 'a noted clown' whose 'shameful stint as Foreign Secretary will cast a shadow over British diplomacy for years to come'. Snell's risk consultancy, Orbis Business Intelligence, was responsible with Christopher Steele, a former MI6 officer, for producing a tendentious report about Donald Trump's unproven activities in Russia years earlier.

Chatham House's director, Robin Niblett, joined the chase. Boris, he would say, was not only shambolic but dangerous, undermining Britain's leadership role and giving succour to right-wing populists such as Viktor Orbán, the Hungarian prime minister. Boris had tweeted congratulations after the anti-Semite's election victory which, said Niblett, 'took Europe to its darkest period'. Not to be left out, John Bercow, the volatile Commons Speaker, encouraged repeated questions in the Commons in order to destabilise the Foreign Secretary. Appearing that afternoon exceptionally shambolic, with his tie askew, trousers slipping and shirt creased, Boris refused to apologise for the Zaghari-Ratcliffe 'gaffe'. 'I accept that my remarks could have been clearer,' he told the Commons. Five days later, under sustained pressure, he uttered his *mea culpa*. 'I apologise for the distress, for the suffering . . . She was there on holiday.' He agreed to travel to Iran to secure her release. Inevitably he failed, just as his predecessor Hammond and successor Jeremy Hunt failed. Britain's politicians had become Tehran's 'useful idiots'.

To the Foreign Office's good fortune, in the midst of the Iran furore, there was another gaffe. In an after-dinner speech to an Anglo-Spanish association in Bath, Boris protested that banning bullfighting in Spain was 'political correctness gone mad'. Based on unnamed Spaniards, the *Mirror* and *Guardian* reported that the whole audience was 'fuming' and Boris was 'a clown'. In truth, many Spaniards applauded his comments.

By the end of 2017, Boris's enemies had accumulated a litany of supposedly disastrous incidents reflecting his incompetence. His admirers said the accusations were contrived to undermine his leadership bid. The real culprit was the Foreign Office, a failing department.

In his official report that year, Simon McDonald did not assess his department's performance in Iran, the Middle East, Africa or the Americas. He rated his principal achievements to be the care of victims of the Caribbean hurricane, protecting Gibraltar and the sale of the British Embassy in Bangkok. With pride, he listed his visits to fifty-nine countries. In one nine-day burst, he swooned, he flew on eight planes to six cities and met seven ministers. He also squeezed in swimming with sharks. The cost of his quest to 'place gender equality at the heart of all we do' was Britain's declining influence across the globe. The Foreign Office's UK–Africa Investment Summit in London attracted the representatives of just twenty-one African countries. A similar summit hosted by the Chinese was attended by all fifty-four African countries, mostly their heads of state. Robin Niblett made no comment about those failures.

To Boris's good fortune, further examination by the media of his gaffes was abruptly halted by a slew of resignations. Two senior ministers were accused of sexual indiscretions: Michael Fallon for touching Julia Hartley-Brewer's knee at a dinner fifteen years earlier; and Damian Green accused of sending 'inappropriate' messages to a journalist. Green's fate was sealed by ex-assistant commissioner Bob Quick. In revenge for his dismissal, Quick revealed that Green had watched pornography on his laptop. Both ministers resigned. The next casualty was Priti Patel, the ambitious international development minister. Her sin was that during a holiday in Israel, she secretly met local politicians without Foreign Office permission. Patel was particularly disliked by Remainers for her strident anti-immigration rhetoric during the referendum campaign. They rejoiced.

May's government was gasping for survival. Since the Tory Party no longer included the fabled men in grey suits to persuade her to leave quietly, she stayed stubbornly entrenched, pleading that only she could keep Corbyn out.

On 4 December, May was back for lunch in Brussels. The problem was no longer money. Britain's departure bill had been reduced to £39 billion. The new hurdle was Ireland's irreconcilable internal politics.

With the encouragement of Leo Varadkar, elected as the new Taoiseach in June 2017, Michel Barnier had invented an Irish conundrum. The previous assumption by both the EU and Britain that some sort of border between Ulster and the Republic of Ireland was inevitable had been abandoned by Barnier. Varadkar's hard-line government insisted that Ulster had to remain part of the EU's single market and customs union – without any border. Without unimpeded traffic between Ulster and the Republic, Barnier and Varadkar sang in unison, the IRA would resume their murderous violence. To win his argument, Barnier not only exaggerated the number of trucks crossing the border and their value to Ulster, but also denied there were any technical solutions. To serve his purpose, he ruled out the use of cameras and computers to monitor trade. Unless Britain agreed to remain within the EU, Barnier said, a border would have to be erected between mainland Britain and Ulster, effectively breaking up the United Kingdom. Adding pressure on May, the EU refused to discuss any trade agreements until Britain committed Ulster to remain in the EU's single market. The clock was ticking to a seemingly irreversible deadline on 4 December. 'Don't rely on your civil servants,' Iain Duncan Smith warned May, meaning that as Remainers and unqualified as negotiators, her officials would prefer to capitulate than walk away with no-deal. As usual she ignored the advice. Buffeted by EU politicians loudly blaming Boris for Britain's incoherent policy, she feared the talks could collapse.

The border had been raised by Simon Coveney, Ireland's new hard-line foreign minister, during Boris's visit to Dublin on 17 November. 'We'll get these issues teased out,' said Boris, leaving

Coveney uncertain whether Boris had fully considered the problem. In public, they did disagree about the length of the transition. Since Ireland's economy was so dependent on Britain, Coveney wanted the transition to last at least five years. Boris told Coveney the maximum would be two years. As usual, Boris was undermined by British diplomats. Foreign Office officials, Coveney told journalists, had told Coveney to 'ignore' what Boris said because he 'went off script'.

Over the following two weeks, Boris was excluded from the hectic discussions in Downing Street about the Irish border. The dilemma was stark. Any agreement separating mainland Britain from Ulster, May knew, would be opposed by the DUP, the Ulster Unionists. Their ten seats in the Commons were critical to her government's survival. But she would also be defeated by the Tory Brexiteers if the agreement on 4 December failed to stipulate the exit of the entire United Kingdom from the single market and customs union.

Nevertheless, May agreed to Olly Robbins' solution, the so-called 'backstop'. In theory, the 'backstop' was simple. If Britain and the EU could not agree to a borderless solution by the end of the transition period when Britain finally left the EU, then the customs union between north and south Ireland would continue indefinitely. In other words, a border would be instantly erected in the Irish Sea. Thereafter, Britain could be permanently tied to the EU, unable to terminate the backstop unilaterally. No date could be set for Britain's final break with the EU. In effect, Britain could be forced to remain as part of the EU's territory – outside the EU but governed by Brussels without any influence or vote over its destiny. Britain would become the EU's impotent colony forever because Dublin could veto Britain's exit from the EU. To May's relief, Hammond and the 'soft' Brexiteers were satisfied by the backstop. Juncker was told that May would fly to Brussels on 4 December and they would jointly announce their agreement including the backstop the following day.

May set off to Brussels aware of an unresolved problem. Knowing that the backstop would be opposed by Boris and the Brexiteers, she had not told her Cabinet about the details of the deal she was about to announce. Similarly, fearful of the DUP's reaction, she had also not called Arlene Foster, the DUP's leader.

Juncker had good reason to feel pleased about May's capitulation. As a bruising Euro-federalist, he had just demanded in his state-of-the-union speech that the EU should completely open its internal borders and end national vetoes. With Britain now impotent within the EU, he expected the Brussels Commission to be given additional powers to levy taxes and issue regulations over Britain. Theresa May was seemingly unaware of Otto von Bismarck's observation, 'He who seeks to buy the friendship of his enemy with concessions will never be rich enough.'

May was just beginning lunch with Juncker, the demon of the Brexiteer's nightmares, when Arlene Foster's telephone call interrupted the bonhomie. The Ulsterwoman had heard about May's capitulation from journalists. 'I'm shocked,' exclaimed Foster. An hour's acrimonious conversation followed. May's myopic secrecy had unravelled. Crestfallen, she returned to the dining room to announce that she needed to return immediately to London.

With the sound of Downing Street's Christmas party in the background, May spent the evening persuading Foster to accept the backstop as a temporary measure and allow the trade negotiations to begin. Just before midnight, she succeeded. She dashed home to sleep in her Maidenhead home before leaving at 3.45 a.m. to fly back to Brussels. The EU leaders accepted her surrender at 7 a.m. Appearing with Juncker and Donald Tusk, the Polish president of the EU Council, May agreed that all Ireland would remain 'in full alignment' until at least 2021. If by then no border agreement had been reached, the backstop would kick in and Britain would be held at the EU's mercy. In Dublin, Varadkar could not believe his good fortune. Ominously, Arlene Foster warned 'We cautioned the prime minister about proceeding with this agreement . . . given the issues which need to be resolved.' For the moment, May appeared triumphant.

'Congratulations to the prime minister for her determination to get today's deal,' Boris tweeted. 'Triumph' hailed the *Daily Mail*.

But serious Brexiteers were puzzled. By the end of that day, May's deal was exposed as postponing a cataclysmic showdown. That would have been the moment for the Brexiteers to remove a duplicitous leader and secure their terms of leaving the EU. But they resisted. Better, they decided, to kick the can down the road because there was no alternative prime minister. May was relieved. In reality, she had exchanged one problem for another. On 13 December, Tory Remain MPs combined with the Opposition and voted to give Parliament powers over the Brexit terms. The government was defeated and landed with yet another constitutional time bomb.

During those nine days, Boris's position was confused. Just twenty-four hours after praising May, he somersaulted. He finally understood the deal, he said. 'We were told it's just a form of words; a temporary and redundant phrase which would never be invoked.' Britain, he continued, must not become a 'vassal state' to the EU. Then he added, 'It's just beyond belief that we're allowing the tail to wag the dog in this way. We're allowing the whole of our agenda to be dictated by this folly.' Tellingly, he failed to understand how May's poisoned chalice would eventually be her undoing and provide him with the chance to be prime minister. At the end of the week, he again readjusted to his loyalty agenda. He praised May for 'a fantastic job'. She rolled her eyes and grimaced.

By then, the Tory hierarchy knew that Boris had started another affair. Carrie Symonds, the high-profile twenty-nine-year-old director of the Tory Party's communications team, was dating Boris. No one on the Tory Party circuit could avoid Carrie, a woman who posted glamorous photos of herself on Instagram and encouraged gushing profiles of a gorgeous, clever, sexy and beautifully dressed political aficionado. Over previous years, she had worked as a party media spokesman, had helped on Boris's 2012 mayoral campaign where they had met, and had been employed as John Whittingdale's special adviser at the Department of Culture, Media and Sport after the 2015 election. In 2016, she supported Gove against Boris but swore loudly after hearing that Gove had double-crossed Boris. By 2017, working for Sajid Javid, the communities minister, she was dubbed a polarising personality. While some praised her sound judgement and loyalty, others in party headquarters described her as manipulative, volatile and aggressive, especially towards women. Some said that she had been appointed as the party's director of communications because of a close relationship with Zac Goldsmith. In 2017, her long-term relationship with a journalist broke up and she began advising Boris. Moody, uncertain and insecure, he needed company and reassurance from yet another new trusted confidante. As a Leave supporter and media relations expert, she encouraged him to trust her judgement. Her critics would say that what started off as a fling became, to match her ambition, a serious affair. Others would say she filled a vacancy.

In the nature of the man, Boris never explained his relationships with women to anyone. But after Marina had forgiven his affairs with Petronella Wyatt, Anna Fazackerley and Helen Macintyre (plus child), and was still unaware of his four-year relationship with Jennifer Arcuri, Boris might have considered the consequence on Marina and their four children once his latest affair with Carrie Symonds was inevitably exposed. Although he loved Marina, he apparently did not care about the hurt he inflicted.

Chapter 24

'God, she's awful'

'I'm increasingly admiring of Donald Trump,' Boris told fellow diners at a Conservative dinner in mid-2018 soon after meeting the president in Washington. 'I have become convinced that there is method in his madness.' The comparisons between the two men were not flattering to Boris. Both were born in New York, became famous on TV and were embroiled in sex scandals. Both were accused of exaggeration, of impatience with the complexities of government and refusal to focus on detail. Critics also accused both men of 'populism', defined as the sin of serving the needs of the working class while ignoring the self-interest of the liberal elites.

As a liberal and an intellectual, Boris dismissed his enemies' comparison but he did appreciate Trump's solution to outmanoeuvre the EU's obstinacy. During their conversation in Washington, the author of *The Art of the Deal* praised Boris's no-deal threat to walk away as the only weapon to defeat the EU's inflexibility. If Trump was negotiating Brexit, said Boris, 'He'd go in hard . . . There'd be all sorts of breakdowns, all sorts of chaos. Everyone would think he's gone mad. But actually you might get somewhere. It's a very, very good thought.' That opinion was not popular in the Foreign Office.

Boris's experience as Foreign Secretary had convinced him about the shortcomings of many diplomats. For more than a year, McDonald's team had failed to exert any influence on the unfolding Syrian tragedy. Indeed, it was hard to find any country where the Foreign

Office had genuinely extended British influence in recent years, or seriously reconsidered British foreign policy after Brexit. Although officials presented the memorandum 'Global Britain – delivering on our international ambition' after February 2018, McDonald's staff had failed to flesh out Boris's ambitions. The most depressing discovery was the inferior quality of the additional diplomats dispatched abroad. Their timidity, unimpressive intellect and limited education inhibited original ideas and initiative. Truly, the Foreign Office was a hotbed of cold feet.

Recommendations by Boris to extend British influence hit brick walls. The unorthodox idea of buying Svarland, a Norwegian island, for $250 million as a spy base was rejected. Similarly, the dispatch of troops to the port of Hodeidah in Yemen to protect food supplies to the starving population was sidelined by officials as too risky, despite Boris's promotion of the idea as 'a no-brainer'. Two minor chances to project Global Britain vanished.

His proposals about causes close to his heart at the Commonwealth heads of government conference were also sabotaged. At the summit, he publicly committed funds to educate girls in Muslim countries and highlighted a forthcoming International Wildlife conference in London to protect elephants and other endangered animals. But after his speeches, nothing happened. By nature, Boris delegated, but without constantly chasing for progress reports, unlike his energetic and responsive team in City Hall, the officials felt no need to undertake the grinding detailed work to implement his initiatives. Instead, the officials whispered that his sole skill was to make big announcements.

'They kept sending him abroad to keep him out of the way and wear him out,' recalled one of his junior ministers. 'He flew nine times to Africa, rubbed happily along with squillionaire Arabs in Saudi Arabia and then was sent to Peru – the first British Foreign Secretary to have visited the country for over fifty years.' Theresa May could only have been bemused to read of him energetically dancing with schoolchildren in a remote mountain village. To his surprise, he discovered that Peru's borders were mapped by Colonel P. H. Fawcett, a distant relative of his mother, who disappeared and was, he colourfully added, presumed eaten. After Boris's visit to neighbouring Chile, David Gallagher, the Chilean ambassador in London, reported that his government welcomed his tour as a triumph. As Foreign Secretary, Boris would report, he had visited fifty-two countries and opened new embassies in twenty-four countries. 'Across the world, the flag is going up, not down,' he said publicly. In private, he muttered, 'I've got no power.'

He also complained about his frustration. Over those months, even Boris's speeches were altered at the last moment by Foreign Office officials, including one about the battle against Islamic extremism and another voicing his criticism of Trump for moving the American Embassy in Israel from Tel Aviv to Jerusalem. If his officials did not interfere, then May intervened. In December 2017, just as her EU negotiations were imploding, she again impeded his planned visit to Moscow to seek a solution to the Syrian tragedy. May distrusted Boris's belief that his force of personality could resolve the problem. But in the end, just before Christmas, she relented. 'No jokes,' she told Boris. After trying to establish a relationship with Sergei Lavrov, the Russian foreign minister, the climax of his meeting in Moscow was an acerbic press conference. In a point-scoring exchange, Boris and Lavrov accused each other of dishonesty. 'Well that didn't work out well,' Boris admitted at the post-mortem in London. Politeness was pointless, he discovered.

He would not make the same mistake three months later. On 4 March 2018, Sergei Skripal, a former Russian intelligence officer living in Salisbury after defecting to the UK, fell seriously ill. British investigators suspected that he was the victim of Novichok, a nerve agent produced by the Russian military. Three days later, before the conclusive scientific evidence had been produced, Boris abandoned his Foreign Office script. At a press conference he accused Russia of 'malign activities that stretch from abuse and murder of journalists to the mysterious assassination of politicians'. Once again, British officialdom sought to embarrass him. This time it was the lead scientist at Porton Down, the Ministry of Defence research laboratory. The scientist said on TV that his laboratory could not identify Russia as the source of the Novichok. Without consulting Boris, the Foreign Office pulled back from blaming Moscow. Six days later, May confirmed that Porton Down's tests proved that the Novichok was manufactured in Russia. Undermining Boris was part of May's survival kit.

Boris summoned the Russian ambassador. Accompanied by his deputy, a KGB officer, the ambassador gave a friendly greeting. 'We know what happened,' snapped Boris. 'This is unacceptable.' The ambassador was speechless. 'He was masterly,' recounted Alan Duncan. 'The buzz around the building praised Boris for his brilliance, for perfectly reading his script and standing up for his country.' Boris also took the credit for organising the expulsion of 153 Russian diplomats from nearly thirty other countries. In fighting form, Boris described the smokescreen orchestrated by Moscow: 'The essence of a Kremlin cover-up is a cynical attempt to bury awkward facts beneath an avalanche of lies and disinformation.' He was tempted to say the same about the EU's stance towards Britain but decided instead to be even more direct.

In the aftermath of Theresa May's Cabinet reshuffle in early January, Boris felt emboldened – because she still did not dare to fire him – and frustrated, because the Brexit negotiations were stuck. Philip Hammond's influence as the shop steward of the Remain opposition was infuriating. With the economy growing faster than predicted and sterling back up at $1.40, the chief architect of Project Fear had become 'a glorious living rebuttal of his own preposterous warnings'. Here was a Chancellor, Brexiteers' allies scoffed, who could not understand the details of his own finance bill. To ruffle feathers, Boris demanded that the government immediately inject £5 billion into the NHS to prove the Brexit premium. Playing giveaway politics infuriated the Remainers when the Cabinet met on 23 January 2018.

Encouraged by Theresa May, Amber Rudd attacked Boris for failing to 'respect the dignity and privacy of Cabinet' by leaking his NHS giveaway. 'I'm talking to you, Foreign Secretary,' snapped Rudd. 'Jealousy,' thought Boris. The £5 billion suggestion, said Jeremy Hunt the health minister, was 'not helpful'. Hunt's reprimand would not be forgotten by Boris. At the end of the discussion, May offered no conclusion. Was it fear of division, some wondered, or had she even listened? Leadership depended on fashioning unity. That eluded May and without a respected leader, no one would follow. The acrimony set the scene for a seven-month battle which climaxed on 6 July at Chequers.

Boris walked back from the Cabinet meeting to the Foreign Office feeling isolated. He had no natural allies, let alone friends, in the Cabinet and, other than the four back-bench MPs who organised his leadership bid, his only reliable parliamentary supporters were the fifty arch Brexiteers, members of the European Research Group (ERG). Yet even that group, led by Jacob Rees-Mogg, were not agitating for Boris to replace May. Despite the plots, feuds, and derision of the prime minister, they feared that without May the Remainers, who were a majority in the Commons, would reverse Brexit. With Labour leading in the opinion polls, May survived only because there was no limit to the humiliation she would accept.

Europe's leaders were similarly not disposed to show May any mercy. At a meeting at Sandhurst with Emmanuel Macron shortly after the Cabinet meeting, May faced an uncompromising French president. Britain, said Macron, could expect no special deals, especially for the City. France would do its best to lure bankers to decamp to Paris and the Commission would formulate proposals to damage Britain. Flights to the UK would be grounded, Britons would not be allowed to drive cars or trucks in Europe, and Britain would be excluded from the Galileo GPS system, despite its major contribution to it. Sniffing that the Brexiteers' fantasies were dissolving in the harsh light of economics and realpolitik, Macron was encouraging Leo Varadkar to exploit the parliamentary splits caused by the backstop. If Dublin pressed harder, Brexit could well unravel. By the end of her conversation with Macron, May was floundering. Two years after the referendum, Britain's incompetence aroused incredulity across Europe.

May's plight encouraged Boris to renew his attack. He prepared to deliver in mid-February a 4,000-word speech about the EU in central London. At the last moment, Jeremy Heywood, the Cabinet

Secretary, forbade him from making the speech. Then, to execute a pre-emptive kneecapping, May's office leaked a part of the speech. But nothing in Downing Street ever worked to plan. Instead, Boris's full call to arms emerged in the *Telegraph*. The government, he said, could not 'frustrate the will of the people'. Bowing to the Remainers would be a 'disastrous mistake' causing 'ineradicable feelings of betrayal'. Britain must take back control of its laws. To abandon Ulster would be 'intolerable'. Crossing the Irish border, he said, was the same as travelling between Camden and Westminster in London. The idea that refined technology could not monitor the Irish border used by just a few hauliers was nonsense. It would be similar to paying the congestion charge or using the Oyster card on the Tube. The backstop, he protested, had become weaponised to stop Brexit. This would impose 'the worst of all worlds . . . out of the EU but still largely run by the EU'. The reply from Brussels hardened the Brexiteers' resolve.

Martin Selmayr, Juncker's aggressive German chief of staff known as 'The Monster', personified the worst of the Eurocrats. Losing Northern Ireland, declared Selmayr, was the 'price' Britain should pay for Brexit. Selmayr's denigration of Britain provoked no response from Olly Robbins or Jeremy Heywood. Their silence confirmed the Brexiteers' suspicions of their partisanship. Both were accused by Boris of using 'dirty tricks' to undermine the referendum. In retaliation, three former Cabinet Secretaries – Robin Butler, Andrew Turnbull and Gus O'Donnell – lined up to attack Boris. The three portrayed the 'rabid' Brexiteers as snake-oil salesmen for suggesting that civil servants were sabotaging Brexit. Buffeted by unceasing disputes, May arranged a meeting of the Brexit committee at Chequers for the end of February. She had faith that her silent chairmanship of the antagonists would produce reconciliation.

In anticipation of those showdowns, Boris increasingly resorted to hyperbolic acclaim to prove his loyalty. Before the Chequers meeting, he praised May's speeches as equivalent to 'the lapidary status of the codes of Hammurabi or Moses'. (Hammurabi was a mighty Babylonian king.)

Even May's admirers would regard that comparison as exaggerated, but the seduction did produce one benefit. In her Mansion House speech, May announced that Britain would leave the single market and customs union and would not tolerate a border down the Irish Sea. 'No UK prime minister could ever agree to it.' Her swing towards the Brexiteers was applauded by Boris. But not in Brussels. Abruptly, Michel Barnier rejected May's proposals to use technology to police the Irish border. With the Remainers' encouragement, the EU refused to discuss compromise over the backstop. The weak British would take what's offered or return to the EU.

Shocked by Barnier's rebuff, May resorted once again to secrecy. Crab-like, hoping Boris and the ERG would not notice, she manoeuvred backwards to satisfy Hammond. She suggested to Barnier that Britain would stay in the single market after all, and in a 'customs partnership' to collect the EU's tariffs. Effectively, Britain would remain in the EU without a vote or influence. Barnier was delighted.

At the beginning of May, the prime minister finally sought the Cabinet's approval for her latest plan. 'Bonkers,' declared Michael Gove. 'The worst of all worlds,' said Jacob Rees-Mogg. 'A crazy system,' said Boris. May became even more distrusted. Rees-Mogg spoke about toppling her and Boris mentioned her resignation.

May was saved just in time by the electorate. In the weeks before the local elections on 3 May, the Tories feared a wipeout in London including the flagship Tory councils in Westminster, Kensington & Chelsea and Wandsworth, not only because of the Cabinet's open warfare but because about 60 per cent of Londoners were immigrants. The revelation that innocent *Windrush* Jamaicans had been deported by the Home Office exposed May, the Home Secretary at the time, as anti-immigrant. Two weeks before the council vote, Fraser Nelson at the *Spectator* warned that the Tories have 'all but given up on London'. Predictions that Labour would 'paint London red', he warned, were accurate. The scare was misplaced. Nationally, the Tories lost just thirty-five seats and retained control over their London flagship councils. Voters were repelled by Jeremy Corbyn, reviled by outspoken Labour MPs and most Jews as Marxist and anti-Semitic – and, in the wake of UKIP's collapse, they were attracted by Boris and Brexit. May out-polled Corbyn 37 per cent to 24 per cent.

The relief for May was short-lived. In early June, warfare resumed in the Cabinet. At stake was getting the European Withdrawal Bill through Parliament within six weeks. As before, the backstop divided the government. The backstop, Boris insisted, must be time-limited. 'I will be prepared to compromise over the time,' he said. 'I will not compromise over the destination.' To appear loyal, he urged the restive ERG group to give May 'time and space' to conclude a deal with Brussels. Their fears of 'betrayal' by May, he promised, were unfounded.

Looking at May, drained and distraught, few believed that she could fashion an agreement at the next round of talks with the EU. In the Commons, there was no majority for any policy except to remain. Now, amid intrigue and recrimination, it was the turn of the Tory Remainers to threaten the government with defeat of the Withdrawal Bill. 'The moment of truth,' admitted Boris facing a dilemma. If he and Davis resigned in favour of no-deal, the Commons would vote to ban no-deal Brexit.

Boris's emollience had lasted just one week. His earlier faux praise of the prime minister was jettisoned. He resumed his attack in public. At a Conservative dinner on Wednesday 6 June, he denounced May for having 'no guts . . . It's beyond belief that the Northern Ireland border has been allowed to dictate policy'. Leaving the EU without a deal was the only solution. There would be short-term disruption, he admitted, but not the 'mumbo-jumbo prophecies of doom' predicted by the Remainers. 'They're terrified of this nonsense . . . I don't want anyone to panic during the meltdown. No panic. Pro bono publico. No bloody panic.' His call to arms was again ignored. As a divisive figure, Boris could not outrightly challenge May because few Tory MPs would support his bid to become prime minister.

Boris's position was further weakened after Rudolf Huygelen, Belgium's ambassador to the EU, reported overhearing a comment during a Foreign Office reception to celebrate the Queen's birthday in Lancaster House. Boris said about the Confederation of British

Industry's attempts to frustrate Brexit, 'Fuck business.' The business community erupted angrily. Boris was accused of creating the chaos of Brexit and, businessmen asserted, was too cowardly to accept any responsibility. This, May thought, was a good opportunity to weaken him.

A bill to permit construction of the third runway at Heathrow was due in the Commons. May knew that in 2015 Boris had pledged to lie down 'in front of bulldozers' rather than allow it to go ahead. Later, like Greg Hands, a junior minister, he had threatened to resign rather than support the legislation. The moment of truth had arrived. A bill was introduced to the Commons and May imposed a three-line whip on a vote. Boris began to squirm. First, he denied that he had threatened to resign. But he had also promised May that he would not campaign against the runway. Unlike Hands who did resign, Boris said that resigning would achieve 'absolutely nothing'. To avoid the vote – and total embarrassment – he decided to escape. On 25 June, he flew to a 'secret' destination. That turned out to be Kabul. The Foreign Office announced that he was to meet the Afghan president. Instead, he had his photo taken with a deputy foreign minister and drove back to the airport. He landed in London the following day. After answering questions in the Commons, he flew to Holland, Denmark and Lithuania.

May had good reason to feel more confident. On the same day as Boris was exposed as unprincipled, the Withdrawal Bill became law. The showdown among Cabinet ministers to finalise Britain's proposals to the EU of their future trade relationship and the backstop was due to be held at Chequers on Friday 6 July.

During the days before that fatal meeting, May promised all factions a new 'magic' plan. With Liam Fox and Michael Gove onside, she believed that she could bounce the Brexiteers to accept her latest deal. Boris, she calculated, had not mastered the detail, lacked the courage to resign and eventually would capitulate. Boris was certainly distressed. Absolutely nothing was clear – or honest.

May's assurance that Brussels would not exercise control over Britain after Brexit was confusing. On the one hand, she had offered the EU leaders on 29 June a customs partnership. But then she told the ERG's leaders she rejected a customs partnership. Either way, it was puzzling because the EU rejected her proposed 'customs partnership' as 'cherry-picking'. Was the prime minister self-delusional, he wondered, or outrightly dishonest? Or was she orchestrating a brilliant diplomatic coup? Thirty-six ERG members led by Rees-Mogg openly challenged May to stage a hard, clean Brexit – just leave the EU. Her supporters tried to suffocate her opponents. 'That's insolence,' said Alan Duncan. 'Shut up,' Nicholas Soames told them. At a summer party, John Major's former Chancellor Norman Lamont urged Boris to defy May. 'Our backs are against the wall,' replied Boris, 'but we're going to fight, fight, fight.' In the countdown to Chequers, nothing was clear except that May was desperate. On Thursday 5 July, the day before the Chequers meeting, she dashed to Berlin to show Merkel her latest proposals. Bemused by her anxious visitor, the German leader said little, deluding May to return to London convinced of Europe's sympathy.

Late that same afternoon, Downing Street finally sent Cabinet ministers a 120-page document – the proposed offer to the EU – entitled 'Facilitated Customs Arrangement'. Boris invited a group of Brexiteer ministers including Gove, Davis and Fox to his office to examine her proposals. For the first time, they read her unequivocal insistence for a soft Brexit. She planned to stay in the single market for goods but not services; and British laws and regulations about employment, aid to industry and consumer protection would remain harmonised with the EU's 'common rule book'. The soft Brexit effectively ruled out Britain concluding separate trade agreements with any country including America. 'It's a big turd,' said Boris, 'which has emerged zombie-like from the coffin.' Unanimously, the ministers in Boris's office agreed that Britain remaining in the single market as a rule-taker was unacceptable. After the meeting broke up, Boris headed to meet David Cameron at White's in St James's. Cameron urged him not to resign. At the same time, Liam Fox went to Downing Street. He revealed to May the reaction of Boris and Davis, and pledged to support the prime minister.

The following morning, the ministers were driven in the chauffeured cars to Chequers for the Brexit showdown. May had ordered that on arrival they should all surrender their telephones. They were also warned that anyone who resigned during the day should call for a local taxi and would have 'a long walk down the driveway' to the gates.

Olly Robbins set the scene in the wood-panelled Hawtrey Room. The twenty-seven EU states were united and, contrary to the original plan, would not be played off against each other. Next, May was emphatic that Britain would need to remain within a limited single market for everything except services. Any other deal would separate Northern Ireland from Britain. Boris's reply was explicit. The plan, he repeated, was a 'big turd'. Looking at May's officials, especially Olly Robbins and the Remainers like Hammond, he concluded, 'I see there are some excellent turd-polishers here.' But he left unclear whether he would actually oppose May. The eagerly awaited contribution was Michael Gove's. After several attempts by Downing Street to secure his support, May was anxious to hear his opinion. He set out both sides of the argument and concluded that despite a lot 'I find hard to swallow . . . we should accept it.' Andrea Leadsom and other Brexiteers also supported May's deal.

'This is an ambush,' David Davis realised. Two days earlier, May had told him directly that she was not proposing that Britain stay in the single market. That morning she said the opposite. She was gambling that no minister would dare to resign. Davis decided to fight but after Gove spoke in May's support, he knew he would lose. With all the other Brexiteers falling in behind the prime minister, Davis alone spoke against May. There were too many concessions to Europe, he said, and after Britain left the EU it would be wrong to be ruled by Brussels. Boris spoke again. He agreed with Davis but had not prepared a detailed critique. What emerged was confusingly about a part-in and part-out plan. To Davis's surprise, the climax was Boris's pledge of support for May. The ministers and officials then went downstairs for dinner. During the meal, Boris toasted the new unity. The government, he said, now had a song to sing.

May looked pleased. Boris had decided not to resign. And Davis, after criticising the weak negotiations and concessions, had also stayed. The rebellion had not materialised. Collective responsibility, she announced, would now be restored. No one could step out of line and remain in the Cabinet. As their discussions continued, a Downing Street spokesman announced that the Cabinet had agreed that Britain would remain within a limited single market. Even before they left Chequers, Saturday's newspapers had been briefed about May's victory and the Brexiteers' surrender. On Sunday morning, Gove appeared on a succession of TV programmes to defend the deal agreed by a united government.

The ERG group was outraged. MPs spoke of 'complete capitulation' and 'a charade intended to dupe the electorate'. They vowed to vote against the government. Boris's performance, said Andrew Bridgen, a leading Brexiteer, was 'waving the white flag of appeasement'. Boris was a 'Chamberlain when we wanted a Churchill'. Rees-Mogg became the Brexiteers' favourite as party leader. 'Your death warrant if you sign up and don't resign,' Iain Duncan Smith messaged to Boris.

David Davis had returned to London from Chequers convinced that he had witnessed an eye-opening watershed. May proposed to surrender British sovereignty indefinitely. The choice was between Britain's humiliation or no-deal. The sixty-nine-year-old former member of the Territorial SAS was an outspoken individualist. He decided to resign but on his own terms.

On that Sunday, he was invited to watch the Formula One race at Silverstone. During the morning, there were repeated calls from Downing Street. 'I'll come and see Theresa at 6 p.m.,' he told Robbie Gibb, her director of communications. 'You can't come,' Gibb replied. 'I will,' insisted Davis. As night fell, Julian Smith, the chief whip, called. 'What about we make you Foreign Secretary?' asked Smith. 'I won't be bribed,' replied Davis. After speaking to May on the phone, it was agreed that his resignation would be announced at 11.30 p.m. – precisely timed to be too late for the morning newspapers but in time for him to appear on live radio and TV in the morning. He would be replaced by forty-four-year-old Dominic Raab, a former lawyer and Foreign Office official.

'I've resigned,' Davis told Boris at 11 p.m.

'Why didn't we threaten her last week?' Boris asked.

'Because it wouldn't have worked,' replied Davis. The impact was bigger, Davis believed, after May had set out her proposals at Chequers.

Boris blustered. Sitting in his official flat overlooking the Mall, he was vacillating, uncertain whether to resign. Never before had he been so conflicted by principle against convenience. As usual, he wanted to believe that his willpower alone could defeat her, but he could not ignore that all the other ministers – Remainers and appeasers including Gove and Fox – had opted for the soft route. He was isolated. To have resigned alone would have been futile and encouraged particularly intense criticism. Now, he wasn't sure that he wanted to be associated with Davis's departure. Davis, brought up in a council house and a grammar schoolboy, was, he thought, unreliable. His attitude – 'It's not working and I'm off' – was, Cameron warned, inappropriate for Old Etonians. As a crowd-pleaser, Boris didn't want to be classed as disloyal. He wanted to fight from within. But Davis was a rival. Now outside, Davis might also run for the leadership. Boris would have preferred to have his cake and eat it. Their conversation ended inconclusively. Shortly after Davis's resignation was announced, Boris mysteriously texted, 'Please don't speculate who might follow you.' Boris was hoping to game it for longer. Constant media questions cut short his brooding.

'Am I doing the right thing?' he asked Will Walden about not resigning. May, he complained, just never listened. Unspoken were his personal conflicts. Being Foreign Secretary was like owning a box of favourite toys. The planes, flunkies, foreign trips, Chevening, Carlton Gardens and all the perks would be lost. On top of all that was the hiatus in his personal life. Marina had discovered his affair with Carrie Symonds. Inevitably there were fierce arguments but after making a full confession he had hoped for forgiveness from his loyal soulmate. She resisted. She was emphatic. She couldn't take his infidelity anymore. He had no sense of loyalty to women, she asserted. She explicitly blamed Stanley. All Boris's worst qualities stemmed from that relationship. The symmetry of Boris and Stanley, the son as the mirror image of his father, could never be broken. Two weeks earlier, Marina had decided to end the marriage. She refused to live with Boris anymore. Before that weekend, she had left Carlton Gardens with the children. Since their house in Islington was rented out, she was searching for her own home. Left alone, Boris lived in an increasingly unpleasant mess.

Boris seems never to have considered the consequences of a permanent break-up, especially that his relationship with the children would be 'toast'. Nor that by jockeying in politics and marriage, his family was splintering. Leo no longer mentioned his relationship with the Johnson family on his website, and nor did Julia, Boris's half-sister. Rachel openly disagreed with her beloved brother. Moreover, Stanley's four oldest children had become estranged from his youngest two. Boris was the catalyst for the distancing. Some blamed Boris for choosing 'hysterical girlfriends'. Others said he chose perfect but temporary companions who could never replace saintly Marina. All, however, would wonder whether he ever considered the consequences of a final split with Marina.

The immediate dilemma he faced was the price of principle. But was it even a principle? he wondered. Resign or stay? In the end, he had no choice. After his dash to Afghanistan to avoid the Heathrow vote, he faced checkmate. He couldn't flee twice or he would be dubbed a coward. Staying would be the kiss of death.

In the morning, Boris telephoned May to tell her that he was resigning. Downing Street announced his departure before he had even finished writing his resignation letter. Once completed, he posted a photograph of himself signing the letter. His tone was predictable: 'That dream is dying, suffocated by needless self-doubt . . . We are truly headed for the status of a colony (sending negotiators) into battle with white flags fluttering above them.' His litmus test was pertinent. Under her terms, Britain would still be unable to change the laws that affected British cyclists' lives. The driver's visibility from a lorry cab would not be improved, an issue that had been important to him since his days as mayor. In conclusion, he reminded May how he had said at the Chequers dinner that the government had a song to sing but 'The trouble is that I have practised the words over the weekend and find that they stick in the throat.' The letter was dispatched. Shortly after, Boris said to Davis, 'You're the man who started all this. If you hadn't resigned, I wouldn't have resigned.' Boris did not leave the official residence. With nowhere to go, he told Jeremy Hunt, his successor, he needed to stay. Hunt was understanding.

No one shed tears or voiced regret about Boris's resignation. His rebellion, thought Tory Remainers, was mad, juvenile and poised to hand power to Corbyn. *The Times* 'warmly welcomed' his departure. Two rats, commented the newspaper, had fled the sinking ship leaving others to clear up the mess. As a 'figure of fun', the newspaper judged, his resignation was the product of his 'own overweening ambition'. May's proposals, concluded the newspaper, were acceptable. Even more concessions, declared *The Times*, could be made to seal an agreement. James Landale of the BBC criticised Boris for failing to convince the world that Brexit did not mean Britain's withdrawal from global affairs. Boris was to blame, he wrote, that Britain's policy towards China, Saudi Arabia and Syria was unclear. The *Guardian* recorded that Boris would be remembered for his gaffes and his failure to spell out his policy on Yemen and Global Britain. Thanks to his 'attention span of a gnat', judged the *Guardian*, Foreign Office officials felt even more 'marginalised'. Those judgements were endorsed by David Howell in his report for the House of Lords International Relations Committee. British foreign-policymakers, stated Lord Howell, had lost their sense of direction. In future, Britain should distrust America, trust China and be ambivalent about Russia. Those who mocked Boris's period were clearly prejudiced. None had any notion about his constant struggle against recalcitrant Foreign Office mandarins. The obituaries of Boris's political career were similarly predictable.

Britain, Max Hastings wrote, had been represented by a 'jester . . . He is a man of remarkable gifts, flawed by an absence of conscience, principle or scruple . . . It is a mistake to suppose Johnson is a nice man. In reality he often behaves unpleasantly. I myself have received some ugly letters from Johnson, threatening consequences for writing about him in terms that he thought unflattering.'

Hastings concluded, that if Boris became prime minister 'a signal would go forth to the world that Britain had abandoned any residual aspiration to be viewed as a serious nation.' That Monday night, eating pizza in the Carlton Gardens flat with friends while watching a football match, Boris was determined to prove his critics wrong.

*

May had appointed Boris as Foreign Secretary in order to destroy him. The opposite had happened. Despite the critics, Boris had gained invaluable ministerial experience and some credibility, especially in the White House. 'Boris is a very talented guy,' said Trump. 'He'd make a great prime minister.' On the eve of coming to London, Trump reportedly called May 'a bossy schoolteacher'. Her days were numbered but her exit scenario was uncertain.

'Let's put a leadership campaign together,' Jonathan Marland told Boris. 'I'll get Lynton.' Scruffy, unshaven, overweight and sweating from his cycle ride, Boris arrived twenty minutes late at Crosby's office. 'You're fucking late again,' the Australian erupted. 'You're fucking around again. I want nothing to do with you. I'll never do anything for you again.' And he walked out of the room. Boris was left open-mouthed.

In Westminster, the ERG group was less sanctimonious. Iain Duncan Smith and Priti Patel arranged that Boris should be surrounded by Brexiteers including Jacob Rees-Mogg and Bernard Jenkin. 'We could not let him drift,' recalled Duncan Smith. He needed support and ideas from a group becoming a party within the Tory Party. At a series of dinner parties organised by Rees-Mogg at his home in Queen Anne's Gate, Boris began to establish a relationship with MPs he barely knew. 'We were feeling our way,' recalled Bill Cash. 'We'd had little contact with him before he declared for Brexit in 2016.' Boris's colourful phrases gave dull politicians hope. 'Britain has gone into battle with the white flag fluttering over our leading tank,' he said about the Chequers plan.

Was he thinking of Churchill, perhaps, wondering how he could save the day?

Invariably arriving late at the ERG's regular Monday morning meetings, the fifty hardcore members gave Boris a solid base. But they were warned by Graham Brady, chairman of the backbenchers' 1922 Committee, that Boris could not get enough MPs' votes to be the leader. Beyond Westminster, the situation was different. Party members were outraged by the Chequers deal. Only 16 per cent of the public polled approved of May. In the fallout, the public sided with Boris against May. But so far, only one third of Tory Party members supported Boris as leader.

So much, Boris knew, depended on the manner of his resignation. Rather than imitate Geoffrey Howe's famous mocking of Margaret Thatcher in the Commons in 1990, Boris decided to speak without jokes, Latin or rhetoric. In a half-empty chamber, he offered no rapier oratory in his description of the 'dithered' negotiations, 'a fog of self-doubt' and May's 'stealthy retreat'. Breaking with convention, May was not on the front bench. 'A futile gesture by a disillusioned man in search of a new start,' mocked one journalist. 'Mrs May was gummed by a toothless lion.'

With good reason to fear the media, Boris delayed his departure from Carlton Gardens while he tried to resolve his future plans. Marina, he still hoped, would forgive him. Simon McDonald emailed that Boris could no longer use the official car and should leave the house within forty-eight hours. Boris asked for more time. McDonald replied he was 'humane' and asked for a timetable. Boris refused to give a departure date. On 13 July, McDonald wrote that he should be out by the 20th: 'Time is passing and I have still not seen a plan. So I'd be grateful for an update please.' Six days later, there was no plan and Boris had not handed over two iPads and his telephone. McDonald gave a deadline of 25 July with the order, 'You must keep a very low profile.' Boris ignored the deadline, and finally left on 30 July, three weeks after his resignation. No one spotted that the family's belongings were divided between two trucks. Marina would live in rented accommodation in Islington while Boris headed for his house in Thame. He could have moved there three weeks earlier.

As the long summer recess began, Boris was marooned. Without a wife and waiting for the inevitable media storm when his latest adultery emerged, he could not imagine his fate in the Brexit turmoil; nor how he would ever return to government. At least, he intended his exile to be lucrative. To maintain his five children and his wife, he reactivated the £500,000 contract to write Shakespeare's biography, told his agent that he was available for speeches for a minimum of £30,000, and resumed his £275,000 *Telegraph* column. In 2014/15, he had earned £224,000 in royalties from the Churchill book.

'I want to get back together again for the leadership,' Boris told Jonathan Marland, a long-standing ally always ready to help Boris.

'You'll have to get Lynton back,' replied Marland, knowing that Boris could not operate without Crosby.

'I've called him,' said Boris, adding that he had texted apologies and promises of good behaviour.

Crosby, a Brexiteer who disliked May, especially after the 2017 election fiasco, finally relented. With an assured group of financial backers including Crispin Odey, an adventurous hedge-fund manager, Crosby teamed up with Boris to 'Chuck Chequers'.

In that battle, Boris was careful not to wholly align himself with the ERG group. He was not present when the group met in Westminster's Thatcher Room to discuss May's removal or join the applause for the MP who said 'She's a disaster and she's got to go.' And he also refused to support the publication of Rees-Mogg's 140-page Brexit manifesto which promised huge tax cuts and a fanciful *Star Wars* missile-defence system. Always the loner, he cut his own path. 'I want to ditch Chequers not May,' he emphasised.

Boris's *Telegraph* column was his best platform to attract attention. In early August, on the eve of leaving for Italy, he spotted a favourite topic. Under the headline 'The lovely Danes have got it wrong – a burka ban is not the answer', he criticised Denmark's decision to fine any woman wearing a burka. 'What has happened, you may ask, to the Danish spirit of live and let live?' the liberal asked. He continued, 'If you tell me that the burka is oppressive, then I am with you. If you say that it is weird and bullying to expect women to cover their faces, then I totally agree – and I would add that I can find no scriptural authority for the practice in the Koran. It is absolutely ridiculous that people should choose to go around looking like letter boxes or bank robbers.' But, he concluded, he opposed Denmark's 'total ban' because that would be interpreted as anti-Islamic, turn the women into martyrs and 'make the problem worse'.

The theme was not new. Five years earlier, as mayor he had opposed young Muslim girls being forced to wear veils and burkas as part of their school uniforms. 'This is against my principles and the principles of liberty that London should stand for,' he had written. 'Female education,' he said about the need to educate Muslim girls, 'is the Swiss army knife, the universal spanner that tackles . . . poverty, social exclusion, gender inequality and radicalisation.' He had also criticised Muslim leaders for failing to prevent some of their young people becoming terrorists. Too often, he wrote, the leaders were 'apologists for terror', blaming Britain and not the Muslim murderers for beheading European hostages. In his book *The Dream of Rome*, published in 2006, he described how Islam, championing 'fatal religious conservatism', had obliterated 1,000 years of Byzantine's glorious culture in Constantinople. That was followed by the Ottoman suppression of democracy, liberal capitalism and even the proscription of printing presses until the mid-nineteenth century. Consistent with his belief in a liberal society, he criticised his local council for forbidding an Englishman to erect a TV dish to watch cricket on the grounds that it was an eyesore. Contrarily, the council did allow TV dishes for people to watch Bangladeshi soaps, Turkish cookery classes and *Blind Date* in Serbo-Croat on the grounds of their 'social needs'. If they live in Britain on welfare benefits, Boris believed, they should learn English. But lest anyone assumed he was a moralising Islamophobe, he reminded his audience that not so long ago Christians had burned books and heretics. In all those comments, he had never advocated imposing a legal ban on Muslim veils. He believed in debate. As a supporter of liberal tolerance and freedom of expression, he was at liberty to oppose Denmark's prohibition of the burka and similar laws in France, Austria, Holland, Belgium and Bavaria. His honesty appealed to the majority of Britons but many Muslims were automatically offended. His use of the 'letter box' and 'bank robbers' jibes gave them the ammunition to attack. Naz Shah, a Labour MP, accused Boris of 'ugly and naked Islamophobia'. Shah was a self-confessed anti-Semite who had proposed 'transporting' Israel to America. She also urged that white girls raped by gangs of Asian men in Rotherham 'just need to shut their mouths for the good of diversity'. By contrast, Maajid Nawaz, the Muslim founding chairman of Quilliam, a counter-extremism think tank, said the burka should be 'ridiculed' as 'the uniform of medieval patriarchal tyranny'.

Tory Remainers were not offended by Boris's liberalism but by his motives. 'Burkagate' had provoked splenetic criticism fixing Boris in the very spotlight his enemies hoped to turn off. Boris Johnson, commented *The Times*, is 'a cynical political opportunist who knows exactly how his remarks will go down with the Tory grass roots'. May said he had 'offended people'. Andrew Cooper, the unreliable Tory pollster, wrote 'The rottenness of Boris Johnson goes deeper than his casual racism and his equally casual courting of fascism . . . His career is a saga of moral emptiness and lies: pathetic, weak and needy.' Female Tory Remainers including Anna Soubry, Ruth Davidson and Heidi Allen piled in demanding an official party inquiry. Camilla Cavendish, a former adviser to Cameron, wrote about an untrusted 'great showman' who 'is surely too smart to have misspoken'. Burkagate, she concluded unconvincingly, was 'not an accident. It is a deliberate bid for the leadership of the Conservative Party – and it may work.' Envy, Boris assumed, fuelled his antagonists. Brandon Lewis, the party chairman and a passionate Remainer, ordered Boris to apologise. Boris refused. Satire was acceptable, he replied, when 'speaking up for liberal values'. His critics should stop trying to shut down legitimate debate. 'Where is the spirit of Charlie Hebdo?' he asked, deriding the Snowflakes. 'We need to fight, gently, for free speech. We need to campaign for the right to make jokes and the right, within the law, to be satirical to the point of causing mild offence', otherwise extremism will flourish. Dismissing his defence, Brandon Lewis ordered an official inquiry. Accused of conducting a witch-hunt, Lewis was criticised for fuelling hysteria against the politician in order to protect May from the eighty Tory MPs opposed to the Chequers plan.

Touring Africa towards the end of August, May was plagued by reports that Burkagate was Boris's ruse to oust her. 'I am in this for the long term,' she replied to questions. The notion that an article about burkas in Denmark written in less than forty-five minutes was a leadership plot was ludicrous, but during the weeks before the party conference she was fretting. She had split the party between no-deal and no-hope. Her Chequers plan had been rejected by Barnier but was supported by Tory Remainers because there was no alternative. Party members, she feared, would hurl abuse at her on live TV. Attacking Boris, she assumed, was her best lifeline, and that included isolating him from Central Office, the party's headquarters.

Within Central Office, the relationship between Boris and Carrie Symonds was well known. Earlier in the year, a notable sighting had been Boris dancing to Abba at Carrie's thirtieth birthday party at her mother's home. Her father, Matthew Symonds, was a founder of the *Independent* newspaper, while her mother, Josephine Mcaffee, was one of the newspaper's lawyers. Boris did not believe Brandon Lewis's decision to abruptly fire Carrie as the party's director of communications in mid-August was a coincidence. Nor, as one journalist wrote, that she had been sacked for being lazy, divisive and submitting questionable expenses. It all reeked of Downing Street's familiar dirty tricks. Boris assumed that May wanted to thwart him before the party conference.

'Bonking Boris booted out by wife' was the *Sun*'s exposé headline on 6 September. The newspaper was allegedly tipped off after Lara, Boris's twenty-five-year-old daughter, told a friend, 'He's a selfish bastard. Mum is finished with him. She'll never take him back now.' Carrie was just five years older than Lara. His daughter would later post on Instagram that the period was 'the hardest and most hurtful year of my life'.

To avoid the inevitable storm, Boris flew to Greece with his children to stay in Stanley's house on the Pelion peninsula. Two days later, Downing Street offered chosen journalists a 4,000-word dossier on Boris's sex life written by Nick Hargrave, the deputy head of May's policy unit. Drawn up during the 2016 leadership election campaign, Hargrave had collected lurid allegations about Boris's adultery and of taking cocaine and other damning assessments of his character. 'It all looks like a sanctioned hit operation as part of an orchestrated campaign to smear him,' wrote one of the recipients.

After seeing the news about Carrie, Bill Cash called Stanley Johnson, a friend from Oxford. 'Buy a takeaway and two beers for yourself and Boris,' advised Cash, 'and show him *Darkest Hour*. Let him see Churchill's moment. Boris is not as tough as Churchill and tell him, unlike Churchill who dodged bullets and bombs, he only faces bits of paper.'

Warfare introduced a new vocabulary into Boris's articles and speeches. 'Humiliation', 'insanity', 'legal servitude', 'democratic disaster' and 'lies' peppered his arguments against the backstop. May, he wrote, had got 'lost in a dither' about a 'myth'. As a result, 'The EU has so far taken every important trick.' Just at the time that his relationship with Carrie Symonds was exposed, he wrote 'We have wrapped a suicide vest around our constitution and handed a detonator to Michel Barnier.' The tabloid language was once again seized by his enemies. 'His words are one of the most disgusting moments in modern British politics,' spat Alan Duncan. Boris was an 'irresponsible wrecker [and] I'm sorry but this is the political end of Boris Johnson. If it isn't now, I will make sure it is later.' Sarah Wollaston, another Remainer Tory, convinced that Boris had used 'disgusting language' to distract from the Carrie revelation, committed herself to resign if Boris toppled May. In reply, Boris asked whether 'the tide of holy feminist rage' would also remove the scourge of female illiteracy, genital mutilation and forced marriages across Africa, the Middle East and Asia. Wollaston did not reply.

Weaponising Burkagate along with Boris's adultery and his tabloid language by those terrified that May could be toppled infected
the *Daily Mail*. The 'reckless and egoistic' Boris and the 'foolhardy
rebels' were denounced by the newspaper for threatening to 'tear
the party apart'. To deflate the panic, Tories were urged by the *Mail*
to 'cling on to Theresa May for dear life'. Only she could navigate
Britain into safe waters. Fraser Nelson agreed with that make-or-
break option. Although May was 'not very inspiring', he wrote,
Britain was best off with her – 'the best woman for the job'. With
many similar endorsements, May was reassured, there was no
alternative to Chequers.

On 18 September, May flew to an emergency EU summit in Salzburg. She had been persuaded by Olly Robbins that the EU would
support her request for concessions to modify the backstop. The
forty-three-year-old official lacked experience in foreign affairs,
Europe and negotiating international agreements. With limited
expertise in disseminating intelligence across Whitehall, Robbins,
a PPE graduate from Oxford, had risen through the Civil Service
without the experience to tell the prime minister that Chequers
would not be approved by the Commons. Nor that half her Cabinet
rejected the backstop. May did not want to hear about the disturbing implications of Dominic Raab's admission that he was unaware
of the importance of the Dover–Calais route for British trade. Once
again, May's lack of emotional intelligence made her deaf to Raab's
limitations. The former lawyer failed to impress on her before she
flew to Salzburg that the EU absolutely refused to time-limit the
backstop.

Insensitive to reality, Robbins and May walked into total humiliation. Without the charisma and skill to persuade the twenty-seven
EU leaders to make concessions, May exposed herself as an over-
promoted junior officer. As predicted, Chequers was comprehensively
rejected as unworkable. As usual, Brussels calculated the Remain
MPs had a majority in the Commons to reverse Brexit. 'Brexit has
shown us one thing,' said President Macron. 'Those who said you
can easily do without Europe, that it will all go very well . . . are

liars.' Pale and wounded, May emerged from the conference with her stubbornness intact. Chequers, she asserted, would survive. She had nothing else to say.

'At last we're arriving at a moment of truth,' said Boris on the eve of the party conference in Birmingham. Blaming 'a collective failure of government, and a collapse of will by the British establishment to deliver on the mandate of the people', he refused to support the government. 'Chuck Chequers and restore basic Conservative values' was his message during the four-day conference. The counter-attack was deafening. Boris, said Philip Hammond, was 'incapable' of grown-up politics. A publicity seeker and a troublemaker, spat David Mundell, the Scottish Secretary. John Major damned the 'princeling fighting for the political crown' who 'deceived' the electorate with 'untruths and half-truths' just to become prime minister. Implausibly, Boris denied he was planning to stand against May. Alan Duncan had the final word: 'He risks bringing everything down and . . . destroy[ing] our prospects for many, many, many years.' Even if MPs voted for him, said Duncan, the party membership would never vote for someone so 'reckless'.

At the end of the conference, Boris had made little progress. While his supporters spoke of May 'entering the killing zone', she remained silent and inscrutable. No one, including her Cabinet, knew her thoughts as the 599-page Withdrawal Agreement which included the unchanged backstop was finalised by Robbins and Barnier. Despite the irreconcilable disagreements between the Remainers and Leavers, the agreement set out the terms of Britain's exit from the EU on 29 March 2019. Renegotiation, rebuked the EU, was impossible.

On publication in early November, May presented the agreement as 'the best that could be negotiated'. In that moment of truth, there were gasps. Nothing had been changed since Chequers. 'An absolute stinker,' said Boris, 'leaving Britain a vassal state, a colony . . . This is not taking back control. It is a surrender of control. Parliament will have even less power than before.' Tony Blair agreed, describing May's deal as 'capitulation, the worst of both worlds'. Out of the blue, Jo Johnson, Boris's youngest brother, resigned as minister of transport on the 9th, damning a 'failure of British statecraft on a scale unseen since the Suez crisis'. Less than a week later, Dominic Raab and three other ministers resigned on the same day. May was told that a majority of the Commons would vote against her deal. Among the few loyalists was Michael Gove, fearful of reigniting suspicions about his character.

In the midst of the latest crisis, Boris went to an ERG meeting in the Commons. Speaking on his behalf during the hour-long meeting, Conor Burns speculated that the prime minister might have to go. Jacob Rees-Mogg revealed that he had already submitted a letter of no confidence in May to Graham Brady, the chairman of the 1922 Committee. Brady would be obliged to hold a vote of confidence once forty-eight MPs had submitted letters. Boris refused to support Rees-Mogg. Others agreed that Rees-Mogg had 'jumped the gun' and had made foolish remarks outside Parliament. Lacking forty-eight votes, the plot collapsed. Gossip about the manoeuvres aroused a cacophony of protests from Tory Boris haters. Among the loudest was Nick Boles, the MP for Grantham. The serially disloyal Wykehamist condemned Boris as a 'plummy-toned Old Etonian trying to bully a conscientious and determined woman out of her job'.

The crisis coincided with the retirement of Paul Dacre as the *Daily Mail*'s long-standing editor. His departure marked the newspaper's shift under the new editor Geordie Greig from supporting Brexit to advocating a soft Brexit. To signal the new editorial policy, Dominic Sandbrook, a columnist, derided the Brexiteer 'pygmies sniping at Mrs May' driven by 'a childish thirst for melodramatic grandstanding and a deep sense of narcissism'. Is there a better deal? he asked. 'Definitely not.' May, he concluded, 'deserves better than to be betrayed by a moral degenerate like Boris Johnson'. As a new member of the Remain church, the *Daily Mail* now sang eulogies to May's deal, blind to the reality.

Standing on the cliff edge, May was paralysed. She had no reply to Boris's repeated speeches damning her pledges about the Withdrawal Agreement as 'a monstrous untruth'. He criticised her promise Britain would retain control over its own laws as 'a stonking, stinking, steaming lie'. No attack evoked a whisper from her.

At that critical moment, he made no ostensible attempt outrightly to challenge May. Surfing, guiding the board as best he could, he had fixed his eye on the destination but retained flexibility about the details so any mistake would not be noticed. Fearful that a slight wave would cause him to fall, he left observers uncertain of his tactics. Listening to his advisers about what to say, when to remain silent and how to vote, he offered a broad sweep leaving no glaring clues about a plot. As the party's internecine battle intensified, his popularity in Westminster fell.

Ensconced in one of Westminster's most unpleasant offices for MPs – he suspected at May's direction – Boris slid into depression. Distressed that half the nation openly despised him for leading a dishonest Brexit campaign, his bitterness about his prospects and the hostile media accelerated. Daily, he grumbled about his plight in the wilderness with his press adviser Lee Cain. The lacklustre former tabloid journalist, paid by a generous donor to work on Boris's staff, listened to his master's regular condemnation of the media. Gradually, as both became convinced that Boris was the victim of spite, the inclusive Boris of the City Hall era was replaced by a man fuelled by suspicion of loathsome journalists. In conversations across Westminster, Cain mirrored his master's sentiments, sowing yet more dislike for Boris amid party members already fearful of their future.

By early December, the Tory Party was in meltdown. David Cameron's prediction in 2015 about a referendum's 'unleashing of demons of which ye know not' had occurred, and May lost control of her party and Parliament. After repeated defeats in the Commons, she postponed the vote on the latest Withdrawal Agreement. The bookies ranked her probable successors as Michael Gove, Amber Rudd or Sajid Javid. Boris was way down. He was damaged by the noise of the battle. He changed tactics.

The ERG group, Boris knew, was on the verge of submitting the forty-eighth letter to Graham Brady that would trigger the vote of confidence in the prime minister. He used an invitation to speak in Amsterdam to eulogise about Churchill and draw what he hoped would be obvious parallels. His hero, he said, was a 'compulsive gambler' who prevailed against his opponents and eventually was proved 'triumphantly right'. He concluded, 'Sometimes you must take the decision which is fraught with risk.' The backlash was nasty. Anthony Seldon, the political biographer, led the ridicule. Boris, wrote Seldon, 'would not heal the nation as did Churchill. It is a fantasy game on his part and we must not let it become a fantasy for the nation.' Deaf to the naysayers, Boris again changed gear.

Unusually well groomed, he appeared on BBC TV on Sunday 9 December to launch his leadership bid. He said nothing new but did forthrightly criticise May in a statesmanlike manner. Two days later, the forty-eighth letter was delivered to Brady. May decided that MPs should vote the following day. That night, as a concession, she told Tory MPs gathered in a Commons committee room that she would not stand in the next general election due in 2022. In return, they should vote for the Withdrawal Agreement. 'God, she's awful,' Boris texted during her speech.

Tory MPs faced a stark choice. Either support the Brexiteers' no-deal with no obvious alternative leader, or continue the division and disarray without a fixed destination. At 9 p.m. on 12 December, Graham Brady announced the result. Only 117 MPs out of 317 had voted against May. With 63 per cent of the vote, she ignored the demand to resign, and furthermore could not now be challenged for the leadership for a year. The coup had failed. As Brady read out the result, Alan Duncan led the cheers. Boris stayed silent. 'Don't play in this arena,' he was advised by Iain Duncan Smith. 'Keep to the margins.'

Despite the collapse of party discipline, the economic news was remarkable. Unemployment was the lowest in forty-three years, wages were rising, a lengthy Treasury analysis admitted that by 2035 the impact of Brexit could be marginal and education was improving. Boris could also bask in Sadiq Khan's poor record as mayor during the past two years. The annual addition of new homes under Boris had steadily risen from 21,000 in 2012/13 to 39,000 in 2015/16. But under Khan, the new homes had fallen back to 32,000 a year. Under Khan, crime had risen. Because Khan forbade stop-and-search, knife crime and the murder of black youths had increased. Boris accused Khan of 'an abject failure to grip the problem of violence'. Stop-and-search was resumed and the epidemic of young black deaths started to fall. Boris's misfortune was that no one reminisced about his achievements as mayor.

In limbo for Christmas, Boris and Carrie hosted a New Year's party in her south London flat and then flew to Greece to stay in Stanley's house. Under her guidance, he was losing weight – off alcohol and late-night binges of cheese and chorizo. Their relationship had taken a course unintended by Boris. If Marina had not terminated their marriage, his fling with Carrie would have abruptly ended. Instead, he was falling under the influence of the woman with whom he was now living.

Chapter 25

Showdown

As an exceptionally polite and well-educated fund manager, Jacob Rees-Mogg's tactlessness surprised some of his colleagues. His invitation on 15 January 2019 to a champagne celebration at his home in Queen Anne's Gate struck some Brexiteers as 'injudicious'. That evening, May's Withdrawal Agreement had been defeated by a majority of 230 MPs including 118 Tories. The majority against the government was the biggest in history. Nearly all the Tory Brexiteer MPs, including Boris, crowded into Rees-Mogg's large house to pledge mutual support. Some felt uncomfortable about celebrating their own party's thrashing. Gulping champagne while Theresa May sat tearfully vanquished close by in Downing Street revealed the Brexiteers' resolute obsession. 'It sends the wrong message,' muttered the sticklers. Boris was not among those complaining. Rather, he happily accepted compliments for his loss of weight. His suit was flapping and there was a gap around his shirt collar. Despite the countdown to Brexit on 29 March, one topic barely discussed that evening was the party's leadership. Another was the ridicule heaped on Boris for speaking about the 'transition' arrangements after a no-deal exit. Without a deal, there would be no transition! His ignorance about realities outraged the Europeans, especially the Germans. In Berlin, no one could understand how the famed British Civil Service and the mother of parliaments could be led by such clumsy, self-deluding politicians. News of Rees-Mogg's champagne party added to the Germans' bewilderment. Berlin's incomprehension spiked three days later. Standing on a JCB bulldozer,

Boris's speech was pitched to the media as an unofficial leadership bid on a One Nation Tory agenda. Few in Berlin could believe that the British could choose Boris as prime minister.

Part financed by Anthony Bamford, JCB's chairman, Boris established a campaign office. With the help of Iain Duncan Smith, it was better organised than in 2016. Grant Shapps, an outspoken critic of May, had joined to manage the spreadsheet, meticulously recording each MP's preference to succeed May. Names were entered after consulting Gavin Williamson, a former chief whip and now the Defence Secretary. Notoriously, Williamson as chief whip was suspected of having recorded every Tory MP's vulnerability. Using his 'black book', he could squeeze any doubters and win their loyalty. Ben Mallet, an American pollster, joined Boris with James Wharton, a well-connected no-nonsense former MP who understood the bigger picture, as his campaign manager. Their office was funded not only by regular £10,000 payments from Bamford but also substantial donations including £50,000 from Jon Wood, a hedge-fund manager, and £23,000 from Lynton Crosby for his services as a loan.

Over the following week, the Brexiteers understood the folly of Rees-Mogg's champagne celebration. With Britain due to leave the EU on 29 March and a majority in the Commons against a no-deal Brexit, they were in danger of losing their prize. 'It's time to compromise,' said Rees-Mogg. As ever, one obstacle was Dublin's refusal to change the backstop. May sought a deal with the Brexiteers.

'What do you want, Prime Minister?' asked Boris.

'You won't find out unless you support us, Boris,' she replied, unable to answer the simple question.

'Will I vote for this backstop?' asked Boris rhetorically. 'No way.'

He was dismissive of those MPs like Matt Hancock, the Health Secretary, who predicted the end of the party under Boris's no-deal Brexit. 'I genuinely think,' said Hancock, 'the deal the prime minister has done is the best on offer.' The majority of Tory Party members disagreed. Sixty-six per cent of members supported a no-deal Brexit.

One week later, on 19 February, three Tory Remainer MPs resigned from the Tory Party. The departure of Heidi Allen, Anna Soubry and Sarah Wollaston hit May hard. Many women MPs, she knew, hated Boris but she assumed she could count on their loyalty. Her demise inched closer. For Boris, three fewer trenchant critics in the parliamentary party was good news. With former UKIP voters joining Tory associations and Nigel Farage creating a new Brexit Party to contest the local elections, Boris was positioning himself as the man to deliver the deal. That intensified the scrutiny of his probity.

Over the previous year, his private income had increased, especially from speeches. Among the most lucrative clients was Golden Tree Asset Management, a US finance firm, who paid £94,508 and a fee of £122,899 from an Indian corporation. He also received £23,000 every month for his *Telegraph* column plus royalties for his books. To his discredit, he was reprimanded by the Commons authorities for failing to declare nine payments totalling £52,722.80. His accountant could easily have avoided that embarrassment. As ordered, Boris apologised but was not grateful to the friendly MP who warned, 'You must take care and not be slapdash.' That critic would not be allowed back in the room. Only those in his close circle were allowed to find fault in him. But he could not control the TV journalist who asked why he had raised the bogus issue of immigration from Turkey during the referendum. 'I didn't say anything about Turkey in the referendum,' Boris replied. Untruthfully or forgetfully remained unresolved. Under relentless pressure, Boris was repeatedly asked during those hectic weeks whose interests he was pursuing: the country's, the party's, or his own?

Oliver Letwin was among those asking that question. In his efforts to find an acceptable solution for the country and party, Letwin had conversations with Boris in the Commons lobby and tea rooms. To his disappointment, Letwin discovered that Boris, mentioning the 'democratic mandate', had hardened against any compromise. Letwin's riposte that only 25 per cent of the electorate voted Brexit and 50 per cent of Britons were non-Brexiteers provoked Boris's silence. Letwin decided that Boris was pursuing his own interests. Boris would reply that he was caring for Britain's interest.

Slowly but remorselessly, the Commons was inching towards the final showdown. A second vote on the Withdrawal Bill was due on 12 March. Despite the turmoil just seventeen days before Brexit, Boris took Carrie for a long weekend to Positano to celebrate her thirty-first birthday. Some feared that political priorities were being forsaken to satisfy Carrie's wishes.

In California, Jennifer Arcuri watched the affair critically. 'She's got far more skeletons than me,' she told a friend. 'Boris got caught at the end of the night by a flirtatious minx. She's controlling him. It drives me insane that there's such a huge difference between me and Carrie. She's just a Type A worker bee, riding a bicycle around the Westminster village.'

In the second Withdrawal vote, David Davis was one of the nine Tories who switched to vote for May. 'The alternative is a cascade of catastrophe,' he explained about a no-deal exit. But seventy-five Tories including Boris voted against the government. Certain to lose, May blamed Geoffrey Cox, the Attorney General. He had delivered a devastating legal opinion that Britain had 'no unilateral means of exiting' the backstop. May's agreement would cast Britain as an EU colony forever, said Boris. She had demonstrated a failure of statecraft. The government lost the second vote by 149 votes. In just seventeen days, May feared, Britain would leave the EU without a deal. Uttering threats in a croaking voice, May retreated from the Commons to her office in tears. 'I'm sorry,' she told her staff. Two days later, MPs voted against Britain ever leaving the EU without a deal. Britain's predicament seemed insoluble. Parliament was paralysed, the major political parties were split, the government was crumbling and the prime minister was losing her judgement. Relieved by the removal of the no-deal threat, the EU's leaders sniggered.

To delay the crisis, May was persuaded, Britain should extend its departure from the EU to 12 April and reintroduce the Withdrawal Bill for a vote in the Commons for a third time. The ERG

Brexiteers, she hoped, would prefer to vote in favour of a bad Brexit rather than no Brexit.

To win the rebels' support, she invited Boris to Downing Street. Would he, she asked, vote with the government if there was another vote. 'No,' he replied, unless the backstop was renegotiated, a condition he knew the EU had rejected. Punctuated by long silences, she explained that if MPs voted against the bill for a third time, Brexit would be delayed. Looking at the broken woman who in the past had enjoyed mocking him, Boris felt little sympathy. Two weeks earlier, he knew, the whips had told her that she would have to resign by the end of the year. 'You need to rule out running again as leader,' he said politely. 'A snap election', she replied, was possible. The threat of bringing down the party in retribution for her own failure exposed her lack of authority. The spectre of Corbyn did not frighten Boris. They sat in silence. At the end of forty minutes, he displayed no hint of dismay when, without any agreement, he left. Theresa May's resignation crept closer. Impetuousness guided her next move.

The following day, Wednesday 20 March, May decided to address the nation on TV. On those rare, invariably difficult occasions, the prime minister seeks to enlist the electors' understanding. That night, even sympathetic Tory MPs were shocked. Defiantly, May blamed MPs for the chaos. Even May's closest advisers in Downing Street finally lost their confidence in her. Impervious to their sentiments, she threw another dice to survive.

To win over her opponents, she invited Boris, Iain Duncan Smith, Dominic Raab, Jacob Rees-Mogg, David Davis and Steve Baker, the ERG's organiser, to Chequers on Sunday 24 March. Before arriving, the MPs had agreed their only purpose was to give May an ultimatum to resign. Electing a new leader before the party conference in the autumn was vital. Meeting on the first floor, she implored the MPs 'Back me or there'll be no Brexit.' Her appeal was sidelined. 'You must set a date for your departure,' said Rees-Mogg. She refused. 'You must set a timetable for resignation,' said another. She talked around it. After the 2017 election, said Boris, 'you said you would only remain as long as you want me'. She remained silent. So did Boris. Finally she snapped 'I'm not resign-ing.' The discussion ground to silence.

'Let's have some tea,' she suggested. 'It's ready downstairs.' As everyone headed for the stairs, Iain Duncan Smith stood with May in an alcove. 'I don't find this easy,' he told her, 'but the honest truth is that the party is not prepared to support you anymore. You must go before the summer break and let your successor sort out the mess.' May's eyes welled up with tears. If she announced that she would resign at the 1922 Committee meeting set for Wednesday, continued Duncan Smith, the ERG group would support the gov-ernment in the third vote. 'The choice is yours,' he concluded and headed down for tea.

After the group left Chequers, they were assured by Duncan Smith that May would announce her departure date at the 1922 Committee meeting of Tory MPs three days later. In advance, she approved the script with the precise words including her departure date. Unexpectedly, before she reached the committee room, she decided to ignore the script and renege on her agreement with Duncan Smith. Uppermost in her mind, was theatrically to stage her exit at the party conference in October. She would gamble that over the following two days, the threat of no Brexit would secure sufficient converts to win the third vote on 29 March. Standing in front of MPs, she delivered her surprise. She would only resign, she said, if her Brexit deal was passed. She gave no date for her resigna-tion. Iain Duncan Smith was furious. But the ERG group was divided.

Boris's ambitions depended on sticking with the ERG group. He noticed that Dominic Raab came to every ERG meeting and his popularity was rising. Over the following forty-eight hours, Boris arrived punctually at meetings to witness the ERG split. As Steve Baker, a key organiser, observed, 'Boris quietly watched to know what was happening with his rivals.' He also witnessed the agony of lifelong Brexiteers. Peter Lilley argued that it was marginally better to leave the EU with vassal status rather than abandon Brexit altogether. In the future, he said, Britain could renegotiate or even renege on the agreement with the EU. Rees-Mogg agreed. 'I apologise for changing my mind,' he would say. He chose to vote for May and abandon the DUP rather than lose Brexit. To avoid the chaos, Iain Duncan Smith also reluctantly agreed. To Steve Baker's surprise, Dominic Cummings urged MPs to support the government. 'You'll be strategic idiots if you don't,' said Cummings.

'You haven't read the bill,' replied Baker.

Over the next two days, Boris was torn. Britain, he still believed, should leave without a deal. On the other hand, loyalty to every institution he had belonged to – his schools, Oxford and City Hall – required him to show similar loyalty to his exhausted party. In a crisis, the priority was to show allegiance to the leader. He had to make himself unassailable among MPs as a flexible leader, willing to reach out to compromise. Even Churchill had voted in 1940 for Chamberlain after the disastrous Norway expedition and became prime minister soon after. He was persuaded by Rees-Mogg to vote for the bill. 'I'm very, very sorry and though it fills me with pain,' he said, 'I'm going to have to support this thing . . . We have got to get this over the line [because] I genuinely think the House of Commons is going to steal Brexit.' Boris's conversion had no influence on the ERG's founders. 'He was a cheerleader and one of us,' recalled Craig Mackinlay, an ERG hard-line member of the self-named Spartans, 'but he did not understand the detail.'

Class divided the ERG. Opposed to the Old Etonians and other clubbable public school MPs who reluctantly supported May, were Steve Baker, Mark Francois, Craig Mackinlay and other non-public school Tories. For them, Brexit was a religion more important than the party. Under no circumstances were they prepared to compromise. To those purists, May's refusal to name her resignation date at the 1922 meeting was a betrayal. Her speech, said Baker, was a 'pantomime' which had 'consumed me with ferocious rage'. Parliament, he said, should be torn down. He would be 'bulldozing it into the river'. Mark Francois, an equally passionate Brexiteer, said he wouldn't back May's deal even if someone 'put a shotgun in my mouth'. Bernard Jenkin was tempted to support May but pulled back because to intend to break an international agreement in the future was wrong. To save Brexit, he would join the thirty

Spartans. That made May's defeat inevitable. A leadership campaign was imminent.

At Lynton Crosby's behest, Boris reached out to the Remainers. 'I agree with Heseltine about One Nation Toryism to make capitalism popular again,' he tweeted. He also pledged support for Dominic Grieve, the leading Remainer who was threatened with deselection after losing a no-confidence vote in his local association. Former UKIP members had infiltrated the local party to sway the vote: 'Sad to hear about Dominic Grieve. We disagree about the EU but he is a good man and a true Conservative.' He did not tweet support for Nick Boles, dubbed by local activists in Grantham as a 'traitor', and also threatened with deselection.

On 29 March, May's third attempt to pass the Withdrawal Agreement was defeated by fifty-eight votes. Thirty-four Tories voted against the government. May's fate was sealed. Remainers feared the Tory Party would become a Brexit party. There was, however, some consolation. Convinced that a Brexiteer could not be a One Nation Tory, they calculated that a majority of party members would not choose Boris.

'There's no "Stop Boris" campaign,' wrote Fraser Nelson, 'because he hasn't even started a campaign.' Surveying the ERG group, Matthew Parris was scathing: 'We're looking at an assemblage of ninnies and rascals here and they're well on their way to being rumbled.' And the Remainer reassured himself, 'So far we are winning.' In *The Times*, Clare Foges wrote 'If Boris were to make it into No. 10, it would be a very bad thing for our country . . . That he is a liar, a philanderer, a reckless stirrer, a man of unconstrained egoism. All this is true . . . what really matters is what Boris lacks: ideas, political purpose, a reason for seeking high office beyond personal ambition.' Finding any support for Boris in the mainstream media was difficult, especially among women journalists. Many were particularly outraged by his character and behaviour.

Cap in hand, May extracted a further extension of Brexit from the EU until 31 October. She intended to garner enough support for a fourth vote. In desperation, she appealed to Jeremy Corbyn to join her in the interests of national unity. May's trust that an anti-Semitic Marxist would negotiate honestly was beyond naive. Corbyn's sole purpose was to intensify the Tory split and that proved successful. Boris spoke for many that her invitation to Corbyn was 'utterly incredible . . . so bad and so disheartening that you can scarcely believe it'. The proof of May's folly was an outburst by David Lammy, the black activist Labour MP for Tottenham. Brexiteers, said Lammy, were Nazis and Boris was 'an extreme hard-right fascist'. Only May failed to grasp that an agreement with Labour was impossible.

With two imminent elections – for local government on 3 May and the European Parliament on 23 May – the Tory Party's split was reflected by a deepening slump in the polls. The biggest threat was from Nigel Farage's new Brexit Party.

The Tory Party's performance in the local elections was the worst since 1995: 1,330 Tory councillors lost their seats and the party lost control over forty-four councils. 'It's the end of the Tory era – like 1997,' Remainer Tories wailed. The party, they cried, faced an existential crisis. 'Bunkum,' replied Boris. Labour's good fortune, he reminded them, was that with the same 28 per cent share of the vote as the Tories, it had lost just eighty-four councillors.

Fearing another bloodbath in the forthcoming European elections, 79 per cent of the party members urged May to resign before her government collapsed. The Queen would be obliged to invite Corbyn to enter Downing Street. As ever, the problem was identifying her successor. Just as in the 2016 referendum, no outstanding Remainer MP had emerged. While Amber Rudd huffed and puffed, casting more insults at Boris and urging voters to reject a Brexiteer spouting 'narrow nationalism' as the next Tory leader, Brexiteers led by Bill Cash began to look seriously at Boris as the party's saviour.

'I'm going for it,' Boris told an insurance brokers' conference in Manchester on 16 May. 'Of course I'm going for it.' Only he could face off Farage and Corbyn and offer One Nation Toryism. The YouGov poll reported Boris with 35 per cent as the clear favourite among party members. Raab was second with 13 per cent. While 31 per cent of Tory members judged Boris as a 'poor' leader, 70 per cent trusted him to win an election. Waiting for just one more calamity, Boris's machine was well organised. By then, over half the Tory MPs had entered his Portcullis House office for their fifteen-minute slot.

Determined to prevent his victory, May urged MPs to get Brexit settled to prevent a Brexiteer inheriting the leadership. To get a Commons majority in the fourth vote, she proposed to make two radical concessions: Britain would agree to remain a member of the single market, and once the deal was finalised there would be a second referendum. May was not only proposing to betray the Tory manifesto but to split fundamentally the party. 'It's hard to recall a time when the Conservative Party was a greater shambles,' *The Times* rightly concluded, and then added the poison: infected by extremism, the Tories should accept May's deal. The newspaper was unrealistic. Exhausted and discredited, May was bust. She had made the Tory brand toxic.

On the eve of the European elections, Andrea Leadsom, the leader of the Commons, refused to present the fourth Withdrawal Bill to the Commons and resigned. In her bunker, May would not meet other ministers. 'The sofa is up against the door,' said Iain Duncan Smith. 'She's not leaving. She refuses to resign.' The electorate fired the fatal shot.

In the European elections, Nigel Farage won 31.6 per cent of the vote. The Tories won just 9.1 per cent, the party's worst result in any election in 200 years. Fifth behind the Greens, the Tory Party faced oblivion. Tearfully, May announced she would step down on 7 June. Even her closest supporters in Parliament and the media were not surprised. The leadership race had officially started.

Boris sprang forward and instantly pledged to take Britain out of the EU on 31 October, 'deal or no deal'. Only by sticking to leave on 31 October, he said, would the Tories recover their voters. And the only way to extract a better deal was to threaten no-deal. The alternative, he said, was the Conservatives 'permanently haemorrhaging support'. Terrified that Corbyn could become prime minister, even some Boris haters agreed. Six months earlier, Iain Martin in *The*

Times had written off Boris as a has-been buffoon, a doomed blond bombshell with a dud fuse. Martin now suggested, 'Boris has to find a way through the wreckage. He must now unite the centre right.' Only Boris haters preferred May to remain. A vote for Boris, Ruth Davidson said, was a vote for Scottish independence. Expecting the EU to abandon the backstop, said Amber Rudd, was a fantasy. Matthew Parris pleaded against opening the door to an 'incompetent scoundrel'. Boris, Parris predicted, would 'rat on his promise to leave the EU'. If elected, his 'reckless caprice, lazy disregard for principle, weak negotiating skills, moral turpitude . . . which has been so destructive of others' lives and failure as Foreign Secretary to achieve anything but an extension of his notoriety beyond these shores' would prove him to be a disaster. Philip Hammond representing the One Nation group predicted that if Boris ignored Parliament and headed for no-deal, 'he cannot expect to survive very long'. Trying to get no-deal through Parliament, forecast Jeremy Hunt, would be 'political suicide'.

For Boris's diehard opponents, Trump's endorsement of him on the eve of his state visit to Britain confirmed the challenger's unsuitability. 'He would do a good job,' said Trump. 'I think he would be excellent.' Rather than meet Trump during his visit in London, Boris spoke to him on the telephone.

After the Brexit Party pushed the Tories into third place in the Peterborough by-election, more Tories concluded that only Boris could save the party. Instead of winning in a Brexit constituency, the Tories lost 25 per cent of their vote. A poll of party members put Boris at 43 per cent. Now, he not only attracted Brexit supporters but also those desperate to defeat Corbyn. Reports by Katya Adler, the BBC's European editor in Brussels, that the EU adamantly refused to reopen negotiations for the Withdrawal Agreement, and were appalled that Boris might renege on the £39 billion 'divorce' payment, only increased his popularity. 'They think he may possess a kind of magic,' Matthew Parris said about party members, and warned, 'The magic, my friends will fade.' Parris urged the re-election of May without a contest 'to unite and heal the party'. His fantasy was shattered by the first real poll: eighty-three Tory MPs had already endorsed Boris, while Jeremy Hunt, his main rival, attracted just thirty-seven MPs.

*

The tension within Boris's campaign headquarters, set up in the home of Tory peer Greville Howard in Westminster's Lord North Street, mirrored the chaos and conflicts of his private life. Behind the street's only double-fronted house, decorated with Howard's wife Corty's elegant window boxes, Lynton Crosby, the trusted strategist, was resolutely in charge. Among his key aides was Gavin Williamson, fired as Defence Secretary by Theresa May for leaking National Security Council information. Each MP was invited for a face-to-face session with Boris not only to make sure their commitment was genuine but also to give them an opportunity to declare their own ambitions. Many like Craig Mackinlay left his office convinced by Boris's assurance of a ministerial post in his administration.

Boris relied on Iain Duncan Smith to bring ERG votes into his camp. In preparation for two meetings with twenty ERG members, he listened to advice about how best to present his policies and explain his complicated private life.

'What line will you take about that sensitive issue?' he was asked during a group meeting.

'I'll say "People are electing me and not my family", and if they persist I'd say that those who cast stones are usually hypocrites.'

Ever since his lie about his relationship with Petronella Wyatt in 2004, Boris had refused to answer any questions about his family. Few in the room thought his prevarication could succeed but as journalists jumped at the opportunity to embarrass him, the team discovered that his stubborn refusal to engage won the public's sympathy. Even when asked, 'How many children do you have?' he refused to reply, triggering the forlorn chase to discover a rumoured unknown child in Bournemouth! Similarly, when asked whether he had used cocaine, he remained mute. The majority of the British public accepted he was a rogue and wanted to move on. During two sessions, Mark Francois and Steve Baker, the ERG's most trenchant activists, demanded specific answers about no-deal. He would not rule out, he said, suspending Parliament to get no-deal Brexit through. At the end of his interrogation, Francois offered his hand to confirm his support. For the moment, other ERG members supported Raab. Simultaneously, to attract Remainer MPs, Boris promised he wanted a deal. As for the rest who disagreed with him, he was coached to make the right noises.

One week into the campaign, long-standing tensions erupted. Crosby was frozen out by Carrie Symonds. Convinced that Crosby had orchestrated her recent departure from Central Office, Boris's girlfriend also blamed Crosby for a run of negative stories in the *Daily Mail*. Unusually, Boris allowed himself to be influenced by Carrie and argued with Crosby. After the split, Boris decided that Dominic Cummings was critical to his campaign and his premiership. Cummings, he knew, would insist on working with Michael Gove. They came as an inseparable pair. Despite Gove's untrustworthiness and his support for May's deal, Boris agreed that Gove should be recruited. Importing Cummings added fuel to the fire. Overnight, Boris's operation was staffed by Vote Leave campaigners. For Iain Duncan Smith and other ERG members who disliked Cummings, that was a breaking point. They left Lord North Street but some still expected to be included in Boris's first government.

In parallel, intimate meetings were hosted across Mayfair by Ben Elliot, nephew of the Duchess of Cornwall, to raise money for the campaign. Renowned as 'a fabulous flirt', Elliot invited hedge-fund managers, venture capitalists and social billionaires to meet Boris and sign cheques of between £10,000 and £20,000. Anthony Bamford gave £89,000.

In the run-up to the first round, Amber Rudd once again dumped on Boris despite his earlier offer of the Chancellorship in his government. 'It is not enough to be told to shut your eyes, cross your fingers, pick up some magic beans and believe in Britain,' she said when endorsing Hunt. 'We need a skilled negotiator and dealmaker, not an instruction for more optimism.' Her words proved to be futile. In a knockout blow in the first round, Boris won 114 votes – one-third of Tory MPs. Several losers abandoned the race and joined Boris. His fight was now focused against Hunt.

Unable to campaign without Crosby, Boris called and apologised. The Australian returned with his colleague Mark Fullbrook. As usual, their tactics included limiting the gaffes. Press conferences would be restricted to six questions and Boris would not agree to a TV debate with Hunt. The challenger retorted that Boris was a 'coward' – and that, Boris decided, sealed Hunt's fate in the event that Boris won. With victory more certain, a transition team including Matt Hancock, Oliver Dowden and Rishi Sunak was established in a Westminster town house owned by Andrew Griffith, a Sky executive. In the next ballot, Boris received 160 votes, equal to more than half the total. He entered the final round – the party members' votes – as the favourite.

On the eve of his runaway success, the *Guardian* contrived an extraordinary scandal. On 21 June, the newspaper reported that Boris and Carrie had been embroiled in a ferocious argument in her flat, a conversion in a Camberwell house. The circumstances and the facts were disclosed to the *Guardian* by their neighbours, Tom Penn and Eve Leigh. In Penn's version, late on Thursday 20 June he heard an argument as he passed Carrie's front door on his way to collect a delivery of takeaway food. He claimed to have heard the argument between Carrie and Boris continue after he returned to his flat. Then Penn did something quite unusual. He claimed to have recorded the argument on his mobile phone. Penn's version, reported by the *Guardian*, was: 'It was loud enough and angry enough that I felt frightened and concerned for the welfare of those involved, so I went inside my own home, closed the door, and pressed record on the voice memos app on my phone.' After the story was published, the builders of the house would say that the walls were too thick to record an argument. Penn, it was suggested, stuck his phone through Carrie's letter box. (This assumes there even was a recording, because the *Guardian* and Penn refused to produce one.)

The key phrases of the argument reproduced by the *Guardian* were Carrie screaming that Boris had spilled red wine on her sofa: 'You just don't care for anything because you're spoilt. You have no care for money or anything.' Then Boris shouted, 'Get off my fucking laptop,' followed by a loud crashing noise of glasses or plates. Then Carrie shouted, 'Get off me', and 'Get out of my flat'.

Soon after, Penn called the police. Arriving just after midnight, the police were satisfied that neither Carrie nor Boris was at risk and left. Penn and Eve Leigh then decided that the public had a right to know about the private argument. 'Once clear that no one was harmed,' Penn said, 'I contacted the *Guardian*, as I felt that it was of important public interest. I believe it is reasonable for someone who is likely to become our next prime minister to be held accountable for all of their words, actions, and behaviours.' The *Guardian* agreed with that sentiment. The same newspaper which campaigned about infringing celebrities' privacy by hacking their telephones decided that publishing a secret recording of an invasion of privacy was different. The newspaper preferred not to mention that Tom Penn and Eve Leigh were political opponents of Boris or about Eve Leigh's internet boast the previous weekend: 'just gave Boris Johnson the finger, this weekend is unstoppable'. Leigh described her theatrical work as an attack against the 'huge ugly edifice of capitalist heteropatriarchy'.

Under the headline 'Police called to loud altercation at potential PM's home', the *Guardian* splashed the allegations. After the event, Carrie told a close friend that she did not shout 'Get off me' and other so-called quotations published by the *Guardian*. The newspaper, she said, had fabricated some phrases. No one disputed there had been an argument, and that fuelled intense speculation about the cause. Some said Carrie was furious that Boris had returned late from seeing Marina, who at the time was recovering from cervical cancer. Others claimed Carrie was angry that Petronella had texted Boris mocking Carrie's 'undignified half-naked' performance on top of a car (she had posted a fun photo of herself on Instagram), and that 'she needs her teeth fixed'. There were claims that he was looking at photos of Jennifer Arcuri. Finally, the internet was awash with a graphic but fabricated account of Boris arriving late home from a sexual encounter in a restaurant with his female barber. The truth was that Carrie, in an emotional outburst, was upset by Boris's spilling a glass of red wine on her sofa: just a domestic tiff. The only question for insiders was whether Carrie, unlike Marina, could cope with Boris's endless needs and bouts of depression.

Because Boris, contrary to advice, remained silent and the *Guardian* refused to release the recording, the truth was never conclusively established but the circumstances were extraordinary. Britain's future prime minister was involved in yet another unseemly affair while camping out in his girlfriend's home. More shocking to many was a photograph of the interior of Boris's car, parked illegally outside the house. That revealed a gruesome mess. Books, newspapers, clothes, coffee cups and food debris were strewn across the passenger seats and inside the boot. That image said more about Boris's character than the tiff. In an attempt to repair the damage, a photo was released of the two holding hands in a pub garden taken from a distance. The suggestion that it was a chance snap taken the previous day was accurately ridiculed by the length of Boris's hair! Asked twenty-six times by Nick Ferrari on LBC when the photo was taken, he consistently refused to answer. In the end, the only result of the *Guardian's* story was that Tom Penn and Eve Leigh ended up 'evicting' neighbours who may not have conformed with their political tastes. Carrie was forced to sell her home.

Two weeks later, another incident undermined Boris. Confidential reports to the Foreign Office from Kim Darroch, the British ambassador in Washington, featured critical judgements about President Trump's administration as 'dysfunctional' and 'inept'. A Foreign Office official had accumulated the messages and leaked them to a newspaper. Darroch was embarrassed, and worse, the president declared that his administration would no longer engage with the ambassador. In an ITV leadership interview, Boris was asked four times whether he supported Darroch and he refused to give a straight answer. Questioned on 12 July by Andrew Neil, Boris again refused to endorse Darroch. Although he did not see either TV interview, Darroch resigned, blaming Boris's refusal to support him. Boris later admitted his silence was mistaken. He had decided there was no advantage in annoying Trump. Boris was the victim of accidents, dirty tricks and fabrication, but his own gaffes were just that – self-made.

In the last hustings for the leadership one week later, Boris was reckless. Vigorously waving a plastic-wrapped kipper in front of a large audience in London, he claimed that EU regulations on kippers had massively increased the costs of export because 'Brussels bureaucrats are insisting that each kipper must be accompanied by a plastic ice pillow.' That was untrue. British rules had introduced the measure. Once again, just like the £350 million on the bus, he used colourful language to secure the Brexiteers' votes. Once again, his self-deprecating smile won him praise as an authentic figure.

On the eve of the final vote, the *Guardian* likened Boris to a ruling-class trickster who 'cynically gambles with the future of their country and the livelihoods of their fellow citizens'. But for his electorate – the Tory Eurosceptics – only Boris could save the party and country from Corbyn at the next election.

*

On the morning of 23 July, the long-anticipated result was announced in Westminster's Queen Elizabeth Hall. Boris won 66 per cent of the members' vote. His victory speech to a packed hall had been worked on for some time but bore the impression of the usual last-minute brainstorm. This was not the moment to be philosophical but punchy: 'Get Brexit done, unite the party, defeat Corbyn and propel the country to greatness' was not a curtain-raiser to a new era but defiantly buried the past three wasted years. 'We'll rise from the slumber and we're going to believe in ourselves again' was positive but nothing could please the pessimists. The speech's gimmicky acronym 'DUDE' – 'deliver, unite, defeat and energise' – fell flat, yet his audience was bursting with relief. After three cataclysmic years, the nightmare of May's premiership was over. But the Brexit crisis remained. Not only would he be leading a minority government unable to pass the law for Britain to leave the EU, but the divided Tory Party was incapable of agreeing to implement its manifesto pledge. The challenge was to bend reality to his will.

As Boris came down from the stage, he walked towards his family in the front row. There was a double kiss for Rachel, a warm glance at Jo, but a firm rejection of Stanley's outstretched hand. More than ever Stanley needed Boris. But at his moment of triumph, Boris refused his father's congratulation, a secret reminder that Stanley ignored his children when he was needed. Without showing a flicker of doubt, Boris walked out of the hall. Never previously in modern British history had a prime minister reached office in similar circumstances, but he believed himself to be exceptional – and now he would prove it.

On his way to meet the Queen at Buckingham Palace, he already knew how he intended to run Downing Street. As in City Hall, he would be the chairman of meetings, encourage a free exchange of opinions, make decisions and delegate to ministers the delivery of his commands. Munira Mirza, the head of his policy unit, and Eddie Lister, his sixty-nine-year-old trusted adviser and chief of staff, would be his key aides. Neither, he knew, had the experience to force Whitehall and Westminster to implement the revolution he planned. Only Dominic Cummings matched his requirements as a strategist to push Brexit through the hostile Commons, and only Cummings would convince Brussels that Boris was ready for no-deal.

Some speculated that Boris was mesmerised by Cummings. That would be an exaggeration. Boris's skill was to identify his own weaknesses and hire the right person to compensate for them. Cummings was not only a master of strategy, able to intensely focus on detail, but like Boris himself, was a rule-breaker. As a kindred spirit, he understood Boris's anarchical spirit. Willpower would demolish their mutual enemies. His most important contribution would be instilling unyielding resolution never to compromise. His determination to march forward and trample the opposition was vital. Boris decided that he could not run Downing Street without him. His initial offers to Cummings to join him in Downing Street had been rejected. So he cycled to Cummings' north London house which he shared with his wife Mary Wakefield (still employed at the *Spectator*, where she had worked during

Boris's editorship), to hear Cummings' list of 'terrorist demands'. He quickly conceded. Cummings' target, they agreed, would be getting Brexit through, win the general election and then reform Whitehall. Civil servants lacking the skills to run a modern government, unable to manage service, procure goods or formulate good policies, would be ditched. Cummings would revolutionise Britain's decrepit government machine, starting with the over-staffed and woefully incompetent Ministry of Defence.

Cummings' more important demand related to his status and terms of work. The Downing Street administrative machine, he said, would be controlled by him. Not only would he appoint or approve the prime minister's private staff but he would be the gate-keeper to control access to Boris himself. The only people he could trust, said Cummings, were the dedicated Vote Leave campaign staff. Those loyalists should come with him to Downing Street. Only through that command structure, said Cummings, could he accept Boris's offer. With no alternative option and probably not realising the consequences, Boris agreed. He never considered the maxim that successful campaigners are not necessarily good administrators. In politics, there is a truism that leaders can be judged by the cronies they select to advise them. Boris's public con-fession that Cummings was the cornerstone of his administration was telling. He failed to calculate that after Benedict Cumberbatch had portrayed Cummings in the feature film *Brexit: The Uncivil War*, his ego had become overblown.

On 24 July, while Boris was inside Buckingham Palace, Cum-mings had arrived in Downing Street. Outside Number 10, the new prime minister strode to the lectern to make a short speech. Brexit, he promised, would be done by Halloween – 'No ifs, no buts . . . We are going to restore trust in our democracy.' 31 October was the target date. He then turned towards the famous black door. Fifty-two years after declaring he wanted to be 'world king', his entry would manifest that dream. As he turned to wave to the cameras, romantics cited Disraeli: Boris had been chosen thanks to 'the sub-lime instincts of an ancient people'. Other admirers intoned, 'Cometh the hour, cometh the man.'

Once through the door, he was welcomed by Mark Sedwill, the Cabinet Secretary. The TV cameras recorded the scene, spotting in the corner by the window a distinctly untidy individual dressed in a grey T-shirt and jeans: Dominic Cummings. In his typically confrontational manner, Cummings wanted his enemies to see his victory. The first people to be horrified by the pictures, as Cummings intended, were the ERG's leaders. 'If we'd known that Cummings would come,' said Bill Cash, 'it would have caused a lot of angst. I was against Vote Leave because of Cummings.' 'The ERG group was appalled,' admitted Peter Lilley, 'but they consoled themselves that Brussels would be more appalled.'

The BBC was clearly appalled by Boris's success. A radio profile called 'Who is Boris Johnson?' featured the well-worn cast of detractors eager once again to portray an ideologically light, shambolic, lazy liar unprepared for public appearances. In the *Guardian*, selected women journalists described him as typical of that breed of 'white men' who 'lash out' and are 'repellently dishonest, xenophobic and politically calculating'. The paper's sketch-writer John Crace could not cope with the result: 'Johnson is the career sociopath [who] doesn't really believe in anything except himself.' Years of their vitriol had failed to frustrate a determined man empowered by an unassailable majority and divided opposition to decide the country's fate.

The trademark of the Johnson administration would be his kitchen cabinet. Automatically invited to join the inner circle and plan his government were the City Hall trustees, Munira Mirza, Eddie Lister, the ever-loyal aide Ben Gascoigne, and Will Walden, the experienced media adviser who would twice refuse Boris's offer to be Downing Street's director of communications. Gathered in an office with the well-used white drawing board leaning against the wall, they sat with Mark Spencer, the chief whip, trusted to nominate the junior ranks.

The Cabinet, Cummings persuaded Boris, should not include any opponents. Critical discussion was anathema to the control freak. Cabinet meetings should be limited to announcements and orders. All their departments would be controlled by himself from

Downing Street. Boris's criterion was the winner takes all. Gavin Williamson and Grant Shapps were rewarded for organising the leadership election. Michael Gove was allowed to become chief operating officer, a boring task to prove his worth. Sajid Javid's fate was in doubt until Carrie Symonds urged his appointment as Chancellor. Reassured by Boris that the chances of leaving the EU without a deal were 'a million to one', Javid accepted. The first to be discarded were those he did not trust or had given him unwelcome advice. The crunch decision was Jeremy Hunt. Normally the defeated opponent would be offered a consolation prize. Hunt wanted to remain in the Foreign Office. Boris didn't trust a Remainer in the Foreign Office. He owed Hunt nothing and did not rate his abilities. In the hope he would reject the offer, Hunt was assigned Defence. Take it on my terms or there's the door, was Boris's ultimatum. Hunt refused the demotion. 'Hunt could not help the government so he and his people were out,' said one adviser. Raab, an ardent Brexiteer, would be more reliable as Foreign Secretary and trusted as Boris's deputy to champion 'Britannia Unchained', a vision for a deregulated state akin to 'Singapore in the North Sea'. Along with Priti Patel as Home Secretary, Javid as Chancellor and James Cleverly, another City Hall loyalist, as party chairman, the Cabinet was noticeably diverse. And Amber Rudd was allowed to remain as minister of work and pensions. She would be a show of political cross-dressing to the One Nation wing of the party. Few thought she would last long.

Allies were shocked that despite the belief that Boris always wanted to be loved, his promises to some key supporters were ignored. Jake Berry, so crucial to Boris after 2016, was not given a major portfolio. 'He didn't fit in the jigsaw,' said one aide. Another disappointed MP was Andrew Mitchell. Four days before the election, Boris had asked 'It's DFID [the Department for International Development] you want?'

'Yes,' replied Mitchell.

'Right ho,' said Boris. 'I'm going to bring you back.'

But Mitchell was overlooked. 'And I've been so loyal to him,' said Mitchell.

As promises went unfulfilled, disappointment spread through the Tory ranks. 'Boris means it only when he says it,' complained another forgotten ally, 'but then changes. He plays fast and loose with the truth.' No longer needed, they blamed 'the London crew'.

The most aggrieved were ERG group members critical to his election. Other than Jacob Rees-Mogg, an Old Etonian, appointed as leader of the Commons, the rest were forgotten. Invited to Downing Street, Steve Baker arrived fuming that Boris had failed to fulfil his promise. During the leadership campaign, Baker assumed that, as the reward for organising the ERG group's support for Boris, he would be the Cabinet minister to negotiate Brexit. 'You're like me,' Boris had told him with apparent sincerity. 'You've got a wild uncontrollable spirit.' Instead, Baker watched compliant Steve Barclay appointed to that Cabinet post. 'The fashionable and clubbable get the jobs,' Baker raged, 'while the difficult, edgy and ungentlemanly don't. I can't laugh at their jokes in Greek and Latin.' Baker later reflected that during their conversations, 'Boris had a playful glint to see into your mind and find out how he can make you like him. And then . . .' Baker was kept waiting for one hour in Downing Street until, just as he was about to leave in anger, he was whisked into the Cabinet Room and offered the job of Barclay's deputy. 'It's a Potemkin job,' shouted Baker. 'I delivered for you.' Boris was startled. For forty-five minutes they argued. 'You've got me wrong,' raged Baker as Boris tried to urge calm. Baker departed without a job and a pledge to settle his grievance. 'The ERG group felt so excluded,' recalled Bernard Jenkin. 'We felt that he doesn't need us. It was galling that he went to the middle ground for support as if we're toxic. Some of us resented that we were called Spartans and sacrificed.'

By the end, seventeen ministers from May's team had been fired. Only those committed to Brexit remained. All were expected to loyally obey. With a Commons majority of just two, Boris could take no risk of a Cabinet split. None of the Cabinet could be classed as wise, experienced politicians. There would be no concessions, only boldness. In truth, not since 1940 had a British politician become prime minister with greater uncertainty. 'He'll be prime minister for either ten weeks or ten years,' said Peter Lilley. 'He'll be a great prime minister or a great disappointment.'

In Oxford, Jasper Griffin, Boris's beloved tutor, was seriously ill. In a lucid moment, he was told that Boris was prime minister. 'Prime minister won't be enough for Boris,' sighed Griffin. 'He wants to be emperor.' Matthew Leeming, Boris's Oxford friend, wrote in congratulation: 'Remember Caesar, you are mortal and all political careers end in failure.' Elsewhere in the city, Oswyn Murray, a Balliol professor, mentioned that he had sent Boris a *renuntiatio amicitiae* – a formal ending of their relationship – in fury about his dishonest championing of Brexit. Roman emperors sent the *renuntiatio*, Boris knew, as an invitation to exile or suicide. Momentarily, he was sincerely hurt but not deflected. He had finally won.

Naturally he was comforted by Cummings' certainty of purpose. He was also reassured by Lee Cain, his new director of communications. The former freelance journalist who had loyally spoken for him during his term as Foreign Secretary, was entrusted with the critical job of managing the prime minister's relationship with the media and the electorate. In Cain's favour was his loyalty to Boris, obedience to Cummings and shared distrust of the media. Downing Street, they agreed, was to operate in secrecy. Staff would be warned not to speak to even trusted journalists. Boris's belief that the man dressed as a chicken during David Cameron's 2010 election campaign and a lowly media official for Vote Leave possessed the necessary intellect and imagination to oversee the government's entire communications operation was a leap of faith.

Everything about the first days of the Johnson administration was unconventional. Prime ministers normally arrive with a spouse, but Boris would invite Carrie Symonds to quietly join him. No prime minister had ever lived in Downing Street with an unmarried partner. Nor had any predecessor been faced by the constant media attention of their personal life disintegrating around them. Facing incoming fire from his closest family, they whispered that he missed Marina and that his affair with Carrie was no more than a fling and not a life choice. His first weekend at Chequers reflected the loner's existence. His guests were friends of Carrie and Michael Gove.

'So the party of family values,' wrote Paul Dacre in the *Spectator*, admitting astonishment about his mistaken predictions, 'has chosen as leader a man of whom to say he has the morals of an alley cat would be to libel the feline species. Thus the Tories, with two women PMs to their credit, have achieved another historic first: scuppering the belief – argued by the *Daily Mail* in my 26 years as editor – that politicians with scandalous private lives cannot hold high office. I make no comment on this, or about the 31-year-old minx who is the current Boris Johnson bedwarmer, but ask you instead to spare a thought for Petronella's abortion, Helen's love child, Marina's humiliation and her four children's agony . . . As for the Minx, mark my words: there will be tears before midnight.'

With that blast, the critics were temporarily silenced. The litany of their dire warnings, smiled Boris, had been ignored.

ACT IV

Triumph and Turmoil

Chapter 26

Total Victory

Seventy days after his appointment as prime minister, on 2 October, the leader's reception at the party's annual conference in Manchester was to be Boris's coronation, with a pledge of ideological renewal and a declaration of war against his opponents. As he walked into the packed hall to the music of The Who, the excited, mostly young audience greeted the star. Their roars of applause as he made his way towards the stage were genuine. He was their saviour.

Just below the lectern Stanley Johnson sat beside Carrie Symonds. Both had waved as they took their seats. The televised pictures of their friendly conversation reignited the division between Stanley and Boris's children. As usual, Stanley was eager for the spotlight. At a fringe meeting the previous night, Boris had spotted Stanley in the audience and invited him onto the stage. The glances between father and son bore a familiar message which no one in the room understood. Noticeably, in his speech to conference the following day, Boris included a reference to his mother whom he had visited before travelling to Manchester. 'My mother taught me the equal importance of dignity and worth,' he said. Only the Johnson family understood that sentence.

'We are the party of capitalism,' Boris told his admirers. The applause was genuine. War, he said, had been declared against Corbyn's 'fratricidal anti-Semitic Marxists' and against the Remainers in the Commons. Britain, he pledged, would be out of the EU by 31 October, just over four weeks later. The spontaneous ovation suggested that the party was united. Boris took strength from Dominic Cummings' conviction: 'Nothing will stand in the way of Brexit.'

Walking out of the hall holding Carrie's hand, Boris's face shone with satisfaction and resilience. In the tumultuous days since he had been appointed prime minister, 'Borisism' or 'Johnsonism' had been born. Contrary to the critics' warnings, there was no evidence so far of racism, no outright lies, and no hard-right populism. But new criticisms had arisen among the Tory Remain MPs. He had won power but could he govern? they asked. In his rush to Brexit, they murmured, he was sacrificing the party's soul and its reputation for 'balance and moderation, all integral to Toryism'. Naturally, he shunned the sceptics. So far, relying on Dominic Cummings had paid off. Now he was ready to take another enormous gamble, entrusting his fate to Cummings' scorched-earth strategy.

As a professional disrupter, Cummings' instinct was to provoke a political and constitutional crisis. In the same manner as his hero Otto von Bismarck, the Prussian Chancellor who plotted to unite Germany's thirty-nine states under the Kaiser by waging successive wars against Denmark, Austria and France, Cummings planned a sequence of anarchic events over the next few months, climaxing in Boris's return to Downing Street after an election with a parliamentary majority. Success relied on repeated attrition – provoking confrontations and overcoming his enemies.

The timetable was precise. First, the Opposition would be ensnared to vote for a general election on 17 October. In parallel, Boris would orchestrate a disorderly Brexit and run down the clock to the deadline of Britain leaving the EU on 31 October; then, to outwit their opponents in the election, the Tories would campaign under the banner 'People versus Parliament' and 'Get Brexit Done'; and finally, while the opposition struggled to make a convincing argument, Britain would threaten the EU that Britain would crash out without a deal. Success, said Cummings, depended on bull-dozing all the resistors. His strategy espoused the 'swerve' methodology – Boris would drive the car as fast as possible towards his opponent and, just as he was spotted, he would throw the steering wheel out of the window. Ideally, Cummings and Boris hoped, alarmed Remainer MPs would support the government and the EU would abandon the backstop, agreeing to a reasonable trade deal. If not, they would be crushed.

The opening shots from Cummings had been fired in early August, soon after Boris entered Downing Street. Private focus groups suggested that Corbyn's leadership had weakened Labour's vote in the Midlands and the north where the majority had voted Leave. Polling also indicated that delivering Brexit would tip the balance towards the Tories. Targeting the Labour heartlands, the government pledged an additional £20 billion funding for the NHS. That enormous sum undermined Labour's traditional anti-Tory battle cry that only they could protect the NHS. The same polls convinced Cummings that the 'out-of-touch London elite' had misunderstood the nation's mood in 2016. Three years later, the Remainers had still not reflected on their mistakes to understand the working class. Instead, Cummings scoffed, they 'just doubled down on their own ideas and fucked it up even more'. He looked forward to defeating them again. The self-publicist enjoyed the fear and loathing he generated, especially among the hard-core Tory Remainer MPs.

Led by Philip Hammond, Oliver Letwin and Dominic Grieve, roughly twenty-five Tory Remainer MPs were alarmed by Cummings' countdown to a no-deal Brexit. On 4 August, the day after Boris handed out the £20 billion, the Tory Remainers threatened to bring down the government if Boris sought to crash out of the EU without a deal. To prove the irresponsibility of no-deal, a former Cabinet minister gave the *Sunday Times* a copy of 'Operation Yellowhammer', Downing Street's blueprint for Britain's survival after Dover and other Channel ports were blocked, medicines became unobtainable and food was rationed. In that moment of truth, Boris believed that the only way to save his divided party from destruction was to remove the Remainers from the Commons and unite around Brexit. That would expose Labour as divided – Brexiteers versus those pursuing a second referendum. He would not resign, he pledged, even if he lost a vote of no confidence.

As a first step, Boris dropped his original self-confident prediction of 'a million to one chance' of a no-deal Brexit. His new vow
was 'a high chance' of getting a deal. Privately, he admitted to be
unafraid of crashing out. His gung-ho attitude alarmed Geoffrey
Cox, the rumbustious Attorney General. Thinking the EU would
abandon the backstop, he warned Boris, was a 'complete fantasy'.
Marking Cox down as another non-believer, Boris preferred Bill
Cash's advice. 'The EU,' Cash told him, 'are not our partners and
allies. They are doing everything to make sure we don't succeed.'
Boris, he was sure, 'could pull off victory because he has Churchill's
frame of mind'.

David Frost, Boris's chosen Brexit negotiator, was dispatched to
Brussels. His offer was uncompromising. The backstop would have
to be abandoned or Britain would leave without a deal. That, Boris
believed, would frighten the Irish government. Next, Boris flew to
Berlin and Paris with the same message. Merkel and Macron needed
to understand that despite his tiny majority, the rebel MPs could
not stop a no-deal Brexit. To win time, Merkel gave Boris thirty
days to resolve the backstop. On his return to London, Boris gave
mixed messages. To prevent the Commons extending Article 50, he
gave the impression to some that there would be a deal. Others
knew there were no proposals to put to the EU. Frost's negotiations, as Cummings admitted, were a 'sham' just to run down the
clock. Boris was solely focused on manoeuvring towards an
election.

At least, Boris reasoned, the Cabinet would be loyal. All his ministers had joined understanding that Britain would threaten the EU
to leave without a deal at the end of October. The problem was
Parliament – paralysed but potent. That August, Cummings' contempt for politicians rubbed off on Boris. In September, he raged,
MPs would return to Westminster to earn their 'crust' by going
through a 'rigmarole' to sabotage the referendum that had been
won three years earlier. The Tory Remainers wanted a second referendum while Labour MPs just wanted to block the government's
negotiations. To extend Article 50 and prevent Brexit on 31 October,
Remain MPs from both sides were co-operating under Hilary

Benn, the Labour MP, and John Bercow, the Speaker, to introduce a short bill, eventually called the Benn Act, to make crashing out of the EU without a deal unlawful.

To prove his macho, Cummings concocted an audacious plan to stifle the Remainers. Usually in the autumn, Parliament was closed or 'prorogued' for one week and suspended by agreement for three weeks during the party conferences. Cummings' plan was to formally close Parliament for five weeks to give Boris unfettered power to threaten Brussels with no-deal. Prorogation, suggested Cummings, would trample on the Tory Remain MPs, a shambolic rabble, he believed, without a sense of mission.

That was a critical moment for Boris. During the leadership campaign, he had said about prorogation 'I'm not attracted to the idea.' Now, he had to gamble whether his opponents would eventually capitulate or whether Letwin and Grieve, both loyal parliamentarians, could unite the Remainers and spawn the spirit of counter-revolution. Relying on Cummings, he was reassured they lacked the courage. Asked in a memo on 15 August by Nikki da Costa, Downing Street's director of legislative affairs, whether he approved the prorogation, Boris scribbled 'Yes' in the margin. Months of plotting ended. Soon after, a civil servant leaked the plan to a newspaper. The secrecy of the plot was lost. 'Cummings,' Letwin later reflected, 'didn't understand the texture of parliamentary politics.'

On 27 August, Jacob Rees-Mogg flew to Balmoral for the Queen to sign the prorogation. In effect, just six days of Parliament were cut. But as a formal prorogation, it was the longest for forty years. Due to return to Westminster on 3 September and with the prorogation to start on Monday the 9th, MPs would not return to Westminster until 14 October. Westminster became convulsed by a constitutional crisis. Remain MPs were left with just four days to extend Article 50. An application was filed at the High Court to declare the prorogation unlawful. The melodrama erupted just as Cummings' true character was exposed.

Boris's acquiescence to Cummings' 'terrorist demands' of total control over Downing Street's administrative machine just before his appointment as prime minister had caused immediate friction. From the outset, Cummings insisted that he approve every minister's special assistant. Not only would he vet their abilities but also their loyalty to himself. At the regular Friday 5 p.m. meetings for special advisers, he assessed whether the person was malleable to his demands or more loyal to the ministers. He also tested the loyalty of those City Hall imports close to Boris. By definition, that group including Munira Mirza, Eddie Lister and Ben Gasgoine was classed as potentially dangerous. Cummings would seek to limit their access to Boris, although they were the prime minister's most trusted advisers. For the moment he could do little about Mark Sedwill, the Cabinet Secretary appointed by Theresa May. Although Sedwill's preoccupation with security and intelligence made him unsuitable to reform the NHS and the Whitehall machine, his tactful diplomacy neutralised Cummings' hostility. Cleverly, Sedwill had approved the prorogation and summoned government lawyers to bless the ruse's legality. But in the initial tussle for influence with Sedwill, Cummings sought to control which submissions drafted by civil servants would be read by the prime minister. Assuming that he was smarter than others, Cummings decided that the permanent secretaries running the machinery of government were best sidelined. Although his interest in and understanding of the machinery of government was growing, Boris agreed to Cummings' rules. He even approved Cummings' control of politicians' access to Boris. Without realising the self-imposed limitations, his advantage as London's mayor of meeting and listening to people was being curtailed.

Demanding total obedience from subordinates was natural for Cummings. By cultivating fear of himself, no one in Downing Street either wanted to annoy him or could be certain what he wanted – except that he would not tolerate any disloyalty. The leak of Nikki da Costa's memo proved the unreliability of some Downing Street officials. His suspicion also fell on Sonia Khan, a twenty-seven-year-old Treasury special adviser to Sajid Javid. Khan, he believed, was in secret contact with Philip Hammond, her former boss. Without informing Javid, Cummings summoned Khan

The three most important women in his life: Regardless of his infidelity, Marina was Boris's loyal wife and consigliere, the rock whom he nevertheless betrayed. His sister Rachel has always been a reliable confidante as well as a rival. His supreme love and care for his mother, Charlotte Johnson Wahl, has become even more important since his divorce from Marina.

Book launch: Boris, Rachel and their mother, Charlotte, attend the launch of his book *The Churchill Factor: How One Man Made History* at Dartmouth House on 22 October 2014.

Action man: Aware of the value of a good photo, Boris always made himself available to prove his sporting prowess and popular credentials. Noticeably, that habit disappeared once he became prime minister.

Going for broke: Declaring his support for the Leave campaign outside his Islington house on 21 February 2016 was a seismic event which permanently changed Britain's history. His conduct during the campaign, especially his misleading suggestion that Britain paid the EU £350 million net every week, aroused huge anger. The Remainers' animosity against him has still not subsided.

Surprise appointment: Despite their mutual antipathy, Boris was appointed foreign secretary by prime minister Theresa May in July 2016. The perception of his poor record there inspired the cartoonist Peter Brookes. Boris's humiliation was aggravated by Simon McDonald (above, right), the Foreign Office's permanent secretary. Their relationship convinced Boris that the civil service needed fundamental change.

The Emperor's New Clothes: Peter Brookes's cartoon in *The Times*, 12 June 2019.

Watching: Ed Lister (right, front row, second from left), Carrie Symonds (front row, third from left), Munira Mirza (left of Boris).

A dream come true: Boris's Downing Street speech on 24 July 2019 after meeting the Queen was the climax of ambition and endurance. Boris was welcomed into Number 10 by Mark Sedwill, the cabinet secretary. The lurking presence of Dominic Cummings in the corner highlighted the imminent peril Sedwill faced.

Overwhelming victory:
Few predicted Boris's
80-seat majority in the
December 2019 election.
His victory was partly
due to an understanding
with the Brexiteers' ERG
group, but the seeds of
future problems were his
two closest aides, Dominic
Cummings and Lee Cain
(right), his director of
communications.

The ERG group,
from left to right:
Steve Baker,
Iain Duncan Smith,
Mark Francois and
Bill Cash, walking
up to Number 10,
16 October 2019.

Unexpected disaster: Covid-19 wrecked Britain and Boris's plans. His total reliance on Patrick Vallance, Chris Whitty, Matt Hancock (all descending the stairs in Downing Street, above) and Neil Ferguson (right) would prove to be a mistake. All except Vallance would be infected by the virus.

Time to clap: Boris clapping for the NHS on the step at Downing Street on 2 April 2020. Three days later, Boris was in hospital, close to death.

An unconventional prime minister: Secretive and shaky, Boris's relationship with Carrie Symonds and Wilfred, their baby son, is the subject of gossip, as is his unusually unimpressive cabinet of 'yes-men'. Combined, they arouse speculation that Boris lacks 'grip'.

and demanded to see her mobile phone. Despite Khan's denials of any disloyalty, Cummings asked a police officer to march her off the premises. 'If you don't like how I run things,' he told the remaining special advisers, 'there's the door. Fuck off.' They stayed, as did Javid. The Chancellor fumed about his humiliation and privately accused Cummings of inventing the issue to damage his credibility. Female special advisers whispered that Cummings had a problem with women.

The shock about Cummings' authoritarianism blended with accusations that the prorogation was the first step towards a dictatorship. Hysterically, Labour MPs called for Parliament to be 'occupied' and workers to hold a general strike. Predictably, Boris had not anticipated how he would convincingly explain prorogation. Throughout his life, excuses for his misconduct had been thin and it was no different in the constitutional crisis. Downing Street's explanation – that the exceptional measure was taken to 'prepare legislation' for the next session – was ridiculed. 'The government,' said Letwin, 'could not give the real reason that prorogation was to prevent the Benn Act and Geoffrey Cox [the Attorney General] refused to lie.' Even Peter Lilley, a Brexiteer, was puzzled: 'I could not understand the purpose. It was so devilishly clever that no one could see that it would not work.' Labour's protests were predictable but those from the right were equally outraged. Tory rebels threatened to forge a breakaway coalition with Labour to bring down the government and veto an early election. 'Boris saw that his legs were cut off,' said a critical Downing Street eyewitness. 'His gamble was certain to fail.' Boris thought the opposite.

On Sunday 1 September, he summoned a council of war at Chequers. Over lunch with Cummings and Mark Spencer, the chief whip, he considered his tactics for the votes leading towards an early election. Going through the list of likely rebels, they came to Nicholas Soames. Churchill's grandson, Boris had been told, had announced at a grouse shoot hosted by Wafic Said, a Syrian financier and philanthropist, that he would never vote against the government or against Boris. Although a great dinner companion, Soames had also predicted that Boris would 'bugger it up'. His bullying manner made him unreliable in the jungle. Next, Dominic Grieve – the barrister, they agreed, was no longer a Tory. Next, Philip Hammond – an outright enemy. Next, Oliver Letwin, a dangerous opponent. Then, Rory Stewart, aka 'Florence of Arabia', whose colourful accounts of his service in Iraq and Afghanistan were disputed by eyewitnesses. Certainly a rebel. Finally, Amber Rudd, more fickle than others and determined to undermine Boris. All in all, they concluded, there would be at least fifteen rebels – fighting blue on blue to assert their moral superiority. Spencer, they agreed, would deliver the individual warnings that night: any MP who failed to support the government and the manifesto commitment to implement the referendum would be expelled from the parliamentary party. Deselection as an MP would automatically follow. The die was cast for a momentous struggle. The hiatus, Boris agreed, was necessary for the revolution.

The ultimatum was repeated the following evening during a drinks party in Downing Street's garden. The only non-combatant running among the MPs was Dilyn, Boris's new Jack Russell dog. That same evening, Boris repeated his intimidation on TV: 'I want everyone to know there are no circumstances in which I will ask Brussels to delay. We are leaving on 31 October, no ifs, no buts.' If defeated in the Commons, he said, there would be an election on 14 October. No other prime minister in the past century had risked his job so early in his administration.

The following morning, fifteen Remainers led by Hammond arrived in Downing Street. All were appalled that Boris's assurance of a 'million to one' chance of no-deal had been reduced to 'touch and go' to conclude a deal. As they waited to enter the Cabinet Room, Cummings appeared. 'I don't know who any of you are,' he said provocatively to the senior MPs. Admitted to the room they knew so well, the discussion quickly became a bad-tempered exchange. Boris urged them to support no-deal as a way to get a deal. In a brash tone, Hammond derided the strategy. Your way, he told Boris, is a 'fantasy'. Your way, countered Boris, will hand power to 'a junta that includes Corbyn'. Hammond dismissed the fear. He threatened to mobilise the Commons to defeat the government.

Readopted by his constituency the night before, Hammond promised 'the fight of a lifetime' if he was expelled from the party after forty-five years' membership. Dominic Grieve was similarly trenchant. If Boris persisted, threatened the former law officer, he would support Corbyn to bring down the government.

Seventy-five minutes later, they departed, furious that Boris was clearly not negotiating a new deal and refused to compromise. Later that day, Greg Clark, the erudite former Business Secretary and a potential Tory rebel, called Cummings to discuss a truce. His ears were burst by Cummings' rant: 'When are you fucking MPs going to realise, we are leaving on 31 October? We are going to purge you.' The common hatred for Cummings, especially his disdain for the Tory Party and Parliament, and the threat of deselection bound the rebels together with a kamikaze spirit.

Unexpectedly, Boris invited Letwin for a chat. 'Despite all the trouble I had caused,' recalled Letwin, 'Boris was so charming.' His message, however, was defiant. 'He would take it to the wire and see if Labour blinked,' Letwin was told. 'He was indifferent to the risk. He was not worried by crashing out of the EU. There could be no compromise and we parted.'

The Commons was packed the following morning for the debate. As Boris spoke, his first statement as prime minister, Phillip Lee, the Tory MP for Bracknell, walked across the floor and sat with the Liberals. Baited by Corbyn that his government's majority had literally disappeared, Boris raised his battle cry: 'Come what may, do or die.' In that afternoon's first vote, the government was defeated by twenty-seven. MPs took control of the parliamentary timetable, a resounding victory for the Remainers and the Labour Party. Twenty-one Tories voted against the government and in favour of what Boris called 'Jeremy Corbyn's Surrender Bill'. The following day, the Benn Bill would inevitably pass into law making it illegal for Britain to leave the EU without a deal on 31 October. 'It means running up the white flag,' Boris shouted. The vote to approve a snap election was also defeated.

Instantly, twenty-one Tories including Hammond, Soames and Ken Clarke, the Father of the House, were expelled from the party.

The uproar, far greater than Boris had anticipated, was deafening. Reacting to the expulsions, John Major accused Boris of 'aggressive bullying' and turning the party into a 'mean-minded sect' while the country was 'torn apart by the divisions of Brexit'. The purge, said Alistair Burt, a Tory MP since 1983 who had also lost the whip, 'risks destroying the Tory Party and [is] a policy of insanity'. Others screeched it was a right-wing populist coup. Boris replied that they had been warned of the consequences of plotting to defeat the government and should nobly accept the price.

Oliver Letwin, one of the expelled MPs, considered the position thoughtfully. While Boris had misjudged the parliamentary strength against a crash-out, Letwin wondered whether the rebels were underestimating the public's support for Boris. The Remainers believed they spoke for the majority, but north of Hampstead, many people were unimpressed by the MPs' antics. After three years of May's inertia, they wanted an effective government. The polls showed a surge in support for the Tories, up from 25 per cent to 35 per cent. Presenting the Benn Bill as the Surrender Bill and shaping up the next general election as People versus Parliament was, Letwin realised, seductive. At the same time, he reassessed Boris, whom he had first met as a pro-European in 2001. To his surprise, Boris had morphed into a genuine Brexiteer. His single-mindedness could not be underestimated. Mentally and physically, when Boris saw a brick wall, he either climbed over it or knocked it down. Characterising him as a lazy, love-me, unfocused man was redundant. The battle to prevent Boris taking Britain out of the EU would be ferocious. Even Letwin's alternatives – a deal or a second referendum – were unacceptable to Boris. Accordingly, Letwin and his fellow rebels pledged, the government would be surprised by their unity and their parliamentary skills. Cummings, 'an unelected foul-mouthed oaf throwing his weight around', would get his comeuppance.

The next morning, 4 September, Boris woke up knowing that the day would be worse than the previous one. The headlines reported his defeat and humiliation. The rebels were promising a bitter battle for the soul of the Tory Party. 'Something mad has taken root in our party,' wrote Matthew Parris, predicting the party's death. 'We are closer to the edge than we may think.' Nicholas Soames agreed about the poison: 'Boris Johnson's experience in life is telling a lot of porkies about the EU and then becoming prime minister.' Joining the backlash, Damian Green accused Boris of being 'monstrously unfair'. Rees-Mogg had rebelled dozens of times and escaped any sanction, he said, while the twenty-one had rebelled at most twice. The airwaves were filled with accusations that Boris had destroyed the centrist Tory Party by embracing right-wing fanaticism. By lunchtime, the twenty-one discovered that the ground was cut beneath them. Hammond was among the first to lose the support of his local association. He was deselected as a Tory candidate. Party members regarded Boris as the only person capable of preventing a Corbyn government. Well-prepared party officials were already listing pro-Brexit candidates to take the rebels' places for an inevitable election.

In the Commons that morning, Boris faced unprecedented embarrassment. He was a minority prime minister who had lost control of Parliament. With the help of the Tory rebels, the Benn Bill was passed forcing him to delay Brexit – or break the law. Defiantly, he shunned Corbyn's carping. Calling him 'frit' and a 'chlorinated chicken' for supporting the 'Surrender Bill', he taunted Corbyn, 'Call an election you great big girl's blouse.' Labour's MPs festered, particularly the women.

Tory MPs were equally annoyed during Boris's appearance later that day at the 1922 Committee meeting of backbenchers. 'It's not for me to interfere with what the whips decide,' he said, feigning innocence about the expulsions. To further provoke his critics, he compared himself to the statesman and military leader Octavius, known as Augustus after he became Rome's first emperor. Augustus was renowned for slaughtering his opponents, gouging out their eyes with his thumb and inspecting their severed heads. He claimed that only by destroying the Roman republic could Rome be saved. And indeed, his reign introduced 200 peaceful years known as the Pax Romana. Boris explained that only by expelling the old Tories could a new One Nation Tory Party be created.

Aligning his personal ambition with Britain's best interests, he, like the emperor, would slaughter his foes and lead the country into a new era.

Exhausted at the end of the day in the Downing Street flat, he answered his mobile. Jo Johnson, his youngest brother, was calling. Jo's return to the government as universities minister had always been fraught. As a Remainer, he had reluctantly accepted the referendum but after that week's rebellion could no longer tolerate a no-deal Brexit. Boris's 'force of personality', he would later say, 'papered over the absence of any deliverable plan'. Brexit had been about taking back control but had become 'incoherent'. Jo told his brother he was resigning from the government. 'In recent weeks,' he would tell the public the following morning, 'I've been torn between family loyalty and the national interest. It's an unresolvable tension.' The torn allegiance was not just to Boris but to his wife, Amelia Gentleman, a *Guardian* journalist. She had joined the Labour Party in protest about the Tory government's treatment of the Jamaicans brought to Britain on the *Windrush*. Jo's resignation confirmed the reality of the Johnsons' splintering. The magic which united the family at Chevening just two years earlier had vanished. In vocal opposition to Boris, Rachel had joined pro-EU groups, while Leo, employed by PriceWaterhouseCooper, remained out of sight. Only Charlotte, his mother, was sincerely loyal. In solidarity, she had voted Leave.

Nine years earlier, Boris had said after David and Ed Miliband turned against each other for the Labour Party's leadership that a similar split was 'absolutely' inconceivable among Tory siblings: 'We don't do things in that way. That's a very left-wing thing. Only a socialist could do that to his brother, only a socialist could regard familial ties as being so trivial as to shaft his own brother.' Days after Jo's resignation, the two brothers met at Charlotte's flat for two hours in the afternoon. 'Boris felt let down by Jo quitting,' recalled Charlotte. 'And Jo felt sensitive about that. We spoke about the family and the problems.' Two days later, Boris stayed away from the celebration of Leo's birthday at Rachel's house. Jo and his wife Amelia were there.

The pressure was mounting. 4 September had been a bad day. The next day was torrid.

Boris headed for Wakefield in West Yorkshire to launch the election campaign at a police college. By the time he arrived, he was besieged from all sides. Ruth Davidson had resigned as the Scottish leader, endangering Tory seats in the country. John Major had called for Cummings, an 'aggressive bully', to be sacked. The referendum, Major believed, should be ignored and Britain remain in the EU. More Tory MPs had announced they would leave Parliament. Boris faced the possibility that after more defeats in Parliament, he would be forced to resign. The Queen would be bound to ask Corbyn to form a coalition government.

Clearly distracted and late, he walked to the lectern placed in front of police cadets. On a hot day, marshalled close behind him, the cadets were sweltering by the time he started to speak. Unable for once to suppress the emotional turmoil pounding in his head, he rambled about Corbyn's refusal to agree to an election. His focus returned after mentioning another spending spree to wrong-foot Labour. 'I'd rather be dead in a ditch,' he pledged, than ask the EU to delay Brexit beyond 31 October. His resolve relied on Cummings. 'We are not going to panic,' said the man accused of destroying Boris's premiership just as it began. 'We're not going to extend [Brexit] and we're not going to resign.' With that defiance, Boris denied lying to the Queen about the reason for prorogation and flew with Carrie north to meet the monarch in Balmoral. In his absence from Westminster, Amber Rudd resigned on 7 September. The deselection of the twenty-one, she said, was 'an assault on decency and democracy'. She also objected to Boris's aggressive language. Hold your nerve, Cummings urged Boris. Everything was going to plan. The Tories had nudged higher in the opinion polls. In public, Boris seemed unflustered. 'We'll get out by October 31, believe me,' he told inquirers. 'We'll break free of the manacles of the EU like the Incredible Hulk. The madder Hulk gets, the stronger Hulk gets.'

To Remainers, Boris's defiance was puzzling. He agreed to abide by the law but still pledged he could ignore the law ordering him to delay departure. Even more puzzling was how he survived over the next days' succession of embarrassments.

During a visit to Luxembourg, he was deliberately humiliated by Xavier Bettel, the prime minister. Boris had declined to attend an outdoor press conference surrounded by anti-Brexit protesters, but Bettel went ahead anyway, standing next to Boris's empty podium. Next, Boris visited Whipps Cross Hospital. He was ambushed by a Labour supporter in front of a TV camera who complained of 'neglect' because of a shortage of doctors. In fact, his child recovered and left the hospital the following day. Three days later, the *Sunday Times* exposed his affair with Jennifer Arcuri. He was accused of abusing his political power and misusing public funds to channel City Hall money to his former girlfriend. Finally, an appeal to the High Court against the government's prorogation had reached the Supreme Court. Accused of acting unlawfully, the government's lawyers were floundering despite favourable judgements in the High Court and Appeal Court.

Both English courts had declared that prorogation was a political decision. Citing the Bill of Rights of 1689, the judges ruled that British courts were forbidden to question proceedings in Parliament. There was no judicial power, said the two courts, to overrule the Queen and declare that the prime minister had abused his power.

Conversely, Scotland's highest court had ruled that the prorogation was 'unlawful' and motivated by an 'improper purpose' to stymie Parliament. Boris, the Scottish judges declared, had not told the Queen the truth. Pertinently, the government had weakened its case by refusing to present a sworn statement explaining why prorogation was necessary, an omission ripe for exploitation by any judge prejudiced against the government.

Brenda Hale, the seventy-four-year-old president of the Supreme Court, was renowned as a feminist campaigner who had rarely concealed her contempt for Boris. Wearing a large spider brooch in the wood-panelled courtroom, she would later star in *Spider-Woman Takes Down Hulk*, a left-wing-funded book. 'Let's hear it for the girly swots,' she would tell a young female audience. As a family lawyer and administrator without any specialist knowledge of constitutional law,

Hale would not allow the previous two judgements of English judges to interfere with her determination to slap down the government. Her hostility was encouraged by John Major. In a statement to the court, Major compared Boris to 'a dishonest estate agent'. Prorogation, he said, was intended to prevent Parliament holding the government to account.

Although Boris had been assured by Geoffrey Cox that the government would win a majority of the eleven Supreme Court judges, the omens were not good when he flew on 23 September to New York to address the UN and meet EU leaders. At 5 a.m. the following morning, after just two hours' sleep, he got up in Manhattan to watch Hale's hostile ruling. Although Parliament was closed down for just one extra week, she described the prorogation as 'an extreme effect upon the fundamentals of our democracy'. To support her decision, she introduced a revolutionary principle into British law: that prorogation had interrupted MPs' 'legal' power to hold the government to account. Naturally, she did not mention that Parliament had just held the government to account in two major defeats – the Benn Act and the vote to prevent a general election. The government lost by eleven judges to zero. Not a single judge agreed with the previous four English judges. Declaring the prorogation 'unlawful' made Hale a hero among Remainers and Boris's enemies. The bias was obvious but Boris obeyed Cox's orders not to criticise the judges.

Before flying back to London, he met Donald Trump in Manhattan. The president had promised a fast trade deal in the event of a no-deal Brexit. Now, with Boris sitting next to him, Trump predicted that British trade with America would quadruple after Brexit. His hyperbolic assurances, Trump noticed, were far from Boris's mind. Referring to that morning's defeat, Trump told the TV cameras, 'He's professional. It's just another day in the office.' Defeats by the US Supreme Court, smiled Trump, were par for the course. In the end, he had beaten the court and so would Boris. With that in mind, Boris flew back to London. Over the Atlantic, he telephoned the Queen to apologise for causing embarrassment. He also heard that MPs had stormed back into the Commons. He was expected to head directly to the chamber from the airport.

Tired but with self-control, Boris entered the Commons just as Geoffrey Cox was arousing fevered anger among Labour MPs. Desperate Labour politicians, unable to solve their own frustration about divisions over the EU and about their leader, were being harangued in a rumbustious scolding. Calling them 'a shower' and 'a disgrace' for refusing to vote for an election to end a parliament which was 'as dead as dead can be', Cox loudly mocked the opposition. Targeting the Lib Dems who were chanting 'Right-wing coup', Cox shouted back, the prime minister was begging for an election. Which dictator demands an election? he scoffed.

As Boris took his seat, Opposition MPs vented their spleen. 'Resign', 'Fraud' and 'He should be in jail', they yelled. Up against the wall, Boris suspected that John Bercow would prolong the session – it would last an unusual three and a half hours. To rally his MPs, Boris denounced Benn's 'Surrender Act' and accused Labour of 'political cowardice' for rejecting an election. Increasingly, several Labour women MPs became agitated. His repeated mention of 'surrender' and 'betrayal' of the electorate aroused their anger. They moved from highlighting the court's damning judgement to attacking Boris in person. Paula Sherriff, the forty-four-year old MP for Dewsbury, rocked unsteadily as she delivered her attack. In a shrill voice, Sherriff pointed at Boris: 'We should not resort to using offensive, dangerous or inflammatory language for legislation we do not like and we stand here under the shield of our departed friend [the murdered Labour MP Jo Cox] with many of us in this place subject to death threats and abuse every single day.' She continued, 'And let me tell the prime minister that they often quote his words Surrender Act, betrayal, traitor, and I for one am sick of it. We must moderate our language.' The prime minister, she said, 'should be absolutely ashamed'. Around her, female MPs sat in tears.

Sherriff's emotional outburst confused several issues but there was no doubt that she had aligned her fate with Jo Cox's. Calmly and politely, Boris replied, 'I have to say that I have never heard such humbug in all my life.' He accused Sherriff of 'synthetic outrage' and 'confected indignation'. In referring to violence, she had forgotten that Jeremy Corbyn had invited members of the IRA to the Commons soon after the Brighton bomb killed and maimed Tories in 1984; she had forgotten, too, that John McDonnell had quoted a supporter who asked, 'Why aren't we lynching the bastard?' of Esther McVey, a Tory MP, and basked in the laughter. The best way to honour Jo Cox, he said was to 'get Brexit done'. Suddenly, the Labour benches rose up. Among the protestors were some women who had not vigorously defended Jewish female Labour MPs against constant threats of violence from members of their own party. Similarly, some of those MPs had not energetically and publicly challenged Jeremy Corbyn after thirteen Labour MPs had resigned in protest against Corbyn's anti-Semitism. To attack the prime minister for the abuse undoubtedly suffered by Labour's female MPs seemed unreasonable.

In the aftermath, some journalists joined in their attack, not least because four investigations had been launched into Boris's relationship with Jennifer Arcuri. To accusations that he had broken City Hall's financial rules, Boris replied, 'Everything was done with full proprieties.' In *The Times*, referring to the Commons uproar, Jenni Russell reported without correction that Boris had invoked the name of Jo Cox. Repeating that inaccuracy multiplied the damage to the prime minister.

Labour's rage did not derail the Tories' celebrations at the party conference in Manchester one week later. Nor did it undermine the confidence of the party's pollsters that the Tories could win a general election. Isaac Levido – a thirty-six-year-old Australian protégé of Lynton Crosby employed by Boris to mastermind the election soon after he arrived in Downing Street – reported that in all three Stoke constituencies, Labour's heartland, Labour's pro-Brexit voters would swing to the Tories. Similar Tory gains would happen, reported Levido, in Wales and in the north. Polling by Michael Brooks, his associate, also showed that Labour voters did not care about the Supreme Court's judgement. They liked Boris's attack on Parliament, they remained concerned about immigration and 58 per cent of voters outrightly distrusted Corbyn. Those Labour voters were prepared to switch to the Tories. Against Boris was age.

Those under thirty-nine, well educated and especially women, were much more likely to vote Labour. By contrast, wealth and class was no longer a barrier to securing Labour votes. Many of the poorest Britons trusted Boris rather than Corbyn. Overall, Brooks's daily polls revealed the vulnerability of 'safe' Labour seats. The Tory grass roots gathering at the Manchester conference had witnessed that shift. Similarly disdainful of Corbyn and his clique of far-left MPs, they were outraged by Speaker John Bercow's partisanship against the government. 'If Parliament were a TV reality show,' Boris told his admirers, 'the whole lot of us would have been voted out of the jungle by now, but at least we would have watched the Speaker being forced to eat a kangaroo testicle.' The audience's laughter encouraged Boris to defy the Remainers and the EU.

Shortly before the party conference, he had met Bill Cash in Downing Street. The MP arrived with a legal analysis compiled by a team of senior lawyers to explain how to remove the backstop. 'The government's lawyers don't understand this,' Cash told Boris. 'They can't understand how to push back the frontiers of the state – and how to get out of the EU.' Although Boris was tired and yawning, Cash was impressed: 'I watched Boris's body language. If his eyes glazed over we were lost. But he was on top of the detail. Top of the game.' Re-energised by the opportunity to resolve the crisis and shape Britain's destiny, he buried his critics' familiar trope of lazy disinterest.

Encouraged by Cash, Boris set out a solution to the backstop in a forty-four-page letter to Juncker. Northern Ireland would stay in the EU's single market but leave the customs union, and the tariffs and single-market regulations would be administered by the UK not at the border but inland. In effect, there would be a border down the North Sea – just what Boris had previously said was unacceptable.

Sent on a secret mission to Dublin, his chief of staff Eddie Lister sought Leo Varadkar's agreement at a sensitive time for the Taoiseach. Facing an election and trailing in the polls, Varadkar was playing a delaying game. He wanted to trigger a second referendum and reverse Brexit. Publicly, he had called for a united Ireland. Not only was Lister rebuffed by Varadkar, but his approach was publicised by the Irish. Barnier also rejected the plan. Britain, he said, needed to improve its offer before the EU summit on Thursday 17 October. In anger, Boris called Merkel to 'get the boat off the rocks'. She refused. He hit a wall. Everyone feared that the road to a deal had run out. In the game of bluff, fuelled by Cummings, Boris was publicly adamant that Britain would still leave without a deal.

That scenario provoked an argument during a Cabinet meeting. Both Geoffrey Cox and Julian Smith, the Secretary of State for Northern Ireland, told Boris that he must obey the Benn Act. His 'do or die' threat was illegal. If no-deal featured in an election manifesto they would resign. Both became marked men. The bluff, Boris was convinced, was working. Merkel and Macron, he had been told, were finally persuaded of their mistake to believe Tony Blair and other Remainers that Brexit could be stopped.

With twenty-four hours to settle the deal, Berlin ordered Dublin to bypass Barnier and agree a fudge. Johnson and Varadkar met on Thursday 10 October in Thornton Manor, a Wirral country estate. 'It was two guys in a room,' Varadkar recalled. 'Sometimes when you do these things without your officials present it's easier. And it was one of those kind of strange conversations, where [Boris] said, "My staff might kill me for saying this but if I said this what would you say back?" And I would go down a similar road, you know, "If I moved on this might you move on that?" And I think we found very quickly that we had shared objectives.' The next stage was secret, intensive negotiations in Brussels to finalise the deal. During those five intense days, Boris became the willing and unwilling star of an extraordinary political – and sexual – pantomime.

Appearing on ITV from Los Angeles, Jennifer Arcuri described how Boris had visited her Shoreditch flat about five times while he was the mayor. They 'immediately bonded', she said, over 'a mutual love of classical literature and particularly Shakespeare'. While she refused to reveal whether they had an affair, she admitted 'He was always a really good friend.' But she showed her anger that her reputation had been traduced. 'I don't understand why you've blocked me,' she said, addressing Boris on TV, 'as if I was some fleeting one-night stand or some girl you picked up at the bar because I wasn't. I'm terribly heartbroken by the way that you have cast me aside like I'm some gremlin.' Boris had good reason to fear Arcuri. When she called to warn him that the media had discovered their affair, he had passed his mobile to an aide. The aide spoke to her in 'Chinese' and then cut the line. Angry, she was now planning a visit to London. If minded, she could seriously embarrass him. Yet he could not risk calling to beg her not to describe their affair.

As the speculation about Boris's private life accelerated, the Queen obeyed his demand that she formally open Parliament. Burdened by ceremonial regalia from the Palace to Westminster, the ninety-three-year-old monarch was forced on 14 October to perform a political gimmick. Looking down at the Lords assembling in the chamber to await the Queen, Quentin Letts in *The Times* spotted that 'Lady Hale sponged up the attention, saying coo-ee to bishops. The only surprise was that she did not plonk herself in the empty throne'. From the throne, the Queen presented the powerless government's election manifesto of a 'One Nation agenda' with twenty-six bills. Accurately, Corbyn called the exercise by a government with a forty-five-seat minority, a 'stunt' and a 'farce'.

That night, as five days of intensive negotiations between the EU and Britain were coming to a successful conclusion, Katya Adler, the BBC's Europe correspondent, pronounced 'the chance of a deal is minimal'. In reality, Barnier had been marginalised and the backstop had gone. In the new deal, Britain would not be the EU's 'vassal state' but Northern Ireland was separated from the mainland.

On 17 October, Boris arrived in Brussels to seal the deal. 'Sell-out', 'Treachery', 'Betrayal' shouted the ten DUP MPs when he returned to the Commons. They scoffed at his assurances that in trade across the Irish Sea there would be 'no forms, no checks, no barriers of any kind. You will have unfettered access.' Asked about the forms which Brussels insisted would be necessary, Boris would later say, 'I will direct them to throw that form in the bin.' No one discovered whether Boris misunderstood the deal he had concluded – or was he outrightly dishonest?

Boris had returned to London to ram the deal through

Parliament and get an election. For one week, the battle of wills was intense. 'We will hammer them day after day after day,' Boris told the Cabinet. Like a battering ram, said Cummings, MPs should be forced to vote every day on Brexit and an election. The Remainers were determined to block Brexit or get a second referendum. Once again, Oliver Letwin offered MPs an amendment to the latest Withdrawal Bill to prevent Britain crashing out of the EU before the whole deal had been considered by Parliament. On 22 October, the Withdrawal Bill was finally approved by 329 to 299 but the government's timetable to legalise Brexit nine days later was defeated by a majority of eighteen. 'I want the House to know,' Boris said in the face of defeat, 'that I am not daunted or dismayed.' To comply with the law, Boris sent the European Commission an unsigned photocopy of the Benn Act to request an extension of Brexit until 31 January. In a separate letter he wrote that this was 'Parliament's delay' and he did not want an extension. Now followed his biggest gamble – to persuade Corbyn to agree to an election in December, despite YouGov's latest poll showing a 15 per cent Tory lead, at 40 per cent of the popular vote. In their daily conversations, Isaac Levido guaranteed that the Tories could win a forty-seat majority.

Corbyn was invited to Downing Street. In the game of bluff, Boris spoke about both parties' equal chance to win an election. This, he said, was Corbyn's opportunity to win power. Boris's enormous luck was to have Corbyn as his opponent. For nearly one week, Corbyn had prevaricated but on 29 October, ignoring Labour MPs' warnings, he succumbed to the temptation. The Commons voted by 438 to 20 to hold an election on 12 December.

The Times called Boris's bid a 'gamble' which risked another hung parliament. Matthew Parris announced that he would vote Lib Dem because the Tories had been taken over by 'a reckless cult'. John Curtice, the psephologist, predicted that the Tories would lose at least twenty seats to the SNP and Lib Dems. The Lib Dems, led by Jo Swinson, posing as the next prime minister, started at 18 per cent, 10 per cent better than in 2017. Pundits forecast that Boris could lose his own Uxbridge seat with a 5,034 majority. Daniel Finkelstein, the Tory peer and journalist, wrote 'There is a very good chance that Jeremy Corbyn will be prime minister.' No party in modern British history, Finkelstein explained, had won a fourth term. Accordingly, despite a 75 per cent dissatisfaction rating, Corbyn would lead a coalition. The Tories, some polls reported, faced a wipeout after being squeezed by Nigel Farage's new Brexit Party. To avoid defeat, Steve Baker urged Boris to do a deal with Farage. Loyal to the party, Boris rejected the offer as suicide.

Soon after Parliament was dissolved on 6 November, the mood began to change. Ian Austin, a former Labour MP and a confidant of Gordon Brown, advised his previous constituents to vote Tory because Corbyn was an 'extremist, unfit to be prime minister'. Other Labour stalwarts echoed the same exhortation.

Boris's challenge was to wrest Labour voters from Corbyn – portrayed as an anti-Semitic, terrorist sympathiser and Marxist – and from Nigel Farage with the promise of 'Get Brexit Done'.

To the Tories' good fortune, Labour's manifesto was a Marxist's dream wish: the widespread nationalisation of industries, the abolition of student fees, a massive increase of pensions, free broadband, the seizure of land and tenanted homes at reduced prices, the restoration of trade union power, the abolition of educational testing and the highest tax burden since 1945. Corbyn's £600 billion plan had already galvanised the exodus of many wealth creators and businesses.

In the first TV debate with Corbyn, Boris was urged to ignore the Marxist agenda and focus on Brexit. To the Tories' delight, that night Corbyn refused eight times to say whether he would campaign to Remain or Leave. Soon after, Nigel Farage announced that his party would not contest vital Tory marginals where a Brexit vote would hand the seat to Labour. The Tories' lead against Labour increased. Three days later, more Brexit Party candidates withdrew from the election to prevent Corbyn winning. Boris's approval ratings increased to 30 per cent over Corbyn. Simultaneously, Jo Swinson's daily appearances discouraged voters and the Lib Dem vote declined. On 24 November, John Curtice predicted the Tories to win with a majority of fifty.

Under Levido's orders, Boris did not lead a traditional election campaign but set off every day for a fourteen-hour stint to deliver a prepared script. Criss-crossing the country, he was encouraged by the party's polls that Labour would be taken by surprise. Briefed to avoid any meaningful interviews with the loathed media, he delivered the same sound bites week after week.

Corbyn's self-destruction was completed during an interview with Andrew Neil two days after Curtice's prediction. Corbyn's visceral anti-Semitism had been highlighted by Ephraim Mirvis, the chief rabbi. A secret Labour Party dossier listing the details of 130 cases of Labour Party members guilty of severe anti-Semitism had been exposed the previous day. Labour Party members were guilty of Holocaust denial, saying that 'Jews represent a viral infection that needs to be completely eliminated' and advocating the 'extermination of every Jew on the planet'. Hundreds of other cases remained uninvestigated. At that moment, Hugh Grant, the actor, was campaigning for Labour, and David Hare, the playwright, had spoken in Corbyn's support. Corbyn, said Mirvis, was not fit to be prime minister. The chief rabbi blamed Corbyn for a 'new poison sanctioned from the top [that] has taken root in the Labour Party'. During his interview with Andrew Neil, Corbyn refused to apologise four times for Labour's anti-Semitism. The following day, YouGov predicted a Tory majority of sixty-eight. Among the Labour MPs expected to be defeated were Dennis Skinner and Paula Sherriff. Like Disraeli, Boris was building a coalition between lifelong Tories and the aspiring working class disgusted by Corbyn's unpatriotic Marxism. Twenty-four hours later, YouGov predicted a Tory majority of eighty-two. Just six months earlier, the Tories faced obliteration after securing 9 per cent of the vote in the European elections. With Corbyn's help, 'Get Brexit Done' had transformed the Tories into a united party, split Labour and devastated the LibDems – the exact opposite to what the pundits had predicted.

Jeremy Hunt could never have persuaded Labour's voters in Sedgefield, Tony Blair's old seat, to switch to the Tories. Boris was different. Filmed eating sausage rolls, doughnuts, crisps and clotted cream, and driving a bulldozer through a wall marked 'GRID-LOCK', working-class Britons across the Midlands and the north believed that Boris could be trusted as a leader because he pulled off the Brexit deal, defied the courts, and kicked out twenty-one Tory MPs. He also promised to sort out the mess in their neighbourhoods after decades of local Labour misrule. They did not care about his boycott of BBC Radio 4's *Today* programme, his refusal to be interviewed by Andrew Neil, or that, after also refusing to appear on Channel 4, he was replaced by a melting ice sculpture. Nor were they persuaded by biographer Sonia Purnell's frequent appearances on BBC broadcasts to describe Boris as 'a liar'. The vituperation of London's liberals did not resonate north of Watford.

London's frustration was best evoked by Nick Boles, as ever the incandescent metropolitan: 'In the blue corner, we have a compulsive liar who has betrayed every single person he has ever had any dealings with; every woman who has loved him; every member of his family, every friend, every colleague, every employee, every constituent. As a senior member of his Cabinet once put it to me: "You can always rely on Boris . . . to let you down." His bumbling braggadocio disguises an all-consuming ego utterly without conscience, empathy or restraint . . . He has sought to defy our courts, neuter our Parliament and deceive our Sovereign. Nothing is sacred. He will betray the NHS in a heartbeat if that is what it takes to get a trade deal out of his role model – Donald Trump.'

Three days before the election, the roller coaster came to a juddering halt. That morning, the *Mirror*'s front page featured a four-year-old boy lying on the floor of Leeds General Infirmary with an oxygen mask at his side. The hospital beds were full. During that day, Boris had been filmed during a visit to Grimsby being shown a photo of the boy on an iPhone by a TV reporter. Inexplicably, Lee Cain, habitually disdainful of the media, had not warned Boris in advance of the *Mirror*'s story. Boris initially refused to look at the photo and put the journalist's phone in his pocket. Prompted, he returned the phone and agreed 'It is a terrible photo.' Unable to think fast on his feet and tell the reporter to ask the hospital's manager for an explanation, the headlines blamed Boris for the boy's plight.

On the 11th, the eve of polling day, YouGov reduced the Tory lead to twenty-six seats and predicted the result could even be a hung parliament. Suddenly there was uncertainty whether Labour voters would switch to the Tories. 'It's not in the bag,' Boris admitted as he started the last day of the hectic campaign delivering milk in Yorkshire. After eating a full English breakfast at a service station on the M1, he put the finishing touches to a pie in Derby, flew to Caerphilly in South Wales to appear at a factory that made Christmas crackers and wrapping paper, then to Southend, and ended the 500-mile dash at a rally in east London. 'It's on a knife edge,' he said.

At 10 p.m. on election day, 12 December, the BBC exit poll gave the Tories a majority of eighty-six. Momentarily, the crowded war room in Central Office was silent. No one could quite believe it. No one in their sweepstake had predicted an eighty majority. Then Boris exploded with joy. Opening beer and wine, everyone chanted 'O Isaac Levido'. At 11.30 p.m., the Tory victory in Blyth Valley, a former mining area and forever a Labour seat, meant victory was assured. The Red Wall had fallen. When Sedgefield declared Tory for the first time since 1931, the war room burst out 'Things can only get better', Tony Blair's campaign song. Clwyd South, the seat Boris had lost in 1997 was a Tory win. All those Tory MPs who had tried to topple him and said he could never succeed were out of Parliament, powerless and pointless. At 3.45 a.m., the victor arrived with Carrie, aka the First Girlfriend, at Uxbridge for the result. His majority increased to 7,210.

Labour's worst result since 1935 meant that the party was probably out of power for ten more years. With 44 per cent of the vote, the Tories had gained forty-eight seats and Labour lost fifty-nine seats. The Tory majority was eighty. Once the delayed boundary review was implemented, the Tories could hope for approximately another twenty seats at the next election. 'Redcar has been turned into Bluecar,' Boris told the party workers at Central Office. Speaking in front of the slogan 'The People's Government', he said 'V must understand now what an earthquake we have created, way in which we have changed the political map of the cou We have to change our own party. We must answer the cha' that the British people have given us.' He appealed to the new centre ground and an end of the Brexit war: 'I urge everyone to find closure and let the healing begin.' Britain was firmly introduced to the Boris Johnson era.

At 4 p.m., on his return from Buckingham Palace, Boris entered Downing Street with Carrie at his side and stood at the lectern in the street: 'To all those who voted for us for the first time, all those whose pencils may have wavered over the ballot, and heard the voices of their parents and grandparents whispering anxiously in their ears, I say thank you for the trust you have placed in us and in me.' Charles Moore was among many to re-evaluate Boris: 'He is one of the few people I have met,' wrote Moore, 'who can be described as a genius.'

That night Rocco Forte, a keen Brexiteer, hosted a victory celebration at Brown's, his luxury hotel off Piccadilly. Then, Boris headed for Evgeny Lebedev's traditional Christmas party in his house overlooking Regent's Park, famous for unlimited caviar and champagne. Boris had unashamedly blocked the publication of the Russia report written by Parliament's intelligence and security committee. Lebedev, according to the gossip, featured in the report. Unknown to Boris, the gossip proved to be wholly mistaken but would clearly be relevant if, as he secretly planned, the Russian was nominated on his recommendation as a peer. That announcement, he knew, would provoke protests of outrage. Lebedev had achieved nothing in London without his father's suspicious money but he had become a trusted friend and that counted for Boris.

The next day, Boris slept off the parties while flying to Teesside a photo opportunity – pulling a pint in Sedgefield, Tony Blair's red fortress. Now he had to prove that he could not only but also govern.

Chapter 27

Covid I

Sunbathing in Mustique in the Caribbean on 2 January 2020, Boris assumed that his world was perfect. For one week, he could enjoy the sun and the sea, and ignore the problems erupting 4,000 miles away. After six months of non-stop campaigning, he was exhausted. Indigo, the three-bedroom villa near the shore, had been obtained by a friend. 'Find me somewhere private,' he pleaded before the election. 'And somewhere for Carrie to relax because she's pregnant.' In Churchillian manner, he had arrived on the island with two PAs – not in order to dictate a book but to stay in touch with London.

For the first time in months, Boris was at peace with himself. Opinion polls reported that the mood in Britain was optimistic. No fewer than 60 per cent of Britons anticipated being better off by the end of the year. Trusting his promise of 'a decade of prosperity and opportunity', the Boris Bounce had encouraged a splurge in holiday bookings, a rise in house prices, record employment and a spurt of manufacturing. In London, Cameron Mackintosh announced a £220 million programme to rebuild the world's most famous theatres. 'It's an extraordinary time,' said the great impresario. Joining the chorus, Britain's world-beating creative industry sang: 'It's a booming market.' Despite the Bank of England's forecast that Brexit would shrink the economy by £14 billion in 2022 – and that estimate would rise a few weeks later to £22 billion – Boris was guaranteed five years as prime minister. No one and nothing could stop the radical 'Brexity Hezza' to, in his words, 'level up' the nation.

In Downing Street on that same day, Dominic Cummings published a blog post of a job advertisement he had written, intended to signal a revolution across Whitehall. Highlighting 'profound problems at the core of how the British state makes decisions', Cummings targeted the nation's civil servants. Besides the 'brilliant' few, he identified the culprits as 'the confident public school bluffers' and the 'Oxbridge humanities graduates' spouting drivel about 'identity' and 'diversity'. Whitehall, he sniped, lacked 'the sort of expertise needed by the PM and ministers'.

His arch villain was Mark Sedwill, the fifty-five-year-old Cabinet Secretary. Unlike his predecessors trained in the Treasury to implement the intricacies of economic and domestic policies, Sedwill was a Foreign Office securocrat with diplomatic service in the Middle East, Pakistan and Afghanistan. Trusted by Theresa May as her permanent secretary while at the Home Office, she appointed him after arriving in Downing Street as both her Cabinet Secretary and the National Security Adviser. His handicaps were stark. Without any mastery of economics or science, Sedwill was ill-fitted to manage Brexit, trade agreements and the Treasury's comprehensive public spending review. Cummings berated him and those departmental permanent secretaries below him for lacking proper understanding of maths, data management and the skills to manage major projects like the proposed HS2 rail network.

Too often, as Michael Gove would explain, in 'the constant whirligig of Civil Service transfers and promotions', careers depended on moving every eighteen months rather than developing deep knowledge to execute policies and procurement. Frowning ⸱aking the initiative, the Whitehall cult incentivised officials to ⸱hold ideas. 'Submissions,' Gove would complain, 'the papers ⸱ prepared to guide ministerial decisions, and which were ⸱ry of our Civil Service, have become in far too many ⸱ overlong, jargon-heavy and back-covering. The ⸱ight, evidence-rich, fact-based argument which ⸱or evade hard choices is critical to effective ⸱ı, the formal hierarchy was sticking to safe ⸱er executing original policies. Too many civil servants, Gove and Cummings agreed, were unable even to communicate in proper English.

Cummings' solution was an appeal for established experts in science and economics to work in Downing Street. His advertisement also called for applications from 'some true wild cards, artists, people who never went to university and fought their way out of an appalling hellhole', 'weirdos from William Gibson novels'. Ideal 'misfits', he suggested, should bypass the formal recruitment process and email him direct. Those chosen would join him in Downing Street to transform radically the machinery of government. 'It will seem chaotic and not proper Number 10 process to some,' he wrote, 'but the point of this government is to do things differently and better.'

Cummings' plan included regular exams for senior civil servants. The trade unions immediately complained. Testing their members' skills, complained a union leader, would cause discrimination on the grounds of age and ethnicity. Success rates in previous exams had been significantly lower for black and minority-ethnic workers and the over thirty-fives. That self-interested protest confirmed Cummings' and Gove's complaint: Whitehall's culture ensured that 'everyone rises to their position of incompetence'. The famed Rolls-Royce machine was worn out. In a crisis, they predicted, it would fail to deliver. Boris was not only convinced by their argument but agreed that fundamental changes should be implemented as soon as possible. Senior officials in all the departments needed to be replaced. As usual, he delegated the task and waited for the results.

On that same day, 2 January, Christopher Whitty, England's fifty-three-year-old chief medical officer, was meeting his deputy, Jonathan Van-Tam, an expert in influenza and respiratory viruses. Appointed two months earlier, Whitty was a physician and epidemiologist who had specialised in controlling infectious tropical diseases. The two met in the Department of Health to discuss a message from the World Health Organisation (WHO) issued on 31 December. The Geneva-based organisation reported that the Municipal Health Commission in Wuhan, a Chinese city with a population of 19 million, had identified an outbreak of an 'unusual pneumonia' coronavirus. The first case was identified on 12 December. Since then, 'a cluster of cases' had developed but none had resulted in death. 'We both agreed that it was something to watch,' Whitty would recall. The potential danger, he knew, should not be underestimated. Any deadly strain of influenza based on high-impact respiratory pathogens which spread through breathing could quickly infect a large number of people. As an experienced epidemiologist, he recalled several global virus alerts in his career – SARS in 2003, swine flu in 2009 and MERS in 2012.

The following day, Whitty told Matt Hancock, the Health Secretary, about his plan to monitor the potential threat called 2019-nCoV. Unknown to Whitty, a Chinese ophthalmologist in Wuhan who had just warned colleagues of the danger was ordered by the local security police not to issue any more 'false comments'.

In blissful ignorance, most of the world's media was focused on America's assassination in Baghdad of Qasem Soleimani, an Iranian general responsible for state terrorism across the region. Boris resisted knee-jerk demands that he return to Britain to respond. Four days later, on 7 January, the prime minister was back in Downing Street. That day, Hancock told him about Covid and that Whitty was monitoring the situation. In his normal manner, Boris expected Hancock and the government's experts to manage any problems. His focus was on Brexit due at the end of the month, a Cabinet reshuffle soon after, and a landmark budget. He planned to remove the deadwood ministers who added neither originality nor electoral appeal to the government, and whose company he found uncongenial. Next, to great fanfare, he would unveil his vision for the future and lay the foundations for his legacy. For once in his life, he had no serious problems.

On 11 January, the Chinese reported the first Covid death. The cause, said the Chinese, was human contact with an infected animal. There was no evidence that the virus could be transmitted from one person to another. Still barred from visiting China for an investigation, WHO endorsed the Chinese report. Nevertheless, as a precaution, Whitty summoned a meeting of the New and

Emerging Respiratory Virus Threats Advisory Group (NERVTAG), chaired by Peter Horby, an epidemiologist already researching the virus with Chinese scientists. The limited function of the committee's fifteen experts was to assess the risk posed by the new virus.

On the basis of the WHO report, NERVTAG concluded that the 'Wuhan Novel Coronavirus does not look to be very transmissible'. In apparent contradiction, they also agreed that a travel ban was worthless. With three flights a week from Wuhan and dozens of flights from other Chinese cities experiencing multiple outbreaks, it was 'unlikely that transmission [of the virus] to the UK could be prevented'. Screening of arrivals at Heathrow, they agreed, where 80 million passengers arrived every year, 'has very low efficacy and the benefit is very unlikely to outweigh the substantial effort, cost and disruption'. The specialists categorised the risk as 'Low'.

Despite the reassurances from WHO, Whitty also consulted Patrick Vallance, the government's chief scientific adviser. Trained as a physician and pharmacologist, Vallance had had a conventional career as head of medicine at University College London and Glaxo before joining the government in 2018. With Vallance now involved, monitoring of the virus was under the control of two clinicians. They agreed to convene immediately the first meeting of the newly founded Scientific Advisory Group for Emergencies (SAGE). Under his chairmanship, Vallance could select about twenty experts from a rich pool. Britain's epidemiologists, life scientists, experts in infectious diseases, behavioural scientists, public health executives and medical statisticians ranked among the world's best. Inevitably those he did not select would feel professional jealousy. To avoid their inevitable carping, SAGE's membership was kept secret. The scientists met with about ten senior Whitehall officials.

Vallance was clear how SAGE would work: 'It is not very useful to ministers or other decision-makers to say, "There are sixteen opinions. Here are all sixteen. Make up your mind." Part of the process is to say in a unified way, "Here is the central view", and then, if there are either dissenting views or a range of uncertainty quantitatively around that, to convey it in a way that is comprehensible to the people who are listening so that they understand the certainty with which the advice is being proffered. If they do not, it is clearly going to lead to bad decision-making. In SAGE, we try to come up with a consensus view, but we are always clear and open about how we arrive at that.'

Vallance probably did not realise the contradiction within his explanation. A 'central view' is different from 'a consensus view'. The issue was whether Vallance fully explained all the options to Boris, made a recommendation but allowed Boris to choose; or did Vallance offer what he considered to be the consensus and simply ask for the prime minister's approval. If Boris heard the competing options around the 'central view', then he would have understood earlier the uncertainty of the science. If presented only with the 'consensus', he would not have understood the alternatives. In the traditional format of British government, Boris should have requested that Mark Sedwill as the Cabinet Secretary was present at Vallance's briefings to offer an impartial opinion. In Vallance's subsequent replies to MPs' questions, he never referred to Sedwill's presence.

On a key issue, Whitty and Vallance were reassured by the Global Health Security Index published in 2019. Britain had ranked as number one in the world able to produce a 'rapid response to and mitigation of the spread of an epidemic'. South Korea was ranked sixth and Germany twenty-eighth. Less encouraging was Whitehall's Exercise Cygnus report published in 2017 about Britain's preparedness for a pandemic. Since both men had been appointed after the report was published, it was not clear whether they had understood its disturbing conclusions. The three-day exercise had assessed the impact of a pandemic influenza outbreak, especially on the NHS. The 'key learning' was that 'the UK's preparedness and response, in terms of its plans, policies and capability, is currently not sufficient to cope with the extreme demands of a severe pandemic that will have a nationwide impact across all sectors'. Operation Cygnus and other plans to cope with pandemics in Britain assumed the cause would be a Covid type of influenza. An attempt two years later, in autumn 2019, to mount a similar exercise to check whether Britain's preparedness had improved, was cancelled. Many of the relevant officials were focused on preparing the country for crashing out of Europe without a deal. Months later, untested by a dress rehearsal, Whitty and Vallance adopted the textbook gospel to cope with a flu pandemic when SAGE held its first meeting on 22 January.

The star was Neil Ferguson, a professor of mathematical biology and the leader of Imperial College's modelling group with over twenty years' experience monitoring viruses. As the leader of SAGE's Scientific Pandemic Influenza Modelling committee (SPI-M), Ferguson's doubts about the Chinese reports were striking. The Chinese government, he said, was under-reporting the extent of the infection and substantial human-to-human transmission was happening. 'Heightened surveillance, prompt information-sharing and enhanced preparedness are recommended,' he stated in his first report. After discussing the potential problems for hospitals and care homes, the group agreed that because of the uncertain data from China, 'a reasonable worst-case scenario (RWCS) cannot be made reliably'.

RWCS has been a critical aspect of 'pandemic influenza planning' by the National Risk Register since 2008. Flu hit Britain regularly every year. In 2017, the National Risk Register estimated that a flu epidemic could kill between 20,000 and 750,000 people. Britain's annual deaths from flu between 2014 and 2018 ranged between 1,692 and 28,330 – making an annual average of about 17,000 people. 'Spanish Flu', the world's worst outbreak between 1918–20, killed between 50 million and 100 million. The participants agreed to rely on the tried and tested plans for a flu pandemic.

Ferguson disagreed. In a report published on Imperial's website the same day, he warned that the outbreak was probably larger than the Chinese had revealed: 'Given the increasing evidence for human-to-human transmission, enhancing rapid case detection will be essential if the outbreak is to be controlled.' Within hours, Ferguson was proved correct.

Early the following day, Wuhan was closed down. The Chinese government told WHO there were 557 cases of Covid and seventeen deaths in the city. The agency did not question the Chinese report. Instead, WHO told the world's governments that the virus was 'not wildly spreading outside China'.

By then, the British embassy in Beijing should have been seeking to discover the truth. Under Simon McDonald, however, the diplomats dispatched to China were not sleuths but focused on trade and championing diversity and human rights. Once again, the Foreign Office was failing to perform its traditional role to discover facts and also failing to match other governments' initiatives and help British nationals to leave Wuhan quickly.

Briefed about the SAGE discussions, Hancock was reassured that the bureaucracy was functioning as planned. In his first Commons appearance concerning Covid, he told MPs that while a few Chinese had died, Britain's experts were monitoring the outbreak.

During the day, Boris appeared in a People's PMQ broadcast from Downing Street. He mentioned his recent discussion in London with Egypt's president Abdel Fattah el-Sisi, a painting by Turner, the tampon tax and the planned EU negotiations after the Withdrawal Bill was given the royal assent the following day. He dodged a question about his shampoo. Although newspapers were reporting the Covid outbreak, Boris did not mention the topic.

The same day, 23 January, *Lancet*'s editor, Richard Horton, called for 'caution' and accused the media of 'escalating anxiety by talking of a "killer virus"' and 'growing fears'. He wrote: 'In truth, from what we currently know, 2019-nCoV has moderate transmissibility and relatively low pathogenicity. There is no reason to foster panic with exaggerated language.' Horton's error would have passed unnoticed had he not later become a vociferous critic of the government and SAGE. In reality, no one outside China, including WHO officials, knew the truth about the Wuhan outbreak. Moreover, contrary to Horton's subsequent criticism of the government, especially about the supposed failure to acknowledge the importance of Public Health England (PHE), the Department of Health had positioned PHE at the front line of Britain's defences. Its senior executives were members of SAGE.

PHE is an executive agency boasting 'operational autonomy' of the Department of Health and Social Care, directly answerable to Matt Hancock. Established in 2013 as part of drastic reform of the NHS designed by Andrew Lansley, the first Heath Secretary in David

Cameron's government, part of PHE's responsibilities were defined as 'maintaining the pandemic influenza stockpile'. That meant buying antivirals, antibiotics and consumables and managing the stockpiles of personal protective equipment (PPE) for use in hospitals. PHE's principal 'stockpile' was stored in a warehouse in Merseyside.

PHE's founding chief executive was fifty-eight-year-old Duncan Selbie, paid £190,000 a year. On his appointment in 2013, Selbie admitted on his Facebook page, 'I am that well-known international expert. You can fit my public health credentials on a postage stamp.'

At seventeen, Selbie had worked as a clerk in the health service, writing prescription pricing cards. At nineteen, he worked as a cashier at the former Queen's Hospital in Croydon. Without medical or academic training, he was rejected for thirteen executive jobs before becoming an NHS lifer at a psychiatric hospital. Despite having no qualifications as a public health professional, he became a survivor of the wreckage unleashed by Andrew Lansley's 'reforms'. Selbie's appointment illustrated the low importance assigned to PHE. Jeremy Hunt, the Health Secretary for the next six years, allowed PHE, cursed by a meagre budget, to exist as the NHS's Cinderella. Selbie's appointment justified Cummings' despair about the qualifications of civil servants.

Selbie would not allow the Department of Health to undermine his self-importance. A glossy brochure boasted: 'PHE plays a key role in planning for and responding to large-scale infectious disease threats locally, nationally and globally . . . It has the capability to respond to a rapid upsurge in activity as a result of outbreaks, epidemics or pandemics of infectious disease, and provides PHE with the resilience to sustain a long-term response to an emerging threat.'

PHE's most relevant claim was: 'Our experts have considerable experience at using contact tracing to prevent and contain outbreaks and to keep the public safe. We remain prepared for future imported cases and for other high-consequence infectious diseases that need to be managed in a similar way. We use our networks, data and capabilities to recognise and manage cases, clusters, outbreaks and incidents of infectious disease.'

To establish its efficacy, in January 2020 the Department of

Health unveiled PHE's match-winning status. The UK, said the department's officials, was well prepared to combat any new diseases because PHE had already produced a diagnostic test for the Wuhan Covid, 'making the UK one of the first countries outside China to have a prototype specific laboratory test for this new disease'. Britain's public health measures, added the department, 'are world-leading and the NHS is well prepared to manage and treat new diseases'.

All those in Whitehall and Westminster not directly involved in health assumed that Britain could rely on Selbie and Chris Wormald, the Department of Health's permanent secretary since 2016. 'Everyone thought they were doing the right thing' because they could trust the health professionals in the Civil Service, Bernard Jenkin would later observe. Unlike the outsiders, in January 2020, Selbie, Wormald, Hancock and other senior departmental officials knew, as did Jeremy Hunt, that the manifest weaknesses exposed by Operation Cygnus in 2017 remained unresolved.

To his credit, Selbie had foreseen in September 2019 'a global pandemic in the coming years, including pandemic influenza and a novel virus, the so-called Disease X'. The hypothetical epidemic, he wrote, is 'a yet to be identified virus or bacteria'. But the country, he wrote reassuringly, could rely on Professor Sharon Peacock, the director of PHE's National Infection Service and a professor of microbiology. Peacock exuded confidence. 'Our mission is to prevent, detect, respond to and reduce the impact of infectious diseases in this country,' she wrote. 'PHE, and its predecessor organisations, have a long track record of using cutting-edge technologies to improve our ability to detect and contain outbreaks and treat people with infectious diseases.'

For obvious reasons, Duncan Selbie was not invited to SAGE's meetings. PHE was represented by Peacock and Dr Yvonne Doyle, the medical director. Both were paid about £250,000 a year, and both would be responsible for testing and tracing the virus across England and Wales.

Assuming that the Wuhan Covid was a strain of influenza, the standard procedure for PHE was to 'contain, delay, research, mitigate'. Since total containment of the infection was not feasible, a balance was to be struck between suppressing the first wave and reducing the country's susceptibility to a second wave. Denied accurate information from China, there was one novel complication unknown to anyone outside China: unlike previous strains of flu, sufferers of Wuhan's Covid could show no symptoms and yet infect other people. Unaware that sufferers could be asymptomatic, SAGE's experts were working unusually blindfolded. 'There is currently little evidence that people without symptoms are infectious to others,' the Department of Health would mistakenly state.

On 24 January, the first Covid case was detected in France. That morning's *Evening Standard* headline was 'Killer Virus: Cases in UK "Highly Likely"'. Tipped that Hancock would chair the first meeting of Cobra to discuss Covid, the newspaper did not report that Boris, like the leaders of the three other nations – Scotland, Wales and Northern Ireland – would not attend. As Nicola Sturgeon rightly assumed, the meeting was for health ministers. Notably, over the next ten weeks, Sturgeon did nothing materially different in preparing Scotland for the virus from the English government.

If the Wuhan Covid reached Britain, Ferguson forecast at the first Cobra meeting, there would be a maximum of 20,000 deaths. Whitty agreed. He told the meeting, 'We think there's a fair chance we may get some cases over time . . . I think we should definitely see this as a marathon, not a sprint. We need to have our entire response based on that principle.' Timing, they knew, was everything. At that stage, no one realised the speed of infection, how far the infection had spread and therefore when to trigger the response.

Vallance presented Britain's defences against the Wuhan Covid along the familiar line as a type of influenza and focused on schoolchildren. Unusually susceptible to getting flu, schoolchildren were prime spreaders of the infection. With the focus on schools, there was no particular provision for the elderly. Care homes were not included in Imperial's model. 'We made the rather optimistic assumption that somehow, as was policy, the elderly would be shielded,' Ferguson said later.

At the end of the Cobra meeting, Hancock was advised that

Covid presented a 'low danger'. In Berlin, Lothar Wieler, the president of the Robert Koch Institute, Germany's centre for disease control, came to the same conclusion.

'Coronaviruses,' Hancock later told the Commons, echoing Whitty, 'do not usually spread if people don't have symptoms – however we cannot be 100 per cent certain.' That would prove to be a serious but understandable error. To signal the government's concern, Hancock visited Porton Down to announce the allocation of £40 million to search for a vaccine. Hancock then went on to promote the government's NHS funding bill in line with Boris's election promise to increase spending by £33.9 billion over five years.

While waiting for the virus to hit Britain, the government's reaction relied on the mathematical models created by Neil Ferguson's team at Imperial College. By any measure, they were controversial. In 1999, Imperial's model had predicted that BSE, or 'mad cow disease', could kill between 150,000 and 500,000 people. In the event, fewer than 200 died. In 2001, advice based on Imperial's model suggested that the cure to a foot-and-mouth outbreak was to cull 6 million healthy cattle, sheep and pigs, at a cost of about £9 billion. An official inquiry criticised Ferguson's modelling as 'severely flawed'. Imperial's model stated in 2003 that SARS posed a '25 per cent chance of killing tens of millions'. Instead, 813 people died worldwide. MERS killed 866 people, although some sources say about 2,000 people. Both viruses disappeared. Nor, contrary to Imperial's forecast, did bird flu kill 200 million people or swine flu in 2009 kill 65,000 people in Britain. Instead, swine flu killed about 150,000 across the world. Called a pandemic by WHO, the organisation was later accused of panicking. In the aftermath, Britain was left with 34 million doses of unused and expensive vaccines. An inquiry called the Imperial's modellers 'astrologers'.

Models were distrusted, not least because the assumptions fed into the programs were questionable. Politicians and officials became reluctant to spend money on preparations for exaggerated scares. 'All these models are forecasts,' Matt Keeling, a professor of life sciences, warned. 'We are used to weather forecasts. We expect them to be right today and maybe tomorrow, but the longer you go on, the more uncertainty there will be.'

Scepticism about Imperial's model was rooted, according to critics, in its age. It was based on a programming code called either 'C' or Fortran that had apparently been used twenty years earlier by NASA for *Mariner 1*. Critics claimed its outdated language and design flaws produced numerical inaccuracies. One file alone contained 15,000 lines of code. Modern industry best practice would use 500 separate files instead. It was 'a tangled, buggy mess which looks more like a bowl of angel-hair pasta than a finely tuned piece of programming', according to one informed critic. One prominent flaw was the code's inability to distinguish between particular people's susceptibility to the virus. An infected nurse in a hospital was more likely to transmit the virus than an asymptomatic child, but the model could not identify the difference.

Critics also discovered that even if they used the same initial set of parameters as Imperial, the model could produce different results if run on different computers. They condemned the results as crude mathematical guesswork.

Mark Woolhouse, a professor of epidemiology specialising in infectious diseases and serving on Scotland's SAGE, was particularly sceptical of the models created to monitor influenza. 'I do not think it was ever possible to predict the course of this epidemic; there were too many fundamental unknowns to do that,' he said. That accusation, which gained considerable traction over the months ahead, was contested by Ferguson: 'You do not really have a flu model – you have models for directly transmitted diseases.' To many, Ferguson's reply was nonsense. His model was focused on the transmission of flu.

Without any sense of alarm, Hancock chaired the second Cobra meeting about Covid on 29 January. Ministers were reassured by Vallance that PHE could contain 'a new infectious disease'. Pertinently, no one commented about the agency's failure to trace the vast majority of the 2,000 people who had arrived earlier in the month at Heathrow from Wuhan. Just two infected Chinese people in York were quarantined and no further transmission was discovered. Nevertheless, Hancock was reassured by PHE: 'The UK is one of the first countries in the world to have developed an accurate test for this coronavirus and PHE is undertaking continuous refinement of this test.' PHE's capacity, Hancock was told, was to conduct 400–500 tests a day. PHE confirmed that it could 'if necessary' scale up testing. Both statements were considerable exaggerations, but in the nature of Whitehall's culture of compliant relationships, no official discourteously questioned that information. Unaccustomed in their brief careers as civil servants to Whitehall's practice of laying effective smokescreens, Vallance and Whitty proved to be equally persuadable. Yet they should have rigorously questioned Peacock and Doyle. If anyone should have outrightly asked how many more tests might be required, however, it was Hancock, but the minister failed to demand more information. In the non-confrontational and uninquisitive mood set by Boris, he was not prepared to vigorously interrogate the scientific experts. Instead, Hancock relied on his officials' assurances, not least that NHS staff would be protected from infection. That was also wishful thinking. At the end of the meeting, the health officers of the four nations raised the risk level to 'moderate'. (Germany would raise the level to 'moderate' five weeks later on 2 March.) Curiously, at the same time but without any publicity, Simon Stevens, the NHS's chief executive, in constant contact with Vallance and Whitty, declared a Level 4 National Incident, the highest level. The next day, WHO declared the outbreak a 'public health emergency of international concern'. BA stopped all flights to China. Boris prepared to celebrate Brexit day in Downing Street.

Anticipating the birth of a new nation, Boris launched a major review of British foreign and defence policy. 'This is a defining moment in how the UK relates to the rest of the world,' he said. The review would assess what manpower and equipment Britain needed to 'address the risks and threats we face'. Boris's address to the nation from Downing Street promised to 'unleash the full potential of this brilliant country . . . This is the moment when the dawn breaks and the curtain goes up on a new act in our great national drama . . . And yes it is partly about using these new powers – this recaptured sovereignty – to deliver the changes people voted for . . . And if we can get this right I believe that with every month that goes by, we will grow in confidence not just at home but abroad . . . And whatever the bumps in the road ahead I know that we will succeed.' On principle, the BBC refused to broadcast the address recorded in Downing Street because the disc of the recording was handed to them without the option of exercising their normal editorial control. His speech was slightly overshadowed by the news that the Britons evacuated from Wuhan were arriving in Brize Norton. They would be compelled to endure two weeks' quarantine. None were found to be infected.

Otherwise, considering the importance, the day was an anticlimax. In the morning, Boris chaired an inconsequential Cabinet meeting in Sunderland, the first town to declare for Brexit in the referendum. During the day, he fired Claire Perry, a former Tory MP, from her post as president of the UN Climate Change Conference for failing to organise properly the conference to be held in Glasgow in the autumn; and that night, unwilling to appear in public with Carrie, he refused to participate in Nigel Farage's street celebration. Considering the wrecked emotions over the past four years, he might have hosted a huge party. But he was both too good-mannered to rub the Remainers' noses in it, and too sensitive to further aggravate his family. Instead, he invited about thirty members of Team Leave to Downing Street. All the food and drink was produced in Britain. The star, Dominic Cummings, dressed in a T-shirt, black tracksuit and trainers, was given the microphone to speak, but was overcome by emotion, while Boris, in a boisterous manner, grabbed a makeshift gong to mark time to 11 p.m. – the Brexit moment in Brussels – because Downing Street's TV circuit had crashed. Then the epic battle was over. As the guests departed, Boris looked like an outsider in his own domain.

*

The first week of February was a milestone for Matt Hancock, the forty-one-year-old former economist. Lacking the serious demeanour of a graduate with a first in PPE from Oxford and an MPhil in economics from Cambridge, few would have realised from Hancock's manner that he had been employed by the Bank of England and later by George Osborne as his chief of staff. In allowing him to continue as Secretary of State despite being a Remainer, Boris had recognised not only a loyal politician but also the unique demands of the Department of Health. Unlike most portfolios, new health ministers needed more than a year to understand the NHS's complexities. Only in the second year could the minister begin to influence the highly paid bureaucrats controlling the NHS's 1.4 million employees. Hancock's efficacy depended on Chris Wormald, his permanent secretary. In his unremarkable Whitehall career, Wormald seemed to have succeeded by remaining low key, as performances before select committees showed. After four years as the Department of Health's senior official, his impact appeared to be imperceptible. During Jeremy Hunt's last two years, the NHS's front-line services had barely improved. He too epitomised Cummings' criticism.

In preparing for the third Cobra meeting on 5 February, Hancock relied entirely on the experts, on 'the very rigorous, well-established and sophisticated policy advice structure that exists within the UK government in crises', as Neil Ferguson described it.

In anticipation of the Cobra meeting, SAGE had met for the second time on 3 February. Although the low-key newspaper reports from China described a limited threat to its economy, everyone at the meeting understood the lurking danger. In Yokohama, Japan, the *Diamond Princess*, a cruise ship hosting 3,711 people, was about to be quarantined after a former passenger was found with Covid-19. At the SAGE meeting, every aspect of controlling the virus was considered: closing schools, social distancing, home isolation, face masks (they were always against them), handwashing and quarantine. They agreed that the Wuhan outbreak was probably ten times bigger than the Chinese admitted and that even cutting travel into Britain by 90 per cent would only delay the virus's arrival by a few weeks. There was also 'very little' benefit from stopping 'large public events'.

While the Chinese government refused to disclose the truth, on

4 February Stanley Johnson – invited as the prime minister's father – stood in the spotlight with Liu Xiaoming, China's veteran ambassador in London, to pronounce a 'China–UK Golden Era' and his confidence that China would defeat the virus. On the same day, Boris met Giuseppe Conte, the Italian prime minister. Two Chinese tourists in Rome had been quarantined after testing positive for the virus. Boris's mind remained firmly on Brexit, however, and it was this rather than Covid that he discussed with Conte. Also on that day, Doyle announced good news: PHE had sequenced Covid's genome. As a 'crucial step', she said, 'we can better understand the roots of this disease, predict its behaviour, and learn how to tackle it'. She also revealed that PHE's testing capacity was limited to just one hundred people a day through its new centralised laboratory in Colindale, north London. But, she said, PHE planned to increase its diagnostic capacity first to 500 tests per day and then to 1,000 daily by creating an extra twelve laboratories across the country. Testing, everyone agreed, was 'essential'. The mechanics for increasing capacity were delegated to Sharon Peacock. Wormald was apparently unaware that Doyle and Peacock felt overwhelmed.

Instead of expanding the service in one huge effort, Peacock decided to focus her efforts on the Colindale laboratory and then enlarge PHE's capacity bit by bit. Asked later to justify her decision, she obfuscated and refused to explain her reasoning. During February, her obduracy was noticed by many directors of laboratories in research institutes, universities and the private sector. Among those who offered their services to PHE was Matthew Freeman of Oxford University's Dunn School of Pathology. Hundreds of the school's staff and students, said Freeman, were ready to use their 119 PCR machines to identify genetic signs of the virus. He never received a reply. Similarly, an executive at the Weatherall Institute of Molecular Medicine at Oxford University offered to carry out 1,000 tests per day but the reply never came. 'You would have thought that they would be bashing down the door,' he later said. Paul Nurse, director of the Crick Institute, said that he had offered his laboratories and staff to the testing effort but he did 'not think that [he] got a reply' until he publicly complained weeks later.

Apacor, based in Berkshire, and other privately owned laboratories also offered to supply millions of tests but there was no response. In total, over fifty laboratories in Britain, in universities and privately owned, could have been approached by PHE. Each had the capacity for between 1,000 and 2,000 tests a day. With expansion, by the end of the month they could have conducted up to 100,000 tests a day. PHE had decided not to trust the private sector or research institutes. By contrast the German government, which relied on sixty private and a few university laboratories under contract to hospitals, began conducting 160,000 tests a day in early February which expanded to 500,000 tests a day.

Utilising that testing capacity depended on directing a team of tracers to find those infected. At the beginning of February, PHE claimed that it could depend on 300 tracers. Neither Peacock nor Selbie explained why they refused to consider employing 5,000 experienced local authority health workers as tracers.

Britain's capacity to test and trace was not raised at the Cobra meeting on 5 February. The responsibility for that misjudgement would be accepted by Whitty: 'We were lulled into a false sense of security by the fact that we were so fast off the mark in developing a test,' he would say. The requirement for PPE was also not discussed at the early Cobra meetings. Without Vallance, Wormald or Doyle mentioning the issue, Hancock would not have known that neither PHE nor the Department of Health had considered the NHS's medical staff's need for special PPE. In those early weeks, Hancock was unaware that PHE's headquarters in Waterloo – his inheritance from Jeremy Hunt – was a building filled with overpaid, squabbling bureaucrats led by a medically unqualified chief executive.

To remedy one failing exposed by Operation Cygnus, the Department of Health had reorganised the responsibility for purchasing PPE. To prevent hospital trusts competing against each other for supplies and to secure the benefit of bulk buying, the responsibility for procuring equipment had been assigned in 2018 to Supply Chain Coordination Ltd, led by Jin Sahota. Paid £200,000 a year, the fifty-two-year-old was answerable to the Department of

Health. Sahota relied on Unipart, a logistical corporation serving the motor industry, to provide the equipment on a just-in-time basis. In February, PHE's guidance about the purchase and use of PPE was still focused on protection against influenza. The equipment would be unsuitable against Covid-19, a more dangerous virus. Reflecting the uncertainty in the SAGE discussions, Vallance remained unaware about the mystery of an asymptomatic infection.

A consensus had emerged among SAGE's scientists and, by its very nature, consensus tended to deter challenge. Neil Ferguson would say that the traditional structures of Britain's government 'may have led to a certain degree of caution in decision-making – balancing evidence, balancing certainty and uncertainty, and being very aware of costs and the risks of second waves'. Confrontational debate was not encouraged by the centralisation in one department of politicians, civil servants and the 1.4 million employed by the NHS. Some would compare the British government's centralised co-ordination unfavourably with that of Germany, a country of sixteen states. The structures – SAGE, Cobra and Whitehall – they complained, had encouraged complacency. Others would say that the lack of argument reflected the nature of the people involved.

The flaws were first revealed on 11 February. PHE had been following up eight separate infections. No one knew how many more cases were undetected or how many people were involved. The only certainty, Vallance and Whitty agreed, was that 'sustained transmission' of the virus was underway in Britain and that at least ten times more people were infected than detected. That proved to be a woeful underestimate. Vallance and Whitty also agreed that the peak of infection was between two and four months away – between April and June.

Over the previous two weeks, Sharon Peacock had considered the governments' reactions in three Asian countries where the virus was already established. She needed to decide whether to massively increase PHE's testing machinery. Based on its experience of combating SARS and MERS, South Korea was well prepared with seventy-nine laboratories. Despite a bad outbreak, it

avoided a national lockdown. Taiwan had introduced mass temperature screening but kept shops and restaurants open. In
Singapore restaurants and schools were open, and working from
home was actively discouraged to protect the economy. In South
Korea, deaths were limited to ten a day. In both other countries,
only two people had died.

As expert epidemiologists in discussion with some of the country's leading scientists, Vallance and Whitty had decided that mass
test and tracing as in South Korea was impracticable in Britain. To
enforce quarantine, Seoul's authorities were empowered to compel
every infected person to move without their family into special
accommodation for at least two weeks. In addition, using facial recognition on CCTV and an app which compromised every citizen's
privacy, the government could rapidly identify anyone possibly
infected by the quarantined person and also order them into confinement. Those like Jeremy Hunt who later advocated that Britain
should adopt the South Korean model never explained how Boris's
government could successfully expect identical obedience from
millions of Britons asserting their human rights. The refusal by 20
per cent of Britons to identify their contacts in the track-and-trace
operation started in May confirmed that Britons would resist Korea-
style regimentation. The challenge was to find a middle way.

Instead, Peacock decided that Britain could not 'accelerate' its
testing capability. The accurate statistics were finally disclosed by
her at a SAGE meeting on 18 February. PHE, she said, could only
track and trace 'five new cases' a week which assumed following
800 contacts. She hoped, she said, to increase her workload to fifty
cases a week which could mean checking 8,000 contacts. There was
a threshold after widespread transmission, she said, when 'contact
tracing would no longer be useful or practical'. Peacock's report
and conclusion were not questioned by her fellow SAGE scientists.
From the mood at the meeting, Neil Ferguson accepted that the
capacity to test was PHE's sole decision and not one that he or the
others could discuss or dispute. In fixing his model, he assumed
there would be no increased testing. Despite Peacock's extraordinary revelation, Selbie had written on his blog four days earlier:

'PHE now has a very extensive and complex contact tracing operation underway with health protection teams around the country
diligently talking to people that might have been in close contact
with carriers of the virus to assess their risk . . . Our experts have
considerable experience at using contact tracing to prevent and
contain outbreaks and to keep the public safe.'

Selbie's self-congratulatory blog coincided with Ferguson's first
alarming report to SAGE. There was, he wrote, a 'realistic prob-
ability' that there is already 'sustained transmission in the UK'.
Because no one knew what was happening in China, and there was
clear evidence that the Chinese government was deliberately providing false statistics, Ferguson's predictions were unsurprisingly
hazy. He speculated that the peak of infection would be in two to
four months (in fact, it would be in just over one month) and he
advised that schools should not be closed, not least because scientists did not know whether children would be infected. Using
unreliable data from Wuhan, he also plundered the available data
from an increasing number of quarantine cruise ships, where passengers were kept in poor conditions, to produce a surprise: only
some passengers were infected. Clearly the majority of passengers
had an unidentifiable immunity. This was unlike any previous
Covid. The reason became apparent only about three months later
as scientists established that people with a particularly tailored
T-cell (a type of white blood cell that helps the immune system
fight off viruses) did not suffer. Surprisingly, SAGE's discussion
about Ferguson's predictions on 18 February ended in just one outstanding disagreement. Opinion was divided whether the virus
had properly arrived or was actually spreading across the UK. In
their view, there was a difference between the virus being present
in one place, or many.

*

That was Europe's last day of innocence. In Codogno, a small town
in Lombardy, north Italy, doctors had just started to treat a man
suffering respiratory problems but had no suspicions that there was

anything unusual. The first case of Wuhan's Covid had surfaced. There was no reason for Boris, like millions of other Britons, not to enjoy a holiday in half-term week. While many headed to ski in the Alps, Boris drove to Chevening with Carrie for a week. (Chequers was closed due to building work.) Their unexpected holiday coincided with his divorce being considered in the High Court. In a private hearing, a judge approved the financial agreement Boris had reached with Marina. The divorce could rapidly follow. The announcement disappointed those friends who had speculated how Boris pined for his wife and hoped for a reconciliation. In their opinion, Boris had always depended on Marina's wisdom and stability. Above all, she was utterly trustworthy and loyal. Carrie, they lamented, was too young and inexperienced to offer the same unconditional friendship. They would blame Carrie's demands in the seventh month of her pregnancy for Boris's absence from London at the beginning of the Covid crisis. Five days after their arrival, Covid infections were erupting across Lombardy. Communes were being quarantined to control a virus that had already killed. But it wasn't Covid that interrupted Boris's holiday; it was Dominic Cummings.

Over the previous weeks, Cummings had not concealed his contempt of civil servants: none properly understood statistical modelling, quantum computation and synthetic biology. They deserved to be 'whacked'. For better project management, he wanted Whitehall to recruit outstanding scientists – not only for their skills but also their absolute certainty based on evidence. Unlike politicians, they did not indulge in endless talk but, like himself, enthusiastically expounded technical ideas. At the same time, he respected overconfident, impatient mavericks, keen to sweep traditions aside. Again like himself, they focused on a goal without noticing or caring about the collateral damage. 'He's the Downing Street version of the Deliveroo guy,' wrote Stefan Collini, a Cambridge professor of English, about Cummings, 'who doesn't care whether you've ordered pepperoni or four-cheese: his job is to make it happen, and if that involves cycling the wrong way up one-way streets then that's probably a plus.' Arcane debate among traditional civil servants aggrieved him. Abandon convoluted arguments, Cummings pronounced. This is what we want, let's get it done.

Among the many who answered his call for 'weirdos' and 'misfits' to join him in Downing Street was Andrew Sabisky. Describing himself as a 'super-forecaster', Sabisky, aged twenty-seven, had advocated giving children a mental performance-enhancing drug and dismissed the risk of fatality as 'probably worth a dead kid once a year'. He had also praised eugenics. 'Intelligence,' he said, 'is largely inherited and correlates with better outcomes: physical health, income, lower mental illness.' He had also argued that black Americans' IQ was on average lower than that of white Americans and so 'you will see a far greater percentage of blacks than whites in the range of IQs 75 or below, at which point we are close to the typical boundary for mild mental retardation'.

Drafted by Cummings onto the Downing Street staff without the usual vetting procedures, Sabisky was immediately assigned to work on Boris's defence review, replacing those described by Cummings as 'has-beens'. Soon after his arrival, newspapers began to report about his unusual background. If Sabisky was the solution to Cummings' problem, the reports implied, then Britain's government was about to fall under the control of extremists. Unease about Sabisky came to a climax after an online post was discovered by *The Times*. Posing as an 'agony uncle', he had told an enquirer that 'Theologically speaking, she is your wife and should submit to you as unto the Lord . . . then it is your place to command her . . . and her place to obey.'

On Monday, Boris called from Chevening and ordered that Sabisky be fired. Cummings refused, arguing that the government should not remove a talented individual because of a media storm. In a second call later that day, Boris was emphatic. Sabisky resigned. Neither Boris nor Cummings realised that an unintended consequence was that talented civil servants and outside experts would be deterred by this episode from joining Downing Street.

Over the following days, Boris was advised to fire Cummings

before more trouble erupted. Boris resisted. After his experience in the Foreign Office, he sympathised with Cummings' antagonism towards the 'Whitehall blob'. When Cummings warned, 'See? They will destroy you. You always need me to sort the bastards out', Boris was grateful.

He had persuaded Cummings to join him in Downing Street for his uncompromising ambitions and methods. He shared Cummings' goals but lacked his insensitivity towards their common foes. Boris's virtue was to identify the qualities he lacked and appoint like-minded people who had those qualities to use them on his behalf. That did not mean he gave those appointed his unqualified trust. Loners required proof of loyalty. Unlike Munira Mirza, Eddie Lister, Andrew Gilligan and Ben Gascoigne, the utterly faithful camp followers from City Hall, he recognised that Cummings' loyalties were shared with Michael Gove, ensconced in the Cabinet Office. While Boris would never forget their treachery in 2016, their capitulation confirmed his victory. Unlike his City Hall friends, the duo were operators on the big stage, sharing an understanding of the obstacles to their agenda of change. Both were committed to revolutionising Whitehall and creating a new Britain. Impatient about any counter-arguments, they had supported his tactics during the Cabinet reshuffle a few days before Boris left for Chevening.

Boris had been looking for a way to remove Sajid Javid, the Chancellor. Javid was resisting Boris's demands to honour the election promises and spend billions in northern England and on the HS2 rail network. Javid, a former banker, was reluctant to spend more than the country could afford. Just as in his private life, Boris had limited concern about profligate spending. Extra money, he had always found, somehow turned up, and he seemed to believe that this happy truth extended to the public purse. With his agreement, Cummings was deeply involved in drafting the new budget to 'level up' the economy and spend on the NHS. Javid's opposition was intolerable. Gossip had also suggested that Javid had been plotting before the election to remove Cummings. Revenge was automatic. In the wake of the dismissal of Javid's adviser Sonia Khan, Cummings insisted that all Javid's special advisers come under Downing Street's control. Javid refused and then resigned on 13 February.

*

In late February, China finally admitted that 2,236 people had died in Wuhan. Two passengers had died on the *Diamond Princess* (by mid-April, fourteen would die), and the first victim had died in northern Italy. New TV pictures from Lombardy's hospitals showed a nation in crisis, convulsed by fear. The latest suggestion was that the virus had been brought to Italy one month earlier by Chinese workers returning from holidays in Wuhan. (In May 2020, water samples suggested that the virus had been already present in December.)

In London, PHE reported that while just nine people in England had been tested positive for the virus, 6,143 people had tested negative. By then, although the infection was much worse than realised, SAGE's scientists were uncertain about the next steps. Every permutation of controls was discussed and, it was agreed, it was too early to do other than adopt a gradual approach while keeping the situation under daily review. School closures were discussed and opposed and there was talk about protecting the elderly.

The most important development was not discussed. On 25 February, PHE noted that with the end of the half-term break, thousands of British holidaymakers returning from skiing in northern Italy could be infected. PHE did not highlight the same dangers of those returning from France and Spain. Research later showed that most of the virus brought into Britain was by those returning from Italy and Spain that week, and not from China. In technical terms, PHE failed in the Case Definition. Convinced that China would be the source of a flu infection in Britain, Sharon Peacock and Yvonne Doyle were slow to realise that Covid-19 was different and that the source of infection would be Europe. Consequently, PHE did take seriously the reality that the returning tourists would carry the infection into every British city, a recipe for a simultaneous mass outbreak.

Vallance and Whitty had long accepted that screening was point-less. Nothing could prevent the virus arriving in Britain but PHE's failure to widely broadcast the danger of the returning skiers was another indictment of Duncan Selbie's agency. The meeting's min-utes reflected no disagreement.

The only voice of dissent on SAGE was John Edmunds, a profes-sor of infectious-disease modelling. Edmunds' model predicted that 370,000 people would die by December 2021 and the NHS would require 220,000 intensive care units (ICU) compared to the existing 4,562 beds. On 21 February, he had suggested that the threat level be raised from moderate to high but he was ignored. Two months later, Edmunds would complain that the government did not listen to 'a small little cadre of people in the middle' like himself who 'absolutely did realise from the beginning that there would be an overwhelming epidemic' in which Britain's health ser-vice was not going 'to get anywhere near being able to cope with it'.

The growing crisis in Italy might have made Boris susceptible to Edmunds' warning but since he relied entirely on Vallance and Whitty he was unaware of any disagreement. In a show of solidar-ity, Downing Street announced that Boris had telephoned Giuseppe Conte and offered his reassurance, but that merely highlighted for a few that the holidaying prime minister was not in control.

On 25 February, with thirteen confirmed cases, PHE declared 'the current position in the UK' was that 'there is currently no transmission of Covid-19 in the community'. PHE also published advice that it was 'very unlikely that anyone receiving care in a care home or the community will become infected'. (That opinion was not withdrawn until 13 March.) On the following day, Hancock chaired the fifth Cobra meeting.

By then, the Cobra meetings had become less important for making decisions – since Vallance and Whitty were personally giv-ing advice to Boris and Hancock – but were vital in trying to ensure that the devolved governments in Ulster, Wales and Scotland acted in unison with London. The meetings were also useful as the refer-ence point for announcements.

Based on Whitty's advice, Hancock told the Commons that

afternoon, 'The public can be assured that we have a clear plan to contain, delay, research and mitigate, and that we are working methodically through each step to keep the public safe.' He also pledged, 'We have put in place enhanced monitoring measures at UK airports.' Britons returning from abroad saw no evidence of PHE officials at the airports. Hancock's reassuring statement reflected self-deception but in the circumstances there was no obvious solution. With Vallance's agreement, testing had not been increased, and the clear need for additional amounts of PPE was the responsibility of Wormald but specifically not Simon Stevens, the NHS's chief executive. Both remained invisible to the public. Neither, it appears, specifically warned Downing Street of any unique problems.

At that critical moment, could a prime minister have been expected to authoritatively ignore Selbie's emphatic statement, endorsed by Vallance, Whitty and Wormald, that there was 'no transmission of Covid-19 in the community'? The experts had either an agreed opinion, or had decided not to disagree. Vallance offered no evidence to Boris that there was a stark dilemma. On what basis could a politician question the experts' apparent unanimity? Perhaps Margaret Thatcher, a chemistry graduate, might have understood the unreliability of scientists, but neither Tony Blair nor Gordon Brown had challenged David King, their chief scientist, when he controversially supported the cull of 6 million healthy animals during the foot and mouth epidemic and advised about the other viruses which followed. Both Vallance and Whitty were sophisticated and experienced. On what basis could Boris have doubted their reassurance?

In the pyramid of Britain's government, the person empowered to advise and expected to urge caution to a prime minister is the Cabinet Secretary. As Whitehall's supreme ruler, Mark Sedwill was Boris's eyes and ears, the official responsible for knowing whether the machinery of government was functioning. Previous Cabinet Secretaries, steeped in Whitehall's folklore after intense periods in the Treasury, were better equipped than Sedwill. Margaret Thatcher had relied on her Cabinet Secretaries but Tony Blair

intended from the outset to ignore his, and also not to rely on the
Civil Service. Persuaded by Jonathan Powell, his shallow chief of
staff, that the Civil Service would sabotage New Labour's mission,
Blair purposely excluded successive Cabinet Secretaries from critical meetings, not least in the run-up to the Iraq War. Blair relied
instead on an army of New Labour supporters imported as advisers
into Downing Street. David Cameron had trusted Jeremy Heywood, his Cabinet Secretary, but had equally relied on the cabal of
friends he had brought into Downing Street. One exception was his
negotiations with the EU. Foolishly, he relied on Foreign Office
officials and ended up with a bad deal.

After his own experience in the Foreign Office, Boris had good
reason to be suspicious of civil servants – but there was a twist. His
predecessors never set themselves a mission to improve radically
Whitehall. Empowering Cummings with that task was, in recent
history, unique. Accordingly, with that inherent scepticism, Boris
did not rely on Sedwill. Nevertheless, the Cabinet Secretary's task
in mid-February was to understand the developing crisis and assess
the advice the prime minister was receiving, especially from the
scientists. By then, Sedwill had good reason to understand Boris's
naivety about the machinery of government. Nevertheless, he
failed to advise Boris to return to London as the Covid infection
spread. The question remains whether Boris himself should have
corrected his own weaknesses: his lack of involvement in the government machine beyond Downing Street, and his failure to
scrutinise Hancock's chairmanship of the Cobra meetings. He did
neither. But with hindsight, the alternative to Boris's overt reliance
on the scientists' advice would have been to announce that he was
deliberately ignoring the experts. That disclosure would have outraged the public and his political opponents. After Donald Trump
openly distrusted his scientific advisers and advocated drinking dis-
infectant to kill the infection, he was loudly criticised. Brazil's
president, Jair Bolsonaro, was equally lambasted for his dismissal of
medical advice. There was no compromise: either Boris could follow the scientific advice or, like Trump, mock his advisers. The
only conjecture is whether Boris, unlike Hancock, would have

spotted the professionals' frailties if he had attended the Cobra meetings in February.

★

26 February was a milestone in Whitehall's planning for Covid. In Italy, twelve people had died of the virus and, amid panic and a new lockdown, many hospitals were overwhelmed. The sick were either lying on hospital floors or abandoned in their homes. Most Britons could still not believe that the plague would arrive. Their incredulity was supported by the refusal of WHO's director general to declare a pandemic. Some would say Tedros Adhanom, an undistinguished Ethiopian public health official, wanted to avoid imposing unjustified fear on the world and a stigma on China. Others, including President Trump, would accuse him of fearing retribution from China's leaders who had supported his questionable candidature. The president threatened to cut off American funding of WHO.

Vallance and the SAGE scientists had no doubt that the virus would arrive in Britain, and that would also have been clear to Ben Warner, Downing Street's representative at the SAGE meeting the previous day. Warner, a digital expert formerly employed by Vote Leave, could report to Cummings that a disaster was coming.

In preparation for the SAGE meeting on the 25th, three papers had been prepared. Ferguson's model, updated by using new data from Italy, predicted that in the classic 'reasonable worst-case scenario' (RWCS), 80 per cent of Britons would be infected and 1 per cent would die. The death toll would be 510,000 people. This was an improvement on Ferguson's earlier assessment that between 2 per cent and 3 per cent would die – up to 1.5 million deaths. Even with mitigation measures, he said, the death toll could be 250,000 and the existing ICUs would be overwhelmed eight times over. The confidence among those at the meeting in Ferguson's modelling was 'low'. Sceptical about RWCS exaggerations, and without any definition of 'reasonable', his forecast was nevertheless accepted as the best available. 'I much prefer to be accused of overreacting than

under-reacting,' Ferguson said. 'We don't have a crystal ball.' Pertinently, although Ferguson hogged the media spotlight, several
other models were used. All came to an alarming conclusion.

In a second paper, the meeting was warned that 'without action,
the NHS will be unable to meet all demands placed on it'. One-tenth
of all infected patients would need an ICU bed. A third paper
expected the peak of infection to be in two to three months and that
3.6 million people would need hospital care, overwhelming ICUs.

Neither Vallance nor Whitty outrightly challenged Ferguson's
model or predictions. By contrast, in a series of messages from
Michael Levitt, a Stanford University professor who would correctly predict the pandemic's initial trajectory, Ferguson was
warned that he had overestimated the potential death toll by 'ten to
twelve times'. 'The problem with epidemiologists,' Levitt wrote, 'is
that they feel their job is to frighten people into lockdown, social
distancing. So you say "there's going to be a million deaths" and
when there are only 25,000 you say "it's good you listened to my
advice". This happened with Ebola and bird flu. It's just part of the
madness.'

Vallance's own presentation left no doubt that the country faced
a severe crisis. His priority was to manage the numbers infected in
the first wave to avoid overwhelming the hospitals' ICUs.

For the first time, the committee considered 'suppression' or a
lockdown. Wuhan's experience proved the immediate benefits of
'suppression' while Lombardy's lockdown on 22 February showed
that Europeans would comply with that draconian measure. Vallance led the consensus that the country should avoid a draconian
lockdown. Gradualism was best: start with a few measures and add
more if required to manage the numbers infected.

In the range of his scenarios called 'contain, delay, research, mitigate', his experts preferred to allow the infection to spread while
providing protection for those over sixty-five and 'special measures
around care homes'. Called managing national immunity, the
choice was ultimately Boris's. Lockdown or not would be 'a political decision'.

At that stage on 25 February, Vallance still professed uncertainty whether immunity to Covid-19 among Britons existed or whether Covid was more complicated than previous coronaviruses. But he did assume that most people in the UK, in the absence of a vaccine, would contract the coronavirus. His only absolute certainty was the graph showing deaths in a second wave: it peaked horrifically high.

Vallance's and Whitty's priority was to keep the virus under control to avoid that second wave. In the 1918 flu pandemic, the second wave killed more people than the first. 'The second wave is the main concern,' Vallance said. 'The more you suppress [the infection] down to zero early on, the more likely you are to get a recurrence at some point. It is a very difficult thing to try to balance.'

If the peak of those infected in the first wave was kept artificially low, Vallance explained, there would inevitably be a second wave. Given the time needed to produce a reliable vaccine, the more Britons with immunity after the first wave, the better Britain was placed for a second wave. That would be proven, according to some British scientists, by their assumption that Germans, unlike other Europeans, had developed an immunity. Chris Whitty agreed. 'The great majority of people who catch this virus,' he would tell MPs, 'will survive it – the great majority: over 90 per cent. It is easy to get a perception that if you are older and you get this virus, you are a goner. Absolutely not.'

Reflecting SAGE's assessment, the National Security Communications Team warned that with 80 per cent of the population infected, 'The current planning assumption is that 2–3 per cent of symptomatic cases will result in a fatality.' That implied that at least 1.5 million would die to establish herd immunity.

In the House of Lords on 26 February, Lord Bethell, a minister at the Department of Health, minimised the validity of those very statistics. 'I do not recognise the numbers,' he told Baroness McIntosh, 'and the government are not yet providing forecasts for the virus. Certainly, the worst-case situation could be of the order that she describes, but that estimate is not based on scientific forecasting.' That was inaccurate: McIntosh's numbers were based on the forecasts discussed at SAGE. But Bethell did admit, 'We simply do not know the behaviours of the virus. We do not know exactly how infectious it will be; we do not know which demographics it will target; and we do not necessarily know how mortal it will be. We hope for the best but are planning for the absolute worst.' He added, 'The public can be assured that we have a clear plan to contain, delay, research and mitigate, and that we are working methodically through each step to keep the public safe.'

At that stage there was no 'plan', only options. The most favoured, Bethell explained, was 'creating some kind of herd immunity, whereby a large proportion of the population has had the virus and is therefore inoculated [which] is clearly the objective – well, not the objective; rather, it is one of the results of the virus passing through, as flu viruses do regularly. It is expected that it will be a one-off experience, so herd immunity will actually provide resistance to future visits by the virus.' Bethell's candour and misinformation reflected the confusion across Whitehall.

On that day, fifteen people in England were registered with the infection. As a result of the global search for information, the experts believed that the virus was transmitted through 'aerosol' droplets in human breath. The unresolved problem was to define the rate of asymptomatic infection. SAGE's scientists assessed the chance between 'rare' and 80 per cent – proof that they could not provide certainty. But they did unanimously agree that stopping international travel and large sports meetings was 'not significant' to stop the infection spreading. Ben Warner returned to Downing Street to report a vacuum while Britain waited.

The newspaper headlines on 26 February were alarming. Schools were closing, £100 billion had been wiped off the value of leading shares the previous day and Ferguson's warning of 500,000 possible deaths was splashed over the tabloids.

In anticipation of the crisis, the prime minister spent four hours discussing preparations with doctors in Kettering Hospital. At that moment, the hospitals relied on PHE to provide testing of patients and staff and issue advice on ordering protective clothing and equipment (just as the three other nations relied on their respective public health agencies). The hospital trust's need for additional supplies of

PPE was not mentioned. Boris returned to London amid reports from Italy of overwhelmed hospitals, fear in Rome and silence from the rest of the EU in reply to Italy's request for help. Soon after, every EU country was acting in its own interest – closing borders and ignoring Brussels. International collaboration was minimal.

In the capital, Boris's performance aroused concern. On Friday 28 February, George Osborne tweeted 'The public is fearful, wants information and needs to know their leaders have got a grip.' The country, he added, should be placed on a 'war footing' and ministers should 'end the boycott' of the BBC. Remarking on Boris's long absence at Chevening and his decision to wait until the following Monday to chair his first Cobra meeting, Jeremy Corbyn called him a 'part-time prime minister'. Boris replied that after a meeting with Whitty and Hancock his best advice was that people wash their hands for twenty seconds. To deflect attention from the criticism, Boris approved the announcement that Carrie was pregnant and their child would be born in early summer – and that they were engaged.

That ruse was swept aside by another crisis. Philip Rutnam, the Home Office's permanent secretary, accused Home Secretary Priti Patel of orchestrating a 'vicious' campaign against him and of 'shouting and swearing, belittling people, making unreasonable and repeated demands – behaviour that created fear and that needed some bravery to call out'. Boris had no sympathy for Rutnam. He was not only the Home Office's senior civil servant when Amber Rudd misled the Commons about immigration targets, but was also at the heart of the *Windrush* scandal. Rutnam personified the officials targeted by Cummings for removal.

Over that first weekend of March, no one doubted that Britain faced a pandemic. According to Ferguson's latest model, the infection was doubling every six days and the peak would be in three to five months. In an attempt to display his leadership, Boris visited PHE's test centre in Colindale. Although the centre was testing only about eighty-five people a day, he announced that it was testing 'thousands and thousands of people for coronavirus'. In reality, the ambition was to complete about 3,000 tests per day across the whole country one week later. Clearly not informed about PHE's failure to fulfil its brief, Boris was also unaware that their tests would not spot asymptomatic Covid carriers.

Next, he visited the Royal Free Hospital in Hampstead, designated a centre to treat the virus. Once again, he was not briefed about the urgent need for PPE. His lack of awareness bred complacency in Downing Street. On his return, there were no fevered demands from his staff to challenge the Department of Health and PHE. His closest advisers' mindset resembled his: rely on the experts and follow the scientists.

Others were more alert. In anticipation, the Care Provider Alliance issued urgent guidance advising care homes to consider restricting visits from all relatives until the outbreak was over.

Recognising the imminent danger, the representative of the care-home industry told members to restrict the use of new agency staff to lessen exposure to the virus, and to isolate residents if they were suspected of being infected. That advice was not endorsed by Whitty. SAGE's advisers, Whitty said, were not keen on stringent measures like banning visitors from uninfected care homes, which would bring misery to the elderly and their relations. Whitty's leniency was ignored by Wales's chief medical officer, Dr Frank Atherton. Sick people were told 'don't go and visit your auntie in a care home'. It would be another ten days before Whitty also advised those who were 'generally unwell' to avoid visiting residents.

In preparation for the next Cobra meeting on Monday 2 March, the first to be chaired by Boris, Ferguson reported to SAGE that the danger had increased. The number of ICUs, he advised, should be doubled or even tripled. All would require ventilators. The statistics were alarming. Up to 570,000, he said, could die and the NHS would need 130,000 ICU beds. That new warning was not highlighted to Downing Street.

In what was still labelled 'the containment phase', Boris was assured that under the Department of Health's 'action plan . . . the UK maintains strategic stockpiles of the most important medicines and protective equipment for healthcare staff who may come into contact with patients with the virus. These stocks are being

monitored daily, with additional stock being ordered where necessary.' Without an expert offering alternative information, there
was no reason for Boris to doubt that assurance. The question is
whether Boris should have appointed immediately an adviser in
Downing Street to query the Department of Health's statements.

The strategic plan, Boris was told by Whitty and Vallance,
remained to 'flatten the curve', slowing the virus's spread so the
NHS could cope at peak infection. The government, said Whitty,
should wait for 'the right time and in the right phasing'. Echoing
Whitty, Vallance added, 'What you can't do is suppress this thing
completely . . . can't and shouldn't . . . timing is so important: right
time, right combination, driven by the data and the science.'

Boris was also told by Vallance that no one on SAGE was recommending that the government should immediately lock down the
country. That advice matched his own instinct that Britons should
'go about their business as usual' and even travel abroad on holiday.
In the meantime, he read the prepared script: 'there will be less
emphasis on large-scale preventative measures such as intensive
contact tracing. As the disease becomes established, these measures may lose their effectiveness and resources would be more
effectively used elsewhere.' Over the next twenty-four hours, the
number of infected people rose from thirty-nine to fifty-one. During the following week, no scientist or politician publicly criticised
Boris's script.

With the media dominated by alarming virus reports, highlighting a total of 107 deaths in Italy, Boris needed to reassure the nation.
In preparing for his first press conference the following day, he calculated that the positive image was for him to be flanked by
Vallance and Whitty. 'The principle that will guide us in all these
decisions,' he told the audience, 'is the scientific advice . . . it's the
science that will help us.' The sight of two medical chiefs agreeing
with the prime minister silenced even Boris's fervent critics. 'Our
country remains extremely well prepared,' he said. 'We already
have a fantastic NHS, fantastic testing systems and fantastic surveillance of the spread of disease.' Both scientists endorsed his
erroneous hyperbole and emphatic advice to the nation: 'We should

all basically just go about our normal daily lives.' He was also clear about the danger: 'Let me be absolutely clear that for the over-whelming majority of people who contract the virus, this will be a mild disease from which they will speedily and fully recover as we've already seen. But I fully understand public concern, your concern, about the global spread of this virus. And it is highly likely that we will see a growing number of UK cases.' Joshingly, he added with injudicious reassurance, 'I was at a hospital the other night where I think there were actually a few coronavirus patients and I shook hands with everybody.' He continued, 'The best thing you can do is to wash your hands with soap and hot water while singing "Happy Birthday" twice.' Echoing his master, Hancock later told BBC TV that handshaking was not dangerous: 'We've taken the scientific advice . . . The impact of shaking hands is negligible . . . as long as you wash your hands more often.' Across the world, every other government warned against shaking hands.

During that same day, SAGE members started to change their minds: 'Government should advise against greetings such as shak-ing hands and hugging, given existing evidence about the importance of hand hygiene.' Instinctively, Boris disregarded that somersault. He refused to follow what was happening in Europe. 'People obviously can make up their own minds,' he told the public, 'but I think the scientific evidence is, our judgement is, that wash-ing your hands is the crucial thing.' With Whitty's support, he was shaking hands at a Downing Street reception that week. Among the guests was Nadine Dorries, a Tory MP. The next morning, she reported Covid symptoms and later isolated herself. Twenty-eight people died that day in Italy. Unknown to the SAGE scientists, the rate of 're-infection' – passing the virus on to another person – was no longer four to six days but had accelerated to two to three days. Although Downing Street's spokesman highlighted 'the biggest crisis the country has faced in our lifetimes', the reaction across the Channel to the oncoming Armageddon was very different than in London. In Paris, President Macron had decided to follow the Asian example and start restricting large indoor gatherings. The first edict on 4 March prohibited more than 5,000 people from meeting in an enclosed space. There was no doubt that Macron intended to eventually impose a total lockdown and end economic activity.

Aware of the tension across Europe, Dominic Cummings attended SAGE's meeting on 5 March. Labour would criticise his presence as likely to interfere with the committee's advice. 'There have been a number of observers at those meetings,' Ferguson retorted, 'who have not interfered with business at all.'

Cummings heard the committee accept their behavioural scientists' advice that it was 'too early in the epidemic' to impose distancing or a lockdown. Without public support, control measures would not work. If people started self-isolating 'too early', Whitty believed, there would be 'no benefit' and it would last too long. There was, Vallance calculated, 'an incredibly difficult balancing act going on. Being too slow to react has potentially dangerous consequences. Overreacting is also potentially dangerous.' The key was not to allow enthusiasm to flag and run out at the peak. People would get fed up being isolated for thirteen weeks just when it was necessary. Mark Woolhouse, the professor of epidemiology on Scotland's SAGE, agreed: 'I would characterise lockdown as a panic measure.' The message Cummings took back to Downing Street was that isolation measures could start in about one to two weeks but the committee was against a total lockdown or banning large sporting meetings.

Whitty's reliance on behavioural scientists would be publicly praised by Deirdre Hine, a public health specialist and the author of a report about pandemics in 2010. But Whitty would be criticised by Stephen Reicher, a psychologist based in Scotland and an SNP sympathiser. Whitty, he complained, took advice from the wrong specialists.

The early disputes among scientists did not trouble Boris. The politician saw no reason to doubt the accumulated wisdom offered by Vallance and Whitty. Even if Boris recalled Churchill's famous quip about having 'scientists on tap and not on top', he was very probably unaware of Richard Feynman's warning in his essay, 'The value of science'. The pathfinding American physicist wrote: 'When a scientist doesn't know the answer to a problem, he is ignorant.

When he has a hunch as to what the result is, he is uncertain. And when he is pretty darn sure of what the result is going to be, he is still in some doubt. We have found it of paramount importance that in order to progress we must recognise our ignorance and leave room for doubt. Scientific knowledge is a body of statements of varying degrees of certainty – some most unsure, some nearly sure, but none absolutely certain.' Oblivious to the nuances of scientists arguing and the groupthink consensus dominating SAGE's scientists, BBC news reporters – the country's principle source of information – copied the politicians and did not challenge the scientists. Instead, the scientists' subjective opinions were repeated as gospel. Lee Cain, Downing Street's director of communications, did not grasp the potential problem of argumentative scientists undermining public confidence.

Whatever their qualifications, the behavioural scientists had not predicted that during that week, as fears of a lockdown loomed, vast numbers of people would storm the supermarkets to stockpile food and huge quantities of lavatory paper. By 10 a.m., supermarket shelves were bare. Similar frenzies did not occur elsewhere in Europe. Even in beleaguered Italy, shoppers behaved normally.

In a crisis, every nation looks to its leader for wisdom and reassurance. Even the Russians in 1941, as the Nazis invaded, put aside Stalin's murderous purges, and trusted him to repel the enemy. Boris's task was much simpler. In those early days of his administration, the majority of Britons trusted his judgement. Long praised as an outstanding communicator with an uncanny ability to read the nation, much depended on Boris's language and tone to maintain public confidence. The first dilemma was whether he should follow Macron and ban mass gatherings. Vallance and Whitty urged resistance. Banning, Whitty told him, was pointless because that would not 'contain' the virus. As the 2011 report recommended, to avoid damaging public morale and economic damage, the government should not 'impose any restrictions'.

To show that normal life should continue, Boris and Carrie joined 82,000 people at Twickenham on Saturday 7 March to watch the England versus Wales rugby match. By then four people had died in Britain of Covid. Boris was still undecided whether Britain should 'take it on the chin, take it all in one go and allow the disease, as it were, to move through the population, without taking as many draconian measures'. On reflection, he thought 'we need to strike a balance'. As a libertarian opposed to any restriction of movement, and also fearful of destroying the economy, he decided that the four-day Cheltenham Festival – attracting about 70,000 racing fans every day, starting on 10 March and worth £100 million to the economy – should go ahead. The bulldog wanted to show the nation that he would not be cowed by an invisible threat. Reassured that he was following Vallance's and Whitty's recommendations, he knew that if he ignored their advice, the presenters on the BBC's *Today* programme would have led the attack. But for the first time, his message divided the country. Many were aghast that Boris had allowed the mass events.

On 10 March, Boris focused on the final details of the new Chancellor Rishi Sunak's budget. (The cornerstone of Boris's election promise to 'level up' northern Britain was to be presented the following morning.) With Ben Warner present, SAGE met the same day amid fearsome news. Italy had been completely locked down the previous day, eighteen days after the first lockdown in Lombardy. Ferguson's model suggested that Britain was four to five weeks behind Italy in the curve. At most, he said, 10,000 Britons were infected. Ferguson's model also predicted that the peak of the infection was ten to fourteen weeks away if no mitigation measures were taken. Otherwise, it could be later. Lockdown was discounted to avoid a serious second wave but held in reserve for two weeks later. As a footnote, the scientists suggested that the government should consider a 'special policy' about care homes but studiously avoided making any firm recommendations.

On 11 March, a few hours before Sunak delivered his budget to the Commons, WHO finally declared a global pandemic. Britain registered 590 cases and ten deaths. In Italy, about 500 deaths had been registered and the death rate was doubling every two days. That afternoon, Donald Trump imposed an international travel ban. On the same day, as 70,000 people enjoyed racing at

Cheltenham, 3,000 Spaniards arrived in Liverpool to watch Atlético Madrid compete in the Champions League. Many commented with bewilderment that the Spaniards had flown in from an infected city which was closing down. Similar events were banned across Europe. Ferguson did not realise the extent of the infection in Europe. Nor did Whitty's deputy Jenny Harries, who explained why mass gatherings were not banned: 'Our experts and modellers basically haven't recommended it because they were still judged "low risk". Those events don't have a big effect.' Boris, she emphasised, was following the science. The 'brilliant modellers' and 'timing' would be critical in determining 'when we should intervene'. Herd immunity 'to flatten the curve', or as Boris called it 'squash the sombrero', remained the agreed policy.

By then, however, the concept of 'herd immunity' had aroused concern. To some, the government planned to let the disease rip through the community as part of a cold-blooded experiment in social engineering. Around this time, according to an alleged eyewitness, Cummings commented approvingly that 'herd immunity' would inevitably mean the premature death of the elderly, a suggestion he later condemned as a journalist's 'fabrication'.

During the day, Vallance was challenged for the first time by some SAGE members for relying on herd immunity. Events in Europe, they said, proved that the virus was out of control. Ferguson's latest model predicted that instead of 20,000 deaths, the infection rate was R3 and 250,000 could die. The committee's mistake, said the critics, was to base British policy on combating traditional flu. While flu sufferers did emerge with immunity against re-infection, there was no evidence that Covid-19's sufferers became immune. Although Vallance would deny proposing herd immunity, Robert Peston, the journalist, was authoritatively briefed about that strategy for an ITV broadcast.

The argument for a 'herd' programme remained credible. The evidence from Italy suggested that those healthy and under sixty were not in danger. Children were probably safe. Only the elderly and those with serious sicknesses were vulnerable. Lockdown in Britain could be avoided if the vulnerable isolated themselves. The elderly and other at-risk groups, explained the behavioural scientist David Halpern on 11 March, should be 'cocooned' and would be released only when the rest of the community had immunity.

Boris chaired Cobra on 12 March. The Italian death toll had risen in just twelve days from 52 to 1,266. PHE had identified about one hundred separate Covid outbreaks and contacted around 3,500 people who were possibly infected. Doyle and Peacock believed the official infection rate was a gross underestimate. They assumed that probably over 100,000 people were infected. In fact, it was worse. The infection rate was about to peak. Regardless, Doyle had realised a critical truth: PHE's assurances about ramping up testing had been false. The reality had to be acknowledged.

At the SAGE meeting the following day, Doyle announced that PHE had abandoned testing in the community. Testing, Doyle said, would be restricted to hospital staff. With a capacity of 1,000 tests a day, that meant PHE could handle only three tests per day in each of Britain's hospitals. After hearing her submission, the experts agreed that PHE's plan to discontinue testing was 'sensible'. Whitty also admitted that 'containment was pointless'. Jenny Harries agreed that community testing was 'not appropriate'. Still relying as an article of faith on the playbook of combating influenza, the scientists assumed that the level of infection could not be limited.

After unilaterally giving up PHE's responsibility for testing, Doyle assigned her responsibilities to the Department of Health's Office for Life Sciences. On 17 March, Vallance told MPs that even 4,000 tests a day was 'not going to be enough'. Because there were thousands of unknown cases, 'contact tracing was a lost cause'. Yet, at the same time, Boris promised 'we will massively scale up our testing capacity in the weeks ahead so we hit 25,000 tests a day'. That was optimistic, to say the least. Even on 23 March, PHE employed just 280 people across the whole country for testing. They needed 280 in every town.

On 25 March Yvonne Doyle chose not to explain to MPs why PHE's testing had stopped. Sharon Peacock also refused to explain why PHE had chosen not to follow South Korea. She undertook to

share 'in the next few days' with the Commons Science and Technology Committee the evidence and analysis on which the decision
to reject South Korea-style mass testing at an early stage was taken.
But despite requests by letter, email and telephone thereafter from
Greg Clark, the committee's chairman, she did not produce the
basis for PHE's decision to scale down testing. Instead, Peacock
sent MPs a study undertaken by the Royal Society describing testing in other countries. Outraged by Peacock's obstruction, Greg
Clark told Duncan Selbie to answer the question. In a jargon-
infected reply, Selbie disputed the accuracy of the SAGE minutes,
and denied that testing and tracing was abandoned because there
was no capacity.

Clark was angry. PHE's failure to publish the evidence about its
testing policy, he wrote, was 'unacceptable'. To restrict testing to
hospitals, he stated, meant that no one knew where the virus was
spreading and who was infected. He suspected that PHE's refusal
to explain meant that 'no rigorous assessment was in fact made by
PHE of other countries' approach to testing. That would be of profound concern since the necessity to consider the approaches taken
by others with experience of pandemics is obvious.'

His irritation was aggravated by Sharon Peacock's proposal to
order 21 million Chinese-produced home-testing kits done by a
finger-prick. In a blaze of publicity, PHE said they would be distributed by Amazon, Boots and other retailers. Whitty's scepticism
proved justified. The product proved to be unreliable and was not
ordered.

The Department of Health's self-confidence was beginning to
unravel. Not only had testing been abandoned but the media was
filled with complaints that hospitals feared an insufficient supply
both of PPE and of ventilators for ICU patients. The government
had changed its advice issued on 1 March. Moving from the 'containment' stage to 'delay', all those infected were asked to
self-isolate.

Among the outside experts condemning the government was
Mark Woolhouse, the professor of epidemiology on Scotland's
SAGE. In an increasingly confusing pattern of contradictions,

Woolhouse rejected Greg Clark's protest about the lack of testing. 'I think the focus on simply the number of tests,' said Woolhouse, 'is extremely unhelpful, and setting targets based on numbers is quite unhelpful. What is crucial is a strategy to which the testing contributes. Why are you using these tests, and what is the goal of that strategy? Some strategies that might be very effective require relatively small amounts of testing and others require extremely large amounts of testing, so it is not the numbers of the tests that count.'

Woolhouse's contribution coincided with Ferguson's latest prediction. In the space of two days, he reassessed the numbers who were infected from 100,000 to 300,000. Ferguson still assumed that the number of cases was doubling every five days. By the end of the following week, about 1 million people would be infected. 'Unless we radically change direction,' warned Clark, 'we will not know where those 1 million cases are.'

The public disagreements fuelled public concern. Governments in Europe had become starkly interventionist. Large public gatherings were banned in Berlin; schools were being shut in Spain and Greece; Ireland had cancelled St Patrick's Day parades; France announced school closures; and Portugal and Spain had ordered complete lockdowns on 14 March. SAGE's behavioural scientists warned ministers that the public would lose trust in the government if measures imposed abroad were not adopted in Britain. 'Not pursuing such routes,' they advised, 'needs to be well explained.' Yet other behavioural scientists doubted that the public would obey restrictions and certainly not a lockdown.

Whitty and Vallance had delayed signalling the whole danger to the public. But on 12 March, they had suggested that the threat level be increased to 'high'. (Germany declared the level 'high' on 17 March.) And they advised Boris to hold his nerve. They were supported by Ian Boyd, a professor of biology and a former government chief scientific adviser. The public, said Boyd, were not ready for a lockdown: 'I think some politicians would have loved to have reacted earlier but in their political opinion it probably wasn't feasible because people wouldn't have perhaps responded in the way they eventually did.' 'Herd immunity', agreed Boyd, was the best policy with warnings to the elderly and vulnerable. 'The only way to stop this epidemic is indeed to achieve herd immunity,' agreed John Edmunds. At the time, Edmunds did not openly criticise SAGE's secrecy and endorsed the credibility of Ferguson's models.

Whitty and Vallance refused to be panicked and follow Europe. Both, however, realised their mistake in initially suggesting they were dealing with a flu pandemic. Covid-19's symptoms were different. Reports from Italy showed it lasted longer and, unlike flu, children were probably not carriers. 'You would normally expect most of the outbreaks to be associated with schools,' Whitty explained, 'yet in the global literature at the moment there is only one documented outbreak.' The evidence for closing schools, said Whitty, 'is quite weak'. Closing schools until there was a 'major epidemic', they advised, would be 'highly disruptive and present an unequal burden to different sections of society'. Parents, especially the poor and those employed by the health service, would have to take on childcare duties or else hand them over to grandparents, recognised as the most vulnerable to Covid and in need of special protection. 'We're not going to trigger draconian measures now,' Boris agreed.

Following the behavioural scientists' advice, Boris had addressed the nation that afternoon. Flanked by Whitty and Vallance, he did not hold back. Adopting Churchill's 'Darkest Hour' tone, he said 'I must level with you, level with the British public, many more families are going to lose loved ones before their time . . . The best scientific advice is that this is now not just to attempt to contain the disease as far as possible, but to delay its spread and thereby minimise the suffering . . . This will help us slow the disease and save lives. The most important task will be to protect our elderly.' Those with symptoms were asked to isolate for seven days. Echoing the scientific advice, he repeated that 'banning major public events such as sporting fixtures . . . will have little effect on the spread' and there would be no lockdown as in Europe. 'So the most dangerous period is not now but some weeks away depending on how fast it spreads.' He did not rule out the gradual introduction of more draconian steps 'at some point in the next few weeks'. At the end, Boris was asked whether he feared catching the virus. With a smile, he replied, 'I am washing my hands, that's the crucial thing.'

Overnight, despite 70,000 enjoying another day at Cheltenham races, the public began to ignore the government's relaxed policies. After the Premier League suspended all games, Jenny Harries was repeatedly asked by Corbyn why Britain was taking a different approach from the rest of Europe. Her answers were unconvincing. On Sky TV, Vallance explained that herd immunity could be an 'important part of controlling [the virus] in the long term'. Experts, he said, estimated that about 60 per cent of the UK's 66 million population would have to contract the virus for effective immunity. In another interview with the BBC, Vallance described the disadvantage of total lockdown: 'If you suppress something very, very hard, when you release those measures, it bounces back and it bounces back at the wrong time.' He added: 'Our aim is to try to reduce the peak, broaden the peak, not suppress it completely; also, because the vast majority of people get a mild illness, to build up some kind of herd immunity so more people are immune to this disease and we reduce the transmission, at the same time we protect those who are most vulnerable to it.' In a conference call that day with health ministers of the G7 countries, Hancock asked the Italian health minister whether Italy was pursuing herd immunity. Brusquely, the Italian replied that sacrificing thousands of excess lives was unacceptable, especially in Lombardy's care homes. There, the fatalities were already horrendous. Hancock was in no doubt about the risk to the elderly. Fearful of the image of ruthlessness, Hancock denied on TV that evening that the government had adopted a herd-immunity plan.

That same night, the public was introduced to a phenomenon which would become increasingly common over the following weeks. Just as Boris emphasised his reliance on scientists, other scientists bitterly disagreed with his trusted advisers. Professor John Ashton, the seventy-two-year-old former regional director of public health for north-west England, denounced Vallance and Whitty on BBC TV for failing to advise Boris to impose a complete lockdown over Britain. 'I don't know where to start really,' he opened. 'I'm embarrassed by the situation in this country. This talk of four stages – and we're now moving on from the containment thing – we've lost the plot here. We haven't taken the action we should have taken four or five weeks ago.' Ashton also damned a herd-immunity strategy as 'pathetic' and 'clinically negligent'. The policy, he warned, would lead to 'huge numbers dying and cata-strophic consequences for the NHS'.

Ashton's qualifications compared to Vallance's and Whitty's were thin. He was not an epidemiologist and he had no deep experience of infectious viruses. Within the profession, Ashton's credentials were challenged. 'The plans are sensible,' said Professor Keith Neal, an emeritus professor in the epidemiology of infectious diseases. 'It is very easy to say more needs to be done but there is little evidence to make any decision which would help contain the spread of the virus.' Ashton, according to Neal, was speaking with the benefit of hindsight. Five weeks earlier, no one had foreseen that Italy would be the centre of the virus, or that tens of thousands of untracked cases would so rapidly spread across Europe. Nor that it would spread so fast across the whole of Britain. Total containment in Brit-ain, the epidemiologist knew, was impossible. Lockdown, added Johan Giesecke, Sweden's virus expert, would do little to prevent the spread of infection and just delay the inevitable – 'just pushing the deaths into the future' was his phrase. By the end of a year, he speculated, most countries would have a similar number of deaths. Professor Matt Keeling, a professor of life sciences, agreed: 'Hind-sight is a wonderful thing when it comes to looking back at epidemics. It is always easier to say that we could have done some-thing slightly different.' Concerned by the outbreak of scientists' warfare, Hancock wrote in a newspaper article, 'We have a plan based on the expertise of world-leading scientists . . . Herd immun-ity is not a part of it. That is a scientific concept, not a goal or a strategy.'

Whatever the warnings, Boris was determined to let life con-tinue as normal. SAGE's advice that outdoor events should not be curtailed matched his own bulldog spirit that the British would not be cowed by any foe. While the Stereophonics played to 15,000 fans over the weekend in Cardiff, he hosted a baby-shower party with Carrie at Chequers for about ten people. That was his last hurrah. On Monday morning, 16 March, he realised that the world had irrevocably changed. The public were no longer prepared to share his appetite for risk or hold their nerve in the face of such uncertainty. Polling showed that two-thirds of people were already avoiding bars and public transport. Airlines were slashing services as people refused to fly. Few wore masks after scientists downplayed their effect. Six hundred academics openly protested about the government's refusal to impose social distancing. They also questioned the scientific credibility of 'behavioural fatigue'. That morning, the mood changed. His inclination to take risks abruptly ended.

Using fresh data from Italy, Neil Ferguson had produced over the weekend new predictions. If the government continued to rely on herd immunity, he reported, 1 per cent of those infected would die, meaning 510,000 people. If the government adopted a policy of 'mitigation', and 'even if all patients were able to be treated, we predict there would still be in the order of 250,000 deaths in GB, and 1.1–1.2 million in the US.' However, with lockdown or 'suppression', he estimated the number of deaths to be 20,000 'or fewer' because the peak was due in two to three weeks and thereafter pressure on hospitals would fall. In reality, the infection had just reached the peak.

In the first serious proposal for lockdown in SAGE, Ferguson forecast that almost one-third of the over-eighties who were infected would be hospitalised and 71 per cent would need intensive care using ventilators. The hospitals would be overwhelmed by at least eight times the usual admittance. Not surprisingly, Vallance and Whitty were shocked by these new projections. Both knew that modelling created serious uncertainties but Ferguson had raised the stakes. Television reports of catastrophe in northern Italy showed harassed doctors being forced to take instant life-or-death decisions. The emotional impact was truly horrific. SAGE's members feared that the underfunded NHS would inevitably run out of

ICU beds and ventilators. Britain had to be protected from similar anguished scenes.

No one on the committee questioned Ferguson's forecast. As they rushed to protect Britain from the horrors seen in Italy, no one mentioned that ventilators were rarely used for the elderly because the patients were often too frail to cope with such an invasive procedure; or that most of those with underlying bad health were destined to soon die from some other cause.

SAGE's secrecy meant that rival modellers would only become aware of Imperial's work later. 'I am surprised that there has been such unqualified acceptance of the Imperial model,' said Sunetra Gupta, a theoretical epidemiologist who led a modelling team in Oxford. Gupta's study disputed the reliance on the tests for antibodies to decide who had immunity or resistance to the virus. She concluded that 68 per cent of Britons were already infected and therefore the projected 510,000 deaths was wrong. In her opinion, fewer than one in 1,000 of those infected would need hospitalisation. The vast majority would suffer mild or even no symptoms, and the death rate would be far lower than Ferguson predicted. Rather than waste money on the NHS, she recommended that people should avoid crowds and that the economy should not be shut down.

Gupta was not alone. The maverick pandemic forecaster at Stanford University, John Ioannidis, called the data collected by Ferguson 'utterly unreliable'. One day, he claimed, it would be dismissed as 'an evidence fiasco'. On the *Diamond Princess* cruise ship, a Covid 'hothouse' of high-risk older people, only 1 per cent had died. The Covid threat, he concluded, was exaggerated. The Swedish government took a similar view.

Anders Tegnell, an epidemiologist and Sweden's chief medical officer, favoured herd immunity. Researchers at Uppsala University told him that on the basis of Imperial's model up to 45,000 Swedes would die from the virus by the end of April if the country relied on herd immunity and not a lockdown. 'The main problem that the Imperial paper has,' Tegnell decided, 'is that it underestimates the number of cases that are light or not severe and that do not bring people to the healthcare system.'

The Cambridge University statistician David Spiegelhalter was almost as sanguine on the BBC's *More or Less* programme. He did not challenge the disease's virulence but suggested it might compress the annual flu death rate into a few weeks – putting intense pressure on hospitals – with the only 'extras' coming from non-vulnerable groups. Yet more scepticism was expressed by a former NHS pathologist, John Lee. He suggested the deaths of elderly people were differently recorded in every country. How many, he asked, were actually dying 'of' Covid-19 rather than of another illness with Covid on top?

Connoisseurs of academic backbiting could enjoy the professional squabble. Eight scientists contacted by the Science Media Centre rubbished Gupta's study, though others hedged their bets. To answer the doubts about his model, Ferguson explained, 'I'm conscious that lots of people would like to see and run the pandemic simulation code we are using to model control measures against Covid-19. To explain the background – I wrote the code [thousands of lines of undocumented C] 13+ years ago to model flu pandemics.'

On 16 March, the death toll in England was seventy-one. Over the previous three days, the sharp rise in hospital admissions confirmed that the virus had taken root. Vallance told MPs that 20,000 deaths would be 'a good outcome'. SAGE would later be criticised for not recommending the lockdown on that day. Whitty and Vallance would reply that the restrictions applied on 16 March were aimed towards the lockdown. But they did not go further. Boris was grateful. The idea, he said, of taking away the ancient, inalienable right of freeborn people of the United Kingdom to go to the pub, would be a huge wrench.

In a sign that Boris finally understood the inadequacy of the Whitehall machine, he summoned a meeting of ministers and key officials which would thereafter gather at 9.30 a.m. every day. Included were Hancock, Gove, Sunak, Vallance, Whitty and Cabinet Office specialists plus Sedwill and Lee Cain. For the first time, Simon Stevens and others from the Department of Health became directly involved with the prime minister. Stevens and Boris had been contemporaries at Balliol and Stevens had been a guest at

Boris's wedding to Allegra. Notably absent were Sharon Peacock and Yvonne Doyle. Boris understood PHE's notable failure to painstakingly monitor the development of the infection in Italy over the previous month. For the first time, questioning, cajoling and deciding, Boris chaired the semblance of a War Cabinet. Boris took charge, ousting the Department of Health. Michael Gove and the Cabinet Office were the supremos.

Later that afternoon on the 16th, after a Cobra meeting, Boris held a televised press conference to sound a more strident warning. The virus, he said, had reached a 'fast-growth stage' and was doubling every five or six days. He did not mention Ferguson's prediction that it would peak at the end of April. No one could tell Boris that the peak of infection was already occurring. That would be calculated later, after the peak of deaths would be fixed on 8 April.

People, Boris said on TV, should avoid pubs, clubs and theatres. Those with the symptoms should isolate for fourteen days and everyone else should stop non-essential travel and work at home if possible. Since the pressure on hospitals would intensify, he announced, he was 'pushing very hard' to increase tests, especially of NHS staff. To answer the outcry that the underfunded NHS lacked sufficient ventilators, he had scrambled an appeal to industry for help. At the time, most of the public grasped the growing danger. Those in doubt would have been convinced the following day.

Overnight, PHE and SAGE's experts realised that their data was inadequate. Ferguson arrived in Downing Street to warn ministers personally that Britain was just two weeks behind Italy. Over the previous three days, he finally acknowledged, the doubling rate of infection had risen to two to three days. Boris returned to the TV briefing room.

Speaking from behind a placard stating 'Stay Home, Protect the NHS, Save Lives', Boris spoke again in 1940 tones: 'We must act like any wartime government and do whatever it takes to support our economy,' he told the country. 'Yes this enemy can be deadly, but it is also beatable – and we know how to beat it and we know that if as a country we follow the scientific advice that is now being given we know that we will beat it. And however tough the months ahead we have the resolve and the resources to win the fight. And, to repeat, this government will do whatever it takes.' Then, with Sunak, he announced unprecedented help to enable working Britons avoid loans, get tax holidays and cash grants for businesses and individuals which would eventually benefit nearly 10 million employees. Wall Street had fallen about 30 per cent to its lowest point since 2008. Financial disaster was beckoning.

In the Department of Health there was increasing activity. Ferguson's forecast that eight times more ICU beds would be needed was alarming. (Later, he would confusingly say that if lockdown had been introduced earlier, England had sufficient ICUs. But there never was a shortage of ICUs.) The headline inspired by Ferguson was that 2 million Britons would need hospital beds – and the NHS had barely 100,000. Many had been awed by the TV reports of China building a huge hospital in Wuhan 'in ten days' (although in fact it took longer). Simon Stevens and the executives at the NHS headquarters decided that the British could do the same. The empty ExCeL Centre in Docklands was appropriated to build a 4,500-bed facility under the army's command. Nine days after Matt Hancock's announcement, the first Nightingale Hospital was opened in London by Prince Charles on 3 April. Eight more would follow across Britain. To match another of Ferguson's forecasts, the government sought 30,000 ventilators. Provisionally, the department ordered 18,000 and finally bought 2,000 through a procurement programme with a budget of £454 million. Simultaneously, within twelve days, the government assembled a network of sequencing centres and analysis groups to understand how the virus was spreading, how it could be controlled and to begin to develop a vaccine.

*

The most important element at that moment was hospital capacity. The Department of Health's priority was to empty the hospitals of non-urgent patients. The largest category were the 30,000 elderly and chronically ill occupying about one-third of the NHS's beds. In past years, NHS administrators had been plagued by the so-called bed-blockers. Unable to persuade local authorities to find suitable care homes, they unnecessarily occupied hospital beds. Now, the emergency demanded that they be ejected.

On 13 March, PHE had withdrawn items of critical advice: that asymptomatic patients could not spread the infection; and that it was 'very unlikely that anyone receiving care in a care home or the community will become infected'. Instead, care homes were urged to 'review' their visiting policy. Obeying SAGE's behavioural scientists, PHE still resisted ordering old people to remain isolated from their relatives.

About 418,000 people in England were living in 11,109 care homes (plus about 4,400 nursing homes) cared for by 1.47 million staff. Over 90 per cent of the care homes were privately owned, subject to control by the Care Quality Commission, an inglorious quango, and local authorities. None were obliged to obey any government regulations for the provision of PPE or staff training. In hindsight, Ferguson would say that he assumed that government policy was to shield care homes and particularly the most vulnerable 'as the top priority'. That had been Boris's assurance on 12 March: 'The most important task will be to protect our elderly and most vulnerable people during the peak weeks when there is the maximum risk of exposure to the disease and when the NHS will be under the most pressure.' But his promise had not been implemented by Whitehall. The government had merely advised the 1.5 million people in England identified as clinically vulnerable to avoid Covid by isolating for twelve weeks. Nothing more.

On 17 March, Amanda Pritchard, the NHS's chief operating officer for England, instructed hospital trusts to discharge urgently all 'medically fit' patients as soon as it was clinically safe, but ideally within three hours. Her directive was endorsed by Hancock, 'to allow the NHS to do what it needs to, and help move people out of hospital as soon as possible to get them back home with the right support'. Some would say that Hancock approved only after consulting Boris.

Pritchard's rapid implementation of the 'discharge to assess' model was targeted to empty 15,000 acute beds by 27 March, and later another 10,000. Even that timetable would be criticised by SAGE's scientists. Immediate action, they warned, would not stop London's ICUs being overwhelmed. Testing patients for Covid was explicitly not required by the government before patients were discharged. The reason was simple: PHE could not provide 15,000 tests over the following ten days. The real danger was asymptomatic patients. Only a test could establish whether they were infected. There was no net to catch them.

Within a day, Pritchard's directive provoked uproar from care-home managers. Key rules, they warned, had been abandoned. 'Unless the NHS ups its game on this and gives us immediate access to the [PPE] we need,' said Martin Green, the chief executive of Care England, 'there will be no discharges from hospitals into care homes.' Green spoke for many who recognised the danger. 'There's a real problem with private care homes refusing to take patients back unless they've been tested for Covid,' a senior director at a London acute trust said. As the *Guardian* reported, the care homes' refusal was widespread. Quoting David Steedman, the manager of Arlington House care home in Sussex, the *Guardian* reported that despite having five empty rooms he had refused to accept people discharged from hospital: 'I'd be mad to let anyone into my home without a test showing they're free of the virus . . . It's my responsibility to keep safe the hugely vulnerable residents who are in my care already.' Steedman's concerns were widespread, yet ignored by many in the business attracted by the government's generous payments. Martin Green blamed Chris Whitty for the consequences: 'Whitty knew our residents are the most at risk but it was all about the NHS. He should've been watching what went on in care homes in Spain and Italy.'

The emergency Covid-19 Bill was introduced in the Commons on 19 March and became law on 25 March. Hospitals were relieved of their obligation to conduct 'eligibility assessments' and the government committed itself to fund all 'out-of-hospital' support packages during the emergency – an inducement to irresponsible care-home owners. The law removed the legal protection for patients to be safely discharged. The requirement to test patients before discharge would be reintroduced on 15 April.

The image later conjured by the *Financial Times* that 25,000 infected patients were dumped into the homes was disputed by Chris Hopson, the chief executive of NHS Providers. The representative of most of England's hospital trusts would claim 'only small numbers of asymptomatic Covid-19 patients may have been discharged into care homes . . . in the first few days after 17 March'. He assessed it was one in twenty, or at most three in twenty if community centres were included. 'Within one or two days [hospitals] quickly became aware of the risk and had developed new agreed discharge arrangements.' Thereafter, he asserted, if a patient could not be tested, they would be isolated in the care home. The department's initiative was a success. Within one week, about 40 per cent of hospital beds were empty.

Within twenty-four hours of Pritchard's directive, Patrick Vallance was under renewed pressure. Without testing, he had no idea about the extent of the infection. Ferguson's predictions, his prime source of information, had pronounced that the 'R' rate of infection was between 2.4 and 4, and would need to fall below 1 to stop the pandemic. Vallance dithered and then, alarmingly, Ferguson revealed he himself was self-isolating with the virus. 'There's a lot of Covid in Westminster,' he said, the day after his Downing Street presentation. Soon after, he tweeted that the virus was more transmissible than he had thought.

The conflicts and uncertainty among the SAGE scientists and those outside should have given Cummings good reason to reconsider his belief that scientists would make better Civil Service administrators than arts graduates. If he had any doubts, they should have been dispelled at the SAGE meeting the same day, at which Cummings asked why the lockdown had not started. (His critics would complain he was interfering. Others viewed his attendance as vital in order to elicit information for the prime minister.) Vallance hesitated. John Newton, a senior executive at PHE, later supported Vallance: 'The infection was entering the exponential growth phase. At this point, access to limitless testing would have made no difference. The decision to enter lockdown would have been the same and would have been taken at the same time.' Professor Keeling, a professor of life sciences, agreed: 'The early assumption was that lockdown probably was not sustainable for more than four to five weeks . . . Lockdown more than a week before we did would have been very difficult to put through . . . We vastly underestimated the general public and how reasonable they can be in the face of such an outbreak.'

Amid all that competing advice, Boris relied on Vallance. 'I think the government have listened to the advice of SAGE very carefully and followed it,' Vallance would say. Asked whether there was any 'significant disagreement between the government and their scientific advisers on anything material', Vallance replied 'No.' But in truth, the prime minister, who was never in total control, surrendered even more to his scientific advisers.

Contrary to his libertarian instincts and under public pressure, on 20 March he agreed to do what he called 'extraordinary'. He ordered hospitality, entertainment and leisure centres to close, banned foreign travel and closed the schools. He no longer had any choice. People were staying at home and parents were keeping their children from school. He also advised Britons abroad to return home. Once again, Foreign Office officials proved themselves incompetent. In India, while German nationals were swiftly repatriated, the British acting high commissioner in Delhi was cursed by desperate British tourists, especially those stranded in Goa, as particularly unhelpful.

The pleas for help by abandoned tourists was drowned out by NHS staff complaints about shortages of PPE. As global demand soared, every country competed for the same products manufactured in Asia. Unlike other countries, Britain no longer had a large-scale textile industry to produce PPE. The NHS's staff protests were brushed aside by Jenny Harries. The few problems in deliveries, she said, had been 'completely resolved' and 'the supply is there' provided by 'an entirely separate PPE oversight and supply chain' in the Department of Health.

The ultimate responsibility was arguably Chris Wormald's, the Department of Health's permanent secretary. Wormald preferred later to shy away from fully answering questions about PPE and the stockpiles and deflected probing on a range of other critical issues of how the health and social care sectors responded to Covid-19 to other officials and advisors. Tiger Eye protectors bought in 2009 and flimsy plastic gowns bearing a 2016 sell-by date were declared unsuitable, but he said nothing. Nor did he personally answer the complaint of Christopher Nieper, the chief executive of a women's fashion company, whose offers to manufacture reusable gowns for front-line workers were ignored. 'We've gotten nowhere at all, absolutely nowhere,' Nieper said after approaching Deloitte, placed in charge of the government's gown procurement under Michael Gove and Theodore Agnew in the Cabinet Office. 'I proposed the exact gown, exact fabric but they're not interested in a reusable product, only interested in disposables,' he said, adding that Deloitte's head of gown procurement 'didn't know how much fabric was required to make one garment'. Jin Sahota, the £200,000-a-year chief executive of Supply Chain Co-ordination Limited, appeared to have disappeared, leaving Simon Stevens to tell MPs that there were sufficient national supplies of PPE – 397 million pieces had been distributed by the army – but he could not explain why commercial procurement and distribution was failing. The media and hence the public were unimpressed by the excuses.

Britain was grinding to a halt. Unusually, the Queen urged the country to unite in face of the crisis, and retreated to Windsor to be joined by the ninety-eight-year-old Prince Philip, who arrived by helicopter from Sandringham. The police were given draconian powers to detain the sick and force the healthy off the streets. Long queues snaked outside supermarkets whose shelves were already bare; school exams were cancelled and interest rates cut to 0.1 per cent, the lowest in the Bank of England's 326-year history.

On 23 March, unaware that his appeals for social distancing, washing hands and closures of social venues had already reduced the infection rate, Boris finally bowed to public pressure and announced a total lockdown. (He refused to use the word 'lockdown' itself, which he thought was 'draconian' and implied 'captivity'.) The nation, he hoped, would rally to yet another TV address with a promise of support, sorrow for those who would die, and an appeal for unity.

'From this evening I must give the British people a very simple instruction – you must stay at home. No prime minister wants to enact measures like this. But at present there are just no easy options. The way ahead is hard, and it is still true that many lives will sadly be lost.' With testing and new vaccines, he said, the virus would be beaten and Britain would return to normal in three months. Unlike leaders in some other European countries, he did not close down the economy. People were expected to continue working from home or in their office. Builders and others could continue to work in the open. He ended with a dose of optimism: 'You are invincible.'

On lockdown day, around 70 per cent of those polled approved of the government's conduct, but Boris was immediately under attack from familiar critics: either for leaving it too late or failing to keep his nerve.

Jeremy Hunt led the charge that the government's response had systemically failed. Had SAGE's advice been published in January, Hunt said, an army of other scientists combined with parliamentary scrutiny could have challenged the abandonment of test, track and trace, and the behavioural assumptions which delayed lockdown. 'We cannot know for certain, but the result may well have been better subsequent advice and many lives saved,' he judged. He would be reprimanded by Chris Whitty for misrepresenting some facts.

Others disagreed. 'I would characterise lockdown,' commented Mark Woolhouse, 'as a panic measure; it was something we did in the UK and was done around the world because we could not think of anything better to do given the information we had available . . . the costs of lockdown may be considerably worse than the disease itself.' Carl Heneghan, the director of the Centre for Evidence-Based Medicine at Oxford University, agreed. The lockdown, he said, was likely to do more damage than the virus. Too much attention was being given to models that often proved to be 'some way out' and there was insufficient testing. Sunetra Gupta criticised the lockdown as a mistake.

Comparisons were quickly made with Germany, which had announced lockdown the previous day – to start the same day as the UK – six days after France where over 1,000 people had already died. Unlike Italy, Spain and France which forced people to stay inside, Germany adopted Sweden's approach, warning people to take care rather than imposing criminal fines on those who left their homes. The difference between Britain and Germany, highlighted by the government's critics, was Germany's comprehensive testing scheme established many years earlier.

That day, Britain announced 136 deaths while Germany reported eighty-three deaths. In total, 802 people had died in Britain, although the official figure was still 336 deaths. Unlike other European countries, British statisticians would honestly revise the death toll. The virus in Germany was not as widespread and the infection rate was starkly lower than Britain's among the elderly but higher among the young who did not die.

Sir John Bell, Regius Professor of Medicine at the University of Oxford, did not believe that Germany's lower mortality was linked only to testing. Germany, he noted, experienced a particularly virulent coronavirus outbreak in 2018–19. Possibly the legacy was a T-cell immunity from Covid-19. 'There is something fundamentally different about Germany which to be honest I don't understand because they have had a pretty easy go of it. I don't think it can all be attributed to the quality of their healthcare system,' he would comment. He also compared London's much higher population density compared to Berlin and other German cities.

'Lockdown Britain' was the *Daily Mail*'s headline, reporting that Spain was about to overtake Italy's 1,444 deaths in just two days and Britain would imminently experience the same. Convoys of trucks carrying coffins through Madrid's empty streets to overflowing crematoria foretold what could happen in Britain. In this context, confidence in Boris was eroded by those scientists excluded from SAGE, who questioned their competitors' advice. The critics blamed SAGE's secret membership and the confidentiality of their working papers for Boris's 'error of following the scientists' advice'. Boris, complained the academics, was 'weaponising' the scientists' advice to protect himself from criticism about delaying the lockdown, the government's reliance on Ferguson and the audacity to consider herd immunity. Boris by then had good reason to doubt Ferguson. On 25 March, the mathematician would predict that Britain's death toll would be 'substantially lower' than 20,000 and he forecast that most of the dead would have in any event died in 2020 from other causes.

Weeks later – with hindsight – Venki Ramakrishnan, the president of the Royal Society, pronounced 'There is often no such thing as following "the" science. Reasonable scientists can disagree on important points.'

That was precisely Boris's problem on the day Britain was locked down. He trusted the scientists but they did not trust each other.

Chapter 28

Covid II

Four days after the lockdown was imposed, Downing Street announced that Boris had 'mild' symptoms of Covid and would self-isolate. At around seventeen stone, he was particularly vulnerable to the virus. Shortly after 1 p.m., Dominic Cummings ran out of Number 10. He had heard that his wife Mary Wakefield was also suffering. That night, the two were fearful that if he also caught the disease, there was no one to care for their four-year-old son. Their solution was to drive 264 miles to Durham and stay in an isolated bungalow near his parents' home. By then, Carrie Symonds had left Downing Street. Soon after, Chris Whitty, Matt Hancock and Mark Sedwill also became victims of the virus. Amid coughing, they had earlier all spent an hour together listening to Neil Ferguson in a closed room in Number 10.

Isolated in his private flat, Boris defiantly refused to concede to any illness. Over the next six days, as he struggled to control his government's response to the virus, meetings and discussions were held by video and telephone. Often, the iPads malfunctioned and the replacement iPads also failed to work. Coughing and sweating, he remained alone in his room, with food left outside the door. No one came to clean the flat or to personally check his condition. Doctors spoke to him on video links while his spokesmen and ministers did not mention his deteriorating health. Statistically, he was not in danger. Only 5 per cent of those infected, the government statisticians had calculated, would need hospitalisation. At 8 p.m. on Thursday 2 April, he was seen tieless and washed-out on

Number 10's doorstep, clapping with the nation for NHS staff. After one minute, he rushed back into his flat exhausted. That day, 563 deaths were reported. 'It's a sad, sad day,' said the prime minister.

On Friday, his condition sharply worsened. Stubbornly, he refused a doctor's advice to decamp immediately to hospital. On Sunday 5 April, the doctor monitoring his health became seriously concerned. Without urgent treatment in hospital, he decided, Boris's life was in danger. By unfortunate coincidence, the Queen was to address the nation on television at 8 p.m. that evening, a rare event (the fourth such occasion during her reign, with the exception of the traditional Christmas Day broadcasts). Boris feared that if the news of his arrival in hospital broke before the Queen's broadcast, the importance of her address would be lost. Throughout that day, he delayed his departure to St Thomas's Hospital, just half a mile away. During those twenty-four hours, 621 Britons would die bringing the total to 4,934. In his debut TV appearance that morning, Keir Starmer, Labour's new leader, had called on the government to publish its 'exit strategy' from the lockdown. The peak of infection would come three days later.

Twenty-four million people watched the ninety-three-year-old monarch tell Britons from Windsor Castle, 'While we have faced challenges before, this one is different. This time we join with all nations across the globe in a common endeavour, using the great advances of science and our instinctive compassion to heal. We will succeed – and that success will belong to every one of us. We should take comfort that while we may have more still to endure, better days will return: we will be with our friends again; we will be with our families again; we will meet again.' Reminding people of Vera Lynn's famous wartime song hit a perfect tone.

Soon after the Queen finished her address, Boris was quietly driven by car – he refused an ambulance – across the River Thames to St Thomas's. Some reflected that if Marina had still been his wife, he would have been at hospital days earlier.

Within minutes of his arrival, the medical team were pumping him with anticoagulants, antivirals, antibiotics and litres of oxygen to save his lungs, weakened years earlier by a dose of pneumonia.

'An hour later,' a doctor subsequently told him, 'and you could have been dead.'

During that first hour, Downing Street's spokesman revealed that Boris was undergoing 'routine tests' as 'a precautionary step'. The spokesman issued a message from the prime minister: 'I'm in good spirits and keeping in touch with my team.'

On Monday, Boris was moved into intensive care. He was fighting for his life. It was touch and go whether he would need to be put onto a ventilator, implying at best a 50 per cent chance of survival. Pericles, he might have recalled, died of a plague that swept Greece in the fifth century BC. The Johnson family were told the truth during the day.

The news triggered another family drama at the Johnsons' farm on Exmoor. Isolated in their separate houses at Nethercote, Stanley and Rachel knew that over the next hours Boris's children should see their father, possibly for the last time. Since Marina refused to speak to Stanley, Rachel needed to make the call. Without a mobile signal, she wanted to use the landline in Stanley's house. An enormous argument erupted about Rachel entering the house. Her trips to London, she was told, risked importing the infection. She should stay away from Stanley's house. Eventually reason prevailed. Marina was given the news. Some of her and Boris's children, still estranged from their father because of his treatment of their mother, went to the hospital to say goodbye. 'It was a terribly scary time for the whole family,' recalled Rachel on LBC radio, 'particularly for his nearest and dearest – his children, his fiancée, everybody who loves him.'

In Downing Street, Boris's closest aides were shocked. Some cried. The news leaked to newspaper editors. 'I fear the worst,' sighed a supporter, convinced the end was just hours away. Obituaries were rapidly commissioned. Dominic Raab, as First Secretary of State and de facto deputy prime minister, assured the nation that Boris was 'in good spirits'.

For three days in intensive care, Boris was bombarded by oxygen and drugs. The ventilator stood ready. 'It was a tough old moment,' Boris later admitted. 'I won't deny it. They had a strategy to deal with a "death of Stalin"-type scenario. I was not in particularly brilliant shape and I was aware there were contingency plans in place.' Three days later, friends were told he had eaten a jacket potato and baked beans. He had survived. Seven days after his admittance to hospital, on 12 April, Easter Sunday, he was driven to Chequers to convalesce. Most people needed two months to recover. Ravaged and thinner, he spoke on TV that night about his gratitude to the NHS staff who had saved his life while 'putting themselves in harm's way, kept risking this deadly virus' and he praised 'so many millions and millions of people across the country obeying the lockdown and so protecting the NHS'. He then slept.

Symptomatic of the hatred felt by many towards Boris, especially among some ardent Remainers, the buzz on social chat sites during that night stated with certainty that the reports of his near death were phoney. Downing Street's news manipulators, some wrote, were creating a 'cult of personality' around a healthy man. Chris Lockwood, an *Economist* editor, tweeted 'something incredibly fishy about the whole business'. A. C. Grayling, the philosopher, tweeted 'Boris the Butcher of Downing Street'. Frances Coppola, an economist and passionate blogger, portrayed Boris's discharge on Easter Sunday as a stunt to draw a direct comparison with the resurrection of Jesus Christ. One scientist, describing Covid to MPs as 'a very deceitful virus', likened Boris to 'an invisible mugger'. To counter the defamers, Downing Street was relieved when Nurse Jenny McGee of St Thomas's told a TV station in New Zealand that she had been unfazed by personally caring for the prime minister. 'He absolutely needed to be there,' she insisted. 'He received the same care as all the other patients.' Chris Lockwood apologised for his tweet. Others didn't.

Ensconced in Chequers with Carrie, Boris called the Queen and then Donald Trump. 'It's like the old Boris,' Trump told the media in Washington. 'Tremendous energy, tremendous drive. He called me pretty close to when he got out the hospital. I think he's doing great. He's so sharp and energetic, pretty incredible. He's a friend of ours, a friend of mine.' Trump had not seen the reality. Exhausted, thinner and bedraggled, many wondered whether the near-death experience had drained the man of his mojo – and his grip. They would not be able to judge for some time.

Across the nation, city centres were deserted. Hotels, pubs and restaurants which normally would be bursting were shuttered. Churches were locked. Few cars were on the roads, only a handful of passengers travelled on a few trains, and Heathrow was operating a skeleton service for 5 per cent of normal landings. Property sales had been stopped and even burglaries were reduced. On the surface, Britain had closed down. The upside was an extraordinary outburst of community help. The very best of Britons' generosity exploded: the young were helping the old, and strangers were caring for their neighbours. A new national identity was being forged. There were other reasons to be cheerful, said the optimists: the number of deaths had peaked and was beginning to decline, the Oxford research group was confident about producing a vaccine, and the government had given £93 million to build a vaccine manufacturing centre near Didcot, Oxfordshire, to limit Britain's dependence on China.

Yet five days after Boris left hospital, the wider situation was grim. Over 10,000 people had died in Britain, and that figure was predicted to rise to 27,000, already classed as the worst in Europe. The failure to obtain sufficient PPE remained a daily scandal, exposing many NHS staff to unnecessary risk. The hospitals were a major source of infection. At least one hundred NHS staff had died, including retired doctors who had volunteered to return to work. The collapse of test and tracing featured daily in the media. The country was plagued by undetected sufferers and faulty tests, especially among NHS workers. The excess deaths among black, Asian and minority ethnic (BAME) people were prompting accusations of racism. Crass police enforcement of the lockdown had provoked outrage. Not only did the police urge snoopers to report those flouting the lockdown – over 200,000 snitchers would call the police – but the deployment of police drones in Derbyshire to shame visitors at local beauty spots, and the use of black dye at the 'Blue Lagoon' to deter sightseers, provoked screams against authoritarian abuse. The redemption was that 750,000 people had volunteered to help those suffering or vulnerable. The biggest disgrace was the fivefold increase in care-home deaths.

On 17 April, Matt Hancock, clearly exhausted, arrived at Chequers to participate in a video conference with other ministers and officials. Rumours of his imminent dismissal, authoritative predictions by the *Guardian* of the underfunded NHS being devastated by overcrowded hospitals, and the alarmists' insistence that Britain would suffer from insufficient ventilators, had all proven to be bogus. Even at the peak of admissions, British hospitals had never suffered the chaos seen in Italy, Spain, New York or even France, where patients were sent by train to Germany for treatment. Furious about the Department of Health's failure to provide even limited testing, Hancock had publicly staked his reputation on 3 April to build a system virtually from scratch for 100,000 tests a day by the end of the month. His pledge had followed two weeks of argument with Roche, the Swiss drug manufacturer, to supply Britain with reagents, a critical component for testing. The Germans had bought the lion's share of Roche's production. Threats by senior politicians persuaded Roche's managers on 1 April to share their production with Britain. Hancock's pledge had aroused scepticism not least from John Newton, PHE's director of public health, tasked to implement Hancock's target. Newton told Greg Clark's Commons committee that the target was Hancock's alone. Shocked that a minister could be deliberately estranged by a senior civil servant, Clark concluded that Newton's attitude was symbolic of the NHS's bureaucracy. Unspoken was the bureaucrats' dislike of Hancock's desire to be the public face of Covid. Constantly, he appeared at the daily press conference to pose as the safe pair of hands. Daily, he demanded that the department produce material for a new announcement. Not only did the hunt for a headline produce errors and inconsistency which undermined the public's trust, but Hancock lacked the reassuring stature to stand in the spotlight.

In Chequers, Hancock met a man who had changed. Boris had met the enemy and respected its potency. Despite the unavoidable effects of the sickness, his directives became considerably clearer. Curiously, Cummings was less involved. With Raab and Hancock, Boris finally took charge again.

During the Chequers video conference, Rishi Sunak's message was bleak. Britain's GDP, feared the Chancellor, would fall by 30 per cent. Government borrowing was ballooning towards £270 billion. Experts were predicting the biggest recession in 300 years. Unemployment was certain to soar. Propping up the economy through the furlough scheme would cost at least £40 billion and probably much more. Even Premier League football clubs and major accountancy firms were taking the taxpayers' money. If an end to the lockdown was not announced soon, the nation might become too accustomed to the comfortable subsidised lifestyle. The pressure to end the lockdown, said Sunak, was growing despite the dangers. This was a critical moment which could be decided only by Boris. Polls showed that the public was divided. Contrary to the behavioural scientists' predictions, the vast majority of the public had obeyed the warnings. Thereafter, people remained more fearful than had been expected and than appeared to be justified. To reverse the mood and mitigate people's ultra-caution would require potent messaging. An overriding complication was the scientists. They were more vocal and divisive than ever; but Vallance and Whitty had been consistent from the outset. The second wave, both had warned Boris, could be more dangerous than the first. Had he not been hit by the virus, Boris would probably have opted to reopen Britain. But he resisted the pressure. He was not yet ready to take that particular gamble. The Chequers meeting ended without Boris's usual optimism.

Complaints were beginning to spread, marginally chipping away at the government's credibility. Based on a PHE source, the *Guardian* reported that 'public health experts had been sidelined' about testing in mid-March. That was clearly untrue – PHE had 'self-sidelined' itself from testing. Relying on John Edmunds, Reuters reported that SAGE had not considered a lockdown until mid-March. In fact, it had been mentioned in February. Reuters also inaccurately reported that the 'government's medical experts' had feared in January that the virus would 'kill hundreds of thousands' but they had not told ministers 'until mid-March'. Hancock saw the first SAGE estimates in January and others throughout February, but had been cautioned by Vallance about reliance on models. Less publicity was given to the new doubts arising during April. Forty per cent of Covid sufferers, scientists now believed, were asymptomatic. That made Covid almost uncontrollable because if lockdown was lifted too early, each infected person without symptoms would on average unknowingly pass the virus to three other individuals.

In that fog of uncertainty, citing anonymous sources, newspapers reported the scientists' criticisms while the experts' own mistakes were minimised. Ferguson had estimated that almost a third of infected over-eighties could be hospitalised and 71 per cent could need critical care. In reality, in the second week of April just 3 per cent of those in critical care were aged over eighty. The experts' predictions of the causes of deaths also proved wrong. Most of the critically sick patients were developing multiple organ failure, requiring kidney dialysis and cardiac care. Few were well enough to be taken to ICUs for respiratory lung support. They died either in A&E or in specialist units. Only 10 per cent of people who died from the virus were admitted to ICUs. At the peak of the crisis over the Easter weekend, 40.9 per cent of acute beds in hospitals were unoccupied – about four times the normal number. None had foreseen that only 6 per cent of all Britons would become infected with the virus and fewer than 0.1 per cent of the population would die, one-tenth of Ferguson's projection.

Hancock's successes – building the Nightingale hospitals and obtaining ample ventilators – had turned out to be worthless. Storerooms were filled with unused ventilators. Instead, 10,000 oxygen masks developed by the Mercedes Benz Formula One facility in Brackley, Northamptonshire, were saving many lives. Only forty-one patients would ever use London's Nightingale hospital. The Nightingale hospitals in Birmingham, Bristol and Harrogate would remain completely empty.

'Something has gone very wrong,' said Carl Heneghan, director of the Centre for Evidence-Based Medicine. 'We would have expected to see an increase in viral pneumonia in people dying of coronavirus but we haven't.' The error costing billions of pounds was SAGE's reliance on a 'reasonable worst-case scenario'. No politician would dare question their credo that 'it is much better to have over-capacity than under-capacity'.

★

Hancock's department was accused of many mistakes, but none worse than the soaring deaths in care homes – thirteen times higher in Britain than in Germany. Long before the Department of Health issued the controversial directive of 17 March that untested hospital patients should be discharged to care homes, the institutions' managers and clinicians knew about the special danger of infection for the elderly. The risk was not only from the discharge of untested hospital patients, Hancock's officials knew, but the movement of agency staff between care homes. Additionally, some care-home managers were failing to properly train their staff to use PPE to prevent infection. On 25 March, Hancock had been warned in the Commons about temporary staff spreading the virus. Untrained care-home workers, he was told, could become infected and carry the virus to another care home and, at the end of the day, also infect their families. That was a particular danger in London, where 67 per cent of the staff were BAME and, a survey discovered, lived in overcrowded and intergenerational housing. Infected at home, they took the virus into the care homes. Hancock had ignored the problem. The reason became clear the following day, during the peak of infection.

Yvonne Doyle was asked by the Commons select health committee whether asymptomatic NHS staff could be transmitting the virus to patients. 'In theory,' she replied, but she did not know for certain. It is unknown when Boris was briefed about the uncertainty – and the threat.

Senior officials in the Department of Health had known about the danger for two years. A report from social care directors published in 2018 about the risks during a flu pandemic had high-lighted those who would be vulnerable. Front-line care workers, the department was told, would need advice about 'controlling cross-infection'. The following year, PHE published 'Infection prevention and control: an outbreak information pack for care homes'. Managers were urged to 'avoid moving staff between homes and floors'. Yet in 2020, the Department of Health's officials ignored all those warnings. Even in April, the department's 'Care Plan' – headed 'Controlling the spread of infection in care homes' – did not mention restricting staff movements. In the nature of questioning by parliamentary committees, Hancock was not asked by MPs whether and when he had been briefed about the dangers by Wormald or any other civil servant. Nevertheless, the care-home managers' outcry after 17 March did have an effect – but only two weeks later.

Officials in the department decided on 2 April that care homes should continue to accept infected people, but only if they could be isolated. The staff were also to be trained to use PPE properly. Negative tests, however, were 'not required', meaning that people without symptoms would not be tested although they could unknowingly be infected and spread the virus. The department's directive was deceptive. Testing was still limited and obtaining PPE was difficult for many care homes despite the government's promise on 13 March to provide free PPE. The department's guidance changed again on 15 April. Every patient, it advised, should be tested. With Hancock's initiative to increase tests, the homes' managers were also told to isolate every new arrival for fourteen days. Only two weeks later did officials belatedly recognise the danger presented by asymptomatic patients and staff. A special alert was issued on 15 May; but the guidance was not properly updated until 9 July. By then about 20,000 people had died in care homes, about 29 per cent of the residents.

In a further sign of the department's dysfunction, researchers tracking the virus's genome in six London care homes made an alarming discovery. Some care-home workers who transmitted the virus had been hired to cover for staff who were self-isolating expressly to prevent vulnerable patients becoming infected. As Boris would later say, too many care homes had not been following the procedures correctly. Telling that partial truth was denounced by care-home managers as 'outrageous'. They blamed the Department of Health for their calamity. Last in line for PPE and testing, the disaffected owners refused to accept that many deaths had occurred in badly managed care homes – where the staff were not properly supervised and trained, and newly arrived patients were not isolated. In 46 per cent of England's care homes, no patients would be infected by Covid. In about 60 per cent of homes there would be no deaths. Poor management in care homes had been quickly discovered by Care Quality Commission (CQC) inspectors. But within days, Martin Green of Care England noticed, 'They stopped their inspections and sat on their hands for weeks.' Kate Terroni, CQC's chief inspector, admitted that she had done no more than 'fifty inspections during lockdown'. There are 11,109 care homes in England.

'Unscrupulous' employers, the trade union UNISON discovered, 'are informing staff that PPE is not to be used until there are confirmed cases of Covid-19 in their workplace, which means they are carrying out close personal care without any protection'. The department's first explanation to care homes about the use of PPE was issued on 17 April and acknowledged as inadequate.

Under attack for the 17 March directive, Chris Hopson of NHS Providers, the group representing most hospital trusts, jumped to the NHS's defence. According to Hopson – a former director of HM Customs and Revenue and Granada Media – the official statistics showed that between one and three in twenty of the 25,000 discharged patients (i.e. between 1,250 and 3,750) went into care homes. Other senior NHS executives insisted that only 2.8 per cent of the 25,000 patients (i.e. 700) went into care homes. The remainder, the NHS insisted, went to homes in the community. Moreover, Hopson insisted, the number discharged into care homes was 40 per cent fewer between February and mid-April compared to January. 'The trust leaders we spoke to,' wrote Hopson, 'strongly resented the suggestion that they had systematically and knowingly discharged known Covid-19 patients to the home-care sector, at increased risk to those individuals and care-home staff.' Unconvincingly, he wrote, 'It is still not clear who is responsible for testing care-home residents and staff.' Hopson was contradicted by care-home managers describing hospital managers using intimidation to force the homes to readmit their infected residents. Even Hopson's limited admission contradicted Hancock's claim to have 'thrown a protective ring around care homes'. Sensitive to the department's early failures, care homes were increasingly inundated with guidance and directives. By 14 May, the department was still sending a fifteen-page letter to re-explain what should have been clear two months earlier.

In the Department of Health, Chris Wormald, the permanent secretary, rejected any criticism. So far as he was concerned, his department's orders to clear out the hospitals and not test the patients were approved and supervised by clinicians. The responsibility for preventing infection in care homes was placed on local authorities and the CQC, not Whitehall. And as for the constantly changing guidelines about testing and PPE – at least forty different versions of PHE guidance on suitable PPE had been issued – he made no excuses. Wormald did not explain why a PHE survey in mid-April warning his department about the danger of agency workers appeared to have been suppressed. It would finally be sent to care-home managers in mid-May.

Wormald also appeared unconcerned by the criticism of Martin Green, Care England's chief executive. Green highlighted that the delivery of PPE and testing had required management consultants and the army. Why, Green asked, could none of the thousands of Wormald's civil servants execute the task? And why had so little of the 'vitally needed' £3.2 billion specifically allocated by the government to care homes been spent? By June, only £194 million had been transferred by the local authorities authorised to dispense the money. Billions of pounds had disappeared in 'red tape and bureaucratic spaghetti', he complained. Green blamed Chris Wormald: 'He's invisible. Behind the scenes he has done absolutely nothing.'

Unknown bureaucrats did not interest the public. The headline that 40 per cent of coronavirus fatalities in England and Wales were in care homes was a recipe for fear. The impression was of people falling dead like ninepins. Hancock disputed the official data. He claimed only a quarter of deaths were in the homes. As the death rate rose, the public's trust in the prime minister and his government fell slightly further. Explaining the reason for the high death rate to the public became critical for the government's credibility. Once again, Lee Cain and Downing Street's communications staff failed. With Boris still convalescing at Chequers, his contact with Downing Street was limited. Every day, he spent hours sleeping and walking to restore his health. In the vacuum, Dominic Raab was focused on defeating the virus, not on defending political rivals. From Chequers, Boris did not issue directions to especially protect Hancock and his department from criticism. And neither Raab nor Cain took the initiative to convincingly explain the challenges to the public.

Without Boris firing demands, no one highlighted the reality of the death statistics. The death rate for those under forty-five was only 1 per cent of the total figure; 89 per cent of those who died were over sixty-five and over 90 per cent of them were suffering from other health issues.

Officially, 12,526 care-home residents died from the virus in England and Wales during the four months to May. Another 10,610 'excess' deaths from other causes were recorded in residential and nursing homes in that period. Explaining all the reasons for the excess deaths was difficult. Since many GPs refused to visit the homes and the homes were discouraged from sending residents to hospital, the managers defined the cause of death on the official certificates without any checks by doctors or pathologists. Some deaths were registered as coronavirus-related based on suspicion rather than proven by a test. Pertinently, Covid-related deaths included people who had died *with* Covid, as well as people who died *of* it.

In ethnic groups, the worst affected were BAME citizens. Those from the Caribbean were twice as likely to die as white people; Bangladeshis and Pakistanis were about three times more likely to die than white people. The Institute for Fiscal Studies reported several reasons, including living conditions, obesity and diabetes. University studies and NHS England reported the obese were three times more likely to die and that 25 per cent of Covid deaths were diabetic. Only 5 per cent of those who died did not have an underlying health issue. In stressing health or genetic reasons for the disproportionate deaths, PHE preferred not to explain that in some South Asian communities referred to, victims lived in overcrowded homes in England's inner cities, often did not speak English and occasionally, according to local PHE officials, ignored leaflets even when written in their own language. In Leicester and elsewhere, many low-paid employees felt compelled to continue working despite their infection with Covid. The reports did not highlight that high population density and social customs went hand in hand with high death rates. PHE was criticised for ignoring structural racism caused by the immigrants' poverty and low-paid employment. Chris Whitty said that no one knew the reason.

Increasingly, the staggering death rates in Britain, seemingly so much higher than those in continental Europe, aroused alarm and blame. Media headlines described chaos. Daily, the media reported the PPE crisis. Descriptions of hospitals on the brink and staff risking death rattled the prime minister. Britain, however, was not unique. Every European government was struggling to obtain protective equipment. Reliant on China, even Germany suffered severe shortages. Mismanaged procurement by the Department of Health made Britain's plight worse. Hundreds of British manufacturers had offered to make protective equipment. Ignored by the Department of Health, they were shipping PPE to Germany, Italy and Spain.

To produce a good news headline, Hancock announced on 18 April that an RAF plane would deliver a consignment of PPE from Turkey. Relying on his officials had been a mistake. Amid repeated delays, Hancock was blamed for not personally ensuring the gowns were loaded onto the plane. Eventually about 400,000 gowns arrived and, contrary to Twitter reports, they matched the approved standard. By then, few believed Hancock could deliver 100,000 tests at the end of the month. The government's credibility was again in doubt.

Belatedly, the convalescing Boris appointed Paul Deighton, a former Goldman Sachs banker and a key organiser of the successful London Olympics, as the PPE tsar. Had he sought to be better briefed, the prime minister would have made the appointment several weeks earlier. By early May, Deighton was overseeing a procurement team delivering 17 million pieces of equipment to 258 trusts on one day. That did not dispel the conviction that a vulnerable, paralysed nation, edging towards bankruptcy, was at the mercy of a leaderless government. Standing in for Boris, Dominic Raab adopted a low-key manner to avoid any whisper of a coup. The resulting image was a vacuum in Downing Street. Although after two weeks' convalescence Boris had still not recovered, he had no choice but to return to London.

Amid headlines of a man who had 'cheated death', was 'raring to go' and was 'taking back control', Boris entered Downing Street on 26 April through the back entrance. Pale-faced, breathing hard and his clothes hanging loose, his PR machine proclaimed 'We're beginning to turn the tide.' Cynics noted that Boris had adopted the title of Churchill's famous book about the Second World War. 'Absolutely no doubt we will beat it,' his statement added. 'We're stronger than ever before.' His optimism was belied by the facts.

Five weeks after the lockdown had been imposed, the economy was crippled. Government borrowing in April had surged to £62 billion, the highest monthly figure on record. Manufacturing had halved and the cost of lost growth was £2.7 billion every day. Airlines were haemorrhaging billions of pounds. Through the furlough scheme, the government was subsidising the wages of about 10 million people. With all the other recipients of state aid, over 26 million Britons were dependent on the state. Over 8 million children in state schools were not being adequately educated. About 2 million operations had been cancelled. Cancer patients remained untreated. High-street retailers faced oblivion in ghost city centres. Mass redundancies in retail and hospitality made high unemployment inevitable. Finding an uncontroversial solution that would be unanimously accepted was impossible. His Cabinet, Boris knew, was divided. Although all had been appointed to agree with him, some sided with the Chancellor that the lockdown should be relaxed with a rapid timetable to its complete removal. Restoring the economy was justified by the behavioural scientists' prediction that after five weeks, lockdown fatigue would start. They were supported by Nicola Sturgeon who demanded that the lockdown be eased.

Two obstacles overshadowed the national recovery. First, mobilising Whitehall to plan the recovery was hampered by Boris's mistrust of the Civil Service. The litmus test was an exchange with Mark Sedwill. 'Who is in charge of implementing this delivery plan?' Boris asked the Cabinet Secretary. There was silence until he asked Sedwill, 'Is it you?' Sedwill replied, 'No, I think it's you, Prime Minister.' Sedwill, he decided, had to go. To improve Downing Street's machine, Simon Case, a taciturn forty-one-year-old Whitehall butterfly who had regularly moved from one department to another, was brought in as the permanent secretary. A hint of Boris's desperation marked Case's promotion from managing Prince William's private office. As a historian, Case personified the conventional civil servant whom Gove and Cummings were determined to expel from Downing Street.

The second obstacle was the negative media. Over the past weeks, Lee Cain had been unable to explain constructively the government's dilemmas. The only respite was the birth of Boris's sixth child on 29 April. Called Wilfred Lawrie Nicholas, Downing Street explained the genesis of the names. Wilfred was after Boris's paternal grandfather, the drunken adulterer; Lawrie was Carrie's grandfather; but the origin of Nicholas seemed less clear. Boris had told Charlotte, his mother, that he would name the boy after Nick Wahl, her second husband. That news provoked uproar in Stanley's home at Nethercote. Any links with Charlotte were declared taboo. Then Boris declared that his son was named after Nicholas Hart and Nicholas Price, the doctors who had saved his life. In the aftermath, the temperature on Exmoor remained high. Postings on social media expressed anger against Boris and Stanley's other elder

children. Others questioned the circumstances of Wilfred's con-
ception in the summer of 2019, before Boris became prime minister
and when friends noticed tension between himself and Carrie. In
the extraordinary roller coaster of Boris's life – divorce, near death
and now an unmarried new father in Downing Street steering the
country though a crisis – few insiders could grapple with the
streams of unpublishable gossip.

After a twenty-four-hour lull, an opinion poll reported that the
government's popularity had fallen from 72 per cent in February to
58 per cent. Boris's hopes of rebuilding trust after Hancock
announced on 30 April that the 100,000 target had almost been
reached were dashed. Despite building fifty regional testing centres, seventy mobile units and three mega-laboratories from
scratch, there was no fanfare. Critics discovered that the '96,000
tests' had been inflated. After the total temporarily fell to 69,463
tests, Boris decided again that the government could not rely on
civil servants. Dido Harding, a former manager at the mobile-
phone company TalkTalk, was appointed to head test and trace and
report directly to Boris. She inherited Operation Charcoal, a trial in
the Isle of Wight of a new tracing app uniquely relying on self-
reporting which ignored local authorities. Experts had accurately
warned the civil servants responsible for pioneering the app that
excluding Google and Apple would make Boris's promise of 'a
world-beating operational system' by 1 June near impossible. With
untrained callers, poor management and technical glitches, the
operation would indeed be derided. The *Daily Mail* called it a 'shambles'. Other officials had approved a home-testing kit with a design
flaw: the swab sticks were too long to fit into the sample bottle.
Amid a myriad of plans for testing for antibodies, infection and
herd immunity, the worst news was that about 70 per cent of those
who tested positive showed no symptoms and most sufferers had
no antibodies. 'This is a disease where we are in the foothills of our
understanding,' Chris Whitty said on 30 April, and 'we are really
still only beginning to understand how we are going to combat it'.
His increasing wariness of scientists was matched by the schism
within the Civil Service.

Chris Hopson, the chief executive of NHS Providers, criticised Hancock's focus on 'an arbitrary number' of tests. 'Too much of April,' wrote Hopson, 'was wasted by focusing on the 100,000 tests by the 30 April target at the expense of other aspects of a clear strategy . . . The testing strategy, if there was one, got hijacked on the basis of just meeting that target when there were lots of other things that needed to be done.' Hopson denied the opinion of Patrick Vallance and WHO that testing and tracing was critical. Hopson also scoffed at Boris's next target – 200,000 tests a day. The disputes presaged the absence of any good news. Fearful of a second wave, the prime minister's only solution was to boost public confidence.

'We can now see the sunlight,' said Boris on 30 April on TV. The deaths that day, 674, suggested that the peak had passed. The total deaths, 26,711 so far, cast a shadow over the government but the R-rate of infection had fallen below 1. Although at least 4,000 people were newly infected every day, over 95 per cent were expected by Whitty to recover without obvious long-term problems. That opinion was contradicted by *Lancet*'s editor Richard Horton, who warned that 20 per cent of those infected would suffer 'severe ill-effects'.

Horton epitomised Boris's problem. His warnings in January that journalists were overdramatising the Wuhan outbreak were clearly discredited. To protect his reputation, he highlighted three months later three papers written by Chinese scientists which he had published online in the *Lancet* at the end of January, shortly after his original admonition to journalists. 'Those papers,' Horton wrote, 'were truly alarming and showed that the disease caused a serious fatal pneumonia . . . The authors of the papers were advocating the immediate provision of personal protective equipment and were urging the importance of testing and isolation.' Horton wrote about his particular anger that neither WHO nor the SAGE experts had recognised the danger at the time. His criticism was unrealistic but signalled the government's problem with self-righteous scientists.

As a fierce political critic of the government, Horton classed the

Department of Health's mistakes – the absence of testing, the failure to procure PPE and the multiple care-home errors – as entirely Boris's responsibility. There were other explanations.

The death rates in Britain, seemingly so much higher than those in Europe, aroused alarm and blame. Yet few questioned how other governments compiled their statistics. In Spain, a death from Covid only counted if it occurred in a hospital, was reported within twenty-four hours of death and was confirmed by a test. That rarely happened. Care-home deaths by Covid in Spain, Italy and Holland were ignored, as were many in France. If the disaster in the care homes was stripped out, Britain's high death rate was explained by the country's high population density and the spread of the infection across the whole country by the returning half-term skiers – unlike in Spain and Italy where the outbreaks were localised. Once the undercounting in Europe was taken into account, the British government was coping as well as most in Europe. But the headlines told a different story.

An alternative explanation about PPE also failed to reach the public. The extreme shortages of PPE exposed the calibre of the individual hospital trust's managers. Many were overpaid and underqualified. While good managers – for example at Chelsea & Westminster Hospital – had averted a crisis, other hospital trusts, notorious for their profligacy and debt, were stricken. Too many hospitals were stockpiling PPE while other hospitals suffered extreme shortages. 'Misuse and waste of PPE equipment,' commented Calum Semple, a professor of healthcare, had become endemic. 'We have kept a huge number of FFP3 masks in reserve for years, but at the current rate, they are being consumed too quickly as people are using them inappropriately. And this is a difficult message to get across.' The wasteful hospitals treated the advice that gowns could be washed and reused as heresy. Still smarting from the Brexit defeat and the Tory's thunderous election victory, Boris's enemies weaponised the Covid crisis as a proxy war. The next battleground was the timing to relax the lockdown.

The Times set the scene, urging the government to lift the lockdown. Just over three weeks after praising Boris for following the science, the newspaper published Matthew Parris's attack on Boris for being 'dishonest and cowardly' for 'hiding behind the science' and relying on Vallance to advise when relaxing the lockdown was safe. *The Times* believed quoting 'the science' was a tactic of 'obsessive secrecy'.

Neil Ferguson had just raised another alarm. Lifting lockdown in the near future, he warned, could cost 100,000 lives by the end of the year. 'Thousands will die,' agreed a group of surgeons, if the lockdown was lifted. Adding to the disquiet, Ferguson told MPs how he knew on 16 March that the epidemic was 'doubling every three to four days before lockdown interventions were introduced'. Dramatically, he added 'had we introduced lockdown measures a week earlier, we would have reduced the final death toll by at least a half'. Those sensational assertions were not challenged, despite being contradicted by the facts. On 16 March, relying on Ferguson, Boris had said at his press conference, 'And without drastic action, cases could double every five or six days'; and SAGE's minutes from their meeting on the same day did not record Ferguson recommending an immediate, complete lockdown or mention his disagreement with Vallance and Whitty. Inevitably, the contradictions did not register among the public. The growing tendency to blame Boris for delaying the lockdown for six weeks, after he had stood alongside Whitty and Vallance on the eve of lockdown with such command and authority, further eroded public trust.

While still feeling justified in imposing lockdown when he did, Boris was certainly torn about lifting it. The experts could not agree about the effect on new infections or even about the lockdown's value. This was a critical moment for Boris to confront both sides and crush the dissenters. Instead, he refused to address the disagreements and convincingly present his conclusion to the public. He decided not to announce a final decision. The result was damaging: a fearful public remained reluctant to go to work or use public transport.

Michael Levitt, the Nobel laureate scientist at Stanford University, blamed the lockdown for causing more deaths than it saved. Calum Semple agreed. 'I am quite pleased that we did not go for a knee-jerk shutdown in the three to four weeks before we did,' he said. 'That period allowed a degree of calmness and preparation to go on at a very important stage . . . The way the government managed information and society this time was far more sophisticated [than the 2009 flu outbreak] and prevented a phoney war and excessive health-seeking behaviour that could have caused an earlier overwhelming of GPs and A&E practitioners.' Karol Sikora, an oncologist, believed that most who died in the spring would have died by the summer anyway. 'It could end up that more people have died because of lack of medical care,' wrote Sikora, because 'facilities have been taken over for Covid. Sloppily, medics put Covid as a cause of death.' Sikora and other lockdown sceptics who were convinced that the virus was killing those who were in any event destined to die were contradicted by David Spiegelhalter, the respected British statistician. Spiegelhalter revised down his estimates of those who would have died during the year in the absence of Covid. The figure, he suggested, was somewhere between 5 and 15 per cent of all deaths. No one will know until the excess deaths over eighteen months have been calculated.

The dispute was fuelled by Sweden's refusal to lock down in favour of seeking herd immunity. By the end of May, Anders Tegnell, the state epidemiologist, estimated that 25 per cent of Swedes were immune, although rival scientists said it was just 8 per cent. No one knew whether the immunity would even last six months or how many needed to become infected to achieve herd immunity. If it took years, the virus might mutate and make immunity pointless. The price Sweden was bearing for the experiment was the highest death rate per capita in Scandinavia, and its economy was as badly hit as in neighbouring countries. Paradoxically for a lauded social democrat country, Sweden's care homes were suffering an exceptionally high death rate. Tegnell was particularly scathing about Ferguson's model which he said had predicted up to 45,000 deaths by 1 May. The actual number was 2,954 deaths. Others still endorsed Imperial's model as reliable.

Then on 5 May Ferguson was exposed for breaking the lockdown, by inviting to his house a married woman who travelled across London to meet him. He resigned from SAGE. 'I accept I made an error of judgement and took the wrong course of action,' he said. 'I deeply regret any undermining of the clear messages around the continued need for social distancing.' Piously, Matt Hancock said he was left 'speechless' about Ferguson's 'extraordinary' breach of the social distancing rules. Boris's critics claimed that Ferguson was a scapegoat. The story of his affair had been released on the day Britain overtook Italy for the highest number of deaths in Europe.

*

The following day, Boris stumbled. At his first Prime Minister's Questions since March he faced Keir Starmer, the newly elected Labour leader, in a semi-virtual House of Commons. Starmer, the fifty-seven-year-old former Director of Public Prosecutions, was a solid lawyer but not the finest legal brain at the Bar. In a typically courtroom manner, Starmer posed precise questions about the government's claim to have scored a 'success' in fighting the virus when Britain's record ranked among Europe's worst, and queried Hancock's failure to deliver 100,000 tests every day – they had fallen back to around 70,000. In the best of times, the great communicator could have easily swotted a lawyer reading his brief. Instead, Boris muffed his replies with bluster and failed to highlight that Starmer, even before the pandemic's peak on 5 April, had demanded that the government produce an 'exit strategy' from the lockdown. No one knew in early April how long the pandemic would last or any of the consequences. But with the latest YouGov poll putting the Tories at 50 per cent and Labour at 30 per cent, Boris felt unthreatened. The public still trusted him.

Making little allowance for Boris's illness, Matthew Parris returned to the attack: 'Is there anyone in the cockpit? It's time to ask whether Boris Johnson is up to the job . . . He was once noisier and bouncier, for sure, but was his ever a good, problem-solving mind? Can you remember any big dilemma of government he ever tackled and sorted? Any unpopular policy he ever won us over to?'

Clearly Parris had forgotten that Boris got Brexit done, won an eighty-seat majority and, contrary to predictions, the NHS had not collapsed but had performed brilliantly. Like so many armchair generals of hindsight, Parris misunderstood the crisis when he praised Vallance and Whitty as having fought a 'Good War', for transcending 'from faceless civil servants to our new overlords'. Both were vulnerable to criticism.

In his flat in 11 Downing Street, Boris was equally vulnerable and was still weak from his illness. The newborn baby cried during the night and Carrie believed Boris should be a modern father and change nappies. His sleep was constantly interrupted. His relationship with his other children and family continued to be troubling. Charlotte, his mother, was the rock but the pressure on the sick man was remorseless.

Tory MPs had become restless about his weak leadership – his poor performance at PMQs, his indecisiveness in the face of squabbling scientists, and the absence of a date to end the lockdown and reopen schools, already handicapped by the mistaken cancellation of all public exams. The Bank of England's prediction of the worst recession in 300 years with at least 2 million new unemployed rattled even the faithful. Fearing a second wave, instead of relaxing the lockdown Boris ordered Priti Patel to impose a fourteen-day quarantine for everyone entering Britain. The nation was baffled. Quarantine had been rejected on 13 March and, on Vallance's advice, Britain's borders were open throughout the height of the pandemic without even screening those arriving. The most informed guess was that only 0.5 per cent of those arriving in Britain on any day were infected with Covid. Boris's order confirmed that his grip was still loose.

Detached, he had overlooked the weakness of his education minister, Gavin Williamson. Throughout the lockdown, private school pupils were getting up to six hours of intensive education with teachers online per day. Most state school pupils had been effectively abandoned. Seemingly unconcerned about denying children their education, the National Education Union, the largest trade union of teachers, opposed online lessons except in 'exceptional circumstances'

on the grounds that it would be unfair to the 7 per cent of children
without access to the Internet. The teachers refused to consider
allowing those few disadvantaged children into school and
obstructed any inventive alternative. Across Europe, most teachers
and their trade unions had worked with governments to reopen
schools with social distancing in classrooms, but British teachers
adamantly rejected Williamson's similar proposals to reopen the
schools on 1 June. The British Medical Association supported the
teachers. Osama Rahman, the BMA's chief scientific officer,
declared that reopening schools was unsafe. Before he joined the
BMA, Rahman was an economics lecturer and worked at the Ministry of Justice. Without any scientific qualifications whatsoever,
Rahman condemned over 8 million children to no proper education. His prejudice was supported by Chaand Nagpaul, the BMA
chairman and a GP, who would authorise an hysterical attack on
the government's and SAGE's management of the crisis. Sending
children to school would 'risk a second spike', claimed Nagpaul,
fundamentally misquoting German research. He ignored David
Spiegelhalter's conclusions: 'More than 1 per cent of those aged over
90 have so far died from Covid-19 in a four-week period. That is
10,000 times the risk of younger people.' The BMA, like the teaching unions, were uninterested in facts. To their glee, keeping the
schools closed was supported by Keir Starmer. While his own children attended school throughout the lockdown because their
parents were classed as 'key workers', Starmer sided with the trade
unions rather than the children. This was a situation on which
Boris could have seized, one which in better days would have been
an open goal for the man who persuaded Britain to vote Brexit and
not to trust Marxist-led trade unions. Instead, he remained silent.

The public argument, like the dispute about relaxing the lockdown, convinced some parents to distrust the government. Public
confidence was eroded by scientists' eagerness to criticise Boris.
John Edmunds, a member of SAGE, said that schools could open
only after a 'well-functioning track and trace' system was 'embedded and working well'. No one knew how long that would take.
Edmunds had not publicly protested when PHE stopped testing on

12 March. Like Nagpaul, Edmunds' protests encouraged parents to ignore Spiegelhalter's report that just one out of 7 million children aged between four and fourteen in England and Wales had died from Covid-19. Children, Spiegelhalter added, carried just a fraction of the viral load compared to adults. That significantly reduced their chance of falling ill or infecting others. Teachers, other scientists on SAGE agreed, were at no greater risk than any other profession. All that reasonable evidence was also drowned out by David King, the former chief scientific adviser to Tony Blair. Anxious to appear in the spotlight, the eighty-year-old forgot his exaggerations about the threat posed by BSE and the foot-and-mouth outbreak during Blair's administration. He attacked Boris and the 'arrogant' British scientific community for getting everything wrong.

The scientists' public dissent added nothing to scientific knowledge but compounded the public's anxieties. Although the death rate in early May had fallen to its lowest level since 24 March – 170 people a day, based on PHE's flawed criteria – and only 20 per cent of the acute beds were treating Covid patients, the death toll was now heading towards 40,000. The nation's fragile self-confidence was not helped by Vallance's inability to give certain advice about lifting the lockdown. John Edmunds did not exercise similar caution. Although the infection rate of Britons had fallen to less than 0.3 per cent, Edmunds led a group of SAGE scientists warning that lifting the lockdown was dangerous. He appeared to be willing for Britain to remain in lockdown until the virus disappeared. The annual cost would be at least a further £150 billion. Edmunds was praised by those like Martin Wolf in the *Financial Times* who admired Australia for 'suppression . . . to eliminate the virus'. 'The real story is that the UK has made blunder after blunder with fatal results,' wrote Wolf. 'With its rushed exit from lockdown, it is taking another gamble.' One month later, a second wave erupted in Melbourne and the city was again in lockdown.

The media pundits were ignored by Boris. He had stopped reading most newspapers. But the immense pressure to relax the lockdown and kick-start the country's economy could not be disregarded, especially in London where the infection rates had plummeted. 'Stay at Home' was no longer either affordable or necessary, Boris was told by some. The country needed to resume working, but there was no easy route. Certainty did not exist. The majority of scientists advising the government dictated gradualism, and much of the country demanded caution. Even selling a slow return was a complicated story, especially since he himself was not convinced. 'I've learned it's much easier to take people's freedoms away than to give them back,' Boris half joked. This was the moment to take a risk. He knew what he wanted and looked to his inner cabal to produce it.

At that critical moment, his congenital neglect of the machinery of government came home to roost. With Cummings absent and denied a masterful chief of staff spreading his tentacles across Whitehall, and lacking an all-seeing Cabinet Secretary, there was no one to pull all the strands together for the prime minister. His illness and continuing physical weakness had allowed confusion to fester in Downing Street. The discipline required for good government had been compromised. None of his remaining advisers could offer a deep understanding of the conflicted mood across the nation, nor provide a credible path through Whitehall's tangled vicissitudes. This was not only the moment requiring a leader's 'vision' but also required mapping a safe route through contradictory uncertainties. In the absence of insightful administrators, Boris was not presented with a master strategy to reassure the country. Instead he relied on Lee Cain and on Isaac Levido, his pollster, campaigners rather than steersmen, both blindsided by opinion polls and gossip, to understand and relay what was happening beyond the bunker. Their advice was that Boris needed to reassert his authority and communicate the country's path from lockdown. A TV address, said Cain, would signpost the end of the paralysis. Everything depended on lucid communication. Boris's first major speech since returning from Chequers required exceptional preparation.

For years, Boris had automatically rewritten the speeches offered by his staff. For authenticity and style, he recrafted their draft to suit his message and delivery. Those contributing to his speech for

Sunday 10 May were supervised by Cain and Levido. The speech's headline suggested by Levido was to replace the slogan 'Stay at Home' with 'Stay Alert'. Downing Street's problem was that no one in the building had composed a seamless message to explain how 'Stay Alert' matched the gradual restoration of normal life. In the absence of a supremo resolving disagreements between the Downing Street team, senior civil servants, Cabinet members and Tory backbenchers, no clarity emerged for the speechwriters to convey into unambiguous prose for Boris to deliver. Instead, Boris was presented with a muddled three-step narrative to reopen Britain. At the final hurdle, his task was to remove the ambiguities to present a simple message.

Years earlier, George Osborne had joked that Boris always dreamt of addressing the nation on TV. In his dreams, Boris could not have imagined that over 27 million Britons would watch him at 7 p.m. on Sunday 10 May. That was more than had watched the Olympic opening ceremony and even William and Kate's wedding. Boris's credibility depended on a similar chorus of approval.

Instead, at 7.14 p.m., the nation was left confused. Few understood whether schools would reopen on 1 June despite the teachers' opposition, how the care homes would be protected, and when (or even whether) the lockdown was ending. 'It would have taken moral courage to tell a frightened populace that their fears are out of all proportion to the actual risk,' wrote Allison Pearson in the following day's *Daily Telegraph*, 'and it's time to start living again. Boris ducked it. This was not his Finest Hour, it was a disappointing thirteen minutes.' Quentin Letts was equally scathing: 'He hesitated to present his scheme as a set plan. It was "a conditional plan", "the shape of a plan", "a sense of the way ahead", "the first sketch of a road map" . . . He called it "this devilish illness" and said that although we had conquered the initial peak "it is coming down the mountain that is often more dangerous".'

Lord Sumption, recently retired from the Supreme Court, joined the fray. He had been resolutely against the lockdown from the outset. The government, he wrote, 'terrified people into submission by giving the impression that Covid-19 was dangerous for everyone. It is not . . . The prime minister's broadcast was supposed to be his Churchillian moment. Instead, we beheld a man imprisoned by his own rhetoric and the logic of his past mistakes. The lockdown is now all about protecting politicians' backs. They are not wicked men, just timid ones, terrified of being blamed for deaths on their watch. But it is a wicked thing that they are doing.' In reality, the government had been ultimately pushed into the lockdown by public pressure but it was easier for Sumption to attack the government than the people.

An Opinium survey taken immediately after Boris's speech reflected his failure. Only 39 per cent supported his management of the crisis. One week earlier, it had been 48 per cent. Nicola Sturgeon somersaulted. Just fifteen days before, she had demanded a route out of the lockdown. Self-interest dictated that she now announce that Scotland would keep the restrictions to 'Stay at Home'. There was no certain scientific basis for her latest decision. A politician could find a scientist to justify every decision. Distancing herself from Downing Street was politically advantageous.

The UK media backlash after Boris's speech generated ridicule across Europe. Foreign newspapers and TV reported that Britain was 'sick', the government was failing and Boris was 'fading'. Although patients had died on the floors of Italian and Spanish hospitals, Britain's record number of deaths was taken as incontestable proof that Boris had lost control. Britain was sliding towards the abyss.

As a little more confidence in the government eroded, hindsight became an even bigger threat to Britain than Covid. Boris's alleged errors empowered his enemies to criticise his decision to follow the scientists, his choice of the wrong science, or even trusting scientists without realising they were grappling with the unknown – and disagreed. *The Times* forgot its endorsement on 30 March of the government's wisdom for following 'good science'.

Typical of those arguing both ways was Ambrose Evans-Pritchard in the *Telegraph*. 'There should never have been a lockdown in the first place,' he wrote, but simultaneously he also argued, 'These deaths could have been held at 1,000 or thereabouts, ideally by Korean methods, or failing that at least by sheer Greek determination. All the other deaths are in essence a policy failure . . . We have both an eye-watering number of avoidable deaths and a staggering amount of avoidable economic damage. The purported trade-off between lives and jobs – always a false choice – has instead spared neither. It is the worst of both.' The notion that Britain under any circumstances could ever have limited deaths to 1,000 was fanciful.

Joining the attack was SAGE's Jeremy Farrar, an epidemiologist and director of the Wellcome Trust. The crucial phase in this epidemic, he said, was 'the last week or so of January and the first weeks of February'. The wrong decisions in those weeks, he said, were 'absolutely critical' to 'why we've subsequently gone on to have an epidemic that at least to some degree could have been avoided'. During those critical five or six weeks, he said, 'Germany reacted more boldly and more courageously, and Britain was slow.' But the SAGE minutes did not record Farrar urging greater boldness in January, February or March because, as he later admitted, there was 'total uncertainty'. Nor had he publicly complained about PHE's failings over previous years. And Germany had not been noticeably 'bold'. As a much bigger land mass with a lower population density, Germany's success owed much to its well-managed care homes and long-established testing industry. Farrar's hindsight in May added to the public's confusion. Schools, Farrar advised, should not be reopened on 1 June because 'we're not confident enough to know whether children are playing an important role in transmission'. Effortlessly, Spiegelhalter's learned opinion was ignored.

Parents' fears were compounded by Professor Martin Marshall, the chairman of the Royal College of GPs. He told Matt Hancock there was a lack of confidence in the government's testing strategy. 'We do not believe that there is sufficient clarity on a joined-up comprehensive testing strategy to prevent a second wave of infections and to secure the overall health of the population.' Marshall had not complained about Britain's lack of a testing industry before Covid struck.

The carping scientists refocused the blame on Boris for every failure: every nurse who still did not receive the right PPE, the failure to achieve a 100 per cent response to test and trace contacts, relatives not getting access to their parents in care homes, and hospitals not resuming non-Covid treatment.

Some Tory MPs mentioned Boris's illness as the cause of his poor television address and the same reason for his lacklustre Commons performance. Watching him at Prime Minister's Questions on 13 May, the MPs were struck by his bluster when Starmer highlighted the government's most vulnerable point. PHE's advice on 25 February and until 12 March, Starmer reminded Boris, was 'it remains very unlikely that people receiving care in a care home . . . will become infected'. The Office for National Statistics figures showed that at least 40 per cent of all deaths from Covid-19 were in care homes. 'Does the prime minister accept that the government were too slow to protect people in care homes?' Boris not only denied this was the case, but also denied the truth about the directive: 'No, Mr Speaker, and it was not true that the advice said that.' 'The lawyer beating the showman hands down this week,' tweeted Laura Kuenssberg, the BBC's political editor.

The following week, Boris again failed to rebut convincingly Starmer's barb that the government had discharged hospital patients without protection into care homes. 'No one was discharged into a care home this year,' blustered Boris, 'without the express authorisation of a clinician.' The number of discharges were down by 40 per cent from January to March, he said. Even if that were true, many blamed Boris for the scandal.

Then his plight got even worse. Asked by Starmer to free foreign caseworkers employed in Britain from paying an NHS surcharge, Boris refused. Britain, he said, could not afford to lose £900 million a year. He had not read his brief properly. The previous year, the charge raised £204 million, a pittance compared to the £200 billion of additional debt, and climbing. 'We cannot clap our carers one day,' said Starmer, 'and then charge them to use our NHS the next.' Pressured by Tory backbenchers, Boris cancelled the payments the following day. 'A victory for common decency,' said Starmer. Prime ministers who change their minds tend not to be applauded for admitting mistakes and rectifying them; Boris, predictably, was criticised for failing to anticipate an own goal, and the first of many U-turns.

Sleep-deprived, humiliated, facing an unprecedented crisis and still not fully recovered from his own bout of Covid, Boris was unsure of his next step. In the tenth week of lockdown, as many in the country became steadily poorer, there was uproar about chaotic quarantine rules and a farcical deadline to open schools. Now Robert Jenrick, the housing minister, was under fire too. He was accused of bias for helping the former pornographer, newspaper proprietor and latterly property developer Richard Desmond avoid a £48 million levy on a £1 billion development in London's Docklands. His decision came after he had sat next to the vulgar developer at a Tory fundraising dinner. Sleaze reeked out of Downing Street, where Desmond certainly had an ally. The next day, 22 May, was a perfect moment for Boris's critics to strike. The exposé had been brewing for six weeks.

Soon after 5 April, the *Guardian* had asked Downing Street to comment about a new discovery: Dominic Cummings had been spotted during the lockdown listening to Abba's 'Dancing Queen' outside his parents' house near Durham. Cummings told Lee Cain to stonewall: 'It'll be no comment on that one,' the *Guardian* was told. Three weeks later, Cummings' wife Mary Wakefield wrote a *Spectator* article about the family's experience of suffering the virus and the lockdown. Soft-voiced, she repeated her account on BBC's *Today* programme to balance the previous day's diatribe against the government by David Hare, the playwright. She made no mention of where the couple had been isolating. Sometime later, a Labour Party member reported that Cummings had been seen on 11 April at Barnard Castle, a River Tees beauty spot twenty-six miles from his family home. The eyewitness, Robin Lees, a retired chemistry teacher, reported that he had seen Cummings, his wife and four-year-old son in the castle car park. Since there was no 'reasonable excuse' for that excursion, Cummings had apparently broken the government's self-isolation and lockdown rules. Foolishly, Downing Street refused to explain the truth.

The facts Cummings and Cain decided to conceal were uncomplicated. Cummings and his wife feared that if both were infected, there was nobody in London whom they could reasonably expect to care for their son for two weeks and possibly be exposed to the virus themselves. Four days after the lockdown was declared, they drove 264 miles to Durham to stay in an isolated family bungalow and be helped by his sister and nieces who lived nearby. The lockdown law stated that a 'reasonable excuse' to gain an 'exemption' to the rules was 'the health of a small child'. After recovering from the virus, Cummings returned to Downing Street on 14 April. His lockdown location remained secret.

By the time the *Guardian* decided to expose Cummings, their accusations had grown. The newspaper's report published on Friday 22 May stated that after returning to Downing Street on 14 April, Cummings had driven back to Durham despite the lockdown for a second time. Once there, he had been spotted on 19 April walking in a bluebell wood near Houghall by Tim Matthews, a jogger, and also by another unnamed witness. The *Guardian* also reported the police had 'spoken to Cummings about breaching the government's lockdown rules'. Unknown to readers, all those additional allegations were totally untrue. There was no evidence of a second trip, which Cummings emphatically denied, and the police had never spoken to Cummings. Matthews later admitted that he had fabricated the second sighting 'for comedy'.

The scenario conjured by the *Guardian* – of not one but two trips, of woodland walks, police disapproval and unnamed witnesses – condemned Cummings as an inveterate lockdown-breaker, brazenly flouting the government's rule: 'Leaving your home – the place you live – to stay at another home for a holiday or other purpose is not allowed.' Over the bank holiday weekend, the stench of hypocrisy overwhelmed the government. While millions of Britons, responding to Boris's appeal to stay at home and protect the NHS, had made painful sacrifices, including the loss of loved ones whom they couldn't be with when they died, Cummings epitomised 'one rule for him, another for us'. Cummings and Cain had woefully misjudged the consequence of their stubborn refusal to tell the *Guardian* the truth or to say anything more than that Cummings refused to resign.

Immediately, nine Tory MPs, led by Roger Gale and followed by Steve Baker, demanded Cummings' dismissal. Growing numbers of Tory MPs during Saturday the 23rd were amazed by an unprecedented wave of protests from constituents. Outside his £2 million house, Cummings was defiant. Asked whether his conduct 'looked good', he replied 'Who cares about good looks? It's a question of doing the right thing. It's not about what you guys think.' Reacting to his contempt, more Tory MPs joined the clamour against a man they loathed. For them, trust in Boris depended on dismissing Cummings. Instant opinion polls showed that the Tory lead had crashed from 19 per cent to at best 10 per cent. Boris's personal rating had fallen from 70 per cent to about 50 per cent.

Against his wishes, Boris had no choice during Sunday but to support the cause of the wreckage – not least because, after Neil Ferguson's resignation, several ministers had mocked the scientist's conduct. But, as he questioned Cummings, Boris's resolve did not waver. He would never sacrifice Cummings to the *Guardian*, especially after he heard about their inventions. Without Cummings, he feared his government would destabilise. The lawyers confirmed that Cummings' trip could be classified as 'exceptional circumstances'. But he did stipulate that Cummings would thereafter maintain total silence. No more provocative blogs or publicity-seeking damnations. In return, he would defend Cummings in an unscheduled appearance at the afternoon TV press conference. Once again, though, Boris misjudged the mood. The tone of his message sounded bland. Boris would not do contrition.

After mentioning Cummings' 'difficult childcare position', Boris told the 5 million TV audience, 'Of course I do regret the confusion and the anger and the pain that people feel [but] it's not like he was visiting a lover . . . I think he followed the instincts of every father and every parent. And I do not mark him down for that.' Compared to the *Guardian*'s 'palpably false' allegations, Cummings had 'acted responsibly, legally and with integrity'.

No explanation or apology would satisfy Boris's opponents,

including the now familiar scientists. Stephen Reicher tweeted: 'I can say that in a few short minutes tonight, Boris Johnson has trashed all the advice we have given on how to build trust and secure adherence to the measures necessary to control Covid-19'; Susan Michie, a professor of health psychology on SAGE, complained that science risked being 'dragged down by association with dishonesty'. Professor Robert West, a health psychologist, accused Boris of 'a shambles with Trumpian levels of deceit'. Richard Horton would write, 'This sad episode shows a regime that has lost its moral compass . . . Every day, government scientific advisers stand next to increasingly discredited politicians, acting as protective professional shields to prop up the collapsing reputations of ministers.' Nicola Sturgeon, who had just accepted the resignation of the country's chief medical officer, Catherine Calderwood, after she visited a second home during lockdown, urged Boris to follow her example.

By Monday, forty-five Tory MPs openly demanded Cummings' resignation. Damian Collins, a thoughtful Tory overwhelmed by his constituents' protests, tweeted 'Dominic Cummings has a track record of not believing the rules apply to him . . . The government would be better without him.' In that unguarded moment, Boris realised that despite his eighty-seat majority, he could no longer be certain of Parliament approving all his legislation and decisions. The party's loyal gratitude could not be taken for granted. To save himself, Cummings agreed to appear at a press conference in the Downing Street garden on Monday afternoon, 25 May.

Dressed unusually smartly in a crisp white shirt, Cummings admitted he had driven to Barnard Castle but had stayed only a short while. He said he was on a test drive to see if his eyesight was robust enough to make the longer journey back to London the following day. In a quiet voice, he denied that he had broken the lockdown rules and added, 'I don't regret what I did . . . I've not offered to resign. I've not considered it.'

'What planet are they on?' screamed the *Daily Mail* headline the following morning. With unremitting hostility, the Tory newspaper devoted ten pages to vitriolic reports with an editorial that

Cummings had 'violated the spirit and the letter of the lockdown'. Durham police's conclusion that Cummings' trip to Barnard Castle 'might have been a minor breach' of lockdown rules but the journey north was permissible within the exemption of a 'reasonable excuse' to care for a child, was ignored by the *Daily Mail* and the public. Boris, wrote Alex Massie in the *Spectator*, was 'a prime minister without clothes . . . He is not up to the job.' He added, 'Any prime minister so wholly dependent on a single adviser, no matter how brilliant he or she may be, is a weak one. If Boris Johnson cannot function without Cummings he is not qualified to be prime minister.' The following evening, Emily Maitlis spoke for the Guardianistas in her opening comments on BBC TV's *Newsnight*: 'Dominic Cummings broke the rules. The country can see that and it's shocked that the government cannot.' She accused Cummings of ignoring the public mood: 'One of fury, contempt and anguish.' No one addressed how the saga had been exaggerated by the *Guardian*.

A reader's letter in the *Guardian* summarised the critics' fury that nothing had changed: 'Johnson says it's time to move on. That's been his mantra all his life. Trash a restaurant as a student – move on. Make a career of lying journalism – move on (but with plenty of money in the bank). Cheat on your wives – deny it, move on. Get your girlfriends pregnant – deny it, move on. Worst Foreign Secretary for a century – laugh, tell a joke in Latin, move on. Campaign for Brexit, which will destroy our economy, unity and position in the world – tell lots of lies, move on.'

Just ten months into his premiership, Boris's administration was battered.

Epilogue

The first anniversary of Boris's premiership on 24 July was muted. There were no cheers, no celebrations and barely any praise. Not only did the media withhold even token compliments, but his own supporters appeared exhausted by the roller coaster of the last year.

Over the previous twelve months, Boris had steered the country through a political crisis, a general election, Brexit, and the worst pandemic in a century. At the same time, he managed his own divorce, watched his family splinter, had come close to death and celebrated the birth of his sixth child.

The media headlines on the morning of his December 2019 election victory pronounced Boris 'unleashed', with a mandate 'to govern as he likes'. That morning, Boris imagined the beginning of a glorious decade. Instead, he quickly learned, the pause for self-congratulation was brief. The hours after his victory were as good as it got. The volume of criticism was to become painful, particularly for an entertainer so dependent on popularity.

To mark his first anniversary, Boris was interviewed in the Downing Street garden by Laura Kuenssberg. The result was a car crash. He reeled defensively, unable to articulate a focused message of even limited success, making it easier for the final edit to be chopped up to suit the BBC's agenda that his management of the pandemic had failed. 'Maybe there are things we could have done differently,' he lamely admitted. 'There will be plenty of opportunities to learn the lessons of what happened.' But he refused to acknowledge specific mistakes or apologise. His enemies would not be handed that sound bite.

The great communicator had not been primed to deliver a convincing explanation about the crisis and his vision for recovery. After the harsh discipline of a year's campaigning, Boris had forgotten the flourish of a witty speech or a charming phrase. Unlike Benjamin Disraeli, he could not deliver a bewitching truism. Rather, he was reduced to uttering colourless sound bites. So much that had been previously taken for granted about a barnstorming orator appeared to have disappeared.

Fatally for a politician, his sense of public opinion was diminished. Isolated in Downing Street, he no longer mingled in the streets as he had as London's mayor, hearing people's complaints and sensing their mood. To the dismay of his admirers, the Brexit prime minister had become a dithering Covid casualty, reluctant to believe that, like his Athenian hero Pericles, his political fortunes could be destroyed by a plague.

His solitariness was self-made. Unlike Abraham Lincoln who appointed his rivals to key posts in his administration after winning the 1860 election because he recognised their superior intellect, Boris had been unwilling to tolerate disagreement and criticism in the Cabinet and Downing Street. With the exception of a handful of trusted allies, he had surrounded himself with second-rate 'yesmen' unable and unwilling to engage in constructive discussions. Self-criticism, the essence of success, was noticeably missing from his inner sanctum. After a year, the weakness of a loner uninterested in the machinery of government and all the institutions of parliamentary democracy – the Whips' Office, MPs, Tory Central Office and the Civil Service – was being slowly exposed. Boris had forgotten King Lear's question, 'Who is it that can tell me who I am?'

Repeatedly over the summer, he was wrong-footed by opponents. The trade unions outwitted him to keep the schools closed; Marcus Rashford, a twenty-two-year-old footballer, forced him to somersault and fund additional school-meal vouchers; the media ridiculed his indecision as to whether masks should be worn and whether social distancing should be reduced from two metres to one; Labour lambasted the government's failure to hit its own track-and-trace targets; migrants crossing the Channel on dinghies made a mockery of his pledge to control Britain's borders; and finally, Boris failed to deliver a defining speech to answer the culture war inspired by the Black Lives Matter movement who had pulled down a statue in Bristol, daubed the word 'racist' on Winston Churchill's statue in Parliament Square, and disputed the traditional interpretation of British history. At critical moments, the student of ancient Greece and Rome was unable or not minded to deliver a memorable oration about his values and his vision. Conflict rather than creativity circumscribed his life. Cometh the hour, cometh the man is the saying which matched Boris's proffered image of being 'pulled like Cincinnatus from my plough' to rebuild Britain. But without an explicit philosophy to govern through a recession, his ambition was threatened by Covid's legacy, especially the vast £2 trillion national debt. That peril of a crisis plunged him into some personal despair.

Surrounded by new and unusual secrecy in order to evade scrutiny, Boris had become unpredictable. Observers seeking to make a rational judgement of him were confused by a man who, unlike at City Hall, offered turbulence rather than stability and encouraged dissension rather than loyalty. Boris had changed.

Before he left for his summer holiday in a remote Scottish cottage, his friends mentioned he was not enjoying the job. Life for him as prime minister, they whispered, had become a disappointment. His triumphalism had waned, no doubt exacerbated by his escape from death. Covid, some believed, had reduced his physical strength and eroded his magnetic ebullience. He was more serious and less spontaneous. Possibly, the enormity of the job had finally made Boris take life more seriously. Had his expensive ambitions to rebuild Britain, many asked, been sapped by the virus? Did he possess the intellectual strength to focus beyond Covid on the wider agenda? Covid was one reason for doubt; another was his new personal life.

Unusually complicated and conflicted, scandal and silence have dogged Boris's bizarre marital relationships for many years. Throughout, he had danced with danger. So often, his ambitions seemed doomed by his amoral behaviour. Condemned to the wilderness several times over the past twenty years, his resurrection always infuriated his bewildered critics. No previous prime minister would have considered living in Downing Street with a woman twenty-four years younger whom he had so far refused to marry despite the birth of their young son. Inevitably, disparaging rumours surfaced about their relationship and their lack of common interests, not least after he decided to abandon modern fatherhood and sleep in another room to avoid being disturbed by Wilfred during the night. The fracturing during the first year of his premiership of relations with Stanley and his family ruled out a repeat celebration of Stanley's birthday at Chequers in August, despite it being a landmark eightieth birthday. The divorce from Marina had destabilised his life. In her absence, his mother Charlotte was his trusted confidante. In the past, Boris's happiness had depended on having a secret best friend. Obedient to the demands of his security, he was denied easy access to any new soulmate in a Shoreditch flat. That glaring vacancy in his life reduced his chance to live in peace with himself. The consequence, some speculated, might persuade him to forgo running for a second term.

The uncertainty caused Tory MPs to fret about the prime minister's grip over Westminster and the government's agenda. The indomitable belief in a cause to glue the government and party together – or Borisism – had frayed. Modern Conservatism was harder to define. The party's ideology – so clearly defined in December 2019 – had become confused by the billions of pounds of state support to mitigate the pandemic's backwash.

Downing Street's poor communications obscured the Tory Party's regeneration. The Red Wall Tories admired Boris's patriotism and positivism. The northerners praised Britain's role in the world, cherished British culture and distrusted the left's damnation of Britain's history. They had grown weary of the perpetual negativism spouted by Labour supporters and the BBC. Those new Tories suspected that Keir Starmer would fail to remove the Corbynistas from the party and fundamentally change the party's left-wing policies on economics, immigration and British values. Unlike Tony Blair after 1994, Starmer has lacked, so far, the bravery to engage the left in a civil war to impose a new, vote-winning vision. Hampered by the poor quality of Labour MPs, he had damned himself among Labour traditionalists for kneeling in sympathy with Black Lives Matter rather than demand the reinstatement as a party member of Trevor Phillips, an outstanding public servant who was suspended from the party on a charge of Islamophobia but in reality for his challenge to Corbyn's anti-Semitism. But those blips were irrelevant to voters irritated by Boris's manner.

Since the election, many Remainers and liberals in the south who had voted Tory to defeat Jeremy Corbyn had switched to Keir Starmer (the Lib Dems had become irrelevant). Relying too often on misinformation, they uncompromisingly condemned Boris's management of the pandemic. Short-sightedly, he had failed to explain the labyrinthine choices he faced in the weeks before and after the lockdown. Carelessly, he had fallen into the trap of confirming his critics' accusation that he was not interested in grasping detail.

Despite their desertion, the Tories continued to poll around 43 per cent during July, the same as in December 2019. Boris remained ahead of Starmer by about 7 per cent. No previous modern Tory leader had maintained that popularity at the end of their first year, including Margaret Thatcher. Both Thatcher, castigated for wrecking the economy, and Tony Blair, vilified for sleaze, understood only at the end of their first year the unique demands of office. Thereafter, both flourished and won successive general elections. To win the next general election, due in 2024, Labour would need a landslide gain of 120 extra seats, including in Scotland where its leader, Richard Leonard, was an unpopular Marxist. The real threat to the government was Nicola Sturgeon's demand for a second referendum. To defeat the nationalists, Boris revamped the leadership of the Scottish Tory Party. Just in time, Ruth Davidson, the popular Scottish Tory, was given a peerage and persuaded by Boris to resume the fight to save the Union. During August, Sturgeon's approval rating rose to plus 50; Boris's fell to minus 15, and Starmer's popularity rose above Boris's. The next battle for Scotland would be decided in the Holyrood elections in May 2021; the Westminster battle was four years away and the odds still favoured Boris. In autumn 2020, he remained the best Britain had. But to survive, he was forced to take a succession of gambles.

His biggest risk was Covid. Under pressure to relax the restrictions despite over 41,000 deaths (revised down from 46,000* after PHE's errors were accounted for), he had pledged at the end of June, 'Our great national hibernation is coming to an end.' Patrick Vallance and Chris Whitty, he knew, opposed a general return to work. From the outset, the clinicians had warned about the danger of a second wave. During July, their caution proved credible. In towns across northern England, distancing rules had been breached, allowing new infections to erupt. Simultaneously, new outbreaks across Europe made crossing the Channel risky, just as in February's ski season. Lockdowns imposed on the towns, and quarantine on returning tourists, were the only protection available for London. If the capital went back into lockdown, the economic consequences would be dire. Boris's dilemma was real. Faced with 2 million more unemployed, the continued shutdown of key sectors of Britain's service economy and billions of pounds of new debt, Boris gambled to reopen Britain. In his favour was the expansion and improvement of testing and tracing, and a steroid, dexamethasone, to limit the number of deaths of those seriously ill. The chance of a vaccine and the purchase of a vast stockpile of PPE equipment improved the odds to prevent another catastrophe.

Boris made his Covid gamble just as his Brexit gamble loomed. Throughout the year, Boris had dismissed Michel Barnier's threat that the timetable to complete a deal was too short. Playing hard ball, he rejected Barnier's offer of a two-year extension to leave the

---

* The number of deaths in June was over 45,000. At the beginning of August, it had risen to over 46,000 but, at the insistence of academic statisticians, it was reduced to around 41,000 in early August. PHE had classified every person infected by Covid who died subsequently as having died from Covid, even if the person was killed by a bus!

EU. Under no circumstances, Boris told Ursula von der Leyen, the European Commission president, would he extend the transition period beyond December 2020. In a game of brinkmanship, the EU was told that Britain would not compromise on its sovereignty and refused to remain subject to the European Court of Justice. If necessary, Britain would leave the EU without a trade deal. Ostensibly, the negotiations were stalled on maintaning the EU's rights to unlimited fishing in British waters and on continuing a 'level playing field' between Britain and the EU. Both demands were rejected by Britain. If Boris's gamble failed and there were no agreement, Britain's trade with the EU would be seriously disrupted. Not only would Britain's fragile economy nosedive but Scottish independence would gain more supporters. Boris was betting that Europe did not want a trade war and problems on the Irish border and, at the last minute, would agree a deal.

His third gamble was discipline within the Tory Party. Weakened in May after the forty-five MPs demanded Dominic Cummings' dismissal, he had been forced by about forty Tory MPs to cancel the agreement with Huawei, the Chinese telecommunications corporation, to build a national 5G fibre network. Despite his eighty-seat majority, he was vulnerable. Tory MPs agreed about Brexit but were disunited on much else. Their loyalty to Boris was limited. His appointment of Chris 'Failing' Grayling as chair of the Intelligence and Security Committee, presumably to suppress a report about Russian interference in British politics, confirmed his plight. Tory MPs were shocked that Grayling was endorsed by Boris. With Labour support on the committee, Julian Lewis, a Tory MP, outvoted Grayling and became the chairman. Boris was infuriated. As usual, the righteous who challenge him are never shown mercy. Petulantly, he ordered Lewis to be kicked out of the parliamentary party. Once published, the vacuous report proved that Boris's fears about embarrassing revelations were unfounded. The prime minister's limited grip over Westminster was exposed.

Over the winter months, Tory MPs suspected, he would be tested by the trade unions. The first battle would be to fully reopen the schools in September. Would teachers succumb to his orders? Boris's confrontation with the teachers resembled Margaret Thatcher's defining war against the miners' leaders in the early 1980s. Without total victory against the teachers' unions, his authority would be diminished. Tellingly, his triumph passed without any gestures.

Doubts about his competence nevertheless persisted following the government's mismanagement of the A level and GCSE examinations in mid-August. Boris's reliance on Gavin Williamson, an inadequate politician, to oversee the awarding of grades proved that Boris had not learnt the lessons of governance from the Covid saga. Just as Boris's Downing Street advisers had failed to monitor and interrogate Public Health England and the Department of Health officials, they had failed to question the executives of Ofqual, the exams regulator, about the algorithm designed to award fair exam grades. Without sufficient thought, Boris endorsed Williamson's guarantees that the system was 'robust'. A cursory examination would have shown the opposite. Invisible throughout a sensational debacle, Boris again risked confirming his critics' damnation that he was lazy and uninterested in detail. Worse, they questioned whether he was a leader with an astute understanding of consensual and practical government. Was he contemptuous of corruption and cronyism? Could he engineer radical but responsible reforms? The questions were asked only after doubts arose.

His answer was the emergence of a political programme despite the Covid crisis. The additional funds for more police, the NHS and education had been delivered. Trusted Tories in the Cabinet Office were implementing plans to level up the north, rebuild the country's road and rail infrastructure and regenerate Britain's commitment to science, not least by investing in a satellite to rival the EU's Galileo programme. New planning laws had been announced to build more houses. Other Tories were conceiving laws to limit the judiciary's abuse of power, protect academic freedom and a plan to rescue the BBC from declining into a shadow of its previous glory. Cummings' threat to Whitehall – 'A Hard Rain's Gonna Fall', he sang after Bob Dylan – had begun with the purge of Simon McDonald from the Foreign Office, Jonathan Slater from the Department of Education, Mark Sedwill as Cabinet Secretary and

Philip Rutnam from the Home Office; and the establishment of a new Downing Street headquarters at 70 Whitehall. Signalling the government's radicalism, Public Health England was closed down and replaced by the National Institute of Health Protection. The proof of PHE's incompetence was Duncan Selbie's belated denial that his organisation was responsible for a 'national testing strategy'. His unrealistic interpretation of the past reflected the general refusal of the civil service unions to agree that their 500,000 members should return to their offices even under safe conditions. Having defeated the teachers, the leaders of the civil service unions were his next foes. Some would criticise the new centralisation and dismantlement of old institutions as dangerous, but Covid exposed the necessity to rebuild the government machine. Modernising Britain after Brexit, Boris believed, depended on a revolution. Many agreed but also wondered whether Boris had the stuff of leadership. The last stages of Brexit were the proof. His decision to challenge Brussels' interpretation of the UK's Withdrawal Agreement, enshrining his opinion in new legislation, and extol the virtues of leaving the EU without a deal was the ultimate adoption of Otto von Bismarck's brinkmanship or Dominic Cummings' 'swerve' as his government's strategy. Gambling the nation's fate was playing for high stakes, but that was always the nature of the man.

Once Brexit was completed, the obvious solution to Boris's woes was to replace Downing Street lightweights with experienced, wise operators and ditch the embarrassing Cabinet no-hopers. Introducing original intellect and astute operators into the government despite the risk of more disgruntled backbenchers was critical. That was a gamble he would need to take by the end of the year. The appointment in September of forty-one year old Simon Case as the new Cabinet Secretary was a risk, clearly targeted at Whitehall's encrusted establishment. Choosing Case also defeated Cummings' search for 'weirdos'.

With the chance to reshape Britain for the rest of the century, Boris is too ambitious to forgo the opportunity to fulfil his dream and become an historic legend. He understands that the country needs leadership to escape from Covid's extremes. In the concluding page of his Churchill biography, he praised his predecessor in Downing Street – 'he alone, made the difference'. Being remembered for making a difference is the dream of all politicians. Unlike his competitors, Boris has the opportunity to improve fundamentally people's lives. To succeed, he will need to step back from the brink, restore calm and re-convince the nation of his vision to build a prosperous, united society. As an intelligent patriot, Boris still retains the goodwill of most Britons. Their loyalty is his to squander. They know him as a loner and a lover. They still wait to see whether he is a leader.

Afterword

At the beginning of September 2020, Boris was in a bad mood. Confidants heard complaints about his dire finances, hardships in Downing Street and how no one cooked good meals for him. Carrie was blamed. Her demands for an expensive refurbishment of their flat had irritated officials. Carrie had run-ins with female civil servants in particular. One at Chequers had caused her special anger after Dilyn, their terrier, had also created a problem. The housekeeper complained that Dilyn was chewing furniture and had damaged a valuable book. After heated discussions between Boris and Carrie, the housekeeper was fired the following morning and the dog survived. On his return to London on Sunday night, Boris's irritation was aggravated by Patrick Vallance's news. The Covid infection rate, he said, was rising. Tourists returning from summer holidays in Spain had brought back the virus. That could seriously derail Boris's plan for the country to return to normality.

The first milestone was the return of schoolchildren and students to their classrooms. Unexpectedly, tens of thousands demanded instant Covid tests. Instead of enjoying Matt Hancock's 'world-beating' £12 billion test and trace programme, they discovered either no tests were available or only at the end of a long journey. Even those tested became distressed after some swabs were dumped in malfunctioning laboratories. Boris had sympathy for Hancock's defence of the indefensible. As for Dido Harding, her appointment had been a gamble. Although Harding had been TalkTalk's chief executive, Boris hadn't realised that her skills did not include data and systems management. However, neither Hancock nor Harding could have anticipated there would be widespread public disobedience. Regardless of his exhortations and the media campaign, large numbers of Britons were flouting the law and spreading the virus.

Only 12 per cent of people with symptoms in some areas asked for the test; and only 18 per cent of those contacted by test and trace agreed to self-isolate. Of those, only half were still isolating at the end of fourteen days. The additional complication, Boris heard, was that one-third of those spreading Covid were asymptomatic. In effect, test and trace, heavily promoted by Jeremy Hunt, was, as a senior NHS executive told Boris, 'a waste of money and an expensive mistake'. Boris could not tell the nation that truth, and by mid-September his optimism was fading.

Patrick Vallance predicted that by mid-October there would be 50,000 new cases and 200 deaths every day. And Chris Whitty forecast there was no hope of a vaccine until spring 2021. Both demanded another lockdown, delicately renamed a 'circuit-breaker'.

Boris resisted. Unquestioningly following the science, he believed, had been a mistake. From the outset, Vallance, Whitty and the SAGE experts had made mistakes. Their worst was to approve Public Health England's abandonment of testing in February 2020 and another was their early opposition to masks. Now, they wanted to close down the economy to avoid what they called 'a very large epidemic with catastrophic consequences'. How much worse could it get, he wondered? Covid had already cut the economy by about 10 per cent and the government's bailout schemes had added about £400 billion to the national debt and generated over £25 billion of fraudulent claims. Yet the left was demanding more restrictions, more self-isolation, more spending and a second lockdown. Boris dug in. His reluctance was supported during a Zoom conference by Anders Tegnell, the Swedish epidemiologist, and Sunetra Gupta of Oxford. Both advised that the current 4,000 cases and eleven deaths a day posed no serious risk. At least sixty Tory MPs agreed. Buffeted from both sides, Boris bought time by imposing piecemeal restrictions across the country: a 10 p.m. curfew on pubs, meetings limited to six people and encouragement to work from home. Tory MPs were still dissatisfied. They accused the prime minister of cluelessness, indecision and riding rough-shod over democracy by not seeking parliamentary approval for his unnecessary controls. Echoing that criticism, Toby Young, his Oxford friend and an opponent of lockdowns, sniped that he had 'given up' on Boris. 'He is no longer fit to be prime minister,' Young wrote, and should resign after Brexit was done. Those bitter arguments fuelled the public's suspicion.

No one could have guessed from Boris's enthusiastic speech to the virtual Tory Party conference in early October that he was beleaguered. Covid, he exclaimed, had not 'robbed me of my mojo'. Covid had only struck him badly because as he said, 'I was too fat.' So far, he had shed twenty-six pounds and there was more to go. His faultless performance did little good. Not only Tory MPs but also Cabinet ministers, senior civil servants and even his fiancée remained hostile. To survive, the Gambler took another bet. So far two bets – the purchase of PPE and test and trace – had delivered one win. The national shortage of PPE was solved, but then complicated by distribution problems – and there was one loss, test and trace. He needed his third bet on a vaccine to be an outright win. He had backed another outsider to deliver the prize.

Kate Bingham, a venture capitalist specialising in biotechnology, had been recruited in the spring to order potentially successful vaccines. Before October, Bingham and her team had sifted through 240 manufacturers and picked seven to deliver 400 million doses. Boris had agreed to pay the manufacturers an unrefundable £914 million without extracting any guarantees of success. Having risked the money and refused to join the EU's vaccination programme, he could only pray.

At the same time he needed a dose of luck in the Brexit negotiations. Ever since his impetuous and unnecessary concession to Leo Varadkar which established a border down the Irish Sea, the EU had heaped humiliating demands on Britain. The answer, Dominic Cummings suggested, was to pitch a last-ditch threat. The insurgents agreed that the government would first announce its readiness to leave with no deal. Second, Boris approved the Internal Market Bill. The law would empower the government to override the

Withdrawal Treaty if the EU imposed controls on Britain's trade with Northern Ireland in 'ways it was never intended', as the treaty stipulated. The presentation of the bill to Parliament was disastrous. The bill, the minister told the Commons, would 'break international law in a very specific and limited way'. The grenade provoked the resignation of Jonathan Jones, the government's senior legal civil servant. Thirty Tory MPs, including Brexiteers, rebelled. Mischievously, they misdescribed Boris's threat as an outright breach of international law rather than the re-enactment of reserve powers existing in section 38 of the Withdrawal Act.

The flawed presentation cast Boris as an outlaw. Not only was he planning to break international law and reduce foreign aid, but he also faced a problem with Priti Patel, the Home Secretary. For weeks, he had suppressed an official report by Alex Allan, a senior civil servant, which declared that Patel had broken the ministerial code by bullying civil servants. Instead of requiring her resignation, he refused to cow to contemptuous officials and the racist left who disparaged self-made immigrants like Patel as coconuts. Finally, he published the report. Patel's behaviour, he said, was 'unintentional'. In protest, Allan resigned. Patel survived but many Tories damned her as lightweight. None of Boris's ministers, they agreed, would have sat in Thatcher's Cabinet. Unbowed, Boris also moved Antonia Romeo as permanent secretary at the international trade department to the justice department. Their professional relationship while he was visiting New York as Foreign Secretary in 2018 may have counted against the former Consul General. Others believe Carrie Symonds may have been a pivotal factor. Boris's puffy face and hesitant replies in the Commons sparked renewed speculation that he would resign in the new year.

Boris appeared to be surrounded by critics. SAGE's scientists, he snapped, were constantly appearing on TV and briefing journalists to embarrass the government: Patrick Vallance forecast that Britain's infection rate would triple to 50,000 cases a day and other scientists predicted that Britain's death rate would be over 100,000. Jeremy Farrar, the director of the Wellcome Trust and a member of SAGE, warned that a vaccine would not be available until the spring. The doomsters, protesting Tory MPs urged the prime minister, should be ignored. After all, the daily death rate was less than one hundred people. Boris tried to hold the line. 'I won't yank kids out of school in a peremptory way,' he pledged. But by the end of October, as the virus spread across Britain, his resistance to the scientists weakened. That made the showdown in Downing Street on Friday 30 October ugly.

That day's death toll was 162 but SAGE predicted deaths would rise to 4,000 a day if the government failed to impose a lockdown. Hancock and Gove supported another lockdown – some believed that both had been 'captured' by the scientists. Rishi Sunak and Boris deplored the idea. Boris wanted to consider his options over the weekend. Some called it dithering but he recalled that Tony Blair's 'decisive decision-making' had approved the invasion of Iraq despite Hans Blix's eyewitness evidence that there were no WMDs. Boris's deliberation was short-lived. To force his hand, that night a Govite leaked the ministers' disagreement. To the anger of over sixty Tory backbenchers, Boris announced on Saturday afternoon the second lockdown from 5 November. Boris's critics seized on the somersault as proof that he had lost control.

For *The Times*, Boris had 'passed the political tipping point'. Amid 'chaos and incompetence', reported the newspaper, he would be ousted by Tory MPs. With undisguised disdain, Rachel Sylvester wrote that Boris had lost forever the electorate's trust. She applauded Anders Tegnell's 'trust-based approach' which had won 'huge praise' in Sweden. 'Trust' in a future vaccine, Sylvester proclaimed, was low. Joining the attack, Gabriel Pogrund in the *Sunday Times* inaccurately criticised Kate Bingham for spending £670,000 on publicists. Castigating her as a 'free-spending vaccine tsar', Pogrund observed that Bingham's 'conduct is worrying Whitehall'. The 'publicists' in reality were communications experts for the vaccine programme – a skill which civil servants lacked. Her appointment, highlighted the *Sunday Times*, was another example of Boris's chumocracy. She and her husband, Jesse Norman, the Tory MP, had holidayed with the Johnsons. Other chumocrats were Tories profiting from the £12.5 billion contracts for PPE. Some of the contracts awarded without competition were to friends of Cabinet ministers. One beneficiary was an acquaintance of Matt Hancock's from their local pub. Another £250 million PPE contract with an American jewellery designer had been brokered by a young Spaniard for a £21 million fee. Boris was portrayed by his enemies as a sleazy loser destined for the dustbin.

The day after the *Sunday Times* piece, 9 November, Britain recorded a total of 50,000 deaths. Boris's outlook looked bleak. Once again luck saved him. On the same day, Pfizer announced a vaccine with 90 per cent efficacy. AstraZeneca was expected to announce its successful vaccine days later. Large orders had been placed by Bingham for immediate delivery of both vaccines. Jonathan Van-Tam, England's deputy chief medical officer, predicted that the current wave of infections would be over by the spring. From his bunker, Boris acclaimed Bingham for delivering the 'scientific cavalry'. His gamble was doubled by the government's investment in new vaccine production factories. Britain was ending its reliance on the EU. And then there was more good luck.

Eighteen months earlier, Simon Stevens, the NHS's chief executive, had designed the mechanism for GP groups to mass-vaccinate their patients. On the morning after Pfizer's announcement, Stevens briefed Boris for one hour in Downing Street about his vaccination plan – twelve hours a day, seven days a week. GPs would be paid £12.58 a jab.

At the end of October, the public could not imagine a successful mass vaccination plan. The headlines had for months described constant government failure. Boris's poll ratings were falling and then another crisis erupted, reminiscent of events at the end of his first year in City Hall.

Since July 2019, Boris's inner sanctum had become contaminated by Dominic Cummings' and Lee Cain's rule. Both wilfully created enemies, isolated Boris from Tory MPs and antagonised the media. Since the election, Cummings had aggressively demanded loyalty to himself and sowed distrust against Boris's stalwarts. Cummings' good ideas produced acrimony, and so as an administrator he was often ineffective. Similarly, Cain was rated as Downing Street's worst communications director in living memory. Yet, during another turbulent week at the beginning of November, Boris decided not to fire Cain but to promote him. Unwittingly, Cain lit the fuse which was to end the chaos.

Cain had proposed that Downing Street should, like the White House, employ a public spokesperson to host a daily media conference. The dubious idea was accepted by Boris. His final choice for the televised event was Allegra Stratton, an ITV journalist. But she was rejected by Cain. Clumsily, the former *Mirror* newspaper's 'chicken' then slipped into dangerous territory. Stratton was supported by her friend Carrie Symonds. 'I love Carrie,' Stratton would say, 'and will do anything for her . . . We are all a nest of singing birds.' Once persuaded by Carrie that Stratton was ideal, Boris also agreed that Stratton should be answerable to him and not to Cain. To avoid that impossible arrangement, the director of communications offered to resign. Fearful of the fallout, Boris offered Cain promotion to chief of staff. In Carrie's version, she now stepped in. Cain, she protested, was unsuitable and worse, he was responsible along with Cummings of endless ridicule of herself as 'Princess Nut Nuts' and 'The Mad Queen'. Both peddled the myth, she claimed, that she made twenty calls every day to the prime minister, even about Dilyn. The two 'Mad Mullahs', said Carrie, spread fear in 'Mafia-speak'. They should be fired. On 11 November, Boris agreed. Cain resigned. Initially, Cummings agreed to remain. Two days later, after confrontations with Boris, Cummings had watched his 'fear factor' evaporate. Having lost control, he staged a dramatic departure from Downing Street carrying a cardboard box. 'The country,' Stratton told the *Observer*, 'does not want to be run by people in Number 10 who treat people discourteously and unpleasantly.'

The two resignations – and more ex-Leave campaigners would follow – placed Boris once again under fire. Downing Street's antics were magnified by another series of gaffes. Boris flipped that Blair's devolution settlement was 'a disaster' – a gift to the Scottish Nationalists. Next, his recommendation of a peerage for Peter Cruddas, a former Tory Party treasurer seriously discredited in a 'cash for access' to politicians scandal, was damned as 'sleazy'. Then, his opposition to Marcus Rashford's demand to extend the £20 per week Universal Credit payments appeared as mean-spirited. Finally, Carrie Symonds' ambitions were again questioned. Having promoted herself as a kingmaker, she was destined to appear as the 'First Fiancée' on *Tatler*'s front cover. The fiery headlines automatically reignited predictions that Boris would be gone by Easter. The critics misjudged the prime minister. His recovery from Covid had prompted a cathartic understanding of decision-making in Downing Street and Whitehall. Boris's strength was his constant evolution, learning and then changing from experience.

AD – After Dominic – liberated Boris. Cummings' control system across Whitehall automatically dismantled. Boris was introduced to Dan Rosenfield, a former Treasury civil servant, to be his new chief of staff. In the background, Carrie simultaneously plotted to insert more friends into Downing Street. Rosenfield's deputy would be Simone Finn, a friend of Carrie's, an old girlfriend of Michael Gove's and a business colleague of Francis Maude. Their company advised foreign governments on improvements to their efficacy. Finn, an experienced Whitehall operator, would be tasked to rebuild Downing Street's relations with MPs and reform Whitehall.

Carrie Symonds' influence confirmed Boris's lack of relationships with talented operators. Besides the City Hall loyalists, he relied on others to find Downing Street's staff. The exception was Michael Gove. 'You're too generous to Michael,' Bill Cash told Boris. Gove's position without Cummings was a problem.

Although articulate, experienced and a master of headlines, Gove's involvement in buying PPE had been unsuccessful. The minister was generating other embarrassments. First was his appointment of Michael Barber to review Whitehall. Barber was an overrated educationist. His delivery unit for Tony Blair's government had been a failure and closed after his resignation in 2005. Official statistics show that England's educational standards had failed to improve in this period. His subsequent employment at Pearson, the educational publisher, and as the chairman of the Office for Students had also been disappointing. Despite his public statements on the issue, the oppression of free speech in universities remained pernicious until his resignation in 2021.

Brexiteers also questioned Gove's preparations for Britain's departure from the EU with or without a deal. He seemed unable to solve the complexities of future non-tariff barriers or recruit the additional customs officials and vets.

Brexiteers did not trust the minister who had supported May's withdrawal agreement and, in David Davis's opinion, 'overestimates his talent'. 'Michael vacillates,' observed Peter Lilley, 'and is good at compromise.' Although Gove claimed to have sealed an agreement with the EU on trade between Britain and Northern Ireland to safeguard supplies of fresh food, the experts knew he was wrong. 'He took positions convenient to himself,' observed Davis. Gove, complained international traders, musicians and fishermen, ignored their requirements to overcome future obstacles. Despite his energy, they forecast, Brexit would still cost £7.5 billion in additional paperwork, VAT complications and incomprehensible rules of origin, all fed into 'Chief', the government's antiquated customs computer. 'Why have you placed your trust in Michael who didn't care about you?' another senior Brexiteer asked Boris. The prime minister sidestepped the question. He could not rebut the Office for Budget Responsibility's (OBR) prediction that non-tariff barriers after Brexit would reduce the UK's economy by 4 per cent within ten years. Gove's curt dismissal of that prediction did not allay anxieties during the Brexit endgame. The spillover for anxious Brexiteers were the never-ending Covid laws. The resisters grouped themselves into the Covid Recovery Group (CRG).

Thirty-three Tory MPs, mostly CRG members, voted against the government's latest restrictions on 3 November. Boris was warned that over sixty MPs would rebel against further controls at the end of the month. 'Too much science and not enough common sense,' complained Craig Mackinlay of the CRG. 'Boris wants to impose nonsensical rules which allow a man to walk across a golf course but not play golf.' Tom Tugendhat, a Kent MP opposed to both lockdowns and Boris, emphatically proclaimed 'The Garden of England doesn't hold the virus.' Kent, he said, should be free of restrictions.

SAGE was blamed for causing confusion. Although in mid-November, Covid deaths rose by 40 per cent in one week, SAGE recommended that the lockdown could be lifted on 2 December because the infection rates in the north-west were falling. Five days later, the same scientists warned that if the rules were relaxed over Christmas, there would be a tough lockdown in January. Boris ignored the warning. Determined to allow a traditional five-day Christmas, he predicted that the majority of Britons would be vaccinated by Easter. The OBR contradicted him. Widespread vaccination, forecast the agency, would not materialise before summer 2021. The constant battle between Boris's optimism and his critics' pessimism suggested that the country was drifting into a permanent crisis.

Even the announcement of a game-changer on 2 December was disbelieved. The regulator's approval of the Pfizer vaccine and the beginning of Britain's £11.7 billion mass vaccination programme on 8 December left the critics unpersuaded. Matt Hancock's assertion that getting Pfizer approved before the EU confirmed the benefits of Brexit was criticised by *The Times* as 'Triumphalism' and 'unnecessary'. Boris's chortle of 'an end in sight' and 'a summer of weddings' was similarly dismissed. Even AstraZeneca's published data promising between 62 per cent and 90 per cent efficacy ignited a sceptical debate. Boris's critics scorned his target to dispense 15 million doses by mid-February and to vaccinate over 20 million people by Easter. The *Sunday Times* predicted that the NHS would miss that target and fail to vaccinate the necessary 2 million people a week. With the army's help, by mid-February, the vaccination rate would be over 3 million a week, and over 20 million Britons would be vaccinated five weeks before Easter. But in early December, the impression among officials in Paris and Brussels was of Boris as weak.

On 3 December Michel Barnier sprang a surprise. At Macron's request, he restricted the terms under which Britain could subsidise its industries. The British would be more limited to grant aid than EU countries. Barnier also demanded unlimited fishing for the EU's fleet. Shocked by Macron's hostility, Boris halted the negotiations and deployed the Internal Market Bill. 'The threatened use of the bill brought them back to the table,' recalls David Davis. 'And they finally understood our demand for sovereignty.' To resurrect the talks, Boris agreed to have dinner with Ursula von der Leyen, the European Commission president, in Brussels on Wednesday 9 December.

In his usual manner, Boris was convinced that good humour would resolve the deadlock over the 'level playing field' and the EU's 'right' to issue instant punishments if the Commission unilaterally decided that Britain had broken EU rules. To ease the tension, Boris had dropped the Internal Market Bill's contentious provision and agreed to reduce Britain's share of fish from 80 per cent towards 60 per cent. His efforts were in vain. During the dinner, Boris spoke into a vacuum. Von der Leyen and Barnier, Boris discovered, had agreed to say little and concede nothing. Boris returned to London chastened. Failure, he knew, would plunge the Tory Party into meltdown. 'We've just got to get out and deal with the problems afterwards,' Bill Cash told him. 'You need to frighten them.' To play tough, Boris announced that no deal was 'a strong possibility'. Next, the government 'leaked' that four Royal Navy boats had been assigned to board French trawlers and prevent any fishing. For the first time, Dublin and Brussels grasped that, unlike Theresa May's government, Tory MPs and the Cabinet unanimously supported Boris's hard line. Another deadline to finalise a deal passed just as Covid infections rose by 50 per cent during the week.

Boris had ignored Vallance's warnings of a new wave. Although 64,000 had died since March, he noted that the death rate was falling. He refused to close schools, abandon exams or cancel the five-day Christmas. Curtailing Christmas, he told Keir Starmer, would be 'inhuman'. On Friday 18 December Boris's optimism crashed. A new variant of the virus, discovered in Kent, was spreading rapidly. The weekly death toll was predicted to rise to 5,000 with 20,000 new hospital admissions. Initially, to protect Christmas, Boris waved the bad news aside until Macron used the variant outbreak as an excuse to close Calais. Within one day 3,000 lorries – some with rotting seafood – were stacked in Kent. Curiously, Boris claimed on the same day that only 174 trucks were waiting outside Dover. The crisis in Kent forced him to surrender. 'It is with a very heavy heart,' he announced, 'that I must tell you we cannot continue with Christmas as planned.' Only limited numbers would be allowed to celebrate for a single day. Downing Street was once again portrayed as rudderless. Reading the barbs about his dithering and confusion, Brussels decided to strike.

'The moment of truth,' declared Barnier. Either Britain made substantial concessions on fish, he threatened, or there would be no deal. For Brexiteers, this was the moment to test Boris's mettle. Boris reassured Bill Cash. 'Boris has got it,' Cash reported.

'I have to say things are looking difficult,' Boris told von der Leyen, rejecting the ultimatum. He would not sign an agreement. The stand-off lasted until two days before Christmas. Then, he lost his nerve about Britain's fishing rights. Boris failed to convince von der Leyen that he was about to walk out without a deal. Instead, he gave way. Although Gove would later claim that Britain got 'about two-thirds of the fish in our waters by 2026', Britain got only an extra 6 per cent in value bringing the total entitlement to about 58 per cent. Boris sacrificed the fishing industry. Damned by the fishery industry as a sell-out, Victoria Prentis, the fisheries minister, admitted she had not read the final agreement because she was arranging a Christmas party.

Getting a last-minute deal mattered more to the Brexiteers and the Remainers than the fate of the fishermen. Within the 1,246-page agreement, Britain had obtained zero tariffs and zero quotas, access to EU markets and the European Court of Justice's authority ceased. Britain's sovereignty was restored. The positive media headlines proved that Boris's doubters had been wrong. At the end of a tumultuous year, Boris was for some a hero. Brexit was delivered and Britain, unlike the EU, had vaccinated during that week nearly 250,000 people. Christmas celebrations were restricted to one day. The government tried to generate optimism. 'We know with a very high degree of confidence,' gushed Hancock on 29 December, 'that we are going to be out of this by spring.' The jabs, promised Boris, meant total freedom by Easter. 'It's the beginning of the end of the crisis,' concluded *The Times*. Britons began booking their summer holidays.

Soon after 1 January, some fresh-food shelves of Northern Ireland's supermarkets were empty, removal vans with domestic furniture sent from London to Belfast were stopped at Liverpool because no customs declaration had been completed, and Ulster's garden centres were forbidden to buy seeds and saplings from Britain. Northern Ireland had become a foreign country. Frictionless trade was a myth. 'There never was going to be a level playing field,' Bill Cash said. The EU, insisted the Brexiteer, was always determined to make the loss of Northern Ireland as the price of Brexit. 'We thought the EU would play nice,' grumbled Craig Mackinlay. 'We were foolish. They're not prepared to be fair.' The EU was determined to harm Britain.

In theory, the EU was breaching Protocol 16 of the Agreement that 'application of this protocol should impact as little as possible on the everyday life of communities in both Ireland and Northern Ireland.' Brexiteers believed that only by threatening to unilaterally abandon Protocol 16 would the barriers be removed. Boris's reliance on Gove to negotiate with the EU aroused anger. 'He's a compromiser and not tough enough,' Cash told Boris. 'I was astonished,' said Davis, 'why Boris even listened to Gove.' Focusing on Gove's character, another critic told the prime minister, 'Michael has an unbelievable sense of himself which transcends the reality. One always senses that he wants you to fail so he can be prime minister.'

Initially, Boris spoke about 'teething problems'. In reality, the cost and complications of trade with the EU had massively increased. British food exporters needed veterinary certificates and multiple forms to establish the origin of their goods; musicians would need work visas to perform in EU countries; the City and financial services were denied 'equivalence' by the EU and operated on even worse terms than the markets in New York and Singapore.

The discontent finally persuaded Boris to replace Gove with David Frost as a Cabinet minister to negotiate a better deal. Unlike Gove, Frost wanted to directly challenge the EU by abandoning many of the restrictions on trade with Northern Ireland. Gove was left nominally in charge of persuading Scots not to vote for independence in the May elections. His reputation did not encourage the Unionists. Boris, they feared, was insufficiently engaged in that life-and-death struggle. But Boris believed that beating Covid would determine his fate. The latest roller coaster looked shaky on 3 January, just as Boris predicted that the lockdown would be over by March.

That Sunday, hospital admissions surged by 30 per cent and new infections were hitting 50,000 a day. Despite the danger, Boris insisted that schools would open the following morning. Infection at schools, said the Education Department correctly, was 'marginal' and 5 million children would be tested during the first week. The teaching unions disagreed and demanded that the schools remain closed. Boris was determined to defeat the unions. Late that Sunday afternoon, Whitty reported that new infections had risen to 70,000 a day. Hospitals were reaching capacity. Pessimistic scientists predicted that another 30,000 would die. Before midnight, Boris surrendered and imposed a third lockdown to last until at least 15 February. The streets emptied and fatigue spread as people faced darkness and isolation. On Monday morning, schools were closed and exams were cancelled. The teaching unions had won. Parents were furious. Public confidence was rattled. Boris's enemies sniped again about his inevitable demise. For ten days, Downing Street was buffeted by bad headlines. Only Venezuelans were enduring harsher controls than Britons. Then, unexpectedly, the Gambler's luck returned.

On 23 January, the government announced that 6.2 million people had already been vaccinated. The critics were astonished by the programme's efficiency. At the same time, the EU's plan to vaccinate its 446 million population was unravelling. On Macron's insistence, the EU had planned to rely on France's Sanofi vaccine. But Sanofi's development had failed and the EU's bureaucrats had bought insufficient doses of Pfizer and AstraZeneca. On the single day that over 340,000 Britons were vaccinated, just fifty in France had been jabbed. Embarrassed by the Commission's failure to protect EU citizens, Ursula von der Leyen not only declared war on

AstraZeneca but, without consulting Dublin, on 29 January invoked Protocol 16 to prevent any vaccines manufactured in the EU crossing from the Irish Republic into Ulster. The unexpected announcement destroyed the Commission's high-minded promise to protect the Good Friday Agreement by preventing a hard border across Ireland. Overnight, the EU's failure to organise vaccinations and its disregard for Ireland boosted the Brexiteers' credibility. About eight hours later, von der Leyen backed down. But the damage had been done and it got worse. French and German politicians quoted bogus facts to scorn the AstraZeneca vaccination as ineffective. Astutely, Boris did not publicly hit back. Instead, he quietly urged EU leaders to reconsider their prejudice. That would take over one month.

The unexpected vaccine success boosted Boris's poll ratings, sufficient to deflect a damaging milestone. 'I'm deeply sorry,' Boris told the nation as the death rate hit 100,000 on 26 January, the worst proportion in the world. Over 75 per cent of the dead were over seventy-five years old, and 95 per cent of the dead had pre-existing health conditions. Pertinently, 31 per cent of the deaths at St Bart's Hospital during the first wave were BAME, although they were just 11 per cent of England's population in the 2011 census. About 60 per cent of BAME citizens were refusing to be vaccinated. Only a few questioned Britain's fluid criteria for a 'Covid death'. Death certificates were issued without supervision and Covid was an imprecise cause of an actual death, if the infection had occurred 'within twenty-eight days of death'.

By 22 February, over 17 million Britons had been vaccinated compared to about 3 million in France. Hospitalisations and deaths were plummeting. Yet a new, cautious Boris announced a four-month road map to end the lockdown in June. Businessmen were outraged but the majority supported gradualism. Caution and the vaccine had restored Boris's poll ratings. He would be judged by the final success of ending the emergency – and restoring the economy and jobs, not the pitfalls on the way.

In mid-April, over 75 per cent of the country was vaccinated. Herd immunity was nearly reality. For the moment, the Gambler had got through the worst. Within twenty months, he had steered the country through a general election, Brexit and Covid. Boris's self-confidence was enhanced by the EU's vaccination failure and his opponents' demise. Inside Downing Street, the relaunch of the government in summer 2021 was focused on transforming Britain into a scientific superpower. The vision embraced huge expenditure, enhanced investment in the north, reform of education, reorganising the NHS and the Civil Service, producing a defence review to fundamentally rebuild the armed forces, properly defining Global Britain, and liberating business and the City from unnecessary regulations. His opponents offered no realistic alternative. His fate also depended on persuading the Scots about the value of preserving the Union and the EU to modify the Northern Ireland protocol. Now, more assured and mature, his turbulent life had prepared him for all that high drama. Always dancing on the edge, he could live no other way.

Acknowledgements

This book was conceived in conversation with Ebury in August 2019. In the course of the year to research and write the book, I received remarkable advice and help from two outstanding editors: Drummond Moir at Penguin Random House and then David Milner. I owe both a genuine debt. I am also grateful to Suzanne Connelly and Joanna Bennett at WH Allen, as well as proofreader John Garrett.

Readers should be aware that Boris Johnson is not a stranger in my home. Veronica Wadley, my wife, has known him as a journalist since he joined the *Daily Telegraph* in 1988. She became the newspaper's deputy editor before later serving for seven years as the editor of the *London Evening Standard*. Their long relationship is one of colleagues rather than friends. She played no part in researching or writing this book.

I have met Boris at parties but we have never engaged in a long conversation. I did not ask him to co-operate in writing this book. However, he did tell others that he would not oppose it. Nevertheless, some people I approached for an interview told me that after Boris had said that he was cool to the idea, they would decline to meet me. By any account, this is an unauthorised biography.

Nevertheless, I interviewed well over one hundred people close to Boris, some several times. Most spoke off the record, others agreed to quotations but did not want to be individually thanked. I think it therefore best not to acknowledge anyone's personal contribution to the text. Suffice to say, I am immensely grateful to them all.

In writing the book, I relied as always on Claudia Wordsworth, a brilliant researcher, especially for the two Covid chapters. They will serve as the first draft of a complicated saga which will define Boris's premiership and Britain's fate.

Those I can personally thank for their contributions are Armand D'Angour, David Blackburn, David Cornwell, Roger Clarke, Miriam Gross, Emma Inglis, Trevor Kavanagh, Matthew Leeming, Quentin Letts, Tom Mangold, Angela Neuberger, Freddie Raphael, Anthony Seldon, Christopher Silvester, Tom Teodorczuk, Michael Waldman and John Ware.

David Hirst was a helpful libel lawyer and, as always, my agent Jonathan Lloyd of Curtis Brown was an outstanding friend.

Brexit and Boris have divided many families and friends, and my home has experienced the same disagreements. To protect our close relationships, we have all agreed to quietly disagree. Despite the obvious conflicts of interest, Veronica Wadley was as always extraordinarily supportive and a true friend.

To all, I say 'Thank you!'

Endnotes

ACT I – ORIGINS

Chapter 1: The Truth

'All his wit, charm and self-deprecation': Prue White, *The Times*, 30 December 2017 • 'I learned from my mother': Stanley Johnson, interview with author • '660 boys stood to attention': *The Sunday Times*, 11 May 2008 • 'swollen head': Stanley Johnson, *Stanley I Presume*, Fourth Estate (2009), p.57 • fed boiled eggs: interview with author • Charlotte blamed herself: Charlotte Wahl, interview with author • Although published, it was not successful: Stanley Johnson, interview with author • He cares far more about other animals: *Mail on Sunday*, 18 January 2017 • 'Total garbage. Honestly': *The Sunday Times*, 30 December 2017 • 'Human relations remain a mystery to me': *The Daily Telegraph*, 31 January 2004 • 'Let's see who can be quietest for longest': *Evening Standard*, 27 February 2012 • drive through the night to a hospital: *The Telegraph*, 11 January 2016 • 'Bring it on, I say': *Boris: The Rise of Boris Johnson*, Andrew Gimson, Simon & Schuster (2006), p.19 • illegitimate daughter of a nineteenth-century German prince: *The Sunday Times*, 3 August 2008 • the 'too rough' Johnsons: Rachel Johnson, *The Sunday Times*, 19 April 2019 • meeting her father for lunch: *Mail on Sunday*, 19 November 2017 • rampantly unfaithful and a serial womaniser: Sonia Purnell, p.34; Andrew Gimson p.27 • 'Freud and the mind is a particular mystery': Stanley Johnson, interview with author • sympathy for Charlotte's illness: Stanley Johnson, interview with author • 'I feel fiercely protective towards my parents': *The Times*, 6 June 2015 • 'your mother disappearing for eight months': *Evening Standard*, 19 March 2013; 'Boris Johnson: The Irresistible Rise', Michael Cockerell, BBC Two (2013) • never leave his beloved mother: *Mail on Sunday*, 27 March 2016 • whether he delivered his children on their first day: Stanley Johnson, interview with author • 'not to have emotional needs': *The Times*, 6 June 2015 • 'I relied on the schools': Stanley Johnson, interview with author • an affair with one of the girls: Stanley Johnson, interview with author • 'lifelong distrust of authority': *The Telegraph*, 26 October 2019

Chapter 2: Effortlessly Superior

'because I never asked them': *The Telegraph*, 31 January 2004; *The Sunday Times*, 31 May 2008 • 'not to say completely unfaithful': Andrew Gimson, p.35 • They handled it brilliantly': Andrew Gimson, p.39 • 'There wasn't much to eat': *The Times*, 6 June 2015 • first hundred lines of the *Iliad* in Greek: *The Telegraph*, 17 March 2009 • 'didn't get the seat': Stanley Johnson, interview with author • 'or told Boris to behave': Stanley Johnson, interview with author • Alex de Ferranti, a school friend of Rachel's: *Mail on Sunday*, 2 December 2019 • 'the network of obligation which binds everyone else': Andrew Gimson, p.43 • 'don't be arrogant': *The Times*, 10 November 2012 • 'the temptations of Oxford life': Andrew Gimson, p.55

Chapter 3: Uncertain Star

uninterested in fame: Andrew Gimson, p.62 • the repetition of old jokes: Tony Young, interview with author • 'Humour is a utensil': Sonia Purnell, p.3 • a future prime minister: Matthew Leeming, interview with author • 'to coddle the self-deception of the stooge': *The Oxford Myth*, Rachel Johnson, Weidenfeld and Nicolson (1988) pp.68–69 • 'Congratulations man': Andrew Gimson, p.64 • 'we became namby-pambies': Sebastian Shakespeare, *Daily Mail*, 20 July 2019 • 'the dinners being incredibly drunken': *The Telegraph*, 28 May 2013 • The article was dropped: Andrew Gimson, p.74 • 'the English genre of bogus self-deception': Andrew Gimson, p.72 • 'you pick up a load of self-knowledge': *The Oxford Myth*, Rachel Johnson • the marriage had already been agreed: Sebastian Shakespeare, interview with author • 'addicted to the joy of hurtling myself down the slopes': *The Telegraph*, 21 February 2011 • 'He's rapacious': Matthew Leeming, interview with author • 'a buffoon and an idler': *The Guardian*, 6 October 2019 • Boris was unaware of the brewing problems: Matthew Leeming, interview with author • 'He put a whole new interpretation on the word "Godfather" ': Stanley Johnson, interview with author

Chapter 4: Awakening

trying to make an impromptu speech: Andrew Gimson, p.87 • 'he would have limped to the altar': Andrew Gimson, p.86 • 'Boris told such dreadful lies, it made one gasp': Andrew Gimson, p.116 • that was inaccurate: Max Hastings, interview with author • a team of people tasked with rebutting negative Boris stories: Sonia Purnell, p.118 • Christopher Booker and Richard Littlejohn: Charlie Pownall, interview with author • 'frightening focus and drive': Sonia Purnell, p.4 • 'He's married to his job': Allegra Mostyn-Owen, *Evening Standard*, 29 May 2012 • 'a manic high' in London: Matthew Leeming, interview with author • the Virgina Woolf-type: Roger Clark, interview with author • At the law school she was seen with a boyfriend: Matthew Leeming, interview with author • offering the 'stolen' gems to Hatton Garden dealers: *Daily Mail*, 4 April 2009 • 'conclusions that the British thought had been explicitly rejected': *The Telegraph*, 16 September 2017 • description of Boris's temper: Sonia Purnell, pp.181, 219, 229, 384 • 'Allegra is too demanding': Charlotte Wahl, interview with author • 'that was the end of the relationship': Andrew Gimson, p.87 • his support of Thatcher was a 'ghastly moment': Andrew Gimson, p.112 • 'the most ruthless, ambitious person I have ever met': *The Sunday Times*, 18 September 2011 • strip away the veto rights of individual states: Andrew Gimson, p.103; Heathcote Williams, p.49; Sonia Purnell, p.128 • Both Hurd and Hastings robustly denied Moore's assertion: Andrew Gimson, p.104 • 'rather weird sense of power': Desert Island Discs, BBC Radio 4, October 2005 • 'Suck and you'll find': Matthew Leeming, interview with author • 'humourless self-deprecation beneath the idiotic flamboyance': Andrew Gimson, p.119 • 'As a virtue, loyalty to friends has its limits': Max Hastings, *Editor: An Inside Story of Newspapers*, Macmillan (2002), p.274 • would destroy the career of any other man or woman in journalism, let alone in government': *The Times*, 19 July 2018 • 'often really I couldn't follow what was going on at all': Desert Island Discs, BBC Radio 4 • people won't be able to tell the difference': *Daily Mail*, 25 March 2013; 'Boris Johnson: The Irresistible Rise', Michael Cockerell, BBC Two (2013)

Chapter 5: Defying the Critics

'I certainly did not attempt to find the address': *Mail on Sunday*, 16 July 1995 • 'a penchant for comedy is an almost insuperable obstacle to achieving high political office': Max Hastings, p.273 • 'temperamental, tiresome and nauseatingly eccentric and simply just obnoxious': *Conrad and Lady Black: Dancing on the Edge*, Tom Bower, HarperCollins (2006) p.144 • 'I love Barbara. I venerate her': *Conrad and Lady Black: Dancing on the Edge*, p.390 • 'entrusting a Ming vase to the hands of an ape': *The Telegraph*, 4 May 2012 • new readers did not rank among those he valued as the elite: Rod Liddle, interview with author • sacked for viewing porn on a school computer: *The Times*, 15 March 2008; *Evening Standard*, 18 June 2010 • 'The blessed sponge of amnesia has wiped the chalkboard of history': Andrew Gimson, p.157 • 'I want to have my cake and eat it': Andrew Gimson, p.156 • 'I have actually been questioned about it on a TV game show': Andrew Gimson, p.142 • he would remain at the Spectator: Andrew Gimson, p.143 • 'I had a wife, beaming up at me from the front row': Boris Johnson, *Lend Me Your Ears*, HarperCollins (2003), p.13 and p.46 • 'the impersonation becomes the man': *Evening Standard*, 14 July 2000 • 'I can't think of a higher compliment': *The Sunday Times*, 27 May 2001

Chapter 6: 'It's all a mess'

'He only agreed to make you happy. He didn't mean it': Toby Young, interview with author • 'I would never, ever, live with a man, let alone get engaged': *Daily*

Mail, 4 April 2009 • 'You are the first woman friend I have ever had': *Mail on Sunday*, 27 March 2016 • 'he wants to be loved by the entire world': *Mail on Sunday*, 27 March 2016 • 'confined' to one woman: *Mail on Sunday*, 27 March 2016 • 'He was right': Boris Johnson, *Lend Me Your Ears*, p.236 • £500-worth of unpaid parking tickets and congestion charges: *Daily Mail*, 3 June 2011 • Four children could not be privately educated on a parliamentary salary: *The Sunday Times*, 15 December 2002; *The Sunday Times*, 19 October 2008 • 'Hey, Dave, what's the plan': *For the Record*, David Cameron, HarperCollins (2019), p.60 • 'Now I have an extravagance that knows no bounds': *Conrad and Lady Black: Dancing on the Edge*, pp.319–320 • Boris, it appeared, was swooning for Mary: Andrew Gimson, p.176 • 'I am a juggler. I can have it all': Andrew Gimson, p.165 • it provoked universal roars of laughter – except from Boris: Fraser Nelson, *The Daily Telegraph*, 4 May 2012 • 'That great prodigious tree in the forest': *The Times*, 25 May 2008 • 'Conrad bought a nice big chocolate cake': Rod Liddle, interview with author • 'I cannot comment on his present predicament': *Evening Standard*, 30 November 2007; *Evening Standard*, 7 December 2007 • 'I'm looking forward to meeting the Ribbentrop brothers': Rod Liddle, interview with author • 'I just felt Boris was running the whole place as a knocking shop': Sonia Purnell, p.247 • She was accused by some of selfishly wrecking Boris's marriage: Andrew Gimson, p.225 • 'There comes a point where you've got to put the dynamite under your own tracks': Conservative Heartland 2001, cited in Andrew Gimson, p.260 • Monogamy did not appeal to him: *Evening Standard*, 8 May 2008 • Boris never fulfilled his threat: *Daily Mail*, 10 October 2012; *Daily Mail*, 1 July 2016 • 'so puffed up with their own egos they end up living in a parallel universe': *Daily Mail*, 11 November 2004 • 'There were things in the papers yesterday': Andrew Gimson, p.219 • 'He regards himself as rather ugly': *Daily Mail*, 8 September 2018

Chapter 7: Downfall and Resurrection

The threat, Boris would recall, forced Cameron to declare his candidacy: *The Telegraph*, 5 April 2010 • 'I am backing David Cameron's campaign out of pure, cynical self-interest': *The Independent*, 5 October 2005 • 'I think British society is designed like that': Desert Island Discs, BBC Radio 4, 30 October 2005 • 'It was as though a cosmic injustice had occurred': *Daily Mail*, 16 July 2010 • 'girly swots who wasted their time at university': *Daily Mail*, 12 June 2013 • Boris is 'not nice': *Daily Mail*, 1 July 2016 • The dent cost £5,000 to repair: *Daily Mail*, 1 June 2007; *Evening Standard*, 31 July 2007 • Marina was doorstepped and Fazackerley resigned from the supplement: *News of the World*, 2 April 2006 • 'It's vastly superior to our approach': *Daily Mail*, 19 July 2007 • 'The political risk for me is considerable. Ken is the favourite': *The Guardian*, 5 July 2007 • a supporter of immigration and diversity: *Evening Standard*, 16 July 2007 • Few gave him much chance against Livingstone's machine: *Daily Mail*, 17 July 2007 • her modern country should not be compared to the Tory party's antics: *The Telegraph*, 5 April 2010 • £1.9 million from Ken Livingstone to build a campaign headquarters: *Evening Standard*, 5 February 2008 • 'the most dismal awakening of my life': *Evening Standard*, 31 August 2007 • 'executed with the scimitar by a beautiful black woman': *Evening Standard*, 24 August 2007 • 'Boris will strip it away from them': *The Guardian*, 17 July 2007 • 'I reserve the right in the course of this campaign to make jokes': *Daily Mail*, 4 September 2007 • 'It's a great utensil for bringing people together': *Evening Standard*, 3 September 2007 • earning money from journalism, TV appearances and after-dinner speeches: *Daily Mail*, 9 November 2007 • 'I want to give Londoners a bus they can be proud of': *The Guardian*, 18 May 2010 • The true cost would be at least £70 million: *Evening Standard*, 13 December 2007 • his appeal to traditional Tory outer-London boroughs: *The Sunday Times*, 12 August 2007 • 'I am laying down my pen and taking up the sword full time': *Evening Standard*, 10 January 2008 • Construction of new homes in 2008 would fall: *Evening Standard*, 23 June 2008 • increased rates by 152 per cent over his eight years: *Evening Standard*, 10 March 2008 • Many were running 80 per cent empty: *Evening Standard*, 17 January 2008 • traffic levels had surged back to pre-charge levels: *Evening Standard*, 11 August 2008 • Boris was told not to speak about social justice: *Evening Standard*, 29 September 2008 • 'You'll always surprise people': *The Times*, 7 May 2012 • 'Not that I know of': *The Telegraph*, 12 April 2009 • three undisclosed children from previous relationships: *Daily Mail*, 4 April 2008 • 'the "democratic right" to insist on its leaders taking no mistresses': *Daily Mail*, 8 September 2018 • Since 2000, the LDA had spent £2.6 billion: *Evening Standard*, 3 April 2008 • enjoyed a holiday to Nigeria paid from public funds: *Evening Standard*, 24 January 2008 • Jasper had given her £100,000: *Evening Standard*, 4 March 2008 • 'There is something chilling and Stalinist about his refusal to comply': *Evening Standard*, 18 December 2007 • 'entirely inappropriate' and 'improper': *Evening Standard*, 16 July 2009 • 'I'm absolutely 100 per cent anti-racist': *Evening Standard*, 28 December 2007 • Johnson suffered only marginal criticism in the newspaper: *The Guardian*, 21 April 2008 • 'I'm working to get Ken unelected': *The Guardian*, 30 April 2008 • the *Standard*'s poll placed Boris 12 per cent ahead of Livingstone: *Evening Standard*, 17 March 2008 • some polls put Livingstone slightly ahead: *The Sunday Times*, 20 April 2008 • reported uncertainty about the outcome: *The Guardian*, 17 July 2019 • Among other Tories who refused to vote for Boris was Michael Portillo: *Evening Standard*, 9 May 2008 • At the end of Boris's speech, his toast was to 'Mayor Leavingsoon': *Daily Mail*, 9 April 2008 • Boris himself still feared he might lose the prize: *The Times*, 27 March 2008 • He pledged to ban alcohol from the Tube: *Evening Standard*, 11 April 2008; *Evening Standard*, 3 April 2008; *Evening Standard*, 16 April 2008 • He also failed to name a single member of his future team: *The Telegraph*, 29 March 2008 • Diamond had earned £21 million in the previous year: *Evening Standard*, 15 April 2008 • Boris would make 'a mess of the whole thing': *The Guardian*, 1 May 2008 • he would try to inherit his son's seat in Henley: *The Telegraph*, 3 May 2008 • Decay, the newspaper predicted, would spread: *The Guardian*, 9 May 2009 • Parker assumed that Boris would cut ribbons: *Evening Standard*, 27 May 2008 • Milton understood how to negotiate with Whitehall:

Evening Standard, 6 May 2008 • 'If you put that I was forced to do it by some fucking Cameron bollocks, I'll be extremely annoyed': *The Times*, 6 December 2008 • 'You get screeds of abuse or praise': *The Telegraph*, 7 June 2008 • 'All the riches, the power and the glory are never quite enough, it seems': Sonia Purnell, p.5 • 'valuable houses or large tracts of land': Sonia Purnell, p.5 • he read Greek poems in the original: *The Spectator*, 10 September 2005

ACT II – 'THE FIRST TIME HE'D HAD TO WORK IN HIS LIFE'
Chapter 8: The Challenge

a warning of the new peril of his life in the spotlight: *Evening Standard*, 12 May 2008 • dogged by allegations of partisanship, chaos, overstaffing and financial mismanagement: *Evening Standard*, 3 February 2009 • phoney 'diversity' projects: *Evening Standard*, 6 August 2008 • 'tens of millions of pounds' had been misspent: *Evening Standard*, 12 November 2008; *Evening Standard*, 16 July 2008; *The Sunday Times*, 8 June 2008 • Beale had authorised Livingstone's first-class air fares: *Evening Standard*, 19 June 2009; *Daily Mail*, 2 April 2012 • Lewis resigned: *Daily Mail*, 5 July 2008; *Daily Mail*, 8 July 2008 • 'I really regretted it': *The Guardian*, 16 April 2011 • 'The autumn will decide whether he can really govern the city': *Evening Standard*, 19 August 2008 • 'an inexperienced blunderer': *The Guardian*, 7 July 2008 • Boris agreed to Parker's departure: *Evening Standard*, 15 July 2008; *Evening Standard*, 19 August 2008 • All those deaths . . . had been 'endlessly ignored': *Evening Standard*, 11 July 2008; *Evening Standard*, 23 April 2009 • 'more intellectually challenging than anything I've ever done': *The Guardian*, 9 August 2008 • 'there is no substitute for me, as directly elected mayor, being in charge': *Evening Standard*, 21 August 2008 • Boris alternated between jokes and seriousness to steady his administration: *The Guardian*, 9 August 2008 • 'My job is to translate into action the ten ideas Boris has while he cycles to City Hall': *Evening Standard*, 8 September 2008 • the only realistic tenant was West Ham, a local club: *Evening Standard*, 10 June 2008; *Evening Standard*, 20 June 2008 • 'No one has broken Britain and no one ever will': *The Telegraph*, 19 August 2008; *Evening Standard*, 20 August 2008 • his eight-times grandfather was George II of England: *Daily Mail*, 21 August 2008 • 'there are times when you have to take a stand': *The Times*, 28 August 2008

Chapter 9: Exposing Vipers

Tony Blair . . . had created London's housing crisis: *Evening Standard*, 16 October 2009 • Charles invited the mayor to Clarence House: *Evening Standard*, 12 June 2008 • 'drab and featureless . . . phallocratic buildings': *Evening Standard*, 24 February 2009 • 'This fetish for tall buildings anywhere and everywhere': *The Sunday*

Times, 11 May 2008 • Was the mayor, some wondered, persuaded by the last person he spoke to?: *Evening Standard*, 6 August 2008 • 'will be wonderful for one hundred years': *The Guardian*, 9 August 2008 • allowed a high-rise luxury development in Doon Street, Lambeth: *Evening Standard*, 25 July 2008; *Evening Standard*, 26 August 2008 • Developers were also burdened by lower house prices and rents south of the river: *Evening Standard*, 6 January 2009 • 'He doesn't do nasty,' Tony Travers realised: *The Guardian*, 9 December 2008 • 'If you're interested in getting something done, by God you focus on the detail': *The Guardian*, 16 April 2011 • 'They would pay taxes,' he explained: *Evening Standard*, 10 March 2009 • 'It's about people who are struggling to put bread on the table': *The Sunday Times*, 15 February 2015 • He even professed enthusiasm for electric cars: *The Telegraph*, 2 December 2008 • His proof in 2009 was to decide the fate of the Metropolitan Police: *Evening Standard*, 29 September 2008; *The Telegraph*, 12 April 2009 • Blair was under suspicion: *Daily Mail*, 28 July 2008 • 'a yank on the steering wheel and that's what I intend to provide': *The Times*, 23 December 2008 • 'because Boris's hair was combed': *Evening Standard*, 2 November 2009 • He would later call the Tory Party 'wholly corrupt': *Evening Standard*, 22 December 2008 • the closure of Green's email address: *Daily Mail*, 28 November 2008 • He'd missed the bigger picture: Len Duvall, interview with author • Stephenson was the 'safe pair of hands' and got the job: *Evening Standard*, 26 January 2009

Chapter 10: Birth of 'Borisism'

They were searching for a new house: *Evening Standard*, 21 January 2009; *Evening Standard*, 28 May 2009 • 'Don't get carried away by neo-socialist claptrap': *Evening Standard*, 23 September 2008; *Evening Standard*, 1 October 2008; *Evening Standard*, 27 October 2008 • he spoke of a rival to the Eiffel Tower: *The Sunday Times*, 25 October 2009 • 'I saw him in the lift': *Evening Standard*, 2 February 2010 • the life opportunities of disadvantaged children were crushed: *The Telegraph*,18 July 2010 • He was to be no longer automatically ridiculed as a buffoon: *The Telegraph*,17 March 2009; *Evening Standard*, 23 April 2009; *The Telegraph*, 26 October 2009; *The Telegraph*, 15 March 2010 • 'has emerged as a more interesting and appealing politician': *The Guardian*, 30 April 2009 • a new headquarters in Newham: Neale Coleman, interview with author • Livingstone had committed the same money three times over: *Evening Standard*, 5 November 2008 • That was Livingstone's legacy to Boris: Ibid • Brown still refused to pay £1.4 billion for the repairs: *Evening Standard*, 24 February 2009 • 'gambling with the fortunes of the capital': *Evening Standard*, 25 November 2008; *The Telegraph*, 25 November 2008 • buy land and underground access along the route: *Evening Standard*, 4 December 2008 • The money should be spent on restoring the Tube: *Evening Standard*, 28 April 2009 • a breach of his election pledge: *Evening Standard:* 4 September 2008 • over 70 per cent *would* be interested: *The Sunday Times*, 15

November 2009 • Cameron could not be ousted, but he could be embarrassed: *The Telegraph*, 25 April 2009

Chapter 11: The Messiah Complex

Goldman Sachs had not been bailed out: *The Telegraph*, 19 October 2009 • 'First they came for the bankers and I said nothing': *Evening Standard*, 12 August 2011 • 'We are hostile to risk and more hostile to reward': *The Telegraph*, 6 February 2012; *The Telegraph*, 20 May 2013 • A trip to Brussels three weeks earlier had aggravated his fears: *The Telegraph*, 27 July 2011 • Neither the Labour government nor Whitehall were combating the EU's grab: *The Telegraph*, 7 September 2009 • No EU country was training Britons to become nurses without payment: *The Telegraph*, 22 March 2010 • 'Thanks a lot for your help this week, you cunt': *Evening Standard*, 9 October 2009 • 'La vendetta è un piatto che va mangiato freddo': *The Times*, 20 October 2009 • 'endlessly trying like wasps in a jam jar to be the survivor': *The Guardian*, 18 April 2011 • 'Messiah complex': *The Times*, 5 October 2009; *Evening Standard*, 5 October 2009 • copy Paris's rent-a-bike scheme: *Evening Standard*, 12 September 2012 • No 'bike file' existed: Kulveer Ranger, interview with author • 6,000 bikes 'at no cost to the taxpayer': *Evening Standard*, 12 August 2009 • 'I'm not very big on self-doubt': *The Guardian*, 18 April 2011 • 'I will change my name by deed poll to Barclays': *Evening Standard*, 11 December 2009 • Builders were going bankrupt: *Evening Standard*, 24 February 2009 • 'I'll stop this madness': *Evening Standard*, 23 February 2009 • 'see the glowing red lights on cranes': Tony Travers, interview with author

Chapter 12: 'I'm standing by to fill the gap'

Cheekily, Boris wrote the following day an article praising Cameron: *The Telegraph*, 12 April 2010 • 'like so many hermaphroditic parrotfish': *The Telegraph*, 17 May 2010 • 'I hope I can survive your endorsement': *For the Record*, David Cameron, pp.357–358 • he was keen to embarrass others to save face: *Unleashing Demons: The Inside Story of Brexit*, Craig Oliver, Hodder & Stoughton (2016) p.34 • 'any delay is a false economy': *Evening Standard*, 6 September 2010 • 'one day the truth will catch up with him': *Evening Standard*, 2 February 2010 • returned to the house to see his children: *Daily Mail*, 18 October 2010 • 'block it and return to your crease': *Daily Mail*, 21 October 2008 • 'the morals of an alley cat': *The Spectator*, 30 September 2019 • 'impossibly far from being prime minister': *Daily Mail*, 16 July 2010 • 'I've got more chance of being reincarnated': *Evening Standard*, 16 July 2010 • a man craving love and attention: *The Times*, 21 July 2010 • 'opportunities for fresh disasters': *The Guardian*, 16 April 2011 • to save £5 billion over four years: *Evening Standard*, 20 October 2010 • 4,232 TfL desks, he claimed, were sold: *The Telegraph*, 5 October 2011 • failing to master the details: *Evening Standard*, 15 June 2010; *Evening Standard*, 17 March 2011 • Boris declared he would run for a second term: *Evening Standard*, 10 September 2010 • about 14 per cent voted to strike: *Evening Standard*, 7 September 2010 • 'A lily-livered government': *Daily Mail*, 5 May 2011 • 'there's always the chance of Boris becoming our ambassador in Pristina, I suppose': *Evening Standard*, 18 November 2010 • he blamed the BBC: *The Telegraph*, 29 October 2010 • 'It's just not important anymore': *The Telegraph*, 8 November 2010 • a £3 billion annual housing budget and 625 hectares of land: *Evening Standard*, 1 December 2010 • 'Everyone thought it was crazy and too expensive': Neale Coleman, interview with author • As a libertarian: *The Telegraph*, 8 March 2010 • He associated his critics with antisocial extremists: *The Telegraph*, 13 September 2010 • British Airways' refusal to allow a female employee to wear her small crucifix: *Evening Standard*, 19 April 2012; *Evening Standard*, 20 June 2011; *The Telegraph*, 25 June 2011; *The Telegraph*, 12 March 2012 • Revisiting his adultery was unappealing: *The Guardian*, 19 July 2011; *The Telegraph*, 19 July 2011 • 'convinced that the gaffe-prone Johnson would make a hash of it': *The Guardian*, 13 May 2011 • 'I think I am very lucky and happy': *Evening Standard*, 27 February 2012 • 57 per cent to 43 per cent: *Evening Standard*, 5 July 2011 • 'mission accomplished': *The Telegraph*, 21 March 2011 • £65,000 plus long holidays and other perks: *Evening Standard*, 9 May 2011; *The Telegraph*, 22 June 2011 • 'Greasing is the key to success in life': *Evening Standard*, 6 July 2011 • 'very distinguished career in counter-terrorism': *The Guardian*, 10 April 2009 • At first, Boris denied making any comments to Cameron: *The Times*, 4 February 2009 • Boris had given the committee false information: *Evening Standard*, 12 February 2009 • he was exposed as unreliable and unwise: *Evening Standard*, 12 February 2009; *Daily Mail*, 13 February 2009; *The Times*, 5 March 2009 • 'I bet that virtually the whole of Fleet Street was involved': *The Telegraph*, 11 April 2011 • Wallis's double relationship with Stephenson was damning: *Daily Mail*, 15 July 2011

Chapter 13: Playing with Fire

'I felt ashamed': *Evening Standard*, 9 August 2011 • They had, he said, performed 'brilliantly': *Evening Standard*, 11 August 2011 • Cameron refused to cancel the police cuts: *For the Record*, David Cameron, p.300 • He blamed London's 'chillingly bad' schools: *The Telegraph*, 15 August 2011; *The Guardian*, 24 March 2012 • 'The best-paid column I've never written': *The Telegraph*, 22 February 2016 • 'I don't think I'll do another big job in politics after this': *The Telegraph*, 5 October 2011; *Evening Standard*, 4 October 2011 • Boris praised Cameron for 'playing a blinder': *Daily Mail*, 19 December 2011 • Cameron swallowed his irritation about being upstaged: *The Times*, 10 January 2012

Chapter 14: 'Jealousies and paranoias'

'It doesn't matter where you come from as long as you know where you're going': *The Times*, 15 March 2014 • They disliked the man and denied there was a message: *The Times*, 5 May 2012 • That, said Boris, was unlikely: *Evening Standard*, 25 January 2012 • his exposure as a hypocrite hit his poll ratings: *Daily Mail*, 27 February 2012 • Boris pulled 6 points ahead in the polls: *The Times*, 12 April 2012 • 'Two arrogant posh boys who don't know the price of milk': *The Guardian*, 24 April 2012 • 'we can't change the country': *The Telegraph*, 14 May 2012 • Boris clasped his enemies close to defuse the antagonism: *Evening Standard*, 18 March 2013; 'Boris Johnson: The Irresistible Rise', Michael Cockerell, BBC Two (2013) • 'It is dismaying that he has become the most popular Conservative in Britain': *Daily Mail*, 5 May 2012 • 'People say I want to be an MP': *For the Record*, David Cameron, p.358 • 'That's the awful fact': *Daily Mail*, 19 June 2012

Chapter 15: 'Alexander the Great'

'The whole thing,' he roared, 'is magnificent and bonkers': *The Telegraph*, 30 July 2012 • The prime minister was a bystander watching the mayor's triumph: *Evening Standard*, 11 September 2012 • 'She will just bulldoze her way into anything because she has that self-belief': 'When Boris Met Jennifer', John Ware, ITV Exposure (2011) • 'Boris is not a prime minister': *Daily Mail*, 3 August 2012 • a 'lachrymose lunch (his tears not mine)': *The Spectator*, 27 July 2019 • 'No point in trying to contain Boris': *Daily Mail*, 8 October 2012 • The war, Boris concluded, was 'a tragic mistake': *The Telegraph*, 16 June 2014 • The children won: *For the Record*, David Cameron, p.247 • 'basically people regard politicians as a bunch of shysters': Boris on CNBC TV • 'Cheque enclosed': *Evening Standard*, 30 January 2013 • a 'welsher, one who does not pay his debts': *Daily Mail*, 1 July 2016 • 'A man's gotta know his limitations': *The Telegraph*, 5 December 2012

Chapter 16: 'Transparently self-defeating policies'

Closer integration of the eurozone nations, she believed, was vital: *The Times*, 12 December 2012 • Leaving 'would not be the end of the world': *Daily Mail*, 17 December 2012 • 'neither particularly necessary nor particularly desirable nor particularly likely': *Evening Standard*, 17 January 2013 • Only the Tories, he said, could deliver UKIP's ambition to leave the EU: *The Telegraph*, 29 April 2013 • Britain's fate depended on renegotiating its relationship with the EU: *The Telegraph*, 13 May 2013 • 'We must threaten to leave if the EU refuses to give us what we want': *The Times*, 10 May 2013 • 'I'd have to declare an interest': 'When Boris Met Jennifer', John Ware, ITV Exposure (2011) • 'terrible confusion about the comments': *Daily Mail*, 16 June 2011 • the BBC was reporting Leveson in approving terms: *The Telegraph*, 18 March 2013; *The Telegraph*, 3 December 2012 • 'blind-eye culture': *The Telegraph*, 5 February 2016 • Patten, demanded Boris, should apologise 'on his knees': *The Telegraph*, 12 November 2012 • he believed that Boris could not be trusted near the nuclear button: *Daily Mail*, 25 March 2013 • 'a private life too baroque for one who aspires to the highest office': *Daily Mail*,

30 March 2013 • 'what's the world coming to?': *The Times*, 26 March 2013; *Daily Mail*, 26 March 2013 • 'Don't give them oxygen': *The Times*, 15 March 2014 • He opposed HS2, the high speed train to the north: *Evening Standard*, 8 July 2013; *Daily Mail*, 27 September 2013 • The annual bill would be £20 million, but the headlines were hopeful: Moore Stephens report 2017 GLA, Budget sub-committee 13 December 2017 p.5 Boris Johnson Briefing • Rose by 65 per cent in 2015: *The Times*, 28 December 2015 • only half were under construction: *Evening Standard*, 16 April 2014 • rents up by 20 per cent in one year: *The Telegraph*, 16 October 2014 • 'Don't collapse in a xenophobic frenzy': *The Telegraph*, 21 October 2013 • 69 per cent of new flats in London were sold to foreigners over the previous two years: *The Sunday Times*, 16 March 2014 • Building statistics, everyone knew, were totally unreliable: *The Times*, 15 March 2014; *The Guardian*, 27 December 2014; *The Guardian*, 26 May 2016 • 256 towers were proposed, approved or under construction: *The Guardian*, 13 March 2014; *Evening Standard*, 4 April 2014 • building over 400 towers: Jenkins, *New London Architecture*; *Evening Standard*, 15 March 2016 • why he had travelled to California and who had accompanied him: Independent review of the Garden Bridge project by Margaret Hodge, London Government, 7 April 2017

Chapter 17: 'A blithering, Bullingdon, Bollinger-drinking buffoon'

'some cut-price edition of David Cameron': *Daily Mail*, 16 October 2013 • Boris posed as the coy, undecided bride: *Daily Mail*, 2 October 2013 • 'We have sold you our offices of the secret service': *Evening Standard*, 14 October 2013 • Cameron and Osborne distanced themselves: *The Guardian*, 28 November 2013; *The Telegraph*, 3 December 2013; *The Telegraph*, 13 January 2014 • Boris hinted that he might after all stand for Parliament in 2015: *Daily Mail*, 24 April 2014; *The Times*, 1 March 2014; *The Telegraph*, 4 March 2014; *Evening Standard*, 14 March 2014; *The Times*, 7 August 2014 • he relied on focus groups and his trusted friends: *The Guardian*, 19 April 2014 • 'It's all going horribly well': *The Guardian*, 22 May 2014 • a press release issued on Boris's orders announcing Gilligan's employment. Len Duvall, interview with author; *The Guardian*, 26 November 2013 • 'pussyfooting and fannying around': *Evening Standard*, 11 December 2013; *Evening Standard*, 22 May 2014 • 'He played a big part in the success of the Tube': *Daily Mail*, 13 March 2014 • Neither mentioned the ongoing problems at the Yard: *The Guardian*, 8 June 2015 • In early 2014, London had 30,085 officers: *Evening Standard*, 5 February 2014 • if domestic crime with an injury was included, the increase was even higher: 5 March 2014, Plenary Policing MQT • cyber crime and fraud, both ignored by Scotland Yard: *The Guardian*, 8 June 2015 • only nine were successfully prosecuted: *Evening Standard*, 23 July 2014 • May's tactics had failed to repatriate large numbers: *The Telegraph*, 29 July 2013 • abandoning the power to force suspected terrorists to move from their homes: *The Telegraph*, 28

February 2015 • May made no comment about the cannons: *Daily Mail,* 7 September 2011 • 'I am keen to ensure that forces have the tools and powers they need to maintain order on our streets': 23 January 2014 • Bookmakers placed her as the favourite as the Tories' next leader: *The Guardian,* 22 May 2014 • The Lib Dems languished at 8 per cent: *Evening Standard,* 20 June 2014 • Boris was assured of a global bestseller translated into thirty-six languages: interview with author • 'He lives by narcissism; he will die by it': *The Guardian,* 18 October 2013 • 'racism, jealousy and political corruption': Tim Shipman, *The Sunday Times,* 4 November 2018 • 'It was bizarre.' *The Times,* 13 June 2019 • mocking Cameron's bid to secure EU reforms: *The Guardian,* 24 June 2014; Anthony Seldon, *Mail on Sunday,* 6 September 2015 • Boris was persuaded to accept an offer negotiated by Wallace: *The Guardian,* 11 August 2014; *The Sunday Times,* 10 August 2014 • 'the first thing he'd do is betray the Tory right': *The Times,* 9 August 2014 • 'Thank you, no,' replied Boris: *The Times,* 28 August 2014 • 'I think we should campaign to come out': *Daily Mail,* 13 October 2014 • 'shows the government's interest in the east London tech cluster': *Business Insider,* 18 October 2019 • she never asked him to speak again: 'When Boris Met Jennifer', John Ware, ITV Exposure (2011) • 'He didn't want any more suspicious gossip being spread': 'When Boris Met Jennifer', John Ware, ITV Exposure (2019) • 'Please put her on the list . . . she has been speaking to Boris': Ibid. • 'to try to play the shots I have as naturally as I can': *The Sunday Times,* 15 February 2015

Chapter 18: 'The next PM will be Miliband if you don't fucking shut up'

'loving twisting the knife': *The Times,* 31 August 2015; 'Cameron at 10' serial, Anthony Seldon, *Mail on Sunday* • admit on Sky TV his aspiration to be the leader: *Daily Mail,* 23 April 2015 • 'That's what worries me': *The Sunday Times,* 3 May 2015 • 'We cannot just shrug at the wealth gap': *The Telegraph,* 8 June 2015; *The Telegraph,* 6 July 2015 • 'Be prepared to walk away if the EU rejects your terms': *The Times,* 2 June 2015; *The Telegraph,* 11 May 2015 • Cameron nevertheless accelerated the referendum to 2016: *The Telegraph,* 14 December 2015 • 'There is much, much more that needs to be done': *The Times,* 3 February 2016

Chapter 19: The Legacy

'I think it comes under the heading of getting the ball back over the net': *Evening Standard,* 18 June 2015 • she had refused to license the three water cannons: *Evening Standard,* 15 July 2015 • Churchill was sixty-five when he became prime minister: *The Telegraph,* 13 August 2015 • he had died in January 2015 before being told he was cleared: *Evening Standard,* 16 October 2015 • Bramall had been accused of participating in an orgy: *Daily Mail,* 19 January 2016 • the crime detection rate falling by 21 per cent since 2008: *Evening Standard,* 24 March 2016 • 'That turned out to be a very grave mistake': *The Times,* 6 March 2019 • the costs of

Whitechapel station were rising by 600 per cent: Crossrail report para2.12 National Audit Office, 3 May 2019 • 'white elephant': *Evening Standard,* 24 September 2015 • 'I fully support the bridge': *Evening Standard,* 5 February 2016 • there was no apparent demand for a footbridge at Temple: *Evening Standard,* 24 September 2015 • the bill by the end of eight years was £195 million: *Evening Standard,* 19 December 2014; *Evening Standard*; 3 December 2015 • 24,000 new homes might have been built: *Evening Standard,* 3 March 2016 • 'The bloated, bulging light-blocking buildings': *The Observer,* 10 April 2016 • Boris's protests against the destruction by Muslim extremists of Palmyra: *The Telegraph,* 28 March 2016 • 'to provide a persecuted people with a safe and secure homeland': *The Telegraph,* 30 October 2017 • His visit to Ramallah was cancelled on 'security grounds': *Evening Standard,* 9 November 2015 • wealthy City denizens stuck in their stationary limousines: *Evening Standard,* 3 March 2016 • Livingstone obtained the funding from the Labour government: *The Times,* 25 March 2019 • 'millions more in cuts than the department had planned to be in its final offer': *The Times,* 8 June 2019 • The last thought would prove to be wishful thinking: *Evening Standard,* 7 August 2016

Chapter 20: 'He's ruined my life'

'a great future outside': *The Telegraph,* 8 February 2016 • Boris was promised a key job in the government, probably Defence: *For the Record,* David Cameron p.653 • uncontrolled accumulation of power against which there was no appeal: 11 February 2016 • 'legitimise the cause and help detoxify the Brexit brand': David Cameron, *For the Record,* p.650 • the idea that Boris's 'opinion matters at all . . . is absurd': *The Guardian,* 17 February 2016 • 'a cast of clowns': *The Sunday Times,* 16 October 2016 • he 'would be a disaster': *Mail on Sunday,* 26 February 2017 • a failing he later admitted: David Cameron, *For the Record,* p.655 • Either way, it was win-win: David Cameron, *For the Record,* p.654 • 'It's just 15 per cent.' *Daily Mail,* 24 March 2016; *The Guardian,* 24 March 2016 • She did not fear dividing the people or her party: *The Telegraph,* 4 May 2009 • That part which laws or kings can cause or cure': *The Telegraph,* 14 September 2009 • The Remain article 'stuck in my craw to write': *The Sunday Times,* 28 February 2016 • 'We got absolutely zilch, effectively': *Daily Mail,* 24 March 2016 • 'He's just gone outside to say Leave': Sunday 21 February 2016 • 'This is the moment to be brave': *The Telegraph,* 22 February 2016 • He departed without making any attempt to justify himself: Peter John, interview with author • inability to 'distinguish truth from fantasy': *The Times,* 25 February 2016 • 'kick it really hard in the balls, in which case it will run away': *Evening Standard,* 22 March 2016 • Michael Heseltine attacked Boris for destroying the City and jobs: *Daily Mail,* 22 February 2016 • 'Unfortunately Bush was bluffing': *The Telegraph,* 30 April 2016 • He also adopted an old habit of speaking without pause: *The Telegraph,* 24 March 2016 • 'This is very hard, very hard': Bernard Jenkin, interview with author • 'If Mr Johnson had the sense of nemesis I suspect he has, he should stop now': *The Times*, 25 March 2016 • Parris saw in the 'zealots a streak of madness': *The Times*,16 April 2016 • motivated by a desire to be loved by more people: *Mail on Sunday*, 27 March 2016 • the referendum's outcome became less certain: *The Times*,14 April 2016 • Boris concluded that Obama was fluent but phoney: 21 October 2008 • America would never accept rule by the EU: *The Telegraph*, 14 March 2016 • 'a disaster for Boris because Obama is pro-British': *Daily Mail*, 23 April 2016; *Mail on Sunday*, 24 April 2016 • could not produce a single report proving that Britain would be richer outside the EU: *The Times*, 23. April 2016; *The Sunday Times*, 24 April 2016; *Daily Mail*, 18 April 2016 • 'The Remainers think the game is over': *The Telegraph*, 25 April 2016 • an increase of support for Leave and more trust in Boris: *The Times*, 28 April 2016 • between £160 million and £248 million a week: *The Times*, 19 September 2017 • claiming he would cut immigration to 'tens of thousands': *The Telegraph*, 13 May 2016; *The Times*, 27 May 2016 • 'Deeply maddening': Craig Oliver, *Unleashing Demons: The Inside Story of Brexit*, Hodder (2016); *Daily Mail*, 25 September 2016 • the longer it is, the more errors are likely': *The Times*, 9 July 2018 • 'The EU is an attempt to do this by different methods': *The Telegraph*, 16 May 2016 • a wholly untrue story was spread: *Daily Mail*, 19 May 2016; *The Sunday Times*, 22 May 2016 • while secretly enjoying an adulterous affair: *Daily Mail*, 6 June 2016 • To his followers, Rudd was desperate: *The Times*, 10 June 2016 • 'Let Thursday be our Independence Day': *The Telegraph*, 20 June 2016 • aligning themselves with liars and racists: Cameron p.687 • 'founded on duplicity': *The Oxford Myth*, Rachel Johnson, p.70 • 'I do not want to be prime minister': *The Telegraph*, 11 October 2012; *The Sunday Times*, 5 June 2016 • FTSE 100 chiefs earned 150 times more than the 'forgotten people': *The Telegraph*, 27 June 2016 • 'inclusive, positive and optimistic message': *The Times*, 2 July 2016

Chapter 21: Leadership and Treachery

'inclusive, positive and optimistic message': *The Times*, 2 July 2016 • 'He's completely untrustworthy': *The Times*, 28 June 2016 • 'forty new trade deals': *The Times*, 15 November 2018 • 'I was a fool to trust him': *Mail on Sunday*, 3 July 2016 • He accused Boles of 'stealing' his phone: *Mail on Sunday*, 23 October 2016 • 'I did not want it': *Daily Mail*, 2 July 2016 • 'if this essentially brutal buffoon became prime minister': *Daily Mail*, 1 July 2016

ACT III – THE CABINET
Chapter 22: 'We're being stitched up'

'I want this to be your opportunity to show you can be the good Boris': *Daily Mail*, 23 May 2019 • 'The Foreign Office has had its limbs amputated': *The Times*,

16 October 2018 • 'Institutionally, the Foreign Office is a bit timid': *Prospect*, 15 October 2018 • 'diplomacy is the art of letting other people have your way': 'Inside the Foreign Office', BBC TV doc, 7 December 2018 • 'need to erase the gaffes': *The Telegraph*, 15 July 2016 • Boris had hoped Leave would lose: *Daily Mail*, 23 September 2016 • Baker assumed that Duncan now wanted to replace Boris: Steve Baker, interview with author • Britain would stay in the single market: *Daily Mail*, 23 November 2016; *The Telegraph*, 5 December 2018 • 'probably' leave the single market: *The Times*, 16 November 2016 • with friends on the Commons terrace: *Daily Mail*, 17 August 2016; *The Telegraph*, 15 August 2016 • only 16 per cent approved of May's performance on Brexit: *The Times*, 30 September 2016 • 'If the ball comes loose from the back of the scrum': *Financial Times*, September 2016 • defended Turkey's right to reintroduce the death penalty: *Daily Mail*, 28 September 2016 • 'I'm Boris's pooper-scooper': *The Times*, 5 November 2016 • 'Complete baloney, absolute baloney': *Daily Mail*, 23 September 2016 • Angela Merkel told Boris publicly he was wrong: *The Times*, 19 November 2016 • 'I was not particularly amused about this': *The Times*, 19 November 2016 • 'a fake foreign minister': *The Times*, 17 March 2017 • 'coming to the end of her tether': *Mail on Sunday*, 20 November 2016 • Niblett avoided finding fault with Simon McDonald: Institute of Government, 4 June 2018 • he supported both for attacking the murderous ISIS groups: *The Times*, 3 August 2016 • 'It is better sometimes to have a tyrant than not to have a ruler at all': *The Times*, 27 January 2017 • Boris supported military intervention but Obama refused: *The Times*, 7 September 2016 • 'Russophobic hysteria': *The Telegraph*, 13 October 2016 • She would not allow the Foreign Secretary to stand on principle: *The Telegraph*, 2 December 2016 • he was cheered by the officials and politicians in the audience: *The Telegraph*, 12 December 2016 • Boris refused to back down: *The Times*, 8 December 2016 • 'It's time to call off the dogs or Boris will snap': *The Sunday Times*, 11 December 2016 • 'any unnecessary risk of meeting Donald Trump': *The Times*, 14 October 2018 • 'There is every reason to be positive about a liberal guy from New York': *The Times*, 16 November 2016 • Boris refused to sign an EU declaration: *The Times*, 17 January 2017 • the negotiations for the exit terms and the future trade relationship should be simultaneous: Bill Cash, interview with the author • 'another pratfall': *The Times*, 13 April 2017 • urging May to call a snap general election: *Betting the House: The Inside Story of the 2017 Election*, Tim Ross and Tom McTague, Biteback Publishing (2017) • 'A buffoon and an idler': *The Guardian*, 7 October 2019 • to urge him to bid for the leadership: *The Sunday Times*, 24 September 2017; *Fall Out: A Year of Political Mayhem*, Tim Shipman, HarperCollins (2017)

Chapter 23: 'Boris is Boris'

unemployment was the lowest for forty-two years: *The Telegraph*, 19 September 2017 • 'In spite of Brexit . . . ': *The Telegraph*, 4 August 2017 • enjoying zero tariffs and frictionless trade: *The Sunday Times*, 18 June 2017 • Boris's chance to be prime minister 'came and went last year': *The Telegraph*, 15 September 2017 • 'Boris seems done for': *The Times*, 13 July 2017 • 'inspires derision among Britain's allies': *The Times*, 14 February 2018 • 'My Brexit Vision': *The Telegraph*, 16 September 2017 • 'Our destiny will be in our own hands': *The Telegraph*, 21 January 2017 • 'Boris is Boris': *The Telegraph*, 19 September 2017 • 'I am wrong. I am sorry': *Daily Mail*, 25 April 2018 • 'me driving 100 mph and crashing into a brick wall': *The Times*, 8 January 2017 • 'a noted clown': Prospect 9 July 2018 • 'took Europe to its darkest period': *The Times*, 16 October 2018 • 'I accept that my remarks could have been clearer': *The Times*, 8 November 2017 • 'I apologise for the distress, for the suffering': *The Times*, 13 November 2017 • Inevitably he failed: *The Times*, 8 December 2017 • she feared the talks could collapse: *The Times*, 24 November 2017 • He praised May for 'a fantastic job': *The Telegraph*, 15 October 2018; *The Sunday Times*, 17 December 2017

Chapter 24: 'God, she's awful'

'It's a very, very good thought': *The Telegraph*, 5 June 2018 • 'an avalanche of lies and disinformation': *The Sunday Times*, 8 April 2018 • could not understand the details of his own finance bill: Craig Mackinlay, interview with author • The three portrayed the 'rabid' Brexiteers as snake-oil salesmen: *Daily Mail*, 5 February 2018 • Their fears of 'betrayal' by May, he promised, were unfounded: *Daily Mail*, 21 May 2018 • 'The moment of truth': *Daily Mail*, 9 June 2018 • 'No panic. Pro bono publico. No bloody panic': *The Telegraph*, 8 June 2018 • Even more concessions . . . could be made to seal an agreement: *The Times*, 10 July 2018 • distrust America, trust China and be ambivalent about Russia: *The Times*, 19 December 2018 • 'abandoned any residual aspiration to be viewed as a serious nation': *The Times*, 10 July 2018 • 'a bossy schoolteacher': *The Telegraph*, 13 July 2018 • one third of Tory Party members supported Boris as leader: *The Sunday Times*, 22 July 2018; *The Times*, 7 September 2018 • 'Mrs May was gummed by a toothless lion': *The Times*, 19 July 2018 • 'I want to ditch Chequers not May': *The Telegraph*, 15 September 2018 • 'looking like letter boxes or bank robbers': *The Telegraph*, 8 August 2018 • 'This is against my principles': *Daily Mail*, 19 September 2013 • 'poverty, social exclusion, gender inequality and radicalisation': *The Sunday Times*, 17 December 2017 • they should learn English: *The Telegraph*, 9 March 2015 • 'just need to shut their mouths for the good of diversity': *Daily Mail*, 9 August 2018 • 'the uniform of medieval patriarchal tyranny': *The Telegraph*, 9 August 2018 • 'a cynical political opportunist': *The Times*, 8 August 2018 • 'It is a deliberate bid for the leadership of the Conservative Party': *The Sunday Times*, 12 August 2018 • 'We need to fight, gently, for free speech': *The Telegraph*, 5 November 2018 • there was no alternative: *Daily Mail*, 11 August 2018 • Attacking Boris, she assumed, was her best lifeline: *The Telegraph*, 28 August 2018 • Hargrave had collected lurid allegations: *The Sunday Times*, 9 September 2018 • 'looks like a sanctioned hit operation': *The Times*, 10 September 2018 • 'this is the political end of Boris Johnson': *The Times*, 10 September 2018 • 'the tide of holy feminist rage': *The Telegraph*, 8 October 2018 • Only she could navigate Britain into safe waters: *Daily Mail*, 13 September 2018 • 'the best woman for the job': *The Telegraph*, 21 September 2018 • 'Chuck Chequers and restore basic Conservative values': *The Telegraph*, 28 September 2018 • 'reckless': *The Sunday Times*, 30 September 2018 • 'trying to bully a conscientious and determined woman': *The Times*, 20 November 2018 • No attack evoked a whisper from her: *The Telegraph*, 17 December 2018 • 'Sometimes you must take the decision which is fraught with risk': *The Telegraph*, 7 December 2018 • 'we must not let it become a fantasy for the nation': *Daily Mail*, 10 December 2018 • 'God, she's awful': Anthony Seldon, *May at 10*, Biteback Publishing (2019), p.510

Chapter 25: Showdown

'It's time to compromise': *Mail on Sunday*, 27 January 2019 • 'No way': *The Telegraph*, 11 March 2019 • 'the deal the prime minister has done is the best on offer': *The Times*, 4 May 2019 • Sixty-six per cent of members supported a no-deal Brexit: *The Times*, 18 May 2019 • Only those in his close circle were allowed to find fault in him: *Daily Mail*, 7 December 2018 • 'I didn't say anything about Turkey in the referendum': *Daily Mail*, 18 January 2019 • Britain, he still believed, should leave without a deal: *The Telegraph*, 25 March 2019 • 'but he did not understand the detail': Craig Mackinlay, interview with author • 'he hasn't even started a campaign': *The Telegraph*, 29 March 2019 • 'So far we are winning': *The Times*, 30 March 2019 • 'what really matters is what Boris lacks': *The Times*, 25 March 2019 • 'so bad and so disheartening that you can scarcely believe it': *The Telegraph*, 8 April 2019 • 'an extreme hard-right fascist': *Daily Mail*, 15 April 2019 • 70 per cent trusted him to win an election: *The Times*, 18 May 2019 • the Tories should accept May's deal: *The Times*, 20 May 2019 • 'He must now unite the centre right': *The Times*, 24 May 2019 • 'reckless caprice, lazy disregard for principle, weak negotiating skills, moral turpitude': *The Times*, 25 May 2019 • also those desperate to defeat Corbyn: *The Telegraph*, 7 June 2019 • 'The magic, my friends will fade': *The Times*, 8 June 2019 • contest 'to unite and heal the party': *The Times*, 2 July 2019 • 'We need a skilled negotiator and deal-maker': *The Times*, 10 June 2019 • he used colourful language to secure the Brexiteers' votes: *The Telegraph*, 18 July 2019 • only Boris could save the party and country from Corbyn: *The Guardian*, 16 July 2019 • 'Who is Boris Johnson?': BBC Radio 4, 23 July 2019 • 'repellently dishonest, xenophobic and politically calculating': *The Guardian*, 20 July 2019 • 'You've got a wild uncontrollable spirit': Steve Baker, interview with author • 'He'll be a great prime minister or a great disappointment': Peter Lilley, interview with author • 'there will be tears before midnight': *The Spectator*, 27 July 2019

ACT IV – TRIUMPH AND TURMOIL
Chapter 26: Total Victory

undermined Labour's traditional anti-Tory battle cry: *The Times*, 3 August 2019 • 'complete fantasy': *The Guardian*, 4 September 2019 • a 'sham' just to run down the clock: *The Guardian*, 4 September 2019 • he would support Corbyn to bring down the government: *The Times*, 16 August 2019 • 'risks destroying the Tory Party and is a policy of insanity': *Belfast Telegraph*, 3 September 2019 • 'an unelected foul-mouthed oaf throwing his weight around': *The Times*, 5 September 2019 • 'We are closer to the edge than we may think': *The Times*, 7 September 2019 • Brexit had been about taking back control but had become 'incoherent': *The Times*, 18 December 2018 • 'The madder Hulk gets, the stronger Hulk gets': *Mail on Sunday*, 15 September 2019 • 'Let's hear it for the girly swots': *The Times*, 5 October 2020 • Repeating that inaccuracy multiplied the damage to the prime minister: *The Times*, 3 October 2019 • 58 per cent of voters outrightly distrusted Corbyn: Opinium poll, 6 November 2019 • 'He was always a really good friend': *Evening Standard*, 7 October 2019 • 'you have cast me aside like I'm some gremlin': *Mail on Sunday*, 17 November 2019 • 'One Nation agenda': *The Times*, 14 October 2019 • 'I will direct them to throw that form in the bin': 9 November 2019 • 'We will hammer them day after day after day': *The Sunday Times*, 27 October 2019 • 'a reckless cult': Matthew Parris, *The Times*, 2 November 2019 • Corbyn would lead a coalition: 6 November 2019 • Hundreds of other cases remained uninvestigated: *The Sunday Times*, 8 December 2019 • YouGov predicted a Tory majority of eighty-two: *The Times*, 29 November 2019 • 'He will betray the NHS in a heartbeat': *Evening Standard*, 11 November 2019 • 'who can be described as a genius': *The Telegraph*, 14 December 2019

Chapter 27: Covid I

'level up' the nation: *The Times*, 1 January 2020; 22 February 2020 • unable even to communicate in proper English: Michael Gove, 'The privilege of public service', given as the Ditchley Annual Lecture, 1 July 2020 • Success rates in previous exams: *Prospect*, 8 November 2019 • 'everyone rises to their position of incompetence': Rachel Wolf, *The Telegraph*, 1 January 2020 • Christopher Whitty . . . was meeting his deputy, Jonathan Van-Tam: Science and Technology Committee, Oral evidence: UK Science, Research and Technology Capability and Influence in Global Disease Outbreaks, HC 136, 24 April 2020, Q.292 • quickly infect a large number of people: 'UK Influenza Pandemic Preparedness Strategy 2011', Department of Health, Social Services and Public Safety, 10 November 2011 • Whitty was monitoring the situation: Government rebuttal to *The Sunday Times*, 19 April 2020; 23 May 2020 • They also agreed that a travel ban was worthless: Lawrence Freedman, 'Strategy for a Pandemic: The UK and COVID-19', 11 May 2020, available at: https://www.iiss.org/blogs/

survival-blog/2020/05/the-uk-and-covid-19) • 'unlikely that transmission [of the virus] to the UK could be prevented': New and Emerging Respiratory Virus Threats Advisory Group (NERVTAG) meeting, 21 January 2020 • 'benefit is very unlikely to outweigh the substantial effort, cost and disruption': NERVTAG meeting, 13 January 2020 • newly founded Scientific Advisory Group for Emergencies (SAGE): *The Conversation*, 24 March 2020; 'Chief Scientific Advisers and their officials: an introduction', Government Office for Science, January 2020; *The Guardian*, 27 April 2020; *The New York Times*, 23 April 2020 • The scientists met with about ten senior Whitehall officials: Correspondence from Patrick Vallance to Greg Clark, 4 April 2020 • 'In SAGE, we try to come up with a consensus view': *The Conversation*, 24 March 2020 • South Korea was ranked sixth and Germany twenty-eighth: Global Health Security Index, October 2019 • Whitehall's Exercise Cygnus report: *The Telegraph*, 28 March 2020 • 'not sufficient to cope with the extreme demands': *The Guardian*, 24 April 2020 • Whitty and Vallance adopted the textbook gospel: Scientific Advisory Group for Emergencies reports and guidance available at: www.gov.uk/government/organisations/scientific-advisory-group-for-emergencies • over twenty years' experience monitoring viruses: NERVTAG meeting, 21 January 2020 • human-to-human transmission was happening: MRC Centre for Global Infectious Disease Analysis, 'Report 2: Estimating the potential total number of novel Coronavirus (2019-nCoV) cases in Wuhan City, China', 22 January 2020 • 'Heightened surveillance, prompt information-sharing and enhanced preparedness are recommended': Ibid. • 'a reasonable worst-case scenario (RWCS) cannot be made reliably': Correspondence from Patrick Vallance to Greg Clark, 4 April 2020 • an annual average of about 17,000 people: Lawrence Freedman, 11 May 2020 • enhancing rapid case detection will be essential if the outbreak is to be controlled: MRC Centre for Global Infectious Disease Analysis, 22 January 2020 • 'not wildly spreading outside China': Lawrence Freedman, 11 May 2020; World Health Organization (WHO), 28 January 2020 • knew the truth about the Wuhan outbreak: 'Coronavirus action plan: a guide to what you can expect across the UK', Department of Health and Social Care (DHSC) policy paper, footnotes 1–12 • failure to acknowledge the importance of Public Health England (PHE): *The Financial Times*, 24 April 2020 • You can fit my public health credentials on a postage stamp: *The Lancet*, 6 April 2013, available at: https://doi.org/10.1016/S0140-6736(13)60787-4 • an NHS lifer at a psychiatric hospital: *The Guardian*, 12 March 2013 • the NHS's Cinderella: *The Guardian*, 31 May 2020 • 'the NHS is well prepared to manage and treat new diseases': Statement from DHSC and PHE, 22 January 2020 • 'Everyone thought they were doing the right thing': 'Bernard Jenkin on the long-term consequences for Whitehall after coronavirus', 30 June 2020, available at: instituteforgovernment.org.uk/blog/bernard-jenkin-whitehall-after-coronavirus • 'a yet to be identified virus or bacteria': 'PHE Infectious Diseases Strategy 2020–2025', PHE, September 2019 •

little evidence that people without symptoms are infectious to others: 'Guidance for social or community care and residential settings on COVID-19', PHE, 25 February 2020 (withdrawn 13 March) • there would be a maximum of 20,000 deaths: Science and Technology Committee, oral evidence, 24 April 2020, Q.300 • 'We need to have our entire response based on that principle': *The Telegraph*, 24 January 2020 • no one realised the speed of infection: 'Considerations for non-pharmaceutical intervention (NPI) policy – timing and sub-national targeting', London School of Hygiene and Tropical Medicine, 5 March 2020; 'Timing and local triggering of non-pharmaceutical interventions (NPIs) to reduce COVID-19 mortality and healthcare demands', MRC Centre for Global Infectious Disease Analysis, 5 March 2020 • Care homes were not included in Imperial's model: Science and Technology Committee, oral evidence, 24 April 2020, Q.827 • 'the rather optimistic assumption': Science and Technology Committee, oral evidence, 24 April 2020, Q.830; Q.838; MRC Centre for Global Infectious Disease Analysis, 'Summary indicative effects of non-pharmaceutical interventions (NPIs) to reduce COVID-19 transmission and mortality', 2 March 2020; Potential impact of behavioural and social interventions on an epidemic of Covid-19 in the UK, SAGE, 9 March 2020 • Hancock was advised that Covid presented a 'low danger': ZDF interview, 29 January 2020 • 'we cannot be 100 per cent certain': Matt Hancock, statement to Parliament, 27 January 2020 • the allocation of £40 million to search for a vaccine: Matt Hancock, statement to Parliament, 3 February 2020 • 'severely flawed': 'Foot and mouth disease 2007: a review and lessons learned', Department for Environment, Food and Rural Affairs, 11 March 2008 • 'the longer you go on, the more uncertainty there will be': Science and Technology Committee, oral evidence, 24 April 2020, Q.895 • 'a tangled, buggy mess': *The Telegraph*, 16 May 2020 (quoting David Richards, founder WANdisco) • crude mathematical guesswork: *The Telegraph*, 16 May 2020; *The Critic*, 19 May 2020 • 'I do not think it was ever possible to predict the course of this epidemic': Science and Technology Committee, oral evidence: UK Science, Research and Technology Capability and Influence in Global Disease Outbreaks, HC 136, 10 June 2020, Q.787; Q.827 • 'You do not really have a flu model': Science and Technology Committee, oral evidence, 24 April 2020, Q.891 • conduct 400–500 tests a day: SAGE reports released 29 May 2020 • 'if necessary' scale up testing: Matt Hancock, statement to Parliament, 27 January 2020 • considerable exaggerations: 'PHE reaches crucial step in fully sequencing novel coronavirus', PHE, 4 February 2020 • that NHS staff would be protected from infection: Matt Hancock, statement to Parliament, 27 January 2020 • raised the risk level to 'moderate': 'Statement from the 4 UK Chief Medical Officers on novel coronavirus', DHSC, 30 January 2020 • declared a Level 4 National Incident, the highest level: 'Incident Response Plan (National)', NHS England, 21 July 2017 • 'public health emergency of international concern': 'Statement on the second meeting of the International Health Regulations (2005) Emergency Committee regarding the outbreak of novel coronavirus (2019-nCoV)', WHO,

30 January 2020 • BA stopped all flights to China: 'Report 6 - Relative sensitivity of international surveillance', WHO Collaborating Centre for Infectious Disease Modelling, MRC Centre for Global Infectious Disease Analysis, Abdul Latif Jameel Institute for Disease and Emergency Analytics, Imperial College London, 21 February 2020 • 'address the risks and threats we face': 'Integrated Review of Security, Defence, Development and Foreign Policy', Boris Johnson, 26 February 2020 • 'the very rigorous, well-established and sophisticated policy advice structure': Science and Technology Committee oral evidence, Q.903 • SAGE had met for the second time on 3 February: Minutes and papers from SAGE meetings held in February 2020 • every aspect of controlling the virus was considered: NERVTAG Meeting 23, 7 April 2020; NERVTAG Meeting 24, 9 April 2020 • confidence that China would defeat the virus: 'Ambassador Liu Xiaoming Meets with Stanley Johnson, Former Member of the European Parliament and Vice Chairman of the European Parliament's Committee on Environment', 5 February 2020, available at chinese-embassy.org.uk/eng/ambassador/t1746350.htm • 'we can better understand the roots of this disease': 'PHE reaches crucial step in fully sequencing novel coronavirus', PHE, 4 February 2020 • creating an extra twelve laboratories across the country: 'PHE novel coronavirus diagnostic test rolled out across UK', PHE, 7 February 2020 • she obfuscated and refused to explain her reasoning: Science and Technology Committee, oral evidence, 25 March 2020, Q.126 • 'You would have thought that they would be bashing down the door': Reuters, 7 April 2020 • he had offered his laboratories and staff to the testing effort: Email from Patrick Vallance to Boris Johnson, 18 May 2020 • 'We were lulled into a false sense of security': Health and Social Care Committee, oral evidence: 'Management of the Coronavirus Outbreak', HC 36, 21 July 2020, Q.652 • 'being very aware of costs and the risks of second waves': Science and Technology Committee, oral evidence, 25 March 2020, Q.903 • had encouraged complacency: *Prospect*, 7 April 2020 • the lack of argument reflected the nature of the people involved: Buzzfeed, 12 April 2020 • PHE had been following up eight separate infections: Matt Hancock, statement to Parliament, 11 February 2020 • between April and June: Minutes from SAGE Meeting 6, 11 February 2020 • could mean checking 8,000 contacts: *The Telegraph*, 31 May 2020; Minutes from SAGE Meeting 8, 18 February 2020 • 'contact tracing would no longer be useful or practical': Minutes from SAGE Meeting 8, 18 February 2020 • he assumed there would be no increased testing: Email from Greg Clark to Boris Johnson, 18 May 2020 • 'sustained transmission in the UK': *Daily Mail*, 25 February 2020 • Chinese government was deliberately providing false statistics: *The Guardian*, 23 April 2020 • Ferguson's predictions were unsurprisingly hazy: 'SPI-M-O: Consensus Statement on 2019 Novel Coronavirus, (2019-nCoV)', 10 February 2020 • scientists did not know whether children would be infected: 'SPI-M-O: Consensus view on the impact of mass school closures', 10 February 2020 • did not suffer: *The Telegraph*, 30 June 2020 • 'doesn't care whether you've ordered pepperoni or four-cheese': *The Guardian*, 6 February

2020 • the first victim had died in northern Italy: Lawrence Freedman, 11 May 2020 • 6,143 people had tested negative: Post to PHE Twitter account, 22 February 2020, available at: twitter.com/PHE_uk • although the infection was much worse than realised: Select Committee on Science and Technology, 19 May 2020 • did not highlight the same dangers of those returning from France and Spain: Tripartite letter, NHS England and NHS Improvement, the Chief Medical Officer for England and Public Health England, 24 February 2020 • by those returning from Italy and Spain that week: Health and Social Care Committee, 5 May 2020 (Vallance at 9.40am) • a recipe for a simultaneous mass outbreak: 'Comparisons of all-cause mortality between European countries and regions: January to June 2020', Office for National Statistics, 30 July 2020 • the NHS would require 220,000 intensive care units: Lawrence Freedman, 11 May 2020 • not going 'to get anywhere near being able to cope with it': Reuters, 7 April 2020 • 'no transmission of Covid-19 in the community': *The Times*, 15 May 2020 • no evidence of PHE officials at the airports: Matt Hancock, statement to Parliament, 26 February 2020 • Blair purposely excluded successive Cabinet Secretaries from critical meetings: Tom Bower, *Broken Vows: Tony Blair, The Tragedy of Power*, Faber & Faber (2016), p.3 • The death toll would be 510,000 people: 'Impact assessment of non-pharmaceutical interventions (NPIs) to reduce COVID-19 mortality and healthcare demand', Imperial College COVID-19 Response Team, 16 March 2020; Addendum to SAGE Meeting 11 on Covid-19, 27 February 2020 • the existing ICUs would be overwhelmed eight times over: Political Thinking with Nick Robinson, 'The Neil Ferguson One', 25 April 2020; https://www.gov.uk/government/publications/spi-m-publish-updated-modelling-summary • nevertheless accepted as the best available: Minutes from SAGE Meeting 10, 25 February 2020 • 'the NHS will be unable to meet all demands placed on it': Addendum to SAGE Meeting 11, 27 February 2020; 'Potential effect of non-pharmaceutical interventions (NPIs) on a Covid-19 epidemic in the UK', SAGE, 26 February 2020 • 3.6 million people would need hospital care: 'Current understanding of COVID-19 compared with NSRA Pandemic Influenza planning assumptions', SAGE, 26 February 2020 • 'It's just part of the madness.' *The Telegraph*, 23 May 2020 • left no doubt that the country faced a severe crisis: 'SAGE's priorities, 26 February 2020', prepared by Sir Patrick Vallance and Professor Chris Whitty. It was considered at SAGE Meeting 11 on 27 February 2020. • 'to avoid overwhelming the hospitals' ICUs: SAGE Meeting 11, 27 February 2020 • Europeans would comply with that draconian measure: *London Review of Books*, 7 May 2020 • whether Covid was more complicated than previous coronaviruses: *The Telegraph*, 3 July 2020 • it peaked horrifically high: 'The effect of social distance measures on deaths and peak demand for hospital services in England', LSHTM Modelling Team, 3 March 2020 (v2) • had developed an immunity: 'Coutts in Conversation: Professor Sir John Bell', 29 May 2020: available at: coutts.com/coutts-in-conversation/professor-sir-john-bell.html; 'Are We Party Protected?', GWK, available at:

https://www.gwm-intl.com/news/are-partly-protected; Coronavirus Disease 2019 (COVID-19) Daily Situation Report of the Robert Koch Institute, 15 July 2020 • 'It is easy to get a perception that if you are older and you get this virus, you are a goner. Absolutely not': Health and Social Care Committee, 5 March 2020 • minimised the validity of those very statistics: *Hansard* LC Deb. vol.802, 26 February 2020 (reply to Baroness McIntosh) • 'herd immunity will actually provide resistance to future visits by the virus': *Hansard* LC Deb. vol.802, 26 February 2020; Science and Technology Committee oral evidence, 25 March 2020, Q.19 • the peak would be in three to five months: also see SAGE meeting, 2 March 2020 • the centre was testing only about eighty-five people a day: Science and Technology Committee, 25 March 2020 • about 3,000 tests per day across the whole country one week later: Ibid. • isolate residents if they were suspected of being infected: *The Telegraph*, 14 April 2020 • bring misery to the elderly and their relations: *The Telegraph*, 3 March 2020 • the NHS would need 130,000 ICU beds: 'The effect of social distance measures on deaths and peak demand for hospital services in England', LSHTM Modelling Team, 3 March 2020 (v2) • with additional stock being ordered where necessary: 'Coronavirus action plan: a guide to what you can expect across the UK', DHSC policy paper, 3 March 2020 • immediately lock down the country: 'Coronavirus (COVID-19) – update following resilience meetings' available at: www.gov.scot/news/coronavirus-covid-19-1/ • 'go about their business as usual': Boris Johnson, speech delivered 3 March 2020 • 'fantastic surveillance of the spread of disease': Ibid. • 'given existing evidence about the importance of hand hygiene': 'SPI-B return to SAGE on the use of behavioural and social interventions', 3 March 2020 • Dominic Cummings attended SAGE's meeting on 5 March: Minutes from SAGE Meeting 13, 5 March 2020 • there would be 'no benefit' and it would last too long: Health and Social Care Committee, 5 March 2020 • 'I would characterise lockdown as a panic measure.': Science and Technology Committee oral evidence, 10 June 2020, Q.808 • Whitty's reliance on behavioural scientists: Scientific Pandemic Influenza Group on Behaviours (SPI-B), 'SPI-B: insights on self-isolation and household isolation', 9 March 2020 • publicly praised by Deirdre Hine: *The Times*, 5 April 2020 • Whitty, he complained, took advice from the wrong specialists: *The Times*, 22 June 2020; 24 June 2020 • that would not 'contain' the virus: UK Influenza Pandemic Preparedness Strategy, 10 November 2011, paras 4.21 & 4.22; Boris Johnson, speech delivered 9 March 2020; Science and Technology Committee, 25 March, p.87 • 'we need to strike a balance': Transcript of Boris Johnson's statements on *This Morning*, ITV, 10 March 2020, available at: https://fullfact.org/health/boris-johnson-coronavirus-this-morning/ • At most, he said, 10,000 Britons were infected: Minutes from SAGE Meeting, 10 March 2020 (possibly, SAGE's minutes mistakenly recorded 10,000 instead of 100,000) • Otherwise, it could be later: Minutes from SAGE Meeting 14, 10 March 2020 • Britain registered 590 cases and ten deaths: Statistics available at: www.england.nhs.uk/2020/04/total-number-of-covid-19-deaths-in-england-by-date-of-death/; Letter from Professor Nick Phin, PHE Incident Director, National Infection Service, 11 March 2020 • Ferguson did not realise the extent of the infection in Europe: Science & Technology Committee oral evidence, June 10 2020, Q.836 • 'when we should intervene': Video posted to Boris Johnson Twitter account, available at: twitter.com/i/status/1237760976482598913; *The Times*, May 27 2020 • 'squash the sombrero': Wired, 12 March 2020; BBC News – David Halpern, behavioural scientists and a member of SAGE, *The Guardian*, 12 April 2020; Minutes of SAGE Meeting 16, 16 March 2020 • would inevitably mean the premature death of the elderly: *The Telegraph*, 22 March 2020 • Vallance would deny proposing herd immunity: *The Telegraph*, 30 May 2020 • Robert Peston, the journalist, was authoritatively briefed about that strategy: Lawrence Freedman, 11 May 2020 • only when the rest of the community had immunity: *The Telegraph*, 30 May 2020 • They assumed that probably over 100,000 people were infected: *The Guardian*, 31 May 2020 • Doyle announced that PHE had abandoned testing in the community: Minutes from SAGE Meeting 15, 13 March 2020, Item 33 • restricted to hospital staff: *The Telegraph*, 31 March 2020 • unilaterally giving up PHE's responsibility for testing: Health and Social Care Committee, oral evidence, 26 March 2020, Q.199; Q.202 • 'contact tracing was a lost cause': *Bloomberg Business Week*, 24 April 2020 • 'so we hit 25,000 tests a day': Boris Johnson, speech delivered 18 March 2020 • They needed 280 in every town: *Hansard*, HC Deb. 23 March 2020, c63 • Yvonne Doyle chose not to explain to MPs why PHE's testing had stopped: Health and Social Care Select Committee, 25 March 2020 • she did not produce the basis for PHE's decision to scale down testing: Peacock letter to Clark, 1 May 2020; Health and Social Care Select Committee, 25 March 2020, Q.122 • sent MPs a study undertaken by the Royal Society describing testing in other countries: 'COVID-19 pandemic: some lessons learned so far', Correspondence from Chair to Boris Johnson, 18 May 2020 • denied that testing and tracing was abandoned because there was no capacity: Sunday Telegraph 7 June 2020; Letter from Duncan Selbie to Greg Clark, 7 May 2020, available at: committees.parliament.uk/publications/1018/documents/8045/default/ • no one knew where the virus was spreading and who was infected: 'COVID-19 pandemic: some lessons learned so far', Correspondence from Chair to Boris Johnson, 18 May 2020 • 'so it is not the numbers of the tests that count': Science and Technology Committee, Oral evidence: UK Science, Research and Technology Capability and Influence in Global Disease Outbreaks, HC 136, Q.817 • 'we will not know where those 1 million cases are.': HC Deb, 23 March 2020, c62 • behavioural scientists doubted that the public would obey restrictions: SAGE Meeting 15, 13 March 2020 • 'because people wouldn't have perhaps responded in the way they eventually did.': *The Daily Mail*, 22 May 2020 • 'The only way to stop this epidemic is indeed to achieve herd immunity', *The Spectator*, 13 June 2020 • children were probably not carriers: *The Times*, 17 May 2020 • 'is quite weak': Select Committee on Science and Technology, 19 May 2020 • 'an unequal burden to different sections of society':

'SPI-B insights on combined behavioural and social interventions', 4 March 2020 • 'We're not going to trigger draconian measures now': Boris Johnson, speech delivered 12 March 2020 • 'The most important task will be to protect our elderly': Ibid. • 'at some point in the next few weeks': *New Statesman*, 1 April 2020; Lawrence Freedman, 11 May 2020 • 'huge numbers dying and catastrophic consequences for the NHS': *The Guardian*, 22 March 2020 • 'It is very easy to say more needs to be done': *The Standard*, 13 March 2020 • 'just pushing the deaths into the future': *The Lancet*, 5 May 2020, available at: https://doi.org/10.1016/ S0140-6736(20)31035-7; Radio New Zealand interview with Johan Giesecke, 17 May 2020, available at: www.rnz.co.nz/national/programmes/sunday/audio/ 2018746794/johan-giesecke-why-lockdowns-are-the-wrong-approach • 'It is always easier to say that we could have done something slightly different': Science and Technology Committee, 19 May 2020, Q.847 • 'That is a scientific concept, not a goal or a strategy': *Sunday Telegraph*, 15 March 2020 • questioned the scientific credibility of 'behavioural fatigue': *Behavioural Scientist*, 16 March 2020 • 'we predict there would still be in the order of 250,000 deaths in GB, and 1.1–1.2 million in the US': 'Report 9: Impact of non-pharmaceutical interventions (NPIs) to reduce COVID-19 mortality and healthcare demand', Imperial College COVID-19 Response Team; *Financial Times* Alphaville, 17 March 2020 • he estimated the number of deaths to be 20,000: Science and Technology Committee, 25 March 2020 Q.24 • thereafter pressure on hospitals would fall: *The Telegraph*, 17 March 2020; Neil Ferguson Twitter account, 26 March 2020, available at twitter.com/neil_ferguson/status/1243294815200124928 • 'I am surprised that there has been such unqualified acceptance of the Imperial model': The Daily Wire, 26 March 2020; *Financial Times* Alphaville, 26 March 2020; The New England Journal of Medicine 2020; 383:303-305 DOI:10.1056/NEJMp2016822 • Gupta's study disputed the reliance on the tests for antibodies: UnHerd, May 21 2020 • the projected 510,000 deaths was wrong: Gupta worked on a 'population-based model'. Ferguson's was an 'individual-based model'. • I wrote the code . . . 13+ years ago to model flu pandemics: Neil Ferguson Twitter account, 22 March 2020 • the restrictions applied on 16 March were aimed towards the lockdown: Science and Technology Committee, oral evidence, 24 April 2020, Q.278 • But they did not go further: Health and Social Care Committee, oral evidence, 21 July 2020, Q.608; Q.638 • right of freeborn people of the United Kingdom to go to the pub: Johnson, press conference 20 March 2020 • should avoid pubs, clubs and theatres: Boris Johnson, speech delivered 16 March 2020 • he had scrambled an appeal to industry for help: Reuters, 7 April 2020 • Britain was just two weeks behind Italy: SAGE meeting 18 March • 'this government will do whatever it takes': Boris Johnson, speech delivered 17 March 2020 • eventually benefit nearly 10 million employees: 'Coronavirus response: social distancing measures and economic support across the UK', Institute for Government, 20 May 2020 • But there never was a shortage of ICUs: Science and Technology Committee Oral evidence: UK science, research and technology capability and influence in global disease outbreaks, HC 136, 25 March 2020, Q.15 • begin to develop a vaccine: Weekly Report 1, COVID-19 Genomics UK (COG-UK) Consortium, 23 March 2020 • PHE had withdrawn items of critical advice: 'Guidance for social or community care and residential settings on COVID-19', PHE, 25 February 2020 (withdrawn 13 March 2020) • About 418,000 people in England were living in 11,109 care homes: 'Later Life in the United Kingdom 2019', Age UK, last updated May 2019; 'Care Homes for Older People UK Market Report', Laing-Buisson, 5 December 2019 • None were obliged to obey any government regulations: 'Care homes market study: final report', Competitions and Markets Authority (CMA), 30 November 2017; Care Homes Analysis (12 May 2020), Working Care Homes Group, published 29 April 2020 • 'as the top priority': Science and Technology Committee, Oral evidence: UK Science, Research and Technology Capability and Influence in Global Disease Outbreaks, HC 136, Q.830; Q.838 • 'when the NHS will be under the most pressure': *New Scientist*, 25 August 2020 • But his promise had not been implemented by Whitehall: Minutes from SAGE Meeting 14, 10 March • ideally within three hours: 'COVID-19 Hospital Discharge Service Requirements', DHSC, 19 March 2020 • empty 15,000 acute beds by 27 March, and later another 10,000: 'Spotlight on Recent NHS Discharges into Care Homes', NHS Providers, 19 May 2020 • would not stop London's ICUs being overwhelmed: SAGE Meeting, 20 March 2020 • 'there will be no discharges from hospitals into care homes.': *Health Service Journal*, 21 March 2020 • the care homes' refusal was widespread: *The Guardian*, 29 March 2020 • 'He should've been watching what went on in care homes in Spain and Italy': Martin Green, interview with author • The law removed the legal protection for patients to be safely discharged: 'COVID-19 Hospital Discharge Service Requirements', DHSC, 19 March 2020 • 25,000 infected patients were dumped into the homes: *Financial Times*, 17 July 2020 • if a patient could not be tested, they would be isolated in the care home: NHS Providers blog, 23 May 2020, available at nhsproviders.org/news-blogs/news/stop-making-the-nhs-a-scapegoat-for-deaths-in-social-care; 'Spotlight on Recent NHS Discharges into Care Homes', NHS Providers, 19 May 2020 • Cummings asked why the lockdown had not started: *The Telegraph*, 29 April 2020 • The decision to enter lockdown would have been the same: John Newton blog • 'We vastly underestimated the general public': Science and Technology Committee, Oral evidence: UK Science, Research and Technology Capability and Influence in Global Disease Outbreaks, HC 136, Q.859; Q.847 • Vallance replied 'No.': Select Committee, 25 March Q.79 & Q.81; 'Scientific evidence supporting the government response to coronavirus (COVID-19)', SAGE, 26 June 2020; 'COVID-19 pandemic: some lessons learned so far', Correspondence from Chair to Boris Johnson, 18 May 2020 • he agreed to do what he called 'extraordinary': Boris Johnson, speech delivered 18 March 2020 • the British acting high commissioner in Delhi was cursed by desperate British tourists: 'Flying Home: The FCO's consular response to the COVID-19 pandemic', Foreign Affairs Committee Report, 28

July 2020 • drowned out by NHS staff complaints about shortages of PPE: 'Spotlight on the Supply of Personal Protective Equipment', NHS Providers, 22 April 2020 • 'an entirely separate PPE oversight and supply chain': Harries, press conference 20 March at 32.43 • Wormald preferred later to shy away from fully answering questions: Public Accounts Committee, Oral evidence: Readying the NHS and social care for the COVID-19 peak, HC 405, 22 June 2020 • 'didn't know how much fabric was required to make one garment': *Financial Times*, 20 April 2020 • he could not explain why commercial procurement and distribution was failing: Health and Social Care Committee, Oral evidence: Coronavirus - NHS Preparedness, HC 36, 17 March 2020; Health and Social Care Committee oral evidence: Delivering Core NHS and Care Services during the pandemic and beyond, HC 320, 30 June 2020 • it is still true that many lives will sadly be lost: Boris Johnson, speech delivered 23 March 2020 • He would be reprimanded by Chris Whitty: Health and Social Care Committee, oral evidence, 21 July 2020, Q.614 • 'the costs of lockdown may be considerably worse than the disease itself': Science and Technology Committee, Oral evidence: UK Science, Research and Technology Capability and Influence in Global Disease Outbreaks, HC 136; Q.808 • and there was insufficient testing: *The Times*, 20 April, 2020 • Sunetra Gupta criticised the lockdown as a mistake: 'COVID-19 Death Data in England – Update 22nd April', Centre for Evidence-Based Medicine, 22 April 2020; • https://www.cebm.net/oxford-covid-19-evidence-service/ Professor Carl Heneghan • Possibly the legacy was a T-cell immunity from Covid-19: 'Coutts in Conversation: Professor Sir John Bell', 29 May 2020; 'Presence of SARS-CoV-2 reactive T cells in COVID-19 patients and healthy donors', Julian Braun *et al*, available at: https://doi.org/10.1101/2020.04.17.20061440; 'How do we know who is immune to COVID-19?', available at: www.gavi.org/vaccineswork/how-do-we-know-who-immune-covid-19; 'Pre-existing immunity to SARS-CoV-2: the knowns and unknowns', *Nature Reviews Immunology* volume 20, pages 457–458, 7 July 2020, updated 17 August 2020; '8 Out of 10 People Not Infected With COVID-19 Protected by Episodes of Colds in the Past: German Study', *Science Times*, 30 June 2020 • the mathematician would predict that Britain's death toll would be 'substantially lower' than 20,000: *The Times,* 26 March 2020; Commons Science & Technology Committee • Statistically, he was not in danger: 'Reasonable Worst-Case Planning Scenario', SAGE, 29 March 2020

Chapter 28: Covid II

'I was aware there were contingency plans in place': *The Sun*, 2 May 2020 • 'He absolutely needed to be there,' she insisted: *Daily Mail*, 23 April 2020 • the number of deaths had peaked and was beginning to decline: SAGE meeting 25, 14 April 2020 • the Oxford research group was confident about producing a vaccine: 'Hancock launches first of three mega-labs for Covid-19 testing', Research Professional News, 10 April 2020 • *The Telegraph*, 17 April 2020 • the government had given £93 million to build a vaccine manufacturing centre: *The Guardian*, 17 May 2020 • already classed as the worst in Europe: *The Telegraph*, 28 April 2020 • Newton's attitude was symbolic of the NHS's bureaucracy: 'COVID-19 pandemic: some lessons learned so far', Correspondence from Chair to Boris Johnson, 18 May 2020; Science and Technology Committee Oral evidence: UK Science, Research and Technology Capability and Influence in Global Disease Outbreaks, HC 136, 8 April 2020 • 'public health experts had been sidelined': *The Guardian*, 1 April 2020; Horton 25 March to Science and Technology Committee. • they had not told ministers 'until mid-March': *Daily Mail*, 9 April 2020 • unknowingly pass the virus to three other individuals: Select Committee on Science and Technology: The science of Covid-19, 19 May 2020 • the experts' own mistakes were minimised: *The Guardian*, 29 April 2020 • 'it is much better to have over-capacity than under-capacity': *The Telegraph*, 2 May 2020 • thirteen times higher in Britain than in Germany: *The Guardian*, 28 June 2020 • Hancock had been warned in the Commons about temporary staff spreading the virus: *Hansard* LC Deb. vol.627, 3 March 2020, question from Liz Kendall • lived in overcrowded and intergenerational housing: Care Homes Analysis (12 May 2020), Working Care Homes Group, published 29 April 2020 • she did not know for certain: DHSC, oral evidence, 26 March 2020 Q.235 • did not mention restricting staff movements: 'New requirement to test patients being discharged from hospital to a care home', Professor Keith Willett and Matthew Winn, NHS England and NSH Improvement, 16 April 2020 • despite the government's promise on 13 March to provide free PPE: '£2.9 billion funding to strengthen care for the vulnerable', DHSC and Ministry of Housing, Communities and Local Government, 19 March 2020 • A special alert was issued on 15 May: 'Spotlight on Recent NHS Discharges into Care Homes', NHS Providers, 19 May 2020 • the guidance was not properly updated until 9 July: 'Coronavirus (COVID-19): care home support package', DHSC, 9 July 2020 • By then about 20,000 people had died in care homes: 'Deaths involving COVID-19 in the care sector, England and Wales: deaths occurring up to 12 June 2020 and registered up to 20 June 2020 (provisional)', Office of National Statistics, 3 July 2020 • had been hired to cover for staff: *The Guardian*, 3 July 2020 • had not been following the procedures correctly: *The Telegraph*, 6 July 2020 • no patients would be infected by Covid: 'Our plan to rebuild: The UK Government's COVID-19 recovery strategy', 11 May 2020; 'COVID-19 and the impact on social care', Office for National Statistics, 9 July 2020; 'Deaths involving COVID-19 in the care sector, England and Wales: deaths occurring up to 12 June 2020 and registered up to 20 June 2020 (provisional)', Office of National Statistics, 3 July 2020 • Care Quality Commission (CQC) inspectors: 'COVID-19 Insight: Issue 3', Care Quality Commission, July 2020 • done no more than 'fifty inspections during lockdown': 'No evidence for Johnson claim that care homes failed to follow Covid procedures', Channel 4 FactCheck, 7 July 2020, available at: www.channel4. com/news/factcheck/factcheck-no-evidence-for-johnson-claim-that-care-homes-failed-to-follow-covid-procedures • 'they are carrying out close personal care without any protection': *Daily Mail*, 16 April 2020, UNISON press release, 4 May 2020, available at: www.unison.org.uk/news/press-release/2020/05/elderly-vulnerable-people-still-risk-poor-advice-care-homes-says-unison/ • acknowledged as inadequate: 'COVID-19: how to work safely in care homes', PHE, 17 April 2020 • 'at increased risk to those individuals and care-home staff': 'Spotlight on Recent NHS Discharges into Care Homes', NHS Providers, 19 May 2020 • 'It is still not clear who is responsible for testing care-home residents and staff.': Ibid. • the department was still sending a fifteen-page letter: Correspondence from Helen Whately, Minister of State for Care, 14 May 2020 • he made no excuses: Public Accounts Committee, Oral evidence: Readying the NHS and social care for the COVID-19 peak, HC 405, 22 June 2020, Q.25; Q.43; Q.90; 'COVID-19: our action plan for adult social care', DHSC, 16 April 2020 • It would finally be sent to care-home managers in mid-May: *The Telegraph*, 19 May 2020; Correspondence from Helen Whately, Minister of State for Care, 14 May 2020 • only £194 million had been transferred by the local authorities: 'ADASS Budget Survey 2020 Part #2 Impact of Covid-19 on budgets', Directors of Adult Social Services, 18 June • 'red tape and bureaucratic spaghetti': 'Readying the NHS and social care for the COVID-19 peak', Public Accounts Committee, 22 June 2020, evidence submitted by Care England • 'Behind the scenes he has done absolutely nothing': Martin Green, interview with author • He claimed only a quarter of deaths were in the homes: *The Telegraph*, 12 May 2020 • the public's trust in the prime minister and his government fell slightly further: 'Response to *Sunday Times* Insight article', DHSC Media Centre, 19 April 2020 • only 1 per cent of the total figure: Office for National Statistics, 'Coronavirus (COVID-19) roundup', updated 26 August 2020. Note: up to 7 August 2020 it was 560 deaths out of 51,879 in England and Wales. • Another 10,610 'excess' deaths: *The Times*, 15 May 2020 • Explaining all the reasons for the excess deaths was difficult: 'The road to renewal: five priorities for health and care', The King's Fund, 16 July 2020 • Covid-related deaths included people who had died *with* Covid: *The Spectator*, 30 May 2020 • Bangladeshis and Pakistanis were about three times more likely to die: *Daily Mail*, 1 May 2020 • including living conditions, obesity and diabetes: *The Critic*, 27 April 2020 • did not have an underlying health issue: *Daily Mail*, 20 May 2020 • felt compelled to continue working: *Financial Times*, 7 May 2020 • immigrants' poverty and low-paid employment: *The Guardian*, 2 June 2020 • Chris Whitty said that no one knew the reason: 'COVID-19 pandemic: some lessons learned so far', Correspondence from Chair to Boris Johnson, 18 May 2020 • Descriptions of hospitals on the brink and staff risking death: *Financial Times*, 29 April 2020 • 17 million pieces of equipment to 258 trusts on one day: 'Our plan to rebuild: The UK Government's COVID-19 recovery strategy', 11 May 2020 • They were supported by Nicola Sturgeon: *The Times*, 25 April 2020 • the government's popularity had fallen from 72 per cent in February to 58 percent: https://yougov.co.uk/topics/international/articles-reports/2020/03/17/

perception-government-handling-covid-19 • a new tracing app uniquely relying on self-reporting: Letter from Niall Dickson, Chief Executive NHS Confederation, 20 May 2020; *Financial Times*, 21 May 2020; *New Scientist*, 25 August 2020 • 'a world-beating operational system' by 1 June near impossible: *The Telegraph*, 4 May 2020 • most sufferers had no antibodies: *The Times*, 29 May 2020 • 'we are really still only beginning to understand how we are going to combat it': Chris Whitty, speech delivered at Gresham College, 30 April 2020 • there were lots of other things that needed to be done: *The Guardian*, 31 May 2020 • 20 per cent of those infected would suffer 'severe ill-effects': Science and Technology Committee, HC 136, 25 March 2020 • 'urging the importance of testing and isolation': Ibid. • the British government was coping as well as most in Europe: 'Number of deaths in care homes notified to the Care Quality Commission, England', Office for National Statistics, updated 25 August 2020 • other hospitals suffered extreme shortages: *The Times* 23 April 2020 • they are being consumed too quickly as people are using them inappropriately: Professor Calum Semple, Professor of Child Health and Outbreak Medicine at the University of Liverpool, and a member of NERVTAG • 'dishonest and cowardly' for 'hiding behind the science': *The Times* 25 April 2020 • quoting 'the science' was a tactic of 'obsessive secrecy': *The Times* 9 May 2020 • could cost 100,000 lives by the end of the year: *The Times* 27 April 2020 • 'we would have reduced the final death toll by at least a half': Commons Science and Technology Committee, Oral evidence: UK Science, Research and Technology Capability and Influence in Global Disease Outbreaks, HC 136, Q.845 • blamed the lockdown for causing more deaths than it saved: *The Telegraph*, 23 March 2020 • could have caused an earlier overwhelming of GPs and A&E practitioners: Strife Blog, Interview with Professor Calum Semple, 2 April 2020, available at http://www.strifeblog.org/2020/04/02/uk-government-policy-in-facing-the-coronavirus-threat-an-interview-with-professor-calum-semple/ • Sloppily, medics put Covid as a cause of death: Planet Normal podcast, *The Telegraph*, 11 June 2020 • contradicted by David Spiegelhalter, the respected British statistician: Winton Professor of the Public Understanding of Risk in the Statistical Laboratory at the University of Cambridge, and formerly president of the Royal Statistical Society. • somewhere between 5 and 15 per cent of all deaths: *Financial Times* Alphaville, 22 May 2020 • Sweden's care homes were suffering an exceptionally high death rate: *The Telegraph*, 28 April 2020 • The actual number was 2,954 deaths: *The Telegraph*, 16 May 2020 • Others still endorsed Imperial's model as reliable: Mike Cates, 'Reflections of a Novice COVID-19 Researcher', 19 May 2020, available at: https://www.trin.cam.ac.uk/news/reflections-of-a-novice-covid-19-researcher/ • the latest YouGov poll putting the Tories at 50 per cent and Labour at 30 per cent: *The Times*, 7 May 2020 • the NHS had not collapsed but had performed brilliantly: *The Times*, 8 May 2020 • 'from faceless civil servants to our new overlords': *The Times*, 16 May 2020 • unfair to the 7 per cent of children without access to the Internet: *The Times*, 7 May 2020 • an hysterical attack on the government's and SAGE's management of the crisis: *The Telegraph*, 30 May 2020; *BMJ* 2020;369:m1932 • Sending children to school would 'risk a second spike': *The Times* 18 May 2020 • That is 10,000 times the risk of younger people: *The Times*, 10 May 2020 • Edmunds had not publicly protested: Sky TV, 20 May 2020 • He attacked Boris and the 'arrogant' British scientific community: *Science*, 11 May 2020, doi:10.1126/science.abc7438 • remain in lockdown until the virus disappeared: *Financial Times*, 4 June 2020 • 'it is taking another gamble': *Financial Times*, 4 June 2020 • three-step narrative to reopen Britain: 'Our plan to rebuild: The UK Government's COVID-19 recovery strategy', 11 May 2020 • the nation was left confused: *The Telegraph*, 11 May 2020 • 'it was a disappointing thirteen minutes': *The Telegraph*, 12 May 2020 • 'He hesitated to present his scheme as a set plan': *The Times*, 11 May 2020 • 'But it is a wicked thing that they are doing': *The Times*, 17 May 2020 • One week earlier, it had been 48 per cent: *Daily Mail*, 17 May 2020 Boris was 'fading': *The Guardian*, 12 May 2020 • 'It is the worst of both': *The Telegraph*, 12 May 2020, extract from Economic Intelligence Newsletter • 'Germany reacted more boldly and more courageously, and Britain was slow': In conversation with Alan Rusbridger in Oxford, 20 May 2020 • 'We do not believe that there is sufficient clarity': 15 May 2020, supported by Keith Neal, professor emeritus of epidemiology of infectious diseases at the University of Nottingham. • 'No, Mr Speaker, and it was not true that the advice said that': *Hansard* LC Deb. vol.676, 13 May 2020 • The number of discharges were down by 40 per cent: Liaison Committee, oral evidence from Boris Johnson, HC 322, 27 May 2020 • 'the health of a small child': The Health Protection (Coronavirus, Restrictions) (England) Regulations 2020, Section 6 • Matthews later admitted that he had fabricated the second sighting 'for comedy': *Mail on Sunday*, 31 May 2020 • 'a shambles with Trumpian levels of deceit': *The Guardian*, 25 May 2020 • 'prop up the collapsing reputations of ministers': *The Guardian*, 27 May 2020 • 'The government would be better without him': *The Guardian*, 26 May 2020 • 'If Boris Johnson cannot function without Cummings he is not qualified to be prime minister': *The Spectator*, 28 May 2020 • 'tell lots of lies, move on': *The Guardian,* 30 May 2020

Epilogue

'Our great national hibernation is coming to an end': 23 June 2020 • opposed a general return to work: *The Times* 17 July 2020; Commons Science a Technology Committee • belated denial that his organisation was responsible for a 'national testing strategy': *The Times*, 17 August 2020

Afterword

The Covid infection rate, he said, was rising: *The Times*, 11 September 2020 • neither Hancock nor Harding could have anticipated there would be widespread public disobedience: Commons Science and Technology Committee, Oral evidence:

UK Science, Research and Technology Capability and Influence in Global Disease Outbreaks, HC 136, Q1318 • and should resign after Brexit was done: *The Spectator*, 19 September 2020 • The presentation of the bill to Parliament was disastrous: *The Guardian*, 11 September 2020 • an outright breach of international law rather than the re-enactment of reserve powers existing in section 38 of the Withdrawal Act: European Union (Withdrawal Agreement) Act 2020, s38(2)(b) • Carrie Symonds may have been a pivotal factor: *Daily Mail*, 27 February 2021 • warned that a vaccine would not be available until the spring: *The Times*, 19 October 2020 • 'Trust' in a future vaccine, Sylvester proclaimed, was low: *The Times*, 20 October 2020 • Pogrund observed that Bingham's 'conduct is worrying Whitehall': *The Sunday Times*, 8 November 2020 • had been brokered by a young Spaniard for a £21 million fee: Comptroller and Auditor General, Investigation into government procurement during the COVID-19 pandemic, Session 2019–2021, HC 959, National Audit Office, November 2020 • 'and will do anything for her . . . We are all a nest of singing birds.': *Mail on Sunday*, 28 February 2021 • England's educational standards had failed to improve in this period: Tom Bower, *Broken Vows: Tony Blair, The Tragedy of Power*, Faber & Faber (2016), pp 368, 417, 476 • would reduce the UK's economy by 4 per cent within ten years: *The Times*, 22 January 2021 • 'The Garden of England doesn't hold the virus.': *Mail on Sunday*, 29 November 2020 • the infection rates in the north-west were falling: *The Times*, 14 November 2020 • there would be a tough lockdown in January: *The Times*, 19 November 2020 • would not materialise before summer 2021: *The Times*, 27 November 2020 • and fail to vaccinate the necessary 2 million people a week: *The Sunday Times*, 3 January 2021 • he noted that the death rate was falling: *The Times*, 16 December 2020 • Boris claimed on the same day that only 174 trucks were waiting outside Dover: *The Times*, 22 December 2020 • 'The moment of truth,' declared Barnier: *The Times*, 18 December 2020 • Britons began booking their summer holidays: *The Times*, 28 December 2020 and 30 December 2020. • just as Boris predicted that the lockdown would be over by March: *The Times*, 16 January 2021 • Over 75 per cent of the dead were over seventy-five years old, and 95 per cent of the dead had pre-existing health conditions: *The Times*, 27 January 2021 and 28 January 2021 • although they were just 11 per cent of England's population in the 2011 census: *BMJ*, 22 January 2021

Bibliography

Cameron, David, *For the Record*, HarperCollins, 2019

Gimson, Andrew, *Boris*, Simon & Schuster, 2012

Hastings, Maxwell, *Editor: An Inside Story of Newspapers*, Macmillan, 2002

Johnson, Boris, *Friends, Voters, Countrymen: Jottings on the Stump*, HarperCollins, 2002

Johnson, Boris, *Have I Got Views for You*, Harper Perennial, 2006

Johnson, Boris, *The Churchill Factor*, Hodder & Stoughton, 2014

Johnson, Boris, *Lend Me Your Ears*, HarperCollins, 2003

Johnson, Buster, *Alas Poor Johnny: A Memoir of Life on an Exmoor Farm*, Matador, 2015

Johnson, Rachel, *The Oxford Myth*, Weidenfeld & Nicholson, 1988

Johnson, Rachel, *Rake's Progress*, Simon & Schuster, 2020

Johnson, Stanley, *Stanley I Presume*, Fourth Estate, 2009

Oliver, Craig, *Unleashing Demons: The Inside Story of Brexit*, Hodder, 2016

Purnell, Sonia, *Just Boris: A Tale of Blond Ambition*, Aurum Press, 2012

Seldon, Anthony, *May at 10*, Biteback Publishing, 2019

Shipman, Tim, *All Out War: The Full Story of How Brexit Sank Britain's Political Class* (Brexit Trilogy 1), William Collins, 2016

Shipman, Tim, *Fall Out: A Year of Political Mayhem* (Brexit Trilogy 2), William Collins, 2017

Picture Credits

Section 2

Index

BJ indicates Boris Johnson.